Second Edition

Elements of Sociology

A CRITICAL CANADIAN INTRODUCTION

John Steckley

Guy Kirby Letts

OXFORD
UNIVERSITY PRESS

OXFORD

UNIVERSITY PRESS

8 Sampson Mews, Suite 204, Don Mills, Ontario, M3C 0H5
www.oupcanada.com

Oxford University Press is a department of the University of Oxford.
It furthers the University's objective of excellence in research, scholarship,
and education by publishing worldwide in

Oxford New York

Auckland Cape Town Dar es Salaam Hong Kong Karachi
Kuala Lumpur Madrid Melbourne Mexico City Nairobi
New Delhi Shanghai Taipei Toronto

With offices in

Argentina Austria Brazil Chile Czech Republic France Greece
Guatemala Hungary Italy Japan Poland Portugal Singapore
South Korea Switzerland Thailand Turkey Ukraine Vietnam

Oxford is a trade mark of Oxford University Press
in the UK and in certain other countries

Published in Canada
by Oxford University Press

Library and Archives Canada Cataloguing in Publication

Steckley, John, 1949–
Elements of sociology : a critical Canadian introduction / John Steckley, Guy Kirby Letts. — 2nd ed.

Includes bibliographical references and index.
ISBN 978-0-19-543166-7

1. Canada—Social conditions—Textbooks. 2.Sociology—Canada—Textbooks. I. Letts, Guy Kirby, 1961– II. Title.

HM586.S84 2010   301.0971   C2010-900907-X

Cover image: Nikada/Vetta Collection/iStockphoto

This book is printed on permanent (acid-free) paper ∞.

Printed in the United States of America

1 2 3 4 – 13 12 11 10

Brief Contents

Contents

PART TWO | SOCIAL STRUCTURES

Chapter 3   Culture   64

Chapter 6   Deviance   152

PART THREE ⏐ SOCIAL INSTITUTIONS

Chapter 7   Family   176

PART FOUR | SOCIAL DIFFERENCE

Chapter 11 Social Inequality: Stratification   294

Chapter 12 'Race' and Ethnicity: Sites of Inequality   322

Chapter 13 Gender and Sexuality 350

PART FIVE | FUTURE PERSPECTIVES

From the Publisher

In preparing this new edition of *Elements of Sociology*, we have, from the start, kept in mind one paramount goal: to produce the most comprehensive yet dynamic and accessible introduction to sociology available to Canadian students.

This revision builds on the strengths of the highly acclaimed first edition and incorporates new features and material designed to make the text even more engaging, more thought-provoking, and more relevant to students and instructors alike. We hope that as you browse through the pages that follow, you will see why we believe *Elements of Sociology* is the most exciting and innovative textbook for Canadian sociology students.

Six Things That Make This A One-of-a-Kind Textbook

A Canadian Textbook for Canadian Students

Written by Canadians for Canadians, *Elements of Sociology* highlights the stories of the figures and events at the heart of sociological inquiry in this country: Dawson and Clark, Porter and Goffman, Dorothy Smith and Daniel G. Hill, the 'Famous Five' and Quebec's Quiet Revolution, the Oka standoff, and much more.

A Visual, Thought-Provoking Approach

Students are challenged on every page to adopt a sociological perspective and see the sociology in everyday life. Carefully chosen photos and captions, provocative critical-thinking questions, and end-of-chapter review questions all invite readers to apply the theory and take a stance.

---

13 | GENDER AND SEXUALITY   373

the 2004 Super Bowl sparked an astonishing level of outrage among scandalized American viewers (not to mention all of those who had merely heard about the incident). Why the big fuss? The sudden appearance in prime time of the sexually objectified black woman experiencing a 'wardrobe malfunction' seemed to have caught a largely white middle-class audience by surprise. Were these viewers right to object? Or is the North American viewing public guilty of a double standard, finding it okay for the sexually objectified woman to appear in videos on MTV, but not on 'family entertainment' on CBS?

The Indian Princess and the Squaw

Aboriginal women have long been subject to the opposing gender/race stereotypes of the 'Indian princess' and the 'squaw'. In the United States, the Indian princess is a heroine that forms an integral part of the American story of how their country was built. She is the beautiful Pocahontas of Disney's

> **QUICK HITS**
>
> **The *Ninauposkitzipxpe*, or 'Manly-Hearted Women', of the Peigan**
>
> *About a third of elderly (sixty years or older) North Piegan women in 1939, and a few younger women, were considered manly-hearted. . . . Such women owned property, were good managers and usually effective workers, were forthright and assertive in public, in their homes, and as sexual partners, and were active in religious rituals. They were called 'manly-hearted' because boldness, aggressiveness, and a drive to amass property and social power are held to be ideal traits for men. . . . [T]he manly-hearted woman is admired as well as feared by both men and women.* (Kehoe 1995: 115)
>
> **What do YOU think?**
>
> How do we in Canadian society tend to characterize women who are bold, aggressive, and career-oriented? Can we say that we think of them as positively as the traditional Blackfoot did?

The daughter of an English mother and a Mohawk father, E. Pauline Johnson played up her mixed heritage in her popular performances, often appearing for the first part of a show in traditional Native costume before changing into a formal evening dress for the remainder of the performance.

worldview, saving the handsome John Smith from certain death, in the process abandoning her people to serve the interests of the incoming colonial power. She is Sacajawea, the Shoshone woman who aided the Lewis and Clark Expedition from 1804 to 1806, helping to open the West to 'civilization' and the eventual reservation entitlement of her people and their Plains neighbours.

The Indian princess is not part of the founding mythology, or master narrative, of Canada. Still, she is found here and there across the country. Emily Pauline Johnson, popular Mohawk poet and novelist at the turn of the twentieth century, was frequently billed as 'The Mohawk Princess' to audiences in North America and Britain, for which she performed her poetry. Catharine Sutton, heroic Ojibwa woman of the nineteenth century, is known in Owen Sound, Ontario, as 'the Indian Princess' (see Steckley 1999).

While the stereotype of the Indian princess has been used as a metaphor for the supposed open, armed acceptance by North American Native people of European colonizers, the squaw is a figure that has been used by white writers (including

---

An Inclusive, Narrative Approach

Sociology is the study of people, and in *Elements of Sociology*, the people tell their stories. Students will read first-hand accounts of what it's like to fast during Ramadan, come out to your family, be Chinese during the SARS outbreak, grow up in a Hutterite community, raise daughters in an era of Lingerie Barbie and La Senza Girl, and be a woman at a professional conference dominated by men.

Coverage of Canada's First Nations

No sociology textbook can claim more extensive coverage of the issues that have affected and that continue to affect Canada's Aboriginal peoples.

---

194   PART THREE | SOCIAL INSTITUTIONS

Telling It Like It Is

A STUDENT POV

Italian Families and Conjugal Roles: Four Generations   POINT OF VIEW

When I think of the topic of gender in an Italian family, I laugh. The struggles between what it means to be male and what it means to be female arise so very often in my family, at every dinner and almost every conversation. The discussions are always split between the three generations because my grandmother lives with my parents and she never misses an opportunity to include her views. As you can probably guess it goes like this: the eldest generation undeniably believes that the female's role in life is to be a complement to her husband; everything she does is based on his needs and his demands. All domestic duties and child-rearing except for punishment are her responsibility. Working outside the home is secondary to household work. The husband makes all decisions, although she can make suggestions. It is the male's responsibility to take care of the family financially.

My parents (second generation) feel similarly, the main difference being the father should be very involved with the children, not solely in areas concerning punishment. Where my grandmother would discourage my father from helping around the house, my mother would welcome the help though not demand nor expect it. In this generation, family decisions are made together; however, household duties are

still very divided, even with my mother working full time outside the home. For the female, post-secondary education and career are second to marriage and family. The main female role in life is keeping a clean house, cooking good homemade food, and keeping everyone happy and healthy. The main male role is to keep the food on the table by providing the family with its main source of income.

The third generation around the dinner table changed things a little. This generation in my family consists of my husband and I, the middle brother and his wife and the 'baby brother', though no longer a baby. Most of us are in agreement that gender roles in the new Italian family have changed. No longer is the female solely responsible for all household duties. Husbands cook, clean, and are physically able to change diapers, something my father had never done even with having three children! The females have post-secondary education and careers and are not a complement to their husbands, but an equal.

I also grew up with a huge double standard that affected me immensely in all areas of my life. It goes something like this: 'This is what boys can do and this is what girls cannot do' (My father's infamous words). Boys can play all day and not help their mothers (girls can't), boys can

Family and Ethnicity

As we'll see in greater detail in Chapter 12, on race and ethnicity, there is a history in Canada of the federal government creating policies that denied family to immigrants. The prohibitively expensive head tax levied on immigrants from China and South Asia in the late nineteenth and early twentieth centuries made it impossible in many cases for married couples or their families to reunite in Canada. Canadian sociologists **Nancy Mandell** and **Ann Duffy**, in their text *Canadian Families: Diversity, Conflict and Change* (1995), noted a

similar connection between government immigration policy and the denial of family for women of colour. They claim:

> [I]t has been a policy of the government not to encourage the possibility of developing families among women of colour who came as domestic workers. Thus, their status as 'single' and as 'temporary' is deliberately organized by immigration policies. (1995: 157).

The policy they refer to was initiated in 1910–11, during one of the country's greatest periods

Three New Chapters

The scope of the new edition has been expanded to provide comprehensive coverage of three critically important areas of sociological research—social roles and organization, religion, and education.

Case Studies and Compelling Viewpoints
Elements of Sociology features dozens of theme boxes—arranged in five different types and scattered throughout the text—to highlight issues, events, and ideas at the centre of sociological debate and investigation.

• Our Stories • • • • • • • •

Our Stories boxes examine the events and contributions that make sociology in Canada unique.

QUICK HITS

Quick Hits sidebars supplement the authors' narrative with relevant lists and examples.

The Point Is...

The Point Is... boxes present case studies and highlight important contributions to sociological research, past and present.

Going Global

Going Global boxes shed light on international issues of interest to sociologists in Canada and around the world.

Telling It Like It Is

EXPERT POVs

Telling It Like It Is boxes feature first-person narratives that give voice to a variety of perspectives informed by a variety of social locations.

Online Resources

Elements of Sociology is but the central element in a comprehensive package of learning and teaching tools that includes resources for both students and instructors.

For Instructors

- Carefully chosen **video clips from the Media Education Foundation**, matched to each chapter and available on DVD, provide unique perspectives on themes and issues discussed in the textbook. Topics include TV and the cultivation of values (Chapter 03 – Culture), the commercialization of childhood (Chapter 07 – Family), advertising in the classroom (Chapter 09 – Education), and the marketing of disease (Chapter 10 – Health and Medicine).
- A detailed **instructor's manual** provides an extensive set of pedagogical tools and suggestions for every chapter, including overviews and summaries, key concepts, teaching notes, homework assignments, and additional print and online resources.
- Newly updated and enhanced for this edition, classroom-ready **PowerPoint slides** incorporate graphics and tables from the text, summarize key points from each chapter, and may be edited to suit individual instructors' needs.
- A comprehensive **test generator** enables instructors to sort, edit, import, and distribute hundreds of questions in multiple-choice, short-answer, and true–false formats.

For Students

- The **student study guide** includes chapter summaries, study questions, self-grading quizzes, and explore-and-discuss exercises to help students review textbook and classroom material.

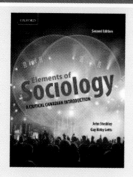

COMPANION WEBSITE

John Steckley and Guy Kirby Letts

Elements of Sociology: A Critical Canadian Introduction, Second Edition
ISBN 13: 9780195431667

Inspection copy request

Ordering information

About the Book

Elements of Sociology: A Critical Canadian Introduction has become a cornerstone of Oxford's domestic sociology list. The first edition, published in 2007, stood out in a crowded market and earned followers in both the college and university markets.

The factors contributing to the success of the first edition of *Elements of Sociology* have been preserved in this new edition. First and foremost of these is the authors' narrative. The tone-conversational, direct, shot through with

Acknowledgements

We would like to acknowledge the following reviewers, along with those reviewers who chose to remain anonymous, whose thoughtful comments and suggestions have helped to shape the first and second editions of *Elements of Sociology:*

- **Fiona Angus**, Grant MacEwan University
- **Tami M. Bereska**, Grant MacEwan University
- **Angela Conti-Becker**, University of Western Ontario
- **Howard A. Doughty**, Seneca College
- **Janice Drodge**, Cape Breton University
- **Laurie Forbes**, Lakehead University
- **Jane W. Haddad**, Seneca College of Applied Arts and Technology
- **Ron Joudrey**, Red Deer College
- **Susan Robertson**, University of Saskatchewan
- **Carolyne Willoughby**, Durham College
- **Amanda Zavitz-Gocan**, University of Western Ontario

From the Authors

Why Write a Sociology Text?

Why write a Canadian sociology textbook when there are so many out there already? We were tired of the dry, conservative bent of other texts, and their general failure to include much or anything about our heroes of the discipline—Dorothy Smith, Michel Foucault, Franz Fanon, Antonio Gramsci, Albert Memmi, and (apart from a perfunctory nod to his sociological imagination) C. Wright Mills. We aimed for a more inclusive approach in covering theories and theorists, including the many women and sociologists of colour who have influenced and redirected the discipline.

> 'We were tired of the dry, conservative bent of other texts.'

An Inclusive Approach

We also wanted to correct what we saw as an inability among introductory texts on the Canadian market to give proper voice to certain perspectives, such as those of Aboriginal and South Asian peoples, among others. We don't claim to have corrected the deficiency, but we hope we have made a significant departure from earlier Canadian sociology textbooks in this regard.

A Narrative Approach

We realized, too, that it wasn't enough to include the work of authors representing different ethnic backgrounds, cultures, and sexualities. We needed to make these other voices heard, and the best way to do that, we felt, was through narratives, which we have incorporated in each chapter. These narratives give voice to a variety of perspectives informed by a variety of social locations—black, Chinese, Italian, lesbian, Muslim, Palestinian, and Portuguese. We strongly believe that the narratives constitute one of the most important features of this textbook.

Breaking Out of the Mould

The narrative approach is just one of many ways in which our textbook is a little different from the rest. Yet the market imperative within the broader political economy of publishing means that there is little interest in doing something different from what has already been done. It wasn't until we began the publishing process that we realized how the conservative elements within the market influenced what materialized as the final product. Little tolerance for difference and little appetite for risk lead to merely reproducing what is known to have worked before. We were fortunate that Oxford, constrained by its own market imperative and logic, has been so supportive of our unique views and approach.

> 'We felt that the best way to make different voices heard was in narratives, which we have incorporated in each chapter.'

Written by Canadians for Canadians

A textbook is typically considered Canadian when it uses Canadian figures, Canadian data, and Canadian research—this despite the fact the text may entirely overlook the history and emergence of sociology in this country. Canadian sociology is quite different from the sociology found in Europe and the US. For instance, the focus of early Canadian sociology was on rural life and the resource economy, which speaks to a society that is not highly urbanized or industrialized. Moreover, the influence of the social gospel movement and social work orients sociology in Canada, more than its counterparts elsewhere, around issues of social justice, even today.

> 'Canadian sociology is quite different from the sociology found in Europe and the US. . . . We are confident that this is the most Canadian introductory sociology textbook on the market.'

We are confident that this is the most Canadian introductory sociology textbook on the market. It is not an adapted American text with Canadian extensions, nor is it a North American textbook co-written by American and Canadian authors. We designed this book, from the ground up, as a text for Canadian students, to teach them about what we—Canadian sociologists—have done, are doing, have failed to do, and hope to do in the future.

Qualitative Methods—Not Just Questionnaires Anymore

While contemporary sociology still engages in foundational methods, there has been an expansion of qualitative methodological approaches influenced by feminism, queer theory, poststructuralism, postcolonialism, and cultural studies, many of which had been ghettoized into other disciplines, like anthropology and women's studies. These methods are not new, but they have not been part of the methodological lexicon in sociology. In order to represent contemporary sociology accurately, we went beyond a conventional discussion of quantitative and qualitative methods to include ethnographic research, case studies, and narratives, as well as content and discourse analysis, psychoanalysis, semiotics, and genealogy. In this way, we hope to introduce students to concepts, ideas, and themes that will recur throughout their education.

Contemporary Theory and Shifting the Canon

An accurate survey of sociology today should stress what is current, what is being done, and who is being studied. The discipline generally and the theory specifically are exciting, yet we feel this message is not conveyed to students, who often see sociology as boring or irrelevant. Sociological theory has shifted immensely, with influences from queer theory, feminist psychoanalysis, postcolonialism, and poststructuralism, as well as people like Foucault, Lacan, Spivak, and Said. Whether the exclusion of these influences reflects the status quo or the belief that they are too complex for our students to comprehend, it is a misrepresentation that benefits no one, and one we have tried to correct.

> 'The discipline generally and the theory specifically are exciting, yet we feel this message is not conveyed to students, who often see sociology as boring or irrelevant.'

A Visual Approach

A casual flip through the text reveals an abundance of photographs and other illustrations. These are not just pretty distractions to keep students looking at the book. They serve a purpose. We have chosen images and have written captions that we hope will, like the numerous critical-thinking questions scattered throughout the chapters, encourage students to adopt a sociological perspective.

Acknowledgements

It takes many people to put together a book of this size and scope. First, I want to thank the people at OUP who made major contributions to this project: David Stover, for suggesting (twice) that I write this book; Nancy Reilly, who signed us on for the new edition; and Jodi Lewchuk and Eric Sinkins, who, with amazing effort and diplomatic skill, got us to the finish line.

I would also like to thank several colleagues at Humber. Les Takahashi, Jim Jackson, John Metcalfe, and Joey Noble all contributed their support and helpful ideas. Librarians Jennifer Rayment and Marlene Beck worked major feats of magic to retrieve obscure articles and books.

Closer to home, my good friend Bryan Cummins saw to it that my pub life at the Toby Jug kept me sane and on track. My dogs—Egwene and Cosmo—proved to be useful distractions and sources of constant emotional support, as did my five parrots—Quigley, Stanee, Lime, Louie, and Finn.

Then, finally, there is my wife, Angie. She supported me through the highs and lows of this project, when I was not the easiest person to live with. When the sands of my life shift, there is always a rock I can depend on.

John Steckley
February 2010

I have used numerous texts throughout my teaching career and have always been at odds with both the representation and the pedagogy that was being advocated. In many ways, the sociology that I read, and that my colleagues and I practise, looks nothing like the sociology found in introductory textbooks. I often wondered why a discipline would represent itself to young adults as something conservative, parochial, and, well, boring, given that the discipline itself is liberating, dynamic, and exciting.

I would like to thank Oxford for giving us the opportunity to attempt something different, and—I believe—exciting. In particular, I would like to thank Nancy Reilly, who believed in the value of what we were trying to do and shared our enthusiasm, and Jodi Lewchuk and Eric Sinkins, for their patience, creativity, and input. I would also like to thank my family, Angela Aujla, Anushka Luna, Indigo West, and our newest addition, Onyx Akash, for tolerating my always 'present absence'. I would like to acknowledge all those who helped me formulate a particular perspective that has allowed me to think critically about sociology specifically and society in general, for which I am eternally grateful. And finally, I would like to acknowledge my students for whom I wrote this text, so we might better understand together this strange thing called life.

Guy Kirby Letts
February 2010

Key Terms

- archaeology of knowledge
- bourgeoisie
- class
- conflict theory (or approach)
- critical sociology
- cultural mosaic
- discourse
- dramaturgical approach
- egalitarian
- ethnography

- ethnomethodology
- folk society
- functionalism
- ideological
- impression management
- latent dysfunction
- latent function
- macrosociology
- manifest function
- melting pot

- microsociology
- narratives
- objective
- policy sociology
- political economy
- professional sociology
- proletariat
- Protestant (work) ethic
- public sociology
- relations of ruling

Introduction to Sociology

LEARNING OBJECTIVES

After reading this chapter, you should be able to

> outline the differences and similarities between sociology and other disciplines;

> describe what the sociological imagination is;

> identify some key ideas of sociology's trailblazers: Durkheim, Marx, and Weber;

> distinguish the three 'functions' identified by Robert Merton;

> outline the differences between two broad categories of sociological approaches: structural functionalism, conflict theory, and symbolic interaction on the one hand, and professional, critical, policy, and public sociology on the other;

> articulate the basic ideas of Michel Foucault and Dorothy Smith; and

> trace the origin and development of sociology in Canada.

- social Darwinism
- social fact
- social gospel
- sociological imagination
- sociological poetry
- sociology
- standpoint theory
- staples
- subjective
- symbolic interactionism

- total institution
- totalitarian discourse
- vertical mosaic

Key Names
- C. Wright Mills
- Confucius
- Ibn Khaldun
- Max Weber
- Charles Darwin

- Herbert Spencer
- Émile Durkheim
- Robert K. Merton
- Karl Marx
- George Herbert Mead
- Herbert Blumer
- Harold Garfinkel
- Erving Goffman
- Michel Foucault
- Dorothy Smith

- Leonard Marsh
- Carl Addington Dawson
- Everett C. Hughes
- Horace Miner
- Harold Innis
- Samuel Delbert Clark
- John Porter

Photo: © Kathy deWitt/Alamy

FOR Starters

Doughnut Shops, Drive-Throughs, and the Value of Sociology

As I live in Bolton, Ontario, unofficial doughnut capital of Canada, it isn't surprising that I am a big fan (both physically and emotionally) of coffee-and-doughnut shops. I them part of my culture. When I go to a doughnut shop, I park my car, walk in, chat with the server, and generally enjoy the social aspect of the transaction. I have never used—and will never use—a drive-through. I feel that pulling up to the drive-through window limits the overall experience—the socializing, the customer service, the ritual of surveying the assortment of doughnuts and then choosing the perfect one. For that matter, it doesn't save any time (I've done an informal study), and it increases the local pollution level.

You can tell I have strong views on the subject, so you probably won't be surprised to learn that I've spent a fair bit of time contemplating why some people use the drive-through. Just who are these people who would rather interact over an intercom and receive their orders through a pickup window? I'd always thought it was either young men whose most significant relationships were with their cars, or else lazy, fat, older men who drive everywhere rather than walk.

My opinion changed, however, because of a student in one of my sociology classes. This is the value of sociology: it can change your opinion. The student carried out his own study, a 'Pilot Assessment of Donut Shop Patronage' in Newmarket, a bedroom community north of Toronto. He spent approximately an hour one morning at a doughnut shop taking note of who was using the drive-through, and who were the 'walk-ins'. Over that period he observed 91 people walk in, and 95 people drive through.

Indeed, he noticed a gender difference in the two groups, but not the one I predicted: for the counter sales, 42 of the customers were women and 49 were men, while of the drive-through patrons, 70 were women and just 25 were men. He also noted that young women were much more likely—by a ratio of nearly 7 to 1—to use the drive-through than were middle-aged or older women. This was different from the group of male drive-through customers, where there was a roughly one-to-one ratio of the two age-determined groups. Another statistic enabled the student to come up with a hypothesis to account for the results of his research: he observed that the cars going through the drive-through were more likely to have child seats in them than were the parked cars of the walk-in clientele. Further, he often identified young children among the passengers of the drive-through cars.

The student's hypothesis, which would apply to that time (between approximately eight and nine o'clock a.m.) and location, was that young mothers with infants and toddlers used the drive-through significantly more because it was easier than going through the complicated process of unbuckling their children and bringing them into the restaurant. To be really convincing, his hypothesis would have to be tested for other times and locations, but it presented a sociological profile that I would not otherwise have guessed.

Introduction to the Textbook

We hope that you'll notice, from this first example on, that this textbook is not like the others. It will offer occasional humour and lots of stories told from the perspective of the writers. In keeping with contemporary sociological terminology, we are calling these stories **narratives**. Narratives make up an important branch of sociological literature, one recognizing that to understand a person's situation requires input from the words, the 'voice', of that person him- or herself. For this reason, every chapter of this textbook will make use of narratives to illustrate key points and concepts.

There are two basic strategies that textbook writers can take. One is to create a kind of reference book that touches on pretty much every conceivable topic within the discipline. This sort of book can be good for students who need support outside of the classroom or away from the professor. The other approach is to write a book that engages the student as a reader and as a student of the discipline (even if only for one semester), and that's what we are trying to do here. Our aim is to hook you on the subject of sociology, and to get you interested in reading and learning about it (we're essentially sociology pushers...).

We feel that—to use a baseball analogy—if you try to round the bases too quickly, you'll get picked off. We'd rather get you safely on base. You may not touch all the bases this inning, but there's a better chance you will in your next at-bat. In other words, we've tried to avoid writing a textbook you will lose interest in because it tries to introduce you to too much, too quickly.

There are precedents for our approach in introductory sociology textbooks. In 1980, Elliott Krause published *Why Study Sociology?*, a book he said was

> designed as a bridge between your everyday understanding of social life and the kind you can develop through the study of sociology. If you do not have a broad overview of all that sociology is doing, by the time you finish this book, I hope that you will have a strong sense of some of the ways that sociology can be relevant to your life. Think of this as the appetizer. Think of any full introductory sociology course you are taking as the main entree. Think of this as the *why*, the full course as the what. (Krause 1980: xi)

The book had just six chapters and was less than 200 pages long. This book is longer and more comprehensive. Think of it as a large, hopefully tasty snack—say, a box of Timbits.

Introduction to Sociology

Sociologists notice social patterns. What's a social pattern? Well, for example, things tend to happen differently to you depending on your sex, age, class, ethnicity ('race'), religion, and sexual orientation. If you are a woman, you pay more in Canada for a haircut and to have your shirt dry cleaned than you would if you were a man (Dunfield 2005). It's not that you're getting more for your money; it's just that your hair and your shirt, because they are designated as 'female', are more expensive to cut and to clean (respectively). If you are a young black man driving in Canada, you are more likely than a white male driver to be pulled over at night by the police (even if you are famous, as in the case of Canadian Olympic boxer Kirk Johnson). You are guilty of the offence known facetiously as 'driving while black' (DWB).

What if you are a young, white, heterosexual male? If you belong to that group, you might think that all the 'other groups' are ganging up on you. Take the education system, for instance. It has a zero tolerance policy for 'fighting', which covers behaviour you might have thought of as just 'fooling around'. You didn't have a male teacher until you were in your middle grades (or maybe later). When you studied English literature in high school, your teachers asked you 'chick' questions about things like relationships and feelings, questions you couldn't possibly have answered as well as your female classmates could. Why didn't they ask you: 'Who killed whom with what weapon, and what was the fight like?' Insurance companies make it very expensive for you (and your parents) to pay for your driving. You read and hear that white males have privilege in terms of getting jobs, but it is often difficult for you to find the jobs that white male privilege is supposed to help you with. If your aim is to be a police officer, you might be discouraged by rumours that only women and visible minorities are being hired. (These rumours aren't true, by the way, although they say something about the older white men who are often the ones spreading them.)

If any of these scenarios describes you, take heart: sociology is here to help you understand your situation. Sociologists investigate and challenge the social patterns that other people perceive. For example, why do so many people,

even those in the medical profession, assume that male nurses are gay? It has never been demonstrated statistically (in part because it would be unethical to ask a male nurse about his sexual preferences. Imagine showing a male RN pictures of attractive men and women and asking, 'Who do you like?'). Sociologists studying the subject would have to investigate the effects of movies like *Meet the Fockers*, where characters played by well-known and well-respected actors (Robert de Niro, in this case) articulate their belief that male nurses are either gay or, at the very least, 'sissies'. Sociologists would look at how the nursing profession is thought of as 'naturally feminine' because it involves caregiving and is a chronically underpaid profession involving duties that we in the West consider less important than the work of (typically male) doctors. They might also look at how male nurses and nursing students might act out their heterosexuality (for instance, by boasting about how many women they have had sex with)

Young, white, and male: is it really all it's cracked up to be?

Photo: © Gabe Palmer/Alamy

in order to combat the perception that they are gay. In short, sociologists would look carefully at the patterns of social behaviour and perceptions associated with male nurses.

Consider another example: politicians who promote conservative social policies often talk disdainfully about the 'liberal media', lumping together print, on-air, and Internet journalists who might disagree with their views. Sociologists can test assumptions about a predominantly left-leaning media by doing a statistics-based content analysis of the political views recorded in popular media on issues in which liberal and conservative positions are clearly established (gun registration and environmental policy are a couple of examples). Sociologists might conclude that the Canadian media in fact leans heavily to the right. We'll talk more about statistical analysis and other kinds of quantitative and qualitative research in the next chapter. What is important to understand here is that sociologists use these kinds of tools to assess and challenge the social perceptions that people hold, views that are sometimes known as 'common sense'.

Sociology and Issues

Sociology can help students understand the issues facing society today. One of the most divisive social issues in recent years is the debate surrounding same-sex marriage. Since July 2005, same-sex marriage has been legally recognized across Canada, although many Canadians remain strongly opposed to the idea; in the United States, same-sex marriage is legal in just a handful of states, and the Defense of Marriage Act, which outlines the federal government's position on the matter, defines marriage strictly as a union of one man and one woman. So what can sociologists tell us about this issue?

Sociology can't say what is moral, or 'right'. There really isn't a scientific way of measuring that. What sociology *can* do is enable us to be well informed about current issues like this. For example, sociology can tell us about who *tends* to be in favour of same-sex marriage: younger people, those with more education, women more than men, French Canadians more than English Canadians. As well, sociology can speak about who *tends* to be against same-sex marriage: those

with fundamentalist religious views versus the more liberal members of Canada's many faiths, and people from rural rather than urban communities. Beyond this, sociology gives us the perspective to document and discuss the many ways that marriage is defined in contemporary cultures around the world, or in Canadian cultures over time, and it can inform a discussion about changes in the relationship that marriage has had with religious institutions through the centuries. In this way, it can help a sociology student avoid making uninformed, generalized statements beginning 'Marriage has always been . . .' or 'Everyone knows that marriage is . . .'. Sociology might also help students understand the impact that socializing influences—parents, the media, even sociology professors—have on their own opinions concerning same-sex marriage. You can have more choice in forming your own opinion when you know what has influenced it in the past.

All of this relates to a question that sociology students often ask: 'How come I received a low mark when it's just an opinion and there are no right or wrong answers?' Ideally, sociology should help students distinguish between a well-argued, informed opinion and an uninformed viewpoint spouted off without careful thought—keep the latter for your blog. While students often say, justly, that everybody has a right to an opinion, it is just as true that people owe it to themselves to become knowledgeable about the issues before offering opinions on them. Sociology gives us the means to form considered opinions on social issues.

Sociology as a Discipline

Academic disciplines such as sociology are artificial constructions. There is nothing 'natural' about the borderlines that separate sociology from other established disciplines such as, say, anthropology, economics, history, psychology, philosophy, or political science. These various fields of interest have much in common, as Table 1.1 shows, and there is a lot of cross-referencing in the books and articles written by specialists in each discipline. Health professionals, for instance, often engage in sociological research that is published in medical journals. And students who have taken courses in psychology,

Table 1.1 Sociology and related disciplines

DISCIPLINE	EMPHASIS
anthropology	the comparative study of human societies and cultures and their development
economics	the production and consumption of wealth, including the distribution of goods and services among individuals and groups
philosophy	major thinkers and trends of thought in particular (usually Western) societies
political science	systems of government and how they serve citizens
psychology	the human mind, the social and biological influences on it, and its functions, especially those affecting behaviour
social work	the application of our understanding of society and individuals to improve peoples' well-being
sociology	the development, structure, and functioning of human society: group interaction, social relations, social institutions, and social structures

anthropology, or philosophy will notice that sociology regularly encroaches on their territory, just as those disciplines often 'poach' on sociology's turf. The people who teach such varied subjects as Canadian studies, communication, criminology, cultural studies, education, Native studies, international relations, and women's studies often have degrees in sociology.

Still, artificial or not, the discipline of sociology does exist and is unique. It has its own history, a distinct vocabulary and set of tools (although some are borrowed from or shared by other disciplines), and a separate department in most colleges and universities in Canada. In order to understand sociology, its weaknesses and strengths, and the ways in which its perspective has broadened over the last few decades, it needs to be understood as a discipline.

So, What Is Sociology?

You may have noticed that so far we have cleverly avoided defining what sociology is. That's because it's not a straightforward thing to do, and in some ways not particularly useful: defining something is very different from understanding it. We could give you a simple (but not terribly useful) definition by saying that sociology is 'the systematic or scientific study of society'. Can you imagine the type of multiple-choice questions that could come from that?

Sociology is:
a) the systematic study of society;
b) the unsystematic study of society;
c) 'statistical stuff and heavy-duty theoretical bullshit' (Mills, see below);
d) all of the above.

The answer could easily be the final one, 'all of the above'. Or we could refer you to the glossary at the back of this book, where we have defined **sociology** as 'the social science that studies the development, structure, and functioning of human society'.

The truth is that giving a precise, all-encompassing explanation of what sociology *is* would be much more difficult than explaining what sociology *does*. This is why we've begun our introduction to sociology by highlighting some of its uses. At this point it is enough to know that sociology involves looking for and looking at patterns in social variables such as age, gender, race, ethnicity, religion, and sexual orientation; in social institutions such as education and justice systems, religions, and family; and in social interactions. By the time you've reached the end of this textbook, you will have formed your own idea of what sociology really *is*.

So, Why Study Sociology?

Studying sociology is useful in order to achieve for oneself, and to generate among others, a greater understanding of the social world. Studying sociology will also help you to better understand yourself in terms of whether you follow or do not follow patterns of social behaviour predicted by sociological variables (think, for instance, of a young Latin woman who likes salsa dancing—quite predictable—and a black youth from the city who enjoys line dancing—not so predictable). Sociology will help you develop an understanding about others around you in our multicultural and generally diverse social world that is Canada, as well as in the smaller worlds of neighbourhoods, chat groups, classrooms, pubs, and the workplace. Thinking more globally, sociology can help you better understand the larger world of nations and their social institutions. You can look, for example, at how the price of oil can affect the relative presence or absence of democratic social practices in oil-producing countries such as Saudi Arabia, Venezuela, and Iraq.

During a strike by Ontario public-school teachers in the 1990s, some strike sympathizers sported a bumper sticker that read: 'If you think education is expensive, just try ignorance.' In a similar vein, we could say, 'If you think sociology is hard, try understanding society *without* it.'

The Heart of Sociology: The Sociological Imagination

While we've managed to excuse ourselves from defining sociology itself, we would be remiss if we avoided defining one of the discipline's most useful instruments: the **sociological imagination**. Developing a sociological imagination is a goal that practitioners and students of the discipline strive for. **C. Wright Mills** (1916–1962), who coined the term, sums it up nicely as

the capacity to shift from one perspective to another—from the political to the psychological; from examination of a single family to comparative assessment of the national budgets of the world. . . . It is the capacity to range from the most impersonal and remote transformations to the most intimate features of the human self—and to see the relationship between the two. (Mills 1959: 4)

Mills argues that when we create and communicate sociological knowledge, our ideas must show not just 'how society works' but 'how society works' in terms of our own personal lives. If you go to buy a good pair of rubber boots (as the spouse of one of the authors did), and the only ones you can get are yellow and relatively flimsy, then you are a woman, and your own frustrating shopping experience reflects the way society thinks of and treats women in general.

What happens when we fail to see the links between individual experience and society as a whole is a subject discussed by culture critic Henry Giroux in *Beyond the Spectacle of Terrorism: Global Uncertainty and the Challenge of the New Media* (2006). Commenting on the lack of sociological imagination in the post-9/11 political posturing of George W. Bush, Giroux warns that 'Democracy begins to fall and political life becomes impoverished when society can no longer translate private problems into social issues' (Giroux 2006: 1). He spells this out in detail in the chapter 'Acts of Translation':

As the very idea of the social collapses into the private realm of the self and its fears, it becomes more difficult for people to develop a vocabulary for understanding how individual insecurity, dread, and misery could be translated into concerns of an engaged and critical citizenry. Instead, they are told that their privately held misery is a fall from grace, a flaw in character that must be suffered in isolation. Poverty, for example, is now imagined to be a problem of individual failing. Racism is rationalized and represented as simply an act of individual discrimination or prejudice. Homelessness is reduced to a freely chosen decision made by lazy people. (Giroux 2006: 4)

The Origins of Sociology

Who Was the First Sociologist?

People have since ancient times contemplated social systems and looked for patterns in human relationships. Perhaps the earliest person whose recorded writings reflect a true sociological imagination is the Chinese philosopher **Confucius** (*c.* 551–479 BCE). A strong proponent of role-modelling—a topic discussed often in sociology today—Confucius believed it was better for leaders to engage in moral practices that modelled the principles they wanted their citizens to follow than to overuse laws to enforce morality. In his words:

> If you use laws to direct the people, and punishments to control them, they will merely try to evade the laws, and will have no sense of shame. (Kaizuka 2002: 126)

Confucius emphasized socialization over social control and stressed that a country's leaders must engage in moral practices which model the type of behaviour that would be desirable in its citizenry. Are politicians, or even celebrities and corporate CEOs, good role models?

We can all think of politicians who would have benefited from following the wise sociological advice of Confucius.

While Confucius touched on some important sociological themes, the first person to carry out a systematic study of sociological subjects and set his thoughts down in writing is most likely the Arab scholar **Ibn Khaldun** (1332–1406), whom some current writers consider the first social scientist. In his book *Al Muqaddimah* (*An Introduction to History*), Ibn Khaldun examines various types of societies—tribes, cities, nations, and dynasties—and their histories, cultures, and economies. Many of his ideas and much of his research are still relevant today. For instance, in *Al Muqaddimah*, he provides insight into the cyclical rise and fall of power and status among desert tribes in the Middle East:

> [W]hen a tribe has achieved a certain measure of superiority with the help of its group feeling, it gains control over a corresponding amount of wealth and comes to share prosperity and abundance with those who have been in possession of these things. It shares in them to the degree of its power and usefulness to the ruling dynasty. If the ruling dynasty is so strong that no one thinks of depriving it of its power or of sharing with it, the tribe in question submits to its rule and is satisfied with whatever share in the dynasty's wealth and tax revenue it is permitted to enjoy. . . . Members of the tribe are merely concerned with prosperity, gain, and a life of abundance. [They are satisfied] to lead an easy, restful life in the shadow of the ruling dynasty, and to adopt royal habits in building and dress, a matter they stress and in which they take more and more pride, the more luxuries and plenty they acquire, as well as all the other things that go with luxury and plenty.
>
> As a result the toughness of desert life is lost. Group feeling and courage weaken. Members of the tribe revel in the well-being that God has given them. Their children and offspring grow up too proud to look after themselves or to attend to their own needs. They have disdain also for all the other things that are necessary in connection

with group feeling. . . . Their group feeling and courage decrease in the next generations. Eventually group feeling is altogether destroyed. . . . It will be swallowed up by other nations. (109)

Replace 'tribe' with 'country' or 'empire', and Ibn Khaldun's observations could have been written any time in the past century.

● ● ● ● ● ● ● ● ● ● ● ● ● ● ● ● ● ● ●

What do YOU think?

1. Why do you think that Ibn Khaldun has only recently been recognized for his contributions to the development of sociology?

2. Change the word 'tribe' to 'country' or 'empire' in the quoted passage from Ibn Khaldun's *Al Muqaddimah*. Do you think the writer has a valid point?

● ● ● ● ● ● ● ● ● ● ● ● ● ● ● ● ● ● ●

The Development of Sociology in the West

Sociology became an area of academic interest in nineteenth-century Europe, specifically in France, Germany, and Britain. It developed in response to the dramatic social changes taking place at that time: industrialization, urbanization, and significant population increases. The economics and especially the politics of the time were also favourable to the growth of sociology. As the American sociologist John Walton comments,

> Sociology was made possible by the French Revolution. The capture of the Bastille on July 14, 1789, and the Women's March on Versailles introduced a new principle into history by demanding political action to redress mass poverty. The authority of king and church that once justified social inequality was challenged by the philosophical notion of the general will come to life among people convinced that their suffering was no longer inevitable. Public opinion became a legitimate method for expressing these social concerns. (Walton 1986: 50)

In the late nineteenth and early twentieth centuries, a similar set of circumstances fostered the

Photo: © Art Directors & TRIP/Alamy

Ibn Khaldun is considered the first sociologist to systematically study the sociohistorical nature of societies. According to Khaldun, as societies acquire more affluence they also become more senile and fall into demise.

growth of sociology in North America. With the influx of millions of immigrants, the development of cities and urban life, and the greater impact of technology upon the daily lives of individuals, North America—especially the United States—became an ideal location for the discipline of sociology to develop.

Max Weber: A Founder of Modern Sociology

No one better illustrates the intellectual force and impact of early sociology than German sociologist **Max Weber** (pronounced VAY-ber; 1864–1920). One of his most important and well-known contributions was his identification of a set of values embodied in early Protestantism that he believed led to the development of modern capitalism; he called this set of values the **Protestant (work) ethic**.

What do YOU think?

1. How might sociology have developed differently as a discipline if the early thinkers had been African, Middle Eastern, Chinese, or South Asian?

2. Why do you think it was that sociology developed in Europe, not in Africa, the Middle East, China, or South Asia?

3. Look at the list of early sociologists in Table 1.2. Why are most of these people men? (Here's a hint: some people foolishly argue that men are better cooks than women, based on the fact that many of the world's most famous chefs are men. Is there a correlation between fame and ability? What role do the opportunities that society provides for certain groups play in this?)

Table 1.2 Early sociologists and their contributions

THINKER (Dates, Nationality)	KEY WORKS	CONTRIBUTION
Auguste Comte (1798–1857, French)	*Cours de Philosophie Positive* (1830–42), *The System of Positive Policy* (1851–4)	Aimed to develop a social science that could be used for social reconstruction.
Harriet Martineau (1802–1876, British)	*Society in America* (1837)	Seen as the first woman sociologist, she also translated many of Comte's works.
Karl Marx (1818–1883, German)	*The German Ideology* (1846), *The Communist Manifesto* (1848), *Das Capital* (1867)	The founder of modern communism, he viewed social change in terms of economic factors.
Herbert Spencer (1820–1903, British)	*Social Statics* (1851), *First Principles* (1862), *The Study of Sociology* (1880)	Social evolutionist coined the term 'survival of the fittest'.
Friedrich Nietzsche (1844–1900, German)	*Human, All Too Human* (1878), *The Gay Science* (1882), *The Genealogy of Morals* (1887), *Will to Power* (1901)	Championed the 'will to power' and the *Übermensch* ('superman') who could rise above the restrictions of ordinary morality.
Thorstein Veblen (1857–1929, American)	*The Theory of the Leisure Class* (1899), *The Theory of Business Enterprise* (1904)	Economist and social critic attacked American 'conspicuous consumption'.
Émile Durkheim (1858–1917, French)	*The Division of Labour in Society* (1893), *The Rules of Sociological Method* (1895), *Suicide* (1897), *The Elementary Forms of the Religious Life* (1912)	Studied society in terms of 'social facts', including ethics, occupations, and suicide.
Georg Simmel (1858–1918, French)	*On Social Differentiation* (1890), *The Philosophy of Money* (1900), *Sociology: Investigations on the Forms of Socialization* (1908)	Father of microsociology studied the way people experience the minutiae of daily life.
Max Weber (1864–1920, German)	*The Protestant Ethic and the Spirit of Capitalism* (1904–5), *Economy and Society* (1914)	Identified a set of values—'the Protestant (work) ethic'—to which he attributed the rise of capitalism.
George Herbert Mead (1863–1931), American	*Mind, Self, and Society* (1934)	Father of 'symbolic interactionism' looked at how the self is constructed through exchanges with others.
Robert Park (1864–1944, American)	*Introduction to the Science of Sociology* (& Burgess, 1921), *The City* (& Burgess, 1925)	Urban sociologist was a founding member of the Chicago School of Sociology.
W.E.B. Du Bois (1868–1963, American)	*The Souls of Black Folk* (1903), *Black Reconstruction* (1935)	Documented the experience of American blacks from a sociological perspective.

The Point Is...

Herbert Spencer: An Early Sociological Contribution

You've probably heard the phrase 'survival of the fittest'. Most people attribute it to biologist **Charles Darwin** (1809–1882), who, in his pioneering theory of evolution through natural selection, claimed that only those organisms 'fit' enough—that is, those individuals or species that have adapted to be most suitable in a particular environment—are destined to survive.

What most people don't know is that the saying itself was coined not by Darwin but by the early English sociologist **Herbert Spencer** (1820–1903). Heavily influenced by Darwin, Spencer was one of a number of scholars who tried to extend the theory of natural selection by applying it to human society as a way to describe the competitive struggle for power, wealth, and general well-being brought about by European industrialization and colonization. Using evolutionary theory in this way to describe social inequalities became known as **social Darwinism**.

Social Darwinists held up natural selection as the basis for claims of European superiority—Westerners regarded societies in Africa, Asia, and the Pacific Islands as more 'primitive' and less evolved—and as justification for colonizing and even enslaving peoples in parts of the world outside of Europe. By the same token, they argued that governments should not intervene to help the sick and the poor in their own societies, as these people were 'naturally selected' to fail. Social Darwinism was used to justify a host of discriminatory practices—sterilization, for example—against a variety of groups, including women, people of colour, and various ethnic groups. For Spencer in particular, evolution guided social change (a notion that runs counter to Marx's idea of class struggle and Innis's notion of technology, which we will examine later in this chapter).

Poverty, as we will see later, is in fact a social problem, not a problem of one's 'fitness'. Notions of superiority and inferiority, and of who should have access to resources, create inequalities and are the byproducts of culture and social history.

Weber's theory was based on a number of related ideas. One is the notion, popular among early Protestants, that there is a predestined 'elect', a group that will be 'saved' during the time of reckoning, at the Second Coming of Christ. Naturally, it was important to early Protestants to be seen as part of this exclusive group. Success through hard work was considered one proof of membership. Another was the accumulation of capital (money and money-producing possessions) through thriftiness. Working hard (remember: 'idle hands are the devil's tool'), making profitable use of your time, and living a materially ascetic (self-denying) life through property acquisition rather than lavish expenditure are all principles of Weber's Protestant work ethic. As he explained,

> The span of human life is infinitely short and precious to make sure of one's own election. Loss of time through sociability, idle talk, luxury, even more sleep than is necessary for health . . . is worthy of absolute moral condemnation. . . . [Time] is infinitely valuable because every hour lost is lost to labour for the glory of God. Thus inactive contemplation is also valueless, or even directly reprehensible if it is at the expense of one's daily work. For it is less pleasing to God than the active performance of His will in a calling. (1904/1930: 157–8)

In a later work, Weber elaborated on how demonstrating these values represents proof of being one of God's chosen few, and how these values supposedly fuelled the rise of capitalism:

> The religious valuation of restless, continuous, systematic work in a worldly calling, as the . . . surest and most evident proof of rebirth and genuine faith, must have been the most powerful conceivable lever for the expansion of . . . the spirit of capitalism (1946/1958: 172).

It's important to note that although the idea of the 'Protestant (work) ethic' took hold firmly enough that the phrase has entered popular speech, it was never sociologically demonstrated that capitalism developed primarily in Protestant rather than in Catholic countries, or that the work ethic Weber associated with Protestantism was somehow missing from Catholicism, or from any religion for that matter. Latin American scholars, for instance, argue that the rise of capitalism began with colonialism, a movement in which Catholic Spain and Portugal were major players from early on. Weber paid little attention to the role that colonialism played in the rise of capitalism as an instrument for exploiting colonized countries and amassing foreign wealth (as when the colonizing Spanish looted Aztec and Inca gold to become, for a time, the richest country in Europe). Weber, by attributing the development of capitalism to the strength of the Protestant will, might have been trying too hard to account for the relatively recent historical superiority of European Protestants. At the same time, he was implying that Chinese and Indian societies somehow lacked a work ethic, a fact he blamed for hampering their economic success.

● ● ● ● ● ● ● ● ● ● ● ● ● ● ● ● ● ● ● ●

What do YOU think?

1. Do you think that Weber would have advanced this theory if he had been a devout Catholic, Muslim, or Buddhist, rather than a liberal Protestant?

2. Does being religious enhance one's ability to become rich?

● ● ● ● ● ● ● ● ● ● ● ● ● ● ● ● ● ● ● ●

The Emergence of Different Kinds of Sociology

As modern sociology developed in nineteenth-century Europe, it did not take on a uniform appearance. Asking *What is sociology?* was no simpler then than it is today, and even its best uses were in dispute. Different social thinkers had their own ideas about what sociology was, what it could do, and how it should be applied. Consequently, sociology developed into several different schools that varied according to the particular applications and perspectives (historical, political-economical, feminist, and so on) of those who were using it.

In this chapter we will explore two ways of distinguishing the various kinds of sociology. The first is based on the approach used; the second is based on the audience and how reflexive or critical the sociologist is. These are by no means the only two ways of looking at sociology, but in our view they are the most useful.

1. Sociology by Approach: Structural Functionalism, Conflict Theory, and Symbolic Interactionism

The traditional way of representing different kinds of sociology in Canadian introductory sociology textbooks is to break sociology into three different approaches:

*   structural functionalism
*   conflict
*   symbolic interaction.

These terms are typically presented in the introductory chapter of the textbook and then repeated throughout most, if not all, of the subsequent chapters. The linguist Edward Sapir said, 'all grammars [i.e. explanations of language] leak.' As a way of illustrating the differences between sociologists, we feel that this particular 'grammar of sociology' leaks too much (imagine a flooded basement) to sustain using it throughout the text. Nevertheless, these distinctions do reveal some key differences, so they are worth explaining and illustrating here.

Structural Functionalism

The **structural-functionalist** approach has deep roots in sociology, especially American sociology. As the name suggests, the approach contains two dimensions. **Functionalism** focuses on how social systems, in their entirety, operate and produce consequences. The work of Émile Durkheim, Talcott Parsons, and Robert Merton represents the functionalist approach.

The functionalist approach was fused with *structuralism* (grounded in the anthropological work of Polish ethnographer Bronisław Malinowski and English social anthropologist A.R. Radcliffe-Brown) as a way of explaining social forms and their contributions to social cohesion. It uses an organic, or biological, analogy for society. How?

Photo: The Canadian Press/Jonathan Hayward

Vancouver's Downtown Eastside is one of the poorest urban neighbourhoods in North America. A functionalist might argue that homelessness is a social consequence produced by our economic system. Would you agree?

Nursing students, when they take the dreaded Anatomy and Physiology course, have to learn all the different *structures* of the human body as well as the *functions* they perform. The structural-functionalist approach treats society in a similar way: *This is the part of society we call organized religion, and this is how it functions . . .*; or *This is the family, which functions like so . . .*

While the structural-functionalist approach has been popular for the better part of sociology's history as a discipline, it has lost favour during the last few decades. It is too much of a stretch, for example, to talk about the *functions* of poverty or inequality. After all, poverty and inequality don't really serve the interests of society at large, just the narrow class interests of those who profit from others' misfortunes. In addition, functionalism is not usually very good at promoting an understanding of conflict or social change. While sociologists still draw on the classic works and essential concepts of structural functionalism, very few contemporary sociologists are committed to the theoretical practice itself.

To get a better sense of the functionalist approach, we'll look at the work of **Émile Durkheim** (1858–1917), who is considered one of the founders of modern sociology. Presenting the highlights of Durkheim's career would fill an entire chapter. Instead of doing that, we'll focus on one of his works as a way of illustrating functionalism. Let's begin, though, with Durkheim's notion of the **social fact**, a term he coined. Social facts are patterned ways of acting, thinking, and feeling that exist outside of any one individual but exert social control over all people. Think about how social characteristics such as gender, age, religion, ethnicity, 'race', sexual orientation, your role as sister or brother, or as student or teacher, all exert a compelling social force over you and lead you to act in sociologically predictable ways. These ways of acting based on social characteristics are social facts.

Every social fact has three essential characteristics:

- It was developed prior to and separate from any individual (in other words, *you* didn't invent it).

- It can be seen as being characteristic of a particular group (young Canadian men, for instance, like to watch sports while drinking beer).
- It involves a constraining or coercing force that pushes individuals into acting in a particular way (like when peer pressure becomes 'beer pressure' among young men watching sports).

You can see how looking for social facts would be a particularly good way for a sociologist like Durkheim to get beyond focusing on individuals to examine larger social forms and how different parts of society function. Hence the birth of functionalism, and in many ways sociology as we know it.

In his groundbreaking book *Suicide* (1897), Durkheim treated suicide as a social fact. Recalling that a social fact exists outside of any one individual, you might find this treatment strange given the intensely personal nature of the act. But Durkheim found that in late nineteenth-century France, certain groups were more likely to commit suicide than others: military officers as opposed to enlisted men, Protestants as opposed to Catholics, unmarried over married people, the rich over the poor and the middle-class. He correlated suicide with the degree to which individuals were connected or committed to society, finding that those having a stronger dedication to society were more likely to commit suicide. Officers are responsible for the soldiers in their charge; an intense sense of honour might make them suicidal when they make a mistake that results in death. On the other hand, Durkheim also concluded that having too weak a connection to society could produce suicide as well. Protestants were then in the minority in France and thus had weaker bonds to both country and culture. Unmarried adults were—as they generally are now—not connected to family the same way that married ones are. And the wealthy were more aloof, much less concerned than others with becoming involved in the affairs of the larger society.

In Canada today, men commit suicide more often than women do. This is a social fact. Why men commit suicide more often than women do is a complicated matter. It has to do in part with the fact that women are more likely to share their problems with other people than to 'suck it up' and remain silent. Women are more likely to have a network of friends with whom they can communicate about serious matters, and they are more likely to go to a therapist with an emotional problem, which lowers their likelihood of committing suicide. Women attempting suicide are also more likely to use less efficient means: pills and slashed wrists over the more deadly male choice of guns.

● ● ● ● ● ● ● ● ● ● ● ● ● ● ● ● ● ● ● ●

What do YOU think?

The authors of this text consider themselves fairly enlightened, with feminist sympathies. Yet a woman reader commented that it was obvious this book was written by two men: women, she pointed out, are less likely to commit suicide because of their childcare responsibilities, not because they're incapable or they 'share their feelings'. Do you agree?

● ● ● ● ● ● ● ● ● ● ● ● ● ● ● ● ● ● ● ●

American sociologist **Robert K. Merton** (1910–2003) identified three types of functions:

- **Manifest functions** are both intended and readily recognized, or 'manifest' (i.e. easily seen).
- **Latent functions** are largely unintended and unrecognized.
- **Latent dysfunctions** are functions that are unintended and produce socially negative consequences.

This last group is often studied using the conflict approach, as we will see, making Merton's brand of functionalism something of a bridge to conflict theory. The three examples in Table 1.3 illustrate the differences among Merton's three functions.

Conflict Theory

Conflict theory (also called the **conflict approach**) is based on the 'four *Cs*': *conflict*, *class*, *contestation*, and *change*. The approach is predicated first on the idea that *conflict* exists in all large-scale societies. The stress lines are major sociological factors, such as gender, 'race' and ethnicity, religion, age, and class. Second, it asserts that in every large scale society *class* has always operated. Third, it contends that the functions of society, as laid out in traditional structural-functional theory, can be

Table 1.3 Examples of Robert Merton's three functions

EXAMPLE 1

Post-secondary Education

manifest function	This provides students with skills and knowledge needed to find a profitable career in order to become productive, self-sufficient citizens.
latent function	This provides a social network that will make the search for employment and a marriage partner easier.
latent dysfunction	From a typical left-wing perspective, this reinforces class distinctions; from a right-wing perspective, it exposes students to socialist ideas.

EXAMPLE 2

Religion

manifest function	Religion fulfills spiritual and emotional needs, and answers important existential questions that many people have.
latent function	Religion creates a social network and marriage market.
latent dysfunction	Religion provides justification for judging outsiders ('non-believers') negatively.

EXAMPLE 3

Canadian Doughnut Shops

manifest function	Doughnut shops provide customers with coffee, snacks, and light meals, served quickly and conveniently.
latent function	Doughnut shops serve as a place to meet and socialize with others.
latent dysfunction	Doughnut shops provide late-night venues for drug dealing.

contested, or challenged, based on the question *What group does this function best serve?* Finally, the approach involves the assumption that society either will or should be *changed*.

A major figure in the early history of sociology was the German economist and political philosopher **Karl Marx** (1818–1883), who, with Friedrich Engels, founded modern communism in the mid-nineteenth century. For Marx, conflict was all about **class**: the division of society into a hierarchy of groups, with each group's position determined by its role in the production of wealth. Beginning with Marx, conflict theory looks at how conflict between the different groups, or classes, leads to change. Marx saw class conflict as the driving force behind all major socio-historical change. He believed that conflict between the class of capitalists (the **bourgeoisie**) and the class of workers (the **proletariat**) would initiate a socialist revolution that would produce a classless, or **egalitarian**, society. A classless society has never really existed in more complex societies, but many of Marx's insights about class conflict and capitalist production are still valid. This is particularly true if you think of transnational corporations in Western societies as the capitalist 'owning class' and underpaid workers in the poorer countries as the ultimate 'working class'.

The limits of conflict theory now stretch well beyond Marxism to incorporate applications in feminist sociology, international political science, personal relations and interaction, and many other fields of study that fit rather neatly into the category of 'critical sociology'. We'll look at critical sociology in greater detail later in this chapter.

Symbolic Interactionism

Symbolic interactionism is an approach that looks at the meaning (the symbolic part) of the daily social interaction of individuals. For example, two male students approach each other and say, 'Yo, wha's up?', lightly bringing their fists together in greeting. What are they communicating to each other about their relationship, their shared interests, and the role models that they identify with?

● ●

What do YOU think?

1. Could you challenge, amend, or add to any of the functions presented? How?

2. What would be the three different functions for
   a) children's organized sports in Canada?
   b) military or police services?
   c) garage sales?

● ●

The symbolic-interactionist method was pioneered by American social psychologist **George Herbert Mead** (1863–1931), who examined the way the self is constructed as we interact with others and how the self allows us to take on social roles, reflect on ourselves, and internalize social expectations (1912–13). Another important figure in the movement was **Herbert Blumer** (1900–1987), a pupil of Mead's and the one who coined the term 'symbolic interaction'. Blumer (1969) argued that social systems are simply abstractions that do not exist independently of individual relations and interactions. In other words, social systems (things like friendship, education, economy) are simply by-products of our personal dealings with one another. The American sociologist **Harold Garfinkel** (b. 1917) founded a method associated with symbolic interaction and known as **ethnomethodology**. Garfinkel developed the technique of ethnomethodology (which means the 'people's method', referring to its focus on practical reasoning or common-sense knowledge) to explain how people use social interaction to maintain a sense of reality in any given situation. While symbolic interaction examines *what kind* of meaning is generated through social

Photo: iStockphoto.com

In this conversation, how is meaning being generated? Words are simply one aspect of constructing meaning in our day-to-day interactions.

Photo: Photo © Bettmann/Corbis

A group of inmates starts boot camp at Sumter County Correctional Institute in Bushnell, Florida. In what ways do you see these men being controlled by a total institution? Could there be similar pictures for elementary school children? soldiers? hospital inmates?

interaction, ethnomethodology looks at *how* meaning is generated through social interaction.

You may have observed that the symbolic-interactionist approach, with its focus on individuals rather than larger social structures, differs from the approaches described earlier in the chapter. In this way it represents one part of another distinction used to differentiate various kinds of sociology, the distinction between **macrosociology** and **microsociology**. When a sociologist engages in research and writing that focus primarily on the 'big picture' of society and its institutions, then he or she is engaging in macrosociology. Weber, Durkheim, Merton, and Marx were all primarily macrosociologists. When our focus is more on the plans, motivations, and actions of the individual or a specific group, then we are taking a microsociological approach.

A good example of how microsociology is used to understand people's actions comes from the work of **Erving Goffman** (which serves equally well as an example of symbolic interactionism). Born in Alberta, Goffman (1922–1982) received his BA from the University of Toronto and his MA and PhD from the University of Chicago. Goffman was a pioneer in microsociology. His work regularly bore the stamp of originality, as evidenced by the many terms he introduced to the discipline of sociology. One example is **total institution**, an expression he coined in his book *Asylums* (1961). A total institution is any one of 'a range of institutions in which whole blocks of people are bureaucratically processed, whilst being physically isolated from the normal round of activities, by being required to sleep, work, and play within the confines of the same institution' (Marshall 1998: 669–70). The term is used to describe psychiatric hospitals, prisons, army barracks, boarding schools, concentration camps, monasteries, and convents—institutions whose residents are controlled, regulated, or manipulated by those in charge.

Goffman carried out his research for *Asylums* in 1955–6, when he engaged in fieldwork at a mental hospital in Washington, DC. He was ahead of his time in stating the importance of learning the subjectivity of people, the views and feelings they have, and especially in the way he denied both objectivity and neutrality in his research methodology. He unequivocally sided with the patients rather than the professionals who managed them in the hospital. He wanted to learn about the day-to-day social world of the inmate. He did this by pretending to be an assistant to the athletic director, and passing his days with the patients:

> [A]ny group of persons—prisoners, primitives, pilots, or patients—develop a life of their own that becomes meaningful, reasonable, and normal once you get close to it, and . . . a good way to learn about any of these worlds is to submit oneself in the company of the members to the daily round of petty contingencies to which they are subject. (Goffman 1961: x)

2. Sociology by Audience: Professional, Critical, Policy, and Public Sociology

Structural functionalism, conflict theory, and symbolic interaction are all different *approaches* to sociology practice and research. The second way of categorizing sociology that we'll present in this chapter is based on the *audience* and how reflexive or critical the sociologist is. The particular distinction we'll present is based on the work of sociologist Michael Burawoy (2004), who divided sociology into four types: *professional, critical, policy*, and *public*. If you'd like to read further on this subject, particularly with respect to professional sociology, we recommend you look at the *Canadian Journal of Sociology*, volume 34, number 3 (2009), which can be accessed online at https://ejournals.library.ualberta.ca/index.php/CJS. This issue contains 11 articles that look at the work that sociologists do in Canada. They are comprehensive and useful.

Professional Sociology

Professional sociology has as its audience the academic world of sociology departments, scholarly journals, professional associations (such as the American Sociological Association), and conferences. The research carried out by professional sociologists is typically designed to generate very specific information, often with the aim of applying it to a particular problem or intellectual question. Consider the following list of articles that

appeared in two 2009 editions of the *Canadian Review of Sociology*:

- from Volume 46, Issue 1 (January)
  - The Pursuit of Postsecondary Education: A Comparison of First Nations, African, Asian, and European Canadian Youth
  - What Do We Do Wednesday: On Beginning the Class as University-Specific Work: A Preliminary Study
  - Gender and Promotion at Canadian Universities

- from Volume 46, Issue 2 (May)
  - Gender Equality and Gender Differences: Parents, Habitus, and Embodiment
  - Rich Sensitivities: An Analysis of Conflict Among Women in Feminist Memoir
  - Canadian Physicians and Complementary/Alternative Medicine: The Role of Practice Setting, Medical Training, and Province of Practice
  - Organizational Self-Sponsorship, Nonprofit Funding, and the Educational Experience

As you can see from the titles, these articles address specific sociological questions, specifically, in these two issues, about gender and ethnicity. Written in technical or specialized language, they target an academic or professional readership, but can usually be read by interested students.

Critical Sociology

The main role of **critical sociology**, according to Burawoy (2004), is to be 'the conscience of professional sociology'. It performs this role in two ways:

> Critical sociology reminds professional sociology of its raison d'être, of its value premises and its guiding questions. It also proposes alternative foundations upon which to erect sociological research. In other words, critical sociology is critical in two senses, first in bringing professional sociology into alignment with its historical mission and second in shifting the direction of that mission. (Burawoy 2004)

Critical sociology, then, addresses the same audience that professional sociology does, but with

Our Stories
Applying Goffman to Research

I have long been a fan of Goffman's research and writing. His books are straightforward and readable, and his concepts are readily adaptable to research, as I discovered in 1972, when I spent a year studying a religious group in downtown Toronto as part of my honours thesis. I needed a theoretical base for my research, and so I turned to Goffman's *Presentation of Self in Everyday Life* (1959). It was an example of Goffman's **dramaturgical approach**, a way of conducting research as if everyday life were taking place on the stage of a theatre. According to an often-told sociological anecdote, Goffman was on the Hebrides Islands off the coast of Scotland, looking in vain for a topic for his doctoral dissertation, when, sitting in a restaurant, he noticed that the wait staff working there acted differently when they were on the 'front stage'—that is, in the public eye—than when they were 'back stage' in the kitchen, away from the dining customers. They presented themselves differently depending on which stage they were on, an example of what Goffman called **impression management**. Impression management refers to the ways in which people present themselves in specific roles and social circumstances. His thesis and his best-selling book were born that day, or so the story goes.

According to my research, the religious group I was studying was managing their impressions for two different audiences. One included street kids and other youthful lost souls who might be in need of spiritual guidance. For this audience, representatives of the religious group put on a hip, anti-establishment face. However, in order to obtain food donations from supermarket chains to feed their flock, and to achieve respectability in the eyes of both corporate sponsors and the neighbouring businesses in their rather exclusive downtown area, they had to present a more conservative face.

I predicted in my honours thesis that the group would split according to the two 'stages', divided by the two audiences to which they were presenting themselves. This in fact happened just a year later, and, thanks to some inspiration from Erving Goffman, I managed to get a pretty good mark in the course.

a different purpose. Its aim is to make sure that professional sociologists do not become so lost in esoteric debates that they lose sight of the issues of fundamental importance to the discipline.

As we stated earlier, much of what we call 'conflict theory' would fit into this category. Two of the giants of critical sociology, Michel Foucault and Dorothy Smith, are known for having examined the production of knowledge in relation to power. Foucault, as we'll see, discusses the conflict between 'scientific experts' and other producers of knowledge, while Smith discusses conflict in terms of gender relations.

The French philosopher and historian **Michel Foucault** (1926–1984) was a major intellectual force in the sociological world. In his

groundbreaking article 'Two Lectures' (1980), Foucault talked about the misleading nature of what he termed **totalitarian discourse** (which other writers have called 'global', 'universalizing', or 'totalizing' discourse). A totalitarian discourse is any universal claim about how knowledge or understanding is achieved. Western science is at the centre of a totalitarian discourse used by those who claim that it is the only legitimate path to discovering 'truth' about the causes and cures for different diseases, while dismissing alternative forms of medicine that are popular and trusted in many non-Western cultures. (For more on this issue, see Chapter 10, on health and medicine.)

'Totalitarian' in this context should be easy enough to understand: it describes a set of beliefs or ideas that dominates all others. The other part of this term, 'discourse', is not as easily understood. A **discourse** can be defined in the following way:

> A conceptual framework with its own internal logic and underlying assumptions that may be readily recognizable to the audience. A discourse involves a distinct way of speaking about some aspect of reality. [Use of the term] also suggests that the item under discussion is not a natural attribute of reality but socially constructed and defined. (Fleras and Elliot 1999: 433)

Calling something a discourse is not necessarily saying it's wrong or false; it's really a way of describing the particular treatment of a topic that has been created through a given set of assumptions, a vocabulary, rules, logic, and so on. However, to call something a *totalizing* discourse is to condemn it as overly ambitious and narrowminded. Consider the commonly made observation that the brain is like a computer. We can create a discourse comparing the functions and capabilities of the brain to those of a computer. Both store memories—sounds, images, video— and both acquire and process 'data'. We can all relate to a time when we felt that our brains had 'crashed'. You can see, though, how this discourse fails when you consider how poorly computers handle translation. (If you haven't experienced this, go to a website where the text is not in English; click on 'Translate This', and what you'll get is something a native speaker of English would never produce.) Computers cannot translate well—not as well as humans—since they cannot deal with the input of social and cultural context. Very few words or phrases from any given language can be translated directly and perfectly into another. Our discourse, then, is problematic: the brain may be similar to a computer in certain ways, but it would be wrong to say that the human brain is just like a computer. A discourse becomes totalitarian when it is promoted by those with power and influence until it becomes widely accepted as the only 'right' interpretation.

In *The Archaeology of Knowledge* (1994), Foucault wrote about the importance of discovering how individual discourses developed as a way of examining their strengths, weaknesses, and limitations. He calls this process of discovery an **archaeology of knowledge**. The sociologist must dig out or excavate a presentation of information considered to be factual (a discourse, in other words) in order to discover how the supposed fact or truth was established or constructed. Through this process of excavation the sociologist may find that some parts of the discourse have been distorted along the way, which affects how people interpret and act upon the discourse. The box on page 23 presents an example of how an archaeology of knowledge can lead us to reassess our understanding of a supposed historical fact.

Foucault's challenge to students of sociology is to understand that knowledge is constructed, and that it is important to investigate the question *How do we know what we know?* Because there are conceptual constraints that both determine and limit our thinking in ways that we are not aware of, there may be other constructions of knowledge on a particular subject that are just as valid or even more valid than our own.

While doing graduate work at the University of California, Berkeley, **Dorothy Smith** (b. 1926) experienced first-hand the kind of systemic discrimination that would become the subject of her first work. Smith moved to Canada in the late 1960s, when she was given a teaching opportunity at the University of British Columbia. Fortunately for the discipline in general and for Canadian sociology in particular, departments of sociology in this country were (in her words) 'scraping the bottom of the barrel'. Her distinguished academic career also includes a tenure of more than 20 years at the University of Toronto's Ontario Institute for Studies in Education.

Smith developed what is known as **standpoint theory** directly out of her own experience as a woman discriminated against by male colleagues in the academic community. Her standpoint theory challenged traditional sociology on two fronts, both relating to sociology's preference for **objective** (depersonalized and distanced from everyday life) as opposed to **subjective** (personalized and connected to everyday life) research and analysis. Her first criticism attacked the traditional position that the objective approach

• Our Stories •

Abandoning Inuit Elders: An Archaeology of Knowledge

Many introductory sociology textbooks assert that among Inuit populations, it was customary to abandon the elders when times got tough, such as during shortages of food (for example, see how this issue is presented by Henslin et al. 2009: 202; Macionis et al. 2009: 237–42). The discourse of abandoning elders, presented as fact, has been reinforced and perpetuated through the disciplines of sociology and anthropology, and internalized within popular culture. By conducting an archeological excavation of this discourse, we are able to unearth both its socio-historical origin and an excellent illustration of the way 'fact' is constructed.

The first step is to check the relevant footnotes and the bibliographies contained in the textbook. Most of the sociology textbooks in question obtained their information from three earlier studies: one on Inuit (Weyer 1932), one on suicide (Cavan 1928), and one on primitive law (Hoebel 1954). When you look at these earlier books, you discover that none of the writers actually did their own research on Inuit; they, themselves, were merely citing the work of other scholars.

Next, track down the works written by those earlier scholars to find out what they actually said. Some researchers studying the people merely assumed that the practice occurred, even though they didn't actually observe it, while others reported that when elders or the very sick were dying, forms of euthanasia were practised; this has also proven to be inaccurate. A few ethnologists mention times when elders were temporarily left behind while others who were more fit went ahead to look for food before returning to feed and resume travel with the elders.

In fact, there is no direct observation or ethnographic account of the practice of elder abandonment, and thus the custom, as it turns out, never really existed. But note that while your archaeology of knowledge has proven a supposed 'fact' to be a distortion, this is only part of the excavation. You can take a further step by examining the underlying structures that informed the interpretation of elder abandonment—structures including mainstream Canadian institutions (such as Canadian mining companies, the Hudson's Bay Company, and the RCMP) that moved into Inuit territory without respecting their aboriginal rights, and the need of sociologists and anthropologists for exotic examples to illustrate the influence of culture (i.e., rather than race) on people's lives.

to research is more scientific and therefore truthful, while the subjective position is **ideological**, based on biases and prejudices, and therefore distorted. According to Smith, knowledge is developed from a particular lived position, or 'standpoint'. Sociology, having developed from a male standpoint, had long denied the validity of the female standpoint and overlooked the everyday lives of women.

Smith's second criticism concerns mainstream sociology's tendency to reinforce what she calls the existing **relations of ruling**. She believes that denying the subjective standpoint further entrenches the dominance of the rulers over the ruled. For example, the Oka crisis of 1990 pitted members of a Quebec Mohawk community against some non-Native members of the community and provincial authorities, represented by the Sûreté de Québec (SQ), the Quebec provincial police force. The emotional standoff between the French-Canadian police and the Mohawk of Kanesatake near the town of Oka needs to be understood in the context of the long history of conflict in the region. But when sociologists deny the subjectivity of the SQ, characterizing the police as neutral agents of society performing their duty to control and punish 'troublemakers', they effectively legitimize the standpoint of the SQ while de-legitimizing the standpoint of the Mohawk (Steckley 2003).

Policy Sociology

Policy sociology is a relatively new term. To a certain extent it replaces the category of 'applied sociology', which is the application of sociological research to social change through various means, including public policy. Policy sociology is about generating sociological data for use in the development of social policy for governments or corporations. Education, health, and social welfare are three main areas that policy sociology serves.

● ● ● ● ● ● ● ● ● ● ● ● ● ● ● ● ● ● ● ●

What do YOU think?

1. How does Smith's standpoint theory fit with Mills's notion of the sociological imagination?

2. Do you agree with Smith's view that sociology developed from a male standpoint? Why or why not?

3. Consider the list of early sociologists and their contributions provided in Table 1.2. How might a greater impact of female standpoint have affected early developments in the growth of sociology?

● ● ● ● ● ● ● ● ● ● ● ● ● ● ● ● ● ● ● ●

Policy sociology has a long tradition in Canada. A classic work of Canadian policy sociology is the *Report on Social Security for Canada*, prepared by **Leonard Marsh** (1906–1982) and issued in 1943. Based on research Marsh had done in the 1930s while acting as research director for the McGill Social Science Research Project, it set the stage for a number of major social policy initiatives that we now take for granted. When you read the following description of the ideas in the report, keep in mind that none of the social policies referred to here existed in Canada at that time. The report, as Antonia Maioni explains, offered

> a dense and detailed plan for comprehensive social programs, constructed around the idea of a social minimum and the eradication of poverty. The realization of this ideal, according to Marsh, meant the recognition that

individual risks were part of modern industrial society, and that they could be met by collective benefits throughout the lifecycle. . . . 'Employment risks' were to be met through income-maintenance programs, such as unemployment insurance and assistance, accident and disability benefits, plus paid maternity leave. . . . 'Universal risks' were addressed through national health insurance, children's allowances, and pensions for old age, permanent disability, and widows and orphans.

> Significantly, practically all of these programs were to be contributory and under . . . federal . . . administration, with the exception of provincial workmen's compensation and medical care. . . . Also significant was Marsh's holistic view of social security that considered health as a central part of the welfare state, rather than a separate item and expense. (Maioni 2004: 21)

The first person to introduce one of Marsh's policy initiatives, health insurance, was Saskatchewan premier Tommy Douglas, who held a degree in sociology from McMaster University.

Public Sociology

Public sociology addresses an audience outside of the academy (i.e. universities and colleges). Herbert Gans, in his 1988 address as president of the American Sociological Association, identified three key traits of public sociologists:

> One is their ability to discuss even sociological concepts and theories in the English of the college-educated reader. . . . Their second trait is the breadth of their sociological interests, which covers much of society even if their research is restricted to a few fields. That breadth also extends to their conception of sociology, which extends beyond research reporting to commentary and in many cases social criticism. To put it another way, their work is intellectual as well as scientific. A third, not unrelated, trait is the ability to avoid the pitfalls of undue professionalism [e.g. an overly cautious style, a tendency to footnote everything and bury analysis in statistics]. (Gans 1987: 7)

Our nominee as the consummate public sociologist is C. Wright Mills, whom we introduced earlier in this chapter.

Professional, Critical, Policy, and Public Sociology: Review

Distinctions between the four types of sociology we've been discussing are not watertight. It is common for individual sociologists to engage in more than one area, even on a single piece of work. Criticisms can flow easily from people who see themselves as practitioners of one form only. Professional sociologists criticize critical sociologists for low professional standards and for being little more than 'troublemaking radicals'. Critical sociologists accuse professional sociologists of being far too conservative, and of taking small bites of data and overanalyzing them, dazzling their reading audience with statistical science while actually saying little. Public sociologists could accuse professional sociologists of speaking only to a very small audience made up exclusively of peers; at the same time they accuse the policy sociologists of selling out their values to corporate and government 'pimps'. But policy and professional sociologists can counter-accuse the public sociologists of being in it just for the publicity, of being no more than 'media whores', 'pop-sociologists', or mere popularizers—a dirty term among many in the academy.

● ● ● ● ● ● ● ● ● ● ● ● ● ● ● ● ● ● ● ●

What do YOU think?

1. Consider the four types of sociology we've just discussed: professional, critical, policy-based, and public. Where do you imagine your sociology instructor would fall in this scheme? (His or her page on the college/university website might give you a clue, or you could simply ask.) Where would you place the authors of this book?

2. Have you ever seen or heard a broadcast interview with a sociologist? If so, what subject matter was being discussed? If you haven't, why do you think this is so? (Think in terms related not to you personally—your radio-listening habits, for instance—but to the way sociological topics are treated in the media.)

● ● ● ● ● ● ● ● ● ● ● ● ● ● ● ● ● ● ● ●

The Development of Canadian Sociology

While there is no distinctly Canadian way to carry out sociological research and practice, the way the discipline developed in this country and its primary focal points are unique. The relationship between French and English, the development of the Canadian West, the connection between class and ethnicity, and a close working relationship with anthropology have all been fundamental to the development of a Canadian perspective on sociology.

As we will see in later chapters, sociology began in this country long before the establishment of departments of sociology in Canadian universities and colleges. Herbert Ames, Leon Gérin, James S. Woodsworth, Carrie Derick, and Colin McKay are just a few of those who practised sociology in Canada before it became firmly established as an academic discipline. However, we will begin here with Canadian sociology as it developed in post-secondary institutions across the country.

McGill University: Dawson, Hughes, and Miner

The first professional, institutionalized sociologist in Canada was **Carl Addington Dawson** (1887–1964). Born in Prince Edward Island, Dawson completed his MA and PhD at the University of Chicago. In 1922, shortly after joining the faculty at McGill, he founded the university's Department of Sociology, an accomplishment that was not achieved without opposition. Senior administrators worried about the left-wing political leanings of sociologists (they still do), and academics in other departments did not want their scholarly territory infringed upon. Dawson succeeded in spite of these objections, and McGill's remained the only independent department of sociology until 1961.

Dawson's work reflected two elements of early Canadian sociology: the **social gospel** movement and hands-on social work. The social gospel movement developed as an attempt by people trained for the ministry to apply Christian principles of human welfare to the treatment of social,

The Point Is...   The Sociologist as Hero: C. Wright Mills

In my first year of university, I was an English major. I wanted to be a writer. But studying English did not appeal to me the way I had hoped it would. Sociology did. The sociologist who captured my imagination that first year was the American C. Wright Mills. He took on the rich and the powerful and challenged his conservative colleagues and his country's government in the staid and stuffy 1950s. His public critique of American society caught the attention of the FBI, who started a file on him. He rode a motorcycle to work, dressed in plaid shirts, old jeans, and work boots. Mills became my first sociologist hero. I can also say that I am two degrees of intellectual separation from him: a teacher of mine was a student of his. (This makes readers of this book and students I've taught his intellectual great-grandchildren.)

During his lifetime Mills published seven books (in addition to others that he co-authored). These include two trilogies and an important stand-alone volume that gave its name to a key characteristic of the very best sociologists and sociology students: *The Sociological Imagination* (1959). His first trilogy, a study of the three main classes in the United States, comprises *The New Man of Power: America's Labor Leaders* (1948), *White Collar: The American Middle Classes* (1951), and *The Power Elite* (1956). It was the last of these that was the most influential of the three. Originally called 'The High and Mighty:

The American Upper Classes' before being given its less inflammatory title, it found a wide and varied audience that included the then young Cuban revolutionary Fidel Castro, who, after he had overthrown the American-backed and possibly Mafia-supported dictator Fulgencio Batista, invited Mills to visit so they could discuss his ideas—something few Americans, sociologists or not, have ever done. After the book was translated into Russian, Mills was asked to visit Moscow.

Mills's second trilogy consists of three best-selling, mass-marketed paperbacks. The first of these was *The Causes of World War Three* (1958), an impassioned plea for an end to the nuclear arms race. The second, and most successful, was *Listen Yankee* (1960). The product of two weeks of interviewing in Cuba and six weeks of writing, it was written in the style of an open letter to Americans from a Cuban revolutionary trying to communicate what life had been like under Batista, what harm American policies were having on the people of Cuba, and what accomplishments in education and health care Castro had achieved during his short term in power. Of the more than 450,000 copies printed, over 370,000 were sold in Mills's lifetime. The third book of the trilogy, *The Marxists* (1962), though it was less popular, was nevertheless translated into four languages. Collectively, Mills's works have been translated into 23 different languages.

---

medical, and psychological ills brought on by industrialization and unregulated capitalism in Canada, the United States, Britain, Germany, and other European countries during the late nineteenth century. Out of the social gospel movement came, among other things, the Social Service Council of Canada (1912), which through various churches carried out the first sociological surveys of Canadian cities, and, in 1914, sponsored the first national meeting to address various social problems.

Dawson's affinity with the social gospel movement was natural—his first degree from the University of Chicago was in divinity—but his inspiration to become involved early on in social work came as well from the methods and philosophy of the 'Chicago School' of sociology. The Chicago School put an emphasis on going out into

communities—what University of Chicago sociologist Robert Park called 'living laboratories'—to observe them. Dawson took this approach and, with his students, applied it to the living laboratory of Montreal. Their research was given a jump-start in 1929, when they were awarded a $110,000 Rockefeller Foundation grant to study unemployment in the city.

That same year, Dawson and Warren E. Gettys became the first Canadians to write a sociology textbook. The text was an instant success: it was adopted by over 150 colleges and universities across North America within a year, and went through three editions (1929, 1935, and 1948). While there was not a great deal of Canadian content, it helped legitimize the study and practice of sociology in Canada. Dawson went on to study

In 1948, in a letter written in praise of a book he had read, Mills coined the term **sociological poetry**:

It is a style of experience and expression that reports social facts and at the same time reveals their human meanings. As a reading experience, it stands somewhere between the thick facts and thin meanings of the ordinary sociological monograph and those art forms which in their attempts at meaningful reach do away with the facts, which they consider as anyway merely an excuse for imagination construction. (Mills and Mills 2000: 111)

A few years later, Mills recast this statement as more of a challenge to sociologists. Responding to a question about sociology writing—specifically, whether or not it could be improved—Mills wrote:

It doesn't look good for two reasons: First, there is no real writing tradition in sociology, as there is, for example, in history. It just doesn't exist. Second, the field is now split into statistical stuff and heavy duty theoretical bullshit. In both cases, there's no writing but only turgid polysyllabic slabs of stuff. So, because that is now the field, no men get trained, have models to look up to; there is no aspiration to write well. (Mills and Mills 2000: 154–5)

While Mills himself, together with a handful of others, has disproved the first point, the second critique stands. Sociologists (and sociology students), your duty is clear: prove him wrong!

Photo: © Yaroslava Mills

Consider this photo of C. Wright Mills: does he look like an educator to you? Why or why not?

and write extensively on settlement patterns on the frontier in western Canada.

Another figure vital to the development of sociology at McGill was **Everett C. Hughes** (1897–1983), whose influence was felt not just in Quebec but also in the rest of Canada and in the United States. Like Dawson, a graduate of the University of Chicago, Hughes joined the sociology department at McGill in 1927 a firm believer in the Chicago School's commitment to community research. For more than the 10 years that he spent in Canada Hughes focused on what he termed the 'ethnic division of labour', a situation that enabled English Canadians to rise above French Canadians, creating a disparity that he badly wished to correct. Out of this research came his classic work, *French Canada in Transition*

(1943; see the chapter on 'Race and Ethnicity'). By the time the book was published, Hughes had already returned to the States to take a position in the faculty of his alma mater. In recognition of his important role in the development of Canadian sociology, Hughes was made an Honorary Life President of the Canadian Sociology and Anthropology Association.

Horace Miner (1912–1993) was another American sociologist who put the study of French Canada at the forefront of the Canadian sociology movement. As a graduate student at the University of Chicago, he came to Quebec to study the parish of St Denis. His book *St Denis: A French-Canadian Parish* (1939) shows the blurred distinction between sociology and anthropology in Canada. His work is best described as an **ethnography**, a study of a community based on extensive fieldwork, whose primary research activities include direct observation and talking with the people observed. Ethnography is the main research method used in social anthropology. Miner described the rural peasants and farmers of his study as a **folk society**, following the model of University of Chicago anthropologist Robert Redfield, who coined the term. The close connection between sociology and anthropology can still be seen today in some Canadian universities where the two disciplines are joined in the same department.

The University of Toronto: Harold Innis and S.D. Clark

As sociology was developing along a particular line at McGill, a very different tradition, that of **political economy**, was emerging at the University of Toronto. Political economy is an interdisciplinary approach involving sociology, political science, economics, law, anthropology, and history. It began in the eighteenth century and looks primarily at the relationship between politics and the economics of the production, distribution, and consumption of goods. It is often Marxist in nature, pointing to the tensions that arise in the extraction and distribution of goods.

A Canadian pioneer in the field of political economy was **Harold Innis** (1894–1952), who joined the University of Toronto in 1920. Innis was more an economic historian than a sociologist, but his work has exerted a strong influence on Canadian sociology. He argued that the availability of **staples**—resources such as fish, fur, minerals, and wheat—shaped the economic and social development of Canada.

Innis was also a mentor to the first person hired at the university specifically as a sociologist, **Samuel Delbert Clark** (1910–2003). Born in Alberta, S.D. Clark received his first two degrees from the University of Saskatchewan before joining the Department of Political Economy at the University of Toronto in 1938. Sociology remained a branch of that department until 1963, when it became a stand-alone department with Clark as its chair. Summarizing his influence in comments in a book published in Clark's honour, Deborah Harrison wrote:

The importance of S.D. Clark within the development of Canadian sociology is universally recognized. Clark's publications span more than forty prolific years, with at least the first fifteen occurring when almost no other sociologists were writing in Canada; he is generally acknowledged as the father of the Canadian approach to the discipline. . . . For reasons of both his scholarly engagement and his articulation of a 'Canadian' sociology, Clark is the most important sociologist Canada has yet produced. (1999)

Clark can be called a sociological historian. To get a sense of what we mean by this, consider the chapter headings of his book *The Developing Canadian Community* (1962):

- Social Organization and the Changing Structure of the Community
- The Farming–Fur-Trade Society of New France
- The Rural Village Society of the Maritimes
- The Backwoods Society of Upper Canada
- The Gold-Rush Society of British Columbia and the Yukon
- The Prairie Wheat-Farming Frontier and the New Industrial City
- Religious Organization and the Rise of the Canadian Nation, 1850–85
- The Religious Sect in Canadian Politics
- The Religious Sect in Canadian Economic Development
- The Religious Influence in Canadian Society
- The Canadian Community and the American Continental System
- Education and Social Change in Canada
- The Frontier in the Development of the Canadian Political Community
- Sociology, History, and the Problem of Social Change
- History and the Sociological Method

As you can see, Clark, like others who would be considered sociological historians, traced the development of different societies, looking in particular at how the resources available to early settlers shaped the growth of regional communities.

Fundamentally missing from the work of both Innis and Clark are the themes of class and

Photo: AP Photo/Kirk Hirota

In 1995, three patrons of this tavern in the agricultural Yakim valley in Washington State were ejected for speaking Spanish. The sign hanging above the door clearly states the position of the tavern's management: 'IN THE U.S.A. IT'S—ENGLISH, OR ADIOS, AMIGO. Is this attitude more characteristic of a cultural mosaic or a cultural melting pot?

ethnicity, which are so persistent in much of Canadian sociology today. These themes received their definitive treatment in what is generally recognized as the best-known work of Canadian sociology, *The Vertical Mosaic: An Analysis of Social Class and Power in Canada* (1965), by **John Porter** (1921–1979). Porter joined the faculty of Carleton University in 1949, becoming the university's first full-time appointment in sociology; he remained at Carleton for most of his career. The title of his book plays on the term **cultural mosaic**, a metaphor frequently used to characterize Canada's multicultural society, especially in contrast to the **melting pot** image often used to portray the more assimilated society of the United States. A mosaic is a type of artwork composed of many small tiles that lend different colours to the picture. A society that is a cultural mosaic is therefore one 'in which racial, ethnic, and religious groups maintain a distinct identity, rather than being absorbed into a "melting pot"' (Lundy and

Warme 1990: 583). By contrast, a melting pot, Lundy and Warme explain, involves the 'rapid assimilation of recent immigrants into their new society, . . . a longstanding ideal underlying immigration policy in the United States' (Lundy and Warme 1990: 586).

Porter coined the term **vertical mosaic** to describe the situation he observed in Canadian society, in which systemic discrimination produces a hierarchy of racial, ethnic, and religious groups. To stay within the metaphor of the mosaic, we can say that Porter's study found that the different tiles were stacked and not placed evenly. White, Anglo-Saxon, Protestant tiles were on top, followed by French-Canadian tiles, the tiles of the more successful ethnic groups (e.g. Jewish, Chinese, and Italian), and finally those of everyone else, with the racially marginalized groups at the bottom. Porter concluded that ethnicity and ranking were linked. The impact of Porter's landmark work can be seen in the number of sociology books and articles that draw upon the title. These include such books as Roberta Hamilton's *Gendering the Vertical Mosaic: Feminist Perspectives on Canadian Society* (1996) and *The Vertical Mosaic Revisited*, edited by Richard Helmes-Hayes and James Curtis (1998), as well as articles like 'The Vertical Mosaic in Later Life: Ethnicity and Retirement in Canada' (in *The Journals of Gerontology*, 1986) by Yameen Abu-Laban.

The Growth of Sociology in Canada

In 1958, there were fewer than twenty sociology professors in Canada, teaching in just nine universities (Clark 1976: 120). Sociology did not become a significant area of study and teaching in Canada until the 1960s and 1970s, as baby-boomers entered universities and colleges. The growth of sociology during that time is astounding. Hiller and Di Luzio, for example, report that 'the University of Alberta had no sociology majors in 1956–57, but a year later had nine, followed by 24 (1957–58), 44 (1959–60), and 62 (1960–61). The number of majors there reached a peak for the twentieth century at 776 in 1987' (Hiller and Di Luzio 2001: 490).

During this era of growth in sociology study and research, most of the sociologists hired to teach in Canadian post-secondary institutions were from the United States and, to a lesser degree, Britain. Of those with doctorates teaching sociology and anthropology in Canada in 1967, 72 per cent had PhDs from the US, 10 per cent from Britain, and only 6 per cent from Canada (Gallagher and Lambert 1971: vii). In 1973–4, 45 per cent of the full-time sociology faculty in Canada was made up of non-Canadians (Hofley 1992: 106). This should not be surprising given that only 22 doctorates in sociology were conferred at Canadian universities between 1924 and 1967 (Gallagher and Lambert 1971: vi).

The lack of Canadian sociologists meant that sociology textbooks, dominated by issues close to the hearts of authors who had grown up or studied sociology outside of Canada, lacked a Canadian perspective. When John Hofley was hired to teach sociology at Carleton University in 1966, he 'found very little about Canada in the sociology texts that were available' (Hofley 1992: 104). It was not uncommon that a textbook used in Canada would be exclusively American. The 1970s saw a big movement to 'Canadianize' sociology textbooks. Today most introductory sociology textbooks used in Canadian schools are either Canadian in origin or 'Canadianized' versions of American textbooks.

● ● ● ● ● ● ● ● ● ● ● ● ● ● ● ● ● ● ● ●

What do YOU think?

How might an introductory sociology textbook written in Canada be different from a 'Canadianized' one originally written in the US?

● ● ● ● ● ● ● ● ● ● ● ● ● ● ● ● ● ● ● ●

Summary

So what have we covered so far? We've tried to give you a sense of what sociology looks like—enough that you could pick it out of a police lineup of social sciences. You likely won't have a really good sense of what sociology *is* until you've reached the end of the book. You've learned a bit about what our approach to writing sociology is like, making this, ideally, a textbook not like the others. We have introduced you to some of the main players that will strut the stage of this textbook in the chapters that follow: Marx, Durkheim, Weber—three of the modern discipline's founders (whose views, incidentally, are often the subject of 'compare and contrast' assignments on tests and exams); Goffman, the Canadian; Foucault and Smith (two more subjects for comparative questions); and Mead. Others we have merely mentioned here, but you will be more fully introduced to them in later chapters.

In addition to familiarizing you with some of the discipline's key figures, we've shown you two different ways of categorizing sociology—by approach and by audience. References to these categories turn up frequently throughout the book. Finally, we have added some Canadian flavour to our overview of the discipline's history. Expect plenty more Timbits and maple syrup in the chapters to come.

Questions for Critical Review

1. Outline the differences and similarities between sociology and other social science disciplines, such as anthropology, political science, women's studies, and Native history. What are some of the places where these disciplines intersect?
2. Identify the key ideas of Durkheim, Marx, and Weber as outlined in this chapter.
3. Distinguish between the structural-functional, conflict, and symbolic-interactionist approaches to sociology.
4. Distinguish between professional, critical, policy-based, and public sociology.
5. Articulate the basic ideas of Erving Goffman, Michel Foucault, and Dorothy Smith as outlined in this chapter.

Suggested Readings

Gutting, Gary (2005). *Foucault: A Very Short Introduction*. Oxford: Oxford UP.

Jacobsen, Michael Hviid, ed. *The Contemporary Goffman*. New York: Routledge, 2009.

Johnson, Allan G. (1997). *The Blackwell Dictionary of Sociology: A User's Guide to Sociological Language*. Oxford: Blackwell.

Kerr, Keith. *Postmodern Cowboy: C. Wright Mills and a New 21st Century Sociology*. Boulder, Colorado: Paradigm Publishers, 2009.

Smith, Dorothy. *The Everyday World as Problematic: A Feminist Sociology*. Boston: Northeastern University Press, 1989.

Turner, Stephen P., ed. (1996). *Social Theory and Sociology: The Classics and Beyond*. Oxford: Blackwell.

Suggested Websites

C. Wright Mills
www.genordell.com/stores/maison/CWMills.htm

Émile Durkheim (Robert Alum, University of Illinois)
www.relst.uiuc.edu/durkheim/

Karl Marx
www.marxists.org/archive/marx/

Max Weber (Albert Benschop, University of Amsterdam)
www.sociosite.net/topics/weber.php

Key Terms

- absolute poverty
- anomie
- best practices
- case study approach
- causation
- content analysis
- correlation
- cultural artifact (or event)
- deliberate restriction
- dependent variable

- descriptive categories
- direct correlation
- discourse analysis
- disjuncture
- ethnography
- experiential
- fact
- free-floating statistic
- genealogy
- hypothesis

- independent variable
- informant
- insider perspective
- institutional ethnography
- inverse correlation
- Low Income Cutoffs
- Low Income Measure
- Market Basket Measurement (MBM)
- narrative
- negative correlation

2

Social Research Methods

LEARNING OBJECTIVES

After reading this chapter, you should be able to

❯ understand the difference between fact, theory, and hypothesis;

❯ distinguish between qualitative and quantitative social research;

❯ recognize the defining aspects of the various qualitative research methods;

❯ discuss the importance of identifying the individual informant in ethnographic research;

❯ explain the importance of narratives to sociological research;

❯ identify the significance of operational definitions in quantitative research;

❯ explain and give examples of spurious reasoning; and

❯ discuss the connection between statistics and rhetoric.

- objective description
- operational definition
- Orientalism
- outsider perspective
- participant observation
- positive correlation
- positivism
- poverty
- poverty line

- psychoanalysis
- qualitative research
- quantitative research
- relative poverty
- research methodology
- ritualization
- ruling interests
- ruling relations
- semiotics

- semi-structured interview
- sign
- signified
- signifier
- spurious reasoning
- statistics
- systematic description
- theory
- third variable

- triangulation
- variable
- voice

Key Names
- Auguste Comte
- Sigmund Freud
- Frankfurt School
- Edward Said

Photo: iStockphoto.com/Mad Circles

^{FOR} Starters

Fact, Theory, Hypothesis, and Wondering Why People Speed Up When I Pass Them

It's easier to *observe* than it is to *explain*. I can observe that people speed up on the highway when I pass them, but I can't really explain why they do it. Is it because the bee-like buzz of my engine wakes them up from a semi-sleeping state? Or is it their competitive spirit that awakens when I—an aging hippie in an old minivan—pass them in their shiny, high-priced, high-powered vehicles?

I believe the idea that people speed up when I pass them is a **fact**: an observation that as far as can be known is true. This doesn't mean it happens all the time, though I have observed it often enough to call it at least a *tentative* fact. But if I want to use important qualifiers such as 'almost all of the time' or 'most of the time', or the easier to prove 'often' or 'frequently', then I have to find a way to quantify this fact—for example, by saying 'I passed 100 vehicles and 37 were observed to speed up.' I should also be more specific about the situation involved, by adding 'on Highway 50 northwest of Toronto; while driving in the slow lane, passing someone who is in the passing lane; while driving home from work, travelling north.' This is how I quantify and qualify my fact: by giving details about how often it occurs and under what conditions.

Now I need a theory. A **theory** is an attempt to explain a fact or observed phenomenon. My theory of why people speed up when I pass them is that I make them aware that they are travelling more slowly than they thought they were. My theory becomes a **hypothesis** when I set out to verify it by providing some kind of concrete test of its validity. What kind of test can I provide for my theory? Obviously I can't pull people over on the highway and ask them why they sped up when I passed them (I would love to have the power to do that). However, I could develop a questionnaire that depends on people's self-knowledge. First I might ask a question such as 'Do you frequently speed up when people pass you on a highway?' It might be followed by a multiple-choice question such as the following:

> What is your best explanation for speeding up when people pass you on a highway?
  a) Being passed makes me realize that I am driving slower than I thought.
  b) I do not like people passing me.
  c) I am very competitive.
  d) Other (explain).

> Then we would proceed to test the hypothesis. What steps would you take? Try jotting down some ideas now, then review the question once you've finished reading the chapter. We bet your perspective will have changed; then again, that's just a hypothesis to be tested.

Introduction

Nothing is more contentious in sociology than **research methodology**, the system of methods a researcher uses to gather data on a particular question. There is an old joke that goes like this:

Question: How many sociologists does it take to change a light bulb?
Answer: Twenty—one to change the light bulb and nineteen to question that person's methodology.

There is no single best way to do sociological research, and many researchers will combine several research methods in their work. In the sections that follow, we'll take a look at some of the different methods used in sociological research, pointing out the pluses and pitfalls of each one as we go.

Sociology's Positivist Tradition

It was the French philosopher **Auguste Comte** (1798–1857) who coined the word *sociology*. The basis of Comte's sociology was **positivism** (later called *logical positivism*), which involves a belief that the methods used to study the natural sciences (including experiment, measurement, and systematic observation) and the supposed objectivity of these methods can be applied just as well to the social sciences with no accommodation made for the biases, or any other aspects of the personal life (gender, age, ethnicity, etc.) of the social scientist. Although the positivist mode of thinking had a long run, many sociologists today do not believe it's possible for an 'outsider' to study a group objectively.

Insider versus Outsider Perspective

One way to contrast the different methods of sociology research is to look at the ways researchers treat the **insider** and **outsider perspectives**. In Comte's view, the outsider was the 'expert' and occupied a privileged position. Most of sociology's history reflects this privileging of the outsider perspective. Of the four audience-based types of sociology discussed in the previous chapter—professional, critical, policy-based, and public—policy sociology is the one tied most closely to the outside expert ideal.

By contrast, critical sociology, particularly feminist sociology, rates the insider view highly while questioning the presumed objectivity of positivism. Dorothy Smith's standpoint theory, which we introduced in the opening chapter, states that such social characteristics as gender, race, ethnicity, age, and sexual orientation will strongly condition the questions a sociologist asks as well as the answers he or she will receive. Michel Foucault, in the first volume of *The History of Sexuality*

(1978), criticized the outsider approach in his discussion of the intellectual model of the 'sexual confession'. According to this model, the subject being studied provides information that comes from his or her subjective experience. But this information is marginalized: it is not recognized as authentic knowledge until it has been interpreted by an 'objective' outsider who, by virtue of being an expert, is in the privileged position of deciding which parts of the account are true and which are fabricated or imagined. The subject is therefore not allowed to have a voice that is heard without translation from the outsider/expert. That means that important sociological messages get lost.

To get a better sense of how an outsider perspective can be flawed, imagine yourself as a sociologist studying a First Nations reserve. Taking an outsider approach, you conduct your study by looking only at various statistics, covering subjects such as unemployment, housing, and crime rate. Not including the voice of the people who live there means that you will miss key elements of interpretation. First, some definitions could be problematic. For instance, is a person who provides for his family when he hunts, traps, fishes, gathers plants for food and medicine, and cuts wood for home heating and cooking 'unemployed'? Technically (and in terms of mainstream Canadian culture) he is, as he does not have a 'job' that pays money. And how do you define 'overcrowding' or 'homelessness' without looking at the particular cultural practices and attitudes of the people you're studying? For example, according to the practice of family sharing, large families may own several dwellings in which individual family members can stay: they 'live' in several houses. If asked 'Who lives in this house?' the respondent might give the names of everyone who, over the course of a year, may spend time living in that house. On the other hand, some people spend a great deal of time in the bush. They are living in no house, so they could be called 'homeless'. Second point: typical statistical surveys of Aboriginal reserves leave unanswered the question of why so many people choose to live on reserves if there is so much unemployment, crime, and overcrowding compared with lower

Mohawk boys play lacrosse on a Six Nations reserve. Do you notice a difference in 'play' when it is constituted as a community activity versus a competitive sport?

Photo: Michael S. Yamashita/Corbis

rates in non-Native communities of comparable size. You need to observe the people you're studying in order to properly answer these questions; you need to hear the people's voice.

Brian Maracle is a Mohawk who left his home reserve when he was five years old but returned as an adult. *Back on the Rez: Finding the Way Back Home* (1996) is his account of the first year of his return to the Six Nations reserve near Brantford, Ontario. This reserve is very different in certain respects from the more troubled reserves—Davis Inlet and Grassy Narrows, for example—that are commonly cited in sociology textbooks. The people of the Six Nations reserve have lived there for over 200 years, since the land (then recently acquired by the British government from the local Ojibwa) was granted to them for siding with the British during the American Revolution. It includes good farmland, which the Six Nations Iroquois, who were farmers long before European contact, were able to take full advantage of. In the introduction to *Back on the Rez*, Maracle points out that reserves can be considered homelands because they function as refuges from non-Aboriginal society:

> The reserves mean many things. . . . On one level, these postage-stamp remnants of our original territories are nagging reminders of the echoing vastness of what we have lost. On another, they are the legacy and bastion of our being. They are a refuge, a prison, a madhouse, a fortress, a birthplace, a Mecca, a resting-place, Home-Sweet-Home, Fatherland and Motherland rolled into one. (Maracle 1996: 3)

Maracle writes of the importance of the reserve as the home of the Mohawk elders, who interpret past traditions and adapt them to the present. In this way, he emphasizes that the reserve is very much the home of Aboriginal culture.

Of course, it is important to see that reserves are not always homeland to everyone. They can be places where men with physical strength and political power can oppress women and sexually abuse children. While recognizing the insider's view is key to effective sociological research, it's important to remember that a range of voices have to be heard.

Our position here is that complete objectivity is impossible whenever one human being studies others. However, complete subjectivity can be blind. A judicious balance of insider and outsider vision is the ideal.

● ● ● ● ● ● ● ● ● ● ● ● ● ● ● ● ● ● ●

What do YOU think?

Think of a community that you are particularly involved in—a club or team, a religious group, your college or university residence, or some other. How easily could it be studied by an outsider looking only at statistics? Which insider voices from your community would an outsider need to listen to in order to get an accurate picture of it?

● ● ● ● ● ● ● ● ● ● ● ● ● ● ● ● ● ● ●

Qualitative versus Quantitative Research

An ongoing debate in sociology concerns the relative merits of qualitative research and quantitative research. **Quantitative research** focuses on social elements that can be counted or measured, which can therefore be used to generate statistics. It often involves working with questionnaires and polls. **Qualitative research** involves the close examination of characteristics that cannot be counted or measured. Unlike quantitative research, which is typically used to find the patterns governing whole structures or systems, communities, and so on, qualitative research may be used to study those individual cases that don't fit into the larger model.

And so the debate begins. Proponents of quantitative research accuse qualitative researchers of relying on data that is 'soft', 'anecdotal', 'too subjective', or 'merely literary'. In turn, champions of the qualitative approach dismiss quantitative researchers as soulless 'number crunchers' operating under the delusion that it is possible for humans to study other humans with complete objectivity. Of course, it's wrong to think that the two methods are mutually exclusive. Good quantitative researchers know that, despite its close historical connection with positivism, their research always has a subjective component to it and always involves choice and some personal bias. Qualitative researchers, similarly, can learn to benefit from using quantitative data occasionally. We'll now take a closer look at different methods of qualitative and quantitative research.

Qualitative Research

When we think of qualitative research, we think of its subjectivity. Qualitative research permits—in fact, often encourages—subjectivity on the part of both researcher and research subject in a way that 'hard' data-oriented quantitative research does not. Among the various qualitative methods are **ethnography** and the **case study approach**, which differ mainly in their breadth of focus. The former takes a broader view by attempting to describe the entirety of a culture, while the latter adopts a narrower focus to study individual cases.

Ethnography

Gephart captures the essence of ethnography when he describes it as relying on

> direct observation and extended field research to produce a thick, naturalistic description of a people and their culture. Ethnography seeks to uncover the symbols and categories members of the given culture use to interpret their world. . . . (Gephart 1988: 16)

A classic example of the ethnographic approach in sociology is William Whyte's *Street-Corner Society: The Social Structure of an Italian Slum*. Beginning early in 1937, Whyte spent three-and-a-half years living in the neighbourhood he called 'Cornerville', following a standard research practice of assigning a fictitious name to the community studied in order to preserve the anonymity of the subjects in the published writeup. During his time in Cornerville, Whyte lived for 18 months with an Italian-American family. His methodology involved **semi-structured interviews**—informal, face-to-face interviews designed to cover specific topics without the rigid structure of a questionnaire but with more structure than an open interview—and **participant observation**, which entails both observing people as an outsider would and actively participating in the various activities of the studied people's lives. Participant observation enables

the researcher to achieve something resembling an insider's view. Researchers engaged in ethnography typically depend as well on **informants**, insiders who act as interpreters or intermediaries while helping the researcher become accepted by the community studied. Whyte's informant was a gang leader in his late twenties who went by the name 'Doc'. Whyte was introduced to Doc by the latter's social worker in a meeting he describes in the book:

> I began by asking him ['Doc'] if the social worker had told him about what I was trying to do.
>
> 'No, she just told me that you wanted to meet me and that I should like to meet you.'
>
> Then I went into a long explanation. . . . I said that I had been interested in congested city districts in my college study but had felt very remote from them. I hoped to study the problems in such a district. I felt I could do very little as an outsider. Only if I could get to know the people and learn their problems first hand would I be able to gain the understanding I needed. (Whyte 1955: 291)

When Whyte stated his research needs, Doc replied:

> 'Well, any nights you want to see anything, I'll take you around. I can take you to the joints—gambling joints—I can take you around to the street corners. Just remember that you're my friend. That's all they need to know. I know these places, and, if I tell them that you're my friend, nobody will bother you. You just tell me what you want to see, and we'll arrange it.' (Whyte 1955: 291)

Doc and Whyte would discuss Whyte's research interests and findings to the point where Doc became 'in a very real sense, a collaborator in the research' (Whyte 1955: 301). Whyte, meanwhile, learned to speak Italian so that he could talk directly to the older generation from Italy. He participated in the second generation's activities of going to 'gambling joints', bowling, and playing baseball and cards. He called his work 'participatory action research' because he wanted his research to lead to actions that would improve the lives of the people studied.

A soup kitchen in the basement of a Montreal church in the 1930s.

Photo: Library and Archives Canada/PA-168131

Whyte's ethnography was typical of the sociology work then being done at the University of Chicago (where Whyte earned his PhD). The American psychologist John Dollard adopted this approach for a five-month study of race relations in a small Mississippi town, the results of which he presented in *Caste and Class in a Southern Town* (1937). In Canada, Whyte's study influenced Carl Dawson's work with Prairie communities, as well as the Quebec community studies of Everett Hughes (*French Canada in Transition*, 1943) and Horace Miner (*St Denis: A French-Canadian Parish*, 1939 and 1963).

Institutional Ethnography

Institutional ethnography is a relatively new method of research, based on the theories of Dorothy Smith. This method of research, as outlined by Marie Campbell and Frances Gregor in *Mapping Social Relations: A Primer in Doing Institutional Ethnography* (2002), differs from traditional sociological research in that it does not reflect the view that a neutral stance is necessarily more scientific

than an approach that explicitly involves 'taking sides' (Campbell and Gregor 2002: 48).

Institutional ethnography recognizes that any institution or organization can be seen as having two sides, each associated with a different kind of data. One side represents **ruling interests**: the interests of the organization, particularly its administration, or else the interests of those who are dominant in society. The data associated with this side are text-based, comprising the written rules and practices of the institution. When the workers in the institution follow these rules and practices, they are activating **ruling relations**— that is, they are helping to serve the needs of the organization, often at the cost of their clients and/ or themselves.

The other side of an organization is that of the informant. In this context, an informant is someone who works in the institution outside of management or the administration, the upholders of ruling interests. The data associated with the informant's side is **experiential**, based on the experience of the informant. Institutional ethnography recognizes that there is a **disjuncture**, or separation, between the knowledge produced from the perspectives of these two sides. In pointing out this disjuncture, institutional ethnographers generate information that they hope will lead to institutional change.

Schools offer a good example of the kind of organization that institutional ethnographers study. Alison Griffith, who currently teaches at York University, asserts that teachers rely on parents (typically mothers) to get school children to do the work and acquire the skills necessary to succeed at school. Campbell and Gregor refer to this reliance on parents as 'downloading educational work' (2002: 43), a practice that serves the ruling interests—those of boards of education and provincial governments—who can then spend less on schools and teachers. Teachers and parents, by complying with the demands of school administrators, are activating ruling relations. At the same time, they are also biasing the system in favour of students from middle-class households, whose parents are more likely to have the resources (including books, a good study space, and time) to best serve this end. Lower-class students are poorly served by the system, as they are more dependent on the school and its resources alone. The problem is made worse in provinces like Ontario, where it has recently become illegal for school boards to pass deficit budgets. Local boards, meeting the ruling interests of the provincial government, have been forced to close pools and cut music and athletic programs, putting the onus for children's health and recreation onto the parents. So there's a second disjuncture—between the provincial government and its boards—in addition to the one between boards and administrators and parents/children. This is the kind of useful finding that institutional ethnography can produce.

Another common subject for institutional ethnography is the hospital. Campbell and Gregor have examined the 'unofficial' hospital duties that nurses perform. These duties include tasks that doctors are responsible for, at least officially. When nurses take on the responsibility for performing these tasks, it keeps the system working smoothly by ensuring that patients' needs are met efficiently. But as the authors point out, nurses who rise to meet the ruling interests may be putting themselves at risk:

They go round in circles fixing the flaws in abstracted (textual) organization of patient care and then cover their tracks in accordance with the traditional gender regime [i.e. in which doctors are typically male and nurses typically female]. When the work they do is not part of the official and textual organization of nursing, it tends to be overlooked, thus not attributable to them as their knowledge, judgement or action. . . . [T]his may create even more trouble for nurses. When it appears that 'the system' runs efficiently on the basis of abstract information, they may find their jobs being cut. (Campbell and Gregor 2002: 21)

● ● ● ● ● ● ● ● ● ● ● ● ● ● ● ● ● ● ●

What do YOU think?

1. Consider the 'sides' involved in institutional ethnography. Which side do you think institutional researchers typically take?

2. Who should be responsible for ensuring that children get the exercise they need: school boards and the province, or parents?

3. According to Campbell and Gregor, how does the extra work nurses do make it more likely that nursing jobs might be lost?

● ● ● ● ● ● ● ● ● ● ● ● ● ● ● ● ● ● ●

The Case Study Approach

British sociologist Gordon Marshall describes the case study approach as

[a] research design that takes as its subject a single case or a few selected examples of a social entity—such as communities, social groups, employers, events, life-histories, families, work teams, roles, or relationships—and employs a variety of methods to study them. . . . Case-studies include descriptive reports on typical, illustrative, or deviant examples; descriptions of good practice in policy research; evaluations of policies after implementation in an organization; studies that focus on extreme or strategic cases; the rigorous test of a well-defined hypothesis through the use of carefully selected contrasting cases; and studies of natural experiments. (Marshall 1998: 56)

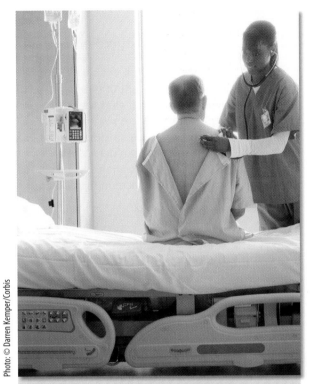

Photo: © Darren Kemper/Corbis

How would each of these two people tell the story of what is going on at this moment? How would each of their narratives add to the story of a sociology of health?

The case study approach is often used to identify and describe **best practices**—strategies with a proven history of achieving desired results more effectively or consistently than similar methods used in the past by a particular organization or currently by other organizations in the same industry. The case study typically begins by introducing an organization or department that exemplifies the best practices under review, before describing the practices in terms of the organization's success. The case study is often geared to finding out whether certain best practices can be applied with comparable success elsewhere in the organization or industry.

The case study in the box on pages 42 and 43 describes policing in a First Nations community. Aboriginal communities generally did not police themselves until the early 1990s, when the federal government put enabling legislation in place to allow band councils of individual Aboriginal communities to establish their own police services, once they had signed a tripartite agreement with the federal and provincial or territorial governments.

Narratives

The **narrative** is perhaps the purest form of the insider view. Narratives are the stories peoples tell about themselves, their situations, and the others around them, and they have long been part of sociology. For example, narratives figured prominently in W.I. Thomas and Florian Znaiecki's five-volume work *The Polish Peasant in Europe and America* (1918–20): of its 2,200 pages, 800 were dedicated to letters, autobiographical accounts, and other narrative documents. Still, the positivism of early sociology and the discipline's more recent emphasis on statistical evidence kept narrative study in a minor role in sociological research until the last 20 years. In 1993, H.R. Maines referred to the growing interest in narratives in a number of different disciplines, including sociology, as 'narrative's moment'. He saw in this trend a dual focus for sociological study, aimed at both examining the narratives of the usual subjects of study and at the same time 'viewing sociologists as narrators and thereby inquiring into what they do to and with their and other people's narratives' (Maines 1993: 17). He suggested 10 propositions on which to base a new narrative sociology:

1. Since all socialized humans are storytellers, they are always in a potential storytelling situation when interacting with or encountering others.
2. The vast majority of all speech acts and self-representations contain at least some elements of narratives.
3. Variation in situation, audience, individual perspective, and power/authority relations will produce the universal condition of multiple versions of narrated events.
4. Narratives and narrative occasions are always potential sites of conflict and competition as well as of co-operation and consensus.
5. All narratives are potentially rational accounts, but because of inherent human ambiguity and variation in linguistic competence, all narratives are ultimately incomplete.
6. Narratives exist at various levels of scale, ranging from the personal to the institutional to the cultural; they exist for varying lengths of time; and they inevitably change.

The Point Is...

Case Study of a Best Practice:
Kitigan Zibi Anishnabeg First Nation Policing

Located about 130 kilometres north of Ottawa, Kitigan Zibi, with a registered population of 2,746 (as of May 2009), is the largest of the nine communities that make up the Algonquin Nation in Quebec. The community first had its own policing services in 1981, when, like other Quebec First Nations, it began operating a community police force under the auspices of the Amerindian Police Service (the APS). The APS is usually seen as a failure by First Nations in Quebec, owing mainly to the fact that Aboriginal officers were given limited, second-class roles as 'special constables'. In 1985, the Kitigan Zibi community moved ahead of other Aboriginal communities by transferring police services to its own independent force.

Following the introduction of the federal First Nation Policing Policy in April 1992, the community entered into a three-year tripartite agreement that allowed the Kitigan Zibi Anishinabeg Police Department (KZAPD) to become a fully functional force, with powers equivalent to those of any non-Native force in Canada. This agreement was renegotiated in March 1995. By 2002, the KZAPD had a chief of police, five full-time officers, and one part-time officer. Community satisfaction with their work has been high. In a survey conducted in 2002, a remarkable 91 per cent of the members of the community surveyed felt that the KZAPD was the best police organization to meet the needs of the community. This compares favourably to the 55 per cent of community stakeholders who, in a First Nations Chiefs of Police Association survey, felt the self-administered police services in their communities were effective.

There are four keys to the success of the KZAPD; unfortunately, two of these keys are unique to the Kitigan Zibi community and cannot be replicated in most other First Nation communities. First, Kitigan Zibi has a very stable political environment. At the time of the study, the chief councillor of the band had been in the position for over 20 years, and during that time there had been few changes in the makeup of the band council. Further, there were no apparent political factions within the community, making it unlike many First Nations communities. Second, there have been no major clashes between the provincial government and Kitigan Zibi, putting it in the minority in Quebec. Largely because of this lack of conflict, the KZAPD has a reasonably harmonious relationship with the Quebec provincial police, a rarity for a First Nations force in Quebec.

7. All social science data are already interpreted data; the uninterpreted datum does not exist.

8. All sociological facts are narrated facts insofar as they have been processed through some form of story structure that renders events as factual.

9. The act of data collection is an act of entering respondents' lives that are partly formed by still unfolding stories. Therefore, in the name of honesty, research subjects will likely tell different stories about the same thing at different times and to different people.

10. A major implication of the above nine propositions is that sociology can only be a science of interpretations and to some extent must constitute itself as an interpretive science. (Maines 1993)

The inclusion of narrative in research is important because it can give voice to people who do not usually get to speak directly in research. **Voice** is the expression of *a* (not *the*) viewpoint that comes from occupying a particular social location (determined by factors including gender, 'race' or ethnicity, sexual orientation, class, professional or academic status, and so on).

Consider the two narratives on pages 44 and 45. Both give voice to viewpoints that are not often heard. In the first, a young Muslim college student talks about life in Canada. His voice is different from the voice of an older person of a different ethnic or religious background. It is also different from the voices of other Muslims—those of young women, for instance, or of local religious leaders. It is not 'the official view', normal or abnormal, representative or strange, but it speaks a truth because it is what the speaker

Two remaining keys to the KZAPD's success offer lessons for other police forces operating in Native (and non-Native) communities to learn from. One is the strong relationship between the KZAPD and the youth of the community. In 1995, the KZAPD took part in a pilot project with Aboriginal youths aged between 12 and 24, who were paired with police officers to ride in cruisers, observe police duties first-hand, and visit the homes of their police mentors. Commenting on the mentoring experience, one officer said, 'I took great pride in seeing the barriers fall and the sense of openness that developed in our communication' (First Nations Policing Update, July 1995, #3). In 1996, Chief of Police Gordon MacGregor stressed

> [t]he importance of being among the people, being visible and approachable especially to the youth and young children. . . . [P]eople see you as being human and as a father, not just as a police figure. (Stewart 1996)

The final key is the KZAPD's dedication to training. One condition of the 1992 tripartite agreement signed with federal and provincial governments was that constables already in the force would earn the basic training equivalency diploma.

This would enable the officers to assume powers equal to those of any other officer in the province of Quebec. All of the KZAPD's officers successfully completed the training. The chief of police even went beyond the qualifications required in the agreement, taking managerial courses for senior officers and additional courses offered at the Canadian Police College in Ottawa. When the Quebec Police Act was amended to include more training for provincial officers, the chief of police prepared a five-year forecast of the training needs of his force.

● ● ● ● ● ● ● ● ● ● ● ● ● ● ● ● ● ● ●

What do YOU think?

1. What indicates that the KZAPD is a good choice for a best practice case study?

2. What factors in the KZAPD's success cannot be readily replicated in other First Nation communities in Quebec? Which ones can?

3. The case study approach combines quantitative and qualitative research. How is that evident in the case study presented here?

● ● ● ● ● ● ● ● ● ● ● ● ● ● ● ● ● ● ●

Photo: All Canada Photos/John E. Marriott

A shawl dancer from the Piikani Nation (otherwise known as the Peigan of the Blackfoot Confederacy) dances a traditional plains dance on the Canadian Prairies at Head-Smashed-In Buffalo Jump National Historic Site and UNESCO World Heritage Site in Alberta. How might her narrative about the shawl dance differ from that of an outsider researcher?

thinks, and it does reflect his life's experience. We value it because it gives the non-Muslim reader a sense of what it is like to be a young Muslim living in Canada. In the second narrative, we hear the voice of a young Canadian of Palestinian background. We are all aware of the longstanding struggles involving Palestinians in the Middle East, but we hear considerably less about Palestinians living in Canada. Consider the factors that shape her point of view: her age, her gender, her ethnic background, her nationality, the site of her upbringing, her current status as a student, even the political climate at the time of writing all contribute to her unique perspective.

If you wanted a more detailed picture of what it's like to be a young Muslim or Palestinian living in Canada, you could gather additional narratives and tie them together through a process known as **triangulation**, which involves the use of at least three narratives, theoretical perspectives, or investigators to examine the same phenomenon.

No matter what your political stripe is, listening to the opinions of those whose views you don't share can be uncomfortable at best. For the person who holds opinions that are outside the political or cultural mainstream, expressing those views can be a very difficult and isolating experience. It's important to recognize that setting down a view you think may be unpopular requires courage. At the same time, recording and publishing the narratives of peoples whose political positions you don't agree with doesn't mean you accept what they say as 'right'. But whether you're expressing what you think is an unpopular view or recording a view you don't agree with, making such views known is an important step in generating

Telling It Like It Is

A STUDENT POV

Fasting

POINT OF VIEW

'Hey Moe, come join us for lunch.'
'I can't guys. I'm fasting.'
'Fasting, what's that?'

This passage, as awkward as it may sound, is quite normal and may be heard every year, asked by anyone and almost everyone. It bothers me to consider that the average person doesn't know what fasting for Muslims is. Fasting is an Islamic tradition practised for centuries, where a Muslim is subjected to no food or drink from sunrise to sunset. This is done to remind Muslims where we came from, as early people, to remind us that we started with nothing. It teaches us to value what we have and to value our gracious religion. There is fasting in almost every religion, yet the people who know the basic term of fasting don't know what type of fasting Muslims commit to. Many people [I have spoken to] were shocked to hear that during Ramadan [fasting month] you cannot only eat, but also drink. Many people thought that

water or gum was allowed in any fasting, but it isn't for the Muslim type of fasting. It surprises me when 26 per cent of the earth's population is Muslim, but non-Muslims don't know what our Eid is. Eid is a celebration. We have two main celebrations. One Eid comes after the last day of Ramadan and the second after the day of pilgrimage. Eid is as holy to Muslims as Christmas and Easter are to Christians.

When someone asks me what fasting is for Muslims, I reply with such fatigue from saying it over and over that I simply reply, 'Well, we (Muslims) basically can't eat or drink anything when the sun is up.' I know that my reply may offend many Muslims since I have not included any significance or talked about the reward given for performing the fast. I simply gave a quick answer because I get that question asked every year, by anyone and almost everyone.'

—Mohamed Abseh

understanding among others who might not agree with the position.

● ●

What do YOU think?

Consider an issue raised in one of the narratives you've just read. How do you think triangulation—the use of at least three narratives—would help you gain a different understanding of the issue?

● ●

Alternative Qualitative Research Methods

Psychoanalysis as Theory and Method

When we think of **Sigmund Freud** (1856–1939), psychology in general and **psychoanalysis** specifically come to mind. You will recall from Chapter 1 the difference between psychology and sociology:

Telling It Like It Is

A STUDENT POV

Palestinian by Culture, Canadian by Birth

POINT OF VIEW

My name is Nadine and I am Canadian-born, but Palestinian by culture. My father was born in Palestine and my mother was born in Egypt to Palestinian refugees. Nowadays, being a Palestinian or of Palestinian origin is quite difficult, especially when you're living in a so-called multicultural nation. I guess it's not as hard for me as it has been for my parents because I am Canadian-born and my parents came to Canada knowing little about the country or what would lie ahead. However, the difficult aspect in my life was that I grew up in a one-cultured town [the predominantly Italian-Canadian town of Woodbridge, in southern Ontario] which was extremely difficult for my brothers and I to fit in. As far as I am concerned, I have never been able to have any close relationship with anyone. Why? I guess that children needed a common ground in order to establish a relationship, and not possessing the same culture as those around me made my assimilation even more difficult. Within homogeneous groups one can be easily singled out and that happened to me. Furthermore, as I grew up it became harder for me to engage in any real relationship with boys or girls because my culture became stronger for me and as well for them, which made us even grow farther apart. Maybe it was because I didn't speak or dress like them, or because I was darker than them, it didn't matter, basically I was just different.

Entering college, it was a bit easier for me to make acquaintances, though I realized how uneducated and ignorant people could really be. It was particularly difficult for me after the events of 9/11 because, automatically, the Arab world would get blamed for it and most people, ignorant as they are, believed everything that the media's propaganda has been telling them. I was in college at that time and explaining to people my point of view was tremendously challenging. Media brainwash had its toll on the majority of those around me. Furthermore getting into debates with individuals about what's occurring in Palestine and my views as a Palestinian was almost impossible. Right now my oppressed and displaced people who have been legitimately resisting occupation since 1948 are the bad guys. Maybe in a couple of years it will be another group, but for me now it's hard because I'm still singled out by my friends and the media. Maybe it would be a little bit easier if individuals would become open-minded about what goes on in the world. Then people could understand who we are and who I am. Knowledge is responsibility and to most, responsibility is a heavy burden to take. It is pretty sad what's going on in the 21st century that people like me, Canadian-born, have difficulties growing up because of who they are and where they're from!

—Nadine Dahdah

psychology focuses on the individual, while sociology generally deals with larger segments of society. Psychoanalysis, though, despite being psychological and highly theoretical, has become a useful research tool for sociologists.

What makes the work of Freud and contemporary neo-Freudian psychoanalysts interesting to sociologists is its potential universality (although sociologists must also be sensitive to the possibility of this being another example of a European perspective sold as universal). Freud believed that childhood developmental stages (which he identified as the *oral*, *anal*, *phallic*, *latency*, and *genital* stages) and the formation of *self* (comprising *id*, *ego*, and *superego*) were culturally universal concepts. And, while they focus on the individual, they also consider the individual's relationship to society. Sociologists, rather than looking at the individual, use psychoanalytic categories and concepts to examine society at a cultural level (Chaitin 1996).

To see how psychoanalysis can be used to examine broader social and cultural institutions, let's turn our attention to architecture. Ian Craib notes that 'crucial aspects of psychoanalysis are concerned with areas of human life that are often manifested in art, literature and religion' (1989: 11). Craib's observation can be extended to architecture: using psychoanalysis as a methodological tool, we can examine various buildings within a larger cultural context. For instance, Toronto's CN Tower, only recently surpassed as the world's largest free-standing structure by the Burj Dubai, is commonly viewed as a phallic symbol—the conscious or unconscious representation of a penis. In Freudian terms, phallic symbols represent not just 'sex' but patriarchy—the domination of society by men, and the exclusion of women from positions of power. The question might arise: why would the source of such civic pride be a structure that also symbolizes male potency and the subordination of women? This isn't to say that the tower's architects were sexist or that Torontonians generally are guilty of gender bias. Montrealers might suggest that it's an act of compensation for the misfortunes of their hockey club. Of course, if you want to build tall, this is one of few choices, and even Freud would concede that sometimes a tower is just a tower. Some have observed that the potent masculinity of the CN Tower is balanced by

The Burj Dubai, in the United Arab Emirates, is now the world's tallest tower. Does size really matter? If not, why would cities compete for bragging rights where size is involved?

Photo: iStockphoto

the Rogers Centre, the domed stadium situated at its base, which is more 'feminine' in shape but also resembles something roundish that you would find at the base of a penis. We're having fun with this, but you get the point: psychoanalysis may be used to 'read' the underlying symbol found in cultural institutions. In this respect, it is similar to semiotics or, as we will see, discourse analysis, though it is much more specific.

Early feminists rightfully criticized Freud's ideas because of theories like that of 'penis envy', the supposed desire among women to have a penis, which Freud felt accounted for certain aspects of female behaviour. But in the late 1970s and 1980s, there was a feminization of psychoanalysis, which turned it into a method that could be used for feminist research. Among those leading the movement was Nancy Chodorow, who has been using feminist psychoanalysis in sociological research on gender, sexuality, and the family for 30 years. In *The Reproduction of Mothering* (1978), her pioneering study of psychoanalysis and the sociology of gender, she wrote that 'Freud's accounts of the psychological destructiveness of bourgeois marriage, gender differentiation, and child-rearing practices remain unsurpassed, and both psychoanalysts and feminists since Freud have deepened and extended his critique' (1978: 40).

Among others who have made noteworthy use of psychoanalysis in sociology research are members of the **Frankfurt School** of social philosophers (Do not comment here about how a 'frankfurter', or hot dog, is also a phallic symbol—we've moved on.) Adherents of the Frankfurt School, which began in the 1920s, applied the work of Nietzsche, Marx, and Freud to their analyses. They were generally critical of fascism, communism, and capitalism as systems that produce social domination. Principal figures of the Frankfurt School include Theodor Adorno, Max Horkheimer, and Herbert Marcuse. Marcuse used a psychoanalytic approach in *One Dimensional Man* (1964), where he argued that, at a cultural level, society had institutionalized elements of the Freudian *id* (which drives us to pursue pleasure in order to satisfy instinctual desires). He believed that these elements had come to displace the *superego* (our conscience, reflecting social standards learned from parents and society) and the ego (which controls the desires of the *id* to meet the demands of 'civilized' society). As a result, contradictory messages are brought together—progress and exploitation, satisfaction and drudgery, freedom and oppression—and made 'normal', producing what Marcuse called the 'happy consciousness'. For Marcuse, the happy consciousness subordinates human freedom, promotes aggressive and immoral social activity, and lays the political foundation for new forms of fascism (1964: 76–9). Here, fascism is not simply a political ideology but an ideology that links erotic pleasure and violence.

We will discuss psychoanalysis and its applications in sociology further in Chapter 4.

Content Analysis

Content analysis involves studying a set of cultural artifacts or events by systematically counting them (to show which ones dominate) and then interpreting the themes they reflect. **Cultural artifacts**

Photo: Ivy Images

Marcuse might have argued that video games like *Call of Duty* and *Grand Theft Auto* are the extension and internalization of fascist ideals, encouraging us to take part in the domination of our own consciousness.

include children's books, billboards, novels, newspaper articles, advertisements, artwork, articles of clothing, clinical records, and even introductory textbooks like the one you're reading. These items all have two distinct properties not normally found in the subjects studied using other types of qualitative methodology. First, they have a natural or 'found' quality because they are not created specifically to be studied. Second, they are *non-interactive*, in that there are no interviews used or behaviours observed to gather the data (Reinharz 1992: 146–8).

Feminist approaches to content analysis attempt to expose pervasive patriarchal ('male-dominated') and misogynist ('woman-hating') culture. Elaine Hall, in her article *One Week for Women? The Structure of Inclusion of Gender Issues in Introductory Textbooks* (1988), demonstrated how women's issues are treated as an afterthought in introductory-level texts, while Judith Dilorio, in a paper presented in 1980, used content analysis to examine scholarly articles on gender role research and found that their methods *naturalized* (made natural or normal-seeming) social facts that diminished women and promoted male-oriented conservatism (as analyzed in Reinharz 1992: 147, 361).

In *Gender Advertisements* (1976), Goffman undertook a content analysis of commercial pictures depicting gender in print media. He demonstrated that women in the magazine ads he examined were overwhelmingly depicted as subordinate and submissive. The magazines Goffman used represented both mass media and popular culture, having been selected on the basis of their availability and the size of their circulation. Taken together, these magazines (available in every supermarket, drugstore, and bookstore) act as cultural objects, reflecting or mirroring the social world. This relationship, however, is not unidirectional but bi-directional: cultural objects like magazines reflect the social world, and the social world in turn is influenced by cultural objects (Griswold 1994: 22–3). With their wide circulation, popular magazines give us both a snapshot of the social world and also, if we look carefully, an indication of how the social world is being constructed through mass media.

Sut Jhally, in his discussion of gender (1990), argues that magazine ads are neither completely true nor completely false reflections of social reality; they are partial truths and falsehoods. Ads depicting gender do not truly or falsely represent 'real' gender relations or ritualized gender displays. Rather, for Jhally, they are 'hyper-ritualizations' or exaggerations that emphasize certain aspects of gender display and de-emphasize others (1990: 135).

Semiotics

Coined by the Swiss linguist Ferdinand de Saussure, **semiotics**, or semiology, refers to the study of signs and signifying practices. To use

Would you say the men and women depicted in this ad are presented as equals?

Ritualized displays of gender often assert stereotypes and speak more to the notion of power relations than to reality. What notions of power relations are expressed in this ad from the 1950s? Are those same notions evident in advertising today?

Saussure's words, it is 'the science of signs'. A **sign** is made up of two parts: a **signifier**, which carries meaning, and a **signified**, the meaning that is carried. Put another way, the signifier refers to the form (dog) while the signified refers to the concept evoked from the form (furry thing with four legs that barks). The interrelationship between the signifier and the signified constitutes a sign.

Signs typically operate together with other signs in a system. It is through the interaction of a system's component parts that meaning is formed. Language, for example, is a system of signs (i.e. words) that express ideas and create meaning when used in relation to one another. All words, after all, are signs. The word *apple*, for instance, is a signifier: it stands for a particular type of fruit that grows on a tree (this definition is the signified). Of course, added to the signified now is a brand name for computers and allied products.

The semiotic approach is not without its critics. Canadian philosopher William Leiss (1988) is among those who have identified some of its weaknesses. He argues, for instance, that the semiotic study of advertising depends too heavily on the skill of the individual analyst. Too often, unskilled analysts state only the obvious. The discrepancy in the skill of various analysts makes it impossible to establish consistency or reliability in the results. Another limitation of semiotic research, according to Leiss, is its inability to derive an overall sense of constructed meanings from even a large survey of messages. He also believes that semiology cannot be applied to all ads with equal success. Notwithstanding these critiques, Leiss grants that the semiotic approach can occasionally be fruitful, citing Goffman's study as an example that demonstrates the capacity of semiology to dissect and examine cultural codes with a sensitivity to the subtle nuances and oblique references within the cultural system (1988: 165–6).

The limitations of semiotics as a sociological method can be overcome with the help of content analysis. Combining a semiotic approach with content analysis reduces concerns about reliability, sample size, and generalizability. Leiss, Kline, and Jhally (1988: 169) identified four main 'descriptors' of a content analysis, criteria by which any legitimate study may be judged:

- **objective description** – an acceptable level of agreement among analysts
- **systematic description** – the same criteria applied to all data

- **descriptive categories** – a specific quantitative procedure permitting a degree of precision in measurement
- **deliberate restriction** – the manifest, or 'surface', content of the message alone is measured.

Like semiotics, content analysis has limitations when used on its own to examine things like advertising. The implication of the fourth descriptor listed above, 'deliberate restriction', is that content analysis can be used to study surface meanings but it cannot really measure deeper meaning, the impact that signs have on an audience (Leiss et al. 1988: 174). What distinguishes Goffman's work is his attempt to look deeper by examining the underlying **ritualization** of the images. A rough grouping of Goffman's categories surrounding women—lying down, body 'cant' (the position or angle of the body), disassociated gaze, childlike innocence—support an interpretative 'reading' of female subordinate and submissive posturing. In this way, Goffman may be considered a semiotician.

Discourse Analysis

There are two types of **discourse analysis** used by sociologists. The first analyzes discourse as it is traditionally defined—that is, as a conversation, a speech, or a written text. A sociologist may examine the 'discourse' found in a given ethnography, in an open-ended interview, or in a narrative. He or she might also focus on things like court transcripts, newspaper stories, and advertisements. As well as applying observational techniques, ethnomethodologists analyze everyday discourse to determine how, through language, people construct, make sense of, and generate meaning about their social world. Foucault's work on totalitarian discourse, which we touched on in Chapter 1, can be considered in terms of this definition of discourse. Foucault himself, you'll recall, defined discourse as 'a conceptual framework with its own internal logic and underlying assumptions that are generally recognizable'.

The second type of discourse analysis focuses more on the methodological practices of genealogy and deconstruction, which we will discuss in the next section. As it is defined in this context, discourse is broader and more all-encompassing. Instead of referring merely to texts and their authors, it refers to entire 'fields'—the field of economics, the field of political philosophy, and so on—and how these fields are constructed and constituted in particular periods. A 'field', then, would comprise all known discourse on a particular cultural concept or idea—'masculinity', for instance. It is the role of the researcher to trace the discourse through time and space, looking at the representation, naturalization, change, and influence of the discursive field. An example of this kind of study would be a discourse analysis of changing popular cultural representations of masculinity in Hollywood films over the past 50 years.

Genealogy

Genealogy in its everyday use refers to the study of heredity for the purposes of genetic or social history, or the study of pedigree and lineage. In the context of discourse analysis, **genealogy** is a method of examining the history of the second type of discourse, as defined above. Foucault, in his later works, used a genealogical method to study the 'heredity' of discourses, to trace the origins and histories of modern discourses as they collide, fragment, and adhere to other cultural practices and discourses over time. Foucault's genealogical work captures the dynamic nature of such discourses as mental illness (1961), the penal system (1975), and sexuality (1978).

To understand the genealogical method, let's consider as our discourse the colour bar in South Asian culture. Any study looking at the social system in South Asia will observe a valuing of skin colour. Darker skin is considered less desirable, while a lighter skin colour is seen as more desirable. This cultural valuing of skin colour leads to prejudice and discrimination. In its origin, this cultural practice of prejudice reproduced and reinforced a caste and class hierarchy in which those who were wealthier stayed inside, and those who were poorer worked in the fields and were, as a result, darker. Skin colour, then, reflected one's social status within society.

A contemporary study of this discourse requires, in addition, an examination of the role British colonialism played in formulating current constructions of this cultural value. The discourse surrounding skin colour initially involved caste, class, social stratification, religion, inequality, gender, and colour, all of which operated within a particular field with its own history and logic. With the advent of colonialism, a new discourse of skin colour, with a history and logic of its own, was introduced into the culture. These two discourses, while distinct and different, grafted onto one another to become a new discourse, one that values and, in turn, privileges those with lighter skin above those with darker skin (Aujla, 1998: 1–5).

Edward Said's classic study of Western attitudes towards Eastern culture, *Orientalism* (1979), offers another example of genealogical research. In the book, Said (b. 1935) acknowledges Foucault's influence, particularly his notion of discourse, which allowed Said to conceive of the genealogy of Orientalism. For him, Orientalism cannot be studied or understood without the concept of discourse:

> My contention is that without examining Orientalism as a discourse one cannot possibly understand the enormously systematic discipline by which European culture was able to manage—and even produce—the Orient politically, sociologically, militarily, ideologically, scientifically, and imaginatively during the post-Enlightenment period. (1979: 3)

Orientalism, in this sense, refers to 'a corporate institution for dealing with the Orient—dealing with it by making statements about it, authorising views of it, describing it, by teaching it, settling it, ruling over it: in short, Orientalism as a Western style for dominating, restructuring, and having authority over the Orient' (Said, 1979: 3). As well as being a form of academic discourse, Orientalism is a style of thought based on the presumed philosophical distinctions between East and West, the Orient and the Occident respectively. Here, we take Orientalism to mean the process by which the 'Orient' was, and continues to be, constructed in western European thinking.

Quantitative Research

Statistics

Sociologists have mixed feelings about **statistics**, a science that, in sociology, involves the use of numbers to map social behaviour and beliefs. Social scientists, like politicians, relish the opportunity to show off by quoting facts and figures. And yet, we are also suspicious of statistics (particularly other people's statistics). There are more jokes about the science of statistics than there are about any other kind of sociological research method—and we can prove that statistically. But here is some anecdotal evidence:

- 'It shames me some to hear the statistics about us in class. The shame burns holes in whatever sympathy I may have for Indians, not my mom though.' – the Native protagonist of Aboriginal writer Lee Maracle's novel *Sun Dogs*, on how sociological statistics portray her people (Maracle 1992: 3)
- 'There are three kinds of lies: lies, damned lies, and statistics.' – Benjamin Disraeli
- '*USA Today* has come out with a new survey: apparently, three out of every four people make up 75 per cent of the population.' – David Letterman
- 'There are two kinds of statistics: the kind you look up, and the kind you make up.' – Rex Stout
- 'An unsophisticated forecaster uses statistics as a drunk man uses lamp-posts—for support rather than illumination.' – Andrew Lang
- 'Smoking is one of the leading causes of statistics.' – Fletcher Knebel
- 'Statistician: A man who believes figures don't lie, but admits that under analysis some of them won't stand up either.' – Evan Esar, *Esar's Comic Dictionary*
- 'Statistics: The only science that enables different experts using the same figures to draw different conclusions.' – Esar

Operational Definition

A key area of quantifiable research, and one in which a sociology student can learn to challenge the research of professionals, is that of **operational definitions**. These are definitions that take abstract or theoretical concepts—'poverty', 'abuse', or 'working class', for example—and transform them into concepts that are concrete, observable, measurable, and countable. This is difficult to do well.

The *Handbook for Sociology Teachers* (1982), by British sociologists Roger Gomm and Patrick McNeill, contains a brilliant exercise that illustrates one of the difficulties of using operational definitions. Students are presented with a table showing the number of thefts that have occurred at each of a number of schools. Included in the table are the following factors which may or may not have some bearing on the number of thefts at each school:

- size of school
- social class of the students
- gender makeup of the school (i.e. single-sex or co-educational).

Students are asked to try to determine whether there is a cause-and-effect relationship between any of these factors (which are called *independent variables*, discussed later in this chapter) and the number of thefts at each school. Once they have arrived at some tentative conclusions, the teacher gives them an additional handout showing that

The Point Is...

So You Think You Know What A Single Parent Is?

Whenever you're gathering or interpreting data from questionnaires, it's critical that you understand the exact meaning—the *operational definition*—of key terms being used. Take a category as seemingly self-evident as 'single parent'. In the following exercise, say who you would count as a single parent, then address the questions below.

Whom Would You Include?

a) a mother whose husband is dead _____

b) a 41-year-old separated mother who lives with her 22-year-old son _____

c) a father whose 4-year-old daughter sees her mother every weekend _____

d) a mother whose 10-year-old son lives with his father every summer _____

e) a father whose two daughters live with their mother every other week _____

f) a mother whose husband lives in the same house but contributes nothing financially or in services to the raising of her children from a previous marriage _____

g) a gay man who, along with his live-in partner, is raising his two sons (his ex-wife is completely out of the picture) _____

h) a mother who along with her son is completely supported by her ex-husband _____

i) a mother whose husband is away at work most of the year _____

• •

What do YOU think?

1. How would you define 'single parent'?

2. Do you think that 'single-parent family' is a category that would be easy to do research with? Why or why not?

• •

each school defined 'theft' differently. With no consistency in the operational definition, their efforts to compare schools were sociologically worthless (although pedagogically rewarding).

To get a sense of how operational definitions are used, let's consider **poverty**, a common focus of sociological study. There is no standard definition for 'poverty' or 'poor'; definitions of these terms vary across the globe. There are, however, various conventional methods of defining poverty. One is to establish a **poverty line**, an income level below which a household is defined (for statistical or governmental purposes) as being 'poor'.

How is a poverty line established? Again, there is no universally accepted procedure, though a few methods are prevalent. One is to link it to the availability of basic material needs: food, clothing, and shelter. Anything below the minimum income level needed to secure these necessities is considered **absolute poverty**. But this, too, will vary, even within countries. Consider, for example, how housing costs vary across Canada. It costs more for a resident of Vancouver to pay rent on an apartment than it costs a citizen of Halifax living in a comparable dwelling.

Since 1997 Statistics Canada has used the **Market Basket Measure** (MBM) to establish a poverty line for different regions across the country. As Giles explains,

> The MBM estimates the cost of a specific basket of goods and services for the reference year, assuming that all items in the basket were entirely provided for out of the spending of the household [i.e. that none of the items were purchased for the householders by family or friends]. Any household with a level of income lower than the cost of the basket is considered to be living in low income. (Giles 2004)

The 'basket' includes five types of expenditures for a reference family of two adults and two children:

- food,
- clothing,
- shelter,
- transportation, and
- 'other' (school supplies, furniture, newspapers, recreation and family entertainment, personal care products, and phone).

The Market Basket Measure (MBM) establishes a regional poverty line for Canada. How would you define poverty? What clues in this picture suggest that this family is not poor?

Photo: © Blend Images/Alamy

Different levels are calculated for 48 different geographical areas in Canada (HRSDC 2003).

Another way to define 'poor' is to use a **relative poverty** scale, which defines poverty relative to the average, median, or mean household incomes. One such measure used in Canada involves **Low Income Cutoffs**, (LICOs) which are calculated based on the percentage of a family's income spent on food, clothing, and shelter. So, for instance, according to Statistics Canada, in 1992 the percentage of total income (before income tax) spent on these three items by Canadians was 34.7 per cent. Any household that spent at least 20 per cent more of its total income (i.e. 54.7 per cent) on these three items could be classified as 'poor'.

Another technique used in Canada to measure relative poverty is based on a mode of calculation that is commonly used across the globe for comparing poverty rates worldwide. The **Low Income Measure** (LIM-IAT) is calculated by identifying those households with total incomes (after taxes) half that of the median income in the country under investigation (with some adjustments made for family size and composition).

What we've seen, then, is that there are three legitimate ways to achieve an operational definition of poverty: the Market Basket Measure, the

• Going Global • • • • • • • • • • • • • •

Defining the World: Labels for Rich and Poor Countries

There are rich countries and there are poor countries. Both have been given various names over the years. For a long time they were known as First World countries and Third World countries. The latter term was coined by French social scientist Alfred Sauvy (1898–1990) in 1952. The First World was seen as including the rich capitalist countries, while the Third World comprised those countries without social or economic power. The USSR and the Eastern European countries under its power (sometimes called the Soviet Bloc or Eastern Bloc) were identified as the Second World.

Somewhat more recent terminology avoids the First World–Third World designation and distinguishes instead between developed nations and developing nations. One problem with this is that not all of the so-called developing nations are necessarily developing. According to the skeptical globalization position, they should really be called 'underdeveloped nations', or perhaps more accurately 'underdevelop*ing* nations', since they are under a constant process of being exploited and running up huge debts incurred as a result of globalization.

More recently, theorists have divided the world conceptually into the North and the South, based on the plain fact that almost all of the powerful and rich nations are in the northern hemisphere, while the less powerful and poor nations are typically found in the southern hemisphere. Of course, this has some flaws, too: Australia and New Zealand, squarely in the southern hemisphere, are not among the world's poorest nations, and a number of the northern hemisphere's central Asian countries are considerably poorer than their immediate neighbours. One of the world's rising economic superstars is Brazil, which technically straddles the equator, though most of it sits below.

Despite the flaws we've just noted, we have, for the most part, used the North and the South to refer loosely to the world's wealthiest and poorest countries. When devising your operational definitions, it's sometimes necessary to rely on conventional categories even though they aren't ideal. The important thing is that you spell out as clearly as possible how you intend each of your key terms to be understood in the context of your discussion.

Low Income Cutoff, and the Low Income Measure. The three methods generally yield similar results:

Using the MBM, in 2000, the incidence of low income for all children in Canada was 16.9%. This number is very similar to the number using the pre–income tax LICOs (16.5%), and slightly above the incidence using the post–income tax LICOs (12.5%) and the LIM-IAT (13.5%).

Note, however, that while the results are similar, the difference of a mere percentage point is a big deal to a statistician, underlying again the importance of knowing the precise meaning of any operational definition you use.

● ● ● ● ● ● ● ● ● ● ● ● ● ● ● ● ● ● ● ●

What do YOU think?

All ways of making an operational definition of poverty have strengths and weaknesses. What do you see as the strengths and weaknesses of the three systems discussed here? How might sociologists employing qualitative research methods define poverty?

● ● ● ● ● ● ● ● ● ● ● ● ● ● ● ● ● ● ● ●

Variables and Correlations

There are a few terms you should know because they are key to understanding and carrying out quantifiable research (and even certain forms of qualitative research). The first one is **variable**.

A variable is a concept with measurable traits or characteristics that can vary or change from one person, group, culture, or time to another. One variable can cause another variable to change, or it can be affected by another. The average temperature of Nunavut's capital, Iqaluit, can be a variable, as can the average amount of clothing a resident of Iqaluit wears. Clearly the first variable can affect the second one.

Sociologists commonly use two different types of variables: **independent variables** and dependent variables. Independent variables are variables presumed to have some effect on another variable. In the example given above, the average temperature of Iqaluit is the independent variable. **Dependent variables** are those that are assumed by the sociologist to be affected by an independent variable. In the example given above, the average amount of clothing worn by the Iqalungiut ('people of Iqaluit') would be the dependent variable. Table 2.1 presents a list of possible independent and dependent variables from examples presented in this chapter.

Another key term is *correlation*. A **correlation** exists when two variables are associated more frequently than could be expected by chance. Both variables might increase together, or one might increase while the other decreases. A **direct correlation** (sometimes referred to as a **positive correlation**) exists when the independent variable and the dependent variable increase or decrease together. Table 2.2 shows some examples. An **inverse correlation** (sometimes referred to as a

Table 2.1 Independent and dependent variable: Three examples

STUDY	INDEPENDENT VARIABLE	DEPENDENT VARIABLE
Opening narrative	car passes another car	The passed car speeds up
Schoolwork	middle-class parents take an active role in children's education	middle-class children achieve better results
Aboriginal policing	political environment is stable	police force is successful
	officers demonstrate commitment to training	competency of managers and officers increases; respect on the part of Quebec police increases and relationship improves*
	mentorship program	relationship with local youth improves

* This has not been measured; it has been assumed based on the lack of problems with the band police.

negative correlation) exists when the two variables change in opposing directions—in other words, when the independent variable increases, the dependent decreases, and vice versa. Table 2.3 gives examples of inverse correlation.

Spurious Reasoning: Correlation is *Not* Causation

You may have noticed that in the correlations above we've said nothing about **causation**, the linking of effects to causes. We may *observe* that people shed layers of clothing as the temperature rises, but we can't assume, based on that correlation, that people wear fewer clothes *because* the temperature rises. That is something we have to prove.

It should be stated clearly that while correlation is relatively easy to prove, causation is usually not. Claiming that a cause-and-effect relationship exists based on correlation alone, without sufficient evidence, is known as *spurious reasoning*.

Spurious reasoning is one of those concepts that's hard to grasp by the definition alone, and sociology instructors are challenged to explain and identify it. It usually takes lots of examples. So we'll begin here with the definition, then move on to examples.

Spurious reasoning, as we mentioned, exists when someone sees correlation and falsely assumes causation. Remember that a correlation is easy to determine; causation is not. The journey from one to the other is long and difficult. It involves proving—or else disproving—the existence of the critical **third variable**, the outside factor that influences both correlating variables.

Here are the examples. Some of them are silly, some serious.

Example #1 Birds and Leaves

There is a correlation in Canada between birds flying south (except for the fat Toronto geese, which seem to travel from York University only as far south as Lake Ontario) and leaves falling. Both

---

Table 2.2   Direct correlation of independent and dependent variables: Three examples

VARIABLE	DEPENDENT VARIABLE
smoking	rates of lung cancer
education level	income level
	tolerance for difference in humans (e.g. regarding race and ethnicity, sexual orientation, etc.)
parents' income level	likelihood of child becoming a doctor or lawyer

---

Table 2.3   Inverse correlation of independent and dependent variables: Three examples

INDEPENDENT VARIABLE	DEPENDENT VARIABLE
average temperature	average amount of clothes worn
a woman's education	the number of children she has
age (of an adult)	support for same-sex marriages

take place roughly at the same time. It would be spurious reasoning to say that the birds see the leaves falling and therefore decide to migrate. If we look for a third factor, we'll find that the angle of the sun's rays affects both dependent variables.

Example #2 Fire Trucks and Fire Damage

This is perhaps the most often taught example of spurious reasoning. There is a direct correlation between the number of fire trucks that go to a fire and the amount of damage that takes place at the fire. The greater the number of fire trucks, the greater the damage the fire causes. It would be spurious reasoning to say that a large number of fire trucks *causes* the extensive damage done at the site of the fire (though some budget-conscious municipal politicians might want us to believe this—they could save a lot of money on fire trucks). Seek out the third variable: the seriousness of the fire affects both the number of fire trucks that appear and the amount of damage that is caused.

Example #3 Older Men and Younger Wives

Older men who marry significantly younger women tend to live longer than the cohort of jealous men their own age. Spurious reasoning would lead us to conclude that marrying frolicsome young women keeps old men active and healthy. But before declaring that we've found the solution for men who want to live long and happy lives, we must look for a third variable. That's when we discover that if the older man is already relatively strong and healthy for his age, then he is both more likely to attract and keep a younger bride and also more likely to live longer.

Example #4 Cohabitation and Divorce

There is a direct (but not strong) correlation between a couple's living together prior to marriage and the likelihood of divorce. People who live together first are more likely to divorce than those who go from living apart to living together in marriage (perhaps the latter are more likely to die of shock, and everything balances out). It would be spurious reasoning to say that a couple's greater likelihood of divorce comes from the fact that they lived together first (for example, they are disillusioned because they find no greater bliss in lawful marriage than they enjoyed in mere cohabitation).

Seek out the third variable and you will find it in social liberalism and social conservatism (the latter possibly a cause or effect of that difficult-to-pin-down social factor 'religiosity'). People who are socially liberal are more likely *both* to live together *and* to leave a marriage if they feel it is a bad one. People who are more socially conservative are *both* more likely to begin living together with marriage, *and* more likely to stay in a marriage, even if it is horrible (our sympathies).

Example #5 Aboriginal Deaths and Christianity

In the seventeenth century some Aboriginal people living in present-day Canada—the Huron (Wendat), the Montagnais (Innu), the Algonquin, and the Ottawa—came into contact with French explorers and missionaries. At that time, there was a definite correlation between Native exposure to European religion (primarily through Jesuit missionaries) and Native deaths from European diseases such as smallpox and influenza. It would be

Photo: PNC/Brand X/Corbis

Spurious reasoning leads us to conclude that this man will live long because he is married to this young woman. What do *you* think?

spurious reasoning to say, as some of the Aboriginal people did, that it was the religion that was causing the death. Seek out the third variable: exposure to priests carrying European diseases to which the Aboriginal people had not naturally developed any antibodies.

Example #6 Divorce and Suicide

Durkheim recorded the following direct correlation between divorce rates and suicide rates during a 10-year period from 1870 to 1880:

Table 2.4 Correlation between divorce and suicide rates in four countries, 1870–1889		
	DIVORCE RATE (per 1,000 marriages)	SUICIDE RATE (per 1 million people)
Italy	3.1	31.0
Sweden	6.4	81.0
France	7.5	150.0
Switzerland	47.0	216.0

Source: Spaulding and Simpson (1951).

So, there appears to be a positive correlation between divorce rates and suicide rates over this period. However, it would be spurious reasoning to say that greater rates of divorce produced higher suicide rates. For Durkheim, the third variable was **anomie**, a societal state of breakdown or confusion, or a more personal one based on an individual's lack of connection to or contact with society. Anomie, concluded Durkheim, was the real cause of increases in both the divorce and suicide rates.

Critical Thinking and Statistics

Sociologist Joel Best, author of *Damned Lies and Statistics: Untangling Numbers from the Media, Politicians, and Activists* (2001), begins an article excerpted from his book with an example that illustrates why we should approach statistics with a critical mind. He was on the PhD dissertation committee of a graduate student who began the prospectus of his dissertation with a questionable statistic meant to grab the attention of the reader. The student wrote the following, which was obtained from an article published in 1995:

'Every year since 1950, the number of American children gunned down has doubled.'

This would certainly gain the attention of those Canadian readers who already think of Americans as gun-toting, trigger-happy rednecks. But wait a minute, said Best: do the math. Say the 1950 figure was the unbelievably low figure of 1. Here is how it would add up to 1995:

1950	**1**
1951	**2**
1952	**4**
1955	**32**
1957	**128**
1959	**512**
1960	**1,012**
1961	**2,058**
1965	**32,768** (there were 9,960 homicides that year)
1970	**1 million +**
1980	**1 billion** (approximately; that's more than four times the total population of the United States at the time)
1983	**8.6 billion** (nearly one-and-a-half times the world's population)
1995	**3 trillion**

What the author of the original article had done was misquote a 1994 document stating that the number of American children killed each year by guns had doubled since 1950; the number itself had not doubled *each year*. If the original number had been one, that would make the 1994 figure two. The unwary dissertation writer simply (and unquestioningly) perpetuated the error committed by the writer of the 1995 article.

After presenting us this cautionary tale, Best warns the reader that bad statistics come to support all political stripes, from the political right wing (our Conservative Party) to the left wing (the NDP), from wealthy corporations to advocates for the poor, the sick, and the powerless. To cite an extreme Canadian example, the Mike Harris Conservative government of Ontario, in the late 1990s, officially stated that the number of people on social assistance in the province had gone down, suggesting that the situation for poor people had improved under their administration. It hadn't. The numbers were down because government-run agencies had closed the 'welfare door' on a number of people. They presented the statistic as though all the people no longer collecting social assistance had obtained jobs and were, as a result, better off; they neglected to include people who had committed suicide (in part because of their poverty), had become homeless, had moved out of the province (to find work, family support, or better provincial assistance programs), had moved in with family members or friends, or had resorted to criminal activity for a living because they were no longer eligible for Ontario's welfare programs.

Best advises us to approach statistics critically. To be critical is to recognize that all statistics are flawed to some extent, and that some flaws are more significant than others. While Best admits that no checklist of critical questions is complete, he does present the following useful series of questions for sociology students to consider when encountering a statistic in a news report, magazine, newspaper, or conversation:

> What might be the sources for this number? How could one go about producing the figure? Who produced the number, and what interests might they have? What are the different ways key terms might have been defined, and which definitions have been chosen? How might the phenomena be measured, and which measurement choices have been made? What sort of sample was gathered, and how might that sample affect the result? Is the statistic properly interpreted? Are comparisons being made, and if so, are the comparisons appropriate? Are there competing statistics? If so, what stakes do the opponents have in the issue, and how are those stakes likely to affect their use of statistics? And is it possible to figure out why the statistics seem to disagree, what the differences are in the ways the competing sides are using figures. (Best 2001)

Abuse Statistic or Statistical Abuse?

We can apply Best's critical thinking to the following example. In 1980, Linda McLeod produced a controversial book, *Wife Battering in Canada: The Vicious Circle*. In it she cited a statistic that has since become what some would call 'free-floating'. A **free-floating statistic** is one that is frequently reproduced without presenting the context—the time, set of assumptions, operational definition, or sample size relevant to how and why the statistic was calculated. McLeod's claim was that 'Every year, 1 in 10 Canadian women who are married or in a relationship with a live-in lover are battered' (McLeod 1980: 21). This was a stunning claim, and commendable as one of the first real attempts to gauge the level of domestic violence against women in Canada. But it's important to look at just how McLeod arrived at this figure.

Two things should be noted from the beginning. First, McLeod clearly stated, as a good sociological researcher often has to, that 'no *definitive* statement about the incidence of wife abuse can be made' (largely due to the lack of reporting; McLeod 1980: 16). Second, her figures were for the year 1978.

Next, we have to take a look at her operational definition for 'wife battering':

> Wife battering *is* violence, physical and/or psychological, expressed by a husband or a male or lesbian live-in lover toward his wife or his/her live-in lover, to which the 'wife' does not consent, and which is directly or indirectly condoned by the traditions, laws and attitudes prevalent in the society in which it occurs. (McLeod 1980: 7)

She generated her statistic first by requesting annual statistics from 71 transition houses or hostels for women. She received data from 47 of these, for a total of 9,688 women (McLeod 1980: 16). She estimated that about 60 per cent of these women would go to shelters because they were 'physically battered', producing a figure of roughly 5,800 (rounded off from 5,813). She then rounded off the number of shelters that supplied data (47/71) as 2/3, and multiplied her estimated number of battered women from these shelters by 3/2 to get roughly 9,000 (the actual figure would be 8,700). She then used a rough statistic that the transition houses could not house 1/3 of the women who contacted them, raising her figure to 12,000. This figure was multiplied by two, as she estimated (from 1976 statistics) that about 45 per cent (which she rounded off to 50 per cent) of the Canadian population was not served by a transition house. Using all these calculations, she arrived at her first major conclusion:

> If transition houses existed across Canada, we can estimate that at least 24,000 Canadian women would request help from them because they were battered by their husbands. (McLeod 1980: 17)

Next, she examined the divorce statistics for 1978. One of the grounds that could be cited for divorce at that time was 'mental or physical cruelty'. She found 2,800 applications for divorce on that basis only, with physical cruelty also included in 17,116 cases where multiple grounds were listed. This gave a combined figure of roughly 20,000.

She acknowledged some flaws with this figure, namely that some of the physical cruelty figures would have come from men's applications, and that 'there is no doubt some overlap between women who stayed in transition houses and those who applied for divorce' (McLeod 1980: 20). Still, she added her two numbers together to say that:

> 40,000–50,000 women in Canada in 1978 suffered sufficient physical and mental abuse to seek outside help. (McLeod 1980: 20)

McLeod then estimated that there were roughly 5 million couples existing in Canada at that time (no source given), leading her to state that,

> One out of every hundred women in Canada married or living in a common-law relationship is battered and has filed for a divorce on grounds of physical cruelty or has approached a transition house for help (given the extrapolation discussed above). (McLeod 1980: 20)

From an examination of what she called 'Miscellaneous Canadian Sources', she concluded that

the number of domestic violence calls were 'far above' the cases she had discussed. She then took an estimate from a 1976 University of Windsor study to say that

> There are *ten* unreported cases for every call by a battered wife to the police. (McLeod 1980: 21)

Multiplying her previous figure of 1/100 by ten, McLeod arrived at the often quoted statistic that,

> Every year, 1 in 10 Canadian women who are married or in a relationship with a live-in lover are battered. (McLeod 1980: 21)

Think of how often the term 'estimate' appeared in the discussion above, and of how many times figures were rounded off. This is a good example of how sometimes the misuse of statistics is used in an attempt to achieve a social good (i.e. the recognition of the profound problem of spousal abuse). The figure for spousal abuse may very well be 1 in 10; subsequent studies by the federal government (1993) put the figure even higher. However, there is no way to verify this statistic based on McLeod's methodology. The flaws in McLeod's statistical calculation are evident. To cite the statistic '1 in 10' without understanding or explaining how one arrived at that figure is irresponsible research.

Abuse of a Statistic

Unfortunately, this statistic was seized upon and used out of context over the next three decades, often by well-meaning organizations aiming to assist in the important goal of reducing the amount of abuse faced by women in Canadian society. Here are a few examples obtained from the Internet in June 2009:

- 'If you've been physically violent against a woman, if you've committed sexual assault, if you've hit, pushed, threatened, kicked your spouse or girlfriend, then you are part of the problem. *One in ten women in Canada [has] experienced this kind of violence from men in the past year.'* (www.eurowrc. org./02.faq/11.men_cando.htm)

- 'Not all abuse is reported, but *at least one in ten women is abused* by her husband, ex-husband, common-law husband, boyfriend or ex-boyfriend in her own home. (www.settlement.org/sys/faqs_detail.asp?faq_id=4000662)
- Myths and Facts About Domestic Violence

Myth	Fact
Family violence is not common	*One in ten women in Canada [are] victims of violence* by conservative estimates

(www.su.alberta.ca/services_and_business/services/student_distress_centre/familyviolence)

What do YOU think?

What have these quotations changed from the original operational definition?

Sociological Research Methods: A Final Word

In this chapter we've introduced a number of ways to carry out sociological research. In all the talk about quantitative and qualitative methods, independent and dependent variables, correlation and statistics, it's easy to lose sight of an important point: the subjects under investigation are people, and the moment you begin to study them, you start a relationship that will not always be equal. Students, soldiers, and inmates of prisons and asylums are often studied because they have little power to say no. If I can ask questions about your life but you can't ask questions about mine, then I have a kind of power over you that you do not have over me. People who are poor, who belong to racialized (e.g. black), or colonized (e.g. Aboriginal) groups when studied by White middle-class researchers have often been studied for purposes that serve more to control or exploit the subjects of research than to give them power over their lives. The Maori of New Zealand have been through that experience. Maori researcher Linda Tuhiwai Smith, in an important work called *Decolonizing Methodologies: Research and Indigenous Peoples* (1999), writes the following:

From the vantage point of the colonized . . . the term 'research' is inextricably linked to European imperialism and colonialism. The word itself, 'research', is probably one of the dirtiest words in the indigenous world's vocabulary. When mentioned in many indigenous contexts, it stirs up silence, it conjures up bad memories, it raises a smile that is knowing and distrustful. . . . The ways in which scientific research is implicated in the worst excesses of colonialism remains a powerful remembered history for many of the world's colonized peoples. . . . It galls us that Western researchers and intellectuals can assume to know all that it is possible to know of us, on the basis of their brief encounters with some of us. It appalls us that the West can desire, extract and claim ownership of ways of knowing, our imagery, the things we create and produce, and then simultaneously reject the people who created and developed those ideas and seek to deny them further opportunities to be creators of their own culture and own nations. (Tuhiwai Smith 1999: 1)

If your interest in sociology comes from a desire to effect positive social change, the bitter tone of this statement might shock you. Let it serve as a reminder: treat research subjects with respect and represent the data fairly, and you will go a long way towards sociology's goal of bringing clarity to social issues.

Questions for Critical Review

1. Distinguish between qualitative and quantitative research. Give examples of each.
2. Explain the importance of narratives to sociological research.
3. Explain spurious reasoning. Furnish some examples of your own.
4. Outline the different methods of sociological research.
5. Identify the importance of operational definitions in quantitative research.

Suggested Readings

Bourdieu, Pierre, et al. (1999). *The Weight of the World: Social Suffering in Contemporary Society.* Stanford: Stanford UP.

Brown, Gillian, & George Yule (1983). *Discourse Analysis.* Cambridge: Cambridge UP.

Feyerabend, Paul (1975). *Against Method.* London: Verso.

Griffith, A., & L. Andre-Bechely (2008). 'Standardizing parents' educational work'. In M. DeVault, *Embodied Workers*, New York: NYU Press.

Hoffer, Lee D. (2006). *Junkie Business: The Evolution and Operation of a Heroin Dealing Network.* Belmont: Thomson/Wadsworth.

Vinitzky-Seroussi, Vered (1998). *After Pomp and Circumstance: High School Reunion as an Autobiographical Occasion.* Chicago: U of Chicago P.

Suggested Websites

Canadian Sociology & Anthropology Association
http://artsci-ccwin.concordia.casocanth/csaa/csaa.html

Doing Research in Sociology (University of Waterloo Library)
http://129.97.58.10/discipline/sociology/research.html

Semiotics (Martin Ryder, University of Colorado at Denver, School of Education)
http://carbon.cudenver.edu/~mryder/itc_data/semiotics.html

Statistics Canada
www.statcan.ca/start.html

Key Terms

- agency
- Algonquian
- authenticity
- contested
- counterculture
- cultural capital
- cultural studies
- cultural relativism

- culture
- decipherment
- dialect
- dominant culture
- dominants
- ethnocentrism
- Eurocentrism
- folkways

- high culture
- hijab
- ideal culture
- indigeneity
- Indo-European
- linguistic determinism (or causation)
- mass culture
- mores

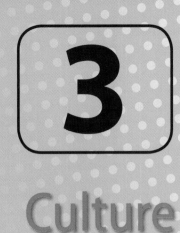

3
Culture

LEARNING OBJECTIVES

After reading this chapter, you should be able to

❯ distinguish between
  - dominant cultures and subcultures/countercultures;
  - high culture, popular culture, and mass culture;
  - reading and decipherment; and
  - folkways, mores, and taboos;

❯ identify the intellectual traps of
  - Eurocentrism,
  - victimology,
  - exoticism, and
  - the biases of Western medicine;

❯ explain what it means for culture to be 'contested';

❯ discuss how ethnocentrism has affected the mainstream sociology's interpretation of the potlatch;

❯ discuss the reasons that Muslim women in Canada elect to wear the hijab; and

❯ contrast the linguistic expectations of speakers of Algonquian and Indo-European languages.

FOR Starters

Culture and Claiming Space

It was all about culture. I saw the conflict coming, but I could do nothing to stop it.

It was 1981. I was in Edinburgh, Scotland, in one of the few decent (according to my refined North American palate) hamburger joints in the city. It was a popular spot, both for locals and for tourists, commanding a beautiful full view of the castle on the top of the hill across the street. I was waiting in line with my Scottish friends when I saw the incident that would precipitate the conflict.

A pair of American tourists set their jackets on two of four chairs attached to a table, and then slowly proceeded the short distance to the lineup. I sensed that trouble was coming. As I stood in line I saw a Scottish couple looking for a place to sit with their meals. Their eyes fixed on the chairs opposite the ones the tourists had laid claim to with their jackets. The couple went over, sat down at the unoccupied chairs, and innocently began to eat.

The tourists had been distracted by the view of the castle. When then turned around and saw the couple at the table, they reacted instantly.

'What are you doing? That's our table. Didn't you see the jackets?' The Scots looked up at them, dumbfounded, but unprepared to move. This was their country, after all, and they weren't prepared to be booted from their seats. My Scottish friends asked me (as a Canadian 'Translantic', an obvious expert in things North American):

'What's wrong with them? Do they think they bought the table? Bloody tourists!'

The tourists continued to argue with the Scots before storming out of the place.

A few months earlier, I might have sided with the tourists, sympathizing with their typically North American sense of space. But having spent time in Scotland, I understood why the Scots were surprised. In Canada, when two people in a bar are sitting at a table with four chairs, and someone asks them, 'Are these seats taken?', the unseated patrons will take the two extra chairs and sit at a vacant table. In Scotland, they will sit down right at 'your' table, perhaps joining you in conversation or else ignoring you altogether.
It's all about culture.

Culture

What is culture?

It's not the meaning used in the punchline to the old joke, 'What's the difference between yogourt and Dull City [or the neighbouring backwater town of your choice]? Yogourt has *culture*.' If anything, the 'culture' referred to in the joke can more properly be called **high culture**. It's what we have in mind when we think of opera, ballet, theatre, fine restaurants. And it's from that idea of culture that we get the adjectives 'cultured'—as in 'refined, having a sophistication of manners and taste'—and 'uncultured'—as in 'Tacos and beer for breakfast? *Awesome!*'

The word **culture** as we use it here is a system of behaviour, beliefs, knowledge, practices, values, and concrete materials including buildings, tools, and sacred items. In calling it a system, we don't mean to suggest that there is total agreement concerning any one culture and its constituent parts, even by those who belong to it. In other words, culture is **contested**: those who are members of a society that has a particular culture disagree about what it does or should include. For instance, as we will see below, the veil is a contested part of Muslim culture.

To illustrate this point, let's talk about hockey. Just about everybody would agree that hockey is part of Canadian culture—but that's where the agreement would end. Does success by Canada's national teams in international hockey mean we've succeeded as a culture? Not everyone would agree there. Is fighting an integral part of the Canadian game? You don't have to be Don Cherry to get into an argument there. In more serious cases, aspects of a culture may be contested when they become instruments of oppression or discrimination.

Anne McGillivray and Brenda Comaskey, in their book *Black Eyes All of the Time: Intimate Violence, Aboriginal Women and the Justice System*, write that it cannot be 'assumed that Aboriginal women subjected to intimate violence [i.e. spousal abuse] will view "cultural" solutions in the same way as Aboriginal men or First Nations political leaders' (McGillivray and Comaskey 1999: 18). Aboriginal justice typically calls for forgiving offenders and reintegrating them into the community; this has been recognized by many observers as a salient part of Native culture. However, most Aboriginal women who have suffered domestic abuse have said, in interviews, that they would prefer that their male abusers spend time in jail to give them time to feel safe again. Under these circumstances, these aspects of Aboriginal justice—forgiveness and keeping offenders in the community—become contested.

One point that often leads to contestation is the subject of **authenticity**. Culture involves traditions but is not confined by them: it is dynamic, changing over time. Authenticity carries the idea of being true to a particular culture, yet think of how broadly the word 'authentic' can be applied and understood: for some, an 'authentic Italian meal' may be something you'd have to fly to Tuscany to experience; for others (including advertisers), it may be a mere phone call away, coming from the North American pizza shop down the street. A word that may be paired with 'authentic' is 'traditional', which is used to imply that only those practices that have been carried on for generations can be true to the culture, while new cultural forms—including those that may incorporate features borrowed from other cultures—are not.

Authenticity becomes a problem when a colonial society studies a colonized culture and claims, having studied that culture's traditions, to hold the key to its authenticity. One of Said's main arguments in *Orientalism* is that Western intellectuals formed their impressions of the Middle East and central Asia from nineteenth- and twentieth-century Western scholarship. Once they had defined what 'the Orient' was, these same scholars and intellectuals negatively compared their rather romanticized (think Aladdin) notion of the Eastern world's traditions with their negative perceptions of its present. In effect, they said: 'You are a corruption of what you used to be. You are no longer authentic.' That would be like someone saying to you: 'I understand you better than you do, and you are not as good as you used to be.' A similar situation occurs when non-Native scholars invoke the stereotype of the noble savage to compare the 'authentic past' of Native culture with what they consider its corrupted, degenerated present state. We'll have more to say about the noble savage myth later in this chapter.

It is a common mistake to think (favourably) of one's own culture as being contested while thinking (less favourably) of other cultures as simple, fixed. 'Canadians enjoy healthy debates on many issues, but Americans as a rule carry guns, hate foreigners, and make obnoxious tourists.' In short, all culture is contested.

What Kinds of Cultures Are There?

The different kinds of cultures that exist within a society can be seen in terms of two oppositions:

>   **dominant culture** vs **subculture**
>   and **counterculture**

>   **high culture** vs **popular culture**
>   and **mass culture**

As we examine each of these oppositions, you will understand why we say that culture is contested.

Dominant Culture versus Subculture and Counterculture

It's not difficult to see that there is a dominant culture in Canada. The dominant culture is the one that through its political and economic power is able to impose its values, language, and ways of behaving and interpreting behaviour on a given society. The people most closely linked with it are sometimes referred to in the literature as **dominants**. Although statistically their percentage has dropped significantly in the last 20 years, it is fairly safe to say that the dominant culture in Canada is white, English-speaking, Christian, and of European stock. It is also fair to say that the dominant culture is middle-class. How do we know what the dominant culture looks like? Think of what culture is typically represented in Canadian morning shows like *Canada AM*, in commercials, and in television programs generally. Think of the expectations they express about what people own, what their concerns are, and how they live.

We can narrow our picture of Canada's dominant culture by looking at the issue from a regionalist perspective. People living in the Atlantic provinces have good reason to suspect that the dominant culture lies in central Canada, where most big companies have their head offices, and where the greatest share of the national population is situated. Likewise, western Canada has several times produced political parties (the Social Credit, Reform, and most recently, the Wildrose Alliance parties, for instance) to protest the West's exclusion from the dominant political culture and its unfair treatment at the hands of institutions dominated by and situated in central Canada (such as banks and agencies of the federal government). Power and wealth tend to be concentrated in large cities, and central Canada is home to the country's two largest metropolitan areas, Toronto and Montreal.

Feminists (both women and men) argue that Canada's dominant culture is male. Think of our most powerful politicians—prime ministers, premiers, cabinet ministers, mayors of large cities. On 8 June 2009, of the 305 members of Parliament (three seats were vacant), only 65—or roughly 21 per cent—were women. The governing Conservative Party had the lowest percentage of women MPs with just 16 per cent. The official opposition party, the Liberals, were but slightly better, with 21 per cent. The NDP and the Bloq Québécois led the way in female representation, with 31 per cent. It seems, then, that the closer you are to power, the fewer women there are. The feminists have a valid point.

Telling It Like It Is

The 'Native' Expert Confesses

I am a white guy who is a 'Native expert'. That has given me a lot of power: I often find myself in the position to declare whether something is or is not 'authentic Indian'. I tend to use 'traditional' rather than 'authentic', but the issue is still the same.

The problem is that I—and outsider experts like me—have too much control over the word 'traditional', and therefore too much say in judging authenticity. What we know are details about the past. But we have no intellectual right to claim that something (for instance, an Ojibwa jingle dress dance performed by a Mohawk) is inauthentic because it isn't how it was done in the past. If a Mohawk does the dance in a way that brings honour to herself and her people, then it is authentic, since that is a traditional role of dancing.

A book I read recently helped me work out this problem. It was called *'Real' Indians and Others: Mixed-Blood Urban Native Peoples and Indigenous Nationhood* (2004). In it, author Bonita Lawrence, a Mi'kmaq woman of mixed heritage and a professor at York University, avoids the term 'traditional culture', using two other terms instead. The first is **primordiality**, which she defines as 'a state of existence in contradistinction to modernity, whereby language, ways of living, and cultural knowledge as manifested by distinct beliefs, traits, and practices, [are] transmitted in relatively unbroken lines from a distant past . . .' (Lawrence 2004: 1). Such a static (i.e. unchanging) construct of culture is what outsider academic 'experts' like me have authority in. It's like knowing the letter of the law. According to a strict primordialist view, a Mohawk performing an Ojibwa dance is not 'traditional', and is therefore inauthentic.

The second, and opposing, term she uses is **indigeneity**, which 'refers less to precolonial states of existence and identity than to a future, postcolonial refashioning of Indigenous identities that are truer to Indigenous histories and cultures than those identities shaped by the colonial realities that continue to surround Native people at present' (Lawrence 2004: 14). This is where the insiders have primary authority. It's a more dynamic view, in which a practice can be informed by traditional culture, but it's not an exact replica. It's like knowing the spirit of the law. From this perspective, a Mohawk performing an Ojibwa dance is honouring traditional Aboriginal culture.

Authenticity is like a river formed by the joining of the two streams of primordiality and indigeneity. Both are authentic. Primordiality tends to be outsider-defined and deals primarily with the details of the past. Indigeneity is mostly insider-defined and deals primarily with the present as reflecting the spirit of the past.

—J.S.

QUICK HITS
Mind Traps in Understanding Culture

Try to avoid these common mind traps in understanding culture:

- thinking that 'culture' refers only to high culture
- thinking that total agreement on what defines a culture can ever exist
- thinking that culture is synonymous with tradition and doesn't change over time
- thinking that 'our' culture is contested whereas other cultures are comparably simple and fixed (for instance, the false but popular notion that Christians differ but that all Muslims, Hindus, Jews, Sikhs, or Buddhists think alike).

We could add age to our portrait of Canada's dominant culture as well. Those who are just starting or have just ended their careers often feel peripheral to the dominant culture. Other factors to consider are sexual orientation, level of education, and overall health (since those with disabilities or chronic medical conditions might feel outside the dominant culture). To summarize, our portrait of Canada's dominant culture looks something like this: white, English-speaking, heterosexual, male university graduate of European background between the ages of 25 and 55, in good health, who owns a home in a middle-class neighbourhood of a city in Ontario or Quebec.

Subcultures are commonly discussed in the culture chapter of sociology textbooks, where they are defined in terms used to describe cultures generally. The beliefs, values, behaviour, and material culture of subcultures are presented and then contrasted with those of a vaguely defined 'larger society' or 'broader culture'. In this way, the term 'subculture' might seem to represent an intellectually 'soft' and socially benign or harmless notion of size difference: the subculture as merely a smaller version of the dominant culture. But this view downplays the imbalance of power—the ability to make political, economic, and social decisions that affect not only oneself and one's family but a good number of others as well—between the dominant cultures and subcultures. For this reason, we find it useful to use the term **subordinate cultures** for those groups who feel the power of the dominant culture and exist in opposition to it, while reserving 'subculture' for those involved in the more neutral cultural contrast often referred to in introductory sociology textbooks: computer nerds, lawyers, sociologists, stamp collectors, and so on. We would then define 'subculture' in terms of a set of minor cultural differences possessed by groups organized around occupations or hobbies, engaged in no significant opposition or challenge to the dominant culture.

Counterculture

Countercultures are defined oppositionally. That is, they are characterized as groups that reject selected elements of the dominant culture (for instance, clothing styles or sexual norms). Examples of

Which of the people in this picture belong to the dominant culture?

Photo: Photodisc

counterculture range from the relatively harmless beatniks of the 1950s and hippies of the 1960s and early 1970s to the dangerous biker gangs that flourish today. A counterculture that is in evidence today is that of the Goths. Descriptions of this counterculture abound on the Internet, from which the following brief description is summarized.

What are Goths? Most people will be able to summon a rough image: dyed black (less often blue) hair, dark clothes, with white makeup that contrasts sharply with clothing and hair colour. When we think of Goths we may think of their supposedly typical fascination with death and with art—especially music and film—that reflects this fascination. But who are the people who belong to this counterculture? What can we add to this picture?

First, they tend to be young. The Goth lifestyle seems to be a phenomenon that is invented and re-invented by the youth cohort of the time. Some bloggers claim that there are three generations of Goths, each not so aware of its predecessors or reincarnations; the 'generation gap' seems a perpetual feature. Second, they are typically white. There are Internet references to black and Asian

Goths, but it appears their numbers are very small. Third, although there has been, to the best of our knowledge, no significant sociological study done of this, they seem to come mostly from middle-class families.

While there is some reason to consider the beatniks the earliest generation of Goths, the oral/Internet history places the origins of the Goth subculture in the late 1970s. The Goth of that period is associated with the song 'Bela Lugosi's Dead', released in 1979 by Bauhaus, and with the look and music of bands such as The Cure and Siouxsie and the Banshees, to mention just two.

The opposition of Goths to dominant culture is expressed most clearly in their dress and overall appearance, but it goes well beyond this visual aspect. The early Goths rejected the Yuppie world of financial self-indulgence and the conservative politics of Ronald Reagan, Maggie Thatcher, and Brian Mulroney; they pursued a life concerned with less world-exploitive politics and cultish small-market arts. Succeeding generations of Goths have taken up different causes, but they carry on the traditional appearance and connection to the arts that their predecessors established.

Photo: Alamy

The Goth 'look' has become popular recently among Tokyo's 'Harajuku girls', whose fashion is inspired by the clothing of Victorian women and girls. Can clothing alone constitute a counterculture or do other values, beliefs, and ideals have to be present?

The Point Is...

Are You Excluded from the Dominant Culture?

Are you excluded from the dominant culture? Here is a simple, informal test.

1. How likely is it that political leaders (prime ministers, premiers, cabinet ministers, opposition leaders, mayors of major cities) are like you in gender, religion, clothing style, language, and parentage?
2. How likely is it that the homes portrayed in most television series look like your home?
3. How likely is it that the lead character in a movie lives a life like yours?
4. How likely is it that your boss is of the same gender, ethnicity, and age as you?
5. How likely is it that in an introductory sociology textbook, there are people like you discussed in every chapter?
6. How likely is it that the authors of an introductory sociology textbook are like you culturally?

7. How likely is it that on reality-based police shows the people who get arrested look like you and your neighbours?
8. How likely is it that people like you are seen demonstrating or protesting something on the TV news or the front page of a newspaper?
9. How likely is it that there are a lot of derogatory slang terms that refer to people like you?
10. How likely are people like you to be called a 'special interest' or a 'designated' group?
11. How often are people like you told you're 'too sensitive' or 'pushy'?
12. How likely are you to be asked, 'Where did you come from?'

For questions 1–6, 'low likelihood' equals exclusion from the dominant culture; for questions 7–12, 'high likelihood' equals exclusion from the dominant culture.

A Theoretical Matter

Just as it is meaningful to distinguish between the dominant culture and subordinate cultures of a single society, it is also worthwhile to differentiate a society's separate countercultures. We could, for instance, draw a distinction among countercultures based on the way each is treated by the dominant culture, as expressed particularly in mainstream media. What we propose to call **dominant countercultures** (i.e. those drawn from the dominant culture) are usually treated with lighthearted criticism and mild restrictions. Think of how Goths are portrayed on television. Different from those are countercultures drawn as subordinate cultures, comprising groups whose class and ethnic background set them apart from the dominant culture. Examples here include the 'gangsta' culture of black youth and, from an earlier time, the zoot-suit culture (see Chapter 6, on deviance).

High Culture versus Popular Culture

The second of our two major oppositions has risen to prominence over the last quarter-century or so. High culture is the culture of the elite, a distinct minority. It is associated with theatre, opera, classical music and ballet, 'serious' works of literary fiction and non-fiction, 'artsy' films (note: *films*, not movies) that may be difficult to appreciate without having taken post-secondary courses on the subject, and a 'cultivated palate' for certain high-priced foods and alcoholic beverages. High culture is sometimes referred to as 'elite culture', which Canadian sociologist Karen Anderson defines as follows:

> Elite culture is produced for and appreciated by a limited number of people with specialized interests. It tends to be evaluated in terms of 'universal' criteria of artistic merit and to be seen as a sign of prestige. Appreciation of elite culture usually entails a process of learning and the acquisition of specific tastes. (Anderson 1996: 471)

French sociologist **Pierre Bourdieu** (1930–2002) coined the term **cultural capital** to refer to the knowledge and skills needed to acquire the sophisticated tastes that mark someone as a person of high culture. The more cultural capital you have, the 'higher' your cultural class.

Popular culture, on the other hand, is the culture of the majority, particularly of those people who do not have power (the working class, the less educated, women, and racialized minorities). Serious academic discussion of popular culture has grown with the rise of **cultural studies** courses and programs. A relatively new field, cultural studies draws on both the social sciences (primarily sociology) and the humanities (primarily literature and media studies) to cast light on the significance of and meanings expressed in popular culture, topics that previously had been mostly neglected by academics.

Mass Culture and Popular Culture

While the terms 'popular culture' and 'mass culture' are sometimes presented as if they were more or less synonymous, there is a crucial distinction: the two differ in terms of **agency**, the ability of 'the people' (i.e. the masses) to be creative or productive with what a colonial power, a dominant culture, or a mass media has given them. Sociologists disagree on how much agency people have. Those who believe that people take an active role in shaping the culture they consume (in terms of the items they buy, the music they listen to, the TV shows and movies they watch) use the term 'popular culture' to describe the majority of those who fall outside the world of the cultural elite. The Internet, particularly sites like YouTube, is a primary vehicle for popular culture since it lets those outside of the cultural elite shape the culture they consume. Those who believe people have little or no agency in the culture they consume are more likely to use the term 'mass culture'. They tend to believe that big companies (Walmart, McDonald's, Disney, and Microsoft, for instance) and powerful governments dictate what people buy, watch, value, and believe. Members of countercultures are predisposed to thinking that those outside their group belong to mass culture.

One feature of mass culture is what French sociologist **Jean Baudrillard** (1929–2007) calls **simulacra**. Simulacra are cultural images, often associated with stereotypes, that are produced and reproduced like material goods or commodities by the media and sometimes by scholars. For example, the Inuit are often represented by simulacra of described practices (e.g. rubbing noses, abandoning elders [see Chapter 1], and wife-sharing) and physical objects (e.g. igloos, kayaks). These images tend to distort contemporary Inuit 'reality'. Consider the way the inukshuk, the Inuit stone figure, has become a Canadian cultural symbol, with models of these stone figures sold in tourist shops across the country. It has such cultural currency that it was incorporated into the logo for the 2010 Winter Olympics held in BC, a province with no Inuit community.

Baudrillard describes simulacra as being 'hyper-real'—that is, likely to be considered more real than what actually exists or existed. If someone were to say to you, 'Save your so-called facts. *I* know what's real—I saw it on television!', you can assume that he or she is heavily influenced by simulacra. Baudrillard illustrates the principle with an analogy of a map. Imagine that you are on a canoe trip and your map indicates that there is a river in a particular place. You paddle your canoe to that place and find only mud. If you keep paddling in search of the promised river because you believe that what the map says is 'more real' than what your eyes see, then the map is a **simulacrum**.

When sociologists encourage their students to be critical of what the media present, they are hoping their students will be able to detect simulacra. The famous 'weapons of mass destruction' that were never found in Iraq are a classic example: governments operated as though these weapons actually existed. The weapons in fact were hyperreal.

The 'Orient', the Western portrait of East Asia and the Middle East described by Edward Said, is a simulacrum. Evidence of Orientalism frequently appears in Western media, and notably in Hollywood representations of the East. A recent example is the 2004 movie *Hidalgo*, discussed in the box on page 74.

British sociologist John Fiske takes the popular culture position. He believes that there is no mass culture, that the power bloc—the political and cultural institutions with the greatest influence on society—merely provides resources that the people resist, evade, or turn to their own ends. He recognizes agency and warns about the dangers of left-leaning sociologists presenting people as mere dupes of mass media. Without using the word, he expresses his concern about the dangers of **victimology**. Victimology has

Why do you think the inukshuk is fast becoming a universal Canadian symbol?

two contrasting meanings in sociology. The first, more general meaning is the study, within criminology, of people who are victims of crime. The second is an outlook that diminishes the victims of crime by portraying them as people who cannot help themselves, who cannot exercise agency. It is in this sense that the term victimology captures Fiske's concerns about the mass culture position of some sociologists.

The Point Is... Aragorn and the Arabs

In March 2004, my wife and I saw the movie *Hidalgo*. Set in the late nineteenth century and starring Viggo Mortensen, the movie tells the supposedly true story of Frank Hopkins, an aging American cowboy and dispatch rider for the US cavalry, who rides his mustang against some of the finest Bedouin thoroughbreds in a 3,000-mile race across the Arabian Desert. We had admired the work of the movie's lead actor in *The Lord of the Rings*, and the trailers for *Hidalgo* made it seem like the type of adventure movie we both enjoy. What we weren't prepared for was the Oriental simulacrum promoted relentlessly throughout the movie. All of the stock features of a romanticized portrait of Arabia were on display: an omnipotent sheik, the Arabs' insatiable thirst for vengeance and callousness concerning the lives of others, Islamic fanaticism and intolerance for non-Muslims, and a veiled Muslim woman willing to be threatened (and rescued) by the heroic Westerner so that she may be freed from the 'oppression' of her veil. She closely resembled the stereotype—another simulacrum—of the Indian Princess (see chapters 12, on race and ethnicity, and 13, on gender inequality).

We appreciated that the hero acknowledged and drew upon his Aboriginal roots, even if his character embodied a few too many clichés. However, the movie was like an old Western, pitting cowboys against Indians—only in this case, the cowboy was part-Indian, and the Indians were really Arabs. Note to the director: Muslims, unlike Orcs, cannot be depicted, one and all, as villains without creating waves in the 'real world' of contemporary politics.

An important distinction between the two positions involves the contrast, identified by de Certeau (1984), between decipherment and reading. **Decipherment** is the process of looking in a text for the definitive interpretation, the intent (conscious or unconscious) of the culture industry in creating the text. For sociologists who believe that mass culture predominates, decipherment is about looking for the message that mass media presents people with, without allowing them to challenge it or reject it by substituting their own.

Sociologists who believe that popular rather than mass culture predominates tend to talk not about decipherment but about reading. **Reading** is the process in which people treat what is provided by the culture industry as a resource or text to be interpreted as they see fit, in ways not necessarily intended by the creators of the text. The sociological technique of reading involves analyzing the narratives of those who are using or have used the text as a cultural resource.

Eric Michaels (1986), describing the way the Aborigines of central Australia received the Sylvester Stallone movie *Rambo*, offers a good example of the difference between decipherment and reading. A mass culture interpretation of the movie would be that it delivers a propaganda message about the triumph of good over evil, of the capitalist West over the communist East. But the Australian Aborigines, who loved the movie, had their own reading of the film:

[T]hey understood the major conflict to be that between Rambo, whom they saw as a representative of the Third World, and the white officer class—a set of meanings that were clearly relevant to their experience of white, postcolonial paternalism and that may well have been functional in helping them to make a resistant sense of their interracial relationships. . . . The Aborigines also produced tribal or kinship relations between Rambo and the prisoners he was rescuing that were more relevant to their social experience than any nationalistic relationships structured around the East–West axis . . . . (Fiske 1994: 57)

Norms

Norms are rules or standards of behaviour that are expected of a group, society, or culture. There isn't always consensus concerning these standards: norms may be contested along the sociological lines of ethnicity, race, gender, and age. Norms are expressed in a culture through various means, from ceremonies that reflect cultural mores to symbolic articles of dress. In the following sections, we'll have a look at the different ways in which norms are expressed or enforced.

Sanctions

People react to how others follow or do not follow the norms of their culture or subculture. If the reaction is one that supports the behaviour, it is called a **positive sanction**. It is a reward for 'doing the right thing'. Positive sanctions can be small things such as smiles, a high five, or a supportive comment, or they can be larger material rewards, such as a bonus for hard work on the job or a plaque for being the 'Innovator of the Year' at college. A hockey player who gets into a fight is positively sanctioned by teammates at the bench banging their sticks against the boards, or by the standing, cheering crowd.

The opposite of a positive sanction is a **negative sanction**. It is a reaction designed to tell offenders they have violated a norm. It could be anything from a 'look' with rolling eyes or a mild joke (like when I hear 'Who are you—Santa Claus?' directed towards me, a middle-aged, well-proportioned sociologist with a big beard) to a nasty note left on the windshield of a car taking up two parking spaces on a crowded street, to the fine you pay at the library for an overdue book.

Folkways, Mores, and Taboos

William Graham Sumner (1840–1910) distinguished three kinds of norms that differ in terms of how seriously they are respected and sanctioned.

The St Louis Blues' Cam Janssen basks in the positive sanction of the home crowd following a fight. Note the Dallas players on the opponents' bench banging their sticks in support of their combatant. Look at the officials: is there any corresponding negative sanction?

Photo: CP Images

He used the term **folkways** for those norms governing day-to-day matters; these are norms that in the normal course of things you '*should* not' (as opposed to '*must* not') violate, and they are the least respected and most weakly sanctioned. The term 'etiquette' can often by applied to folkways. If you want to think of folkways with an example from popular culture, think of George Costanza on the TV show *Seinfeld*. He continually violates folkways: double-dipping chips and fetching a chocolate éclair out of the garbage come immediately to mind.

Mores

Mores (pronounced like the eels—*morays*) are norms that are taken much more seriously than folkways. They are rules you '*must* not' violate. Some mores—against rape, killing, vandalism, and most forms of stealing, for example—are enshrined in the criminal code as laws. Violation of some mores, even if they are not laws, will meet with shock or severe disapproval. Booing the national anthem of the visiting team prior to a sporting event is likely to cause offence among supporters of the visitors and even anger or embarrassment among fans of the home side. Violations of this kind can be complicated and contested. For example, some fans at Toronto Blue Jay home games did not stand during the playing of 'God Bless America', which was mandatory at all Major League Baseball ballparks for a short period during the US's 'War on Terror'. Is this an unforgivable breach of mores or a justifiable negative sanction of American foreign policy?

Mores of cleanliness, too, are in the cultural eye of the beholder. In Britain, dogs are allowed in pubs; in Canada, they are not. This does not mean that bars in Canada are more sanitary than those in Britain. Many readers of this textbook will be able to think of bars restricted to human rather than canine patrons that have appallingly unsanitary conditions, particularly in the washrooms. Differences in mores of cleanliness can lead to serious problems when, for instance, an overdeveloped Western sense of what is hygienic jeopardizes the health of a hospital patient (see the example of the Hmong study in Chapter 10, on medical sociology).

Like folkways, mores can change over time. A young woman sporting a tattoo would once have been seen as violating the mores of acceptable behaviour for a lady. Today, many women have tattoos and display them without arousing the kind of shock or condemnation generally produced when mores are violated.

What do YOU think?

Recently, the cultural more of shaking hands has been challenged by the atmosphere of fear surrounding H1N1. Do you think that this could affect the practice in the future? Will it be replaced by something perceived as more hygienic (like bumping elbows)?

Taboos

A **taboo** is a norm so deeply ingrained in our social consciousness that the mere thought or mention of it is enough to arouse disgust or revulsion. Cannibalism, incest, and child pornography are examples that come immediately to mind. Taboos affect our dietary habits: for instance, eating dogs, cats, or other animals that might be considered family pets is taboo in North American culture, and there are religious taboos surrounding the consumption of certain foods—pork by Jews and Muslims, beef by Hindus. Some cultures recognize gender taboos, such as those aimed at women 'interfering' with or partaking in typical male activities. Consider the following from Anna Reid's *The Shaman's Coat* (2002). The speaker is an older woman of the Nivkh people of Siberia:

> Everything about men was sacred; everything about women was dirty. If a man was sitting down it was wrong to step over his legs—it would bring bad weather when he was out hunting. If I or my sisters just touched a gun, we'd get such a scolding. I remember once, my father went out to check his traps, and didn't come back for a long time. We all sat there holding our heads, wondering what we'd done wrong. (Reid 2002: 155)

Symbols

Symbols are cultural items, either tangible (i.e. physical) or intangible, that come to take on tremendous meaning within a culture or subculture of a society. Symbols can be material objects, as illustrated

The Point Is...

The Jackrocks Story: A Narrative about the Power of Symbols

In the fall of 1989, I travelled through rural Virginia on a short lecture tour, having been invited by staff and students of Southwest Virginia Community College who had attended a lecture of mine during their spring break. I spent the first night of my stay at the home of the college president. It was elegant, finely furnished, with everything in its place. While there, I noticed something that surprised me. In a glass case—the kind normally used to hold curios and objets d'art, such as glass and china figurines—I saw two 6-pointed objects, each one made of three nails. They reminded me of the jacks I had played with as a child. Why had these mean-looking items been placed on display?

The next night I stayed with a coal-miner's family. It was a fascinating evening. Among the things I learned from them are that moonshine drunk from a mason jar can disconnect your brain from your feet, and that the term 'cakewalk'—a surprisingly easy task—comes from a game resembling musical chairs, in which the winner receives a cake as a prize. During a more serious conversation I learned about the dynamics of a months-long coalminer's strike in the one-industry area. I was taken on a tour of the strike centre, where bunk beds were being built to accommodate the families of striking workers who had been thrown out of their homes for failing to pay the rent. The people I met there were friendly, but the long strike was crushing their spirit.

The mining company was owned by people from outside the area—foreigners, in the eyes of the locals. But then, even the state capital of Richmond was considered foreign, much like Halifax is by people who live in Cape Breton. The company owners had circumvented the picket lines by trucking the coal out at night, but striking miners in camouflage had found ways to thwart their efforts. One of my cherished souvenirs of the trip is a camouflage T-shirt with 'Holding the Line in 1989'. I wore it with pride during a strike at Ontario community colleges that same fall.

The next day, at Southwest Virginia Community College, I spoke to a sociology class about symbols. Near the end of the class, I asked whether there were any local symbols. One student piped up, 'Jackrocks.' When I asked what 'jackrocks' were, I got a description of the 6-pointed objects I had seen in the president's glass case, as well as a bag full of jackrocks handed to me by a student who went to his car to get them. I was told that one of the tactics used to keep the coal trucks from shipping out the coal was to toss these jackrocks underneath the tires. The jackrocks had become symbols of resistance. They appeared in store windows in the town nearest the mine, and I was given a pair of small, aluminum jackrock earrings—another souvenir. I then understood why the college president kept the two jackrocks in the glass case. He was from Florida, and therefore a 'foreigner' to the area. By keeping the jackrocks in a place of honour, he was expressing solidarity with his students and their community.

● ● ● ● ● ● ● ● ● ● ● ● ● ● ● ● ● ●

What do YOU think?

1. What meaning did the jackrocks have for the local people of southwestern Virginia?

2. Why do you think the college president kept jackrocks in his glass case at home? Do you think he fully appreciated their significance?

● ● ● ● ● ● ● ● ● ● ● ● ● ● ● ● ● ●

in the narrative on this page, or non-material objects such as songs or the memory of events.

Symbols of Ethnic Identity

Canadians travelling abroad often wear pins with little Canadian flags on them or display the Maple Leaf on their backpacks. A flag is one symbol of ethnic identity. For Americans, the symbolic significance of the flag is even more firmly entrenched: it is the subject of their national anthem; in schools, they pledge allegiance to it; and many support a law that makes it illegal to burn or otherwise desecrate it. In Zimbabwe, the national currency bears the symbol of a bird carved in stone; the image represents the birds found in the Great Zimbabwe, the large stone ruin after which the country was named. Scottish people show a great emotional attachment to songs about battles fought in the early fourteenth century against the English. These are all symbols of ethnic identity: items that contribute to a people's sense of national or ethnic identity.

The Veil as a Symbol for Canadian Muslim Women

Few clothing symbols have a greater power to evoke emotions than the Muslim veil, or (in Arabic) **hijab**. For many in the West, it is a symbol of patriarchal domination by weapons-waving misogynist young men of the Taliban, similar in effect to the full-length, screen-faced *burqa* that hides Afghan women from the world of opportunities and freedom, and to the *chador* that Iranian women are forced by law to wear. Former British prime minister Tony Blair condemned it as a 'mark of separation' that made others feel uncomfortable and that discouraged the integration of Muslims with mainstream British society.

It is important for readers of this textbook to understand some of the reasons why women of various cultures—especially in Canada—choose to wear the veil. For this information there can be no better source than the community of Canadian women of Middle Eastern background who have considered the choice themselves. We will get to specific reasons in a moment, but in the meantime, one point must be emphasized: for a significant number of women in Canada, as for those women in France who opposed a law that would ban the veil in French schools, the veil is a matter of choice, not command.

To hear the perspective of Canadian Muslim women on this subject we are drawing upon a groundbreaking study carried out by Iranian-Canadian anthropologist Homa Hoodfar (2003) in Montreal during the mid-1990s. The voices Hoodfar recorded speak compellingly of their choice to wear the veil as a way of opposing restrictions placed on them (and not their brothers) as teenagers by parents concerned that their daughters will fall prey to the irreligious sex-, alcohol-, and drug-related behaviours of North American culture. Some saw veil-wearing as a step, together with Qur'anic study and banding together with Canadian Muslim women of different cultural backgrounds, down a path of opposition to some of the patriarchal mores of their specific cultures. In addition, taking the veil gave some of them the opportunity to defend their faith against the ignorance and ethnocentrism of some of their fellow Canadians. The three examples in the box on page 79 are particularly instructive.

Photo: Graham Bibby/CP Photo

A Muslim woman wearing a hijab passes a Paris clothing store, as symbols of beauty and identity face each other. How you interpret the look she is giving the picture might depend on your cultural background.

Telling It Like It Is

The Hijab as Worn by Young Canadian Muslim Women in Montreal

POINT OF VIEW

1. Narrative of a 19-year-old Palestinian-Canadian Woman

The veil has freed me from arguments and headaches. I always wanted to do many things that women normally do not do in my culture. I had thought living in Canada would give me that opportunity. But when I turned fourteen, my life changed. My parents started to limit my activities and even telephone conversations. My brothers were free to go and come as they pleased, but my sister and I were to be good Muslim girls. . . . Life became intolerable for me. The weekends were hell.

Then as a way out, I asked to go to Qur'anic classes on Saturdays. There I met with several veiled women of my age. They came from similar backgrounds. None of them seemed to face my problems. Some told me that since they took the veil, their parents know that they are not going to do anything that goes against Muslim morality. The more I hung around with them, the more convinced I was that the veil is the answer to all Muslim girls' problems here in North America. Because parents seem to be relieved and assured that you are not going to do stupid things, and your community knows that you are acting like a Muslim woman, you are much freer. (Hoodfar 2003: 20–1)

2. Narrative of a 17-year-old Pakistani-Canadian Woman

Although we did not intermingle much with non-Indian-Canadians, I very much felt at home and part of the wider society. This, however, changed as I got older and clearly my life was different than many girls in my class. I did not talk about boyfriends and did not go out. I did not participate in extracurricular activities. Gradually, I began feeling isolated. Then my cousin and I decided together to wear the veil and made a pact to ignore people's comments, that no matter how much hardship we suffered at school, we would keep our veils on.

One weekend we announced this to our surprised parents. They . . . consented, though they did not think we would stick with it. . . . At first it was difficult. At school people joked and asked stupid questions, but after three months they took us more seriously and there was even a little bit of respect. We even got a little more respect when we talked about Islam in our classes, while before our teacher dismissed what we said if it didn't agree with her casual perceptions. (Hoodfar 2003: 28–9)

3. Narrative of Mona, an Egyptian-Canadian Woman

I would never have taken up the veil if I lived in Egypt. Not that I disagree with that, but I see it as part of the male imposition of rules. . . . The double standard frustrates me. But since the Gulf War, seeing how my veiled friends were treated, I made a vow to wear the veil to make a point about my Muslimness and Arabness. I am delighted when people ask me about my veil and Islam, because it gives me a chance to point out their prejudices concerning Muslims. (Hoodfar 2003: 30)

4. A Muslim Student from Montreal Reacts to the Examples

The young women in these articles claim that wearing the hijab, overall brought them joy and happiness. However, look at the reason they decided to wear the hijab. In the first example, it was because her parents were not letting her go out and be free like her brothers. So she wore it to gain her own freedom, not to appreciate anything about the culture. In the second, it was because they did not talk about going out or boyfriends. Big deal! Many people do not talk about those things. It was their own minds that made them feel isolated, not the culture surrounding them. And the third example, I feel she did it for more right reasons than any of the others. Nevertheless, to prove a point???

I do not wear this 'veil', but have relatives that do. It does not make me a 'poor' Muslim woman. Even if a girl has this 'veil' on she can still do bad things and be persuaded to do bad things just like anyone else.

—Ferita Haque

Values

Values are the standards used by a culture to describe abstract qualities such as goodness, beauty, and justice, and to assess the behaviour of others. Values have long been a topic of great interest to sociologists. Max Weber's identification of the Protestant work ethic is but one early example of a sociological study of values. But in spite of these studies, values remain difficult to understand and to represent accurately. What makes the issue especially puzzling is that the values that people claim to have are not always the ones they act upon. Do we recognize, then, the value that is professed or the value that is reflected in human action? Is the person who preaches a value but fails to honour it in his or her daily life necessarily a hypocrite?

The issue revolves around the distinction between **ideal culture** and **real culture**, the former more talked about, the latter more acted upon. A person might speak passionately at a community meeting about the place of environmentalism in an ideal culture, then drive three blocks home in a gas-guzzling SUV. The same person might not always put recyclable garbage in the recycling bins because he or she is 'in a hurry'. And sometimes we feel we don't have a choice. We might hate the idea of driving to work, but if we live in a small town with no bus or train service to the big city we work in, we have no option but to drive. The society does, but the individual in this case really does not.

There can be value contradictions in what people say and do that are different from the contradictions of ideal and real culture. Holding a double standard can be a value contradiction. We see this in examples of racism. Nineteenth-century Canadian governments, whose members no doubt believed strongly in individual freedom, created policies that put tight restrictions on Native people and limited the freedom of black refugees who fled slavery after the War of 1812 to come to supposed freedom and opportunity in Nova Scotia (see Chapter 12, on race and ethnicity). Patrick Henry, the American patriot and revolutionary who famously declared, 'Give me liberty or give me death,' owned slaves.

Canadian and American Values

Canadians will regularly compare themselves with Americans on anything from foreign policy to curling prowess. In fact, some Canadians like to define themselves by what an American is *not*, making statements like, 'A Canadian is an unarmed American with health insurance.' But how much do these two neighbouring societies really differ in their values?

Michael Adams, of the Environics Research Group, has been conducting and publishing polls since the early 1980s. One of the things he has done in this capacity is to measure and track 100 'social values' of Canadians. In *Fire and Ice: The United States, Canada and the Myth of Converging Values* (2003) he draws on his own findings, as well as those of American sociologist Seymour Martin Lipset (1990), to contrast the values of Canadians and Americans. His thesis is that Canadians and Americans are becoming more different rather than more alike in their values. It certainly seemed so in 2003, when the American military was heading into Iraq and Canada was not, and when a modest majority of Canadians supported gay marriage and the liberalization of marijuana laws, two social changes that were not on the radar screen of American values. The following discussion deals with a number of the divergent trends Adams claimed were taking place.

Adams based his findings not on informal research or anecdotal evidence but on data from polls conducted by Environics in the US and Canada in 1992, 1996, and 2000. Still, it's always important to look at the data critically. For one thing, the polls prompted respondents to 'talk' about their values. Remember the difference between professed and real values—are these kinds of responses likely to yield data accurate enough to identify actual cultural differences? Another point: is the time period—from 1992 to 2000—long enough to produce evidence of what he calls 'long-term shifts'? Remember, too, that all of this data was gathered before 11 September 2001; Adams is quick to point this out, though he argues that the events of that day would only make the differences he identified greater. We will look at one of the value clusters Adams identified—**patriarchy**—leaving out his interpretation and leaving you, the reader, to put in your own.

Even Canadian and American flags reflect different cultural values. The Canadian flag, handed down by the government in 1965 (we had to look that up), features a leaf that is not native to most of the country. First sewn by Betsy Ross, the American flag emerged as a powerful symbol during the American Revolution and is still the subject of the country's national anthem.

Photo: iStockphoto

Adams used two statements to measure patriarchy:

1. 'The father of the family must be master in his own home.'
2. 'Men are naturally superior to women.'

Respondents were asked whether they agreed with these two statements. Table 3.1 presents the results.

Note the increase in the difference after each four-year period. It's worth observing that even the ranges of the two countries do not intersect: agreement with this statement among Canadian respondents ranged from a province-wide low of 15 per cent (in Quebec) to a high of 21 per cent (in the Prairie provinces) in the 2000 poll; agreement among US respondents ranged from 29 per cent in New England all the way to 71 per cent in the Deep South (Adams 2003: 87).

The percentage of difference between Canadian and American agreement on the second question was less than on the first (see Table 3.2), but notice how the difference again increased over each four-year period.

Table 3.1 Percentage of respondents agreeing with the statement 'The father of the family must be master of his own home.'

YEAR	CANADA	UNITED STATES	DIFFERENCE
1992	26	42	16
1996	20	44	24
2000	18	49	31

Source: From *Fire and Ice* by Michael Adams. Copyright © Michael Adams, 2003. Reprinted by permission of Penguin Group (Canada): 50–1.

Table 3.2 Percentage of respondents agreeing with the statement 'Men are naturally superior to women.'			
YEAR	CANADA	UNITED STATES	DIFFERENCE
1992	26	30	4
1996	23	32	9
2000	24	38	14

Source: From *Fire and Ice* by Michael Adams. Copyright © Michael Adams, 2003. Reprinted by permission of Penguin Group (Canada): 50–1.

What do YOU think?

1. The findings in tables 3.1 and 3.2 appear to support Adams's thesis that American and Canadian social values are becoming less alike. How convincing do you find them?

2. What do you think the cause of the growing difference might be?

3. Could the difference be caused by the greater participation of Americans in organized religion? If so, do you think the use of values likely to be shaped by religion is a fair way to measure Canadian–American social difference?

Ethnocentrism

Ethnocentrism occurs when someone holds up one culture (usually, but not always, the culture of the ethnocentric individual) as the standard by which all cultures are to be judged. It follows a simple formula: 'All cultures like the gold-standard culture (usually, but not always the one "I" belong to), are good, praiseworthy, beautiful, moral, and modern. Those that are not are bad, ugly, immoral, and primitive.' Ethnocentrism can manifest itself in many forms. It can entail saying that business should be run in only one way—the way of the cultural model—that policing should take only one form, or that progressive policies should concentrate only on certain ideas.

Ethnocentrism is often the product of ignorance. For instance, there are North American websites reporting that Chinese people eat aborted fetuses. This idea, which has become an urban legend, may have its origins in the idea that in some cultures, a mother who has just given birth eats a piece of the placenta, in an act that combines symbolism and tradition with beliefs about the nutritive value of placenta.

Hmong refugees living in the United States have had to contend with this kind of ethnocentric ignorance. They have been targeted because of their supposed practice of stealing, killing, and eating dogs. Lack of evidence or truth does not deter an ethnocentric public from spreading these stories about a 'foreign' culture. According to Roger Mitchell, the false stories follow particular themes:

[Rumored] methods of [dog] procurement vary. Some are coaxed home by Hmong children. Some were adopted from animal shelters (until those in charge noted a high rate of adoption). Others are strays. The most common accusation is theft, often from backyards, sometimes leaving the head and collar as mute testimony to Rover's passing. . . . The dog is usually an expensive one, often owned by a doctor. The theft is observed, the license plate number is marked down. When the police check, the dog is already in some Hmong family's pot.

The supposed proof varies. That fixture in the urban legend, the garbage man, reports the presence of canine remains in Hmong garbage cans. Carcasses are seen hanging in the cellar by meter readers, salesmen, or whomever. Freezers are said to be full of frozen dogs. A bizarre touch is that the dogs are supposedly skinned alive to make them more tasty. (quoted in Fadiman 1997: 190–1)

On a larger scale, ethnocentrism has played a role in the colonizing efforts of powerful nations that have tried to impose their political, economic, and religious beliefs on the indigenous populations of lands they 'discovered'. European missionaries arriving in present-day North America found a large indigenous population they regarded as uncivilized, uneducated, and badly in need of Christianity to replace their pagan spirituality. European ideas stemmed from the belief that their god—the Christian God—was the only true god. This kind of ethnocentric treatment of North American Aboriginal people did not end there, as succeeding generations of religious, government, and social leaders laboured to impose European values on the Native population. The church-run residential schools for Native children are a well-known example of how misguided such ethnocentric beliefs can be and what tragic results they can produce. The following discussion highlights another example of how Canada's First Nations were forced by an ethnocentric government to abandon a traditional custom.

● ● ● ● ● ● ● ● ● ● ● ● ● ● ● ● ● ● ● ●

What do YOU think?

While in Canada dogs are seen as pets, in other cultures they are seen as edible meat. Western ethnocentrism informs the protests to stop the consumption of dog meat in other cultures; it is called 'barbaric' and 'insidious'. But is there any difference between eating a dog and eating a chicken, pig, lamb, or cow?

● ● ● ● ● ● ● ● ● ● ● ● ● ● ● ● ● ● ● ●

The Potlatch Act of 1884

The **potlatch** is a traditional ceremony of the Northwest Coast Native people. It revolves around the acquisition or affirmation of hereditary names. During the ceremony, the host of the potlatch demonstrates his social, economic, and spiritual worthiness to be given the hereditary name. An important aspect of the event is the telling, singing, and acting out of stories. In this way, potlatches affirm the possession of the stories, songs, dances, carved and painted images, masks, and musical instruments used by the hosting group to celebrate the cultural history of the name and those identified with it. These hereditary names carry more than just symbolic significance: they are connected with rights to fish, hunt, or forage for plants in a particular territory, and with the responsibility to conserve the living entities within that territory. Potlatches go a long way in maintaining the strength and social unity of the group.

Another important aspect of the potlatch is the giving away of gifts and possessions. One way for a high-ranking man to prove he was worthy of his position was to give away many gifts. The hierarchical nature of Northwest Coast culture made this very competitive, as those holding or aspiring to high rank gave away as much as they could afford. The level of competition rose after European contact, in part because of the availability of European manufactured goods, but also because of the toll European diseases took on the Native population. The population of the Kwakiutl of Vancouver Island, for example, dropped from roughly 8,000 in 1835 to around 2,000 in 1885. When diseases decimated lineages entitled to important names, more distant relatives would vie for prestigious family names. In some cases, competition could become socially divisive, and there were even incidents in which property was destroyed as a show of wealth ('I am so rich, that this property means nothing to me'). Such incidents appear to have been rare, but over-reported in the literature. And by its very nature, the potlatch encouraged the circulation of wealth throughout the community, for one could be a host on the giving side at one potlatch, a guest on the receiving side of the next.

In 1884, the Government of Canada, under pressure from church leaders opposed to 'pagan practices' and fearful of the Native population because of rumoured Métis, Cree, and Blackfoot hostility on the prairies, made the potlatch illegal:

Every Indian or other person who engages in or assists in celebrating the Indian festival known as the 'Potlatch'. . . is guilty of a misdemeanour, and shall be liable to imprisonment for a term of not more than six nor less than two months in any gaol or other place of confinement, and any Indian or other person who encourages, either directly or indirectly, an Indian or Indians to get up such a festival or dance, or to celebrate the same, or who shall assist in the celebration of same, is guilty of a like offense, and shall be liable to the same punishment.

In 1921, 45 of the highest ranking Kwakiutl were arrested, and 22 were sentenced to prison terms of two to three months. For the community, the tragedy was twofold: first, they had lost their leaders; second, they lost many sacred potlatch items that were taken as a condition for the release of community members arrested but not charged. The items became the property of the Minister of Indian Affairs, who distributed them to art collectors and museums.

In 1951, the potlatch ban was repealed. But it wasn't until 1975 that the National Museum declared it would return the sacred items—provided they be kept in museums. The Royal Ontario Museum returned the items it had in 1988, and the National Museum of the American Indian in New York repatriated some of its holdings in 1993. Some items will never be recovered.

We see ethnocentrism here at several levels. Northwest Coast ceremonies were not respected because they differed from Western ceremonies. They involved dance, drums, masks, and other elements not typically found in Christian churches. If there were parallels in Western culture, they were not recognized.

Ethnocentrism is not a phenomenon confined to the West, or to white people. When the Japanese seized control of its northern islands from the Ainu, the indigenous people of those islands, they developed and implemented ethnocentric policies that rival any laws enacted by the governments of Canada and the United States to limit the freedoms of the North American Native people.

Eurocentrism

It is easier, and perhaps more enlightening, to say what **Eurocentrism** *involves* than what it *is*. It involves addressing others from a broadly defined 'European' (i.e. western and northern European, and North American) position and assuming that the audience is, or would like to be, part of that 'we'. It can be seen in historical references to the 'known world'—that is, the world as it was known by Europeans—and, of course, to

An Indonesian boy sleeps on a piece of cardboard in a Jakarta slum. Cultural globalization contributes to the loss of cultural identity in favour of a homogenous culture based on Western icons and values.

Photo: AP Photo/Ed Wray

Going Global

Observing Cultural Globalization in Taiwan in 1997

As a product, and critic, of Western culture, I am always shocked when, travelling abroad, I see signs of Western popular culture.

On a recent trip to Taiwan, I was struck by evidence of cultural globalization all around me, on two occasions in particular. The first occurred as I was walking on the outskirts of an orange grove in what was, for all intents and purposes, a reserve of the local indigenous people (the Amis, an Austronesian people). In the distance I saw an old woman by herself, picking oranges. She was wearing one of those broad, conical 'coolie' hats made of straw, the kind that is so identifiable as a 'Chinese hat'. It made me feel, as I did more than once on that trip, that I was culturally a long way from home. Yet I felt much closer to home as I neared her and saw that she was wearing a T-shirt emblazoned with the Nike swoosh and the caption 'Just Do It'.

The second time cultural globalization struck me in Taiwan was in the Taipei night market. As I was looking for clothes, in a somewhat distracted way, I turned a corner and was jolted by the sudden appearance of a tall black man. As my mind and eyes adjusted, I realized first that he looked familiar, second that it was none other than Michael Jordan, decked out in his familiar Chicago Bulls uniform. It was merely a life-sized cardboard cutout, used for promotional purposes, but it was a shock nevertheless.

A few days later, talking to a high-school class, I asked what their favourite sport was. I was expecting it to be baseball, given Taiwan's enviable international record in Little League baseball. I was surprised, though, to hear most of them reply, 'Basketball.'

While writing up this narrative, I checked on some statistics (one of a sociologist's favourite activities), and I noticed something interesting, which may be significant. While Taiwan had been very successful at all age levels (9–12, 14–16, and 16–18) throughout the 1970s and 1980s, that success was not repeated from the mid-1990s, when the profile of Chicago Bulls forward Michael Jordan and, later, Chinese centre Yao Ming became international. Could Taiwan's baseball program be a victim of 1990s cultural globalization, with basketball being promoted more than baseball?

Photo: CP/AP/Ng Han Guan

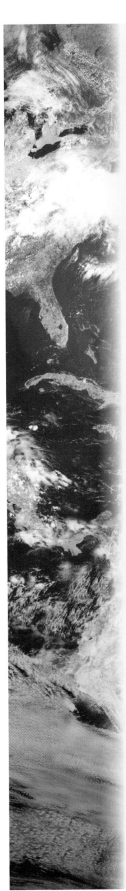

Basketball's popularity in China got a boost when the NBA's Houston Rockets drafted Chinese centre Yao Ming. But why are sports such as soccer, cricket, rugby, and lacrosse still not very popular in North America?

Christopher Columbus 'discovering' in 1492 continents that were already home to millions of people, whose ancestors had settled more than 15,000 years earlier. It involves a tendency to foreground discoveries and contributions that are Western, and background those that are not. It involves promoting the cause of historical heroes and heroines who are European or who acted to benefit a European cause. For example, it is a Eurocentric tendency to downplay or ignore the fact that Native agriculture gave the world many crops—arguably the most, by volume, of all the crops currently grown: corn, squash and pumpkins, most beans, peppers (hot and sweet), potatoes, tomatoes, and sunflowers, to mention just some.

Cultural Globalization

Manfred Steger defines cultural globalization as 'the intensification and expansion of cultural flows across the globe' (2003: 69). The concern here is with what some have called the 'Americanization' of the world, or with what can more broadly be termed the danger of a one-directional flow of culture. Think of the factors. First of all, English has emerged as by far the most prominent language of science, of the Internet, and of other powerful media. Second, American movies and television are seen in almost every country in the world. But to label this 'American' culture is perhaps giving it too broad a scope, when you consider that it is just a small number of transnational companies—AT&T, AOL/Time Warner, Universal, Viacom, General Electric, and Walt Disney in the US, as well as the European companies Bertelsmann and Vivendi, and Sony in Japan—that control most of the media. Not only do these companies reap enormous dividends by exporting their respective brands of Western culture to consumers across the globe, but as Steger points out, they draw audiences abroad away from the culture of their own countries into a global 'gossip market' that revolves around the 'vacuous details of the private lives of American celebrities like Britney Spears, Jennifer Lopez, Leonardo DiCaprio, and Kobe Bryant' (Steger 2003: 77).

It's worth noting as well that the interpretation of globalized items of American culture are not necessarily the same abroad as they are in the US—remember the Aborigines and their reading of *Rambo*. The classic study of a cultural reading by a non-Western audience of a Western cultural item is described by anthropologist Laura Bohannan in her article 'Shakespeare in the Bush' (1966). In it she describes her experience of telling Shakespeare's *Hamlet* to the Tiv of West Africa, and the spin they put on it. The article concludes with the words of a Tiv elder. After admitting that he had enjoyed Bohannan's story, told 'with very few mistakes' (which he corrected), the elder said:

> Sometime…you must tell us some more stories of your country. We, who are elders, will instruct you in their true meaning, so that when you return to your own land your elders will see that you have not been sitting in the bush, but among those who know things and who have taught you wisdom. (Bohannan 1997: 47)

Reverse Ethnocentrism

Not to be confused with **xenocentrism**—a preference for foreign goods and tastes based on the belief that anything foreign must be better than the same thing produced domestically—**reverse ethnocentrism** involves assuming, often blindly, that a particular culture that is not one's own is better than one's own in some way. Reverse ethnocentrism sets an absolute standard that one's own culture does not or cannot match. In the United States, liberal Americans who blame their own country's cultural values and foreign policy for terrorist attacks on Americans at home and abroad are sometimes accused of reverse ethnocentrism and anti-Americanism by more conservative thinkers. Sometimes the myth of the **noble savage** is seen as an instance of reverse ethnocentrism. The term 'noble savage' refers to any idealized representation of primitive culture that symbolizes the innate goodness of humanity when free of the corrupting influence of civilization. It was a theme especially popular in literature of the seventeenth and eighteenth centuries, when European explorers were encountering the indigenous populations of foreign lands. The image of the noble savage, which is frequently invoked today by opponents of globalization, is largely drawn by matching the perceived flaws of Western civilization—pollution, consumerism, exploitation, warfare—with their opposites: environmental balance, subsistence economy, fair trade, peace.

A strong sense of reverse ethnocentrism is sometimes felt by the children of immigrants, who may turn their backs on their parents' cultural roots in an attempt to fit into their adoptive culture. Children of families that have immigrated to the West can be bombarded by messages implying that the cultural ideal is not their own, not the one of their parents or grandparents. When these first-generation Canadian children achieve positions of linguistic power by having 'better

Going Global

Pioneer Global Village

I was asked to help guide Indonesian science teachers on a bus trip to a few of the educational sites near my college in northwestern Toronto. We went to Crawford Lake Conservation Area, where they have reconstructed fourteenth-century Iroquois longhouses. These were easy to explain to my visitors, who knew of cultures in their own country that had lived in similar dwellings. I was aware of this connection, and it made my explanations that much simpler.

The next sight we were going to visit would, I thought, be more difficult to contextualize. We were going to Black Creek Pioneer Village, a reconstructed nineteenth-century settler community where historical interpreters dressed in period costume demonstrate various aspects of pioneer life to school groups and tourists. As we approached the site, I was frantically searching my mind for points of connection that would make this part of the trip understandable.

I needn't have bothered. For as I entered the park with my Indonesian teachers, and they all looked out in interest, one loud voice suddenly piped up, 'Hey, it's just like *Little House on the Prairie*.' That television show, based on the Laura Ingalls Wilder novels depicting life in the American West during the 1870s, had been shown from 1975 to 1982 in North America, but had lived on in reruns around the world—including Indonesia.

My visitor's ready reference to a classic American television show caught me by surprise, but then the American Midwest of the nineteenth century has no less to do with Indonesia than turn-of-the-twentieth-century Prince Edward Island has to do with Japan, where Lucy Maud Montgomery's heroine Anne of Green Gables flourishes as a cultural icon. Should we feel proud, as Canadians, that one of our literary figures has been embraced halfway around the globe or unnerved that a piece of cultural property has been bought and transformed to serve the global marketplace?

Photo: © Nippon Animation Co., Ltd 1979

Sailor Moon meets Anne of Green Gables.

English' than their parents, and when peer pressure makes them want to be like 'real Canadian' children, pre-teens, and teens, they can easily succumb to reverse ethnocentrism.

Cultural Relativism

Cultural relativism is an approach to studying the context of an aspect of another culture. It can be spoken of as existing at two levels. One is the level of understanding. Because of the *holistic* nature of culture—because everything is connected in a system—no single thing can be understood outside of its social, historical, and environmental context. Every aspect of culture has strings attached. Just as you can't understand a single part of a car without understanding the system of which it is a part, so you must understand individual aspects of culture within their cultural context.

Unlike what Spock used to say in the original *Star Trek*, logic (as a pure entity) does *not* dictate. Logic is a cultural construct, and every culture has its own cultural logic. Any explanation of a cultural practice or belief must in some way incorporate this logic. This is especially important in medicine. Western medicine is dominated by a kind of ethnocentric logic that states that nothing worth knowing comes from non-Western traditions. Yet in order to cure or to heal, it's important to respond to the way the patient envisions the healing process. This point comes across with striking clarity in the award-winning book *The Spirit Catches You and You Fall Down: A Hmong Child, Her American Doctors and the Collision of Two Cultures*, by Anne Fadiman (1997). The book describes American doctors and nurses failing to respect, among other things, the Hmong people's spiritual connections to medicine, the importance of encouraging their belief that a cure is available, and the role this belief plays in the curing process.

The second—and more contested—level at which cultural relativism operates is that of *judging*. One viewpoint suggests that individuals should not be judged by the practices of their culture. They have relatively little choice in what they do. After all, they no more invented those customs that might be objectionable than they invented their more laudable practices. Consider the Maasai, an African people with a strong warrior

tradition, who have a custom in which boys, at the onset of puberty, are circumcised. It is frightening and painful, but it is an important initiation ceremony: only once he has gone through the ceremony is a Maasai boy treated as a man and permitted to have sex with women. It is easy for Canadians to judge this custom negatively, to be critical of those who perpetuate what they consider a cruel and barbaric ritual. But is that right?

Cultural Relativism, Ethnocentrism, and Smell: Two Stories

Our senses are conditioned to a certain extent by our culture. Our perception of beauty is affected by culture. Many North Americans have a skinny model (or skinny models) in their minds when they think of female beauty. And, if sales and commercials are anything to judge by, they set a great deal by the whiteness of a person's teeth. What we hear as either 'music' or 'noise' is conditioned by our experience—our ears are not totally our own. The same applies to our noses.

Describing his experience working in the Peace Corps, an organization of volunteers working in developing countries, Tom Bissell noted how difficult he found it to share a bus in the central Asian country of Uzbekistan with people who were overdressed for the weather, and smelly. He made the following observation:

> When I was in the Peace Corps, one of my least favorite things was when my fellow volunteers complained about Central Asian body odor, even though most people in Central Asia did indeed smell really bad. But Gandhi probably smelled bad. Surely Abraham Lincoln smelled, as . . . did . . . King George, and Henry IV. William Shakespeare was, in all likelihood, rank. . . . Most certainly Jesus and Julius Caesar and the Buddha all smelled terrible. People have been smelly for the vast majority of human history. By gooping up our pheromonal reactors with dyed laboratory gels, could it be that we in the West are to blame for our peculiar alienation? Might not the waft from another's armpit contain crucial bioerotic code? Could it be by obscuring such code we have confused otherwise very simple matters of attraction? (Bissell 2003: 98)

Telling It Like It Is

A Sociologist Sees Beauty in Taiwan: Reverse Ethnocentrism

POINT OF VIEW

It was my first trip to Asia, and not a moment passed when I wasn't aware I was no longer in Canada. The streets of Taipei, capital of Taiwan, buzzed with the sound of scooters; small feral dogs roamed the sidewalks; rooftop gardens crowned many of the buildings with lush greenery; and everywhere my whiteness drew gawks and stares from the locals. A group of school kids in the museum pointed to me more often than to the exhibits. A young girl, brimming with fragile self-confidence, walked up to me, and with her best English looked at the painting I was viewing and said, 'Beautiful, isn't it?'

Late one evening, I think it was the third night we were there, we decided to go to the Shilin night market, where food and clothing is sold at hundreds of stalls. For a special price, you can have the tourist special: 'freshly killed snake'. Weighing just over 200 pounds (okay, *well* over), I often find it hard to get well-fitting clothes in Canada, and at the night market, where I was something of a curiosity because of my size, it was even more difficult. It was fascinating, nevertheless, to visit the clothing vendors, to be encouraged by entire families to buy from their family stall.

During the tour I saw something strange, and my sociological spider senses began to tingle. After noting it once I began to look for it, and I saw it again and again: the mannequins in the clothing stalls were modelled after Europeans. I did not see one 'Chinese' mannequin, either there or anywhere I went the entire week-and-a-half I was in Taiwan.

What does a sociologist make of this? While I was in Taipei, I read an article in one of the English-language newspapers questioning whether the Taiwanese people admired the West too much. What I had found was an example. Mannequins, which we, as prospective customers, are meant to admire for their beauty, are in Taiwanese terms 'not us'. Beauty is 'not us'. It couldn't be economics dictating this move. These couldn't be spares for the Western market. They must be for the domestic market.

Then I remembered a beautiful young Italian-Canadian woman, a former student of mine, who made money in Japan as a model. She had remarked to me that a number of her colleagues in the Japanese modelling industry were white. I also remembered reading about how, during the Vietnam War, some South Vietnamese prostitutes

A woman browses current fashions in a shop in Chongquing, China. What ideas of beauty are conveyed by the mannequins?

Photo: Alamy

would have eye operations on their epicanthic folds (the technical term for the distinctive skin and fat tissue that makes most Asian people distinctive) to make themselves look 'more White'. I thought of Japanese animé characters with big eyes—Sailor Moon comes to mind.

Are these examples of 'beauty is not us', of a prevailing belief that standards of beauty come from another culture, of reverse ethnocentrism? I think so, but some of my students do not agree with me (particularly the White students, which is interesting in itself). What do you think?

—J.S.

What do YOU think?

1. Summarize the author's experience of reverse ethnocentrism in Taiwan. To what standard did this relate? Do you agree with the author that the prevalence of European mannequins in Taiwan can be attributed to reverse ethnocentrism?

2. Do you think that Canadians sometimes subscribe to reverse ethnocentrism? When, or under what circumstances?

In a very different setting, Emma LaRoque, a Métis writer from northeastern Alberta, came to a similar conclusion:

Several summers ago when I was intern-teaching in a northern reserve, one of the teachers told me how she 'had to get used to' the smells of the children. She insisted it was not just stuffiness, but a 'peculiar odor'.

It was a beautiful summer, a summer northern Natives enjoy. There were fishes to be caught and smoked. There was moosehide to be tanned, and as always pesky mosquitoes to be repelled with smudge [smoke]. Oddly enough, the 'peculiar' smell was a redolent mixture of spruce, moosehide, and woodsmoke. All the while this teacher was complaining about the smell of the children, the children reported a 'strange' odor coming from the vicinity of some of the teachers and their chemical toilets. And it never seemed to occur to the teacher that she could be giving off odors.

More to the point, both the teacher and the children attached value judgements to unfamiliar odors. As a friend of mine noted, 'to a person whose culture evidently prefers Chanel No. 5 or pine-scented aerosol cans, moosehide and woodsmoke can seem foreign.' The converse is true, I might add. (LaRoque 1975: 37)

As we have seen, ethnocentrism and cultural relativism are opposing ways of looking at cultures,

both our own and those of others. Ethnocentrism is laden with negative judgment, while cultural relativism is characterized by a greater appreciation for context in understanding and evaluating culture. This is not to say that everything is relative, or that there are no standards, as some sociology students seem to conclude after learning about the two concepts. Some things, such as female genital mutilation, the use of land mines, and the torture of political prisoners (are you listening, George W.?) can be considered universally bad.

The point to take from this is that it's important to realize how easy it is to make an ethnocentric assessment of a different culture. It is important to try to understand why different cultures do what they do. And, while true appreciation of aspects of other cultures might not always be possible, it is worth the trip to take a few steps down that path.

Sociolinguistics

Sociolinguistics is the study of language as part of culture. Language exists at the centre of communication between individuals and between groups. It is a source both of understanding and of misunderstanding. It is also the main vehicle for transmitting culture, and a culture cannot be understood without some sense of the language(s) it uses and the fit of language with other aspects of culture. Sociolinguistics thus looks at language in relation to such sociological factors as race, ethnicity, age, gender, and region.

Dialect as a Sociological Term

A **dialect** is a variety of a language, a version that is perhaps different from others in terms of pronunciation, vocabulary, and grammar. To the sociologist, the distinction between dialect and language is interesting because it can be as much a product of social factors as of linguistic ones. Dutch and German, for instance, are considered separate languages, although based strictly on linguistic criteria they could be called dialects of the same language. For some German speakers living near the Netherlands, Dutch is easier to understand than dialects of German spoken in Austria or Switzerland. Dialects, unlike languages, are often evaluated according to whether they represent proper or improper, casual or formal, even funny or serious versions of a language; these judgments usually depend on the social status of the dialect's speakers. In Britain, the 'Queen's English' is an upper-class dialect, more highly valued in written and formal communication than are regional dialects like that of the city of Manchester. The latter is often heard spoken by characters of TV shows like *Coronation Street*, where it signifies that the characters using it are 'real people' rather than aristocrats. A recent commercial for a Nissan SUV featured a voice-over spoken in a Newfoundland accent. The accent here is used to put the audience in a receptive mood by evoking the famed good nature and affability of the people of Newfoundland and Labrador. You would not hear that accent extolling the marketable features of a Lexus.

Sometimes differences in dialect reflect religious differences. This is generally true for the dialect pairs shown in Table 3.3. In such contexts, saying you don't understand someone when they speak can be as much a social as a linguistic commentary.

Linguistic Determinism and Relativity

The relationship between language and culture is usually discussed in terms of the **Sapir-Whorf hypothesis**, which suggests that **linguistic determinism** (or **causation**), exists. In other words, the way each of us views and understands the world is shaped by the language we speak. Like theories of biological or social determinism, the Sapir-Whorf hypothesis can be cast either as strongly or weakly deterministic—that is, language can be seen to exert either a strong or a weak influence on a person's worldview. We favour a weak determinism. We feel that linguistic relativity is a valid form of cultural relativity, that exact translation from one language into another is impossible, and that knowing the language of a people is important to grasping the ideas of a people.

Typically, when sociologists discuss this topic, they drag out a particular old example: there are 'x' number of words for snow in Inuktitut, the language of Inuit (we say 'x' because this number changes); each one differs subtly in meaning from the others and cannot be translated exactly into other languages. That there are so many different words for snow in Inuktitut reflects—supposedly—an important aspect of Inuit experience. Such references to vocabulary are not really very useful in proving the deterministic force or influence of language. They do help to make the point that there are no 'simple' languages with small vocabularies (i.e. vocabularies with less than tens of thousands of words). The Inuit have developed a large, sophisticated vocabulary without resorting to all the terms that Europeans have for their cultural features. That is important to know in terms of respecting the languages and their speakers, but it does not really help much in discussing relativity.

Table 3.3 Religious differences as reflected in dialect: two examples

LANGUAGE	DIALECT	RELIGION	VOCABULARY SOURCE	SCRIPT
Hindustani	Urdu	Islam	Arabic	Arabic
	Hindi	Hindu	Sanskrit	Sanskrit
Serbo-Croatian	Serbian	Orthodox	Old Church Slavonic	Cyrillic
	Croatian	Catholic	Latin	Roman

Noun Classes and Gender

The different noun classes that exist in a language can reinforce the beliefs its speakers have within their culture. English speakers in Canada have some awareness of difference in noun classes through the presence of gender exhibited by the Romance (i.e. based on Latin, the language of the Romans) languages—French, Italian, Portuguese, Spanish—to which they are exposed. Students struggling through French classes may wonder why every French noun has to be masculine or feminine. Why are the words for 'tree' (*arbre*) and tree species masculine (avoiding any Freudian interpretation), while the parts of trees—roots, leaves, branches, bark, blossoms—are feminine?

While it does not have noun classes labelled as 'masculine' or 'feminine', English does have a certain degree of grammatically mandated gender, with our use of *he, him, his*, and *she, her, hers*. Take the following two sentences: *One of my sisters is called Ann. She is younger than I am, and her hair used to be the same colour as mine.* In the second sentence, the words 'she' and 'her' are grammatically necessary but do not add any new information. Am I am assuming that you are stupid, and have forgotten the gender of my sister? We already know from the nouns 'sister' and 'Ann' that the person spoken about is female. English, French, all the **Indo-European** languages—the family of languages that includes almost all the languages of Europe plus Farsi (Iranian) and the languages of Pakistan and northern India—all impose gender grammatically in some way.

Algonquian languages, which together make up the largest Aboriginal language family in Canada and the United States, have no grammatically mandated gender, in either the French or the English sense. They have no pronouns meaning 'he' or 'she'. They are not alone, nor strange in that respect. In fact, almost every Canadian Aboriginal language does not recognize gender. Interestingly, they share this feature with the non-Indo-European languages of Europe (such as Finnish, Estonian, Hungarian, and Basque). Does this mean, as some sociolinguists have suggested, that Algonquian speakers were traditionally more flexible about gender roles than their European contemporaries, that there was a greater degree of equality between the sexes? The latter was certainly true at the time of contact, but whether that can be related to the absence of grammatical gender in their language is difficult to determine.

A Final Thought

Sometimes the terms that a language *doesn't* have tells you something significant about the culture. Take the following case. In translating for the upcoming movie *Whispers Like Thunder*, one of the authors (J.S.) several times found that he was asked to translate concepts for which there were no corresponding words in the Aboriginal language Wendat (Huron). A few examples are enough to provide plenty of insight into the differences between Aboriginal and European cultures. There are no Wendat terms for 'guilt' or 'guilty', 'innocence' or 'innocent', 'pride' or 'proud' (though there is a word for 'arrogance'). There are terms for 'good' and 'very good', but no terms for 'better' or 'best'. Likewise, the Huron have terms for 'bad' and 'very bad', but not for 'worse' or 'worst'. What do you think might be the cultural implications of these 'holes' in the Wendat lexicon?

Conclusions

If we could summarize this chapter in a statement or two, we would say this: not only do cultures differ—which should be fairly obvious—but cultures are viewed and lived differently by people who occupy different social locations (i.e. different gender, races, ethnicities, sexualities, and so on). Similarly, although humans, as intensely social creatures, cannot live without culture, they can also feel oppressed by their culture, if their social location is not one of power and influence. The final point: remember that all culture is *contested*.

Questions for Critical Review

1. Differentiate the following: *high culture*, *mass culture*, and *popular culture*.
2. Differentiate the following: *dominant culture*, *subculture*, and *counterculture*.
3. Differentiate the following: *folkways*, *mores*, and *taboos*.
4. Identify and give examples of Eurocentrism and ethnocentrism.
5. Contrast the linguistic expectations of speakers of Algonquian and Indo-European languages.

Suggested Readings

Adorno, Theodor W. (1991). *The Culture Industry*. J.M. Bernstein, ed. London: Routledge.

Anderson, Benedict (1983). *Imagined Communities*. London: Verso.

Benedict, Ruth (1934). *Patterns of Culture*. New York: Mentor Books.

During, Simon, ed. (1993). *The Cultural Studies Reader*. London: Routledge.

Geertz, Clifford (1973). *The Interpretation of Cultures*. New York: Basic Books.

Rose, Steven, R.C. Lewontin, & Leon J. Kamin (1984). *Not in Our Genes: Biology, Ideology and Human Nature*. Harmondsworth: Penguin Books.

Steckley, John (2007), *White Lies About the Inuit*, Toronto: University of Toronto Press.

Suggested Websites

Institute for Intercultural Studies
www.interculturalstudies.org/IIS/index.html

Multicultural Canada
www.pch.gc.ca/progs/multi/evidence/contents_e.cfm/

Postmodern Culture
http://jefferson.village.virginia.edu/pmc/

Six Nations of the Grand River
www.geocities.com/Athens/Olympus/3808

Key Terms

- agency
- agents of socialization
- bar mitzvah
- bat mitzvah
- behaviourism
- behaviour modification
- bopi
- branding
- broad socialization

- confirmation
- culture and personality
- degradation ceremony
- desensitization theory
- determinism
- ego
- eros
- game stage
- generalized others

- generation gap
- habitus
- hurried child syndrome
- id
- internalize
- Law of Effect
- longitudinal study
- looking-glass self
- narrow socialization

Socialization

LEARNING OBJECTIVES

After reading this chapter, you should be able to

> outline and assess the basic ideas of Freud;

> discuss the application of oversocialization to the concepts of Mead and Cooley;

> compare/contrast social and biological determinism;

> distinguish between agency and determinism;

> explain the roles of various agents of socialization;

> discuss critically the effects of television violence; and

> contrast narrow and broad socialization.

- national character
- observational learning theory
- oversocialized
- packaged rebel
- peer group
- peer pressure
- play stage
- preparatory stage

- primary socialization
- reproduction
- resocialization
- risk behaviour
- rite of passage
- role-taking
- secondary socialization
- significant others
- superego

- swaddling hypothesis
- thanatos
- total institution
- vision quest
- XYY males

Key Names
- Edward Thorndike
- John B. Watson

- Sigmund Freud
- George Herbert Mead
- Charles Horton Cooley
- John T. Hitchcock
- Ann Leigh Minturn
- Pierre Bourdieu

Photo: Joseph Sohm/Getty Images

FOR Starters

Small-Town Socialization 'In the Hood'

I live in Bolton, just north of Toronto. It's a largely white, middle-class bedroom community, inhabited by well-off suburbanites who commute to jobs in the city. It's also home to a strangely large population of white teenaged boys from middle-class homes who walk around as if they were black urban youths. They've got the loose-hanging, load-in-the-drawers pants, the brooding slouch, the rhythmic, side-to-side walk, the hoodie done up tight in even the warmest weather, the hat worn crooked or backwards, and the light fist-to-fist greeting reserved for peers and initiated members of the Bolton white boys' fraternity. They didn't learn that at home. No Bolton parents would socialize their kids that way. Could you imagine?

> 'Come, Jackson, my little homeboy, do put a little more *Kanye* into your shoulders—you aren't slouching nearly enough. And get some rocks in your pockets so I can see your Boxers—you don't want to look like the wiggas down the street, do you?'

So if Jackson's parents didn't socialize him in the ways of African American youth, who or what did? Well, music videos, movies, and video games are all powerful socializing agents. Friends and older teenagers who have been socialized previously and are considered cool can act as agents as well. Jackson has probably been practising his act in front of a mirror, since socialized skills and mannerisms generally need to be rehearsed before they are performed in front of an audience.

A more puzzling question: if you're a white teenager from a middle-class suburb who has never been a part of black urban culture, why act black? As the American comedian Jon Stewart quipped, 'You might as well talk like a pirate.' One of my former students, a young filmmaker who happens to be black, has been working on a documentary exploring the question of why, when he goes to hip hop shows, the performers are black, but the majority of the audience is white. He has yet to figure it out.

As a sociologist, I have a few theories. For one thing, African Americans have long led the way in popular music—jazz, rock and roll, soul, all began with black musicians playing for black audiences, before non-blacks caught on and the performers became more and more white. Pop music artists are typically 'cool', and appearing cool is important to teenaged boys. I know it was important to me. Just talking like a musician has a lot of cool to it. The first band I was in was named The Shropshire Lads (thanks to the father of our bass player; the reference to the 1896 poetry collection by A.E. Housman was lost on us), and we spoke with British accents too generic (and pretentious) to resemble the Liverpudlian cadences of the Beatles.

Another thing, hip hop is an identity that white, middle-class teenagers can slip into easily (unlike, say, a Scottish kilt or a pirate shirt). It's got a look that will help you fit in rather than stand out. When I was a teenager, long hair, faded jeans (just grind a lot of cigarette ash into them), old military shirts from the army surplus store, and blue pea jackets were indispensible parts of the image that I and my friends (particularly my fellow band members) cultivated. We carefully observed what the British rocker bands wore, and we emulated their identity.

Many companies, from clothing stores to soft drink sellers, invest huge amounts of time and money trying to socialize teenagers and younger children (the all-important 'tween' demographic) through **branding**, getting them to use brand-name products by linking the product to their identity. Many products are marketed to consumers of hip hop culture. Individual performers have their own lines of jewellery (are we still saying 'bling'?), clothing, and fragrances, all designed to socialize young people concerning what to wear and what to smell like.

The walk and the gestures aren't sold with the brand, but they are part of the package deal, thrown in for free. The **packaged rebel** has long been a treasured image among Western youth: an identity that says, 'I swim against the tide,' is readily available for sale at any mall, making it something of a capitalist oxymoron. (An oxymoron, like 'jumbo shrimp', brings together contradictory elements—in this case, a desire for nonconformity and a susceptibility to mass merchandising.) The snowboarder image, for example, is packaged as that of a rebel, but you need middle-class parent money and brand-name gear to carry off this rebel look with authenticity. Repeat after me: 'We will all think for ourselves.'

Will they grow out of it—the white boys of Bolton acting black? My money says they will, as they become resocialized as adult members of society, earning a living, paying their taxes, mowing the lawn, raising children, and trying to fit in where they work. Part of the package may remain. I no longer use my faux British accent, but I still look like a hippie, albeit an aging one.

Introduction

Socialization is an area of sociological study that brings the discipline close to psychology. The intersection of sociology and psychology is clear from the fact that a good number of the leading socialization theorists are psychologists. Socialization is a learning process, one that involves development or changes in an individual's sense of self. This applies both in the earliest socialization that an individual undergoes in childhood, generally known as **primary socialization**, and in socialization that occurs later in life, which is sometimes known as **secondary socialization**.

Determinism

Any discussion of socialization needs to cover the topics of determinism versus free will, and biological determinism versus social determinism. When we speak of **determinism**, we are talking about the degree to which an individual's behaviour, attitudes, and other 'personal' characteristics are *determined*, or caused, by a specific factor. There are 'hard' and 'soft' versions of determinism: proponents of the former claim that we are, in essence, programmed by our biology or our culture, while champions of the latter believe there is some room for free will or the exercise of **agency** in one's life. Agency involves personal choice above and beyond the call of nature or nurture.

Biological Determinism

Biological determinism (representing nature in the old 'nature versus nurture' debate) states that the greater part of what we are is determined by our roughly 26,000 genes. Biological determinism has become a popular subject of discussion and debate in the mainstream media, owing in large part to the rise of human genetic research generally and, in particular, the Human Genome Project, which involves a painstaking count of the number of genes we have and investigation into what each of those genes actually codes for.

Certain abilities seem to fall into the 'nature' category. We all know of people who are 'naturally good' (or 'naturally bad') at sports, music, art, and so on. However, we have to be very careful in making even tentative statements about biological determinism. A notorious research study into the **XYY males** that began in 1962 provides a cautionary tale. Men are genetically XY in their chromosomes, women XX. The first studies were done by looking at the populations of hospitals for dangerous, violent, or criminal patients with emotional/intellectual problems, first in England, then in the United States and Australia. A certain percentage of the men were found to be XYY, and the 'criminal gene' was hastily declared. The problem was that the researchers had neglected to study non-criminals. When the study was extended to the general population, they discovered that roughly the same percentage (about 1 in 1,000) were XYY. There remained some well-documented associations of XYY males with above-average height, with a tendency to have acne, and with somewhat more impulsive and antisocial behaviour and slightly lower intelligence, but it is impossible to conclude that XYY males are genetically determined criminals.

Softer forms of biological determinism focus on predispositions that people have (for shyness, for aggressiveness, and so on). These findings tend to have a stronger foundation and are easier to support than the more sensational claims of hard determinism—the ones beginning '*We have found the gene for _____*'—that sometimes make the news. What we are comes from too complex a mixture, even too complex a genetic mixture, for one gene to be an absolute determinant of behaviour or personality.

Social or Cultural Determinism: Behaviourism

Behaviourism is a school of thought in psychology that takes a strong cultural determinist position. It emphasizes the causative power of learning in the development of behaviour. For the behaviourist, the social environment is just about everything in the creation of personality, while nature and free will count for very little. One cautionary statement about this school of thought is that much of the research on which it is based involves nonhuman

Photo: Robert W. Allan; reprinted with permission

A pigeon in a Skinner box. Behaviourism asserts that behaviour is the product of stimulus and response. Are human beings simply the byproduct of their interaction with the environment?

animals: Pavlov and his dogs, Thorndike and his cats, B.F. Skinner and his rats and pigeons. One unkind nickname for the behaviourist school is 'rat psychology'. If you've watched enough reruns of the television shows *Cheers* and *Frasier*, you'll recognize that Frasier Crane's ex-wife, Lilith, is a caricature of a behaviourist. Critics say that the theory disallows the existence of choice, of agency, even for a dog, pigeon, or rat.

One of the earliest principles developed in behaviourism is the **Law of Effect**, introduced by **Edward Thorndike** (1874–1949) in his book *Animal Intelligence* (1911). The Law of Effect has two parts. The first one says that if you do something and it is rewarded, the likelihood of your doing it again increases; this behaviour is said to be *reinforced*. On the other hand, according to the second part, if you do something and it is punished or ignored, then the likelihood of your doing it again decreases. It boils down to the idea of the carrot (reward) and the stick (punishment). Accordingly, if the screaming child in the grocery store lineup is given a chocolate bar to be quiet, the reward reinforces the screaming—expect it to happen again.

There are debates about what constitutes a reward for an individual, and about what behaviour is or is not being rewarded. For example, if you punish a child who is acting out at school by making her sit in the corner and the objectionable behaviour persists, could it be that she sees the 'punishment' as a reward? Is she getting attention, and is that her goal? If you pick up a baby who is crying, does that teach him that he can get anything he wants by crying? Or, does it reward communication, which, once he learns to speak, becomes words and not tears? Attempting to change someone's behaviour using this kind of approach is called **behaviour modification.**

Hard social determinism claims that just about any behaviour can be taught and learned. A powerful expression of this view comes from **John B. Watson** (1878–1958), the founder of behaviourist psychology, who, in his book *Behaviorism* (1925), declared:

> Give me a dozen healthy infants, well-formed, and my own specific world to bring them up in and I'll guarantee to take any one at random and train him to become any type of specialist I might select—a doctor, lawyer, artist, merchant, chief, yes even a beggarman and thief, regardless of his talents, penchants, tendencies, abilities, vocations, and the race of his ancestors. There is no such thing as an inheritance of capacity, talent, temperament, mental constitution and behavioral characteristics. (Watson 1925: 82)

It is hardly surprising that a person who felt that manipulating humans was so easy would (after being fired for having an affair with his laboratory assistant) become involved in advertising—selling, among other things, baby powder (by playing on the guilt of young mothers)—and in writing articles for the popular media.

● ● ● ● ● ● ● ● ● ● ● ● ● ● ● ● ● ● ● ●

What do YOU think?

How much of your own behaviour do you think is influenced by your social environment—by friends, family, your charismatic sociology professor—and how much were you simply born with? Think about it in the context of one or two specific habits or tendencies that you have.

● ● ● ● ● ● ● ● ● ● ● ● ● ● ● ● ● ● ● ●

Sigmund Freud: Balancing the Biological and the Socio-cultural

The thinking of **Sigmund Freud** (1856–1939), father of psychoanalysis, involves socialization and the balancing of biological and social aspects of human personality. He believed the mind had three parts. Think of it as a team of three players: the id, the superego, and the ego. The first two are the most involved with socialization. The **id** is motivated by two **i**nstinctive **d**rives (or **i**nner **d**emons, for those who have a difficult time remembering which of Freud's players is which) that we are born with as part of our unconscious mind: they are eros and thanatos. **Eros** (related to the word 'erotic') is the drive that tends to be stressed by Freud's fans and critics (and Freud himself, to be fair). It is a 'life drive' or instinct that involves pleasure—particularly, but not exclusively, sexual pleasure. **Thanatos**, the less celebrated of the two drives (at least by TV pundits

Photo: © imagebroker/Alamy

This image socializes the reader into the prevailing Western view that (a) heart = love and/or sex; (b) large breasts = love and/or sex; and (c) sex = love. If there were a sign like this meant to attract women, what would it look like?

Agency

Canadian sociologist Dennis H. Wrong, in an important article entitled 'The Oversocialized Conception of Man in Modern Sociology' (1961), stressed that it was important not to view humans as passive recipients of socialization programming. His point was similar to the argument we made in Chapter 3: just as the culture and symbols of a society can be contested—that is, spark disagreement among groups or individuals about the nature of the former and the meaning of the latter—so, too, do individuals contest their socialization. Wrong didn't actually use the word 'contest', but he did argue that people do not naturally conform to the lessons of their socialization, automatically doing what socializing agents like parents, peers, and the media dictate. They can decide to be different, to resist their socialization. This was an important point to make at the end of the 1950s, a time of relatively great conformity to norms in North America. It remains important in the branding days of the twenty-first century, when advertisers try to socialize children at younger and younger ages into social acceptance through their products. It's also worth considering this point in terms of the debate, discussed in the last chapter, between proponents of mass culture (who see individuals as passive recipients of cultural messages) and of popular culture (who view individuals as having a role in interpreting culture).

Luis M. Aguiar, who teaches sociology at Okanagan University College in British Columbia, offers another view of the conflict between agency and socialization. Born on the island of São Miguel in the Azores, off the coast of Portugal, Aguiar experienced the 'working-class socialization' of his parents, who encouraged him to adopt a trade rather than pursue a post-secondary education. The very idea of finding a 'career' was incomprehensible to Aguiar's parents (Aguiar 2001: 187–8). They considered boys who preferred mental to physical work 'sexually suspect' and 'unmanly', and Aguiar's father even supplied him with examples of men who 'became insane as a result of too much reading and studying' (180).

Ultimately Aguiar did go to university, demonstrating agency by overcoming his parents' attempts to socialize him into entering a trade. However, he was not unaffected by their efforts,

and pop psychologists), involves a 'death drive', an instinct for aggression and violence.

The **superego**, also part of the unconscious, is your conscience. It takes in the normative messages of right and wrong that your parents, family, friends, teachers, and other socializing agents give you, and *internalizes* them—in other words, it adopts them as something like a personal code of moral behaviour. Picture, if you have trouble remembering this one, a caped crusader with a big 'S' on his chest, saying 'Don't hit your sister or want to have sex with your mother—that's wrong!'

Needless to say, id and superego often come to blows in conflict that can take years of psychotherapy to resolve. If one is too strong, the individual is either too unrestrained or too controlled. The **ego**, meanwhile, mediates between the conscious and unconscious while trying to make sense of what the individual self does and thinks. It can interpret well if the individual is aware of what is going on in his or her unconscious with information from dream analysis, talks about childhood, inkblot tests, hypnosis, and 'Freudian slips' ('Today, we'll be talking about Sigmund Fraud'). If it is weak or lacks self-awareness, there will be serious problems.

The article by Dennis H. Wrong discussed in the following section began with the insights of Freud, who, like Wrong, would not have thought that socialization could control the individual.

which left him with feelings of guilt since he could not, because of his long-term education, help provide for the family until relatively late in life:

> Today I still feel terribly guilty because of my selfish educational pursuits that deprived my parents from owning a home or car or having some higher level of comfort in their retirement years. My parents never complained about my lack of financial contribution to the family, but my sense is that they are extremely disappointed at not achieving the immigrant dream of owning their own home. To my mind, only immigrant students of working-class background feel this heavy load of class guilt. (Aguiar 2001: 191)

Agents of Socialization

In the case of Luis Aguiar, his parents were among the most influential **agents of socialization**—the groups that had a significant impact on his socialization. There are many agents of socialization that can affect an individual, but seven in particular readily come to mind:

- family
- peer group
- neighbourhood/community
- school
- mass media
- the legal system
- culture generally.

The impact of each of these agents is severely contested, both in the sociological literature and in the day-to-day conversations of people in society.

Significant Other, Generalized Other, and Sense of Self

The American psychologist and philosopher **George Herbert Mead**, introduced as a symbolic interactionist in Chapter 1, developed a twofold categorization of agents of socialization: 'significant other' and 'generalized other'. He believed that children develop their sense of self from being socialized by the 'others' in their lives. They **internalize** norms and values they observe, incorporating them into their way of being.

Significant others are those key individuals—primarily parents, to a lesser degree older siblings and close friends—whom young children imitate and model themselves after. Contrary to common usage, your spouse or partner is not really your sole significant other. Somewhere in your mind right now there should be a picture of a mother or father doing yardwork with a young child imitating the practice (for instance, clearing leaves with a toy rake). Later on the child comes under sway of **generalized others** and begins to take into account the attitudes, viewpoints, and general expectations of the society she or he has been socialized into. In Freudian terms, we would say that the individual's superego had internalized the norms of society.

Mead identified a developmental sequence for socialization. It begins with what he called the **preparatory stage**, which involves more or less pure imitation. The next sequence is the **play stage**, where pretending is involved. The child at this stage engages in **role-taking**, assuming the perspective of significant others and imagining what those others are thinking as they act the way they do. The third stage is the **game stage**, in which the child considers simultaneously the perspective of several roles. In terms of baseball, for example, this is when a child, fielding the ball at shortstop, might be able to consider what the runner and the first baseman are thinking and doing.

Photo: © George Simian/Corbis

This is a common image in North American culture, one you've likely seen in TV commercials or in a scene from a movie. Why isn't the image of a mother and daughter shaving their legs or doing their makeup as common?

Significant others and generalized others continue to exert strong socialization influences later on in the life of an individual, with significant consequences for the individual's self-concept. Mentors and other role models can become important significant others for the adolescent or adult individual. Later still, a generalized other may be a social group or 'community' that has an impact on the individual's sense of self. Think of television commercials. Whenever a star athlete, a famous actor, or any other major celebrity is chosen to endorse a product, the marketing team behind the advertising is banking on the fact that the person will be viewed as a significant other by the group the product is being marketed to. When an athlete transgresses the moral norms of a society, that person loses his or her marketability as a significant other. Evidence of this is Tiger Woods, who was quickly shunned by his corporate sponsors after details of his extramarital affairs became public. When an Old Navy commercial presents a group of young, attractive, and well-dressed people dancing and having a good time, the advertising agency is trying to tell you that this is what your cool, young community likes, and you should, too.

Another symbolic interactionist and a colleague of Mead's, **Charles Horton Cooley** (1864–1929) put forth the idea of the **looking-glass self**. This is a self-image based on how a person thinks he or she is viewed by others. In Cooley's poetic words, 'each to each a looking glass / Reflects the other that doth pass' (in Marshall 1998: 374). The looking-glass self has three components:

(1) how you imagine you appear to others;
(2) how you imagine those others judge your appearance; and
(3) how you feel as a result (proud, ashamed, self-confident, embarrassed).

A good example of this is the relationship between body image and self-esteem, especially in young women. Harvard educational psychologist and respected feminist thinker Carol Gilligan noted how the self-esteem of girls declines during their teenage years (Gilligan 1990). Studies show that this happens more with girls and young women than with boys. The harsher standards of body type that we apply to women has rightfully been associated with this difference in self-esteem.

Mead's and Cooley's ideas are very much like those of behaviourism, in that they exaggerate the influence of the social environment and downplay the role of individual input into the construction of self. Wrong would speak of their sense of self as '**oversocialized**'. However, by taking a less deterministic approach to these symbolic interactionist ideas, we can find some interesting aspects about the role the environment plays in shaping behaviour.

Family

The family is the first agent of socialization, and often the most powerful one. It is important to recognize that just as the family is different across cultures, so are the means and goals of the family in socializing the child. Consider the means and goals as they are outlined in the narrative on page 103 It comes from research on the Rajput community of Khalapur in northern India, carried out by anthropologist **John T. Hitchcock** (1917–2001) and social psychologist **Ann Leigh Minturn** (1928–1999) in the early 1960s. Their work was part of a classic study of cross-cultural socialization, Beatrice Whiting's *Six Cultures: Studies of Child Rearing* (1963).

Socialization and Culture: Inuit Socialization as Morality Play

In her book *Inuit Morality Play: The Emotional Education of a Three-Year-Old*, psychological anthropologist Jean Briggs records the findings of her intense six-month study of an Inuit toddler, a little girl she called 'Chubby Maata', in the Baffin Island community of Qipisa, a year-round camp of about sixty Inuit. She paid particular attention to how Chubby Maata's mother and her other caregivers engaged in the process the Inuit call *issummaksaiyuq*, meaning 'cause (or cause to increase) thought' (Briggs 1998: 5). They did this by challenging the child with difficult questions like 'Are you a baby?' and 'Who do you like?', and by prefacing instructions and explanations with the phrase 'Because you are a baby . . .'. They would also use commands such as 'Say "ungaa" [a term closely associated with baby-talk].'

Briggs called these techniques 'morality plays', borrowing the term for the medieval drama in which the characters—personifications of abstract qualities—delivered lessons about good

Telling It Like It Is

The Rajputs: Child Rearing and Personality in a North Indian Village

Although Rajput infants will be picked up and attended to when they are hungry or fussing, for the most part they are left in their cots, wrapped up in blankets.... Except for anxieties about a baby's health, it is not the centre of attention. A baby receives attention mainly when it cries. At that time, someone will try to distract it, but when it becomes quiet, the interaction will stop. Adult interaction with babies is generally aimed at producing a cessation of response, rather than stimulation of it. Infants and children of all ages are not shown off to others.... Children are also not praised by their parents, who fear that this will 'spoil' them and make them disobedient.

Rajput children . . . are never left alone, yet neither are they the center of interest. The child learns that moodiness will not be tolerated. Few demands are put on Rajput children; they are not pressured or even encouraged to become self-reliant. Weaning, which generally occurs without trouble, takes place at two to three years; but if the mother does not become pregnant, a child may be nursed into its sixth year. There is no pressure for toilet training.... Babies are not pressured, or even encouraged to walk. They learn to walk when they are ready, and mothers say they see no reason to rush this. . . . Village women do little to guide children's behavior by explaining or reasoning with them. There is also little direct instruction to small children. Small children learn . . . the customs and values of the group through observation and imitation. In the first five years of life, the child moves very gradually from observer to participant in village and family life.

. . . [C]hildren are not encouraged in any way to participate in adult activities. The chores a child is given are mainly directed to helping the mother. . . . There is little feeling that children should be given chores on principle in order to train them in responsibility. . . . Rajput children take little initiative in solving problems by themselves. Instead, they are taught whom they can depend on for help in the web of social relations of kin group, caste, and village. . . . Although chores increase somewhat as the child gets older, it is not a Rajput custom to require children to work if adults can do it. Children are not praised for their work, and a child's inept attempt to do an adult job is belittled. Thus children are reluctant to undertake what they cannot do well.

—J.T. Hitchcock & A.L. Minturn

What do YOU think?

1. How would this be interpreted by a behaviourist?

2. What values are being taught with this form of socialization?

conduct and character. Chubby Maata's caregivers used these techniques to teach Chubby Maata important social lessons such as the difference between -*kuluk* ('charming, lovable') and -*silait* ('undesirable, foolish') baby behaviour, while slowly encouraging the child to grow out of being a baby. Their teaching was directed towards helping Chubby Maata develop the personal characteristic called *ihuma* or *isuma* (the first element of the word *issummaksaiyuq*), which relates to strong self-control. This is a quality that, as Briggs argued in an earlier work (Briggs 1970), is a prized trait in adults.

What do YOU think?

1. How is this family socialization different from that found among the Rajputs?

2. Why might the two cultures socialize their children differently?

Culture and Personality

It is reasonable to argue that the impact of family socialization in its different forms has been over-emphasized since it became a source of interest to sociologists. During the first half of the twentieth century, sociology, together with anthropology and psychology, was involved in what is called the **culture and personality** school of thought. The culture and personality school attempted to identify and describe an idealized personality or 'personality type' for different societies, both small and large, and attach to it a particular form of family socialization. During World War II and in the early years of the Cold War standoff between the United States and the Soviet Union, the scope of these studies broadened to examine **national character**, the personality type of entire nations. David Riesman's *The Lonely Crowd: A Study of the Changing American Character* (1950) is an example. These studies typically drew conclusions about how the primary socialization of child-raising is linked with the country's national character.

An illustrative example of national character research is *The People of Great Russia* (1949), in which authors Geoffrey Gorer and John Rickman proposed the **swaddling hypothesis**. They identified moodiness as a supposedly typical Russian character trait, citing extremes of controlled and out-of-control behaviour (evidenced, for example, in intense alcoholic bingeing), and attributed it to the fact that the country's people were tightly *swaddled*—as in bundled up—as infants. Similar theories were proposed for the Germans and the Japanese (see, for example, Ruth Benedict's *The Chrysanthemum and the Sword*, 1946). Needless to say, theories that attempt to generalize about such large populations are extremely difficult to prove.

The swaddling hypothesis and studies attempting to link child socialization practices to national character could very well be sitting on the dusty shelf of old theories that no longer affect us if it weren't for a persistent preoccupation with trying to understand overarching personality traits of certain populations. Since 11 September 2001, there has been much focus in the media and even among American political and military leaders on the 'Arab mind'. In fact, Raphael Patai's book of this very title, first published in 1973 and revamped in 1983, was reprinted not long afterwards, in 2002. Each edition has sold well, and *The Arab Mind* is currently enjoying considerable influence in upper military circles in the United States. It replicates all the excesses of the national character study publications, both by oversimplifying the psychological makeup of very sociologically diverse peoples (for instance, portraying them all as lazy and sex-obsessed) and by tying that broad portrait to overgeneralized child-raising practices (a significant portion of the book is devoted to, in the words of the publisher, 'the upbringing of a typical Arab boy or girl'). As one critic writing on a Muslim website says,

> It is hard to see how Patai's findings can apply equally to a Saudi prince and a Tunisian fisherman, to a Libyan Bedouin [a nomad in the desert] and a Kuwaiti commodities-broker, to an Egyptian soldier and Moroccan 'mulla', to a wealthy Palestinian businessman in Qatar and an impoverished Palestinian migrant-worker from Ghazzah, to a child who is growing up in the hills of Syria and the one doing so in coastal Yemen, to a woman who is an executive director of the Cairo museum and one who farms field in northern Iraq, to a Marxist in Aden and a Christian in Beirut, a 'muadhdhin' in Marrakesh and a musician in Muscat, and so on. (www.Muslimmedia.com)

Different cultures do socialize their children differently, but it is important to remember that in no culture is there complete uniformity of socialization. Think of the arguments made for and against 'spanking' or 'corporal punishment' that appear in Canadian newspaper editorials and letters to the editor. This is no different from what we know about cultures generally. We know that our own culture is not uniform, yet we easily slip into thinking that other cultures are different in that regard. The Arctic anthropologist Diamond Jenness was guilty of making this assumption in his observation of Inuit child socialization, discussed in the box on page 105.

Peer Group

An important agent of socialization is the **peer group**, a social group sharing key characteristics such as age, social position, and interests. The term is usually used to talk about children and adolescents of the same age. In some societies

• Our Stories •

Diamond Jenness Learns Exceptions to a 'Rule' of Inuit Family Socialization

Early in his career of studying Northern populations, Diamond Jenness was told by his predecessor Viljamhar Stefansson that an Inuit child was considered the reborn soul of an ancestor or recently deceased family member, and that the older soul became the infant's guardian spirit, or *atka*. According to Stefansson, this belief influenced the way Inuit raised their children. As quoted by Jenness in his diary:

> The atka protects the child, guarding it from harm. A little child is wiser than an adult person, because its actions are inspired by its atka—the wise old man or wise woman who died. Consequently a child is never scolded or refused anything—even a knife or scissors. (Stuart Jenness 1991: 7)

Perhaps as the tenth child of fourteen, Jenness had a hard time accepting that the latter statement could be true, because he would soon come to challenge the point. On 5 October 1913, he made the following observation:

> The boy was allowed to play with the scissors or anything else that caught his fancy. He had his father's watch and began to hammer it on the floor; the father remonstrated very mildly. (Stuart Jenness 1991: 14)

The son of a watchmaker, Jenness must have found this incident particularly upsetting, since he refers to watches later on in his account.

Two days later, Jenness wrote about a young boy being addressed as 'father', 'apparently on the "atka" theory' (1991: 17). By 25 November of that year, he was directly criticizing Stefansson's theory:

> I noticed the children were scolded several times, and twice slaps were administered severe enough to make them cry—which contradicts what Stefansson told me. (1991: 63)

Three days later he develops his criticism further:

> I have been watching their treatment of the children rather closely, in view of what Stefansson told us on September 27th. It is true that they are allowed to play with many things—scissors, watches, etc, which a European child would never be allowed; it is true to that their whims and caprices are often humoured and given way to; but it is not true—with these two families at least—that they are never scolded or slapped, nor that they are invariably allowed to have their own way. (1991: 67)

Jenness's entry for 1 December brings more critical comment. The violence of the imagery is perhaps telling:

> Stefannson's theory about little children never being hit received its death blow as far as these families are concerned. Aksiatak's baby boy (about 15 months old) was tugging at Pungashuk's hair.... Aksiatak hit him lightly two or three times with the stem of his long pipe, then as he [the child] did not let go, he struck him a sharp knock, which made him run screaming to his mother. Aluk's wife Qapqana also gave her son a slap, which made him cry. (Stuart Jenness 1991: 70–1)

Even after the 'death blow', there is one more hit, on 11 December. It is noteworthy that Jenness criticizes not just Stefansson with this statement but also any notion that children should be treated with a light hand. His reporting betrays some cultural bias, especially with his use of the word 'deserved':

> Pungasuk received rather deserved punishment this evening—three slaps as hard as Aluk's wife could inflict. Aksitak's little boy was worrying him so he gave him a slap which made him cry. Stefansson's dictum about little children not being punished does not apply here in the least. (Stuart Jenness 1991: 81)

Do these episodes add up to sufficient evidence to contradict Stefansson's theory?

the peer group of children is more formally recognized than in others. For example, among the Mbuti pygmies of the central African country of Zaire, as studied during the mid-twentieth century by anthropologist Colin Turnbull, the social world of the **bopi**, or children's playground, was almost exclusively the territory of children from the age of three to puberty, with adults and teenagers made to feel unwelcome.

The term **peer pressure** refers to the social force exerted on an individual by his or her peers to conform in behaviour, appearance, or externally demonstrated values (i.e. not appearing excited about something that isn't deemed acceptable or 'cool').

A classic sociological study that argues for the influence of the adolescent peer group is Paul E. Willis's *Learning to Labor: How Working Class Kids Get Working Class Jobs* (1977). Willis and his colleagues studied the informal culture of a group of 12 teenaged boys attending a working-class, all-male school in the industrial town of Hammerstown, England. The question Willis wanted to address was why working-class boys settled for labouring jobs rather than directing their energies to getting the kinds of jobs obtained by middle-class kids in their cohort. He believed the boys were not passive recipients, through socialization, of the informal working-class culture. Rather, he speculated that,

as an act of minority-culture resistance to the dominant culture, they were active participants both in the creation of this culture, with its belief and values systems and rules of behaviour, and in socializing newcomers into the culture. Among the evidence Willis found to support his theory were vocalized disdain for and humour directed against more conformist middle-class peers, ridicule of the 'effeminate' nature of the mind-centred work done in school and in offices, and denunciation of middle-class values in general. The minority-culture resistance also involved manipulating the classroom (by controlling attendance and the level of work done, for example) and educational figures of authority in ways that the youths would repeat in the 'shop floor' environments of factories and warehouses and with the middle-management figures they encountered there. Their classroom behaviour prepared them for their future.

● ●

What do YOU think?

1. Do you think the peer group had the power it did because it was a single-gender school?

2. Do you think the peer group had the power it did because all of the students were from working-class families?

● ●

Can you imagine the chain of events that led to this moment? How do you think the two girls differ in their attitudes towards smoking? Do you agree with the statement that *how* a teenager smokes is almost as important as *whether* she smokes?

Photo: © Angela Hampton Picture Library/Alamy

This isn't an ideal route for children walking to school, but what if you don't have a choice? What do you think the frequent sight of police cars and caution tape teaches these children about their neighbourhood, and about life?

Photo: Andrew Wallace/GetStock.com

Community and Neighbourhood

Community and neighbourhood can be important agents of socialization on a child. It's one of the reasons parents debate whether they should live in the city or move their family to a town or suburb outside the big city where they work. It's also why urban planners are concerned about creating mixed-class city neighbourhoods rather than ghettoizing the poor into government-assisted housing projects. Toronto, for example, is currently witnessing the planned change of one of its most notorious housing projects, Regent Park, into a mixed social environment. Studies have shown that youths living outside large cities are at lower risk of becoming involved in crime and drug and alcohol abuse. J.J. Arnett's cross-cultural study of adolescents in Denmark and the United States is one such study showing a correlation between risk behaviour and city size.

Mass Media

Questions about the role communication for the masses plays in socializing young people go back at least as far as the ancient Greek philosopher Plato, who felt that art (in his day, plays) aroused primal instincts, stimulating violence and lust. Plato's student Aristotle believed that violence depicted in art actually produced among those viewing it an experience of *catharsis*, a relief from hostile or violent emotions, leading to feelings of peace.

Does mass media today—through action movies that make heroes out of vicious criminals, video games that promote war and crime, and TV shows that glorify death and murder—socialize young people, especially adolescent males, into committing violence, or at least into being desensitized to violence and the pain of others? Or does it provide a safe outlet for pent-up hostile emotions? The two sides of this contentious debate are taken up by contemporary writers in the following excerpts. First, arguing for a link between media violence and criminal activity, are psychologists Brad Bushman and L. Rowell Huesmann:

> True, media violence is not likely to turn an otherwise fine child into a violent criminal. But, just as every cigarette one smokes increases a little bit the likelihood of a lung tumor someday, every violent show one watches increases just a little bit the likelihood of behaving more aggressively in some situation. (Bushman and Huesmann 2001: 248)

Telling It Like It Is

Experiencing Peer Pressure

Growing up, everyone is exposed to peer pressure, and how we respond to the powerful influence exerted by our peer group helps to mould us into the adults we become.

When I was 10, I had a small group of classmates I hung out with. I felt they were 'cooler' than I was, so I was fairly susceptible to peer pressure from them. I pride myself in my independence of thought, action, and appearance, but I certainly didn't show those characteristics then. I was up for anything they suggested, even when I knew they weren't the wisest things to do. We never did anything seriously wrong. We begged candy from a local candy manufacturer and stole candy from the neighbourhood drug store. We played 'chicken' with trains on the railroad tracks. We threw snowballs at passing cars and apples at cars idling in the local lovers' lane. Peer pressure made me do things I would never have done otherwise, and you can probably remember petty crimes of your own youth that cause you to blush—or to chuckle—today.

But it's important to recognize that, while leading us to do some pretty silly things, peer pressure plays a vital role in forging personality. Peer pressure hits us hardest when we're insecure adolescents striving for acceptance among people outside our immediate family. By encouraging a degree of conformity, peer pressure helps children develop friendships and find acceptance among others their own age, fostering both self-confidence and independence. I belonged to a class of smart kids culled from various schools in the district, and it was easy to feel separate, different. But through our lunch-hour pranks and hijinx, my classmates and I formed a close circle from which we all gained a sense of belonging. It also gave us a safe place to test norms and values. I don't throw snowballs at passing cars anymore—I figured out then that it wasn't right. And perhaps, by remembering these stories, I will be less likely to judge younger people who do the same things.

—J.S.

Arguing for the other side is communications professor Jib Fowles, in his controversial book *The Case for Television Violence*:

> Television is not a schoolhouse for criminal behavior. . . . Viewers turn to this light entertainment for relief, not for instruction. Video action exists, and is resorted to, to get material out of minds rather than to put things into them. . . . Television violence is good for people. (Fowles 1999: 53 and 118)

Having whetted your appetite for the debate, we'll take a closer look at how Huesmann and Fowles arrived at their views.

Huesmann's Longitudinal Studies

Huesmann's pioneering work on the effects of television violence on children involved a **longitudinal study**, which examined data gathered on research subjects over a long period. His first was a 22-year study of 856 youths in New York State. At the beginning of his study the participants were all in Grade 3, about 8 years of age. Huesmann followed up by interviewing them again when they were 19, and then again at 30 (Huesmann et al. 1986). For male subjects, the relationship between viewing television violence and engaging in aggressive behaviour roughly 10 years later was both positive and highly significant—in other words, there was a link and it was a strong one. These findings were consistent for males of different class, IQ, and level of aggressiveness at the start age. When the subjects were checked again at age 30, the relationship among males between violent television viewing and aggressive behaviour—both self-reported and documented in criminal records—was just as strong.

In another major study (2003), Huesmann and his colleagues studied 557 Chicago-area children from Grade 1 to Grade 4, beginning in 1977. Fifteen years later they interviewed as many of them (and their spouses and friends) as they could, and also looked at public records and archival material. They were able to gather reasonably complete data for 329—roughly 60 per cent—of the original research participants (153 men and 176 women, all then in their early twenties). The results of this study were similar to those of the earlier study, with the only difference being that the link between TV violence and aggressive behaviour was evident among women as well as among men. The researchers concluded their study with the following statement:

> Overall, these results suggest that both males and females from all social strata and all levels of initial aggressiveness are placed at increased risk for the development of adult aggressive and violent behavior when they view a high and steady diet of violent TV shows in early childhood. (Huesmann, et al. 2003: 218)

Huesmann proposed two theories to explain the data. The first one, **observational learning theory**, states that children acquire what he termed 'aggressive scripts' for solving social problems through watching violence on television. The second, **desensitization theory**, states that increased exposure to television violence desensitizes or numbs the natural negative reaction to violence.

Fowles's Defense of Television Violence

Jib Fowles, author of the second statement, cited on page 108, argued that sociologists and others who condemn violence on television are really using TV violence as a pretext to tackle other issues: class, race, gender, and generation. He calls television violence a 'whipping boy, a stand-in for other clashes':

> The attack on television violence is, at least in part, an attack by the upper classes and their partisans on popular culture. In this interpretation, . . . the push to reform television is simply the latest manifestation of the struggle between the high and the low, the dominant and the dominated. (Fowles 2001: 2)

Fowles draws upon the work of **Pierre Bourdieu** (1930–2002), a French sociologist, anthropologist, and philosopher best known for his work on the connection between class and culture. In

Which is more likely: that these boys are becoming desensitized to violence, or that they are ridding themselves of aggression?

Photo: © Kenneth James/Corbis

particular, he draws upon two of Bourdieu's key concepts: habitus and reproduction. **Habitus** (related in origin but somewhat different in meaning from the English word 'habits') is a wide-ranging set of socially acquired characteristics, including, for example, definitions of 'manners' and 'good taste', leisure pursuits, ways of walking, even whether or not you spit in public. Each social class has its own habitus, its set of shared characteristics. **Reproduction**, in Bourdieu's definition, is the means by which classes, particularly the upper or dominant class, preserve status differences among classes. As Fowles phrases it, 'the reproduction of habitus is the key work of a social class' (Fowles 2001: 3). In one of his classic works, *La Reproduction* (1970), Bourdieu argued that educational systems reproduce the habitus distinctions of the classes.

Fowles's main point, then, is that sociologists and other academics who condemn television violence are merely fighting proxy wars aimed at reproducing the habitus of the dominant class by condemning the habitus of the dominated class. It is somewhat ironic that he uses Bourdieu's writing to do this, as Bourdieu himself (1996) was a severe critic of television.

● ●

What do YOU think?

1. Do you think that Fowles's arguments are valid?

2. What other criticisms of mass media might be challenged using this kind of approach?

● ●

Education

Education can be a powerful socializing agent. For example, schools often are the first source of information that children receive about a social group other than their own. Teachers, curriculums, textbooks, and the social experience of being in the classroom and in the playground all play a part. We will focus here on the role teachers play in the socializing function of education.

What we call the 'social location' of the teacher—his or her gender, age, ethnicity, and so on—can have an effect on the educational socialization of the student. The fact that the early years of schooling are dominated by women teachers will have a different effect on female and male students. The fact that science and math courses in high school are usually taught by men and English courses by women will also have a different effect on girls and boys. Being of the same ethnic background as the teacher can have a positive effect on a child's socialization experience, as Kristin Klopfenstein points out in her article 'Beyond Test Scores: The Impact of Black Teacher Role Models on Rigorous Math-Taking'. She notes in the introduction to her article that:

> Poor [in terms of income] black students, amongst whom teachers are often the only college-educated people they know, are in particular need of role models who (a) are interested in their educational progress; (b) understand the school system as an institution [in the sociological sense of being located in the middle class and more in 'white culture' than in 'black culture']; and (c) actively encourage academic excellence and the pursuit of challenging curriculum. Culturally similar teachers may take more interest in mentoring black students and have more credibility with those students. Given the importance of a rigorous mathematics curriculum and that math is frequently a gate-keeper subject for black students [i.e. success in math determines whether or not they will advance to post-secondary education], same-race math teachers play a potentially vital role in preparing black students for their academic and working futures. (Klopfenstein 2005: 416)

Klopfenstein's paper looks at the correlation between having a black math teacher in Grade 9 and the likelihood that a black math student will choose to enrol in a more challenging or 'rigorous' math class in Grade 10. Her findings, not surprisingly, are that having either male or female black teachers increases this likelihood, and that black students have a greater chance of post-secondary entry and success.

The socialization effect of having black teachers does not end there. Klopfenstein quotes P.R. Kane and A.J. Orsini's assertion that 'Teachers of color are important role models to white students, as they shape white students' images of what people of color can and do achieve' (Kane and Orsini 2003: 10).

Girls do better at language and boys do better at math. In terms of gender differences, how much is the result of our genes and how much is the result of our socialization?

What do YOU think?

How do you think the social location of a teacher might affect a student's socialization? Give some examples. How do you think this might differ for male and female students especially during the early years when, typically, all the teachers are women?

Issues of Socialization

In what follows, we will look at two issues of socialization, both involving adolescents, and both involving a complex combination of agents of socialization.

Male Readers

Traditionally, school-aged boys do better in maths and sciences, while girls fare better in writing and reading. Sociologists and educators today recognize that this is partly a result of socialization: boys have always been encouraged more in the former area of study, girls in the latter. In fact, beyond a lack of encouragement, there has been outright discouragement, as girls struggling in these supposedly male subjects have often been told not to worry: 'You aren't expected to do well in math,' or 'You won't need to know it.'

A lot has been done to improve female performance in the 'male preserve' of math and science, including the institution of all-girls classes in these subjects and the conscious promotion of role models such as astronaut Julie Payette. On average, boys still tend to perform better in these areas, but the difference has been lessened.

The same cannot be said for male–female differences in performance when it comes to reading and writing, as a 1999 federal government report, based on studies done in 1994 and 1998, makes clear. The following is an excerpt:

> Girls score substantially higher than boys in language skills and this gender difference is already pronounced by the age of 13. Boys and girls do not differ in mathematics achievement at the age of 13; however a gender gap in favour of males, particularly in problem-solving skills, seems to emerge by the time students are in their last year of secondary schooling. . . . It appears nevertheless that any gender differences in numeracy are substantially smaller than such differences in literacy. Hence, with respect to skills attainment, by the end of secondary schooling, girls should be in a somewhat better competitive position than boys. (Government of Canada 1999)

This raises a number of questions. To what extent is socialization to blame for gender differences in learning? Which agents of socialization might be having the greatest effect? How might educators and administrators change their approach to socialization in order to diminish the gender differences in literacy skills? The following editorial, which appeared in a small-town paper, offered several intriguing suggestions:

BOYS MUST READ TO CATCH UP TO GIRLS?

So boys—are you prepared to let girls be considered smarter than you? Parents—do you know that more boys drop out of high school than girls and fewer attend post-secondary school?

Head Argo coach 'Pinball' Clemons and other Argo players joined Premier Dalton McGuinty and Education Minister Gerard Kennedy last week to publicize these disturbing trends and issue the rallying cry—boys should read more! . . . In his direct and pointed way, Pinball Clemons challenged boys to 'be champions and read to keep learning and having fun.'

Test scores from Ontario and across Canada show that boys lag behind girls in reading and writing. For example, province-wide testing of Grade 6 English-language students in 2003–4 showed only 51 per cent of boys met the provincial standard in reading, compared to 65 per cent of girls. . . .

What to do?

As research shows that positive role models can successfully encourage boys to read, the Argo team members have been enlisted to spread the message publicly. But at home, dads and older brothers can show young boys that they read themselves to keep informed and for pleasure—the newspaper, magazines, work-related manuals and novels.

Make sure your boy has available something he likes to read. Boys often like to read science fiction and fantasy, books with action and humour, and magazines, comic books or even the sports pages of the newspaper. Take him to the library or bookstore and encourage him to choose his own reading materials.

Encourage the boy in your family to set aside time for reading every day. If he finds reading a struggle or a chore, try reading to him at bedtime, or alternating chapters; you reading one—him reading the next chapter himself . . .

Some parents even set up some kind of 'reward' system for reading; buying a treat after each book finished, or taking their reluctant reader to a movie based on a book he's just read.

And all parents and teachers can rely on the time-honoured 'negative reinforcement' idea to push boys to read books—they can't possibly want the girls in their class to seem smarter than they are! Get cracking, boys! Cracking open those books! (*Caledon Enterprise*, 26 January 2005)

What do YOU think?

1. What agents of socialization are stressed in this editorial? What agents of socialization are not mentioned that should be?

2. What do you consider to be the most important agents of socialization in this matter? What is the role of school in all of this?

3. The editorial is 10 years old. Are the writer's suggestions still valid? Has anything happened since it was written to change the prospects for male readers?

Adolescents and Risk Behaviour

One of the leaders in studying the socialization of adolescents is Jeffrey Arnett. A developmental psychologist, he has extensively researched **risk behaviour** (driving at unsafe speeds, unsafe sexual activities, drug and alcohol abuse, etc.) among adolescents. While he recognizes that there is a biological component to such behaviour, related to genetically 'inherent' individual traits like egocentrism and sensation-seeking, Arnett stresses that socialization plays a very large role in this area. He makes an important distinction between **narrow socialization** and **broad socialization**, describing them as follows:

Telling It Like It Is

Branding Consciousness, Selling Pretty

In an era in which feminism has made many legislative gains toward gender equity, and more women are entering into professional and non-traditional fields for their gender, the world of children's media seems unable or unwilling to keep up. Most toys are still marketed along strongly demarcated gender lines of what constitutes femininity and masculinity. Through pervasive marketing campaigns of many different toy brands, girls are compelled to obsess, and enjoy obsessing about, clothes, makeup, shopping, boys, and babies. They are also given the message that to be physically attractive you must also be sexy.

Through product lines and advertising, the gender roles young girls are frequently and repeatedly labelled with include Diva, Princess, Angel, and Pop-Star. These roles are not usually seen by parents as part of gender socialization, and girls who are labelled as such are often seen by parents as sweet, cute, and girly; however, these roles embody and encourage traits such as vanity, self-centredness, and an 'all about me' attitude, while encouraging, normalizing, and rewarding girls' preoccupation with their bodies over their minds.

Marketing toward young girls is not just stuck in the past; in many ways, it is worse than in the past. The Bratz doll has emerged as a hypersexualized version of Barbie, Mattel upped the ante with 'Lingerie Barbie', and there is an array of T-shirts that objectify and impose an adult sexuality on toddlers and young girls through slogans like 'Future Trophy Wife', 'Hot Tot', 'Made You Look', and 'Born to Shop'. Costume stores feature many provocative costumes for preteen girls, one of which is 'Major Flirt'—a provocative 'military' uniform complete with high, black leather-look boots with a platform heel, kilt-style mini-skirt, and studded black leather belt and choker.

Everywhere they turn—family, toys, advertising, media, and school—girls learn that beauty, narrowly defined and sexualized, is of utmost importance. This definition of beauty is also dependent on the consumption of beauty aids and products. 'Salon' and 'spa' birthday parties aimed at little girls as young as three years old are gaining popularity, providing a venue for girls to indulge in a range of services from manicures and pedicures to full makeup and hair extensions. One website for such services (replete with descriptors such as 'diva' and 'little princess') suggests that such experiences 'build confidence', a statement reflecting the sad reality of girls who are taught that their self-worth is dependent on validation they receive from others in response to their physical and sexual attractiveness.

–Angela Aujla

In cultures characterized by *broad socialization*, individualism and independence are promoted, and there is relatively less restrictiveness on the various dimensions of socialization. This allows for a broad range of expression of individual differences on the developmental tendencies (such as sensation seeking) that contribute to risk behavior, and leads to higher rates of risk behavior. Cultures characterized by *narrow socialization*, in contrast, consider obedience and conformity to the standards and expectations of the community to be paramount (enforced through the parents and the school as well as through members of the community), and punish physically and/or socially any deviation from the norm. The result is greater obedience and conformity, a narrower range of expression of individual differences, and low rates of antisocial adolescent risk behavior (although risk-taking tendencies may be directed by such cultures into avenues that serve a culturally approved purpose, such as warfare). (Arnett and Balle-Jensen 1993: 1843)

In a cross-cultural study of adolescent socialization, Arnett and colleague Lene Balle-Jensen

The Point Is...   Culture as an Agent of Socialization

David Elkind is an American sociologist who specializes in investigating some of the negative effects of the ways children growing up in the last 25 years or so have been socialized. In his best-known work, *The Hurried Child: Growing Up Too Fast, Too Soon* (1981, 1988, and 2001), he discusses the effects of the stress on children whose lives have been over-programmed by their parents, with little free time for spontaneous play. He calls this the **hurried child syndrome**. In 2003, he wrote an insightful article, 'Technology's impact', in which he discussed the effects of technology on child growth and development. Addressing the question 'What is it like growing up in a high-tech world, and how does that differ from growing up at an earlier time?', Elkind offers the following response, in which he expresses his concern about how the modern child's comfort with new technology is creating a **generation gap** (a significant cultural and social difference complete with an equally significant lack of understanding between generations):

> Part of the answer lies in the fact that the digital youth has a greater facility with technology than their parents and other adults. As a result, there is a greater disconnect between parents and children today, and some adolescents have even less respect for the knowledge, skills and values of their elders than they did a generation ago (hard as that may be to believe). . . .

> Independence from parents and adults means greater dependence on peers for advice, guidance and support. The availability of cell phones and immediate access to friends through instant messaging has only exaggerated this trend and quite possibly worsened the divide between children and their parents. (Elkind 2003)

With reference again to the hurried child syndrome, Elkind in this article also expresses his concerns about how children's sense of time has changed. Digital communication enables us to do more, faster, giving us a false feeling that we can accomplish much more than before. We extend this to our children, putting pressure on them to take part in more after-school activities, play more organized sports, do more homework, and learn languages and other academic subjects at an earlier age. This, Elkind feels, adds to the stress and guilt that children feel. We could argue, as well, that this pressure contributes to the sometimes crippling apprehension that post-secondary students feel about deadlines and their career—'I'm 21 and I don't know what I want to be.'

Elkind goes on to talk about how technology is changing the 'traditional culture of children' in ways that may affect personal autonomy and originality:

> [The] traditional culture of childhood is fast disappearing. In the past two decades

investigated the effects of socialization on adolescents in Denmark. While that country, like other Western countries, has a tendency towards broad socialization, the researchers noted ways in which Denmark has narrower socialization than the United States and Canada. For example, they cite the fact that the legal age for driving a car in Denmark at the time of the study was 18, reflecting, according to Arnett, narrow socialization elements in the legal system and in the cultural belief system. It reflects, too, a different cultural consensus concerning the balance between ensuring the individual autonomy of the teenager who wants to drive a car and the good of the community,

through fewer traffic fatalities and fewer cars on the road. This narrower socialization means, according to Arnett, that in Denmark fewer adolescents engage in the risk behaviour of unsafe driving than in North America.

Another example of Denmark's narrower socialization is community size. As Copenhagen is the only large city in Denmark, Danish children are more likely than North American children to grow up in small cities or towns. The researchers discovered a correlation between larger city size and several types of risk behaviour, including sex without contraception, sex with someone known only casually, marijuana use, cigarette

alone, according to several studies, children have lost 12 hours of free time a week, and eight of those lost hours were once spent in unstructured play and outdoor pastimes. In part, that is a function of the digital culture, which provides so many adult-created toys, games and amusements. Game Boys and other electronic games are so addictive they dissuade children from enjoying the traditional games. Yet spontaneous play allows children to use their imaginations, make and break rules, and socialize with each other to a greater extent than when they play digital games. While research shows that video games may improve visual motor coordination and dexterity, there is no evidence that it improves higher level intellectual functioning. Digital children have fewer opportunities to nurture their autonomy and originality those engaged in free play. (Elkind 2003)

Parents reading this are nodding their heads, kids are shaking their heads. Can this be considered, at least in part, like Fowles's discussion of media violence: an attack of one generation, growing older and losing power, on the habitus of a younger generation?

Does technology change social relations and the ways in which children experience everyday life?

Photo: E. Sinkins © 2009

dependency, and shoplifting. However, statistics for the United States did show evidence of narrower socialization than Denmark in some areas. For instance, in the US, as in Canada, there was and is a fairly extensive anti-smoking media campaign, unlike anything that existed in Denmark at that time. Perhaps as a result, Denmark has higher rates of smoking among adolescents than does North America.

In the conclusions to this study, the researchers stressed that that there significant agents of socialization (peers, school, neighbourhood/community, the legal system, the mass media, and the cultural belief system) that operate beyond the family.

Resocialization

Resocialization takes place whenever an individual shifts into a new social environment. It typically involves both unlearning and learning. In its extreme form, the individual unlearns all of the behaviours, attitudes, and values that were appropriate to his or her earlier social environment while learning those that make it possible to fit into the new situation.

A particularly explicit process of unlearning values was experienced by the bestselling religious author Karen Armstrong, who, as a teenager in the 1960s, joined a strict order of nuns in Britain.

In the following passage she recollects what the Mother Superior said to her and others who had just joined the order as postulants:

> Novices and postulants are kept in a particularly strict seclusion. They may not speak at all to seculars [i.e. to those who are neither nuns nor priests]. If a secular speaks to you, you must never reply. It is only by severing yourself absolutely from the world that you can begin to shed some of its values. Again no novice or postulant may ever speak to the professed nuns unless she is working with them and those few necessary words are essential for the job. The professed are in contact with the world, and even that indirect contact might seriously damage your spiritual progress. . . .
>
> You have to be absolutely ruthless in your rejection of the world, you know, Sisters.

Telling It Like It Is

A FIRST-HAND POV

Resocializing the Mi'kmaq

POINT OF VIEW

Shubenacadie school was a residential school in Nova Scotia, where Mi'kmaq suffered abuse at the hands of the staff. Their goal was to resocialize students by beating their traditional culture out of them— literally, if necessary. The abuse is illustrated graphically in the words of another ex-student, anthropologist Isabelle Knockwood, who tells the following story of a little Mi'kmaq girl caught speaking in her native language:

The nun came up from behind her and swung her around and began beating her up. . . . then the Sister pinched her cheeks and her lips were drawn taut across her teeth and her eyes were wide with terror. . . . Then the nun picked the little girl clean off the floor by the ears or hair and the girl stood on her tiptoes with her feet dangling in the air . . . The nun was yelling, 'You bad, bad girl.' Then she let go with one hand and continued slapping her in the mouth until her nose bled. (Knockwood 1992: 97)

The Shubenacadie Residential School. Notice that the boys have more freedom in what they can wear than the girls do. Why do you think that was so?

Photo: Copyright © Sisters of Charity, Halifax: Congregational Archives image #1693B

So many of its attitudes, even in really good people, are permeated with selfish values that have nothing at all to do with the self-emptying love of God. You yourselves are riddled with these ideas; you can't help it—it's not your fault. (Armstrong 1981: 92–3)

Resocialization can be voluntary or involuntary. Voluntary resocialization occurs when someone starts school or moves to a new school, when someone begins a job with a new company, when someone retires from work, or when someone undergoes a religious conversion (which can also, in extreme circumstances, be involuntary, as with cults). Associated with this kind of resocialization is the **rite of passage**, which is a ritual marking a change of life from one status to another, typically following some form of training. A wedding is a rite of passage; so is a funeral. Other examples include the Christian practices of baptism and **confirmation**, and the Jewish **bar mitzvah** (for boys) or **bat mitzvah** (for girls), when adolescents become 'adults in the faith' after a period of instruction.

Involuntary resocialization occurred in Native residential schools, like the one in Shubenacadie discussed in the box on page 116 where the language, religion, and customs of First Nations children were brutally beaten out of them. Other examples include being drafted into military service, being thrown in jail, being committed to a psychiatric hospital, and being subjected to mandatory retirement. Goffman (1961) calls institutions where involuntary resocialization takes place **total institutions**, as they regulate all aspects of an individual's life. A significant part of the unlearning process associated with involuntary resocialization is what has been termed a **degradation ceremony**, a kind of rite of passage where a person is stripped of his or her individuality. Hazing, whether of Grade 9 students, first-year college or university students, or rookies on amateur and professional sports teams, is a degradation ceremony in which being made to perform acts of minor (sometimes major) humiliation informs the initiates that they are in a new social world where they are mere beginners.

Sometimes voluntary and involuntary resocialization can occur together. Consider, for instance, programs for treating alcoholism or obesity, which begin with the sufferer's decision to change his or her lifestyle but then involve a strict and rigorous regime that is imposed for the duration of treatment.

'Incorrigible': The Resocialization of Velma Demerson

From 1913 to 1964, thousands of women in Ontario were put into reformatories under the *Female Refuge Act*. Among the 'offences' for which young women (especially teenagers and women in their early twenties) would be placed in these institutions was being sexually active outside of marriage. This kind of behaviour and the women guilty of it were branded 'incorrigible'.

In 1939, Velma Demerson, 18 years old and white, became sexually involved with a Chinese man. They intended to get married. When she became pregnant, her parents reported to the authorities that she was being 'incorrigible'. Velma was arrested and sent first to a 'home' for young girls, then to the Mercer Reformatory. The following is her account of her degradation ceremony:

> I can see that the girls ahead of me in line are getting large cotton dresses, aprons, underwear, white cotton stockings, and black shoes. When my turn comes, I put on a large faded old-fashioned dress. It's extremely wide and reaches my ankles. However, when I put on the full apron with its long ties I can see that it will hold the dress in, making it look like it almost fits. The thick cotton stockings are about two inches too long at the toes but are easily stuffed into the shoes, which are also several sizes too large.
>
> Each girl has quickly been handed a bundle without reference to size. We learn that we can expect to be issued standard Mercer attire in our own size later. What we've been given is the garb provided to all new inmates, to be worn for the first few weeks. In the months to come we are always able to recognize a new inmate by her initiation clothing. To girls already in a state of anxiety, the code of silence and humiliating dress further the subjugation. We are young women, aware of fashion. We know that large cotton dresses and wide aprons belong to a past era of drudgery on the farm. (Demerson 2004: 5)

The Point Is...

The Vision Quest: A Modern Aboriginal Rite of Passage

A traditional rite of passage for Aboriginal peoples is the **vision quest**, which in the past was reserved primarily to mark the passage from childhood to adulthood. After receiving months of informal instruction from elders, the Native individual would embark on a journey away from the home community to an isolated location. Then he or she would fast for days, and possibly go without sleep, in the process of seeking a vision. A vision could be a song that comes to mind, or the appearance in dreams of an animal or other spirit who instructs the dreamer and initiates a connection with him or her that will continue until death.

More recently, adults have used the vision quest as a way of resocializing themselves with traditional ideals following a period of difficulty. The following is a generalized example of the Ojibwa vision quest as it has been practised recently in northeastern Ontario (Steckley and Rice 1997: 226–7). It begins in a sweat lodge, a dome-shaped structure built around overlapping willow poles, covered with skins or tarpaulin and used as a kind of sauna. The participants throw sacred tobacco on the fire to thank the Creator. They are told the story of how the sweat lodge came to the people from a little boy who was taught about healing from the seven grandfather spirits. Water is put onto the seven stones that represent those spirits. The Elder sings ceremonial songs.

After the sweat, the participants are led to their own small lodges, where they fast and meditate. The Elder visits them and asks about their spiritual experiences.

The participants fast for three nights and four days. What they learn changes with each night:

The first is described as the night of doubt, where participants pray but are uncertain about what will happen. Hunger is mitigated by a feeling of excitement. The second night is one of fear, sometimes known as the dark night of the soul. Participants realize that their bodies are beginning to weaken, and they may question their resolve. The third night is the night of the spirit. It is often said that if something meaningful is going to happen, it will occur between the beginning of the spirit night until the fast is finished. (Steckley and Rice 1997: 226–7)

After the final sweat there is a feast with gift-giving to the Elder and to those who have assisted the individuals in their resocialization.

Following this, she was led to her cell, which was seven feet long and four feet wide, equipped with one bare light bulb, a cot, a cold water tap and basin, and a covered enamel pail to be used as a toilet.

Hazing as Resocialization

Hazing is a particular way of resocializing new members of some group or organization, such as a high school, a university fraternity, a sports team, or a military unit. It is like a test in which the initiate must demonstrate, by successfully undergoing a demeaning or uncomfortable experience, that he or she is 'tough enough' to be a member. In sports, hazing typically involves some form of ritual humiliation of the rookies, imposed by the veterans who, as first-year members, had to go through the same trial to become full-fledged members of the team. Usually this kind of hazing is fairly minor: male players might have to shave their heads, or wear women's clothing or dress like a chicken in a public place. Sometimes, however, it crosses the line in ways that can harm the individual being hazed, particularly when the activity involves nudity and sexualized activities. In 2005, sports hazing made national headlines when a member of the McGill University football team quit after he and other rookies were forced to participate in a hazing ritual: nude and gagged, they were made to bend over while being prodded up the backside with a broom. This was nothing less than sexual abuse. At around the same time, a 16-year-old rookie on the Windsor Spitfires of the Ontario Hockey League became the subject of media attention after refusing to go through a hazing ritual called the 'sweat box'. This entailed crowding, naked, with other rookies into the washroom at the back of the team bus, with the heat turned up high enough to make the participants perspire.

Traditionally hazing in sports and elsewhere has been much more a male than a female activity. Establishing one's toughness has long been viewed as a manly thing to do. But this may be changing. In September 2009, the Carleton University's women's soccer team was suspended by the university for holding a rookie initiation party that ended up with a player becoming so drunk that she had to be rushed to hospital by ambulance. Interestingly, while the suspension made the national news, the ensuing decision to reduce the suspension to just two games did not.

● ● ● ● ● ● ● ● ● ● ● ● ● ● ● ● ● ● ●

What do YOU think?

1. Why does hazing often 'cross over the line' into abusive acts?

2. Is proving toughness an inherent part of sports? An inherent part of being male?

3. Do you think it's fair to draw parallels between hazing rituals in women's sports and the increasing acts of violence by girls and young women?

● ● ● ● ● ● ● ● ● ● ● ● ● ● ● ● ● ● ●

Photo: CP Photo/Winnipeg Free Press - Ken Gigliotti

Members of the CFL's Winnipeg Blue Bombers tape the team's athletic therapist to a goalpost as part of a hazing ritual. Does it surprise you to see this kind of incident associated with professional sport? Do you think you would react differently to the image if it featured university players? High school players?

Questions for Critical Review

1. Outline the basic ideas of Freud as they relate to socialization.
2. Outline the basic ideas of Mead and Cooley as they apply to socialization.
3. Explain the difference between the following: *social determinism*, *biological determinism*, and *agency*.
4. Identify at least five different agents of socialization and outline their roles.
5. Contrast *narrow* and *broad socialization*.
6. Do you believe the following areas are more socially or more biologically determined: career, clothing, hobbies?
7. Consider one or two situations in which you have been resocialized (for instance, starting a new school, moving to a new neighbourhood or city, entering or leaving an intense relationship). What did you have to learn? What did you have to unlearn?
8. In terms of socialization, what do you feel has been the impact of television, video games, movies, and the Internet on your life?

Suggested Readings

Armstrong, Karen (1981). *Through the Narrow Gate: A Memoir of Spiritual Discovery*. New York: St Martin's Griffin.

Barthes, Roland (1972). *Mythologies*. London: Paladin.

Davis-Floyd, Robbie, & Joseph Dumit (1998). *Cyborg Babies: From Techno-Sex to Techno-Tots*. New York: Routledge.

Erwin, Lorna, & David MacLenna (1994). *Sociology of Education in Canada: Critical Perspectives on Theory, Research and Practice*. Toronto: Copp Clark Longman.

Freud, Sigmund (1953). *On Sexuality: Three Essays on the Theory of Sexuality and Other Works*. New York: Penguin.

Rousseau, Jean-Jacques (1911). *Émile*. B. Foxley, trans. London: Everyman.

Steinberg, Shirley R., & Joe L. Kincheloe, eds (1998). *Kinder-Culture: The Corporate Construction of Childhood*. Boulder: Westview Press.

Suggested Websites

http://www.

FreudNet
www.nypsa.org

Jean Piaget Society
www.piaget.org/

Media Studies (College of Education, University of Oregon)
www.aber.ac.uk/media/Functions/mcs.html

National Longitudinal Study of Children and Youth
www.statcan.ca/english/research/89-599-MIE/2005002/about.htm

PART TWO | SOCIAL STRUCTURES

Key Terms

- achieved
- agent
- ascribed
- back stage
- chaos theory
- character classes
- complexity theory
- control
- cosmology
- critical management studies
- definition of the situation
- disenchanted

- dramaturgical approach
- efficiency
- egalitarianism
- eugenics
- field of discourse
- formal rationalization
- formal social movement organizations
- front stage
- general systems theory
- impression management
- institutionalized

- labelling theory
- marginal man
- marginalization
- master status
- matrilineal
- McDonaldization
- organizational behaviour
- organizational culture
- organizational studies
- organizational theory
- paradigm shift
- passing

5

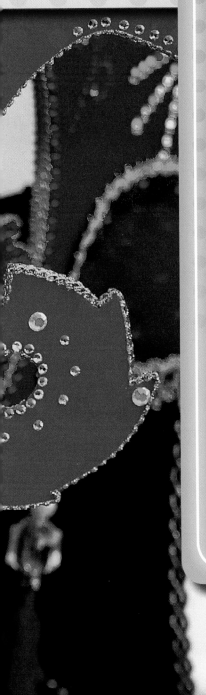

Social Roles, Interaction, and Organization

LEARNING OBJECTIVES

After reading this chapter, you should be able to

› distinguish between the various kinds of statuses that an individual holds at any one time;

› discuss the impact of role conflict, role exit, and role strain on the life of an individual; and

› discuss the impact of bureaucracy and formal rationality on the lives of Canadians.

Photo: A. Steckley

FOR Starters

Learning to Be a Stepfather

In one of my favourite novels, *David Copperfield*, Charles Dickens describes a truly evil stepfather for young David. That character was the model I hoped to avoid when I acquired the status of stepfather in the early 1990s, with stepsons who were seven and eight. During my first years as stepfather I felt that it was the *status* that caused me the most grief: I couldn't sort out what my responsibilities were, because they weren't clearly defined. I wasn't their 'dad', and yet I felt I was expected to take on many of the responsibilities that go along with being a father of sons. I had previously walked away (well, *run* away) from a potential relationship because the woman I was almost involved with had three sons from her just-ended marriage, and that was way too much for me at the time.

Much of the time I felt as though I was making up my job and status as stepfather as I went along. What do you do when a seven-year-old boy grasps your hand and walks with you in public? What do you do when a 10-year-old won't go out the front door because there's a bee outside? I wished there were a manual—Stepfathering for Dummies—that I could consult. At first, I was anxious to win them over by acting like the uncle I already knew how to be—the one who spoils nephews and nieces with candy, craziness, and presents, then leaves Mom and Dad to deal with their rambunctious children now jacked up on sugar and gifts, and my very physical humour. But I didn't want to be like a stepfather I had once met whose stepson could get away with anything. I had stayed with this acquaintance's family for a few days, and the boy soon learned that I wasn't soft like his stepfather. When he wouldn't wash his face, as part of the routine I was asked to supervise, I took a cloth and gave him a good, hard scrub; next time, he did it himself. But then, I wasn't emotionally attached to him or his mother. I had nothing to lose.

In this new relationship, I had to be more like a father, strict but fair—not an easy path to take for a 'live and let live' kind of guy. But I didn't initially take to the 'dad' label. When their mother and I got married, and the boys asked if they should call me 'Dad', I rather thoughtlessly replied, 'You already have a father.' I didn't feel that 'Dad' was part of my stepfather status. It was a good thing that I loved sports, like they did. I went to all of their hockey, baseball, and lacrosse games. I coached Rob in baseball, and drove Justin all over the countryside when he made the local rep baseball team. I was glad that they weren't girls. Conjuring up a hideous stereotype, I just couldn't imagine myself going shopping in a mall with a stepdaughter. She'd have to love sports or I wouldn't know what to do.

I felt self-conscious becoming close to the boys. I worried that people are sometimes suspicious of stepfathers, as though they're child abusers just waiting for the right opportunity. And when the school called or I went for parent–teacher interviews, I felt that my status was being assessed. Sometimes, after explaining the nature of my relationship to the boys, I perceived a 'that explains it' look in the eyes of teachers, principals, and office staff.

Now that both boys are in their twenties, I am finally becoming comfortable with my stepfather status. I confidently refer to them as 'my sons' (most of the time). When Rob had a near-fatal car accident and he asked me to drive him home, I was moved to tears. One of Justin's co-workers calls me 'Justin's dad', and I'm happy with that. I might just write a 'stepfather for dummies' book—although I know I made lots of mistakes, I also feel I finally know what it means to have the status of 'stepfather'.

● ●

What do YOU think?

1. Why, according to the author, is the status of stepfather a complicated one? What does this status entail?

2. Imagine the narrative the author's step-sons might write in response to this. Do you think they would have found the status of stepson just as complicated?

● ●

Introduction to Social Interaction

When we interact with other people, and they interact with us, much of what goes on both in thoughts and in behaviour relates to the statuses we hold and the way we perform the roles attached to those statuses. The interaction may be relatively simple when the expectations are well understood by both parties. But if a status is more complex because the set of expectations attached to it is not well established, the exchange may be more difficult. Such is the case with stepparents and stepchildren, as the opening box suggests. Sometimes, too, the expectations associated with one status interfere with those of another, as we will see.

Erving Goffman

In the opening chapter we introduced Alberta-born sociologist **Erving Goffman**, who can be considered an early leader in the development of theory related to social interaction. We looked at his *Presentation of Self in Everyday Life* (1959), a landmark work and an example of his **dramaturgical approach**. This is a way of approaching sociological research as if everyday life were taking place on the stage of a theatre, with a **front stage** for public display and a **back stage** for private, personal, or more intimate encounters. **Impression management** is Goffman's term for the strategies we adopt when presenting ourselves publicly. You can think of impression management as it applies to the social interaction of politicians, particularly those on the national stage. Goffman would have had a great time studying Stephen Harper, who exercises a great deal of impression management with every tie, every sweater, every cowboy vest he pulls from his closet, not just for his appearance at public events but for his communication with his cabinet. So careful is he in managing impressions that it became a major political incident when an internal memo intended for an all-Conservative 'stage' was leaked to the broader stage of Canadian media. When front stage meets back stage, impression management has gone awry.

Social Status

Status and role: it sounds like a quick order for lunch, but these two concepts are central to sociology. A **status** is a recognized social position

that an individual occupies. It contributes to the individual's social identity by imposing responsibilities and expectations that establish the individual's relationships to others. You don't have just one status; in fact, you can have several at once—daughter, mother, wife, CEO, volunteer board member, soccer coach, and on and on. The collection of statuses you have is your **status set**. If you are a man, you could have the statuses of son, brother, uncle, teacher, drummer (for your band), neighbour, citizen, white person, all at the same time and with little effort. We gain statuses as we age, and we also possess, however briefly, dozens of statuses throughout our lives.

One way of classifying our many statuses is to distinguish between statuses that are *achieved* and those that are *ascribed*. A status is considered **achieved** if you've entered into it at some stage of your life, but you weren't born into it; a professional position (assuming it's not a job in the family business), a role in a hobby or recreational activity ('avid wakeboarder'), an academic standing ('college graduate' or 'Master of Arts')—all of these are achieved statuses. They assume some

Imagine writing an essay with one hand, and only part of your mind on the subject. What role conflict do you think this student has to go through?

Photo: MorganLane studios/iStockphoto.com

kind of personal ability, accomplishment, or voluntary act, although very few statuses are completely achieved (for instance, an accomplished wakeboarder has to have had *some* natural ability).

An **ascribed** status is one that you were born into ('female' or 'male', 'daughter' or 'son', 'sister' or 'brother', etc.) or one you have entered into involuntarily ('teenager', 'elderly person', 'cancer survivor'). Circumstances trump choice in ascribed statuses. For a long while there, it looked as though being president of the United States was always going to be an ascribed status—white, male; others need not apply. Of course, the degree to which a status is achieved or ascribed depends on how free a society is and how much **social mobility** exists. In a society where a small ruling elite dominates, the statuses of lawyer, politician, doctor, professor, or rich business owner can be more ascribed than achieved. There is little vertical mobility from the lower, labouring classes into the elite. On the other hand, while 'race' is for the most part ascribed, a person from a racialized group who wants to avoid discrimination and whose appearance does not clearly put them into one group or another can successfully claim dominant racial status; this process is known as **passing**. It is not unusual for Aboriginal people in Canada to pass for white, or at least to try, particularly in big cities.

Sexual Orientation and Status: A Problem Area

We would argue here that sexual orientation is primarily an ascribed status. Heterosexuality is natural for some, and homosexuality is natural for others. There are those who believe that homosexuality is simply a 'lifestyle choice', one that can be overcome with heavy doses of therapy, drugs, religion, or conservative politics. Remember, homosexuality was against the law in Canada until 1969. The scholarly literature strongly argues that sexual orientation is a physical/psychological predisposition, which may or may not be acted upon at some point. According to this definition, regardless of whether you live in a gay or lesbian relationship, you are homosexual if your sexual fantasies are overwhelmingly about people who are of the same sex as yourself.

Of course, sexual orientation, as we will see in Chapter 13, is much more complicated than this. One problem with labelling it either an achieved or an ascribed status has to do with the way one's own sexuality is recognized by others. Someone who is gay but who marries into a heterosexual relationship because of social pressure would not be socially recognized as homosexual. In terms of statuses, that would mean the status of sexual orientation is, at least partially, achieved because it is a lifestyle choice based on what society recognizes. Status, then, lies in what you do, not in what you feel; in this case, choice can trump circumstances.

'Indian Chief' and Status

As the preceding section shows, the issue of achieved versus ascribed status isn't always cut and dried. But does it really matter whether a status is achieved or ascribed?

In short, it does. In fact, the consequences can be quite serious when people incorrectly assign ascribed status to a position that has a strong achieved component. The status of the word 'chief' (an English word, and, in Canada, a defined status in the eyes of the federal government), as applied to the leader of an Aboriginal group, is one such case. Consider, for example, the 'peace chiefs', or **sachems** (an Algonquian word for 'leader'), of the Confederacy of the Haudenosaunee or Iroquois. There were 50 sachems, each member appointed, by tradition, according to lineage within a clan. Because the clans are **matrilineal**, the leading women in the clan had the power to suggest both who should receive the title of chief and who should have this status removed. If you belonged to the right lineage—if, say, your mother was the sister of the previous chief or you were the brother of the previous chief—you would be eligible to become chief. However, you could not be chosen and awarded this status unless you were seen by key members of the clan as having demonstrated the abilities necessary for a sachem—abilities in listening, speaking, and compromising, for instance.

When the Canadian government disallowed the traditional government of the Iroquois—violently, in the case of the Six Nations and in the Mohawk community of Akwesasne—one of the reasons they used to justify their position was that First Nations government was undemocratic. Federal leaders assumed that being a hereditary chief meant that the position automatically went from father to son (or, more accurately in a matrilineal society, from mother's brother to sister's son), with no input from the community. In other words, they saw the status of sachem as ascribed rather than achieved. In fact, as we've just noted, there was a strong achieved component to the status. The government's misguided assumptions resulted in forcing an unwanted form of government on the Iroquois people. Ironically, they did so in the name of the British king, the holder of an ascribed status.

Master Status

Everett C. Hughes introduced the concept of **master status** in *Dilemmas and Contractions of Status* (1945), published after he had left McGill University for the University of Chicago. He applied the term in the context of 'race' in the US:

> Membership in the Negro race, as defined in American mores and/or law, may be called a master status–determining trait. It tends to overpower, in most crucial situations, any other characteristics [i.e. statuses] which might run counter to it. (Hughes 1945: 357)

The term 'master status' as it is used today signifies the status of an individual that dominates all of his or her other statuses in most social contexts, and plays the greatest role in the formation of the individual's social identity. You can learn a lot about people by asking them what they consider their master status to be. Canadians, upon being introduced to someone, will often ask the new acquaintance: 'What do you do?' This implies that a person's occupation is his or her master status. It isn't always the case, though: ethnicity and gender can be master statuses, even when an individual doesn't want them to be. If you met Barack Obama at a dinner party (say you crashed it) and asked him, 'What do you do?', he would probably inform you, politely, of his status as leader of the most powerful nation on earth and recent winner of the Nobel Peace Prize. Nevertheless, during his presidential campaign, his master status was that of a black man. It will be interesting to see whether the status of president will override the status of 'race' in the future.

Sociologist **Howard Becker** (b. 1928) developed **labelling theory** in the 1960s. It deals with the negative effects on self-identity and behaviour of people outside of the majority (i.e. deviants) when they are assigned a name or label that has negative connotations. Part of this theory, first expounded in his work *Outsiders: Studies in the Sociology of Deviance* (1963), states that when negative connotations are attached to a status, a powerful master status can be created and internalized by both the individual and others, regardless of other positive statuses exhibited. The process is well portrayed in the following excerpt from Hanson, which describes the master status of 'druggie':

> [I]f people who are important to Billy call him a 'druggie' this name becomes a powerful label that takes precedence over any other status positions Billy may occupy. Even if Billy is also an above average biology major, an excellent musician, and a dependable and caring person, such factors become secondary because his primary status has been recast as a 'druggie'. Furthermore, once a powerful label is attached, it becomes much easier for the individual to uphold the image dictated by members of society, and simply to act out the role expected by significant others. Master status labels distort an individual's public image because other people expect consistency in role performance. (Hanson et al. 2006: 76)

In this sense, a label like 'criminal' becomes a master status that can follow a person for his or her entire life, despite efforts to change it. Moreover, the internalization of a master status can determine individual behaviours and actions based on what is expected from society and oneself. It's like a self-fulfilling prophecy: 'If I've been branded a criminal, then I suppose I should act like one.' Labelling theory has also been used to look at how negative, racialized statuses within education affect self-esteem, educational performance, and educational outcomes.

Status Hierarchy

Statuses can be ranked from high to low based on prestige and power; this ranking is referred to as **status hierarchy**. For each of the basic sociological categories of gender, race, ethnicity, age, class, sexual orientation, and physical ability, there is a scale in which one status tends to be ranked more highly than another or others. For example, in Canadian society we rank male over female, white over black or brown, British over Eastern European, elite over middle and working class, heterosexual over homosexual, and able-bodied over disabled. Age is more complicated: power is concentrated in the hands of those who are middle-aged, yet because we live in a society that promotes the cult of youth—the desire to look, act, and feel young—youth also has some prestige. The middle-aged often abuse their bodies, injecting poison (Botox) into their faces and fat into their buttocks, undergoing facelifts, and fighting to hold onto their youthful appearance through fitness regimes and the masking effects of makeup. We could also call this a form of *passing*, as those who engage in such rejuvenating practices are trying to achieve higher status by 'passing' for younger.

Not all of the social categories align in all people, and this can result in social tension. You may find yourself with a high-ranking gender or ethnic status but a lower-ranking class status. As it happens, there are a fair number of people who have the complete favoured set of being male, white, British, rich, heterosexual and able-bodied. Federal and provincial parliaments seem to be clubhouses for people with that status set. Likewise, there are a lot of black or Native women living at or below the poverty line, and who are lowly regarded. **Status consistency** is the result when all of the social status hierarchies line up; when they do not—when one is highly ranked in one status category but not in others—the condition is called **status inconsistency**.

Michaëlle Jean, the twenty-seventh governor general of Canada, exemplifies status inconsistency. She was raised in a middle-class home in Haiti, where her father, the principal of a prestigious preparatory school in Port-au-Prince, taught philosophy. However, her family was forced to

What statuses are displayed in this image? Which would you consider to be the master status? Could the master status be one that isn't visible in the picture?

Photo: © Kris Timken/Blend Images/Corbis

emigrate to Canada after her father was imprisoned in the mid-1960s during the Duvalier dictatorship. Shortly after coming to Canada in 1968, Jean's parents split up, and her mother was forced to work at low-income jobs. The experiences of racism and poverty that Jean faced in Canada, having come from a country where she belonged to the racial majority, further added to her status inconsistency. Jean excelled at university, winning a number of scholarships, and went on to obtain a Master's degree. She taught at university and went on to become a prize-winning journalist and social activist, honoured several times for her work with women's shelters. When she was appointed governor general in 2005, there was a significant amount of social tension surrounding her appointment. She was a black woman and an immigrant, whose first language is French. (Indeed, she came very close to exemplifying the mythical black, disabled lesbian who is awarded a plum position owing to affirmative action and politically correct hiring committees. In Ms Jean's case, however, it is safe to say, based on her accomplishments, that her status is achieved rather than ascribed. Her low status as Haitian may have been raised as she may have been seen as representing an intelligent, compassionate face for Canada during the earthquake in Haiti in January, 2010.)

Hughes noticed that when people of 'lower' status moved into occupations associated with more favoured statuses, they became targets of certain strategies others used to reduce the apparent inconsistency. One strategy was to modify the stereotype surrounding the lowly regarded status; this would result in the upwardly mobile individuals being alienated both from people sharing their low ascribed status and from people defined by the more highly regarded achieved status. Referring to sociological data gathered during his research for *French Canada in Transition* (1943), Hughes wrote:

> [I]n Quebec the idea that French-Canadians were good only for unskilled industrial work was followed by the notion that they were especially good at certain kinds of skilled work but were not fit to repair machines or to supervise the work of others. In this series of modifications the structure of qualities expected for the most-favored positions remains intact. But the forces which make for mobility continue to create marginal people on new frontiers. (Hughes, 1945: 356–7)

This situation, where individuals live in a kind of limbo—partly in the old world of stereotypes and prejudices assigned to one status, partly in the new world of achieved occupational status—characterizes what Robert E. Park (Hughes's colleague at the University of Chicago) referred to as a **marginal man**. The male bias implied in the term, which was inspired by Hughes's work, is the main reason it's no longer used; however, it is historically important because it led to the coining of the commonly used term **marginalization**, which refers to the process by which groups are assigned into categories that set them at or beyond the margins of the dominant society.

Another strategy that Hughes referred to was **social segregation**, which he illustrated in the following passage:

> The woman lawyer may become a lawyer to women clients, or . . . may specialize in some kind of legal service in keeping with woman's role as guardian of the home and of morals. Women physicians may find a place in those specialities of which only women and children have need. A female electrical engineer was urged by the dean of the school . . . to accept a job whose function was to give the 'woman's angle' to design of household electrical appliances. The Negro professional man finds his clients among Negroes. The Negro sociologist generally studies race relations and teaches in a Negro college. (Hughes 1945: 358)

In this way, social segregation is both the outcome of being marginalized as well as a strategy to deal with marginalization.

● ●

What do YOU think?

In what situations do you think 'race' is still a master status in Canada?

● ●

SOCIAL ROLES

A **role** is a set of behaviours and attitudes that is associated with a particular status. A particular status may be associated with more than one role, and roles attached to a status may differ across cultures. For example, people holding the status of elder in traditionally minded cultures in China, Africa, and North American Aboriginal communities are expected to have acquired a certain level of wisdom that is then shared with those who are younger. The same expectations seldom exist in mainstream Canadian culture, where the status of elder has few positive role expectations attached to it; the status is more 'old person' than it is elder. (Indeed, one reason why Western social scientists were slow to question the myth of Inuit elder abandonment—discussed in Chapter 1—is that Western culture lacked its own positively defined role of elder, making the myth much more credible in their eyes.)

Robert Merton (1968) developed the idea of the **role set**, which comprises all of the roles that are attached to a particular status. As professors, we have the role of teacher to our students, but we are also colleagues to our peers, employees at our schools, and, of course, trouble-making underlings to our administrators. Students have a peer role with classmates in addition to their student role with instructors. To the college or university, they are paying customers.

Role Strain

Role strain develops when there is a conflict between roles within the role set of a particular status. For example, if a student complains to his instructor about another class, the instructor is placed in a conflict between her role as educator, in which she has the student's best interests at heart, and her role as colleague, in which she must be loyal to the professor teaching the other class. Similarly, a student who catches a classmate cheating on an exam is at once a member of the academic community with a responsibility to report the offence and a member of the student body who wouldn't rat out a peer. Role strain can even affect a single role. Consider the parent who feels more at ease with one of his children than with the other, but tries to balance his attentions between them. (Heaven forbid they should wind up on opposing hockey teams!)

Role Conflict

Another useful concept for understanding social tensions is **role conflict**. Role conflict occurs when a person is forced to reconcile incompatible expectations generated from two or more statuses he or she holds. If you are both a mother and a student, then you know all about role conflict. Imagine: it's the night before the big exam and you need to study—part of the set of behaviour expectations attached to being a college or university student; however, your daughter needs help with her homework, your son is ill, and your husband (working late, as usual) is pretty useless in terms of nurturing skills. These clashing sets of expectations illustrate role conflict. We see cases where people turn down promotions because they do not want to begin reporting to a manager who is also a friend: this is role conflict. If you have ever lost a friend because you became their boss, you understand all too well the nature of this conflict.

Role Exit

Role exit is the process of disengaging from a role that has been central to one's identity, and attempting to establish a new role. Helen Rose Fuchs Ebaugh (an ex-nun turned sociologist) has studied role exit processes extensively; some of her findings are summarized in *Becoming an EX: The Process of Role Exit* (1988). According to Ebaugh, who wrote not just about ex-nuns but about ex-priests, ex-convicts, and recovering alcoholics, role exit involves shifting your master status. If you were forced to retire having always defined yourself by what you did ('I am a nurse'), you might feel uncomfortable when asked, 'What do you do?'. If you are a stay-at-home mother and your children move away, your identity needs to be reformed beyond 'empty nester' or 'housewife'. If you are a father and your parental role is reduced

Photo: CP/AP Photo/Mike Roemer

NFL quarterback Brett Favre announces his retirement from the Green Bay Packers on 6 March 2008. Does it look to you as though he's struggling with role exit? Would it surprise you to learn that he returned to the NFL the following season with the Minnesota Vikings?

because your ex-wife gains primary custody of the children, then becoming a part-time dad may feel like a role exit.

The role exit of married people who become single through separation, divorce, or death of a spouse is always difficult, as it entails shifting from 'we' to 'I'. Previous relationships with friends and family change and, in the case of divorce, people take sides. Some people you've been close to might start avoiding you, treating your divorce like something contagious and you as a carrier of the failed relationship virus. On the other hand, others might begin to pay you more attention, and in ways you haven't been used to. After all, if you're still reasonably young, you are expected to be 'out there' meeting eligible singles, even if you have always enjoyed staying at home. Role exit, as uncomfortable as it might be, is something we will all experience throughout our lives.

The Thomas Theorem

In Chapter 2 we introduced the symbolic interactionist William I. Thomas, whose work with Florian Znaniecki, *The Polish Peasant in Europe and America* (1918–20), illustrates the important part that narratives play in defining situations. Thomas showed, as much as his later work did, that people's own interpretation of their lives was an important sociological element. This idea eventually became the **Thomas theorem**, the notion

that the 'situations we define as real become real in their consequences' (1966: 301).

The Thomas theorem influenced other developments in symbolic interactionism, including the concept of **definition of the situation**. This states that given a particular situation, different individuals will define the situation differently and in contradictory ways, based on their own subjective experiences. In order to understand an individual's actions and responses to particular situations, you need first to understand how he or she defines the situation. This is a very important consideration when it comes to issues in healthcare. If, say, a psychiatrist views 'treatment' as the patient working through his own problems, but the patient views 'treatment' as the psychiatrist providing a cure without the patient doing any work, then therapy will be ineffective (Alison Harold, personal communication, 1980). Anne Fadiman's work on how Western medicine failed to address the problems of a young Hmong girl with epilepsy (see Chapter 10) concludes with a consideration of eight key questions, first posed by Arthur Kleinman, that Western doctors should use when they interact with patients who have different cultures of medicine (see Quick Hits below). The purpose of the questions is to determine, from the point of view of the patient and her family, the definition of the sickness and healing situation. This approach ensures that problems that may arise around opposing situational definitions based on cultural differences can be mitigated.

QUICK HITS
Arthur Kleinman's Eight Questions

1. What do you call your illness? What name does it have?
2. What do you think has caused the illness?
3. Why and when did it start?
4. What do you think the illness does? How does it work?
5. How severe is it? Will it have a short or long course?
6. What kind of treatment do you think the patient should receive? What are the most important results you hope she receives from this treatment?
7. What are the chief problems the illness has caused?
8. What do you fear most about the illness?

Introduction to Social Organization

When we think of the term 'social organization', we might think of the way a society and its institutions—family, law, religion, polity, economy, and so on—are organized. What we seldom consider is that the basis for social organization, whether imagined or real, rests on a particular set of principles. In the sociological literature, 'social organization' is rarely defined, and when it is, it's often conflated (i.e. blended together as being considered the same thing) with the terms 'social structure' or 'social institution' as though they are all synonymous.

They are not. While social institutions are social structures and are socially organized, social structures and social organization are not social institutions. So, what is 'social organization'? We take **social organization** to be the social and cultural *principles* around which things are structured, ordered, and categorized. In this way, we are able to speak about the social organization of cultures, social institutions, or corporations. For example, a culture may be organized around the principle of **egalitarianism** (society based on equality) or hierarchy, and further organized in terms of the type or form that the egalitarian or hierarchal structure takes: that is its social organization.

Organizational Structure

Under the European system of feudalism, one's allegiances were to God first, king next, and country last. As European societies moved from **theocracies** (religious states) to **secularism**, monarchies to democracies, and countries to nation-states, the nation-state became the main locus of allegiance and loyalty. When we go to war, we no longer fight for God or our sovereign or prime minister, but for our country. And, despite the emotional feelings—pride, loyalty, sentimentality, etc.—that are aroused when we sing the national anthem or win an Olympic gold medal, 'Canada' is an imaginary geopolitical space in which a diverse population is constructed as an 'imaginary community' through symbols such as the anthem and flag. Canada, then, is not a 'natural' thing but rather, a socially organized manifestation based on certain collectively shared principles. Culture and the organizing principles it's based on imposes

Photo: CP Photo/Chris Young

Prince Charles, visiting Toronto in November 2009, inspects troops from the Toronto Scottish Regiment during a ceremony in which he presented new Regimental Colours.

what is seen as 'natural'. In this way, organizing principles are upheld by shared cultural beliefs and maintained through a network of social relations.

At the heart of organizing principles are the ways in which a culture produces knowledge about the world based on a particular **cosmology** (the study of the universe—religion, philosophy, and science). Cosmologies and corresponding myths are seen as a high form of truth.

The Point Is...

Dungeons and Dragons: Virtual and Real Status

Before video games, the virtual battling worlds of Warcraft and Warhammer, and the escapism of Second Life, there was E. Gary Gygax's Dungeons and Dragons (D&D), the first worldwide **role-playing game**. Millions of copies were sold in the 1970s and 1980s as a pen-and-paper, sit-at-the-table game before it joined the computer world. D&D was populated by creatures such as elves, trolls, gnomes, dreaded orcs, and wyverns, all borrowed from Tolkien's *Lord of the Rings* and the fantasy works of Michael Moorcock, H.P. Lovecraft, and Roald Dahl. What does D&D have to do with status and role? For a generation of adolescents—almost exclusively boys—their D&D characters formed a status that was recognized by other players, and that was as significant as traditional statuses such as son, brother, friend, and student. The roles played in D&D games were more engaging than those occupied in real life, though some real-life 'truths' were learned through playing.

A good introduction to D&D is Mark Barrowcliffe's *The Elfish Gene: Dungeons, Dragons and Growing Up Strange—A Memoir* (2008). Barrowcliffe, known as 'Spaz' to his peers, grew up in working-class Coventry, England, and began playing D&D in 1976 at the age of 12. Barrowcliffe, explaining his fascination with the game, notes that he and his

D&D was played with dice and a map sketched on a sheet of graph paper, typically around the dining room table. How do you think that would affect the status formation of those who played? How might it differ from the experience of participants in today's online gaming community, who may never meet one another face to face?

friends didn't aspire to their parents' simple and (from their perspective) dull lives, characterized by predictability and stability. Instead, they sought the kind of magic that was missing from their lives and their world. They were, in Barrowcliffe's estimation, intelligent (particularly in the many mathematical calculations necessary to be a successful player), but not necessarily school-smart. They certainly were not jocks or tough guys, and they weren't concerned with fashion or appearance.

Aboriginal cosmologies are rooted in the belief that all matter, both inanimate and animate, are interdependent: everything is connected. They emphasize the interdependence of humans and nature, Judaeo-Christian-Islamic cosmology emphasizes human dominion over nature as decreed by God. Western culture's sense of the privileged position of humans in nature, together with the emergence of modern science dating back to the Enlightenment, has led to a knowledge based on control. Unlike Aboriginal cosmology, modern science is based on a logic in which knowledge is deduced by analyzing the various parts of a given phenomenon—think of dissecting a frog for your Grade 10

science class—as opposed to studying the whole phenomenon in its totality.

Here, it might be useful to introduce another of Foucault's concepts, the **field of discourse**. The dominant field of discourse, according to Foucault, is inseparable from institutional practices and relations of power and authority that privilege some forms of knowledge over others. Understanding a particular field of discourse and how it constitutes a domain of knowledge requires an examination of the institutions that are linked to ways of thinking and speaking about the natural and social world (Mills & Simmons 1995). The dominant field of discourse relating both to organizations and to

That might be why they weren't popular with girls. The D&D world of Barrowcliffe and his peers was definitely male. As Barrowcliffe writes, 'the game at its height was played by millions of boys and two girls around the world' (2008: 1), adding that 'Girlfriends are generally poison to a committed life in D&D' (2008: 242).

The statuses adopted by players were all members of different **character classes**. Initially, these were simple: fighter (warrior), cleric (priest), and magic-user (wizard). As the game evolved, however, the number of character classes grew to include alchemists, assassins, berserkers, druids, ninjas, paladins (holy warriors), and female characters such as witches and the bizarrely sexual houris—'a cross between sorcerers and prostitutes' (2008: 227). By rolling dice and recording the results, players would know precisely the strength, magical ability, charisma, and intelligence of their characters, and they would speak and act as they imagined their characters would. According to Barrowcliffe:

> People . . . identified very strongly with their characters. . . . This is where it differs from a computer game. You can't reboot if your character is killed. In D&D if the character dies, he's dead, which . . . is a serious threat to his future. Losing a character that you've had for . . . years can be a major emotional experience. At fourteen years old it can be the first real grief you've known in your life. It's like

having an imaginary friend but one you get to actually look at, that other people will discuss as if they're real and may even attempt to kill. (2008: 35)

Barrowcliffe's main characters were Alf the Elf, Foghat the Gnome, and Effilc Worrab, an elf warrior with the head of a mule, who eventually became his favourite. As for the dungeons, they really weren't dungeons but settings invented by the person acting as the 'dungeon master' (DM). You could call the DM a sort of referee, but for Barrowcliffe, 'To call the DM a referee is a bit misleading. His role is nearer to that of a god. He creates a world, sets challenges for players' characters, and rewards or punishes them according to the wisdom of their actions' (2008: 32).

The game socialized young males, giving them self-knowledge, opportunities to exercise creativity, and experience in the competitive world of adults, lessons other males might learn through their statuses as goalies, drummers, long-distance runners, or high-school students.

● ● ● ● ● ● ● ● ● ● ● ● ● ● ● ● ● ● ●

What do YOU think?

What lessons did participating in the game produce? Does it matter that they were learned while playing out fictional rather than real statuses?

● ● ● ● ● ● ● ● ● ● ● ● ● ● ● ● ● ● ●

organizational theory, as we will see, is very much a privileged form of knowledge.

The Study of Organizations

To recap: organizational principles are based on our knowledge or understanding of the world, which is informed by our cosmology. These principles determine not just how our culture and society are organized but how other social bodies are organized, whether we're talking about social institutions like the family and education, or bureaucracies and corporations, or community-based organizations.

What is important in the study of organizations is distinguishing both the level of organization and the level of analysis.

There was increased interest in the sociological study of organizations after Weber conducted his detailed work on bureaucracy, and again when the study of organizations filtered into the business sector and commerce degree programs that emerged in the 1980s. The study of organizations shifted from the examination of social institutions to the examination of business corporations in order to uncover more effective and efficient management practices. This led to an explosion in the fields of **organizational theory** and **organizational behaviour** (see Mills & Simmons 1995). During the last 20 years, the study of organizational behaviour has expanded by integrating approaches from other disciplines. Anthropology, for instance, has contributed to the study of organizations through its understanding of corporations as communities in which an **organizational culture** with 'organizational rituals' and 'symbolic acts' is an aspect of organizational dynamics. An anthropologist may also study the informal organization of a company to determine how decisions are made or how information actually flows, which may be quite different from the mandated, formal structure of the organization itself.

With the spread of globalization, there has been increased study of cross-cultural organizations, which are of particular interest to businesses and those who study organizational behaviour. In the 1980s, organizational structures based on models derived from the productive corporate culture of Japan were implemented in North America. They failed, however, in part because they did not account for the organizational principles of Japanese culture, which are more collectivist than the individualist organizational principles favoured in Canada and the US. Organizational structures based on a collective model, in which employees work in teams, did not have the same success when applied to the competitive

individualism found in North American business culture and society generally. Think of the TV show *The Apprentice*, where, on the one hand, competing cast members are asked to co-operate and work in teams, yet there can be only one winner in the end. There is no real commitment to the team; the commitment is only to oneself.

There were other attempts to implement cross-cultural business organizational practices in North America. Canadian Airlines, for instance, studied the business culture of Korea in the hopes of increasing customer satisfaction and market share. They also examined the organizational structure and practices of Middle Eastern banks in developing strategies for capital expansion under globalization. Banking practices in many Muslim countries are different from those of the West because **usury** (lending money with interest) is seen as immoral, and so Middle Eastern banks tend to be not just lenders but also partners in whatever business venture they have invested in.

Much of the increase in **organizational studies** has been fuelled by Western capital invested by companies in an effort to find ways to increase profits by managing organizational structure and employee behaviour and practices in a more managerially efficient manner. This has led to questions about the ethics of controlling worker behaviour, not to mention the inherent ethnocentric and

Compare these two working scenarios, the one from a Japanese boardroom, the other from a New York stock-trading office. What organizational differences do you notice?

Photos: (l) © Dex Image/Corbis; (r) © James Leynse/Corbis

capitalist assumptions in organizational theory given the context of global culture. These critiques have led to the rise of **critical management studies,** which are critical of traditional theories of management. Two such theorists, Mills and Simmons (1995), have challenged the assumptions of mainstream accounts of organization. They point out that there is little in the organizational theory and behaviour literature that deals with race, ethnicity, class, or gender, despite the high participation rates of women and people of colour in the British and North American labour force. Even after a Canadian Royal Commission on Equity in Employment (1984) concluded that employment opportunities in Canada were severely restricted owing to widespread systemic discrimination against Native people and visible minorities, as well as disabled people and women, mainstream organizational theory continues to ignore issues of inequality within organizational structures. Mills and Simmons also note that there is little attention given in this literature to the impact organizations have on the social and psychic life of individuals and groups affected by organizations. Despite the demonstrated link between organizational life and lack of self-esteem, a sense of powerlessness, segregated work life, stress, physical injury, pay inequality, sexual harassment, and racism, organizational theory and behaviour studies continue to ignore it (Mills & Simmons 1995).

Feminist Organizations

Organizational structure and process have been a major focus for the contemporary women's movement. Whether the structure is based on networks and coalitions, or at the level of individual organizations, feminists have always been concerned with the form of the organizations they create. In some instances, feminists have developed organizational forms that differ from mainstream forms as an expression of feminist politics. Because of their political and symbolic importance, issues surrounding organizational structure like the internal distribution of power and control, the division of labour, and decision-making rules can make it difficult for feminist coalitions to maintain their organizational cohesion.

While feminist organizations are generally organized around principles different to those found in traditional patriarchal organizations based on hierarchy, it would be a mistake to think that such organizations are without internal conflict. Carol Mueller (1995) studied feminist organizational form and conflict orientation, and found that generally speaking the type of organization itself would either mitigate or facilitate conflict. Mueller identified three types of feminist organizational form:

1. **formal social movement organizations,** which are professionalized, bureaucratic, inclusive, and make few demands of members;
2. **small groups or collectives,** organized informally, which require large commitments of time, loyalty, and material resources from its members; and
3. **service-provider organizations,** which combine elements of both formal and small-group organizations.

Mueller found that these organizational forms varied in terms of the degree to which feminist organizational principles such as inclusivity and democratic participation were practised, and were combined in a variety of structural configurations ranging from coalitions to complex social movement communities.

Organizational conflict can also vary depending on whether it is orientated internally, toward other members, or externally, toward other organizations, the state, or civil society. When conflict is directed internally—typically around issues of identity or ideology—it can cause fracturing within the organization. When conflict is directed externally, internal divisions tend to be minimized, and there is often increased solidarity in the face of a common threat. On the other hand, external-directed conflict can create a combat-orientated climate that often legitimizes hierarchical divisions of labour. However, whether defensive or offensive, external conflict heightens participation and increases pressure for action to defend those values under attack.

Mills and Simmons (1995) believe that feminism has had a growing presence in organizational theory, where it challenges the male domination of organizations and calls attention to the absence of gender analysis in organizational theory.

The Point Is...

Feminist Organization at Work

The Teaching Support Staff Union (TSSU) represents teaching assistants, tutor markers, and sessional instructors at Vancouver's Simon Fraser University. Certified in 1978, the TSSU began as Local 6 of the Association of University and College Employees (AUCE). AUCE was a feminist trade union movement that developed out of the Vancouver Women's Caucus in the late 1960s and early 1970s. The feminist roots of TSSU make it strikingly different from more conventional unions. From its start, the AUCE rejected the traditional form of organization found elsewhere in the Canadian union movement, which tends to be based on hierarchical structure and centralization. It successfully organized large numbers of women working in underpaid positions, mostly as clerical and teaching support staff. But since AUCE's inception, all of the AUCE locals, with the exception of Local 6, joined larger, more mainstream unions, such as the Canadian Union of Public Employees (CUPE); Local 6, now the TSSU, has continued to maintain its independent status.

The TSSU today is a grassroots union that is no longer affiliated with any other larger union or umbrella organization. All of its decisions come from the general membership. There are three salaried officers who are part of the larger executive committee and who handle the day-to-day operation of the union. The officers, as well as all members of the executive committee, are also members of the union itself, an arrangement that ensures that executives are in touch with issues of concern to the broader TSSU membership. Executive positions come up for re-election annually, and no member is allowed to occupy a position for more than two years consecutively. This practice encourages skills development among the general membership and prevents the concentration of knowledge in the hands of a few members. The executive meets every two weeks, and meetings are open to all TSSU members.

General meetings (GMs) of the membership take place three times every semester, and a minimum of 20 members must be present before decisions can be made. The membership has control of union resources and must approve the annual budget, financial statements, and most expenditures of the union. Committees and executive members make regular reports to the GM, guided by the motions put forward at these meetings. Any member can bring forward a motion at a GM.

The TSSU maintains a global vision. Not only does it fight to improve the working conditions of its own members, it also actively fights for labour rights and social justice locally, nationally, and internationally. The TSSU has supported CUPE's University Bargaining Sector, the BC Teachers' Federation, and other striking teachers from Hamilton, Ontario, to Oaxaca, Mexico. They have also initiated a Social Justice Committee to expand the scope of the union's advocacy, with a mission to fight the root causes of injustice, inequality, and poverty.

Complexity Theory

A framework based on **systems thinking** has been fundamental to organizational studies and organizational theory. **General systems theory** was the first theory aimed at modelling and designing human organizations. More recently, another systems-based model, **complexity theory**, has been used to examine organizations in various ways in the natural and social sciences and in the humanities. Scientific proponents of complexity theory champion it as a new 'theory of everything', capable of explaining biological evolution, consciousness, weather patterns, earthquakes, revolutions, social change, and the stock market (Waldrop 1992).

Chaos theory, a precursor to complexity theory, examines the unstable states within systems. Chaotic systems are collections of multiple orderly subsystems, which are flexible because they can switch rapidly and unpredictably between many different states. However, while chaotic systems may be unpredictable, they are also deterministic—that is, if two identical systems have the same initial conditions, they will produce the same effect. The classic example of a chaotic system is the weather, which, despite sophisticated modelling, still defies prediction beyond days or even

Vancouver received record snowfalls in the winter of 2008–9. Weather frequently defies prediction. Does this look like chaos to you?

hours into the future. Complexity theory, on the other hand, is concerned with how ordered, complex systems spontaneously emerge out of chaotic systems. This spontaneous emergence of forms is often referred to as **self-organization**, or **emergent complexity**. Complex systems, then, are not merely complicated, static objects, but spontaneous, self-organizing, systems. A prime example is life: out of a primordial soup of inorganic elements emerged a rich and ever-changing diversity of life forms.

The adaptiveness of complex systems is critical, as Peter Allen points out:

> [Complexity] is about 'adaptability' and the capacity to become aware that circumstances have changed and to produce new solutions. Not only that, it is also true that this ability to produce innovation and change will drive circumstances of others and drive evolution itself. . . . (Allen 1994: 584).

Rather than passively responding to events, complex systems interact with their environment.

Indeed, complexity is characteristically found in systems that are able to exist at the boundary between order and chaos, where it strikes a balance between two points that is never quite stable and never quite turbulent. As M. Mitchell Waldrop has described it, 'the edge of chaos is the constantly shifting battle zone between stagnation and anarchy, the one place where complex systems can be spontaneous, adaptive, and alive' (1992: 12).

Fundamental to the process of increased complexity and the emergence of spontaneous self-organization is the role of the **agent**. In complexity theory, a system is made up of a network of agents that act in parallel. It is important, here, to think of agents as plural—that is, agents can be either individuals or collectives. For example, households, cities, provinces, or countries can all be seen as agents, depending on what level or system is being examined. Regardless of the category, the environment of the agent is produced through interactions with other agents within a given system. In other words, agents are constantly acting and reacting to what other agents are doing in the system. Because of this, the environment is always dynamic, fluid, and unfixed. Moreover, the agents themselves have to be dispersed (as opposed to being centralized) if there is to be any coherent behaviour in the system. The notion that coherent behaviour can arise only out of competition and co-operation among agents themselves is central to complexity theory (Waldrop 1992).

Finally, in any adaptive, complex system there are many levels of organization wherein agents at one level serve as the 'building blocks' for agents at a higher level. For instance, individual workers make up a department, several departments make up a division, and several divisions make up a company, and so forth. Adaptive, complex systems continually revise and reorder building blocks as each level of organization gains more experience similar to the modification, reorganization, and adaptation that occur. Whether we are speaking of cells, neurons, organisms, politics, or economics, the processes of learning, evolving, and adapting are the same within each level of organization (Waldrop 1992).

To sum up, complexity theory seeks the unpredictable and creative emergence of order out of chaos in natural, cultural, and social systems. Generally, adaptive self-organization takes place in a population of independent agents. Through the exchange and interaction of co-operation and competition, these agents become increasingly interdependent, resulting in the spontaneous emergence of new structures. The emergence of novel structures not only raises a system's complexity to a 'higher' level but provides the foundation necessary for the emergence of yet another level of complexity.

Complexity theory, then, can be used in a variety of ways in the study of social organization(s) and social systems. However, in organizational studies, the systems approach has been used to develop techniques for studying systems in holistic ways that have supplemented traditional methods. The systems approach relies on achieving negative entropy through openness and feedback within organizations, and gives priority to interrelationships rather than to the elements of the system itself. It is from these dynamic interrelationships that new properties of the system emerge.

Bureaucracy

The Origins of Bureaucracy

As sociologist Amitai Etzioni points out, 'organizations [and bureaucracies] are not a modern invention' (1964: 1). Bureaucracies arose out of the formation of states and writing systems some 5,000 years ago. The development of a sophisticated system of administration in early Sumerian cities led to the invention of writing. The earliest bureaucrat is found in the scribe. Sumerian script was so complicated that it required scribes who had trained in the discipline of writing for their entire lives. These scribes had considerable power within Sumerian society because they held a monopoly over record-keeping and inscriptions.

As empires emerged and grew, administrative bureaucracies expanded at a pace to match imperial expansion. In the Persian empire, the central government was divided into administrative provinces: in each one, a royal secretary was posted to keep records and supervise troop recruitment. Royal inspectors were sent out to the provinces to report on the local conditions. In Han Dynasty China (fifth century BCE), the bureaucratic system developed out of Confucius's concern with creating social stability which required a system of administrators to ensure good governance. Administrators were appointed based on the merit of examinations (i.e. written tests). What became known as the imperial examination system continued until the early twentieth century.

While the idea of bureaucracy has existed since ancient times, the term itself originated in eighteenth-century France and comes from the word *bureau* meaning 'writing desk', or the place where officials work. The cumbersome processes of bureaucracies is sometimes referred to as 'red tape', which dates back to nineteenth-century Britain, when government officials used red tape to tie up official documents until they were needed. Red tape, then, is used to refer to the slow procedures associated with acquiring and dispensing information. Most of us have encountered bureaucratic red tape in our federal, provincial, or municipal agencies—when applying to replace a lost passport or driver's licence, for instance—but the situation is far, far worse in many developing nations that

IT'S A 300 PAGE GOVERNMENT QUESTIONNAIRE ABOUT CUTTING BACK ON BUREAUCRACY!

Photo: © Fran/www.CartoonStock.com

are choked by bureaucracy and red tape, a legacy of colonial administration. As we will see, despite the inefficiencies and the difficulties in changing bureaucratic organization to meet individual and societal needs, bureaucracies are necessary for the successful functioning of complex societies.

Marx and Bureaucracy

In **Karl Marx** and **Friedrich Engels**'s theory of historical materialism, the origin of bureaucracy comes out of *religion*, *state formation*, *commerce*, and *technology*. Initially, they showed, bureaucracies were made up of religious clergy, officials, and scribes, as well as armed guards, all of whom worked to maintain social order. The shift from egalitarian society to civil society 10,000 years ago marks the beginning of 'the state', a political body in which authority was increasingly centralized and enforced. With the emergence of political 'states' came the introduction of laws, taxes, mediating conflicts, and the defence of territory, all of which require officials performing various functions. The growth of trade and commerce called for a distinctive form of bureaucracy involved in keeping accounts, recording transactions, and enforcing legal rules of trade—as markets increase, complex systems of record-keeping, management, and calculation are needed. Eventually, the total amount of work involved in commercial administration outgrows the state's administrative role. Technologies involved in mass production require standardized routines and procedures, as well as people to design, control, and operate machinery.

Rather than serving society, technologies create wealth and maintain power for a particular class. In this sense, a technological bureaucracy, or **technocracy**, controls power through specialized technical knowledge and information.

Marx viewed state bureaucracy not as creating wealth but as appropriating wealth, through fees, licensing, levies, and taxes. The role of bureaucracy, he believed, is to control, coordinate, and govern the production, distribution, and consumption of wealth. The cost of bureaucracy to society is offset by the formation of a social order that is maintained and enforced through the rule of law. A central theme in Marxist socialism is the idea of workers' self-management, the idea that workers would internalize morality and self-discipline, making bureaucratic supervision and control redundant. This would also entail a reorganization of the division of labour that currently exists. Moreover, if the role of bureaucracies is to mediate conflicts through existing laws, then bureaucracies would become redundant if conflicts disappeared with the equal distribution of resources under socialism.

Bureaucracy and Formal Rationalization

Max Weber's extensive work on bureaucracy is still frequently cited and used today. It was part of his larger study of the process of rationalization, specifically, his examination of **formal rationalization**. Rationalization is a term we frequently hear in business reports, where it is almost a euphemism for cutting jobs in an effort to cut costs and become more efficient. Formal rationalization, with its emphasis on forms, differs from other models of rationalization like **substantive rationalization**, which involves the substance of values and ethical norms. With formal rationalization, form trumps substance.

According to Weber, formal rationalization has four basic elements:

- **efficiency**,
- **quantification**,
- **predictability**, and
- **control**.

These are discussed in detail later in the chapter.

Weber was critical of formal rationality and bureaucracy, arguing that formal rationality led to the 'irrationality of rationality' and that bureaucracy was dehumanizing by nature. Expressions such as 'cog in the wheel' or 'brick in the wall' emerged to characterized the worker's role as bureaucratic organization of various companies and political bodies began to increase. 'You can always be replaced' is another common statement that workers in bureaucratic organizations often hear. We may feel similar effects even when we're not part of the bureaucracy. When you're told, 'Your call is important to us,' you know that it isn't—a point summed up nicely in Laura Penny's, *Your Call is Important to Us: The Truth About Bullshit*. These examples speak to the dehumanizing feelings we experience daily through our interactions with bureaucratic organizations.

The irrationality of rationality involves the 'disenchantment of the world', an important concept in Weber's writing. Weber believed that with the increase in formal rationalization, the West was becoming increasingly **disenchanted**—lacking in magic, fantasy, and mystery—which could only lead to further alienation. Enchantment is a quality that cannot be efficient, quantified, predicted, or controlled. Disney's 'Magical Kingdom', for instance, is anything but magical: it is a rationalized system of pre-packaged enchantment commodities. Weber worried and warned about the oncoming danger of the 'iron cage of rationality', a world in which every aspect of life is controlled by the formal rationalization of bureaucracy, a world dehumanized and over-controlled.

The Evolution of Formal Rationality

The Industrial Revolution, which occurred in the late eighteenth and early nineteenth centuries, was the starting point for the development of formal rationality. **Sir Francis Galton** (1822–1911), considered the father of both modern statistical analysis and the racist/classist field of **eugenics** (which led to the sexual sterilization of 2,800 people in Alberta, and thousands more around the world), was praised for his use of quantification to measure the capabilities and productivity of individuals. He had a natural love of numbers. An example: he spent many hours getting the quantities (temperature, volume, etc.) just right

for the 'perfect' pot of tea (he was English, after all). While studying at Cambridge University, he informed his sister, in exacting detail, how much he loved the pictures she had painted for him:

> I am, on average, 5 minutes dawdling in getting up, 10 minutes . . . going to bed. During this time I . . . look at one side of the room or the other. . . . [A]t least . . . 10 minutes will be daily spent in looking at your pictures, besides this I am always awake about ¼ of an hour before getting up, when I cannot help seeing them as they are just before my nose, that makes 25 minutes a day, or twelve hours nearly a month or 156 hours or 19 ½ days of 8 hours each yearly! (Brookes 2004: 32)

While we might expect this sort of behaviour from a statistical analyst, Galton's description of his day suggests the extent to which formal rationality was a part of everyday life.

Along these same lines, **Frederick W. Taylor** developed what he referred to as **scientific management**. Based on 'time-and-motion' studies, scientific management became known as **Taylorism** because Taylor's aim was seen as the *one best way* of doing any given job. He and his team of 'efficiency experts' studied the time, methods, and tools required for a proficient worker to do

An assembly line at a Ford plant in Montreal.

Going Global

Economic Globalization and Formal Rationality

One of the pillars of economic globalization is a belief in liberalizing trade by reducing or eliminating protective tariffs. The view that poor countries of the developing world will abandon inefficient industries that have been supported by protective tariffs in favour of more productive industries is heavily influenced by the principles of formal rationality. But as Joseph E. Stiglitz argues in *Globalization and Its Discontents* (2003), policies designed to enhance a country's income by forcing resources from less to more productive uses often fail in countries where, because of conditions imposed by global loan-granting agencies like the International Monetary Fund (IMF), those human and capital resources are altogether lost through diminished productivity and job loss:

> It is easy to destroy jobs, and this is often the immediate impact of trade liberalization, as inefficient industries close down under pressure from international competition. IMF ideology holds that new, more productive jobs will be created as the old, inefficient jobs that have been created behind protectionist walls are eliminated. But that is simply not the case. . . . It takes capital and entrepreneurship to create new firms and jobs, and in developing countries there is often a shortage of the latter, due to lack of education, and of the former, due to lack of bank financing. The IMF in many countries has made matters worse, because its austerity programs often also entailed such high interest rates . . . that job and enterprise creation would have been an impossibility even in a good economic environment such as the United States. The necessary capital for growth is simply too costly. (Stiglitz 2003: 59–60)

Haiti, often referred to as the poorest nation in the world (and now more than ever, in light of the crippling devastation of the January 2010 earthquake), provides an excellent but depressing example of how economic globalization can harm a country in the developing South. Haitian scholar Patrick Bellegarde-Smith explains:

> High unemployment, low wages, political repression, and high productivity—the very same factors that render the country politically unstable—make Haiti a manufacturer's paradise. Corporations 'can count on a profit margin of at least 30 percent, and sometimes as much as 100 percent, from their Haitian operations'. The low investment rates; the absence of restriction on profit 'repatriation' [returning to the country of investment origin], a primary feature of the Haitian model; and low labor costs make these high profit margins possible. Government policy has led to foreign business opportunism and a domestic lack of opportunity. Haiti has, in a sense, become the 'land of opportunism'. (Bellegarde-Smith 2004: 153)

In 2004, a bill with the self-congratulatory name HERO (Haiti Economic Recovery Opportunity) was proposed in the United States, designed to expand certain preferential trade treatment for Haiti. While this was hailed by its supporters as being long overdue aid for long suffering Haitians, it just meant, in essence, that foreign-run companies in Haiti would get better trade agreements, with the lion's share of the benefit going to the foreigners, not the Haitians. Extended to the global scale, the policy of formal rationality, with its emphasis on efficiency and control, benefits the wealthy nations of the north at the expense of developing nations of the south.

a particular job. His objective was to eliminate wasteful or 'inefficient' (slow, non-productive) motions or movements. Frank Gilbreth, a follower of Taylor's, undertook an intensive study of a bricklayer's job and reputedly reduced the number of motions involved in laying a brick from 18 to just 5. Assembly line work also used Taylor's methods to the maximum efficiency, though Henry Ford is credited with making the assembly line an industry standard.

One of the weaknesses of Taylorism/scientific management is that it didn't allow the individual worker to develop a broad set of skills because he or she was asked to perform a single set of actions over and over again. Workers often became alienated from their work, with little sense that they had anything to do with the overall manufactured product.

Taylorism, slightly modified, was practised in North America during the 1980s and 1990s. At that time, the success of Japanese auto manufacturing prompted North American businesses to implement Japanese business practices in their training sessions. The **team approach** incorporated worker input and the idea that workers could be involved in several stages of the manufacturing process, generating a greater sense of product ownership. This approach was first adopted by car manufacturer Saturn, which, until the downturn in the automotive sector in 2008, was very successful.

The McDonaldization of the World

George Ritzer, in *The McDonaldization of Society* (2004), draws on Weber's concept of formal rationality in his conception of the **McDonaldization** of the world. What is McDonaldization? Similar to Disneyfication, Walmartitis, or Microsoftening, it is, according to Ritzer, 'the process by which the [rationalizing] principles of the fast-food restaurant are coming to dominate more and more sectors of American society as well as the rest of the world' (2004: 1).

Ritzer applies the four fundamental elements of Weber's formal rationality—efficiency, quantity, predictability, and control—to his examination of contemporary fast-food restaurants. **Efficiency** relates to the streamlined movement in time and effort of people and things. This efficiency is achieved largely by breaking up larger organizational tasks into smaller repeated tasks performed by individuals who are separated from each other by a division of labour. Smaller tasks are often performed later by machines rather than people. It should be noted that efficiency has different meanings in the different layers of a social organization. What is efficient for a college administrator might not be efficient for a college professor (for example, the former finds efficiency in the networking of printers, rather than allowing the prof to use his own little printer and not wait in line when print requests are heavy—personal experience here). And being efficient in this way is not the same as being *effective*, although it's possible for a process to be both efficient and effective. Think of the potential differences between being an efficient teacher—one who teaches quickly and articulates a great number of concepts—and an effective teacher—one who successfully communicates to students all or almost all that is taught. A teacher can be one or the other, both, or none of the above. At college and university, the multiple-choice test is a classic example of bureaucratic efficiency—questions are often provided with the textbook, and they can be marked quickly using a computer.

Second, formal rationality in bureaucracy involves the **quantity**, or quantification, of as many elements as possible. The efficiency or 'success' of the process is measured by the completion of a large number of quantifiable tasks. For instance, the success of call centres is primarily measured by how many calls are handled rather than how many clients were satisfied. When educational administrators pressure instructors to quantify the type and exact percentage of tests on a course syllabus, this is a type of formal rationality—the logic being that if courses are equally quantified, then students are equally served. With bureaucratic education, administrators and instructors can quantify the number and length of interactions between students and professors through computer platforms that monitor such things as number of e-mails and the number and length of 'chats'. In the classroom, instructors can monitor students by having them use electronic clickers to respond to questions, which is an attempt to counteract the impersonal nature of large, 'efficient' lectures with increased and quantifiable electronic interaction.

Next, **predictability** means that administrators, workers, and clients all know what to expect from employees, underlings, colleagues, and companies; this is the 'uniformity of rules'. A Big Mac in Moscow is the same as a Big Mac in Calgary. You can wake up in a Holiday Inn anywhere in the world and know where you are until you look out the window. Hollywood, too, is all about predictability—if you've seen one Will Ferrell movie, you've seen them all. With the advent of rationalized, bureaucratic education, teachers are replaceable in the delivery of predictable, pre-packaged courses, and creative, innovative input is minimal. Students who have already taken a course can tell others almost exactly what to expect and what will be taught. Pre-packaged online courses cut down on lesson preparation time, thus making class preparation more 'efficient,' leading to what might be called the silicon cage of rationality. However, in a recent lecture, culture critic Henry Giroux (currently teaching at McMaster University) noted that it is the value of the indeterminate in education—in effect, the value of the unpredictable—and the free-flowing 'don't know where this is going' instructor–class discussion that makes for an inspiring classroom experience. This creative process, however, is lost through formal rationality and the imposition of predictability.

Finally, **control** is always hierarchical. Ritzer characterizes the hierarchical division of labour in the following passage:

> Bureaucracies emphasize control over people through the replacement of human judgment with the dictates of rules, regulations, and structures. Employees are controlled by the division of labor, which allocates to each office a limited number of well-defined tasks. Incumbents must do the tasks, and no others, in the manner prescribed by the organization. They may not, in most cases, devise idiosyncratic ways of doing those tasks. Furthermore, by making few, if any, judgments, people begin to resemble human robots or computers. (2004: 27)

This control is exercised over both workers and clients. People who work at McDonald's are taught exactly what they have to do, while customers have their selection controlled by the menu board.

Even the uncomfortable seating is part of the process, helping to control how long customers stay in the restaurant. With bureaucratic education, interaction between teacher and student is severely controlled by the use of computer platforms like Blackboard or WebCT. Even when such technologies are inefficient (i.e. when students cannot access their instructor), the technology is still in control of the interaction. As well, professor performance is controlled through the course outline 'contract' (if significantly changed, the contract between teacher and student is invalid), including fixed percentages of 'objective' (multiple-choice) and 'subjective' (essay questions) testing.

We can see the formally rationalized, bureaucratic package at its most extreme in the following overview of material from a 1958 copy of the McDonald's operations manual, cited in John F. Love's *McDonald's: Behind the Arches* (1986):

> It told operations *exactly* how to draw milk shakes, grill hamburgers, and fry potatoes. It specified *precise* cooking times for all products and temperature settings for all equipment. It fixed *standard* portions on every food item, down to the *quarter ounce* of onions placed on each hamburger patty and the *thirty-two slices per pound* of cheese. It specified that french fries be cut at *nine thirty-seconds of an inch* thick. And it defined quality *controls* that were unique to food service, including the disposal of meat and potato products that were held more than *ten minutes* in a serving bin. (quoted in Ritzer 2004: 38)

As with people who have only ever eaten french fries from McDonald's, never real 'chips' cut and prepared on site, students experiencing today's increasingly bureaucratized education might become less able to judge the quality of what they are receiving.

Organizational Change

Social organization and social stability are fundamental aspects of the human condition. To dispense of all social organization would be the pursuit of 'nothingness'. However, the foundational principles and forms of organization

Telling It Like It Is

AN AUTHOR POV

Little Boxes: Mass Produced Suburban Communities

POINT OF VIEW

After the end of World War II, which marked the start of North America's 'baby boom', there was a fairly severe housing shortage in both Canada and the United States. One response was the development of mass-produced suburban communities. The first and standard-setting effort in this regard was the series of 'Levittowns' built in the eastern US. Between 1947 and 1951, Levitt and Sons built 17,447 houses on Long Island, New York, creating an instant community of about 75,000. This would be soon reproduced in Pennsylvania and then New Jersey. The company began by building warehouses for their supplies, their own workshops for wood and plumbing manufacture, and gravel and cement plants. Ritzer describes the rationalization of the house-building process in the following excerpt:

Photo: Toronto Star/GetStock.com

The planned community of Don Mills.

> The actual construction of each house followed a series of rigidly defined and rationalized steps. For example, in constructing the wall framework, the workers did no measuring or cutting; each piece had been cut to fit. The siding for a wall consisted of 73 large sheets of Colorbestos, replacing the former requirement of 570 small shingles. All houses were painted under high pressure, using the same two-tone scheme—green on ivory. . . . The result, of course, was a large number of nearly identical houses produced quickly at low cost. (Ritzer 2004: 36)

The owners of the construction company knew that their employees did not enjoy many of the intrinsic rewards experienced by skilled independent tradespeople, but they felt that the *extrinsic* rewards of money would make up for that:

> The same man does the same thing every day, despite the psychologists. It is boring; it is bad; but the reward of the green stuff seems to alleviate the boredom of the work. (A. Levitt 1952, quoted in Ritzer 2004: 35–6)

In the Toronto area, the suburb of Don Mills, constructed during the early 1950s, became known as 'Toronto's first planned community'. I grew up there beginning in 1956. It had the first shopping centre in the city, with the first Country Style doughnut shop and the first Shopper's Drug Mart. (As a teenager, I was a 'plaza boy'—a term for someone who spent his leisure hours hanging around the mall.) Famous Canadians from this community include Rick Green (of *The Red Green Show*), 'Martha' of the 1980s band Martha and the Muffins, and singer Dan Hill ('Sometimes when we touch,' the music gets too much). It also produced an outstanding Canadian sociologist: Neil Guppy. And yours truly, of course.

—J.S.

What do YOU think?

Think of a suburb you're familiar with. What aspects of it do you think reflect formal rationality or 'McDonaldization'? Do you think these qualities are beneficial or not?

themselves can have a profound effect on society and the lives of individuals, and so they deserve to be critically examined and questioned. As we have seen, social organization affects everything from environmental degradation through our relationship with nature, to the dehumanizing effects of formal rationality in bureaucracies and business corporations. Instead of organizations serving the interests and needs of people, they can often dictate our values and interactions. In other words, we become servants to organizations, instead of the organizations serving us.

Organizational structure, then, produces social order. Here, **social order** refers to social cohesion and how organizations and systems are held together. This cohesion is maintained either through **social control**—in which overt or covert coercion is used to ensure that norms and values are obeyed and supported—or the predictable patterns of behaviour and experience that are induced by the organization or structure itself. However, repressive elements such as patriarchy, racism, and classism can be woven into the structural fabric of organizations, and these in turn reproduce social oppression.

The way in which a society organizes social life and organizations can enable those who are the dominant group in the society to oppress others.

Social oppression is a concept that describes the dominant–subordinate relationship involving groups or 'categories' of people, in which the dominant group benefits directly from the systemic abuse, exploitation, and injustice directed toward the subordinate group. While an individual who is part of the dominant group may not participate directly in oppressive behaviour towards subordinate groups, he or she may still benefit from the general oppression of others. In colonial Rwanda and Burundi, the colonizing Belgians and the native Tuutsi aristocracy directly oppressed the Hutu through such measures as labour taxes, in which unpaid labour (on roadwork, for example) was exacted. The Tuutsi 'peasants' did not, by and large, participate in the oppression, but they benefited from things like the Hutu-built roads without having to work on them themselves. In this sense, all members of both dominant and subordinate categories are a part of social oppression regardless of their individual attitudes and behaviours. Social oppression is **institutionalized** when the oppression has become so embedded into the everyday workings of social life that it is not easily identified as oppression or interpreted as an overt act of discrimination (Fanon 1967). In such cases where social life becomes devalued, it becomes necessary to challenge, resist, or change social organization(s).

Do you agree that organizational structure produces social order? How does this play out in organized religion? In what way do churches represent Etzioni's normative form of organization?

Photo: Alex Nikada/iStockphoto.com

In his landmark text *A Comparative Analysis of Complex Organizations*, sociologist Amitai Etzioni (1975) examines a wide range of social organizations, from prisons, hospitals, and schools to communes, churches, and business corporations. He identifies three main types of organizations (Etzioni 1975: 455):

- coercive (example: prisons)
- normative (example: churches)
- utilitarian (example: businesses).

He concludes his study noting:

> Society and its organizations [have] alienating elements—and while people are truly involved only in normative organizations, there are signs of a yearning, and of a secular trend, toward greater reliance on normative organizations and less on coercive and utilitarian ones. (470)

Etzioni believes that organizations can fulfill and satisfy human demands and needs if there is a greater reliance on symbolic normative compliance instead of compliance being 'inauthentically manipulated to deflect pressures toward higher satisfaction [that] sustain the current centrality of material production and consumption and the use of force' (470). However, instead of moving toward more normative organizations that would promote self-actualization, we have increasingly become more reliant on coercive and utilitarian ones. Etzioni draws on the work of William H. Weber to make this point. Weber argues that human needs in educational organizations like the university could be fulfilled by shifting away from a logical-empirical tradition to a humanist intellectual model. In this way, education would provide the basis for self-actualization. Weber goes on to say that while universities used to be normative organizations, pursuing intellectual goals considered morally beneficial, the impact of faculty unions and the emphasis on research have increasingly made them utilitarian organizations wherein faculty are treated as 'hired-hands', deans as 'foremen', students as 'consumers', and the university itself a 'knowledge factory' (Etzioni 1975: 471).

Since the publication of Etzioni's work in 1975, universities and other organizations have generally become more utilitarian and coercive.

Is Etzioni's belief that organizations, especially bureaucratic ones, can change fundamentally to meet the demands of humanity a realistic goal? Long before Karl Marx's critique of bureaucracy, Baron Grimm, in 1765, wrote:

> The real spirit of the laws in France is that [of] bureaucracy. . . . [H]ere the offices, clerks, secretaries, inspectors and intendants are not appointed to benefit the public interest, indeed the public interest appears to have been established so that offices might exist (quoted in Albrow 1970: 16).

And, while Weber long ago warned of the disadvantages of bureaucracy and formal rationality, the problems associated with bureaucratic rationality have only intensified, if we use Ritzer's work on McDonaldization as an indicator. The inefficiency of efficiency seems to dominate organizations from the military and businesses to hospitals and post-secondary institutions. Red tape, long lineups, quantity over quality, apathy, and even violent reactions (going 'postal', road rage, fighting with the registrar's office or school board) have become the norm both within and outside of organizations and bureaucracies. Grimm's comments reflect the broader critique that bureaucracy has lost sight of the 'greater good' through a perversion of means and ends in which the means become ends in and of themselves. Left unchecked, organizational bureaucracies become increasingly self-serving and corrupt.

Michel Crozier's work *The Bureaucratic Phenomenon* (1964) is a critical examination of Weber's ideal bureaucracy in contrast with how bureaucracies actually operate. For Crozier, bureaucratic organization is not the expression of rational efficiency that Weber claimed, but a form of organization incapable of change. According to Crozier, '[a] bureaucratic organization is an organization that cannot correct its behaviour by learning from its errors' (1964: 187). Perhaps the non-reflexive character of bureaucratic organization, along with its inability to respond quickly, is part of the reason organizational change has not been forthcoming. This, along with the cultural organizational principles that inform organizations, makes them less likely to change without changing the fundamental cultural narratives, beliefs, and behaviours that inform them—a point illustrated by Mills and Simmons in their discussion of organizational racism, sexism, and classism.

There is always something both absent and perverted about the application of organizational theory in business. Despite the introduction of a 'new' organizational model—whether it's the corporate cultural perspective of anthropology or complexity theory—utilitarian organizations never become more human and never become more efficient beyond a certain level. Recalling our discussion on the level of organizational analysis, changing an organizational model within the context of a higher level of organization will not yield any change, as higher levels of organization subsume, inform, and direct subordinate levels based on the very nature of their organization. Any real change in bureaucratic organization has to be at the institutional level, if not the cultural.

Social movements are sustained, organized collective efforts that focus on some aspect of progressive social change. Unlike **reform movements**, which involve changing the conditions within an existing social order, **revolutionary movements** are about trying to change the fundamental character of the system itself by changing the basic cultural and structural aspects of the reigning social order The word 'revolution' means a complete turning over of some element, either socially, as in the Industrial Revolution, or physically, as in the revolutions per minute (RPMs) of your car. A revolution is not necessarily an armed insurrection, but it can be and often is a '**paradigm shift**'—a fundamental change in the way we think collectively. Our use of the term 'organizing principles' mirrors the point made by Mills and Simmons that all organizations are a part of history and culture within their respective societies, and that as such they should be studied within the context of the broader society. Paradigm shifts are most often not artificially imposed by social planners, but are to a significant extent emergent phenomena, coming to being or emerging from that broader context.

Conclusions

While there is a lot to learn in this chapter, a lot of terminology to remember, we would stress one basic thing. There is more choice involved in both social interaction and social organization than what might seem to be 'out there'. Often that choice is between oppressive forms that have been practised over years and less oppressive, and more empowering, ways that have been little tried, or that have come from groups outside the mainstream. The oppressive forms are not as 'natural' as they may seem.

Questions for Critical Review

1. Why and how might the status of stepmother be more complicated and difficult than that of stepfather?
2. Why do you think that the federal government disallowed the traditional Aboriginal status of 'chief'?
3. Why can it be said that, generally speaking, the larger the organization, the less well it serves the needs of its customers/clients/students?
4. Do you think men or women are more likely to have virtual statuses? Why?
5. An American science fiction writer and social essayist has proposed what is referred to as 'Pournelle's Iron Law of Bureaucracy', which states that: 'In any bureaucracy, the people devoted to the benefit of the bureaucracy itself always get in control and those dedicated to the goals the bureaucracy is supposed to accomplish have less and less influence, and sometimes are eliminated entirely.' How would this apply to big business and government bureaucracies?

Suggested Readings

Barrowcliffe, Mark (2008). *The Elfish Gene: Dungeons, Dragons and Growing Up Strange.* New York: Soho.

Kanigel, Robert (1997). *The One Best Way: Frederick Winslow Taylor and the Enigma of Efficiency.* New York: Viking.

Mills, Albert J., & Tony Simmons (1995). *Reading Organization Theory: A Critical Approach.* Toronto: Garamond Press.

Penny, Laura (2005). *Your Call Is Important to Us: The Truth About Bullshit.* Toronto: McClelland & Stewart.

Ritzer, George (2004). *The McDonaldization of Society.* Thousand Oaks, CA: Sage.

Suggested Websites

'Erving Goffman', by B. Diane Blackwood
www.blackwood.org/Erving.htm

The Governor General of Canada: Her Excellency the Right Honorable Michaelle Jean
www.gg.ca/document.aspx?id=41

Teaching Support Staff Union - SFU
www.tssu.ca/

Society for Chaos Theory in Psychology and the Life Sciences
www.societyforchaostheory.org/

Amitai Etzioni Notes
http://blog.amitaietzioni.org/

George Ritzer Room
www.angelfire.com/or/sociologyshop/RITZER.html

Key Terms

- assimilate
- bodily stigma
- conflict deviance
- contested
- corporate crimes
- covert characteristics

- delinquent subculture
- deviant/deviance
- dominant culture
- essentialism
- hallucination
- heteronormative

- ideology of fag
- impression management
- marked terms
- misogyny
- moral entrepreneur
- moral stigma

6

Deviance

LEARNING OBJECTIVES

After reading this chapter, you should be able to

> avoid some of the leading misunderstandings of the term 'deviant';

> distinguish between *overt* and *covert* characteristics of deviance;

> discuss the reasons that deviance is sometimes associated with ethnicity, culture, race, gender, sexual orientation, and class; and

> talk about the contested nature of deviance.

- multiculturalism
- negative sanctions
- non-utilitarian
- norm
- normalized
- occupation crimes

- overt characteristics
- patriarchal construct
- positive sanctions
- racializing deviance
- racial profiling
- relations of ruling

- Other
- social constructionism and social resources
- status frustration
- stigma
- subculture

- tribal stigma
- unmarked terms
- vision quest
- warrior frame
- white collar crimes

Photo: © John Steckley

^{FOR} Starters

Gordon Dias, 1985–2001

If deviance involves acting against the values of a society, then perhaps suicide is the ultimate act of deviance. It takes the gift society values most—life—and withdraws all value from it. Explaining this act of deviance has been a part of sociology ever since Durkheim's *Suicide* was published in 1897.

It has been almost 10 years since my nephew, Gordon Dias, committed suicide at the age of 16. He hanged himself from a tree in front of his high school. As a sociologist, and as his uncle, I struggle to understand why he did this.

Gordon was a young, single man. This made him part of the social group most prone to suicide. He was on the margins of society in several ways. He was the youngest of three children, a child whose brother and sister demanded attention by their actions and by their achievements. His older brother was the first-born grandchild and nephew on both sides of the family, a position that brought him ready attention. His older sister is simply brilliant, a very hard act to follow. In my earliest memory of Gordon talking, he is straining to be heard above his siblings.

He was a person of colour, the product of a mixed South Asian and Caucasian marriage, living in a very white Canadian city. He was very close to his South Asian grandmother, so much so that when he left home for a while, he went to live with her. It could not have been easy in that city to have made that choice.

He was artistic. It is not easy for a young man to express himself artistically in our culture, not without presenting some counterbalancing signs of macho behaviour. Perhaps that's one reason why he sought the social company he did. According to his parents, my sister and brother-in-law, he had been hanging around with guys who regularly got into trouble. This eventually got him into trouble at school, and he was suspended. Zero-tolerance policies don't leave a lot of time for even temporary allegiances with groups of kids who act out. For him, I guess, that was the final piece of the puzzle, and the picture he was left with led him to suicide. He did care enough about his education that he left his only suicide note at school.

There was nothing inevitable about Gordon's suicide. Suicide is a personal act. Yet it's an act that reflects the society that alienates the victim.

Introduction: What Is Deviance?

Many people, when they hear the word *deviance*, think immediately of behaviour that is immoral, illegal, perverse, or just wrong. But deviance is better thought of as a neutral term. It means straying from the norm, the usual. However, it does not mean that the deviant—the one engaging in deviance—is necessarily bad, wrong, perverted, 'sick', or inferior in any way. These could all be qualities that characterize the norm, in which case the deviant is none of these things. Deviance, then, comes down to how we define 'the norm'. It's also about the power of those who share the norm to define and treat others as inferior or dangerous. And we must recognize that just as the norm changes—over time and across cultures, so does deviance.

Revisiting Terms from the Culture Chapter

Understanding deviance depends to a certain extent on concepts and terms presented in Chapter 3, on culture. The first is **dominant culture**, the term used for the culture most represented in the media, the one with the most power. As you read through the different sections of this chapter, keep in mind the dominant culture we asserted exists in Canada. It is white, English-speaking, European-based, Christian, male, middle-class, middle-aged, urban, and heterosexual. To a certain extent it is true that to differ from the dominant culture is to be deviant—to repeat, though, that doesn't make it wrong.

Another term to revisit here is **subculture**. This is a group existing within a larger culture and possessing beliefs or interests at variance with those of the dominant culture. Albert K. Cohen used this concept in his study of teenage gangs (1955). His model of what he called the **delinquent subculture** combines class and gender. In this model, young lower-class males suffer from a **status frustration**: failing to succeed in middle-class institutions, especially school, they become socialized into an oppositional subculture in which the values of the school are inverted. For example, the youths he studied engage in delinquent stealing that is primarily **non-utilitarian**—in other words, the objects aren't stolen because they're needed for survival but because the act of stealing is respected by peers in the delinquent subculture. Cohen stresses that becoming a member of the delinquent subculture is like becoming a member of any culture. It does not depend on the individual psychology of the individual, nor is it invented or created by the individual. When members grow up and leave the gang (to join adult gangs or mainstream society), the subculture persists. In Cohen's terms:

> [D]elinquency is neither an inborn disposition nor something the child has contrived by himself; that children *learn* to become delinquents by becoming members of groups in which delinquent conduct is already established and 'the thing to do'; and that a child need not be 'different' from other children, that he need not have any twists or defects of personality or intelligence in order to become a delinquent. (1955: 11–12)

We can use Cohen's model to review other ideas presented earlier in the textbook. First, the **norms** of the subculture—the rules or expectations of

QUICK HITS

Getting Deviance Straight

- **Deviant** just means *different from the norm, the usual.*
- **Deviant** *does not mean bad, wrong, perverted, sick, or inferior* in any way.
- **Deviant** is a category that *changes with time, place, and culture.*
- **Deviance** is about *relative quantity*, not quality.
- Definitions of **deviance** often *reflect power.*

behaviour—would be different, at least in part, from those of the main culture. The difference, according to Cohen, comes from the inverting of norms. In Cohen's words, 'The delinquent's conduct is right, by the standards of his subculture, precisely *because*, it is wrong by the norms of the larger culture' (Cohen 1955: 28). Likewise, there is an inverting of the **sanctions**, the reactions to the behaviour of the individuals. The **negative** sanctions of non-gang members—negative reactions to their behaviour—can be seen as **positive sanctions** from the delinquent gang's perspective, and vice versa.

What do YOU think?

Why do you think it can be misleading to think of a delinquent subculture as being created only by opposition or inversion?

Overt and Covert Characteristics of Deviance

When looking at deviant behaviour it's important to separate the **overt characteristics** of deviance—the actions or qualities taken as explicitly violating the cultural norm—from the **covert characteristics**, the unstated qualities that might make a particular group a target for sanctions. It is like the difference between manifest and latent functions, the first being obvious and stated, the other being hidden and undeclared. Covert characteristics can

Some would call this deviance, while others see it as art. What other forms of art might be considered deviant?

include age, ethnic background, and sex. In the example presented in the box on page 158 the overt characteristics are the zoot suit clothing and hairstyle. The covert characteristics are age (the groups involved were mostly teens) and ethnicity (they were mostly Latino or African-American).

The Importance of the Cultural Component in Deviance

It is important to note that what gets labelled 'deviant' differs across cultures. Take the **vision quest** in Aboriginal culture. As we discussed in Chapter 4, it is traditional for young Aboriginal people to go on a vision quest at around the time of puberty. They leave on their own, they fast, and they typically go without sleep in the hopes of having a vision. In this vision, they might learn songs that will give them strength in difficult times. They might find objects that will connect them with spiritual power. And, if they are fortunate, they will identify a guardian spirit during the experience. This important rite of passage represents the major step in becoming an adult.

In the dominant culture of North America, the experiences surrounding a vision quest might be considered 'normal' only among specially defined groups like artists (musicians, dancers, writers, and so on) or perhaps Olympic athletes in training. Otherwise the experience might strike members of the dominant culture as suspect and deviant. They might be tempted to characterize the vision as a **hallucination**, an image of something that is not considered to be 'objectively' there. They might want to label the person undergoing the experience as mentally ill. However, it is important to recognize the long-held spiritual significance of the vision in North American Native culture.

Arthur Kleinman warns students of sociology not to fall into the trap of linking what is considered a normal practice in one culture with a similar practice, deemed deviant, in another. He asks his readers to suppose that ten sociologists have interviewed ten different adult Aboriginal people who have experienced the death of a loved one. If they discover that nine out of the ten individuals interviewed reported having heard or seen the recently deceased family member in a vision, the ten researchers can conclude that their findings are reliable. However,

> . . . if they describe this observation as a 'hallucination', that is, a pathological percept indicative of mental illness, which it might be for adult non-Indian Americans, they would have an empirical finding that was reliable but not valid. Validity would require the qualifying interpretation that this percept is not pathological—in fact it is both normative and normal for American Indians since it is neither culturally inappropriate nor a predictor or sign of disease—and therefore it could not be labeled as a hallucination. Rather it would require some other categorization . . . in order for the observation to be both reliable and valid. (Kleinman 1995: 73–4)

All of this is to say that what is considered deviant will differ from culture to culture. This has unfortunate sociological effects when one of those cultures is dominant, the other a minority, in the same country. The dominant culture's definition then might condemn as deviant not just the practice of the minority culture but the minority culture itself.

The Contested Nature of Deviance

Not only will definitions of deviance differ *across* cultures, they will vary *within* cultures. It is true that the culture defines deviance—that deviance is essentially a social or cultural construct—but it is important to remember, as we mentioned earlier in the chapter, that there is seldom total or even near total agreement within a culture as to what is deviant. In other words, deviance, like other elements in a culture, can be **contested**, meaning that not everyone agrees.

When deviance is contested in any given area, we have a situation known as **conflict deviance**. Conflict deviance is a disagreement among groups over whether or not something is deviant. The legality of marijuana is a good example. In Canada, the possession of marijuana for recreational use is

The Point Is...

The 'Zoot Suit Riots' of the Early 1940s: Clothes and Ethnicity as Deviant

An unusual, and yet instructive, instance of deviance labelling and sanction is the case of the 'Zoot Suit Riots' that occurred in June 1943 in Los Angeles. The targets were racialized groups—African-American and Latino males—who made convenient scapegoats for wartime tension.

In the early 1940s, Los Angeles was undergoing rapid change. The city's population was growing and its demographics were changing, with large numbers of Mexicans and African Americans coming to the city. Teenagers made up a high percentage of the population, as older men and women had gone off to join the war effort, and with a surplus of well-paying jobs left available by older brothers and sisters drafted into the military, the young people who remained behind made money to spend on music and clothes. These teens—black and Latino males in particular—adopted a unique style of dress, a distinctive haircut (the 'duck tail', also known as the 'duck's ass' or DA), and a musical style that were countercultural. The music was jazz, rooted in the African-American experience and only slowly gaining acceptance among the conservative elements of the United States. The dancing (the jitterbug) was more sexual than dancing of the 1930s. The clothing was the zoot suit: a jacket with broad shoulders and narrow waist, ballooned pants with 'reet pleats', 'pegged cuffs', and striking designs. Zoot-suit culture swaggered with a distinctive bold strut and posing stance, and distinguished itself from the older set with a host of new slang words unknown to parents and other adults.

How did the zoot suit become deviant? Through the media. The main vehicle was the comic strip *Li'l Abner*, by Al Capp. In a time before television, comic strips were a major part of popular media, and *Li'l Abner*, with maybe 50 million readers a day, was one of the most popular strips in this golden age. It's difficult to overstate its influence. If you ever attended a high-school 'Sadie Hawkins' dance, named for the comic strip's man-chasing spinster, then you've experienced a small bit of the influence of *Li'l Abner*.

Al Capp identified the zoot suit as a target for his negative sanctioning humour. From 11 April to 23 May 1943, the strip presented the story of 'Zoot-Suit Yokum', an invention of US clothing manufacturers bent on taking over the country politically and economically. They conspired to create a national folk hero (Zoot-Suit Yokum), who would popularize their zoot suits by performing feats of bravery clad in this signature costume. This was the fictional start of 'Zoot-Suit Mania', which was soon defeated when the conservative clothing manufacturers, determined to preserve their market share, found a Zoot-Suit Yokum doppelganger to act in a cowardly way. The triumph of conservative clothiers was proclaimed in the third frame of the 19 May strip, which displayed the mock headline: 'GOVERNOR ISSUES ORDER BANNING ZOOT-SUIT WEARERS!!' (Mazón 1984: 35).

Beyond the pages of dailies carrying the *Li'l Abner* comic strip a very real hostility emerged between mainstream society and the zoot-suit counterculture. One LA newspaper even ran a piece on how to 'de-zoot' a zoot-suiter: 'Grab a zooter. Take off his pants and frock coat and tear them up or burn them. Trim the "Argentine ducktail" that

Courtesy of Denis Kitchen Art Agency; used by permission of Julie Cairol, Stout Thomas & Johnson NYC

Los Angeles police round up zoot-suit suspects, 11 June 1943. Do these zoot-suiters look like trouble-makers to you?

goes with the screwy costume' (Mazón 1984: 76). Whether it was intended with humour or not, instructions for the negative sanctioning of zoot-suiters were carried out in a very real way by some of those opposed to the counterculture. The conflict reached a climax in early June 1943, when thousands of young white men—soldiers, marines, and sailors on weekend leave from nearby military installations—launched a campaign to rid Los Angeles of zoot-suiters by capturing them, buzzing their hair down in a military style, and tearing or burning their clothing. Still, as riots go, they were relatively harmless. As Mauricio Mazón points out in his now-classic study of this phenomenon, 'riot' is a bit of a misnomer:

> They were not about zoot-suiters rioting, and they were not, in any conventional sense of the word, 'riots'. No one was killed. No one sustained massive injuries. Property damage was slight. No major or minor judicial decisions stemmed from the riots. There was no pattern to arrests. Convictions were few and highly discretionary. (Mazón 1984: 1)

The conflict lasted just under a week, and was brought to an end with two acts. First, the military reined in their troops. More significant, on 9 June, Los Angeles City Council issued the following ban:

> NOW, THEREFORE, BE IT RESOLVED, that the City Council by Resolution find that wearing of Zoot Suits constitutes a public nuisance and does hereby instruct the City Attorney to prepare an ordinance declaring same a nuisance and prohibit the wearing of Zoot Suits with reet pleats within the city limits of Los Angeles. (Mazón 1984: 75)

This, the culmination of a series of increasingly explicit and punitive sanctions, shows how humour with a social edge and a large audience can be used against a particular group.

● ● ● ● ● ● ● ● ● ● ● ● ● ● ● ● ● ● ●

What do YOU think?

1. Why do you think the zoot-suiters were targeted?

2. Do you think there are any parallels between zoot-suiters of the 1940s and any group today?

● ● ● ● ● ● ● ● ● ● ● ● ● ● ● ● ● ● ●

against the law, and is therefore deviant. However, results of a 2002 survey conducted by the Canadian Community Health Survey suggest that three million people aged 15 and older use marijuana or hashish at least once a year, which goes a long way towards normalizing the practice. Further complicating the issue is the fact that possession of marijuana for medicinal purposes is legal. The recurring debate over whether possession of small amounts of marijuana for recreational use should be legalized is proof that smoking up, though deviant, is a focal point for conflict deviance.

Gay marriage is another issue of conflict deviance. Even though gay marriage was made legal in all provinces and territories during a two-year period from 2003 to 2005, Canadians are still far from having a consensus as to whether or not marriage for gays and lesbians is deviant.

Social Construction versus Essentialism

One of the reasons deviance is contested has to do with the differing viewpoints of social constructionism and essentialism. **Social constructionism** puts forward the idea that certain elements of social life—including deviance, but also gender, race, and other elements—are not natural but are artificial, created by society or culture. **Essentialism**, on the other hand, argues that there is something 'natural', 'true', 'universal', and therefore 'objectively determined' about these aspects of social life.

When we look at any given social element, we can see that each of these two viewpoints applies to some degree. Alcoholism, for instance, is a physical condition, so it has something of an essence or essential nature, but whom we label an alcoholic and how we as a society perceive an alcoholic (i.e. as someone who is morally weak or as someone with a medical or mental health problem) is a social construct, one that will vary from society to society.

The interplay between social constructionism and essentialism receives excellent treatment from Erving Goffman in his study of stigma and deviance, *Stigma: Notes on the Management of a Spoiled Identity* (1963). A **stigma** is a human attribute that is seen to discredit an individual's social identity. It might be used to identify the stigmatized individual or group as deviant. Goffman believed there were three types of stigmata (the plural of *stigma*):

- **bodily stigmata**
- **moral stigmata,** and
- **tribal stigmata**.

He defined them in the following way:

> First there are abominations of the body— the various physical deformities. Next there are blemishes of individual character perceived as weak will, domineering or unnatural passions, treacherous and rigid beliefs, and dishonesty, these being inferred from a known record of, for example, mental disorder, imprisonment, addiction, alcoholism, homosexuality, unemployment, suicidal attempts, and radical political behavior. Finally there are the tribal stigma of race, nation, and religion, these being stigma that can be transmitted through lineages and equally contaminate all members of a family. (Goffman 1963: 4)

So while bodily stigmata exist physically, definitions of 'deformed' can be and often are socially constructed—think of descriptions such as 'too fat' or 'too thin'. People in a variety of societies 'deform' their bodies (by dieting to extremes, by piercing and tattooing their bodies, or in certain cultures, by putting boards on their children's heads to give them a sloping forehead) to look beautiful according to social standards. People who hear voices and see what is not physically present may be considered religious visionaries in some cultures, just plain crazy in others. Racializing is another social process, national identity a social construct open to change over time, and different religions are privileged in different societies.

In this textbook, we have adopted a view of deviance that is more social constructionist than essentialist. Following Howard Becker's classic work *Outsiders* (1963), we will tend not to speak of deviance as being inherently 'bad', conformity to a norm being inherently 'good'. Instead, we will generally follow the rule that

> social groups create deviance by making the rules, whose infraction constitutes deviance, and by applying those rules to particular

Photo: © M-J Milloy 2006

The Marijuana Party Book Store in Vancouver. The political party runs on a single platform: the campaign to legalize marijuana. If recreational use of marijuana becomes legalized, does it cease to be deviant?

people and labelling them as outsiders. . . . Deviance is *not a quality* of the act the person commits, but rather a consequence of the application by others of rules and sanctions to an 'offender'. (Becker 1963: 8–10)

The Other

An important word used in contemporary critical theorizing about deviance in sociology (as well as in other disciplines), is '**other**', or 'otherness'. Difficult to define and even harder to use, it intersects with such concepts as ethnocentrism, colonialism, stereotyping, essentialism, and prejudice.

The 'other' is an image conjured up by the dominant culture within a society or by a colonizing nation of the colonized. When the United States took over Haiti (1915–34), Hollywood and the Catholic Church helped to make deviant the indigenous religion of the Haitians by casting it as an element of the 'other' culture. Voodoo and zombies became familiar figures of reported Haitian deviance from 'civilized' norms. Along with sympathy and aid for Haiti following the January 2010 earthquake came criticism of Haitians, mostly

in the conservative media, for their 'fatalistic' or 'superstitious' views and adherence to voodoo, which, critics argued, made the people incapable of helping themselves. The image created of the other can be mysterious, mystical, mildly dangerous, but somehow it is ultimately inferior. Edward Said, in his discussion of Orientalism, characterizes the West's image of the Middle East as the creation of an other. The dominant culture in Canada includes 'Aboriginal' as 'other'. English Canada has portrayed French Canada that way. In 'slacker movies' written and directed by men and aimed at young men, 'woman' seems to be constructed as an other. For Emily Murphy, discussed below, Chinese men were the other.

'Race' and Deviance: To Be Non-White Is Deviant

To racialize deviance is to link particular ethnic groups with certain forms of deviance, and to treat these groups differently because of that connection. We see this in movies and television shows that portray all Latinos as involved with

• **Our Stories** •

The Warrior Frame: How Intro Soc Texts Cast the Mohawk as Deviant 'Other'

The 1990 Oka land dispute in Quebec pitted members of several Mohawk communities against the Quebec provincial police (the Sûreté du Québec, or SQ) and the Canadian army. Media reports portrayed the confrontation as a clash of interests: those of the mainstream dominant culture, represented (and upheld) by the police and the army, versus those of the Mohawk, cast as an 'other', a deviant and insurgent culture. Since that time, the crisis has been dissected and analyzed in a number of introductory sociology textbooks (14 published between 1991 and 2002 alone). What is alarming about the textbook treatment of the situation is that it differs little from media representations of the event, perpetuating stereotypes about Aboriginal people through the use of what can be called a **warrior frame**.

The warrior frame gives a narrow view of the Oka situation, making any sociological explanation partial, vague, and disconnected from any 'big picture' examination of the event. It is a good example of Dorothy Smith's **relations of ruling**: the sociological presentation essentially serves the federal government's public relations campaign to vilify the Mohawk, to defend its own inaction on the Kanesatake land question, and to downplay its failure to live up to its responsibility to stand up for Aboriginal people in conflicts with the province when it failed to call into question the highly questionable actions of the Quebec government, especially its police force.

The warrior frame, as it is reproduced in the introductory sociology textbooks, generally has seven parts:

1. reproduction, without contextualization, of the famous picture of the Mohawk warrior confronting a soldier
2. portrayal of the Mohawk warriors as deviant criminal outsiders
3. depiction of the Mohawk warriors as uniformly belligerent
4. exclusion from the frame of the important role of women
5. presentation of a false picture of Aboriginal unity
6. depiction of the Sûreté du Québec as a 'neutral' organization
7. underrepresentation of acts of non-Aboriginal violence.

The warrior frame begins with *the* picture. It appeared first on television and was often reprinted in newspaper and magazine articles; at least three textbooks include it. It shows a masked Mohawk warrior, his facial expression concealed, glaring at a young soldier who looks guiltless but resolute. The picture is never contextualized with a discussion of the sociological message it conveys. It is presented as if it constitutes part of a neutral or objective depiction of the events that took place, rather than being an example of how non-Aboriginal media came to distort the discourse of Oka.

Another key part of the warrior frame is that it casts the Aboriginal participants at Oka as criminal outsiders—as Americans, as Vietnam War veterans, or as criminals. In fact, the vast majority were Canadian, had never fought in a war, and had no criminal record. None of the 14 introductory sociology texts attempted to refute the outsider image; 2 actually supported this stereotype.

The warrior frame plays up a popular impression of the war-like nature of Aboriginal men. Like the Hollywood Indian, the warrior seeks out battles and does not acknowledge pain or gentler feelings. This part of the warrior frame leaves no room for contradictory images of Aboriginal maleness or any representation of women, who were important actors in the protest from beginning to end.

The warrior frame presents the Mohawk position as a unified stance. In fact, the confrontation and the events leading to it were marked by differences of opinion, both among the Mohawk and among Aboriginal people generally. Not everyone was in favour of the protest (see Monture-Angus 1995: 84–5). But the textbooks manage to tie together the Mohawk and Aboriginal people generally with mystical connections of unity that appear to deny that any divisions could exist within their ranks.

You can't have Aboriginal warriors without the cavalry riding to the rescue. Our introductory textbooks all accept the role of the Quebec police as neutrally 'serving the people', in spite of the fact that the Sûreté du Québec includes many Francophone officers who have been raised in a culture that views the Mohawk as the great enemy of the classical period of New France. The SQ relationship with the province's Aboriginal people in general (see Dickason 2002: 332) and with the Mohawk in particular has a colonialist history forged over nearly a century. However, the SQ, by name, remains almost anonymous in the introductory sociology textbooks; most of the time they are referred to as merely the 'Quebec police', the 'provincial police', or 'the police'. There is no mention of the bad relationship between the SQ and all three Quebec Mohawk communities, and there is no discussion of the role of the SQ in the long history of hostility between the province's French and Mohawk communities.

The warrior frame makes it easy to portray the Mohawk as the antagonists in the confrontation, with local French residents as the victims. The actions of the Mohawk appear deviant. But it's important to recognize the depth of animosity and illegal behaviour on both sides. When the Mohawk blocked the Mercier Bridge, opposition grew quickly as commuters living on the South Shore of the St Lawrence River faced a three-hour commute to bypass the barricade. The nature of the angry response reflected its several causes: commuter frustration, mob dynamics, and racism. However, the last of these is not mentioned in the introductory sociology textbooks. Crowds of as many as 4,000 people demonstrated their anger, some yelling obscene and racist remarks. As the summer moved into August, the protesters grew more violent. At nightly demonstrations, effigies of Mohawk were burned, United Nations observers were blocked from going to the Mohawk community of Kahnawake, and journalists were threatened with violence. One night, 200 of the demonstrators stormed a local police station where one of their leaders was being held; they broke windows and destroyed two squad cars. In August, a convoy of 75 vehicles left Kahnawake, evacuating Mohawk children, women, and elders who feared racial violence. A French radio station reported the convoy, and about 500 local residents came out to impede its progress. Some threw rocks at the cars, injuring at least six Mohawk.

How was this series of events represented by introductory sociology textbooks? Five make mention of it. Not one mentioned that the bridge was on Mohawk land. Not one referred to anyone being hurt. Not one used the words 'racism' or 'racist' or 'criminals' in the description. The actions of the non-Aboriginal people are dismissed merely as examples of crowd or mob behaviour, provoked by the deviant actions of the Mohawk.

What do YOU think?

What factors do you think affect the way a textbook author might present an incident like the Oka standoff?

Emily Murphy made effective use of photos to illustrate her argument that Asians and blacks were luring white North Americans—especially women—into lives of illicit drug use. This photo from *The Black Candle* bore the ominous caption: 'When she acquires the habit, she does not know what lies before her; later she does not care' (Murphy 1973 [1922]: 30–1).

drugs, all black males as involved in street crime, and all Italians as involved with the mafia. Part of **racializing deviance** is making ethnic background a covert characteristic of deviance, as though all people of a particular ethnic group were involved in the same supposedly deviant behaviour.

Despite the public promotion in Canada of **multiculturalism**—the set of policies and practices designed to promote respect for cultural differences—the pressure to **assimilate** (i.e. become culturally the same as the dominant culture) is persistent ('You're in Canada now, why don't you just wear normal clothes?'). Immigrants who have experienced the embarrassment of having Canadians stumble over their names—sometimes deliberately for supposed comic effect (as when Don Cherry mispronounces French and Russian names)—may have felt pressure to Anglicize their names to make themselves more 'Canadian'.

A classic Canadian instance of racializing deviance comes from the 1922 book *Black Candle*, a collection of articles written by Emily Murphy, many of them originally published in *Maclean's* magazine. A journalist, activist, and self-taught legal expert, born of a prominent and wealthy Ontario family, Murphy was a gender heroine of first-wave feminism, becoming, in 1916, the first woman magistrate not just in Canada but in the British Empire. She would later play a role in the historic 'Persons Case' (1928), which ended with the Supreme Court ruling that women were not 'persons' eligible to hold public office; the decision was appealed to the British Privy Council and overturned the following year.

Murphy's four books of personal sketches, written under the pen name 'Janey Canuck', were already well known when she published *Black Candle* to expose the insidious details of the Canadian drug trade. *Black Candle* cast Chinese Canadians as the main villains in the trafficking of illegal drugs—particularly opium, heroin, and cocaine—although blacks were also singled out for censure. The main theme was that Chinese men—those bachelors who, because of the restrictive head tax on Chinese immigrants, could not be reunited with their wives or find companionship among women 'of their own race'—were corrupting white women through drug dealing, 'ruining them' and making them accomplices in their dealing. The following quotation, from the chapter on 'Girls as Pedlars', is typical:

> Much has been said, of late, concerning the entrapping of girls by Chinamen in order to secure their services as pedlars of narcotics. The importance of the subject is one which warrants our closest scrutiny: also, it is one we dare not evade, however painful its consideration. (Murphy 1973 [1922]: 233)

Murphy believed that the 'yellow races' could use the drug trade to take over the Anlgo-Saxon world, and she warned North American readers to be wary of these 'visitors':

> Still, it behooves the people in Canada and the United States, to consider the desirability of these visitors . . . and to say whether or not we shall be '*at home*' to them for the future. A visitor may be polite, patient, persevering, . . . but if he carries poisoned lollypops in his pocket and feeds them to our children, it might seem wise to put him out.
>
> It is hardly credible that the average Chinese pedlar has any definite idea in his mind of bringing about the downfall of the white race, his swaying motive being probably that of greed, but in the hands of his superiors, he may become a powerful instrument to this very end.
>
> In discussing this subject, Major Crehan of British Columbia has pointed out that whatever their motive, the [drug] traffic always comes with the Oriental, and that one would, therefore be justified in assuming that it was their desire to injure the bright-browed races of the world.
>
> Naturally, the aliens are silent on the subject, but an addict who died this year in British Columbia . . . used to relate how the Chinese pedlars taunted him with their superiority at being able to sell the dope without using it, and by telling him how the yellow race would rule the world. They were too wise, they urged, to attempt to win in battle but would win by wits; would strike at the white race through 'dope' and when the time was ripe would command the world. (Murphy 1973 [1922]: 187–9)

Black Candle had a huge impact on the perception of the drug trade and on drug legislation in Canada. Chapter XXIII, 'Marahuana—A New Menace', was the first work in Canada to discuss marijuana use. It contained a lot of damning half-truths and anecdotes, and led to the enactment of laws governing marijuana use. In fact, if you do an Internet search on the words, you will find that proponents of legalizing marijuana continue to target the book as an opponent.

Emily Murphy can be seen as an example of what is called, following Becker (1963), a **moral entrepreneur**. This is a person, sometimes a member of a group, who tries to convince others of the existence of a particular social problem that the group or individual has identified and defined. The moral entrepreneur labours to create consensus on an issue on which there is no pre-existing consensus; at the very least, the individual or group tries to foster sufficient agreement among policy-makers to ensure that the action the moral entrepreneur desires takes place. Examples of moral entrepreneurs can include opposing groups, such as pro-life and pro-choice activists or the gun and the anti-gun lobbies.

Racial Profiling

Racial profiling is one way in which deviance is racialized. The Ontario Human Rights Commission offers a thoroughgoing definition on their website. According to the OHRC, racial profiling is

> any action undertaken for reasons of safety, security or public protection, that relies on stereotypes about race, colour, ethnicity, ancestry, religion, or place of origin, or a combination of these, rather than on reasonable suspicion, to single out an individual for greater scrutiny or different treatment.

Age and/or gender can also be factors in racial profiling.

This type of profiling assumes that the personal characteristics of an individual are indicative of his or her actions or of a tendency to be engaged in illegal activity. This

differs from criminal profiling, [which] relies on actual behaviour or on information about suspected activity by someone who meets the description of a specific individual.

Profiling can be committed 'in many contexts involving safety, security, and protection issues'. Racial profiling may govern actions

- by law enforcement personnel, such as police and border control agents;
- by security personnel, for example, private security guards;
- by employers, for example, in conducting security clearances of staff;
- in housing accommodation, for example, if landlords assume that certain applicants or tenants will be involved in criminal or other illegal activity;
- by service providers, for instance, if taxis do not stop at night for certain persons; and
- in the criminal justice system, such as in courts and prisons.

Photo: Photodisc

When you look at this picture, do you see a man behind bars looking out or a free man looking in? What factors in society might have contributed to the way you interpreted the photo?

The Point Is...   Crossing the Border While Black

I was part of an EdD (Education doctorate) cohort in a class on community college leadership. It was a high-powered group, including faculty members, middle administrators, and presidents of three colleges. We were going on a class trip from Toronto to Monroe Community College in Rochester. It was the summer before September 11, so 'home security' was not the issue it would become in a few months' time.

The car I was in was driven by one of the administrators, who was white; the passengers, both faculty members (I was one), were also white. I looked like an extra in a Cheech and Chong movie, but the others were dressed respectably. We passed through customs with no problems and few words exchanged with the friendly border guards.

The same was true for the other white travellers in our convoy: no delays, no problems.

But there was one exception. One of our cars carried two black men. One was an upper-level administrator, well dressed, a distinguished-looking gentleman (streaks of white in all the right places in his hair) from the Caribbean. The other was a faculty member, younger, also well dressed, very articulate, with an American accent. They were stopped and asked to get out of the car. Their trunk was searched carefully. It would be an understatement to say that they were not treated with the respect due to people of their standing in the community. It took them over half an hour to cross the border. They were guilty of crossing the border while black.

Gender and Deviance: To Be Female Is Deviant

Feminists have taught us that in a patriarchal society (one dominated by men), the concept of 'male' is treated as normal, while the concept of 'woman' is seen as inherently deviant. Male values are **normalized** (i.e. made to seem 'normal', 'right', and 'good') through customs, laws, and cultural production. Two related concepts are important here: misogyny and patriarchal construct. **Misogyny** means literally 'hating women'. In a patriarchal or male-dominated society, the images of women are constructed in ways that contain and reflect misogyny. **Patriarchal construct** refers to social conditions being thought of or structured in a way that favours men and boys over women and girls. Think, for example, of highly prized and well-paying jobs—corporate lawyer, investment banker, emergency room doctor—that have been constructed so that the job-holder is forced to place family in a distant second place to employment. This gives advantages to men, who in Canadian society are expected to fulfill fewer domestic and childrearing duties than are women.

Casting the woman as deviant is not a new phenomenon; in fact, it may be as old as human life itself. A particularly interesting example surrounds the witch hunts waged in Europe and, later on, in colonial America from about the fourteenth to the seventeenth centuries. Those who were identified as witches were tried and, if found guilty, executed. This for several reasons makes the witch hunts an intriguing case for the sociological study of deviance. For one, the deviance was fictitious: while the people tried may have committed criminal acts, their powers and connections with Satan were not real (although often believed by both accuser and some accused).

Photo: The Granger Collection, New York

This nineteenth-century lithograph depicts the trial of a witch in Salem, Massachusetts, 1692. Look at the faces of the men in the courtroom. Do you think the artist believed in the validity of the witch trials?

Second, the vast majority of those accused were women (the figure usually cited by authorities on the subject is 85 per cent). The word 'witch' itself is closely associated with women, conjuring up traditional negative images of pointed black hats, old warty faces with pointed noses, and flying broomsticks: bad clothes, bad looks, and bad use of a female-associated cleaning implement. In a patriarchal society, this image of deviance is very much associated with femaleness,

Telling It Like It Is

A POET'S POV

Age and Deviance: To Be Over 50 Is Deviant

POINT OF VIEW

Warning, by Jenny Joseph (b. 1932)

When I am an old woman I shall wear
    purple
With a red hat which doesn't go and
    doesn't suit me.
And I shall spend my pension on brandy
    and summer gloves
And satin sandals, and say we've no
    money for butter.
I shall sit down on the pavement when
    I'm tired
And gobble up samples in shops and
    press alarm bells
And run my stick along the public railings
And make up for the sobriety of my youth.
I shall go out in my slippers in the rain
And pick the flowers in other people's
    gardens . . .

This poem, written by British poet Jenny Joseph, was recently voted the most popular poem of the twentieth century in a poll conducted by the British Broadcasting Corporation. Among other things, this poem is about how many women, particularly middle-class women, spend their lives having to conform, to avoid deviance, and how they desire to be free of the pressures of conformity once they have reached older age. How would you generalize the acts of deviance that the author intends to commit here? What has she been forced to do that she wants to do no longer? What is being encouraged in the following lines, which end the poem?

But maybe I ought to practice a little now?
So people who know me are not too
    shocked and surprised
When suddenly I am old, and start to
    wear purple.

There is a Red Hat Society for women over 50 that began in North America and now has thousands of members in a number of different countries. Do you think the existence of something as formal as a club undermines the deviant tendencies expressed in the poem? Or is joining the club an act of solidarity in deviance?

In order to give voice to the male 50+ set, I've written my own poem (my first work of deliberately sociological poetry):

The Old Men's Deviant Society

When I am an old man,
I will wear any colour I want,
I will enjoy flowers, poetry,
and other unmanly pleasures
that I have secretly enjoyed for years
and maybe even talk about them
in my favourite bar.
I won't care or talk about
what car I drive
(as long as it is reliable),
whether or not I can fix it,
how fast it can go,
what my lawn looks like,
how big my barbecue is.
And I won't comment on
whether what other men wear or do
makes them look, smell, or act
like sissy boys.
It's my 50th birthday party,
and I'll cry if I want to.

Are there ideas here that challenge the norm for male behaviour? What signs of deviance do you find here? Are they parallel to the deviant acts promised in 'Warning'? How so?

its opposite—normalcy—with maleness. Harley puts it well when he states that

> Women were associated with witchcraft because of the nature of Renaissance thought, which divided things into opposite categories. In the classifications that related to social order and morality (God/Devil, good/evil, normal behavior/witchcraft) the category 'female' was associated with witchcraft because it was unthinkable not to associate the category 'male' with normal behavior. (Harley n.d.)

In this context, it's worth noting the Australian Aborigine language Dyribal. The language offers up another example of how femaleness is associated with deviance in a patriarchal culture, where nouns classified as 'feminine' include poisonous or dangerous fish, plants, and insects.

Class and Deviance: To Be Poor Is Deviant

Poverty can be considered a covert characteristic of deviance. Marginally illicit activities like overindulgence in alcohol are more likely to be considered deviant in poor people than in middle-class or 'rich' people. Jeffrey Reiman is a professor of philosophy at the American University in Washington, DC, but he thinks like a good sociologist. In his bestselling book *The Rich Get Richer and the Poor Get Prison: Ideology, Class, and Criminal Justice*, which had its eighth edition in 2007, he argues that the criminal justice system has a distinct class bias. This bias appears in many ways: in the way we define what constitutes a crime, and in our processes of arrest, trial, and sentencing. Each step biases against the poor. As Reiman explains:

> [T]he criminal justice system keeps before the public . . . the distorted image that crime is primarily the work of the poor. The value of this to those in positions of power is that it deflects the discontented and potential hostility of Middle America [the American middle class] away from the classes above them and toward the classes below them. . . . [I]t

not only explains our dismal failure to make a significant dent in crime but also explains why the criminal justice system functions in a way that is biased against the poor at every stage from arrest to conviction. Indeed, even at the earlier stage, when crimes are defined in law, the system primarily concentrates on the predatory acts of the poor and tends to exclude or deemphasize the equally or more dangerous predatory acts of those who are well off. (Reiman 1998: 4)

This is how behaviours associated with poverty and criminality become synonymous with deviance while criminal activity associated with wealth and celebrity is often labelled 'good business'. Martha Stewart, for instance, was convicted of contempt of court and yet received a standing ovation from a mostly supportive public and press following her trial.

Class bias is at the centre of what is known in the literature as the 'schools-to-prison' hypothesis: this is the idea that in schools located in poorer, often racialized neighbourhoods there is a biased application of practices such as 'zero tolerance', which increases the perception of higher crime rates in these communities. There are greater rates of suspension and expulsion, a higher number of random locker and student searches, and anti-violence measures like the installation of metal detectors, the hiring of security guards, and even period police raids.

While most of the literature and statistics relate to the American situation, the school-to-prison hypothesis can also apply to urban Canada. In a 6 June 2009 *Toronto Star* article, 'Suspended Sentences: Forging a School-to-Prison Pipeline?', authors Sandro Contenta and Jim Rankin reported that Ontario's Safe Schools Act, in force from 2001 to 2008 produced startlingly high numbers of suspensions and expulsions. The *Star*'s analysis, which examined school suspension rates for 2007–8 with sentences and postal code data for inmates in Ontario provincial jails, showed that the highest rates of suspension tended to be in those areas that also had the highest rates of incarceration. This is a positive correlation, which suggests that punishing youths from the city's poorest neighbourhoods with zero-tolerance measures reinforces the higher incarceration rate in those areas.

Photo: Bill Ivy Images

Do you think that imposing negative sanctions (i.e. making homelessness illegal) is a good response to this kind of deviance?

'But wait,' I can hear you say; 'Isn't it possible that low-income neighbourhoods naturally produce crime, and that greater rates of true crime, not increased levels of scrutiny or harsher application of zero-tolerance policies, are responsible for higher incarceration rates corresponding to these neighbourhoods? Indeed, lower-class people are overrepresented in the statistics on criminal convictions and admission to prison. That means that per population they are more often convicted and admitted to prison than are middle- and upper-class people, and this contributes to the idea that all lower-class people are deviant. However, a closer look at the statistics helps us see why they do not give us an accurate picture of the lower classes.

'Lower class' is a designation that is often established by looking solely at recorded income, but it covers a broad and far from homogeneous set of individuals. Some are part of the working class, labouring for long hours with little financial reward. Others are on welfare. These two sub-groups of the lower class are probably not significantly more involved in criminal activity than are middle-class or upper-class people. In fact, it's a separate sub-group, representing a small minority of the lower

class, that is responsible for a high percentage of the crimes. These people are lumped together with the first two groups statistically because of their low reported income, giving a misleading forensic picture of the working poor.

Another reason for the overrepresentation of the lower class in crime statistics has to do with **social resources**. In this context, the term refers to knowledge of the law and legal system, ability to afford a good lawyer, influential social connections, and capacity to present oneself in a way that is deemed 'respectable'. Lower-class individuals generally have access to fewer social resources than middle- and upper-class people do, and this makes them more likely to be convicted of charges people from the wealthier classes might be able to avoid. Tepperman and Rosenberg explain the importance of social resources:

> Social resources help people avoid labelling and punishment by the police and courts. For example, in assault or property-damage cases, the police and courts try to interpret behaviour and assess blame before taking any action. They are less likely to label people with more resources as 'criminal' or 'delinquent' and more likely to label them 'alcoholic' or 'mentally ill' for having committed a criminal act. (Tepperman and Rosenberg 1998: 118)

The authors make use of Goffman's concept of **impression management**, which they define as 'the control of personal information flow to manipulate how other people see and treat you' (Tepperman and Rosenberg 1998: 118). The upper classes are better at managing impressions than are people who belong to the lower class. Therefore, they conclude,

> Official rule-enforcers (including police and judges, but also social workers, psychiatrists and the whole correctional and treatment establishment) define as serious the deviant acts in which poor people engage. On the other hand, they tend to 'define away' the deviant acts of rich people as signs of illness, not crime. They are more likely to consider those actions morally blameless. (Tepperman and Rosenberg 1998: 118–19)

White Collar Crime

It was in a speech to the American Sociological Society in 1939 that Edwin Sutherland introduced the term **white collar crime**. He defined it as 'crime committed by a person of respectability and high social status in the course of his occupation' (1949: 9). His article 'White Collar Criminality' was published the next year in the *American Sociological Review* (Sutherland 1940), and he would later devote an entire book to the subject (*White Collar Crime*, 1949). Sutherland's work was an important step in the sociological study of criminology. Previous work had focused on the poor and the crimes they committed, creating at the very least a biased sample. But his definition is not flawless. Associating certain kinds of criminal behaviour with a particular class reflects a class bias and a misleading view of the situation. After all, you don't have to be a person of 'high social status' to commit identity theft (making copies of bank or charge cards), which tends to be included in the category of white collar crime. The implication in Sutherland's original definition is that only people of the higher classes are capable of planning and carrying out crimes that are essentially non-violent. In this way it fails to recognize that industrial accidents caused by unsafe working conditions that are allowed to exist by a negligent owner are in a real sense crimes of violence. Even the term itself reflects this class bias: the use of the qualifier ('white collar') to the word 'crime' suggests that most crime, ordinary crime, is not committed by people of 'high social status', in much the same way that the term 'white trash' carries the implication that it is unusual for whites to be 'trash', unlike people of other ethnic backgrounds.

More recent works have refined the definition of white collar crime to remove the class bias associated with Sutherland's original definition. Clinard and Quinney (1973) went further, breaking white collar crime into two categories by distinguishing between what they called **occupational crimes** and **corporate crimes**. They defined the former as 'offenses committed by individuals for themselves in the course of their occupations [and] offenses by employers against their employees' (1973: 188). The latter include 'offenses committed by corporate officials for their corporation and the offenses of the corporation itself' (1973: 188). The difference is one of beneficiaries and victims: occupational crimes benefit the individual at the expense of other individuals who work for the company; corporate crimes benefit the corporation and its executives at the expense of other companies and the general public. This latter definition, by placing less emphasis on the individual, hones in on the negative aspects of corporate culture and the way that individuals and corporations work together to commit illegal acts against consumers and the common public.

The announcement in the spring of 2001 that the energy giant Enron, the seventh largest company in the United States, was declaring bankruptcy had devastating effects on the company's employees and shareholders and on the US economy as a whole. The creative legal financing and letter-but-not-principle-of-the-law accounting schemes of the executives involved, taken together with the multi-million-dollar salaries and perks they were paying themselves, constitute white collar crime of both varieties. Their crimes were occupational in that they took from the economic viability of the company, causing its bankruptcy. They also caused the personal bankruptcy and economic hardship of thousands of employees by encouraging them to sink their life savings into Enron stock. At the same time, their crimes were corporate in that they had a profound negative impact on the American economy (particularly the financial sector) and were a major cause of the energy crisis that occurred in California.

It would be wrong to think smugly that this kind of crime is far more common in the US than in Canada, where we think of ourselves as more

Table 6.1 Occupational and corporate crimes

OCCUPATIONAL CRIMES	CORPORATE CRIMES
sexual harassment	industrial accidents
embezzlement	pollution
pilfering	price-fixing

financially conservative. Reporter Charles Davies, in a December 2009 edition of Metronews, disabused readers of this notion:

> If PriceWaterhouseCoopers' annual survey is an accurate indicator, economic or 'white collar' crime in Canada is growing at a disturbing rate, and far faster than in other developed countries.
>
> The accounting giant, which has been toting crime statistics in 26 nations for the past five years, finds that in 2009, 56 per cent of Canadian companies surveyed reported instances of fraud, a 10 per cent increase since 2003. Globally, only 30 per cent of companies reported frauds this year compared to 37 per cent in 2003.
>
> The accounting firm's survey focuses on the various types of fraud—asset theft, accounting offences, money laundering, bribery, and corruption—that are either perpetrated on companies by their own employees (59 per cent of the cases in 2009) or by outsiders, including customers and suppliers (38 per cent of cases). (Davies 2009)

● ● ● ● ● ● ● ● ● ● ● ● ● ● ● ● ● ● ●

What do YOU think?

Those who study linguistics distinguish between **marked** and **unmarked terms**. The unmarked term is the usual or standard one, while the marked term has a label added to it to distinguish it from the common term. 'Field hockey' (as opposed to the usual brand of hockey played in Canada), 'light beer', 'white chocolate', and 'decaffeinated coffee' are all marked terms. 'White collar crime' is another example. By distinguishing this variety of upper-class criminal activity, are we implying that most crime is committed by the lower or working class?

● ● ● ● ● ● ● ● ● ● ● ● ● ● ● ● ● ● ●

Sexual Orientation and Deviance: To Be Gay Is Deviant

It comes as no surprise that homosexuality is defined as deviant across the world (although not in every culture). This particular social construction

Photo: G. Letts

Do you think that, on the whole, the men in your class would react more negatively to this picture than the women would?

of deviance does differ among cultures in terms of how and what kind of social sanctions are applied. At the beginning of 2003, sexual activity between consenting adult homosexuals was still against the law in 13 US states (Alabama, Florida, Idaho, Kansas, Louisiana, Michigan, Mississippi, Missouri, North Carolina, South Carolina, Texas, Utah, and Virginia). In June of that year, in the case *Lawrence vs Texas*, the Supreme Court voted 6–3 against the constitutionality of the Texas law. That ruling effectively rendered anti-homosexuality laws in the other 12 jurisdictions unconstitutional also. This is a big step, to be sure, although same-sex marriage remains illegal in the United States under the Defense of Marriage Act (DOMA). It's important to note that even in Canada, where same-sex marriage has been legal nationwide since 2005, the issue remains one of conflict deviance.

In Britain, homosexuality is addressed in Section 28 of the Local Government Act. It reads:

A local authority shall not:
1) intentionally promote homosexuality or publish material with the intention of promoting homosexuality;
2) promote the teaching in any maintained school of the acceptability of homosexuality as a pretended family relationship.

It would interesting to find out how accurate information about homosexuality might be conceived of as 'promoting' it.

In looking at how laws concerning homosexuality differ across the globe, it is interesting to note that former British colonies or protectorates are high on the list of those countries in which male homosexuality (and in some cases female homosexuality) is against the law: Grenada, Guyana, Jamaica in the Caribbean; Botswana and Zimbabwe in Africa; and Bangladesh, Bhutan, Brunei, India, Malaysia, the Maldives, Myanmar, Nepal, Pakistan, Singapore and Sri Lanka in Asia. Those Asian countries appear to have carried on from colonial times with different versions of an act passed in British India in 1860. They differ from Asian countries such as China, Japan, and Thailand, which were never colonized, and countries colonized by other European nations (e.g. Cambodia, Laos, and Vietnam, colonized by France; Indonesia,

The Point Is... The Criminalization of Sexuality

Even though lesbians, gays, bisexuals, and transgender (LGBT) rights in Canada are some of the most progressive in the world, the laws regarding sexual activity and sexual regulation continue to reflect a **heteronormative** bias. In Canada, acts of sodomy and buggery (which comprise any sexual activity that does not lead to procreation, such as oral sex and anal sex) was punishable by death until 1869. In 1892, any homosexual activity by men was deemed 'gross indecency' under criminal law. And in 1948 and 1961, changes to the criminal code branded those who engaged in homosexual sexual activity as 'criminal sexual psychopaths' and 'dangerous sexual offenders', who could be charged with an indeterminate prison sentence. In the mid-1960s, just 40 years ago, George Klippert, after being charged and convicted of gay sexual activity, was labelled a dangerous sexual offender and sentence to life in prison (McLeod 1996).

Today, Canadian law does not prohibit anal sex if it is between consenting parties over the age of 18 and provided there are no more than two people present. However, for all non-anal sex, the age of consent is 16 regardless of the sexuality of the participants. While both homosexuals and heterosexuals engage in sodomy and anal sex, there remains a legal double standard that continues to target gay male sexual activity over heterosexual sexual activity (Kinsman 1995).

Photo: goldenticket/flickr

'Bobbies Kissing', a wall mural by British graffiti artist Banksy. Why do you think certain kinds of sexual activity between consenting participants continues to be criminalized? Should they be?

colonized by the Netherlands; the Philippines, colonized by Spain). In some Muslim countries—Afghanistan, Pakistan, Saudi Arabia, Sudan, the United Arab Emirates, and Yemen—laws against homosexuality carry the death penalty, although in some of these jurisdictions (Afghanistan, for instance) it has rarely been applied. Ironically, it is not uncommon in Muslim countries for a young heterosexual man to have his first sexual experience with another young male, which, if it is discovered, is less likely to bring dishonour upon the families involved than would a sexual relationship with an unmarried woman.

In communities where homosexuality is regarded as deviant, negative sanctions can have a powerful influence on behaviour. In Canada, young men can influence the behaviour of other young men by sanctioning them with statements such as 'that's so gay', or 'you're gay'. This practice, sometimes referred to as the **ideology of fag**, is a way of influencing people to behave according to gender role expectations, particularly young males.

It is interesting to note that the attitude towards homosexuality as deviant is, on a global scale, more strict concerning men than women. There are 30 countries in the world in which only male homosexuality is condemned (Armenia, Jamaica, Nigeria, Sri Lanka, and Uzbekistan, to name just a few).

Summary

We have tried to make several key points in this chapter. First, deviance is largely socially constructed, and it can vary from culture to culture. The social construction is often contested or challenged within the culture. The dominant culture's definition of deviance (in North America, a predominantly white, male, English-speaking, middle-aged, middle-class definition) can override the definitions of deviance that come from people less powerful in the same society. This can happen in ways that socially sanction or punish members of minority cultures and people with 'alternative' lifestyles.

Questions for Critical Review

1. Describe with examples what is meant by the term 'deviant'.
2. Outline how deviance can be associated with ethnicity, culture, race, gender, sexual orientation, and class.
3. Explain with examples what 'conflict deviance' is.
4. Explain how the Mohawk were cast as deviant by the Canadian media (including sociology textbooks) during the Oka standoff.
5. Identify with examples what 'white collar crime' is.

Suggested Readings

Coleman, James William (2002). *The Criminal Elite: Understanding White-Collar Crime*, 5th edn. New York: Worth Publishers.

Contenta, Sandro, & Jim Rankin (2009), "Suspended sentences: Forging a school-to-prison pipeline?, *Toronto Star*, 6 June, 2009, www.thestar.com/Article/646629.

Goffman, Erving (1963). *Stigma: Notes on the Management of Spoiled Identity*. Englewood NJ: Prentice-Hall.

Greenberg, David F., ed. (1993). *Crime and Capitalism: Readings in Marxist Criminology*. Philadelphia: Temple UP.

Hill, Stuart L. (1980). *Demystifying Social Deviance*. New York: McGraw-Hill.

Reiman, Jeffrey (2007). *The Rich Get Richer and the Poor Get Prison: Ideology, Class, and Criminal Justice*. 8th edn. Boston: Allyn & Beacon.

Rigakos, George S. (2002). *The New Parapolice: Risk Markets and Commodified Social Control*. Toronto: U of Toronto P.

Suggested Websites

American Society of Criminology (Critical Criminology/ Feminist Criminology).
www.critcrim.org/index.php

Kohlberg's Theory of Moral Development (Robert Barger, University of Notre Dame).
www.nd.edu/~rbarger/kohlberg.html

New Journal of Prisoners on Prisons.
www.prisonactivist.org/pipermail/prisonact-list/1995-December/000098.html

Socioweb (Criminality and Deviance).
www.socioweb.com/directory/sociology-topics/criminology-and-social-deviance

Key Terms

- cluttered nest
- common-law (or cohabiting)
- companionate conjugal roles
- complementary conjugal roles
- complex household
- conjugal roles
- crude marriage rate
- delayed life transitions
- dynamic
- empty nest
- endogamy
- eugenics
- exogamy
- extended family
- fecundity
- gender roles
- gender strategy
- general intelligence

7

Family

LEARNING OBJECTIVES

After reading this chapter, you should be able to

❭ characterize the diversity of the Canadian family;

❭ explain the ways that family in Quebec is different from family in the rest of Canada;

❭ discuss eight major changes taking place in the family;

❭ identify the different forms that conjugal roles can take;

❭ describe the varying impacts of endogamy on different racial and ethnic groups in Canada;

❭ identify how immigration patterns can affect family development; and

❭ outline and comment on the argument that Aboriginal families were 'under attack' during the twentieth century in Canada.

- genocide
- intelligences
- joint conjugal roles
- matrilineal
- nuclear family
- occupational segregation
- patrilineal
- replacement rate
- residential schools
- scientific classism
- scientific racism
- segregated conjugal roles
- simple household
- Sixties Scoop
- total fertility rate
- work interruptions

Key Names
- Rod Beaujot
- M. Reza Nakhaie
- Nancy Mandell
- Ann Duffy
- Daniel Moynihan

'One of these days, Alice . . .' Audrey Meadows and Jackie Gleason spar in *The Honeymooners*, one of the first television sitcoms to explore the tensions of married life.

Photo: Ivy Images

FOR Starters

Family and the Negative Sanction of Humour

Wherever tension exists in a culture, there is humour. Humour gives us a way to address everyday issues that cause tension with an openness that doesn't come easily when the same issues are discussed more seriously. In North American culture, family life is often a target of humour, whether that humour comes from a stand-up comic's routine, a co-worker's rant about her mother-in-law, or one of the many sitcoms that revolve around family dynamics. That's because there is tension in the family, between people living the roles of husband and wife, parent and child, spouse and in-laws.

Looking at a culture's humour can tell us where the tension is. But remember that humour is rarely sociologically 'innocent': we can also learn about whose perspective has power. I'll bet that if you came up with 10 jokes about husbands and wives, most would take the perspective of the husband. Jokes can be (and often are) sanctions, hinting that what someone is doing is not approved of. Look at each of the following jokes and see if you can find the subtle message for husbands and wives.

> **Q:** If a man speaks in the forest, and his wife isn't there, is he still wrong?
> [*subtle message, from a male perspective: don't nag your husband—he is the head of the family and should not be challenged.*]
>
> **A:** That would depend on whether or not he's talking about sports or cars.
> [*subtle message, from a female perspective: men have a narrow scope of expertise; women are more broad-minded.*]

> A woman took her husband to the doctor. After the examination, the doctor went out to talk to the wife. 'How is he?' the wife asked.
> 'You're going to have to fix his meals three times a day, every day. You must keep his clothes in order, bathe him, put his pajamas on, and comfort him every night, or he will die.'
> So the wife went inside to see her husband. 'What did the doctor say?', the husband asked.
>
> a) The wife looked at him and said, 'You're going to die.'
>   [*subtle message, from a male perspective: wives don't work hard enough to give their husbands comfort and support.*]
> b) The wife looked at him and said, 'Well, the good news is that we don't have to make any changes in our lifestyle.'
>   [*subtle message, from a female perspective: wives work like slaves for their husbands; husbands should do more or at least recognize how much they depend on their wives.*]

> In a flashback sequence in the popular syndicated sitcom *Everybody Loves Raymond*, Raymond and Debra Barone are discussing their wedding plans. Raymond asks Debra why she's planning the wedding so soon. Debra replies that she has been planning their wedding ever since she was 12. When Ray (foolishly) comments that they only met when he was 22, Debra tells him he was merely 'the last piece of the puzzle'.
> [*Which gender perspective do you think this was written from?*]

Diversity of the Family

The opening line of Russian novelist Leo Tolstoy's famous, tragic romantic novel *Anna Karenina* reads, 'Happy families are all alike; every unhappy family is unhappy in its own way.' We disagree. Happy families, functional families, good families exist in many forms, and are alike only in their success at serving basic purposes: providing emotional support for family members, taking care of elders, raising the next generation, and so on. In most other respects, happy families are diverse.

The family in Canada, as elsewhere, has existed in many forms historically, and still does today. Before the arrival of Europeans, there was diversity among Aboriginal families. Some Native bands were **patrilineal** (determining kinship along the *male* line), some were **matrilineal** (determining kinship along the *female* line); some lived in societies structured around family-based clans, while others did not. The period of European exploration and resource exploitation brought other diverse and changing forms. Fur traders sometimes had European wives in New France

(Quebec) and Aboriginal wives in the West. Loggers and fishers spent such long periods away from their home communities that they were visitors when they returned. Age at marriage has varied in Canada, rising and falling with changes to the country's economic prosperity and the availability of jobs. Women, who in the late nineteenth century worked for pay only when they were unmarried, have become more and more immersed in the workforce throughout the twentieth century and into the twenty-first, and men, if statistics are to be believed, are taking on a greater share of responsibilities around the home.

It would be wrong to say that any one form or structure is consistently better or worse than any other for its members. And yet newspapers, other media, and even snippets of day-to-day conversation we might overhear on the street are filled with judgmental remarks about contemporary family forms. Even traditional sociology is not free from this bias. If you were presented with the terms **nuclear family** (which includes a parent or parents and children) and **extended family** (which might include, in addition, grandparents, aunts, uncles, and cousins), you might be led to believe that the former is 'normal' and the other some kind of modification or perversion of the regular model; you might even associate it with a particular ethnic or immigrant population. Such is not the case. For some cultures, historical and current, calling the nuclear family by the name 'family' would be as odd as referring to an arm as the whole body.

The Huron language of the seventeenth century had no terms for 'nuclear' or 'extended' family. Instead, the noun root -ndat-, meaning 'place', was used to refer to those people who lived in the same small section of a longhouse (a dwelling that might house up to 60 people). This would be roughly equivalent to what we today call a nuclear family, although a better modern translation is 'household'. The more common way for the Huron to refer to family was through the noun root –hwatsir-, meaning 'matrilineage', or the verb root -yentio-, meaning 'to belong to a matrilineal clan'. Matrilineage is the line of descendants that follows the mother's line. A woman, her sisters and brothers, and their mother would belong to

the same matrilineage. A longhouse may be dominated by one matrilineage, with married sisters and their husbands and children forming the nucleus of the people living in one house. Thus, the most common term for 'family' in the Huron language referred to a model we would probably brand with the term 'extended family', a variation of the model contemporary sociologists have deemed normal.

More useful, perhaps, than 'nuclear family' and 'extended family' are terms proposed by Frances Goldscheider and Regina Bures in their study of intergenerational living arrangements in white and black households of the US. They favour the terms 'simple household' and 'complex household'. A **simple household** consists of unrelated (by blood) adults with or without children. Conversely, a **complex household** includes 'two or more adults who are related but not married to each other and hence could reasonably be expected to live separately' (2003). A simple household tends to consist of a single adult or married adults living with or without children; the most common example of a complex household

Would you call this a typical Canadian family? How many families do you know that look like this?

today is one in which adult children live at home with a parent or parents.

Using census data from 1940 to 1990, Goldscheider and Bures demonstrated that there was a 'crossover' in household patterns between black and white families. From the 1940s to 1960s, black families were less likely to live in complex households than were white families. By 1990, the pattern had reversed: white families were significantly more likely to live in simple households, black families more likely to live in complex ones.

(As we will see below, a similar change occurred in Quebec during the same period.) The study illustrates a very important principle about family. It is **dynamic**—that is, like other social institutions it changes, adapting to changing circumstances.

We should point out that when sociologists talk of a family's diversity, they may mean one of two things. Some mean 'diversity' in the sense that there are different family structures: dual-earner, single-earner/two-parent, lone-parent. We use 'diversity' here and throughout this text in a broader sense

• Our Stories •

The Crestwood Heights Family

During the period from 1948 to 1953, John Seeley, R. Alexander Sim, and E.W. Loosley studied a white, upper-middle-class neighbourhood in northern Toronto, to which they gave the fictitious name 'Crestwood Heights'. The following is a brief introduction to their chapter on the family:

> The family of Crestwood Heights . . . consists of father, mother, and two (rarely more) children. The children are healthy, physically well developed, attractively dressed, and poised as to outward behavior. The mother, assured in manner, is as like an illustration from *Vogue* or *Harper's Bazaar* as financial means and physical appearance will allow. The father, well tailored, more or less successful in radiating an impression of prosperity and power, rounds out the family group.
>
> This small family unit is both lone and love-based. It is, more often than not, formed by the marriage of two persons from unrelated and often unacquainted families . . . who are assumed to have chosen each other because they are 'in love'. Other reasons for the choice (perpetuation of property within one family, the linking of business or professional interest, an unadorned urge to upward social mobility and so on), even if influential, could not reputably be admitted as grounds for marriage.
>
> This family unit is not embedded in any extended kinship system. The newly formed family is frequently isolated geographically and often socially from the parental families. It is expected that the bride and groom will maintain a separate dwelling removed by varying degrees of distance from that of each set of parents. . . . The isolation of each family acts to decrease the ability of the family to transmit traditional patterns of behavior, which might otherwise be absorbed from close contact with, for instance, grandparents. The absence of kinship bonds also tends to concentrate the emotional life of the family upon a few individuals. . . . (Seeley et al. 1956: 159–60)

• •

What do YOU think?

1. How many families do you know that conform to the Crestwood Heights model?

2. In what respects does your own family differ, if at all, from the description given here? In what respects does it resemble this model?

• •

that includes not just differences in structure but also cultural and ethnic differences as well as different beliefs in conjugal and **gender roles**. The discussion of the family in Quebec later in this chapter highlights this broader sense of diversity.

Changes in and Questions about the Canadian Family

There are a number of changes occurring in the makeup and behaviour of Canadian families today. It is interesting to note that in a number of these areas where change is occurring, families in Quebec are leading the way. This is not to say that they are 'farther ahead' in some kind of modernist progressive model but that they offer the clearest evidence of certain general trends.

1. The marriage rate is decreasing while the cohabitation rate is rising.

A quick look at crude marriage rates will tell a sociologist if it's true that fewer people are getting married these days. The **crude marriage rate** is the number of marriages per 1,000 people in a population. Crude refers to the fact that no statistical wizardry has been used to 'refine' the rate (to use an oil analogy). It doesn't mean that the marriage is crude (although there are crude marriages). Since the population keeps rising, the crude marriage rate will give a better indication of trends than the overall number of marriages alone. If the number of marriages was the same for 1991 and 2001, the actual rate would have to be decreasing, and our sociologist could conclude that fewer people indeed are getting married these days.

The crude marriage rate has fluctuated over the years in which it has been calculated. In 1920, it was relatively low at 6.1, probably because so many young men had died during World War I and the Spanish flu epidemic that followed it. When I (J.S.) think of that statistic I think of two of my great aunts who were young then—Aunt Nell the nurse, Aunt Margaret the teacher—both of whom I got to know very well. They were gifted, intelligent women adored by the children and grandchildren of their married brothers. Neither of them ever married.

The marriage rate rose to a peak of 7.9 marriages per 1,000 people in 1950, representing a post–World War II marriage boom that would precede (and contribute to) the post-war baby boom. My sister and I, and our many cousins, are all products of the baby boom.

After dropping a little, the marriage rate remained fairly high over the next three decades, peaking at 8.0 in 1980 (a year before my second marriage, for those of you who are keeping track). That was just before the recession hit. Since then, the rate has dropped rather steadily, plummeting to 5.5 in 1995 and 4.7 in 2001, where it remained until 2003. After that a directly comparable figure became harder to obtain, as laws allowing same-sex marriage were passed in British Columbia and Ontario (next to Quebec the most socially liberal provinces). They were, not surprisingly, the only two provinces that year in which the number of marriages increased. (The rate also rose in Yukon.) The lowest crude marriage rate was in Quebec, with 2.8 marriages per 1,000 population; it was the only province (along with Nunavut and Northwest Territories) where the marriage rate was below the national average. The marriage rate for the other nine provinces (BC and Ontario included) averaged about 5.3 in 2003.

Of course, fewer marriages does not mean fewer *couples*. The number of **common-law** (or **cohabiting**) unions has risen since 1980. Precise figures are difficult to track, since society doesn't mark the beginning of such relationships the way it records marriages. Still, we do know that the percentage of all couples that are common-law or cohabiting has risen from 0.7 per cent in 1976 to 18.4 per cent in 2006. The cohabitation rate in the United States is always lower than that in Canada (for instance, the US rate in 2001 was 8.2 per cent, just over half the Canadian rate of 16.0 for that year). Can you think of why that is? Here's a hint: Quebec (with a 2006 cohabitation rate of about 35 per cent of all couples, which accounts for roughly 46 per cent of all cohabiting couples in Canada) skews the Canadian figures here. Now can you guess? Our discussion of Quebec later on may give you some help.

There are a number of other good questions that can be addressed concerning common-law or cohabiting couples. For instance, is cohabitation replacing marriage? Does cohabitation benefit

Compare this photo with the one on page 180. Is this family any less typical of the families you know? What factors in our culture might lead us to view one family as more conventional than another?

Photo: Queerstock Inc./Alamy

men more than women? How does cohabitation, versus marriage, affect children?

One of my favourite questions concerns the following fact, which seems to generate a considerable amount of spurious reasoning: people who cohabit prior to marriage are more likely to divorce than those who go straight from living apart to marriage. A survey done in 1990 found that after 10 years of marriage, the breakup rate was 26 per cent for those who had cohabited first and 16 per cent for those who had not (Le Bourdais and Marcil-Gratton 1996: 428). When students are asked to propose reasons, they often come up with false causation: something happens during cohabitation, or else cohabiting couples became tired of each other during marriage, and so on. A better answer that they seem to miss is that people with more liberal values are both more likely to cohabit and also more likely to leave a bad marriage. Another possibility: people who are afraid of commitment are more likely to cohabit and to leave a relationship.

2. The age of first marriage is rising.
The average age of first marriage has been rising recently (see Table 7.1) but is not out of step with the age in earlier times. In 1921, the average age of first marriage for brides in Canada was 24.5 and 28.0 for grooms. It is important to see that these figures are not very different from those for 1991, which were 25.7 and 27.7 respectively. The numbers rose slightly during the Depression-era 1930s, dropping slowly again in the 1940s. Then the drop became more dramatic in the 1950s and 1960s: in 1965, 30.8 per cent of first-time brides were under 20 years of age (Beaujot 2000: 102). By 1971, the average ages of first-time brides and

Table 7.1 Average age of first marriage for brides and grooms, 1991, 1996, 2001		
YEAR	FIRST-TIME BRIDES	FIRST-TIME GROOMS
1991	25.7	27.7
1996	27.3	29.3
2001	28.2	30.2

grooms were 22.6 and 25.0 respectively. (My first marriage was in 1973: my wife was 22, I was 24.) The questions here are these: has this figure peaked, reaching levels that are only slightly higher than during the 'strange times' of the 1950s and 1960s? Is this figure becoming increasingly meaningless as the cohabitation rate increases?

Naturally, the averages are different for various provinces. In 2003, the lowest average age of first marriage was in Saskatchewan, where it was 27.0 for first-time brides and 29.3 for first-time grooms; for Quebec, the comparable figures were 30.4 and 31.9 respectively.

3. More women are having children in their thirties now than in earlier years.

The number of women in their thirties giving birth for the first time is increasing. In 1987, just 4 per cent of women aged 35 and older gave birth for the first time; in 2005, the percentage rose to roughly 11 per cent. Likewise, women in their early thirties giving birth to their first child increased from 15 to 26 per cent over the same period. What is important to consider here is the factor known as **fecundity**—that is, a woman's ability to conceive.

Photo: Catchlight Visual Services/Alamy

Why do you think many North American women today are waiting until they are in their mid- to late-thirties before having their first child?

This ability changes during a woman's fourth decade. It is estimated that 91 per cent of women at the age of 30 are physically able to become pregnant. This drops to 77 per cent of women at the age of 35 and just 53 per cent of women at 40 (Rajulton, Balakrisnhan, and Ravanera 1990). Do you hear the clock ticking? Do you think that this could have a significant effect in lowering the total fertility rate?

4. The number of children per family has dropped to below the 'replacement rate'.

The **total fertility rate** is an estimate of the average number of children that a woman between the ages of 15 and 49 will have in her lifetime if current age-specific fertility rates remain constant during her reproductive years. The **replacement rate** is the number of children that a woman must bear if the population is to continue at the same level. The replacement rate is 2.1, meaning that for each woman aged 15–49, 2.1 children must be born in order for the population to hold constant.

You can see how things have changed by looking at the following contrasts. Of women born between 1927 and 1931, 31 per cent had five or more children. Compare that with women born between 1952 and 1956, of whom just 1.3 per cent had five or more children. Among the latter group, 38.3 per cent had just two children, and 33.7 per cent had one child or no children, meaning that a total of 72 per cent of women born in 1952–6 had two children or fewer, compared with 42.7 per cent of women born in 1927–31. Table 7.2 shows the total fertility rate for select years between 1941 and 2007.

In 2005 the total fertility rate in Canada was 1.54, so it seems to have bottomed out. But consider this: rates for the 100 most populous countries in the world in 2003 ranged from 3.86 to 6.98, with the top 10 fertility rates all being in Africa. Those countries with fertility rates below Canada's include the former communist countries of eastern Europe, ranging from the Czech Republic (1.18) to Georgia (1.51); some Mediterranean countries, including Italy (1.26), Greece (1.35), and Portugal (1.49); and several East Asian countries—Singapore (1.24), Hong Kong (1.32), Japan (1.38), South Korea (1.56), and Taiwan (1.57). In each of these countries, the population is expected to fall. Why do you think their fertility rates are

Table 7.2 Total fertility rate for select years, 1941–2007

1941	1951	1961	1971	1976	1981	1986	1991	1996	2001	2007 (est.)
2.8	3.5	3.8	2.2	1.8	1.7	1.7	1.8	1.6	1.5	1.6

Source: Adapted from Beaujot 2000: 85–9.

so low? Is it just economics (at the national and family level), or is some pessimistic sense of the future involved as well?

So what do you do if your national fertility rate is below the replacement rate of 2.1? Sociologists and politicians will answer that Canada makes up for its low fertility rate with high levels of immigration—take note, however, that immigrants from countries with higher fertility rates soon begin to reproduce at a rate consistent with the fertility rate here in this country. Are there ways to boost the fertility rate? Would government incentives (such as those offered in Quebec) help to offset the cost of having and raising children? Would a system of universal daycare, similar to what exists in Quebec, change things significantly? Recent studies in the US suggest that women are willing to have more children when their husbands are willing to take a greater share of responsibility for childcare and general housework. How significant a factor do you think that could be?

5. There are more divorces.

Analyzing divorce statistics can be complicated. If you ask a group of people whether they think the divorce rate is rising or falling (as I have often done in class), they will typically say that it's going up. This is not the case. The rate has jumped on several occasions over brief periods of time, but we can account for these, in part, by looking at changes to the legislation surrounding divorce.

In 1961, there were 6,563 divorces in Canada, producing a divorce rate of 36.0 per 100,000 population. In 1968, the grounds for divorce were expanded in most of Canada: no longer was adultery the sole basis to sue for divorce. Between 1968 and 1971, the numbers shot up from 11,343 to 29,685, representing rates of 54.8 and 137.6 per 100,000 population. By 1982, the numbers had peaked (at 70,346, or a rate of 285.9); in fact,

they were dropping slowly. Then in 1985, the Divorce Act was changed again, allowing marital breakdown as legitimate grounds for divorce. By 1987, the numbers had peaked again, this time at 90,985 (339.5 per 100,000 population). By 2002, the numbers were back down to 1982 levels: 70,155 divorces for a rate of 223.7, the lowest rate since the 1970s.

From 1999 to 2003, the number of divorces stayed about the same: 70,910 in the first year and 70,828 in the last. During that period the number of divorces went down in every province and territory except for Ontario and Alberta.

What do YOU think?

1. Do you think that divorce rates will increase when they include the breakups of same-sex married couples? (Consider the social pressure placed on same-sex married couples and what that might do to divorce rates.)

2. Do you see a relationship between falling divorce rates and the increasing rates of cohabitation? Is the second causing the first?

6. There are more lone-parent families than before.

The number of lone-parent families in Canada has been increasing since 1966 (which followed a 35-year period of decrease from 13.6 per cent during the Depression year of 1931). In 1966, 8.2 per cent of all families were single-parent families; since then, the figure has risen to 12.7 in 1986, 14.5 in 1996, 15.7 in 2001, and 15.9 in 2006.

People often speculate about the negative effects on children of living in lone-parent households, particularly with regard to school dropout rates and criminal activity. They need to be cautious here, as most lone-parent households began

Photo: Sophia Fortier © 2009

What social conditions (e.g. the social network of the lone-parent, or readily available daycare) do you think need to exist for a child to thrive in a lone-parent household?

as two-parent households. It is hard to determine whether the bad conditions that may have existed in the pre-divorce or pre-separation family—conditions that include an abusive parent or, at least, parental fighting—weren't the real causes of children's crime or truancy.

There is, however, a strong connection between lone-parent families and poverty, especially where the mother is the family head. Beaujot (2000: 348) uses an interesting statistic when he compares child poverty rates among lone-parent households for various countries before and after taxes have been deducted and transfer payments (social assistance) distributed. The countries include Canada, the US, Australia, Israel, and a number of European nations, all studied over a 10-year period from 1982 to 1992.

Before taxes and transfer payments, Canada has the sixth highest rate of child poverty in lone-parent households, with a 1991 pre-transfer payment rate of 68.2. What is more shocking is that Canada moves up to third on the list when the after-tax-and-transfer totals are considered. Canada, with a poverty rate in lone-parent households of 50.2 per cent, falls behind only the US (59.5 per cent) and Australia (56.2). This suggests that Canada is not doing enough—less, certainly, than the other countries studied—to help children living in poverty in lone-parent families. What (if anything) do you think can be done to change this?

7. There are more people living alone than before.

In 1996, of the entire Canadian population aged 15 and over, 12 per cent were living alone. Contrary to what you might think, this rate is highest for those over 85 (48 per cent), and lowest for those younger than 55 (10 per cent or less; Beaujot 2000: 117).

A Statistics Canada publication offers an interesting comparison. In an examination of the changing percentages for 1-person and 5+-person households, the authors note:

> In 2006, there were three times as many one-person households as households with five or more people. Of the 12.4 million private households, 27% were one-person households, while 9% were large households of five or more people.
>
> In 1941, 6% of houses were comprised of one person, while 38% [more than six times as many] were comprised of five or more people. (Statistics Canada 2009)

Interestingly, and strangely, we build larger houses now on average than we used to, but house fewer people in more households.

● ● ● ● ● ● ● ● ● ● ● ● ● ● ● ● ●

What do YOU think?

Which do you think is the more significant cause of the statistics noted above: the aging population or marriage delay among people under 30? What other figures might help you address this question?

● ● ● ● ● ● ● ● ● ● ● ● ● ● ● ● ●

8. Children are leaving home at a later age.

The term **cluttered nest** is sometimes used to describe the phenomenon in which adult children continue to live at home with their parents (the opposite, **empty nest**, describes a household in which children have moved out of the home). Statistically, we see that 'at age 20–24, 50.4 per-cent of women and 64.3 percent of men were living with parent(s) in 1996, compared to 33.6 and 51.4 percent respectively in 1981' (Boyd and Norris 1998, cited in Beaujot 2000: 98). Causation is fairly easy to establish: it takes more time and education nowadays to establish a career. And with a higher cost of living, rising house prices, and a number of costs that earlier generations didn't have to face, it's more difficult to set one-self up on one's own. With couples marrying later and later in life, it takes that much longer to set up a dual-earner household, the only model that is financially viable for some people who want to move out of their parents' home.

Delayed Life Transitions

In an interesting piece called 'Delayed Life Transitions: Trends and Implications', University of Western Ontario demographer **Rod Beaujot** links together some of the trends we have just been dis-cussing as part of a phenomenon he calls **delayed life transitions**. We go through a number of major life transitions in our lifetime—getting a full-time job, going out to live on our own, getting married, having children, retiring. During the prosperous socioeconomic times of the 1950s, 1960s, and early 1970s, people went through what we could call 'sped-up life transitions', making these major life changes at a relatively young age. The situa-tion has changed considerably, and people today are making these transitions later and later in life.

Several questions arise here. To what extent is our current speed of life transition 'delayed' and to what extent is it simply 'normal' (whatever that might mean)? What are the implications for today's generation of college and university students of having parents who went through life transitions at a much more advanced speed, perhaps one that was 'less normal' than now.

Family in Quebec

By just about every statistical measure you can come up with, the family in Quebec is socio-logically distinct from the family in other parts of Canada. For a snapshot of the differences, con-sider that in 1996, Quebec was the province with

- *the highest cohabitation rate*: 20.5 per cent of all families, almost twice the next high-est rate in Canada (New Brunswick, at 10.9 per cent);

How long do you think it will be before this 'college senior' moves out of her parents' basement and gets a job? More seriously, what are the social benefits to be gained from attending college or university as an adult? Is this kind of delayed life transition good for younger students at the school? Society in general?

- *the lowest marriage rate*: 3.1 per 100,000, significantly lower than the next lowest rate, British Columbia's 5.2;
- *the highest divorce rate*: 45.7 per 100 marriages, a little ahead of BC's 45.0; and
- *the highest number of divorces* (per 100 marriages) among couples married less than 30 years, with 47.4 in the year 2000 (Alberta's rate of 41.5 is the next highest).

In 2001, Quebec led all provinces with an abortion rate of 19.6 per 1,000 women or 421.5 per 1,000 live births (trailing only Northwest Territories in the latter statistic). In 2002, Quebec was the province with the greatest number of total births by single (never married) women; by percentage (55.3 per cent), they trailed only Nunavut. The province also had the greatest percentage of births to women who were divorced (2.1 per cent).

Another feature unique to Quebec is the province-wide support for same-sex marriage (see Table 7.3). In a poll conducted among 10,015 Canadian adults in August 2003, residents of Quebec showed the greatest support for changing the legal definition of marriage; in March 2004, it became the third province (following Ontario and BC) to legally recognize same-sex marriage.

In the 1995 Bibby Report, Quebec was also shown to have the highest rate of approval for premarital and extramarital sex (Bibby 1995: 76),

with 88 per cent supporting the former (compared with 82 per cent, the next highest, in BC) and 24 per cent supporting the latter (compared with 14 per cent, the next highest, in the Prairies).

Quebec residents also show a difference when it comes to parenting, as indicated by a *Globe and Mail*/CTV poll of 648 Canadian parents conducted by Ipsos-Reid and published in the *Globe and Mail* on 10 April 2004. The poll noted the following results:

- The percentage of parents who said they spanked their children for disciplinary reasons:

Alberta	60%
British Columbia	52%
Saskatchewan/Manitoba	46%
Ontario	45%
Atlantic Provinces	42%
Quebec	**22%**

- The percentage of parents who agreed that using flashcards at an early age makes kids smarter:

British Columbia	71%
Saskatchewan/Manitoba	67%
Alberta	63%
Ontario	60%
Atlantic Provinces	57%
Quebec	**25%**

Table 7.3 Support for changing the definition of marriage to include same-sex unions, by region, 2003

	AGREE SOMEWHAT	AGREE STRONGLY	TOTAL
Quebec	**36**	**25**	**61**
British Columbia	26	25	51
Atlantic Provinces	19	26	45
Ontario	19	23	42
Prairies	16	17	33

Source: TNS Canadian Facts, http://www.tns-cf.com/news/03.09.05-samesex-charts.pdf, 2003. The study was conducted by TNS Canadian Facts (formerly NFO CFgroup), one of Canada's leading full-service marketing, opinion and social research organizations.

Telling It Like It Is

Telling Your Family You're Gay

Growing up in the small town of Whitby, Ontario, I never felt the negative effects of discrimination. I am an English-speaking, Caucasian female and had never been a part of a minority group, in any sense of the word. At the age of 21, this changed and I became aware of how easily people are judged. I am a lesbian, and from the moment I became open about my sexual preferences, I felt first-hand what it feels like to be viewed based solely on one aspect of your life, and not as an entire person. When meeting someone new in my life it was as though I was wearing a sign on my forehead reading, 'I am gay', and it was perceived as 'I am gay . . . that is everything you need to know about me.' Once this information is divulged, almost instantly people form opinions on who I am as a person and who I should be. They develop expectations that quite often are illogical and unrealistic. By writing a paper such as this one, I am being given the opportunity to address a few of these numerous stereotypes and prejudiced beliefs. Hopefully, I can educate some to stop these beliefs from spreading.

From my experience, the original thought that people tend to have when finding out that I am gay is that it is simply a phase I am going through, a time of experimentation and rebellious behaviour. My brother's reaction was as such. He believed that it was just a phase and

that it would pass. He continued to express this for an entire year after I had told him. He realizes otherwise now. . . . When telling my mother (who along with the rest of my family is extremely supportive of me), I was shocked to hear her initial reaction to what I had told her. After a moment or two of silence, she . . . said, 'But I thought you wanted to get married and have kids one day.' The thought of these dreams possibly fading away is what seemed to unsettle her the most. I found two things wrong and rather presumptuous about this statement. To begin with, the idea that a woman must want/need a husband and children to live a fulfilling life is old-fashioned and a step backward from the times we live in today. I figure, why can't a woman who is independent and who has a satisfying career be considered to lead a successful, happy life, despite the fact that she has no family to raise. Furthermore, my mother was correct in assuming that I did want a family, but it was not the family that she had in mind. Marriage and children are a large part of my future plans, and, with adoption, and artificial insemination, this is a very feasible option for lesbian couples. Simply because a woman falls in love with another woman, it does not mean that she didn't grow up with the same desire for nurturing children and caring for a home and family that a lot of heterosexual girls do.

What should we make of all of this? First, it is important to note that a number of the statistical indicators discussed show a major change from the situation in Quebec prior to the Quiet Revolution of the 1960s. Take divorce, for example. Prior to 1968, if you were living in Quebec and you wanted a divorce, you had to seek it through Parliament (the situation was similar in Newfoundland). A growing separation from the Catholic Church has been cited (especially by religious officials) as a possible explanation for the rising divorce rate. Yet in the 2001 census, Quebec had the third-lowest

number of residents declaring they had 'no religion' (a rate of 5.8 per cent, compared with the national average of 16.5 per cent). Of course, having an affiliation with the Church and being influenced by that affiliation can be two different matters. The Catholic Church considers suicide a sin, but Quebec, the most Catholic province, has the highest suicide rate in Canada, especially among men: in 1999–2001, the suicide rate for Quebec males was 30.7 per 100,000, compared with 16.1 in the provinces of Ontario, Alberta, and British Columbia.

Can we say, as more right-wing or conservative interpreters would, that family life is falling apart in Quebec? One statistic we haven't presented might be seen as supporting that view: in 2002, Quebec had the highest rate of one-person households, about 30 per cent. But from our perspective, a more likely interpretation is that Quebec went through more rapid modernization and outright change during the last 40 years than any other province. The falling away of old structures does not mean the falling apart of the institutions. Quebeçois are perhaps best seen as a people who are reinventing family as they are reinventing other institutions—political, religious, educational, and so on.

Conjugal Roles

Conjugal (or *marital*) **roles** are the distinctive roles of the husband and wife that result from the division of labour within the family. The first important sociological study done on this subject was British sociologist Elizabeth Bott's *Family and Social Networks* (1957), in which she differentiated these roles as being either **segregated**—in which tasks, interests, and activities are clearly different—or **joint**, in which many tasks, interests, and activities are shared. The study was set against a backdrop in which men were primarily responsible for the financial support of the family, while women were primarily responsible for the housework and childcare.

Earning and Caring: Changes in Conjugal Roles

In 2000, Canadian demographer Rod Beaujot published an important book on the Canadian family: *Earning and Caring in Canadian Families* (2000). Winner of the 2000 Canadian Sociology and Anthropology Association's prestigious John Porter Award for outstanding scholarship, Beaujot aimed to discover 'how to better understand the changing links between earning and caring'. What did he mean by that? He wanted to study how conjugal roles were changing from a situation in which they were more or less complementary to one in which they were companionate. **Complementary roles** (like Bott's model of *segregated roles*) cast men primarily as earners, breadwinners, doing paid work, with women involved primarily in the unpaid work of childcare and housework. In **companionate** relationships (like Bott's *joint* relationship) the roles overlap.

Beaujot notes that the shift is far from complete, which is not to say that complete overlap is possible or even desired. Genders roles are different to a significant extent because, biologically, men and women are different. But there is a point to which we may be able to say that a basic fairness or justice has been reached, and we are far from that point. As Beaujot—like others before him—several times documents, married women do more total work per day than married men do, even though married women are more likely to work part-time. Married women, especially those who are the mothers of small children, do much more unpaid work. And while women have entered new roles in the work world, men have not gone as far in entering new roles at home. This has created an imbalance in conjugal roles, leading some women to view their lives in terms such as 'double burden', 'double ghetto', or 'second shift'. The difficulty of correcting this imbalance in households with small children has led some women to conclude, pessimistically, that 'childlessness is the easiest route to equality' (Beaujot 2002: 81).

In 1995, sociologist **M. Reza Nakhaie** published 'Housework in Canada: The National Picture', a summary of his study demonstrating that gender was the single most important factor—above relative income and amount of available time—determining how much domestic labour or housework an individual did. The author's most striking discovery concerned the relationship between gender, hours of paid work, and share of the housework. Nakhaie found that there is an inverse relationship between the hours of paid work a man does and the size of his share of the housework: the more paid hours he has, the smaller his share of the housework. However, the same is not true for women. In fact, a direct, rather than inverse, relationship seems to exist over a particular number of hours of work: an increase over 30 in a woman's hours of paid work per week correlated to an *increase* in her contribution to housework.

The key to correcting the imbalance, as Beaujot and a number of other sociologists see it, is to recognize that gender roles are not carved in stone

"Gotta run, sweetheart. By the way, that was one fabulous job you did raising the children."

and handed down by society. Rather, they are products of what Arlie Hochschild terms a '**gender strategy**', which is 'a plan of action through which a person tries to solve problems at hand, given the cultural notions of gender at play' (Hochschild 1989: 15). These 'problems at hand' include the fact that small children have to be taken care of. From the studies that Beaujot cites, it is clear that the typical strategy for infant care is for the mother to take time off, then to work part-time as the infant matures towards school age, and eventually to try to go back to full-time work.

The responsibility for care of children is the main reason that married women are much more likely to work part-time than are married/unmarried men or unmarried women. It is also the cause of what Beaujot calls the **occupational segregation** of men and women. Women choose occupations in fields such as education and healthcare, which have the greatest flexibility in terms of childcare-related **work interruptions** (which include staying home to care for a sick child or taking a longer-term leave to care for a newborn). Beaujot makes an interesting argument that this is something of a chicken-and-egg scenario: women seek out jobs in employment areas that offer greater flexibility, but part of the reason these jobs tend to offer greater flexibility is that they are dominated by women. Is it possible, then, that if women were to enter other occupations in large numbers, a similar flexibility might develop? What do you think?

The Ethnic Factor in Conjugal Roles

One weakness of Beaujot's work is that he completely ignores the ethnic factor, clearly a mistake. The classic study looking at the division of conjugal roles among North American immigrant groups is Sathi Dasgupta's 'Conjugal roles and social network in Indian immigrant families: Bott revisited' (1992). Although the article was written over 15 years ago about South Asian immigrants in the United States, the findings it sets out have a general applicability to the situation in Canada today. Dasgupta studied 25 couples and found that *segregated* conjugal roles dominated. The men were invariably the primary breadwinners and made virtually all major decisions affecting the household, while the women, with few exceptions, were full-time homemakers and primary caretakers of the children. Interestingly, however, there were aspects of joint conjugal roles among the immigrant families that would not be nearly as well accepted back in India: joint discussion of the children's education and of the couple's social life (with joint leisure activities the norm).

Change will come, as immigrants to North America adopt a more 'Western' approach to

Photo: Image Source/Corbis

I love a clean house.

What does this image tell you about our perception of the gender roles handed down by society?

dividing conjugal roles, but the ethnic factor still must be considered in any study of gender roles in the Canadian family.

Endogamy and Ethnicity

Endogamy means 'marrying within'. It is the practice of marrying someone of the same ethnic, religious, or cultural group as oneself. My mother's mother wanted me to be religiously endogamous and marry a Protestant, not—God forbid—a Catholic. My cousin married a Jew, and I married a Protestant the same year; my stock rose, his fell. My mother, a woman of great understanding and respect for all people, once gave me a very earnest talk about why I should not marry a black woman. I can't hold it against her—there is a strong tradition of endogamy in many cultures, where 'marrying in' is seen as the only way to preserve the purity of one's group.

The opposite of endogamy, marrying *outside* of one's group, is **exogamy**. Support for exogamy, once quite low in Canada, is increasing, according to findings published by Bibby (1995; see Table 7.4). I believe that this set of statistics gives a picture that is more positive than real. It seems more an expression of ideal culture than an indication of probable practice. Contrast it with the series of comparable exogamy rates from the 1996 census shown in Table 7.5.

Table 7.4 Canadians' approval of intergroup marriage (%), 1975–1995

	1975	1980	1985	1990	1995
Whites and Natives	75	80	83	84	84
Whites and Asians (Orientals)	66	75	78	82	83
Whites and East Asians (Pakistanis)	58	66	72	77	80
Whites and Blacks	57	64	72	79	81
Protestants and Catholics	86	88	89	90	92
Protestants and Jews	80	94	84	86	90
Roman Catholics and Jews	78	81	82	85	89

Source: Bibby (1995).

For all of the groups shown in Table 7.5, the vast majority of the people marry within their own group. Do you think that this situation has changed significantly in the past decade? Do you think it will change? What about those examples in which there is a meaningful gender difference—with South East Asians (Thais, Cambodians, Laotians, for example) and Filipinos? The difference among Filipinos may be attributed to the pattern of early immigration of women coming to Canada to obtain jobs in the health sciences and childcare (see Chapter 13). What do you think the reasoning might be for the South East Asians?

Table 7.5 Rates of exogamy for men and for women, by ethnic group, 1996

	HUSBANDS	WIVES
Aboriginals	25.8	31.6
East Asian	7.5	5.8
Chinese	6.4	8.4
South East Asian	8.1	23.3
Filipino	6.7	28.6
Vietnamese	10.6	12.2
South Asian	7.4	5.8
African	25.3	15.1
Caribbean & Bermuda	23.3	18.7
Jewish	19.2	12.7

What do YOU think?

1. Consider Table 7.4. Do you think that Canadians' attitudes towards exogamy are different now than they were 15 years ago?

2. Have you ever been involved in a relationship with someone from a different ethnicity or culture? If not, could you imagine yourself in such a relationship? What challenges do you think you might face?

3. Have you noticed that commercials on Canadian television commonly portray white men with Asian partners but never Asian men with Caucasian spouses. Why do you think that is?

Photo: Eamon Mac Mahon © 2005

Under Canadian miscegenation laws, interracial marriages were illegal. However, intergroup marriage approval has been on a steady increase since 1975. Today, Vancouver has the highest rates of interracial marriage in Canada.

Telling It Like It Is

A STUDENT POV

Italian Families and Conjugal Roles: Four Generations

POINT OF VIEW

When I think of the topic of gender in an Italian family, I laugh. The struggles between what it means to be male and what it means to be female arise so very often in my family, at every dinner and almost every conversation. The discussions are always split between the three generations because my grandmother lives with my parents and she never misses an opportunity to include her views. As you can probably guess it goes like this: the eldest generation undeniably believes that the female's role in life is to be a complement to her husband; everything she does is based on his needs and his demands. All domestic duties and child-rearing except for punishment are her responsibility. Working outside the home is secondary to household work. The husband makes all decisions, although she can make suggestions. It is the male's responsibility to take care of the family financially.

My parents (second generation) feel similarly, the main difference being the father should be very involved with the children, not solely in areas concerning punishment. Where my grandmother would discourage my father from helping around the house, my mother would welcome the help though not demand nor expect it. In this generation, family decisions are made together; however, household duties are still very divided, even with my mother working full time outside the home. For the female, post-secondary education and career are second to marriage and family. The main female role in life is keeping a clean house, cooking good homemade food, and keeping everyone happy and healthy. The main male role is to keep the food on the table by providing the family with its main source of income.

The third generation around the dinner table changed things a little. This generation in my family consists of my husband and I, the middle brother and his wife and the 'baby brother', though no longer a baby. Most of us are in agreement that gender roles in the new Italian family have changed. No longer is the female solely responsible for all household duties. Husbands cook, clean, and are physically able to change diapers, something my father had never done even with having three children! The females have post-secondary education and careers and are not a complement to their husbands, but an equal.

I also grew up with a huge double standard that affected me immensely in all areas of my life. It goes something like this: 'This is what boys can do and this is what girls cannot do' (My father's infamous words). Boys can play all day and not help their mothers (girls can't), boys can

Family and Ethnicity

As we'll see in greater detail in Chapter 12, on race and ethnicity, there is a history in Canada of the federal government creating policies that denied family to immigrants. The prohibitively expensive head tax levied on immigrants from China and South Asia in the late nineteenth and early twentieth centuries made it impossible in many cases for married couples or their families to reunite in Canada. Canadian sociologists **Nancy Mandell** and **Ann Duffy**, in their text *Canadian Families: Diversity, Conflict and Change* (1995), noted a similar connection between government immigration policy and the denial of family for women of colour. They claim:

> [I]t has been a policy of the government not to encourage the possibility of developing families among women of colour who came as domestic workers. Thus, their status as 'single' and as 'temporary' is deliberately organized by immigration policies. (1995: 157).

The policy they refer to was initiated in 1910–11, during one of the country's greatest periods

fight and play rough (girls can't), boys have to do well in school (girls don't have to), boys can go out whenever they want (girls can't), boys have to play sports (girls don't have to), boys can stay out late (girls have to come home early).

'This is what girls must do and this is what boys do not have to do.' Girls must cook and clean (boys do not), girls must learn the traditions (boys do not), girls must be good always (boys do not), girls must stay home to take care of the family (boys do not), girls must not be left alone with their boyfriends (boys can live with their girlfriends). I fought with my younger brothers fairly consistently growing up. The words, 'that is not fair' were spoken often. I actually disliked one of my brothers for years and it was not until he got a family of his own that we began to grow closer together. We even talked about the jealousy we felt for one another over different family issues and how the double standards we grew up with had a great deal to do with it.

Needless to say my family's views on gender have had a great impact on my life. It has carved me into the woman I am today. Much to my parents' chagrin, I cannot cook, I hate house cleaning, run away from tradition whenever I can, I am constantly in school working on a career, and even though I am married, I frequently go out with my friends and stay out late! Being married

has been difficult at times also. I always have an intense instinct to run from the gender roles that surround me, and yet I realize that in many circumstances they are needed to preserve peace in a family. I now have many concerns for my daughter. I know she will not be faced with an obvious double standard, as I do not have any sons and I am fully aware that being completely opposite of the Martha Stewart-like woman is not anything to be proud of. Something in the middle would be nice. Since little girls are greatly influenced by their mothers, I know I must be really careful to set a positive female role in our family. I truly hope the difference for my daughter will be the ability for her to choose the woman she wants to be instead of madly running away from what I demand her to become.

—Alina Mucci

● ● ● ● ● ● ● ● ● ● ● ● ● ● ● ● ● ●

What do YOU think?

1. Do you think the narrative writer's brothers would write a different story about conjugal roles?

2. Do you foresee any gender role conflict concerning the writer and her daughter?

● ● ● ● ● ● ● ● ● ● ● ● ● ● ● ● ● ●

of immigration. About a hundred black women from the Caribbean islands of Guadeloupe came to Canada to work as domestic servants, but when authorities discovered that many of the women were not as 'unattached' as they had claimed to be—many had children they had been forced to leave behind—they were sent back.

Between 1955 and 1967, a number of women from the Caribbean—primarily Jamaica—were allowed to come to Canada to work as domestics. They had to be young, of 'good character', and single (in other words, not married or in a common-law relationship). They were given the status of

landed immigrants, but they could not seek other work until they had served at least a year of domestic duty. Roughly 300 Caribbean women came to Canada each year between 1955 and 1960, the number rising to about 1,000 a year during the 1960s (Bolaria and Li 1985: 178). Many of them agreed to work as domestics, even though they were trained as teachers or secretaries; many, in order to be 'single', left family behind, all because it was the only way they could enter the country.

Naturally, those immigrants who had left husbands and children in the Caribbean wanted to sponsor their families to join them in Canada, but their efforts were blocked by immigration officials. In 1976, seven Jamaican women applied to sponsor their children to come to Canada; instead, they were ordered to be deported for having failed to report their children on their applications to come to Canada (Leah and Morgan 1979). Their cases were highly publicized, and after an intense struggle that involved community and labour groups, the seven women won their appeals and were allowed to stay in Canada.

Attacks on the Aboriginal Family

Immigrant families are not the only ones that have been touched by restrictive Canadian legislation. The Aboriginal family also has long been a target

of federal policy and government agents. The following passage describes how, during the early twentieth century, an Indian Agent used the Blackfoot community's need for food rations as a tool to ensure that the people remained monogamous:

It may be remembered that, in my last report, I expressed thankfulness that there had been no plural marriages during the preceding year. That report was barely out of my hand when I learned that three members of the band were dissatisfied with one wife each and had taken another. I immediately directed that the rations of these families be withheld until such time as they saw fit to obey the rules in this respect. One family missed one ration,

---

The Point Is...

Blaming the Victim: Daniel Moynihan and Black Families in the United States

In 1965, American sociologist **Daniel Moynihan** (1927–2003), acting in his capacity as assistant secretary of the US Department of Labor, compiled an ambitious document called *The Negro Family: The Call for National Action*. In it he presented a statistical profile of black families in the United States and outlined a plan to address what, in his determination, was a growing problem in need of repair. Moynihan's plan was eventually scrapped as unworkable, but its influence persists. Every 10 years, the conservative media celebrate the anniversary of the document's publication by arguing vociferously that Moynihan was right.

One of the strongest opponents of the approach and policy implications of what came to be called 'The Moynihan Report' was William Ryan. His critique formed the basis for his most famous work, *Blaming the Victim* (1971). In a chapter facetiously titled 'Mammy Observed—Fixing the Negro Family', Ryan summarized what he felt were the five essential elements of Moynihan's work:

First, the Negro family, as a major institution within the Negro subculture, is weak and unstable, tending toward a matriarchal form. Second, the present status of the Negro family is rooted in the experience of slavery. Third, the distortions in Negro

family structure have been maintained by Negro unemployment that has continued at disastrously high levels for many decades. Fourth, the weakened Negro family produces children, particularly sons, who are so damaged by their family experience that they are unable to profit from educational and employment opportunities. Fifth, therefore efforts to achieve formal change in such social institutions as ghetto schools and discriminatory employment practices will have little effect on present patterns of inequality of status; the ending of inequality and poverty will not, and cannot, be achieved until something is done to strengthen and stabilize the Negro family. (Ryan 1971: 66–7)

● ● ● ● ● ● ● ● ● ● ● ● ● ● ● ● ● ● ● ●

What do YOU think?

1. Why can this be called 'blaming the victim'?

2. Why would conservative thinkers and media support such a position?

3. Can this position be reconciled with the growth of the complex household in black families in the United States referred to earlier?

● ● ● ● ● ● ● ● ● ● ● ● ● ● ● ● ● ● ● ●

and then decided that it was better to abide by the rules. The other two families held out for several rations, and then they succumbed and put away wife No. 2. (in Dosman 1972: 52–3)

As outrageous as it sounds—withholding food rations to control marriage choices—this incident is not atypical of the kind of treatment Native families suffered at the hands of government agents.

It's important to point out that actions like this were often products of well-meaning agencies and their representatives. With the benefit of modern perspective, we can see just how misguided—and, frankly, racist—these policies were. The following section looks closely at three policies aimed at controlling Native families. In some cases, as we will see, the same strategies have targeted other groups that governments have felt they needed to manage, including certain cultural and ethnic groups as well as people with physical or mental disabilities.

Residential Schools

Among the institutionalized instruments of control devised to manage the lives of Canada's Native populations, the establishment of residential schools tops the list for the devastating effects it has had on Aboriginal families. Officially started in 1910 but existing as 'industrial' and 'boarding' schools before then in the nineteenth century, **residential schools** were created with the almost explicit objective of keeping Aboriginal children away from the harmful influences of their parents and their home communities. Families were ripped apart as parents reluctantly signed over legal guardianship of their children to school principals, then watched their children leave for the state- and church-run boarding schools, where they would live for most, if not all, of the year. Parents were discouraged from visiting, and those who did were closely monitored. Brothers and sisters were kept apart, sometimes not seeing each other for months on end. Many families were never reunited.

Historian J.R. Miller, tells the story of a Cree woman who went to a residential school that was just 19 kilometres from her reserve, though it might as well have been on another planet. For hours on end, she would stand at the corner of a fence that surrounded the school property:

She would put her hand through the fence, because that meant she was closer to her home and family by the length of her arm and watch for her parents. She would say to herself, 'the next black horse that comes along' will be drawing her parents' wagon on a visit. Disappointment only led to repetitions of the childlike incantation, a wish and a prayer that never seemed to come true. (Miller 1996: 338–9)

Physical, emotional, and sexual abuse by residential school employees demoralized the students. And as those who have been abused so often become abusers, many Aboriginal children grew up to bring the abuse they learned at school to their home community.

Sexual Sterilization

In its official definition of **genocide**, the United Nations includes attempts to destroy a people by imposing measures designed to prevent births within the group. This describes certain policies that hit, among and above other groups, Canada's Native population during much of the twentieth century. For instance, in 1928, the United Farmers Party of Alberta passed the Sexual Sterilization Act, with the intent of sterilizing 'mental defectives' so that their 'bad genes' would not be passed on. The act reflects the early twentieth-century belief in **eugenics**, the flawed notion that a single gene responsible for intelligence was absent in 'stupid people', who would be capable of having only 'stupid children'—in other words, children inheriting their parents' defective intellect. We know now that there is a complex relationship between a number of yet-unidentified genes and the various aptitudes that make up the biological potential known as intelligence. It would be more be accurate to say that we have **intelligences** of various kinds and levels (for instance, I have a talent for writing, but I am inept in drawing). This complexity makes the degree to which intelligence is inherited uncertain; we just don't know.

Eugenics has rightly been called a kind of **scientific racism**, as it was used to justify prejudices based on the supposed genetic inferiority or 'feeble-mindedness' of certain groups of immigrants to North America—particularly those coming from eastern Europe (see Gould 1981 and 1983)—as well as of black people and Native people. Since it was used to support prejudice against the poor and homeless, it could also be held up as an example of **scientific classism**. The traditional yardstick for measuring intelligence is the intelligence quotient test. We're all aware that a high IQ suggests a high degree of intelligence, but the test has been criticized for its bias against people representing certain language and culture groups. As well, the test perpetuates a myth that we all have a **general intelligence** to which a single number can be assigned.

During the history of Alberta's Sexual Sterilization Act, which lasted from 1928 to 1972, some 2,832 people were sterilized, most of them women. Sterilizations of Métis and First Nations people account for a disproportionately high number of the total, an estimated 25 per cent (roughly 10 times their percentage of the total population). Not surprisingly, eastern Europeans (Ukrainians, Russians, etc.)—people whose English language skills and cultural capital were low—were also represented in high numbers in the sterilized group.

The province of British Columbia passed an act similar to Alberta's Sexual Sterilization Act in 1933, the same year that the notorious Law for the Prevention of Genetically Diseased Offspring was passed in Nazi Germany. Recently there have been accusations that, following both racial and religious prejudice, hundreds of non-Christian Aboriginal people were sterilized by a United Church missionary doctor in a church-run hospital in the BC coastal community of Bella Bella, and that a good number of young Aboriginal women made pregnant by residential school staff, clergy, and visiting officials were coerced into having abortions. While numbers are being contested in the courts, there seems little doubt that the practices did take place.

The Sixties Scoop

The UN's definition of genocide also includes attempts to destroy a people by forcibly transferring children of the group to another group. This characterizes what has been referred to as the **Sixties Scoop**, a program, which began in the

1960s, of removing large numbers of Aboriginal children from their families, their communities, and the Aboriginal world. Children could be taken from their families by government-affiliated agencies for a variety of reasons: some were children of parents judged to be alcoholics, some were newborns needing hospital care taken to the nearest city (and in many cases never returned), some were living in crowded or 'sub-standard' homes. In 1964, the number of children of all backgrounds removed from their families was 4,228; 1,446 of these—roughly 34 per cent—were Aboriginal children.

Between 1971 and 1981 in Manitoba, where Aboriginal families were hardest hit, over 3,400 Aboriginal children were removed from their homes. Many were taken from the province, and more than 1,000 of them were sent to the United States, where American child welfare agencies could get as much as $4,000 for each child placed. The province later launched an investigation into the practice, led by Justice Edwin Kimelman. In his summary of the investigation, *No Quiet Place* (1985), he stated:

> [C]ultural genocide has been taking place in a systematic routine manner. One gets an image of children stacked in foster homes as used cars are stacked on corner lots, just waiting for the right 'buyer' to stroll by. (in Fournier and Crey 1997: 88)

But statistics and judges' reports do not give a real sense of the suffering of those affected. The following statement comes from a research report on the emotional return of children to their families, communities, and people:

> I was sixteen years old when my daughter was taken from me. My partner at the time was drinking and at eighteen he went to prison. I had no way of looking after her and felt very alone. The social worker told me that my daughter would be better off with a 'nice, normal family'. I thought that I would at least be able to visit her sometimes, but she was placed in Pennsylvania and we did not meet her again until she was 20 years old. I took a bus to Windsor and that is where we

met. I was alone and scared. She looked just like me when I was twenty, but with a very different attitude. She had suffered sexual abuse in her adopted home and she blamed it on me. She had a little girl of her own, but she would not let me meet her. I wish there was someone who could help us get past this pain. (Budgell 1999: 6)

Summary

As we said at the outset, good families exist in many forms in Canada, and always have. They differ in terms of ethnicity, structure, size, qualifications for membership, and sexual orientation, and the model continues to change. Perhaps it is better to say that it is evolving, adapting to specific circumstances. From this standpoint, there is good reason to be optimistic about family in Canada.

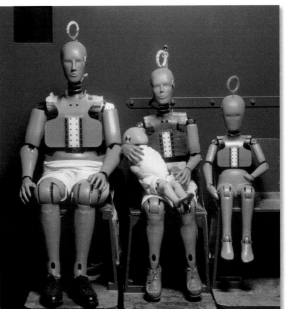

Having read the chapter, how would you define the Canadian family today?

Photo: Louie Psihoyos/Science Faction/Corbis

Questions for Critical Review

1. Describe the diversity of the Canadian family, both culturally and historically.
2. Describe how family in Quebec is different from family in the rest of Canada. Give some examples as well as possible explanations.
3. Outline eight major changes taking place in the Canadian family today.
4. Identify the different forms that conjugal roles can take.
5. Outline some of the measures used to place Canadian Aboriginal families 'under attack' during the twentieth century.

Suggested Readings

Duffy, Ann, Nancy Mandell, & Norene Pupo (1989). *Few Choices: Women, Work and the Family*. Toronto: Garamond Press.

Giddens, Anthony (1992). *The Transformation of Intimacy: Sexuality, Love and Eroticism in Modern Societies*. Stanford: Stanford UP.

Hunter, Mark, ed. (1997). *The Family Experience: A Reader in Cultural Diversity*, 2nd edn. Boston: Allyn and Bacon.

Lasch, Christopher (1997). *Women and the Common Life: Love, Marriage, and Feminism*. E. Lasch-Quinn, ed. New York: W. W. Norton Co.

Luxton, Meg, ed. (1997). *Feminism and Families: Critical Policies and Changing Practices*. Halifax: Fernwood.

Risman, Barbara J., & Pepper Schwartz (1989). *Gender in Intimate Relationships: A Microstructural Approach*. Belmont, CA: Wadsworth Publishing.

Suggested Websites

Guide to the Sociology of the Family (Michael Kearl)
www.trinity.edu/~mkearl/family.html

PFLAG (Parents and Friends of Lesbians and Gays)
http://pflag.ca

Vanier Institute of the Family
www.vifamily.ca/

Via-à-vis (National Newsletter on Family Violence)
www.ccsd.ca/viasvis.html

Key Terms

- Abrahamic religions
- age group
- agency
- aid evangelism
- androcentrism
- base communities
- Catholic-Traditionalist

- cohort
- collective consciousness
- ecofeminism
- essentialist
- false consciousness
- god = society
- haram

- herd morality
- Islamaphobia
- jihad
- jihad-i-akbar
- jihad-i-asghar
- liberation theology
- misogynistic

8

Religion

LEARNING OBJECTIVES

After reading this chapter, you should be able to

> outline Émile Durkheim's sociological approach to religion;

> discuss the relationship between organized religion and gender roles;

> talk about how the sociological profile of religion is changing in Canada;

> analyze the relationship between organized religion and family;

> describe the impact of religion on the lives of Hutterites in Canada; and

> describe the impact of Christian religious colonialism upon the Aboriginal people of Canada.

Photo: iStockphoto.com

FOR Starters

The Postmodern Altar: An Ethnography of the Church of Religious Science

Our **postmodern** world is a jigsaw puzzle in which old fashionably mixes with new and many different cultural traditions are brought together. What would a postmodern religion look like? Read on.

Mrs X was extremely flattered when I asked her if I could go to her church to do an ethnography for a sociology class. She picked me up one Sunday morning at 9:45 a.m., and we drove downtown through the silent streets and sleeping skyscrapers to the Alberta Theatre Project complex. We parked nearby and walked into the Max Bell Theatre, where I was greeted at the foot of the stairs with a smile, a program, and a song book. Across the top of my program it read, 'Calgary Center for Positive Living', and below it was a picture of two Koala bears hugging entitled, with the caption 'HUGS'. As I entered the lobby, I noticed people scurrying around to prepare coffee, set out books, line up CDs, organize the visitors table, and arrange various pamphlets for display on another table. Four long tables were stacked with various metaphysical and self-help books, with titles like *Your Thoughts Can Change Your Life*.

At 10:30 I entered the theatre to catch the pre-service Meditation. On the stage sat three female 'practitioners' (licensed by the church to do spiritual mind-prayer-treatment work) with their eyes closed, while soothing music rounded the painted marble pillars. Five minutes had passed and about 30 people had amassed for the Meditation before Reverend Carol Carnes came on stage. With her head slightly tipped down and her eyes closed, she began the Meditation:

> In the only way we can, through the conscious use of our own mind, and by allowing our attention to move to that inner knowing where the truth resides. That is the sacred place within us, the secret place of the most high. It is that essential self the core of our being, the heart of our heart, and the mind of our mind; it is a point of attention. From this point I speak this treatment outward. . . .

The Meditation goes through five steps:

1. It Is (spirit, or God)
2. Unification (I am that I am)
3. Desire (what you want)
4. Thanks (that you have already received)
5. Let It Go (release it).

It is designed as a general treatment for those who are receptive. The meditation lasted about 20 minutes and then, as quietly as she had entered, Reverend Carnes left the stage.

I went back to the lobby to find it bustling with a great many more bodies than when I had left. Like any church gathering, people were dressed up, and socializing. They made their last comments to each other as they shuffled toward the doors and into the theatre for the 11:00 service. I followed, and took my seat.

Reverend Carnes, a handsome, smartly dressed woman in her fifties, entered and greeted the congregation with a resounding 'Good Morning, Everyone,' which prompted a collective 'good morning' in return. She started the services with an opening affirmation:

> There is One Life . . . And that's the way it is!

We then opened our song books and began to sing, 'It's in Everyone of Us'. Later in the service, when we sang 'How Great Thou Art', (a traditional Christian hymn) Mrs X must have noticed a puzzled look on my face, for she whispered, 'We change some of the words.'

The 'lesson of the day', which was called 'Prosperity One, Two, Three', started with a riddle much like 'Is the glass half full or half empty?' Concluding the story, Reverend Carnes posed the question: 'Is there anyone here who wouldn't welcome a simple formula for being more prosperous?' Looking around at the 250 or so members in attendance, I suddenly noticed that an overwhelming majority were middle-aged women there on their own, many of whom, I found out later, were divorced. The Reverend continued to speak, addressing her own question: 'The answer to all our questions is in the universe.' She went on to describe the simple workings of the universe ('one plus one equals two'), noting that the universe was designed that way because life was meant to succeed, and that we are not separate from the power of life but are all prosperous beings by our nature.

The Reverend quoted the teachings of Dr Ernest Holmes (founder of Religious Science) for prosperous living: first, receive the gift; second, use the gift; third, extend the gift. During the service some took notes, while others chuckled at the humorous stories. Reverend Carnes continued her talk on material spiritualism, explaining that in a spiritual system, money is a symbol of a spiritual idea, the abundance of being, and that giving and participation are necessary to receive the gift. Money is a symbol of wealth: if we have a wealthy life, then we will receive the symbol of wealth, money; if we don't have prosperity, it's because we are denying our nature. Love, power, peace, vitality, intelligence, radiance, joy—all these components are necessary to becoming prosperous and having money. Our nature is to prosper; we must be in harmony with that nature and willing to change in order to be richer in all aspects of life. Reverend Carnes concluded the sermon with this advice: 'Receive the gift, utilize it, extend it, make prosperity your life right know—God has given us every good thing. . . . God has given us its *being*ness, and that is prosperity.' After the applause, the liturgy closed as it had begun, but this time with an affirmation of prosperity.

The church's postmodern eclecticism borrows from a range of influences, from Protestantism, Buddhism, and Jungian psychology to Utilitarianism, Sufism, and quasi-science, all of them coming together as a jigsaw-puzzle whole. If religious fundamentalism is a rejection of the postmodern, complicated world, then the Church of Religious Science is its embrace.

Introduction

In the introductory chapter, we spoke about Max Weber and the **Protestant (work) ethic**. It was based on the common Protestant belief that there was a predestined 'elect' who would be saved during the second coming of Christ; a person demonstrated that he or she belonged to this elect group by working hard and achieving material success. According to Weber, this religious/cultural influence spurred people to accumulate wealth, which was a key factor in the rise of capitalism. Another aspect of this Protestant belief was that a person who was predestined to be saved could do anything without fear of divine punishment, a theme explored by the Scottish novelist James Hogg in his eerie book *The Private Memoirs and Confessions of a Justified Sinner: Written by Himself. With a detail of curious traditionary facts and other evidence by the editor*; this book is said to have been the inspiration for Robert Louis Stevenson's *The Strange Case of Dr Jeckyll and Mr Hyde*. While the phrase 'Protestant work ethic' is still with us, its cultural and religious origins have been undermined by consumer society bent on immediate gratification.

According to Karl Marx , religion serves ruling-class interests by dissuading the working class from organizing around their own self-interests, which would challenge the inherent inequality of initially the feudal, and later the capitalist system. Marx used the term **false consciousness** to describe the belief that class-based hierarchy was justified on religious grounds (i.e. that is the way that God planned society to be), and that by simply toiling away, even under oppressive conditions, members of the lower class were really acting in the best interests of their class. They would be rewarded in the 'next life'. Yet as we will see in Chapter 11, religion in certain circumstances brings a kind of 'revolutionary possibility', exemplified in Canada by the **social gospel** movement and the progressive politics of people like J.S. Woodsworth and Tommy Douglas, who were both trained as ministers, but later were involved in the development of policies, such as socialized medicine, that improved the lives of working class people.

The Sociocultural Elements of Religion

One of the earliest sociological insights into religion came from the Greek philosopher Aristotle, who wrote:

All people say that the gods also had a king because they themselves had kings either formerly or now; for men create the gods after their own image, not only with regard to form, but also with regard to their manner of life. (*Politics* i.2.7)

In part, Aristotle was claiming that a society with a powerful king or emperor would likely have, in its religion, a commanding authority figure. In other words, if a society is less hierarchical, then there will also be a spiritual society of gods and spirits that is more egalitarian, in their relationships both with one another and with human beings. The language people use to describe human relationships is also used to describe their relationship with their god or gods. In this way, the gods we worship are a mirror, reflecting our own social conditions and our own cultural beliefs, values, and ideals.

You can see something of this insight by comparing the religious and social practices of the French Jesuit priests and the Huron (or Wendat) with whom they lived and did missionary work during the seventeenth century. The Jesuits had a powerful king and, likewise, an omnipotent God. The language they used when speaking of either political or spiritual figures was one of great respect, with frequent reference to commanding and obeying. By contrast, the Huron of the early seventeenth century were formed by an alliance of four member nations, or tribes. Each of the separate nations had a tribal leader who could recommend actions but not give orders. The word used to refer to the leader can be translated as 'we cause him to be a principle to imitate'—in essence, 'he who is our role model'. There were no words that meant 'order' or 'command'. As for religion, the Huron recognized a series of spiritual figures, including Yaatayentsik, the first woman on earth who fell from the sky, and her twin grandsons, Ioskeha and Tawiskaron, who transformed the earth, which was built on the shell of the Great Turtle. These and other spirits did not *command* people; rather, they *inspired* them in visions or plagued them with curses. This isn't meant to suggest that the Huron or other societies without strong political hierarchy had no sense of a creator or god above all other gods. It simply means that the relationship between people and spirits was more in line with the relatively egalitarian relationships between humans.

Of course, by the late nineteenth century, this idea of the link between social and spiritual relationships became set in a **social Darwinist**, or evolutionary, model. According to this model, the

The Jesuit missionary St Francis Xavier baptizes a Native North American. Is the missionizing work of the conversion of 'pagans' ethnocentric by its very definition?

'primitive' people had pesky spirits; 'barbarians' had nasty but ultimately impotent gods. Only 'civilized' people had a Supreme Ruler. Herbert Spencer, the early sociologist who coined the expression **survival of the fittest**, articulated such a position.

● ● ● ● ● ● ● ● ● ● ● ● ● ● ● ● ● ●

What do YOU think?

How do you think a social Darwinist would have characterized the gods and level of civilization of the seventeenth-century Huron? How might that kind of characterization have affected the relationship between Native people and mainstream Canadians?

● ● ● ● ● ● ● ● ● ● ● ● ● ● ● ● ● ●

Photo: The Art Archive/Alamy

Émile Durkheim: The Elementary Forms of the Religious Life

Despite the fact that he was not a particularly religious man, **Émile Durkheim** (1858–1917) has had a profound effect on how sociologists view religion. Although his father and grandfather were both rabbis, he felt no religious call himself. His great work in the area of religion is *Les Formes élémentaires de la vie religieuse: Le système totémique en Australie*, published in 1912. In 1915, two years before Durkheim died, it appeared in English as *The Elementary Forms of the Religious Life*. He was a believer in *la science positive*, which can be translated a little too easily as 'positive science' but is better interpreted as 'empirical science': a type of study based on data that may be concretely perceived. Durkheim is famous for having taken sociology into areas where at first glance it did not belong, areas such as suicide—surely the realm of psychology—and religion—certainly the realm of theology. Both suicide and religion were seen as being firmly rooted in the individual, not in the group or society, and there was strong resistance to his ideas by people studying religion at the time. According to Karen Fields, the French sociologist Raymond Aron 'described the immediate reaction to [Durkheim's work] in France as *violent*' (1995: xxii).

Durkheim's aim was to identify and examine the basic elements of religion. He believed he could do this by studying the religion of the most fundamental, most basic society then being discussed in the ethnographic literature: the Aborigines of Australia. Through this study he hoped to develop a sociological model of religion that would apply to all religions.

What Is Religion?

Here is how Durkheim defined religion:

> A religion is a unified system of beliefs and practices relative to sacred things, that is to say, things set apart and forbidden—beliefs and practices which unite into one single moral community called a Church, all those who adhere to them. (Durkheim 1995: 44)

As Fields puts it, Durkheim's view was that 'religion is social, social, social' (Fields 1995: xxxiv). In his use of the term **moral community**, the word 'moral' 'specifies that the groups are . . . made up of individuals who have mutually recognized and recognizable identities that set them, cognitively and normatively, on shared human terrain' (Fields 1995: xxxiv). It's clear from this why he deviated from his contemporaries, who considered religion as experienced by the individual rather than the larger community. We examine Durkheim's ideas on religion in more detail in the sections that follow.

Three Key Elements of Religion

There are three key elements in Durkheim's analysis of religion. The first is the well-known but often misinterpreted equation: **god = society**. Durkheim formulated this idea in the context of the totems of the Australian Aborigines, so to understand what Durkheim might have meant by god = society, we should begin by looking at the word 'totem' itself.

Totem is a word that came into English in the late eighteenth century from the Ojibwa language of the Anishinabe people living in Quebec, Ontario, Manitoba, Saskatchewan, and BC, and the northern border states of Michigan and Minnesota. In Ojibwa the word means 'clan', and it's used to

The images here are culturally stylized versions of the totem animals of clans (e.g. killer whale and raven) of the artist's First Nation. Remember that the expression 'bottom of the totem pole' is an English expression that probably has little to do with Aboriginal culture.

Photo: Chris Cheadle/All Canada Photos

identify an organization of peoples as diverse as Scots, Somalis, and the Seneca. In contemporary usage, when Anishinabe people introduce themselves in formal situations, they often follow the statement of their name by saying something such as *waawaashkesh ndotem*, 'deer is my clan.' In this way, they are telling something about their identity and who they are. Edward Benton-Banai, a respected Anishnabe fish clan member elder and the author of *The Mishomis Book: The Voice of the Ojibway*, identified seven original clans of the Anishnabe people. In the book, he explains that traditionally each clan was associated with a specific function and certain ideal characteristics of the people belonging to the clan, characteristics that connect with the totem animal:

Crane and Loon Clans	chieftainship, leadership
Fish Clan	settling disputes, meditation, philosophy
Bear Clan	protecting the community, medicinal plants
Marten Clan	warriors, war strategists
Deer Clan	poets
Bird Clan	spiritual leaders (Benton-Banai 1988: 75–7)

If you're familiar with the word 'totem' from the idea of 'totem poles' (which are found in British Columbia among First Nations other than the Anishinabe), you can appreciate how the carved structures represent different clans of the village where they were erected by displaying the animals associated with them.

Having some sense, then, of what totem means, we can look at Durkheim's famous explanation of the god = society equation:

[The totem] . . . symbolizes two different . . . things. [I]t is the outward and visible form of . . . the totemic principle or god; and . . . it is also the symbol of a particular society that is called the clan. It is . . . the sign by which each clan is distinguished from the others, the visible mark of its distinctiveness, and a mark that is borne by everything that in any way belongs to the clan: men, animals, and things. *Thus if the totem is the symbol of both the god and the society, is this not because the god and the society are one and the same?* How could the emblem of the group have taken the form of that quasi-divinity if the group and the divinity were two distinct realities? Thus the god of the clan, the totemic principle, can be none other than the clan itself, but the clan transfigured and imagined in the physical form of the plant or animal that serves as totem. (Durkheim 1995: 208)

In other words, cultures and societies fashion deities represented as having characteristics like the people themselves; these characteristics are then projected back onto both the culture and individuals.

Collective Consciousness and the Sacred and Profane

Durkheim in his analysis focused primarily on the collective or group experiences and rituals of people belonging to a particular religion; these sacred experiences foster what Durkheim called

Photo: Israel Images/Alamy

Muslims pray at the Noble Sanctuary in Jerusalem during Ramadan. How do you think prayer generates a sense of collective consciousness?

a **collective consciousness**. In Muslim countries, the cry of the Muzzin (the religious caller) over the loudspeaker calling the faithful to early morning prayer, followed by the collective deep bowing of people who are similarly dressed, is a very compelling example of collective religious experience.

Durkheim distinguished between objects and acts that are **sacred** and those that are **profane**. Sacred objects and acts are set apart from more ordinary (profane) ones as being positively regarded, holy, and therefore deserving of reverence or respect. Sacred objects include prayer beads, crosses, flags, and items in the medicine bundle of an Aboriginal shaman; sacred acts include prayer and keeping kosher. But Durkheim used the term 'sacred' also for those objects and acts that are forbidden or tabooed. The Arabic term used in Islam, **haram**, applies here. In Canadian

The Point Is... Religion and 'Football'

In Scotland there is a long history of religious conflict between Catholics and Protestants. This has not had the explosive violence of the same conflict in Ireland and Northern Ireland, but it certainly exists, and has since the mid-nineteenth century, when many Irish Catholics came to Scotland because of the starvation brought on by the potato famine.

One arena in which the animosity is apparent is that of football (or soccer, if you prefer). Two of the dominant teams in Scotland are Rangers and Celtic, both based in Glasgow. Rangers is the Protestant team. In the early 1980s, when I lived in Scotland, there was an unwritten rule that no Catholic would play for Rangers. I say 'unwritten', but the rule was widely recognized. I remember, for instance, a comedy routine of the time (by Rikki Fulton) in which a new team executive had foolishly signed a Catholic to the team; the comedian was acting out the part of the coach who was trying to change the player's mind, saying things like 'You really don't look good in blue [the Rangers' team colour]'. It wasn't until 1989 that an openly Catholic, former Celtic player was signed by Rangers.

Celtic (wearing green and white) are the Catholic team. Although they could and did have Protestants on the team, these players were considered traitors by Rangers fans. When you went into a pub in Glasgow, you looked for football pictures on the walls so you knew which team the locals supported, which side to discuss in conversations with strangers.

In Edinburgh, where I lived, the Protestant team was Hearts (short for Heart of Midlothian, a novel by Sir Walter Scott), and the Catholic team was Hibs (short for Hibernia). My then brother-in-law was Catholic and therefore a Hibs fan. I was a Hearts fan, not for religious reasons (I'm not that

religious), but because I liked the idea, as a writer, that a team was named after a book. We never watched football together.

The religious tensions were displayed in bridge graffiti, where you could see 'Rangers Rule' spray-painted alongside 'F**k the Pope.' Fans, whether at the games or in the pubs, glorified their team with sectarian songs, like 'The Billy Boys' (a reference to the Protestant William of Orange, whose defeat of the Catholic James in 1690 made him king of Britain)—that song was banned in 2002. There was also the 'Famine Song', (which included the line 'The famine is over. Why don't you go home?'). The away colour (or stripe) of the Rangers fans was orange (as in William of Orange), but has recently been changed to something less likely to start fights. However it's worth asking whether overt changes, like the banning of provocative songs, can really erase or even minimize the underlying animosity rooted in religious differences.

● ● ● ● ● ● ● ● ● ● ● ● ● ● ● ● ● ● ● ●

What do YOU think?

1. Sports rivalries exist among many teams— Oilers and Flames, Red Sox and Yankees, Ti-Cats and Argos. Do you think that, today, religion is really the cause of the animosity between fans of Rangers and Celtic animosity, or is it just a pretext for a sports rivalry?

2. In what other sports—at the local, national, professional, or amateur level—are religious 'proxy wars' carried out? (Think, for instance, of international sports such as cricket.)

3. In what other areas of life are there religious wars by proxy?

● ● ● ● ● ● ● ● ● ● ● ● ● ● ● ● ● ● ● ●

writer Haroon Siddiqui's *Being Muslim*, he lists the following prohibited objects and practices:

Haram Foods: Pork and its byproducts, carnivorous animals (those that tear their food apart with claws, such as lions), almost all reptiles and insects, animals that died before being properly slaughtered, blood, and all alcoholic or intoxicating drinks.

Haram Lifestyle: Gambling, including lotteries; all drugs that cause intoxication, alter sensory perception (hallucinogens) or affect one's ability to reason and make sound judgments; and paying and accepting interest. (Siddiqui 2006: 80)

Durkheim argued that objects were not sacred by nature, but acquired the status of 'sacred' as they were either set apart or forbidden by social groups.

What do YOU think?

Consider the totemic principle equating god and society. Do you think this is the same as the connection of the cross, Christ, and Christians?

Photo: Chris Pole/iStockphoto

Photo: Jeremy Richards/iStockphoto

The Kandariya Mahadeva temple, a Hindu holy site in Madhya Pradesh, India. Close inspection reveals its erotic reliefs. Sacred or profane?

Canadian Society and Religion

The last year that questions about religion were asked in the Canadian census was 2001 (20% sample). Table 8.1 summarizes some of the data from that census.

Trends in the Data

The trends in the data worth noting in particular are the categories that show the greatest increase and decrease. Those with the largest increases in percentage are Pagan (281.2 per cent), Muslim (128.9), 'Christian not included' (121.1), Serbian Orthodox (109.5), Hindu (89.3), Sikh (88.8), and Buddhist (83.8). There are several points to observe. First, Canada is not 'going Pagan', although Wicca, the largest group that can and has been called 'Neopagan', is growing. Even though that category has the highest percentage increase, the respondents giving that answer are going from a low number to another low number. That is one reason why a good sociologist—professional or student—does not go by percentage alone when looking at change. The raw numbers themselves are also important. Immigration from countries in South Asia is a major factor in the increase of Muslims (primarily from Pakistan), Hindus, and Sikhs. War refugees have increased the numbers for some religions, notably Serbian Orthodox (from the former Yugoslavia) and Islam (from Somalia). The growth of Canada's Tibetan population, owing to the oppression of Tibetans by the Chinese government, has caused the Buddhist number of increase. (Westerners have also been 'discovering' Buddhism recently.) The 'Christian non included' numbers rose in part because of people from the West Indies joining local independent churches in relatively large numbers.

The decreases in percentage are also important sociologically. One important correlation to observe is that between median age and decrease in percentage. It also relates to lack of immigration The Presbyterians have the highest median age and the highest decrease in percentage. Presbyterianism is a long-established religion in Canada, one connected with Scotland, which is no longer a major source of Canadian immigration. The

decrease would be even sharper were it not for immigration from Korea, which for decades was a major centre of Presbyterian missionary work. The Anglican Church falls in the same category: an old religion in Canada, connected with Britain, another area of decreased immigration. But here is the other half of the 'check the raw numbers as well as the percentage' factor: as the category with the third highest number, a small loss in percentage brings with it a fairly large loss in terms of absolute numbers.

Age Group versus Cohort

Statistical studies consistently demonstrate that young people (teens and those in their early twenties) are less religious (whatever operational definition is applied) than are older people. The danger with looking at a study like this in isolation is that we may take it to mean that overall levels of participation in religion are falling, that as these young people age, there will be fewer and fewer religious people in Canada. The mistake here is seeing an **age group** difference (i.e. a consistent difference between old and young) and assuming that it is a **cohort** difference (i.e. a difference between people born in two different periods). Young people may not attend church because they are too busy with schoolwork and social activities. They may reject religion if they feel it has been forced upon them by parents and other members of the older generation. However, they may very well take up religion later in life— for instance, when they reach marrying age and decide to have a church wedding, or when they become older still and turn to a local church as a way to become more involved in the community, either through charity work or one of the many social clubs typically situated in churches.

Old and Established Churches

Canadian census data for 2001 includes, in addition to the breakdown of the population by religion presented in Table 8.1, figures showing the median age for each religious group and the change in number of followers (by percentage) since 1991. By combining the two numbers we can verify that the religious groups with the highest median ages are also those that are dropping

Table 8.1 Population by religion, 2001

		PERCENTAGE	CHANGE FROM 1991	MEDIAN AGE
Total Population	29,639,030	100.0%	9.8%	37.3
No Religion	4,900,090	16.2	43.9	31.1
Pagan	21,080	0.1	281.2	30.4
Roman Catholic	12,639,035	43.2	4.8	37.8
Protestant	8,654,850			
United Church	2,839,125	9.6	−8.2	44.1
Anglican	2,035,500	6.9	−7.0	43.8
Christian Non-Included	780,450	2.6	121.1	30.2
Baptist	729,470	2.5	10.0	39.3
Lutheran	606,590	2.0	−4.7	43.3
Protestant Not Elsewhere	549,205	1.9	−12.7	40.4
Presbyterian	409,830	1.4	−35.6	46.0
Pentecostal	369,475	1.2	−15.3	33.5
Mennonite	215,175	0.6	−7.9	32.0
Jehovah's Witnesses	154,750	0.5	−8.1	38.7
Mormons	101,805	0.3	8.4	28.7
Salvation Army	87,790	0.3	−21.9	39.3
Christian Reformed Church	76,670	0.3	−9.5	32.3
Adventist	62,880	0.2	20.1	35.5
Hutterite	26,295	0.1	22.3	22.2
Methodist	25,730	0.1	6.1	43.9
Brethren in Christ	20,590	0.1	−22.0	38.2
Christian Orthodox	479,620			
Greek Orthodox	215,175	0.7	−7.1	40.7
Orthodox Not Included	165,420	0.6	79.9	35.4
Ukrainian Orthodox	32,720	0.1	−5.1	45.8
Serbian Orthodox	20,520	0.1	109.5	34.8
Ukrainian Catholic	126,200	0.4	−1.7	45.0
Muslim	579,640	2.0	128.9	28.1
Jewish	329,955	1.1	3.7	41.5
Buddhist	300,345	1.0	83.8	38.0
Hindu	297,200	1.0	89.3	31.9
Sikh	278,410	0.9	88.8	29.7

Source: StatsCan.

the fastest in numbers, and that the religious groups with the lowest median ages are those that are growing the fastest in numbers. Among the former group are the long-established Protestant churches that, despite their declining participation rates, continue to have the highest overall numbers; examples include the United, Anglican, Lutheran, and Presbyterian churches. An interesting exception to this trend is the Baptist Church, which has a long history in Canada and a relatively high median age (39.3), but which experienced a 10 per cent increase in followers between 1991 and 2001. These gains occurred not in those provinces where the median age of Baptists was higher—Newfoundland and Labrador, where the median age of Baptists is 39.7, actually experienced a 10 per cent decline—but in the provinces where the median age is lower, especially Quebec (median age 33.1), which saw a 28.9 per cent jump in Baptist following between 1991 and 2001. Similar increases occurred in Manitoba and Alberta as well. Only British Columbia bucks the trend of a lower median age of Baptists translating into growing participation rates.

Based on these statistics, you might guess what is happening. The 'Christian not included elsewhere' group is relatively young (median age 28.2) and growing rapidly (156.9 per cent). It includes evangelical and fundamentalist Christian groups. Some Baptist groups call themselves evangelical or fundamentalist, so they may be gaining in numbers and, as a result, lowering the median age.

● ● ● ● ● ● ● ● ● ● ● ● ● ● ● ● ● ● ● ●

What do YOU think?

1. Why do you think younger people are turning to less established Christian denominations?

2. Why else do you think people might identify themselves as 'Christian not included elsewhere'?

● ● ● ● ● ● ● ● ● ● ● ● ● ● ● ● ● ● ● ●

Religion and the Family

Religion and the Marginalized Family

Religion is discussed in the context of 'family values.' Indeed, if we revisited Merton's three kinds of functions (introduced in Chapter 1), we might be tempted to identify 'strengthening the family' as a manifest (i.e. intended and recognized) or at least a latent (i.e. largely unintended and unrecognized) positive function of religion. Yet throughout history, family and religion have been set in opposition to each other, particularly in situations where officials representing the State (and, typically, organized religion) have deemed a family situation bad or harmful. Normally these situations involve families belonging to cultures other than European. The destruction of family then becomes a latent *dys*function of religion.

A case in point is the story of Kateri Tegakwitha, who stands to become the first Aboriginal saint. She is a significant figure in the religious history of Canada and a powerful role model for Aboriginal

Photo: Mary Evans Picture Library/Alamy

How does this artist's rendering of Kateri Tegakwitha idealize the life of a Native convert to Christianity? Consider in this regard that she had suffered from smallpox as a young child, and the marks left on her face were permanent.

Catholic women and girls in North America. One eighteenth-century historian called her a Canadian Joan of Arc, and Leonard Cohen made her the central figure of his most important novel, *Beautiful Losers*, about a man obsessed with her life.

Kateri Tegakwitha was born in 1656 to an Algonquin mother and Mohawk father. She died in 1680 at the age of 24, the victim of a weak constitution after surviving smallpox as a small child. A convert to Christianity, she regularly subjected herself to the religiously motivated discipline of whipping herself until she bled, and shortly before her death, she lay in a bed of thorns, repeating the practice of an early Christian martyr who had done so.

She was raised by her uncle—the brother of her father, whom, following traditional Mohawk cultural custom, she would have called *rakeniha*, 'my father'—and his sister. Traditional Christian accounts paint him as a villain, though little is known about him; it is typical, in the Christian literature, for the 'badness' of Kateri's family and culture to be used to highlight her 'goodness'. Jesuit missionaries first visited her community in 1667, in accordance with a peace treaty imposed after French troops attacked the village in 1666. In 1676, Kateri was baptized in a ceremony described by a Jesuit writer of the time as a form of adoption into a lineage that would exist in heaven (Steckley 1999: 39). The Jesuit missionaries strongly believed that religion was more important than family, and this belief set up a conflict that divided many children from their parents. As she became a young woman, Kateri was pressed by her family to get married. She refused, however, having been taught the symbolic value of virginity by the missionaries. At the age of 21, she rejected her family and community and ran away from home to the recently established Christian Iroquois community of Ganawage, near Montreal, which was run by Jesuits. She was encouraged and aided by Iroquoian Christians from Ganawage, who considered her 300-kilometre trek from family and home an 'escape'.

The story of Kateri Tegakwitha is but one of many examples of how religion was used to sever Aboriginal family ties. We have seen, earlier in the textbook, accounts of how during the twentieth century church-run residential schools separated children from their families, removing them from the culture-carrying influence of parents:

> Children were taken from the parents and extended families for periods of time that often lasted the whole school year, even when the residential schools were located in the students' own communities. Parental visits, when they were permitted, were typically closely monitored in a special 'visiting room'. Brothers and sisters were often kept apart in strict sexual separation, sometimes meaning that the children could only communicate with each other by waving from one building to another or through secretly arranged meetings. (Steckley and Cummins 2008: 194)

Residential schools had a strong detrimental effect on Aboriginal parenting skills. Raised under the strict and often abusive authority of underpaid, underqualified, and poorly screened teachers and administrators, whom historian J.R. Miller describes as the 'devoted and the deviant' (1996: 321), three generations of Aboriginal parents had only these harsh role models on which to base their own parenting techniques.

Imports from Britain

It would be easy to assume, based on these accounts, that the attack of religion on the marginalized Aboriginal family flows exclusively from the ethnocentrism and racism of the bearers of the religion. These are definitely factors. However, practices like the establishment of residential schools were not based exclusively on racialized differences. In her 1995 book *Empty Cradles*, British social worker **Margaret Humphreys** describes how thousands of British children—the vast majority of them born to parents who were either poor or socially marginalized as single parents—were shipped to Australia to live in church-run orphanages. While it would be misleading to deny that any of these children benefited, it is true that the children, many of whom had been living in orphanages in Britain, were often told that their parents were dead, and were subjected to the same degree of hard labour and abuse that Aboriginal children experienced in Canadian residential schools. The following testimonial comes from a woman who was shipped out to Perth in Western Australia when she was just eight:

> Do you think I've got any family? Cousins, anybody. I'm not fussy. Anybody. They told me that my parents were dead. Do you think that's true? . . . I don't know anything about myself. Until I married, I didn't even have a birth certificate. I felt ashamed. . . . What did we do wrong? . . . Can you find out why they sent me? What did I do wrong? . . . (Humphreys 1995: 14)

Humphreys collected a story of a five-year-old girl who had long, curly, blonde hair when she entered the Australian Catholic orphanage named Goodwood:

> After being at Goodwood a few days, she packed all her possessions in a bag and ran down the drive in her nightie. The nuns followed her and dragged her back. The next morning, all the girls were made to line up in the year and watch her being punished. . . . Two of the nuns held the little girl down, while another started cutting off her hair with garden shears.
>
> Her struggles and cries went unheard. When they had finished, there was just an inch or two of hair left on her head. 'God wants her punished more than that,' one of the nuns said, and she produced a pair of secaturs [small pruning shears]. She started cutting again and didn't stop until the young girl's hair was gone completely and her scalp was bloody with cuts. (Humphreys 1995: 125)

In looking at the treatment of English orphans and North American Aboriginal children, we can see several common themes that characterize this discontinuity between religion and family:

- the marginalized (in terms of race, class, and even sexual behaviour) backgrounds of the families from which the children were taken
- the statistically deviant choice made by religious workers such as missionaries, priests,

and nuns to opt for 'religious life' over 'normal' family life in their own society
- the strict hierarchical nature of religion operating in institutions such as religious orders, residential schools, and church-run orphanages
- the strict codes of discipline that are associated with religious-based institutions
- the ease with which religious concepts such as 'sin' can be associated with negative judgment and used to justify harsh punishment.

Hutterites: Religion and Family

The preceding sections illustrate some of the situations in which religion and family come into conflict, with damaging results. In contrast to these accounts is the strong positive connection between religion and family found in the Hutterite communities in Canada. The Hutterites are the religious group with the youngest median age (22.2). Children aged 0–14 make up 37 per cent of their population, while young people aged 0–24 make up 54 per cent—well over half—of their total population. Their fertility rate, even though it has declined somewhat in recent decades, approaches the maximum fertility rate possible for a single community and is famous in the sociological literature (see, for instance, Nonaka, Miura, and Peter 1994). The high fertility rate is attributed to several sociology factors, including the following:

- cultural norms opposing contraception
- farming as the main industry, requiring a large population of strong, young farmhands
- the practice of communal living, which ensures that childcare, a shared responsibility, is always available.

We must also consider that it is when young people are aged 19–25 that they must decide whether or not to become baptized as full members of the community, a decision that involves a very critical testing of the individual (Kirkby 2007: 184). Young adults in their mid-twenties electing to leave the fold could keep the median age down.

Hutterite boys on a farm in Alberta. More than a third of Canadian Hutterites are below the age of 15. Do you think this means their population is on the rise?

Photo: Tyler Olson/Alamy

The Hutterites are named after Jacob Hutter, who was the leader of a radical Christian movement during the 1520s and 1530s. Along with Mennonites, they were part of the Anabaptist ('rebaptizers') religious movement. What made them radicals? For one, they opposed the class linkages between the established Church, the state, and the rich. They were also pacifists, who adhered strictly to commandment, 'Thou shalt not kill.' As Anabaptists, they believed that people should be baptized as adults, when they're old enough to make a mature choice, not as infants. This was against the rules of the Catholic Church, and therefore against the law in Austria, where the Hutterites first formed. Hutter was tortured and killed for his ideas.

The Hutterites were driven, because of their radical beliefs, from one European country to the next until they eventually emigrated from Orthodox Russia to the United States during the 1870s. In 1889, the Canadian government, wanting sturdy farmers to exploit the agricultural potential of the Prairie West, offered them exemption from military service if they moved to Canada. During the First World War, many Hutterite communities, fearing persecution in the US, moved from the American Plains to the Canadian Prairies.

The social organization of the Hutterites involves three communal groups (called 'Leuts', meaning 'people'): Lehrerleut, Dariusleut, and Schmiedeleut. Each forms a moral community in Durkheim's sense. In Canada, the Lehrerleut and Dariusleut are found mainly in Alberta, Saskatchewan, and BC, while the Schmiedeleut are in Manitoba. The differences between them are slight, a measure of how conservative or liberal each is. In **Mary-Ann Kirkby**'s *I Am Hutterite* (2007), she lists some of the differences in the following, somewhat amusing, way:

The cultural and religious differences between the three groups were minor, confined more to dress code than religious principles. To an outsider the discrepancies would hardly be discernible, but to the Hutterites they were so significant that intermarriage between the groups was rare. The

Dariusleut in Saskatchewan were committed to simple buttons on their shirts and jackets, but the Schmiedeleut in Manitoba considered buttons too flashy and opted for invisible hooks, eyes, and snaps. The Lehrerleut were the most conservative, insisting the zipper of a man's pants be at the side rather than the front, in case some unmindful man forgot to zip up. All three groups did agree on one thing; pockets on the back of a man's pants were far too worldly. Store-bought pants with 'ass pockets' were strictly off limits. (2007: 5)

The three groups exist among roughly 300 farming colonies in Canada, each comprising 60 to 150 people who share a 'community of goods', except

Telling It Like It Is

The Minister's Role in a Hutterite Community

AN EXPERT POV

POINT OF VIEW

The following passage comes from a study of the Hutterite community of Pincher Creek, Alberta, published by historian David Flint in 1975.

Hutterites look to their religion when making both small decisions, such as how to dress, and large ones, such as the election of their minister, who is the single most important member of the community. Not only does he attend to the spiritual needs of the colony, but his advice is often asked on everything from when the pigs should be marketed to the price that should be charged for eggs. He is the colony leader, and his election is the most vital decision the colony makes in affecting its future nature. . . .

Hutterites expect the minister, even though he has been closely identified with them all their lives, to set standards and demand conformity, and to guard the traditions and values of their religion, and they readily obey him. If the minister is easy-going about slight deviations in dress, the colony will reflect his attitude. On one new colony there was not yet a minister in residence. Dress became sloppy—women went around in summer without kerchiefs and shoes and socks. When asked about this, one embarrassed man replied, 'When the cat's away, the mice will play.' He admitted that there was laxity and confessed that this would change when the minister arrived. . . .

In the week-by-week, year-by-year operation of the colony, group consensus and Sunday-evening meetings play a vital role in maintaining solidarity and discipline. It is an accepted practice to bring pressure to bear on those adults who do not conform to the will of the community. It is considered ethical and necessary to report an individual's misdoings to the colony meeting, and this is accepted for the common good and in recognition of the weakness of human nature. Usually the minister will first caution any person who is stretching the colony regulations too far—for instance by showing too much interest in photographs or pictures (considered to be vain), by being overly concerned with one's flower garden (over-watering taxes the limited water supply), or by frequent outbursts of anger. If change is not evident in the person's behaviour, then the preacher and the elders will decide on a punishment. The commonly accepted practice is to have the guilty party stand during church service, or kneel in front of the entire congregation and confess guilt, or sit with the children. . . . In cases of minor transgressions against colony rules, the minister, as the elected official responsible for maintaining colony discipline, needs deep human understanding to know when and where to draw the line.

Source: David Flint (1975), *The Hutterites: A Study in Prejudice* (Toronto: Oxford).

for small personal possessions. During their years in Canada, they have frequently encountered opposition to their communal farming practices from other farmers and, in the past, from provincial governments as well. The Hutterite system gave them several advantages over single-family farms, like those of contemporary 'factory farms'. By pooling their resources, they could amass greater funds for equipment and supplies, and secure large contracts for their agricultural products, supplied by a large, well-trained, and comparatively cheap workforce.

Other characteristics separate the Hutterites from the general population. The primary language of the community is an Austrian dialect of German, which is taught in schools along with a more useful and widely used form of High German and English. They live an austere and conservative lifestyle. They wear dark clothing—black headscarves with white polka dots, long-sleeved blouses and dresses, and long skirts (never pants) for the women. They are not permitted televisions, radios, snowmobiles (for recreational rather than work use), jewellery, makeup, dancing, or swimming (nakedness here is an issue). Each colony has its own school on colony land. They have a strong sense of spiritual superiority over the mainstream that appears in such phrases as the following, posted on churches: 'Whoever cannot give up his private property as well as his own self will cannot become a disciple and follower of Christ. The ungodly go each their own egotistical way of greed and profit. To such we should not be conformed' (Kirkby 2007: 5).

Religion and Gender

Organized world religions are characterized by patriarchal power structures; as a result, women tend to have subordinate roles that marginalize their participation. During the **second wave** of feminism in the 1960s and early 1970s, women in North America and western Europe became increasingly critical of Christianity and Christian practices. They viewed Christianity's imbedded patriarchy as an influential cultural factor in the reproduction of gender inequality. Consider, they said, just a few examples from the Bible:

- 'Man' was created in God's image, while 'woman' was created from spare parts (a rib, we are told) to be his companion (Male and female humans have the same number of ribs).
- The first woman, Eve, is blamed for having all humans banished from the paradise Eden after she succumbed to temptation by eating an apple supplied to her by the devil.
- The most memorable female characters in the Bible—those whose names are recognized even by non-Christians—are associated with sin and destruction; among them are Mary Magdalene, who is customarily identified as a prostitute; Delilah, who brought about Samson's downfall; and Jezebel, who was denounced for introducing the worship of rival gods into Israel, and whose name is synonymous with immorality.

Add to these points the Christian tradition of a wife's obedience, subservience, and even belonging to her husband, and you have some powerful examples that inform, transmit, and reproduce patriarchal structures of inequality, including **androcentrism** (from *andro* meaning 'man') and sexism. This same patriarchal inequality is blamed for numerous instances of women's oppression in society, from the denial of voting privileges and work opportunities to sexual objectification and male violence. In this sense, Christianity—in fact, all **Abrahamic religions** (including Islam and Judaism)—has much to answer for from a feminist perspective.

Gender Construction among the Hutterites

Mary-Ann Kirkby's *I Am Hutterite* (2007) gives a good sense of what it was like to be a young girl growing up as a Hutterite in the 1960s. As in other strong religious societies, gender roles were (and continue to be) clearly delimited. Girls and women cook, sew, and take care of children and aging elders. Girls between the ages of 11 and 14 may be chosen by a new mother to take on the role of *Luckela* ('baby holder') for the first year of the child's life. It is a society in which the 'community raises a child', though 'community' in this case

In the Buddhist tradition, Mara is a demon who attempts to seduce Buddha with visions of beautiful women; here the demon is subdued by Buddha. Why do you think the theme of women trying to tempt or seduce gods runs through so many ancient religions?

Photo: Historical Picture Archive/Corbis

means 'female community'. If a woman in her prime childbearing years is pregnant and finds the care of her toddler difficult, that child can be shared out for a while to another mother in the community.

Boys and men, meanwhile, learn their traditional roles of raising crops, managing livestock, running and repairing engines, and exercising primary decision-making for the colony. The colony is led by a male Head Minister, who guides the *Stübel*, or men's meeting, to make community decisions. The connection between male authority and strong religion, aided by the absence of alternative models of authority from mainstream society, can foster dictatorial patriarchal power. Kirkby describes how such power was exercised in her colony:

> In spiritual terms, [the Head Minister] . . . was 'shepherd of the flock', providing doctrinal guidance, administering discipline, and settling disagreements. He was . . . involved in every aspect of community life. No purchase was made without his knowledge or the approval of the council which he headed. . . .
>
> If you were out of favour with him, he had the authority to prevent you from leaving the colony to go to the doctor, to town on business, or for a Sunday visit. [His] . . . sweeping powers were enough to keep most of the men in line and agreeable, but his political manoeuvrings did not impress my father. He often found himself . . . at odds with [the minister's] . . . tactics. (Kirkby 2007: 62–3)

Women Priests in the Anglican Church

The Church of England (otherwise known as the Anglican Church or, in the US, the Episcopal Church) is the largest Protestant denomination in the world, with an estimated membership of between 76 and 84 million. Over the past half-century the battle for women to take on the orders of deacons, priests, and bishops has been long, hard, and accompanied by very emotional dialogue that has at times seriously divided the Church. Of the 38 individual provinces that make up the Anglican Church, the first two to be permitted to ordain female priests were the United States and Canada, in 1976. In Canada, on 30 November 1976, six women were ordained almost simultaneously (so that no one would be considered the first), in four different dioceses.

The situation in the United States is not as clear. While the General Convention has passed a resolution stating that 'no one shall be denied access' of ordination into the three orders (deacons, priests, bishops) on the basis of their sex, another resolution protects bishops who oppose women priests in their dioceses. As late as 2004, there were still three (of one hundred) dioceses whose bishops would not allow the ordination of women. One opposed bishop, Bishop Jack Iker, of Fort Worth, Texas, expresses his resistance in the following question:

> Are we a culturally conditioned church, trying to keep up with the times, and changing practices and teachings to conform with the times, or are we a part of the historic biblical church of the ages? (Iker 2003)

It wasn't until 1998, when the Japanese province voted to ordain women priests, that most Anglican provinces accepted female clergy. The 'mother church' in England began permitting ordination of women only in 1993, four years after the first female bishop was ordained, in New Zealand. The first women to become an Anglican bishop in Canada was Victoria Matthews, who was ordained in her Edmonton diocese in 1994. She had been made a deacon in 1979 and a priest the next year.

The thirteenth Lambeth Conference, a convention of Anglican bishops worldwide held every ten years, was attended by 11 women bishops, all of whom had been ordained as priests between 1978 and 1984. In the words of Louie Crew, a powerful champion of acceptance within the US Episcopal Church:

> Nearly all can tell tales of painful marginalization, even, in a few cases, of being spat upon, shouted at, verbally abused. . . . With each bishop, however, such tales are told only rarely and then reluctantly, and usually, only to illustrate how much progress has been made. (Louie Crew)

As of the beginning of 2009, only fourteen Anglican provinces allowed the ordination of women bishops, with just four—Canada, the US, Australia, and New Zealand/Polynesia—actually having one. Parishes that have reluctantly accepted women bishops have what are termed 'flying bishops', men who can step in as needed to serve in place of the woman bishop.

The resistance to women holding positions of authority within the Church is not restricted to Anglicans. It remains the official position of the Roman Catholic Church, as well as some fundamentalist Christian groups in Canada and the US, that women should not be ordained as ministers or priests.

Why is there such opposition? Much of it comes back to Christianity's embedded patriarchy, which is extremely difficult to overcome in an institution that derives much of its meaning from its history and traditions. Many Church leaders still justify their opposition to the ordination of women on the grounds that Jesus had no female disciples. Of course, in the patriarchal culture in which Jesus lived, there would have been strong social opposition to his having female disciples. He was revolutionary enough in the respectful way in which he treated women. And he did have a good number of women followers who dedicated their lives to learning from him, with his approval (see Mary, sister of Martha, in Luke 10: 38–41).

The negative attitude of the disciple Paul, as expressed in his letters to the Corinthians, is another reason given for opposing women in authority, and reflects the cultural attitude towards women at that time:

> As in all the churches of the saints, the women should keep silence in the churches. For they are not permitted to speak, but should be subordinate, as even the law says. If there is anything they desire to know, let them ask their husbands at home. For it is shameful for a woman to speak in church. (1 Cor. 14: 33–35)

A similar attitude is expressed in Paul's correspondence with Timothy:

> Let a woman learn in silence with all submissiveness. I permit no woman to teach or to have authority over men; she is to keep silent. For Adam was formed first, then Eve; and Adam was not deceived, but the woman was deceived and became a transgressor. Yet woman will be saved through bearing children, if she continues in faith and love and holiness, with modesty. (1 Tim. 2: 11–15)

It should come as no surprise that Paul never married. His role in the Bible was to take the ideas of Jesus and organize them into a structure. That the role itself was patriarchal reflects the culture of his upbringing and experience.

What do YOU think?

1. Why do you think the Anglican Church took so long in ordaining women?
2. What should the role of sociological analysis be in discussing the position of women in the social structure of religions in Canada?
3. Do you think it's fair to say that Paul's statements were (to use the bishop's phrase) 'culturally conditioned'?

Ecofeminism and Spirituality

What is and isn't considered a religion is a subject of debate in sociological studies. Traditionally, some sociologists were reluctant to call Buddhism a religion, as it made no overt reference to a central God; they preferred to call it a philosophy, like Confucianism, instead. (We disagree, believing that definition to reflect a monotheistic—lit.'one god'—bias in the West.) More controversial is a social/political/spiritual movement such as **ecofeminism** (short for 'ecological feminism'). We'd like you to read the following and decide for yourself.

The term *ecofeminism* was coined in 1974 by Françoise d'Eaubonne to refer to the linking of environmentalism with feminism. Ecofeminists argue that there is a strong parallel between the subordination of women and the degradation of nature through male domination and control. Ecofeminists also explore the intersections between sexism, the domination of nature, racism, animal rights, and other aspects of social inequality. Contemporary ecofeminists argue that the capitalist and patriarchal systems that predominate throughout the world create a triple domination of women, nature, and the global South, or Third World (both men and women) (Ruether 1993).

QUICK HITS
The Myth about Islam and Women

While it can be argued that there is a tendency, in all countries where organized religion is strong, for women to be oppressed, the countries of the Middle East where Islam is the dominant religion have been singled out as especially oppressive and **misogynistic**. It is part of a generalized and uncritical targeting of Islam by the conservative Western media, a targeting that is related to deeper Eurocentric cultural beliefs that reproduce **Orientalism** and **Islamaphobia**. When examining Islam and the rights of women, it is important to separate those anti-female practices that are specifically Muslim from those practices that happen to occur in Muslim countries but that are not supported by the faith. We have used **Haroon Siddiqui**'s book *Being Muslim* (2006) to compile the following list.

- The practice of honour killings (killing female relatives for alleged sexual misconduct that brings dishonour upon the family) in countries such as Pakistan, Turkey, and Jordan is *not* an Islamic tradition.
- The practice of female genital cutting (FGC) in North and Central Africa is *not* condoned by Islam. (At the First Islamic Ministerial Conference on The Child, held in Morocco in 2005, FGC was condemned as un-Islamic.)
- The number of cases of polygyny (one man having more than one wife) in Muslim families in Western and Muslim countries is greatly exaggerated. Most Muslim marriages involve couples.
- Most Muslim women around the world do not wear a hijab or head-covering. (Siddiqui: 96-125).

What do YOU think?

What contributes to the distorted view that prevails in the West of the way women are treated under Islamic law and tradition?

Ecofeminism argues that the connection between women and nature is based on their shared history of oppression in patriarchal societies. Culturally, there is a common symbolism in the idea of 'man' being pitted against nature, wherein nature is feminized and women are assumed to have a profound affinity with the natural world (Rochelau et al. 1996). Ecofeminists point to the linguistic links between the oppression of women and the oppression of land in such phrases as 'rape the land' and 'virgin territory'. Nature is frequently constructed as feminine through the pronoun 'she' and the term 'Mother Nature'. Many ecofeminists argue that the European witch hunts of the seventeenth century represented a patriarchal triumph of 'male knowledge' over the nature-based wisdom of female herbalists and midwives. Vandana Shiva (1988) argues that globally women have a special connection to the environment through the simple actions of their daily lives, like making and washing clothes, and buying or growing foods.

Irene Diamond and Gloria Orenstein (1990) identify three strands in ecofeminism. One strand emphasizes that social justice has to be achieved in concert with the well-being of the environment, since all human life is dependent on the Earth. Another emphasizes the need to maintain a balance between using the Earth as a resource and respecting the Earth's needs. The third strand is spiritual and emphasizes the idea that the Earth is sacred unto itself. It is the last of these three strands that is of interest to us here. The desire to recover female 'pagan' wisdom, typically identified with pre-Christian Europe, as a means of liberating women and nature from patriarchal destruction was the basis for a spiritual revival. Central to this revival is the belief that spirituality is the life-force in everything, connecting women to each other, to other life forms, and to the elements (Adams 1993; Mies and Shiva 1993).

Janet Biehl (1991) has criticized ecofeminism as being idealist, focusing too much on the idea of a mystical connection with nature and not enough on the actual social and material conditions of women. However, this criticism does not apply to most contemporary ecofeminists, who reject both mysticism and **essentialist** ideas about the 'natural' connection between women and nature. These more materialist, anti-essentialist

Many women who believe in a spiritual life-force connecting humans to nature turn to Wicca, a shamanistic nature religion sometimes called modern witchcraft. Why do you think the number of Wiccans is on the rise in Canada?

ecofeminists discuss economical and political issues while drawing only metaphorically on the spiritual doctrines of Gaia, or 'Great Mother Earth' (Mies & Shiva 1993; Starhawk 1979, 1982, 2002).

Religion and Social Change

Religion has been a primary agent of change throughout history. Both the emergence and spread of new religions—like Islam—and the loss of indigenous religions—like those of the Mayans have brought about and reflected significant social and cultural change. Examples from earlier chapters include the Protestant ethic, which influenced cultural normative structures, and the European missionary movement, which was used to convert and subjugate populations as part of the broader aims of colonialism. And while religion has been used to submit populations to the will of authority, it has been used to emancipate populations as well. Take, for instance, figures like Gandhi, Mother Teresa, Martin Luther King, Malcolm X, and Desmond Tutu, all of whom were instrumental in using religion as a point of social change for the purposes of social justice. Marx, you will recall, claimed that religion pacifies people and stifled movements for change, as it encouraged citizens to put up with their worldly hardships because of the promise of better fortunes that await in heaven. However, religion has been a driving force behind anti-imperial and anti-colonial liberation movements, anti-racism and anti-discrimination movements, struggles against poverty, and democratic reform throughout the nineteenth and twentieth centuries. During the same time, however, every major religion has been used, at least in part, as an excuse to hate others and to justify terrorism.

Religion is not merely a social institution that is in the service of either progressive social change or social repression. According to **Friedrich Nietzsche** (1844–1900), history, in ways we are often unaware of, determines who we are and the values we believe in. While we may think of ourselves as independent-minded, ahistorical beings, the influence of Christian morality in Canadian society, whether we are Christian or not, informs our notions of free will, responsibility, guilt, sin, and what constitutes 'goodness'. Modern morality in Western societies, then, is essentially Christian, like the social movements mentioned above. Nietzsche's criticism of Christian morality, in whatever form, is that it is based on slave values and **herd morality**, which attracts individuals who are pessimistic and timid, encourages the repression of instincts, thwarts creative energies, and produces societies that are dull, static, and conformist. While herd morality answers the needs of the weak and insecure, it simultaneously obstructs human potential and achievement. In this sense, war, climate change, environmental degradation, and global poverty, to a large extent, are the result of hostility and a sense of entitlement based on the 'resentment' found in slave morality. For Nietzsche, Christian values had lost their relevance, and the various 'faiths' replacing

Christianity, such as the worship of science and progress, were equally bankrupt and would lead to a form of pessimistic **nihilism**. When he famously said 'God is Dead,' Nietzsche was referring specifically to the principles by which we determine moral values. Nihilism, based on the Latin word *nihil*, meaning 'nothing', is an extreme form of skepticism in which traditional principles of morality are rejected because there are no universal truths to base them on. People who adhere strongly to traditional religions think of **postmodernism** as a kind of nihilism.

What do YOU think?

1. Do you think that Nietzsche would argue that the negative elements found in herd morality outweigh progressive, Christian-based movements for social change?

2. What do you think a Nietzschean critique of the US civil rights movement might look like? Remember that the 1950s and 1960s movement was led by religious figures such as Christian minister Dr Martin Luther King.

Christian Religious Colonialism and its Impact among the Aboriginal People of Canada

As we mentioned earlier, religion is not just a social institution promoting social order: it is also a force for social change. When missionaries brought Christianity to Canada's Native people, their actions were an integral part of colonization, designed to make the people more like Europeans, not just in beliefs but in other social areas such as gender roles (see Karen Anderson's *Chain Her By One Foot*), and, of course, in their obedience to the Crown. But the people also had **agency**—that is, they were not merely victims of colonially imposed religions. As Native prophets reacted to the new world of Christian beliefs and ensuing political turmoil, they began to promote innovative religious beliefs. For example, the early nineteenth-century Seneca prophet Handsome Lake (*c.* 1735–1815) combined elements of traditional belief with what his people had learned from Quakers who had spent time among the Seneca. What was known in English as the Code of Handsome Lake combined traditional aspects

• Going Global •

Jihad: A Misunderstood Term

A religious practice often connected with terrorism is the Arabic word **jihad**. Movies, websites, 24-hour news channels, radio phone-in shows, and even dictionaries and encyclopaedias typically lead us to believe that *jihad* means 'holy war'. Yet if you look in English copies of the Koran, the Muslim holy book, you will find the Arabic word translated as 'struggle, striving, endeavour'. The following is an example taken from the Koran:

> Those who believe, and emigrate
> And strive with might
> And main, in Allah's cause
> With their goods and their persons,
> Have the highest rank
> In the sight of Allah:
> They are the people
> Who will achieve (salvation) (9: 20)

There are actually three types of jihad: personal, community, and martial. In his insightful book *Global Islamic Politics*, **Mir Zohair Husain** explains these different types in the following way:

> The personal jihad or **jihad-i-akbar**, is the greatest jihad. It represents the perpetual struggle required of all Muslims to purge their baser instincts. Greed, racism, hedonism, jealousy, revenge, hypocrisy, lying, cheating, and calumny [false and malicious accusation] must each be driven from the soul by waging jihad-i-akbar, warring against one's lower nature and leading a virtuous life. . . .
>
> Likewise, **ummaic jihad** addresses wrongs within the community of Muslims, whether by the written word or by the spoken word. Ummaic jihad represents the nonviolent struggle for freedom, justice and truth within the dar-al-Islam [Muslim world]. . . .
>
> Marital or violent jihad is referred to in Islam as **jihad-i-asghar** (lit., the smaller, lower, or lesser jihad). Martial jihad ideally represents a struggle against aggressors who are not practicing Muslims. . . . Martial jihad should be used to protect and to promote the integrity of Islam and to defend the umma [community] against hostile unbelievers, whether they are invading armies or un-Islamic internal despots. (Husain 1995: 37–8)

Muslim college students asked for examples of jihad in their lives have given answers as varied as the following:

- donating money to a charity rather than spending it on yourself
- studying for an exam rather than watching television
- working hard at a job you don't like because your family needs the money
- avoiding temptation in all forms (similar to the Christian avoidance of the seven deadly sins).

What do YOU think?

1. How do the three types of jihad differ?
2. Why do you think non-martial forms of jihad are not well known outside the Muslim world?

of the Great Law of Peace, which had brought the initially five nations (Mohawk, Oneida, Onondaga, Cayuga, and Seneca) of the Iroquois together into one confederacy, with Quaker elements such as a strong opposition to witchcraft, sexual promiscuity, and gambling. The nineteenth and early twentieth centuries saw the rise of other such figures as social disturbance and the imposition of Christianity moved west.

More interesting, perhaps, are the cases in which the people developed new forms of Christianity by integrating European-based religion into their own belief system and practices (Gray 2006; Valentine 1995). In many instances, these adapted forms of Christianity enabled the people to preserve or return to the cohesiveness of Durkheim's moral community that had existed in pre-contact times. In *Ta'n Teli-ktlamsitasit (Ways of Believing): Mi'kmaw Religion in Eskasoni, Nova Scotia* (2005), Angela Robinson uses the term **Catholic-Traditionalists** to refer to Mi'kmaq who adopted Catholicism but incorporated non-Christian elements into their religious practices (2005: 143). Mi'kmaq scholar and writer **Marie Battiste** (1997) offers the following description of how her people claimed Catholicism as their own to give strength to their community:

In 1610 the Mi'kmaq people entered into a compact with the Holy Roman Empire when our Chief Membertou and 140 others were first baptized. While our alliance with the Church was more political than spiritual, it was solidified in daily rituals when the French priest Father Antoine Maillard learned Mi'kmaq and began addressing the spiritual questions of the people. . . . Following the expulsion of the French priests [by the English] . . . [the] Mi'kmaq people held to their strong spiritual rituals in the Catholic church by conducting their own services. They had prayer leaders who led Sunday prayers, baptized children, accepted promises of marriage, and provided last rites for the dying. . . . These Catholic rituals continue today in many communities, and elders still play an important role in them, although a priest in the community offers the primary services. (157–8)

Photo: Yannick Luthy/Alamy

An Omoto altar in Hiroshima, Japan. Omoto is one of a number of Japanese religions that became prominent after World War II, though it was established, by a Japanese housewife, in the late nineteenth century. Since then, many of its spiritual leaders have been women. Why do you think this might be?

During the late nineteenth and early twentieth centuries, Christian missionaries along with federal officials in Canada and the US took aim at important Aboriginal ceremonies that were conducted, in part, to nourish a strong, cohesive sense of community. These ceremonies were the heart and soul of 'religious competition' for missionaries, and a form of resistance to political domination for the government officials. In Chapter 3 we examined the potlatch and the circumstances surrounding its banning. Here we will look briefly at the Sun Dance, the main ceremony for indigenous groups living in the Prairies. Sun Dance is an English term introduced by non-Natives. The Blackfoot, who live in southern Alberta, termed the ceremony *Okan*, after the pole at the centre of the ceremony. The Okan was initiated, sponsored, and presided over by a woman:

> The decision to hold a Sun Dance was made by a pure woman . . . who had a male relative in danger of losing his life. A husband might be ill or a son may not have returned from a raid. The woman made a public vow that if the person's life was spared, she would sponsor a Sun Dance. Then, if her prayer was answered, she began preparations for the summer festival. (Dempsey 1995: 392)

This ceremony was quite different from anything found in Christian religions. The following statement from Montana governor John Rickard, speaking in 1894, illustrates the typical sentiments of Christian culture to non-Christian religious practices:

> Investigation . . . convinces me that it is not only inhuman and brutalizing, unnatural and indecent, and therefore abhorrent to Christian civilization, but that its aims and purposes are a menace to the peace and welfare of communities. My information . . . leads me to regard the proposed exhibition as wholly inconsistent with Christian civilization. (Quoted in Dusenberry 1998: 219)

One aspect of the ceremony gave Canadian government officials an excuse for issuing a complete ban on the Sun Dance in 1895. Sometimes, as a spiritual offering, young men inserted leather thongs through their chest or back muscles, attaching the other end either to a pole or to the skull of a buffalo. They would then dance until the thongs ripped free—a painful process, as you can imagine. Section 114 of the Indian Act was amended to include a provision making it an indictable offence to take part in any ceremony 'of which the wounding or mutilation of the dead or living body of any human being or animal forms a part or is a feature'. Technically, this would have made the 'mortification of the flesh' (self-flagellation, or whipping oneself) illegal, even though it was associated with Christian religious dedication and was practised throughout most of Christianity's history (and is still practised in parts of Latin America and the Philippines). Little Bear, a Cree leader who had moved with his band to Montana, is reported to have stated that he was willing to remove that part of the ceremony in the spirit of getting along with colonial authorities (Dusenberry 1998: 220). However, the entire ceremony was deemed uncivilized, and there was no room for negotiation; this prompted the following response by one Blackfoot:

> We know that there is nothing injurious to our people in the Sun-dance. . . . It has been our custom, during many years, to assemble once every summer for this festival. . . . We fast and pray that we may be able to lead good lives and to act more kindly towards each other.
>
> I do not understand why the white men desire to put an end to our religious ceremonials. What harm can they do our people? If they deprive us of our religion, we will have nothing left, for we know of no other that can take its place. (Quoted in Nabokov 1991: 225)

The ceremony continued to be held in secret, and participants who were discovered were arrested for dancing. The Sun Dance did not return publicly in Canada until 1951. However, the damage to traditional religious beliefs had already taken its toll, and the ceremony never recovered its former prominence.

More recently, religious revival among Aboriginal people has gained popularity. Termed **neo-traditionalism** by some observers, it involves the reinterpretation of traditional beliefs and practices in ways that incorporate elements unique to one's own culture and others borrowed from Native cultures elsewhere. The sweat lodge, the drum, and the medicine wheel are examples of elements used in neo-traditionalist practice. The recovery of traditional customs has been very important in helping Aboriginal peoples find and strengthen their identity, and neo-traditionalist practices are often used in the rehabilitation of people in prison or in treatment for substance abuse. In this regard, Aboriginal religious leaders in some communities have finally achieved status equal to that of prison chaplains and addiction councillors.

The Missionary Position

It would not be wrong to say that the primary role of missionaries is to change people, to make them leave the religious path they are on and walk a new one, one that often bears the mark of a different culture. But it is also important that missionaries exemplify the values that are at the core of the religion they represent, particularly the principle of charity. Here the sociologist needs to ask: Do the two aims clash? Can there be a kind of role strain between conversion and charity? This is a question that a number of people in religious organizations, for example the World Council of Churches, are eager to address in terms of religion-based aid organizations and their workers. The practice of sending missionaries into developing countries in need of financial assistance is sometimes called **aid evangelism**. The financial assistance is a kind of **tied aid**—money that comes with purse strings attached. Often when countries (including Canada) spend money on aid, it is given with the condition that the people receiving the assistance must spend at least some of the money on products and services that come from the donor country. Another term for this is **phantom aid**, which captures the idea that the aid is not real but rather a form of investment.

So, do religious-based aid workers and the religious communities that sponsor them sometimes see aid as a form of investment in conversion? Aid evangelism has taken various forms over the last few decades. Some American fundamentalist groups delivered thousands of 70-pound food packages to starving people in Iraq; the packages were covered with biblical verses written in Arabic. More seriously, following the disastrous Boxing Day tsunami that hit southern Asia on 26 December 2004, the 2,000-member Antioch Community Church, based in Waco, Texas, sent 'aid workers' to Sri Lanka to stage children's plays about Jesus and hold Christian prayer services for those suffering from the devastating effects of the flood. Sri Lanka is primarily a Buddhist country, though Hinduism and Islam are also practised. The Christian element is small, but still a presence. An essentially Buddhist backlash to perceived aid evangelism caused vandalism and threats to local Christian groups, even to the point of attacking the offices of the Christian aid agency World Vision, which had no apparent connection with the missionary practices in question. In Indonesia, the world's largest Muslim country, the government blocked the move of American religious-based aid agency World Help to settle 50 Muslim children from the flooded Aceh province to a Christian orphanage, as they suspected that conversion was the cost of the aid.

● ● ● ● ● ● ● ● ● ● ● ● ● ● ● ● ● ● ● ●

What do YOU think?

What do you think is the motivation behind attacks on Christian aid agencies and government intervention against Christian charity?

● ● ● ● ● ● ● ● ● ● ● ● ● ● ● ● ● ● ● ●

Liberation Theology

Liberation theology is a progressive school of Christian thought that advocates social justice for the poor. It takes as its model the life of Jesus as being politically opposed to privilege. It is very much like the **social gospel** movement put forward by Protestant ministers of the late nineteenth and early twentieth centuries (see Chapter 11), except that it is rooted almost exclusively in the Catholic Church, particularly in Latin America, and especially among members of the Jesuit and Maryknoll religious orders. Liberation theology is a kind of Christian socialism, opposing the oppression of the poor by the corrupt, ruling class in developing and underdeveloped

A small service at a Christian base community in São João de Meriti, Brazil. Compare the photo of Muslims praying at the Noble Sanctuary in Jerusalem (p. 209). Do you think this setting is better suited to what Durkheim called the collective consciousness of religious experience?

Photo: Mike Goldwater/Alamy

countries. Its proponents emphasize social practices that improve the situation for the poor. These practices are devised based on input received from the poor, not from the rich who, historically, have supported the 'monarchic and pyramidic' system of hierarchical authority of the Catholic Church (Russell 2001). There has been strong opposition to this prioritization from conservatives within the hierarchy of the Catholic Church, particularly those bishops in Latin American countries who had been appointed from the elite class. Advocates for the poor argue that these bishops are conscious of their own class interests, and act upon these interests over those of the poor. Pope John Paul II and Pope Benedict VI, both socially and politically conservative, have been opponents of liberation theology and have barred 'offending' priests from holding mass.

The Sandinista National Liberation Front (known by its Spanish initials FSLN) was a Marxist revolutionary group in Nicaragua that began in the 1960s and overthrew the right-wing dictator Anastasio Samosa in 1979. The Sandinistas stayed in political power until 1990 despite an ongoing battle with the United States, specifically the counter-insurgency Contras, who were backed by the US Central Intelligence Agency. The Sandinistas supported priests who worked to benefit the poor. The Catholic hierarchy in Nicaragua had supported the dictatorship of Samosa. In an official statement made in 1950, Nicaragua's conservative bishops said:

> [A]ll authority comes from God. God is the Author of all that exists, and from the Author comes Authority; [faithful Catholics] should remember that when they obey the Political Authority, they do not dishonor themselves, but rather they act in a way that basically constitutes obeisance to God. (Quoted in Gilbert 1988: 131)

Priests working with the poor and who believed in liberation theology became members of the FSLN. When the Sandinistas came to power, some priests took political office, but were quickly reprimanded by Pope John Paul II and the Vatican hierarchy. One such priest was Father Miguel D'Escoto, who became the Foreign Minister for the Nicaraguan government. In 2008, he was elected as the President of the General Assembly of the United Nations.

Brazil is the largest Catholic country in the world, with well over 130 million people, yet it has a chronic shortage of priests. It has been estimated that in Latin America, there is one priest for every 7,000 Catholics, versus one for every 880 in the United States (Russell 2001). One social strategy to overcome this shortage supported and implemented by liberation theologists is the establishment of **base communities**, estimated to number as many as about 75,000 in Brazil alone (Russell 2001). Within the base communities, which average 10 to 30 members each, the focus is on shared religious instruction and prayer as well as communal self-help. Though local priests provide

Telling It Like It Is

AN AUTHOR POV

The Golden Compass and Religious Censorship

POINT OF VIEW

Around Christmas 2008, I saw the television premiere of a movie I had watched and enjoyed a year earlier in the theatre. It was *The Golden Compass*, based on the first novel of Philip Pullman's bestselling trilogy *His Dark Materials*, starring Nicole Kidman and Daniel Craig. I knew that a sequel had been planned, so I did a Web search to find out when it was scheduled to come out. It wasn't. The movie had been the target of a strong religious-based boycott in the US, which had limited its American profits to just $70 million, although it had grossed a solid $300 million worldwide. The reason for the religious opposition to the movie was that the 'bad guys' in the film, the evil Magisterium, were suspected to have been modelled on the Catholic Church and its hierarchical organization. I didn't pick up on that in the film, but then I wasn't looking for it either. I just thought that it was a big evil, over-controlling administration (something I see in a lot of things). The books, I've been told, are fiercely anti-religion and anti-hierarchy, and the author is both a declared atheist and a social anarchist.

If my reading of the religious criticism is correct, it is not so much that the movie supports an atheistic or anti-Christian position, but that it poses a threat to children who, if they enjoy the movie, will want to read the books and in turn may be turned off of religion to a life of atheism. And then there's the sex . . . but that's another story.

I am of two minds about the boycott. I hate that the sequel will not appear because of religious opposition mounted by what I would call narrow-minded people. However, it is a democratic right to boycott a film, and I could not oppose that action without being a hypocrite. I, too, read into the meanings of movies that I don't like—such as *The Fast and the Furious* franchise and all the bloody *Saw* films—and consider the damaging effects such movies may have on young people; I'm even concerned about the mindless Disney movies, which I fear will turn little girls into pouty, pink-clad princesses. Is there any real difference between my stance and the position taken by opponents of *The Golden Compass*?

In my mind, the difference is that *The Golden Compass*, and the books it is based on, encourages young people to imagine and think and makes their minds grow. It encourages people to challenge convention and, hopefully, be creative and original in the worlds they create as adults. Religion is often, in my opinion, overly concerned with conformity and blindly following the paths of the past. I believe that a rich religious life is one that involves addressing the big questions of life, and perhaps answering a few of them. The movies I don't like are typically those that I believe don't encourage people to really think at all.

guidance to community leaders, the principal focus of the groups is on relating the lessons of the Bible to the day-to-day activities of their members, whether they are urbanites, slum-dwellers, or rural campesinos.

At a typical base community in the town of Campos Eliseos, 14 miles northwest of Rio de Janeiro, 30 local residents meet every Friday night in a cinderblock home to read the Bible and discuss their problems. Antonio Joinhas, a 44-year-old railroad signalman, relates how one study session inspired a local public health centre:

> After reading how one biblical community helped another to overcome a problem, we decided to work together too. We all supplied the manpower and raised money for materials from the community. Now we've got a health center, and it came from the Bible. (Quoted in Russell 2001)

Summary

Religions touch the spiritual, and address needs that appear to be universal. This aspect of religion is, for the most part, outside the critical eye of sociology. However, religions have social organizations and practices that are directly connected with the domain of the sociologist. They are intimately linked with other aspects of society—hierarchy, gender roles, and colonialism, to name just a few—that sociologists regularly analyze. From that link comes the very critical approach that we have brought to this chapter.

Questions for Critical Review

1. What is the social tension that exists between hierarchy and egalitarianism in organized religion?
2. What would a feminist critique of organized religion look like?
3. How does religion link with colonialism?
4. Why do you think that there is such a misunderstanding about the Muslim faith in the West?
5. Why are many sociologists critical of organized religion?

Suggested Readings

Margaret Humphreys, *Empty Cradles*, 1995, London: Corgi Books: London

Isabelle Knockwood, *Out of the Depths: the Experiences of Mi'kmaw Children at the Indian Residential School in Shubenacadie, Nova Scotia*, Halifax: Fernwood Publishing, 2001.

Haroon Siddiqui, *Being Muslim*, Toronto: Groundwood Books, 2006.

Suggested Websites

Elizabeth G. Sullivan Memorial Collection on Eco-feminism and Related Materials
www2.cnr.edu/home/library/resources_ecointro.htm

Key Terms

- access
- access without mobility
- adjunct professor
- alienation
- anomie
- assimilation
- capitalist correctness

- Christian correctness
- college correctness
- commodification
- corporate correctness
- credentialism
- critical education
- cultural capital

- cultural racism
- cultural reproduction
- cultures of education
- disenchantment of the world
- disqualified knowledges
- docile body
- Eurocentric

9

Education

LEARNING OBJECTIVES

After reading this chapter, you should be able to

> outline the positive and negative effects of 'streaming' (or 'tracking') in elementary and secondary education;

> discuss the positive and negative effects on post-secondary education of increasing reliance on adjunct instructors, online education, and corporate sponsorship of research and infrastructure;

> provide a comprehensive sociological examination of plagiarism in post-secondary institutions;

> assess the value of schools run by and for marginalized groups such as Aboriginal people and blacks

> describe the types of political correctness that have an impact on post-secondary learning; and

> discuss how education can reproduce the class structure of a society.

- (the) examination
- hidden curriculum
- hierarchical observation
- human capital thesis
- indigenous knowledges
- institution
- institutional racism
- instrumental education
- intellectual property
- legitimation of inequality
- McJob
- meritocratic
- neoliberal
- normalizing judgment
- patriotic correctness
- plagiarism
- political correctness
- relative deprivation
- reproduction of class structure
- role models
- significant others
- social distance
- tracking
- underemployment

Key Names
- Jean Anyon
- Jeannie Oakes

FOR Starters

Exploit U and the Academic Underclass:
Take a Good Look at Your Professor

Student of sociology, take a good look at your instructor, professor, or TA—quick, right now, while she or he isn't looking. What do you notice? Is she relatively young? Does he always seem to be running late, to be hurrying in or out, to be distracted before or after class? When your instructor tells stories of her teaching experience, are these stories about some other college or university? Does your prof also teach at another school? Is the secretary unsure of whom you're speaking when you say your instructor's name? Do you know the status of your professor, her official title, her place in the hierarchy of your college or university?

   If your instructor is teaching an Intro to Soc course, chances are that he's been hired only for a session, a semester, or a year; he probably isn't a full-time, long-term, tenured member of the department. He likely falls into the category of 'contract faculty' or 'sessional staff', or maybe he's an 'adjunct professor', which sounds a bit loftier but still means that he's teaching courses and students—particularly lower-level ones—that the permanent staff doesn't want to deal with. Technically he's long-term part-time, though that makes it sound better than it actually is—my *Canadian Oxford Dictionary* (we've got to push our publisher) defines 'adjunct' as 'an assistant or a subordinate person, esp. one with a temporary appointment only'. The person teaching you may well be fully qualified but an academic gypsy, part of a post-secondary underclass that is growing in Canada and the US. They get paid less for teaching you and often don't receive any benefits, even though their knowledge is current and up-to-date, and they likely put more work into their lectures than do their 'full-time' colleagues.

What do YOU think?

1. Do you think that you can tell the difference between a prof who is full-time and one who is adjunct? Do you have any sense of what percentage of your instructors are adjunct?

2. What are the positive and negative aspects of being taught by an adjunct professor?

Introduction

The social institution of education is one of the most important institutions in contemporary postindustrial, industrial, and industrializing societies because of the multiple influences it has on everything from socialization and status to social order and economic productivity. Remember from Chapter 5 that an **institution** is an enduring set of ideas about how to accomplish goals that are deemed important within a society or culture. The degree to which social institutions are formalized depends on the nature of the society or culture. Since the inception of public education, children spend more time at school than they do with their parents. Your child is raised by a stranger and, simultaneously, your child becomes in some senses a stranger. This is a consequence of modern societies and their institutional structure, one that reflects elements of Durkheim's **anomie** (for example, in parents' frequent disconnect with the school system, influencing their children) and Weber's **disenchantment of the world** (for example, in the increasingly rationalized, controlled curriculum that takes away from the mystery and magic of self-driven education). Nevertheless, the time and duration of schooling has a significant impact on our sociability and socialization. At school, behaviours are modified, skills are developed for future employment, social interaction and conflict are negotiated, notions of social reality are defined, and structures of inequality (classism, sexism, heterosexism, and racism) are reproduced. Schools prepare us to be productive citizens and obedient subjects. How we do in school plays a significant role in determining our potential social mobility. These are a few of the issues we will explore throughout this chapter.

The Emergence of Public Education

Before the Industrial Revolution in Europe and the United States there was little interest in educating the masses. On the contrary, it was in the best interest of the ruling elite to keep the population ignorant and illiterate so its authority could not be challenged. With the rise of industrial capitalism, companies demanded more from their labour force. Specifically, as industry became more complex, it required a more disciplined, trainable, and literate workforce that would be more economically productive. Industrialization and public education, then, became interdependent in the same way that labour is dependent on capital and capital on labour. This symbiotic relationship still exists, and is seen in the correlation between industrial 'development' and an educated population. For instance, one of the main objectives of developing nations is to establish an educational base that ensures increased economic and social stability by producing a broader, middle-class foundation, which requires a literate, educated population.

The Rise of Public Education in Canada

As early as 1846, education in Canada was seen as a means of achieving economic modernization. Liberal reformers like Egerton Ryerson (after whom Toronto's Ryerson University is named) promoted the idea of a school system that would be universal, free, and compulsory, in order to advance social justice and industrialization in Canada. According to Schecter (1977), the aims of Ryerson's public education model went beyond economic growth and social justice: it was also a means by which the state could save the bourgeoisie from itself. Education was not simply a method of producing social *order* but one that procured social *control* by subverting potential social conflict and animosity from the influx of the labouring Catholic class. Ryerson himself, speaking of the unskilled, potato-famine afflicted Irish Catholic migrants, warned: 'the physical disease and death which have accompanied their influx among us may be the precursor of the worst pestilence of social insubordination and disorder' (quoted in Schecter 1977: 373). Education was seen as a means to avert the threat of discontent from the impoverished Catholic labourers by assimilating them into the dominant Protestant culture.

Schecter (1977) argues that education has never contributed as much to prosperity and social mobility as it has legitimized social inequality. He explains that the implementation of state-run education is premised on centralization and uniformity, instruments of social control to be used on the emerging working class. However, to ensure the uniformity of education—from textbooks to teachers—it became necessary to establish provincial boards that could act as executive bodies to set up and maintain large systems of 'normal schools' (the old and very significant name for teacher's colleges). School boards were able to enforce codes of discipline and enact hierarchical authority relations that placed both students and parents in positions subordinate to the place of the teacher. Such practices, according to Schecter, were used to cover up both the overt school curriculum and the hidden agenda of subordinating the working class.

It may sound cynical to suggest that the state-run school system was born of a need to discipline

The cover of *Le Petit Journal*, dated 5 December 1897, shows Eugénie Bonnefois, the daughter of a puppeteer, who set up a school for the children of travelling performers so that they would not miss out on the education she never gained. What difference do you think this kind of education might have made to their lives?

the growing labour force for industrial capitalism and legitimate the social order. However, it's important to bear in mind that at the time public education systems were established in the latter half of the nineteenth century, many social reformers were warning of the 'motley Americanism' and civil disorder that might result from a disgruntled working class. This only perpetuated pre-existing middle-class fears of downward mobility, the loss of property, and of the 'lower' classes themselves. Even the ruling classes were uneasy with the ambiguity surrounding the emerging capitalist society, which promised wealth but also the possibility of social conflict and misery. With the newly solicited support of Canada's middle class, reformers were able to instill the need for school reform and, after numerous debates, several reversals, and considerable time, implement a public school system.

Capital Expansionism and the Human Capital Thesis

> Thus, wherever I hear the masses raise the cry for an expansion of education, I am wont to ask myself whether it is stimulated by a greedy lust of gain and property, by the memory of a former religious persecution, or by the prudent egotism of the State itself.
>
> —Friedrich Nietzsche, 'The Future of Our Educational Institutions', 1872

The Canadian economy after World War II required a workforce that was better educated than it had ever been before, as well as new training centres for men returning from war. This sparked an unprecedented expansion of colleges and universities across Canada to match the economic boom that peaked during the 1960s. Most scholars situate the historic period of economic and post-secondary expansion between 1946 and the early 1970s. This period coincides with an overall expansion of the role of government, which began providing essential services including education as a means of subsidizing capitalist reproduction. Government officials may have championed the expansion of post-secondary institutions as increasing access to education, but historians like Newson and Buchbinder (1988) maintain that economic considerations were the driving force.

The perceived relationship between educational expansion and economic growth is part of what is often referred to as the **human capital thesis**. The human capital thesis asserts that the human worker is similar to a piece of machinery, one of many forces of production. Just as industrial societies invest in factories and equipment to attain greater efficiency, they also invest in schools to enhance the training, knowledge, and skills of their workers. When applied to social inequality, the concept of human capital theory argues that marginalized groups earn less money than dominant groups because they possess less human capital in the form of education, skill and experience.

QUICK HITS
The Father of Canadian Education's Illegitimate Child

'There is a need to raise the Indians to the level of the whites . . . and take control of land out of Indians' hands. The Indian must remain under the control of the Federal Crown rather than provincial authority, that efforts to Christianize the Indians and settle them in communities be continued . . . that schools, preferably manual labour ones, be established under the guidance of missionaries. . . . Their education must consist not merely training of the mind, but of a weaning from the habits and feelings of their ancestors, and the acquirements of the language, art and customs of civilized life.'

—Egerton Ryerson, in an 1847 report to Indian Affairs

The forms of production in the economic sphere dramatically changed in Canada after 1975. Decreases in the taxes charged to corporations contributed to decreases in educational funding between 1970–1 and 1990–1, and cuts to government funding of post-secondary institutions have continued since then. This has allowed the corporate sector to form stronger ties with cash-hungry colleges and universities who, in return for corporate finance, have made concessions to corporate capital. This is most evident in increased advertising on campus, visible everywhere but in the classrooms (coming soon?). Academic research has become more closely tied into corporate agendas and control, especially in such areas as medical/pharmaceutical and agricultural product research.

Discipline, Punishment, and Evaluation

Discipline is a large part of education and is often referred to as part of the **hidden curriculum**, the unstated, unofficial agenda of school system authorities. In primary school, discipline is focused on the body, restricting movement, impeding interaction, and normalizing confinement. Children are encouraged to use their 'inside voices', to raise their hands before they speak or

The recently opened Rogers Communication Centre at Ryerson University. Corporate funding made the facility possible. What are the drawbacks to this kind of corporate-university relationship?

Photo: Bill Ivy Images

ask permission to go to the bathroom, to sit quietly in their seats, to line up, to be punctual, and so on. Secondary school continues to enforce corporeal behaviours, though there is an increased focus on cognitive discipline: disciplining the mind, more than the body, is the main goal as this stage.

What is common at all levels of education is the external and internal 'routinization' of the individual. As with all rules that govern behaviour, punishment is enacted if the rules are not followed—it may be a 'time-out' (we were given the strap until corporal punishment was abolished when I was in Grade 2), a detention, or a poor grade on a report card. You will recall from Chapter 3 that rules are enforced through sanctions when norms are broken. Poor and good grades are sanctions regarding behaviour, designed to either negatively or positively reinforce norms that are ignored or obeyed. Teachers, like police, are the ones responsible for managing behaviour to a large degree.

While discipline can be enabling as well as inhibiting—many young students require and thrive off of a formalized structure of rules and routines—much of the discipline within the public school system is excessively punitive and repressive. Two of my neighbour's children who have been home-schooled their entire lives thought they would like to attend public school. They lasted less than two weeks before they returned home, complaining that they could not sit that long between breaks. It is not simply the body that is curtailed in its movement but also the mind. Children are by nature curious. Curiosity is the basis for asking questions, which is essential in the process of learning. Yet we are taught with adages such as 'Curiosity killed the cat' and 'Don't rock the boat' or 'Don't make waves'—all of which mean, essentially, don't ask questions. By the time we reach college and university, not much curiosity is left. Post-secondary students too rarely ask questions with respect to ideas (other than 'Is this on the exam?').

In many respects, public education creates what Foucault termed the **docile body**, a group that has been conditioned, through a specific set of procedures and practices, to behave precisely the way we want it to (Foucault 1977). Docile bodies are produced through three, decisively modern forms of disciplinary control:

1. hierarchical observation,
2. normalizing judgment, and
3. the examination.

The idea behind **hierarchical observation** is that people are controlled through observation and surveillance. While Foucault used prisons as an example of hierarchical observation, the principle applies as well to schools, offices, factories, and malls—all places where our movements and activities are micromanaged and under constant surveillance within a society based on hierarchical structures and configurations.

Educational institutions are based on a hierarchical structure in which authority figures—namely instructors and administrators—scrutinize the behaviour of students through observational surveillance. For Foucault, hierarchical observation works on the psychology of the observed

individual as much as it governs his or her specific movements. It works, then, to transform individuals and take hold of their conduct. When a person assumes that he or she is always being watched, it induces a state of self-consciousness—an awareness on the part of the individual of his or her permanent visibility—that enhances the power of the authority (Foucault, 1977: 172).

Normalizing judgment is another instrument of disciplinary control that produces docile bodies. Under this model, individuals are judged not on the intrinsic rightness or wrongness of their actions but on how their actions rank when compared with the performance of others. Children are ranked at school, schools are ranked against one another, provincial education is ranked, and the level of education among countries is ranked. Normalizing judgment is a pervasive means of control because regardless of how one succeeds, a higher level of achievement is always possible.

The **examination** combines hierarchical observation with normalizing judgment. Foucault described it as 'a normalizing gaze [that] establishes over individuals a visibility through which one differentiates them and judges them' (1977: 184).

The principal reprimands a student at Toronto's C.W. Jeffreys school. Which form of disciplinary control does this represent? What other examples can you think of?

Photo: Tara Walton/GetStock.com

It is, in his view, the locus of power and knowledge, because it combines and unifies both 'the deployment of force and the establishment of truth' (1977: 184). How? Exam and test scores are documented and recorded, and provide detailed information about those individuals examined. Based on these records, various categories, averages, and norms are formulated by those in control, and these become the basis of knowledge. In this way, power remains invisible, while those constructed as deviant become highly visible: those students with the thickest files are scrutinized by scores of anonymous, invisible functionaries (Foucault 1977: 189). Remember that deviance, rather than simply being negative, reflects positive elements as well. In this sense, both Lisa and Bart Simpson have the thickest files at school, but for different reasons.

Educational Models

Assimilation Model in Education

Education in Canada, albeit informally, has historically been based on a monocultural model that emphasizes **assimilation**. English Canada was viewed as a white Protestant nation into which people outside this dominant culture were assimilated. One trouble with the assimilation model was that it failed to recognize the racial bias and discrimination, both inside and outside the school system, that prevented assimilation. According to Henry and Tator (2006), the emphasis on monoculturalism formed a pervasive and coercive ideology that 'influenced the training of educators, the practices of teaching, the content and context of learning, the hiring and promotion practices of boards, and the cultural values and norms underpinning all areas of school life' (213). Students, regardless of their backgrounds, were expected to leave their cultural, religious, and ethnic identities at the door.

The assimilationist approach continues to be a strong influence in Canadian education today (Dei 1996; Dei & Calliste 2000). My daughter, for instance, after two years of kindergarten, is already well versed in European fairytales and folklore, and Judeo-Christian traditions and values. It's not so different from my experience at college, where I became intimately acquainted with Western philosophy and English literature. Prior to attending college I was reading, in translation,

Tolstoy, Dostoevsky, Kafka, Camus, and Hessen. When I enrolled in an English literature course I inquired why we weren't reading any of those authors; I was told the course was 'just English'; apparently, great works of literature translated into English didn't count. English then, is really English cultural studies. As a discipline, it represents an assimilationist and monocultural perspective, despite the facts that Canada is officially a multicultural society, and that only 10–15 per cent of the population is actually of British ancestry. Implicit in all of this is the underlying notion that English culture is somehow superior, the only thing worth learning. We are told that Shakespeare is the greatest writer in history, while the German Goethe, the Italian Dante, the Spanish Cervantes, the Russian Dostoevsky, and the Bengali Tagore tend to be neatly swept into the dustbin of history.

Multicultural Education

The federal government implemented its official policy of multiculturalism in 1971 to preserve and promote cultural diversity while removing the barriers that denied certain groups full participation within Canadian society. The idea was to create a learning environment that was respectful to all learners. School boards launched initiatives to study and celebrate the lifestyles, traditions, and histories of diverse cultures (Henry and Tator 2006). These initiatives were based on three fundamental assumptions drawn from a key study of multicultural education in six countries:

1. that learning about one's culture will improve educational achievement;
2. that learning about one's culture will promote quality of opportunity; and
3. that learning about other cultures will reduce prejudice and discrimination.

After two decades of multicultural education in Canada, these untested assumptions began to be undermined. Not only did teachers themselves have very little knowledge or understanding of other cultures, but the classroom focus tended to take a museum approach to the study of culture instead of exploring the complexity, subtlety, and vitality of culture. Educators focused on the historical material, as well as 'exotic' aspects of different cultures, including food, festivals, and

A teacher takes attendance outside of Canada's first Africentric public school, which opened in Toronto in September 2009. Does establishing alternative schools for students of specific ethnic backgrounds help by enlightening those students on their history and culture? Will Africentric schools lead to an improvement in the coverage of Canadian black history throughout the public school system, making all students more enlightened on the subject?

Photo: Tara Walton/GetStock.com

folklore; they overlooked the values and beliefs—those found in racial, linguistic, religious, gender, and regional differences—that are fundamental to shaping cultural identity (Dei 1996).

Francis and Tator argue that the most glaring weakness of multicultural education was its failure to acknowledge that racism was systemic in Canadian society. While the superficial aspects of 'other' cultures were being studied, the problem of racial inequality was ignored (2006: 213–14). Both monocultural and multicultural educational models, then, overlooked the role of the institution in generating and reproducing racism and ignored the reality of racism as a powerful and pervasive force that shapes all Canadian social institutions.

Anti-Racism and Anti-Oppression Education

Anti-racism and anti-oppression education is meant to eliminate institutional and individual barriers to equity. It is intended to create a classroom environment where

- stereotypes and racist ideas can be exposed;
- sources of information can be examined;

- students become equipped to look critically at the accuracy of the information they receive; and
- alternative and missing information can be provided and the reasons for the continued unequal social status of different groupings can be explored.

The aim of this model is to change institutional policies and practices, as well as individual attitudes and behaviours that reproduce social inequality.

Anti-racism and anti-oppression education first appeared in Canada in the 1980s, when some school boards introduced new policies to promote the model; these policies included changes to teacher education, new criteria for reviewing and evaluating the practices of educators, greater analysis of teacher placement procedures, employment equity strategies, and resource and curriculum development (Henry and Tator 2006). In 1992, the Province of Ontario introduced two measures directed at meeting the growing demands for racial equality on the part of racially marginalized communities. First, the government legislated that boards of education develop and implement anti-racist policies—though no additional funds were allocated. Second, the government launched a new de-streaming process to end the practice of separating Grade 9 students into different groups according to their abilities. However, just three

Telling It Like It Is

Eurocentric Curriculum and the University

POINT OF VIEW

Despite Canada's multicultural character and state-legislated multicultural policy, a patriarchal, **Eurocentric** curriculum still dominates our institutions of 'higher learning'. Such a curriculum offers a narrow view of the world. Many minority and non-minority students whom I have mentioned this issue to have expressed concern or outrage at the Eurocentricity of what we learn. I fail to see an excuse for the exclusion of other points of view when there is a wealth of literature about non-European cultures by non-European academics. These works are not inferior to those of Europeans, but are works that are integral to the attainment of a fuller, more encompassing education in which knowledge and ideas are derived from a wider, culturally diverse range of sources and perspectives. They are particularly useful in dispelling the racist assumptions and myths placed upon 'others' by Western society.

In their inadequate attempts to be more inclusive, many of the professors I have encountered take a 'just add and stir' approach to the inclusion of Natives, women, and 'otherized' groups which simply does not work; an anthropology professor of mine once commented that this approach is 'like throwing a bunch of radishes into a salad'. Just as they are treated as asides or special interest groups in society at large, women, Native people, and ethnic groups are often merely added on to Week 13 readings—if, that is, they are included at all. It was not until I experienced a course taught by a progressive, culturally sensitive anthropology professor who incorporated a multitude of perspectives that I became aware of the partial and limited view of the world which I had previously been subjected to. Those who perpetuate the mainstream academic curriculum seem to have fallen into a state of historical amnesia, whereby the contributions and, indeed, the very presence of non-Europeans have been omitted from Canadian history. Though Chinese, Japanese, and Indian immigrants arrived in Canada at the same time as early European immigrants, one could pass through the entire school system from kindergarten to university without being aware of the fact. Many students emerge from the school system rightfully well versed in the works of Shakespeare, Plato, and Marx, but how many students come out of university knowing anything about feminist theory, the cultural genocide of Native peoples, or slavery in Canada?

I am concerned that the exclusion from postsecondary curricula of minority groups, their perspectives, and their writings perpetuates a view of the world taken through a Eurocentric lens. This exclusion is also dangerous because it may lead some students to believe that since little is studied from 'other' cultures, then perhaps those cultures have nothing of benefit to offer, or else they are inferior to European thought.

The courses I have found the most valuable and educational are those that, though not designated as courses specifically about multiculturalism, women, or Native people, still incorporated a variety of cultural perspectives into the reading materials, films, and seminars. A culturally diverse curriculum and alternative critical forms of pedagogy can also have a positive effect on the academic achievement of minority students, whose experiences and interests are not validated but are typically marginalized or excluded from the existing curriculum.

It is my opinion that the education of all students and faculty would be deeply enriched through a more culturally diverse and inclusive curriculum, one that reflects the multicultural society in which we live.

—A.R. Aujla, 1996

years later, the Conservative government dismantled all anti-racism and anti-oppression initiatives. As Henry and Tator point out:

> While lip service is paid to . . . ensure equality of opportunity for all students in the classroom, in reality, individuals, organizations, and institutions are far more committed to maintaining the status-quo, that is the cultural hegemony of the dominant culture with which most educators identify. (2006: 223)

The Hidden Curriculum

Earlier in the chapter we mentioned the hidden curriculum, which is a common topic in the sociology of education, though its definition varies depending upon the specific issue being discussed. We find it useful to consider in terms of Robert Merton's three functions, introduced in the opening chapter. Using his terms, we could define the hidden curriculum as the latent—not openly stated on a course outline or syllabus—curriculum of an education system, institution, or course. Whether or not it is the latent function or dysfunction depends on the interpreting sociologist. A conservative structural-functionalist sociologist might say that the hidden curriculum helps to teach the norms of society (concerning the value of work, for instance, or the need to obey authority and to use one's time efficiently); it therefore performs a latent function. A conflict or critical sociologist might say that the hidden curriculum reproduces the class system, hindering class mobility; it is therefore a latent dysfunction.

A concept that is often mentioned in discussions of the hidden curriculum is Pierre Bourdieu's **cultural capital**, which we touched on in Chapter 3 (p. 72). As Bourdieu employs the concept, it has to do with the reproduction of the class structure, mostly through differences in consumption patterns and taste (e.g. in the arts and in sports). According to Bourdieu, the 'taste culture' (or 'symbolic culture') of the upper classes gives them advantages in education that benefit them in their subsequent careers (Bourdieu and Passeron 1977).

In Britain, cultural capital can be seen in speech patterns and sports. The use of 'more educated' speech associated with the upper class can cause a student to be treated with greater respect by

Photo: © Ace Stock Limited/Alamy

What signs of cultural capital do you see in this image?

teachers and employers. Having an 'Oxbridge' (combining the names of the prestigious British universities Oxford and Cambridge) accent can further a person's career in the executive boardrooms of Britain. Having gone to an exclusive 'public school' (in Britain, an expensive private school) can also help, especially for the student who shares the 'old school tie' with an employer or influential colleague. The sports played in British schools have tended to reflect and reinforce class divisions. Soccer, played mostly in working-class schools, has been called a gentlemanly game played by hooligans, while rugby (played mostly in 'public schools' including Rugby) is a ruffian's game played by gentlemen.

Jean Anyon: Social Class and the Hidden Curriculum of Work

A useful study of the **reproduction of class structure** is Jean Anyon's 'Social Class and the Hidden Curriculum of Work' (Anyon 1980), based on an ethnographic study of five elementary schools in New Jersey in 1978–9. Two of the schools she studied she identified as working-class. Most of the fathers had semi-skilled or unskilled jobs (assembly line work, auto repair or assembly, maintenance work); 15 per cent of the fathers were unemployed, and less than 30 per cent of the mothers worked. According to Anyon, schoolwork in these schools

> . . . is following the steps of a procedure. The procedure is usually mechanical, involving rote [drilled memorization] behavior and very little decision making or choice. The teachers rarely explain why the work is being assigned, how it might connect to other assignments, or what the idea is that lies behind the procedure or gives it coherence and perhaps meaning or significance. . . . Most of the rules regarding work are designations of what the children are to do; the rules are steps to follow. . . . The children are usually told to copy the steps as notes. These notes are to be studied. Work is often evaluated not according to whether it is right or wrong but according to whether the children followed the right steps. (Anyon 1980)

Students at a third school, which Anyon identified as middle-class, had parents working in skilled, well-paid trades (as carpenters, plumbers, construction workers, and so on) or as professionals (such as fire fighters, teachers, accountants) or small business owners. Schoolwork here was all about 'getting the right answer':

> One must follow the directions in order to get the right answers, but the directions often call for some figuring, some choice, some decision making. For example, the children must figure out by themselves what the directions ask them to do and how to get the answer: what do you do first, second, and perhaps third? Answers are usually found in books or by listening to the teacher. Answers are usually words, sentences, numbers, or facts and dates; one writes them on paper, and one should be neat. Answers must be given in the right order, and one cannot make them up. (Anyon 1980)

A fourth school, which Anyon termed 'affluent professional', had students whose parents were em-

ployed as corporate lawyers, engineers, and advertising executives. At this school, the work involved

> . . . creative activity carried out independently. The students are continually asked to express and apply ideas and concepts. Work involves individual thought and expressiveness, expansion and illustration of ideas, and choice of appropriate method and material. . . . The products of work in this class are often written stories, editorials, and essays, or representations of ideas in mural, graph, or craft form. The products of work should not be like anybody else's and should show individuality. . . . One's product is usually evaluated for the quality of its expression and for the appropriateness of its conception to the task. (Anyon 1980)

The fifth school Anyon studied she called 'executive elite', as most of the students' fathers held positions as presidents and vice-presidents of major corporations. In this school, work involved

> . . . developing one's analytical intellectual powers. Children are continually asked to reason through a problem, to produce intellectual products that are both logically sound and of top academic quality. A primary goal of thought is to conceptualize rules by which elements may fit together in systems and then to apply these rules in solving a problem. (Anyon 1980)

If there were a sociology class offered at the school level Anyon studied, daily activities in each category might look something like this:

working-class	copying down and memorizing the instructor's notes from the board
middle-class	reading the textbook and finding the right answer
affluent professional	finding information on an assigned topic and writing it up in one's own words
executive elite	analyzing social systems and looking for strengths and weaknesses

Cultural Reproduction Theory

There are two opposing positions on education and social mobility. One is that education is **meritocratic**: according to this position, school performance reflects natural ability (i.e. merit), and the system provides mobility for lower-class and minoritized students who work hard to succeed. The opposing position, that of **cultural reproduction**, argues that the education system reinforces and reproduces the inequality of the surrounding society.

An influential work grounded in cultural reproduction theory is **Jeannie Oakes**'s *Keeping Track: How Schools Structure Inequality* (2005), which addresses the issue of **tracking** (also called 'streaming') in junior and senior high schools. Oakes defines tracking as 'the process whereby students are divided into categories so that they can be assigned in groups to various kinds of classes' (Oakes 2005: 3). Tracking is hierarchical, with both classes and students being labelled according to different levels of aptitude and projected outcomes (for instance, whether or not students are expected to pursue a post-secondary degree). Oakes studied 297 classrooms in 25 schools in the late 1970s and early 1980s. Her work demonstrated that sorting is based as much or more on class, race, and ethnicity as it is on perceived ability. She also showed that lower tracks offer lower quality of education than the higher tracks do, and that, as a consequence, the American tracking system reproduces inequality.

Oakes argued that the disproportionate representation of lower-class and non-white students in the lower track reflects the cultural biases of testing and the prejudices of counsellors and teachers. The inferior quality of lower-track education came partly from the reduced expectations for the students in the lower track. For instance, lower-track English courses emphasized basic punctuation and form-filling as opposed to great works of literature; lower-track math courses emphasized basic computational skills rather than problem solving, critical thinking, and abstract logic; lower-track vocational courses focused on clerical skills, not the managerial and financial skills taught in the higher-track courses.

Another important finding had to do with differences in classroom time spent on instruction and learning activities versus administrative routines and discipline. According to data supplied by teachers, the average amounts of classroom time spent on instruction in English and math courses in the higher track were 82 per cent and 77 per cent; the comparable figures for lower-track instruction time were 71 per cent and 63 per cent.

From a cultural reproduction standpoint, it is also important to look at relationship differences between teachers and students, among students, and between students and the institution generally. Samuel Bowles and Harold Gintis point to the 'close correspondence between the social relationships which govern personal interaction in the work place and the social relationships of the educational system' (1976: 12); in other words, in terms of social relationships, the education system trains students in the lower track to become lower-class workers. Oakes summarized their position as follows:

> These [lower-class] workers will be subordinate to external control and alienated from the institutions but willing to conform to the needs of the work place, to a large extent because of the way they were treated in school. . . . Bowles and Gintis suggest that the absence of close interpersonal relationships is characteristic of both lower-class work environments and classroom environments for lower-class children. In contrast, upper- and middle-class students, destined for upper-status and middle-level positions in the economic hierarchy, are more likely to experience social relationships and interactions that promote active involvement, affiliation with others, and the internalization of rules and behavioral standards. Self-regulation is the goal here rather than the coercive authority and control seen as appropriate for the lower class. (Oakes 2005: 119–20)

Oakes found that teachers were more punitive in lower-track classes, while higher-track classes fostered more trusting relationships between teachers and students. In her words, '[t]rust, cooperation, and even good will among students were far less characteristic of low-track classes than of high. More student time and energy were spent in hostile and disruptive interchanges in these classes' (2005: 132).

Key to cultural reproduction theory is the **legitimation of inequality**. According to this idea, if students accept that their differential tracking placement is fair, this legitimates the inequality reproduced by the education system. Oakes found that 'students in low-track classes tended to be saying that school's all right, but I'm not so good. In contrast, students in high-track classes were feeling pretty good about both their schools *and* themselves' (2005: 143–4).

Overall, Oakes believes that with the deep class, ethnic, and racial distinctions existing in mainstream American society, a tracking system can only reproduce inequality. She argues for more of a common curriculum shared by all students, and for more mixing of students of different ability levels.

QUICK HITS
Student Examples from Oakes's Study

What is the most important thing you have learned or done so far in the class (in terms of subject matter)?

High Track
Vocational Education, Junior High
'We've talked about stocks/bonds and the stock market and about business in the USA.'

English, Junior High
'Learned to analyze famous writings by famous people, and we have learned to understand people's different viewpoints on general ideas.'

Social Studies, Junior High
'The most important thing is the way other countries and places govern themselves economically, socially, and politically. Also different philosophers and their theories on government and man and how their theories relate to us and now.'

Low-Track
English, Junior High
'Learns to fill out checks and other banking business.'

English, Junior High
'to spell words you don't know, to fill out things where you get a job.'

English Senior High
'I learned that English is boring.'

Source: Oakes 2005: 68–71.

What do YOU think?

1. The strongest opposition to detracking comes from those involved with education of the 'gifted'. Why do you think they are more opposed to detracking than those involved with low-track education?

2. If you were the principal of a high school, would you support or reject streaming? Would your answer depend such social factors as the class, ethnicity, and overall demographics of your school?

Disqualified Knowledges: Aboriginal Voices and the Politics of Representation in Canadian Introductory Sociology Textbooks

Textbooks form an important and influential part of education, and yet they remain an understudied topic in the sociology of education. For my doctoral dissertation, I examined 77 Canadian introductory sociology textbooks concerning their representation of Aboriginal people. What I discovered was a serious and progressive lack of Aboriginal voice. Aboriginal writers were not represented as a significant source of information on their own people. In Michel Foucault's terminology, theirs were **disqualified knowledges**—'knowledges that have been disqualified as inadequate to their task or insufficiently elaborated; naive knowledges located down on the hierarchy, beneath the required cognition of scientificity' (Foucault 1980: 82). Foucault might have argued that Aboriginal writers were not included because they were not scientific or 'objective' enough for the writers of sociology textbooks. Yet their viewpoints offer a legitimate alternative to standard sociology knowledge. They represent **indigenous knowledges**, described by George Dei et al. as 'the common-sense ideas and cultural knowledges of local peoples concerning the everyday realities of living. Those knowledges are part of the cultural heritage and histories of peoples' (Dei et al. 2000: 49).

The 'disqualification' of Aboriginal voice has been a growing, not diminishing, trend. Early Canadian introductory sociology textbooks

The Point Is...

Education, Employment, and Disabled Women

Most evidence shows that the more education you have, the better your chances are for finding employment. But this does not necessarily follow for disabled women.

A report on disabled women published in 2005 found that disabled women in Newfoundland and Labrador were less likely to attend trade and technology schools than disabled men, though they had higher high-school completion rates and higher participation levels in colleges and universities.

Almost twice as many women as men with disabilities graduated from university. Yet despite the fact that disabled women had higher levels of education than their male counterparts, unemployment and underemployment, according to figures cited in the study, are the major causes of poverty among disabled women.

While disabled women reported increased levels of self-esteem when they had more education, they still had lower employment rates than disabled men, able-bodied women, and able-bodied men (Murdoch 2005).

---

entailed collections of readings. As sociologists were not studying Aboriginal people then, contributions written about Aboriginal people were typically authored by outsiders to sociology, including Inuit leader Abraham Okpik, Ojibwa author Wilfred Pelletier, and Cree politician and scholar Harold Cardinal. When sociologists began studying Aboriginal people in urban settings in the early 1970s, the Aboriginal voice was lost from sociology textbooks: the only coverage of Aboriginal people came from non-Aboriginal sociologist writers. Excluded were works by important Aboriginal writers such as Howard Adams, George Manuel, Emma Laroque, Maria Campbell, Patricia Monture-Angus, and Lee Maracle.

Aboriginal Education: Best Practices in British Columbia

Sociologists have been criticized for concentrating on Aboriginal people only as social problems while neglecting some of the more influences they have on society. This is true of sociological discussions of Aboriginal education, which tend to focus only on the horrific stories of the residential schools, and the poor academic performance of Aboriginal students since. An alternative perspective comes from *Understanding the Aboriginal/Non-Aboriginal Gap in Student Performance: Lessons from British Columbia* (Richards, Hove, and Afolabi 2008). Summarizing the results of a study that examined Aboriginal student performance in non-Aboriginal public schools, the authors identified the following five 'best practices' that are key to student success:

- collaboration between school district personnel at all levels and local Aboriginal communities
- commitment by administrators and teachers to incorporating Aboriginal content into the curriculum
- creation of influential positions (such as full-time teachers and school trustees) dedicated to Aboriginal education
- relationship-building between Aboriginal and non-Aboriginal communities in the district
- willingness of school district authorities to share responsibility for making decisions with Aboriginal communities.

Interviews conducted by the study's authors revealed that non-Aboriginal teachers often presented obstacles to Aboriginal involvement in their classrooms. While it is easy to say that personal racism is involved, sociologists also look for institutional barriers. The Canadian education system overall teaches very little about Aboriginal people. This means that most Canadian teachers are ill prepared to work with an Aboriginal curriculum. They are ignorant of Aboriginal history, language, and culture generally—not through individual bias, but because they are products of a school system that has failed to adequately cover issues relating to Canada's Native people. This is a form of **institutional racism** that is self-perpetuating.

● ● ● ● ● ● ● ● ● ● ● ● ● ● ● ● ● ● ● ●

What do YOU think?

What problems do you think might exist in terms of adopting the best practices referred to in this study?

● ● ● ● ● ● ● ● ● ● ● ● ● ● ● ● ● ● ● ●

Credentialism

Credentialism is another factor that often blocks Aboriginal attempts to improve education. It is the practice of valuing credentials—degrees, diplomas, certificates—over actual knowledge and ability in the hiring and promotion of staff. Community college departments in faculties of social science and humanities practise credentialism when they refuse to consider candidates for instructors' positions unless they have a PhD; having 'just' an MA isn't enough, regardless of the candidate's experience. Degrees do not measure teaching ability; and teaching is stressed over research at colleges.

In many Aboriginal communities, elders are deeply involved in educating children and young adults (Haig-Brown et al. 1997). However, elders do not typically carry paper credentials. Their qualification comes primarily from community recognition. Elders are people recognized in Aboriginal communities as being experts in traditional knowledge, such as hunting, fishing, spirituality, healing, childcare, and crafts. Most teachers coming from non-Aboriginal communities are

• Our Stories • ●

Plains Indian Cultural Survival School

Dropout rates for Aboriginal students are highest in Grade 9 and Grade 10. In regions of the country where there is no local Aboriginal high school, the first day of high school outside the Native community may be a young person's first direct experience with mainstream society. At an age when there are intense social pressures, Aboriginal youth in the public school system frequently encounter racist attitudes and behaviour, from both students and teachers, undermining their self-esteem.

Some Canadian cities have seen the establishment of Native Survival Schools, designed to meet the needs of Native students in urban centres. They offer academic programs that meet provincial curriculum standards while incorporating elements of Native cultural traditions, language, and spirituality.

The Plains Indians Cultural Survival School (PICSS) was established in 1979. It was the brainchild of Howard Green, a teacher in Strathcona, Alberta, who was alarmed by the high dropout rates among Aboriginal students. At the time, 95 per cent of Native children who started school never graduated, with 84 per cent of Native students having dropped out by Grade 9. PICSS became the first urban junior and senior high school in Canada initiated and controlled by the Aboriginal community. In its first year of operation, it had 53 students; today, there are over 450.

The school's stated mission is 'the successful education of all children . . . [which] centres around . . . the development of a positive self concept, a belief in one's own worth, . . . [which is] crucial to academic and social progress' (PICSS information sheet). Its aim is achieved through courses emphasizing Native culture. Although many of the courses are taught by non-Natives, all cultural courses and programs are taught exclusively by Aboriginal teachers. The school provides instruction for students aspiring to graduate with either a general or an advanced diploma. Because two-thirds of the students are 'mature' students over the age of 20, PICSS has introduced job-training programs, in partnership with Calgary businesses.

Although the academic courses follow provincial guidelines, the school board openly invites Native input because of its unique academic and cultural curriculum. The curriculum replaces many traditional optional courses with ones that are more culturally relevant to the student body; examples

Photo: © David Leadbitter/Alamy

Children enter an elementary school at Alert Bay, BC. What do you think are the best strategies to ensure that the Aboriginal voice is heard in Canada's classroom?

include Blackfoot or Cree as a second language, wilderness survival in physical education, drumming in music, and stone carving and bead work in art. Wherever possible, Native culture has been integrated as much as possible into the mainstream academic programs; for instance, courses in English literature study only Native authors or books about Native peoples.

Elder Lloyd Ewenin, a guidance counsellor and the culture director of PICSS, became involved in the school when he moved to Calgary and enrolled his children. He soon went from being a parent to being a PICSS Society board member and, after serving a five-year term on the board, an employee. Ewenin, who has extensive training in counselling through Native-run organizations such as the Nechi Institute, notes that prejudices in the non-Native education system produce a general mistrust of the system among Aboriginal students, as well as a negative self-concept that contributes to the high drop-out rate. In a personal interview, he explained that many of the students at PICSS have 'a lot of anger' in them stemming from bad experiences in the public school system. As a result, PICSS attempts to defuse any resentment towards authority by creating an atmosphere that is non-institutional and based on a model of understanding and support, with minimal restrictions and pressures. Students are free to work at their own pace, and a student who is absent for a month, for whatever reason, may resume his or her studies upon return—though, Ewenin admits, chuckling, this often frustrates the teachers.

PICSS is in a difficult financial position because it is not on a reserve and therefore does not receive any direct financial support from band, federal, provincial, or municipal governments. Although the local school board and the provincial government do allocate funding to PICSS, they are not legally required to do so, which makes this source of funding tenuous. The provincial government and school board assign PICSS a low priority, leaving it subject to cutbacks. Such was the case in 1993, when the local school board announced it would pare back its funding of the school, which resulted in the loss of five full-time teaching positions and one part-time position. Ewenin notes that he regularly stresses the importance of education to his students as a 'vital component to Native survival', something both the school board and province failed to learn.

not familiar with elders because the role of elder is not assigned significant status in mainstream Canadian society.

● ●

What do YOU think?

In what other areas of education might credentialism pose problems? Credentialism seems to flow from anonymity and social isolation; people do not know you so they need to see your 'papers'. Do you think that makes it inevitable?

● ●

Issues in Post-Secondary Education

Post-secondary education in Canada has changed dramatically over the last 30 years. Most of the changes have not been positive, having been driven primarily by shifts in economic policies. In spite of the fact that more students than ever are enrolled in post-secondary institutions, tuition fees have risen while funding of public education has been steadily cut back. There has been an increase in part-time faculty, and in some areas a rapid move away from actual in-class instruction towards online program and virtual colleges and universities. Grade inflation and plagiarism are both on the rise. Amidst all of these changes there has been very little informed public dialogue about how these trends are affecting schools, students, and society. In the sections that follow we will take a close and critical look at many of these issues and how they affect the quality of education in Canadian classrooms and society in general.

Long-Term Adjunct Instructors: A Social Class within Post-secondary Education

The growing ranks of long-term adjunct instructors in post-secondary institutions is the product of several economic and social factors, including the increasing number of post-secondary students, the reduction of government investment in post-secondary education, the increasing levels of private corporate funding (through sponsorships and advertising), and the rising influence of a corporate culture that regards education just like any other business. The trend of turning full-time teaching positions into long-term adjunct posts is not unlike contracting out skilled jobs (think of IT professionals, for instance) to avoid having to grant the benefits or long-term commitment that come with full-time work.

Names for this class of education workers differ. They are commonly referred to as **adjunct professors**, following the American convention, but you may have heard them called sessionals, contract staff, part-time instructors (a particularly misleading term, since many put in more hours than do full-time instructors). In Canada, the term 'adjunct' is used to refer specifically to an experienced instructor who, because of seniority, is the first in line to take the courses full-timer instructors don't want. Originally, adjuncts were typically professionals who had careers elsewhere—usually in business or in law—and who taught for the prestige and the extra money. This group still exists, but they are now greatly outnumbered by those whose intended career is teaching. Contract teaching used to be a first step towards a full-time job or a tenure-track position (in other words, a full-time, nearly impossible to lose job). Now that path is often blocked.

Ghosts in the Classroom: Stories of College Adjunct Faculty—and the Price We All Pay, edited by Michael Dubson, is a collection of narratives from adjunct professors working at colleges and universities in the United States. Almost all of the contributors are English instructors—not surprising, given that many of them teach writing for a living, and English departments are large, with lots of temporary work for adjuncts. There is a lot of competition for jobs in this area, illustrated in the writers' frequent use of the phrase 'dime a dozen' to refer to their competitive position. One of the topics raised again and again in the collection is the low pay, which is especially tough to swallow given that salaries for full-time staff are well over double what adjunct instructors are paid. One of the collections contributors speaks eloquently of the sense of **relative deprivation** felt by many adjuncts:

I work half a semester before I ever see a dime. [Full-time instructors] get pay-checks every week or every other week. . . . If I teach eight courses in an academic year, I make approximately $16,000. They teach eight to ten courses during an academic year and make, on the average, $40,000. I must horde my money and pinch my pennies for I must live on it during the semester breaks. Full-time teachers get paid all year long, whether they work or not.

Because the pay is so poor, . . . I must string together collections of adjunct course assignments from several different schools. I have taught six, seven, eight classes a semester at three or four different schools. . . . I have worked other jobs and taught on the side. I have split my time between teaching four or five courses, a full-time load, and another job. (M. Theodore Swift 2001: 2–3)

Working conditions are often commented on in the collection. Conditions range from sharing a desk or not even having a desk to having restricted use of departmental photocopiers—all factors contributing to relative deprivation. Jody Lannen Brady's description of working conditions is typical:

I shared a dingy office with twenty other instructors, and some semesters I was lucky to find a chair to perch on during my office hours. I often met with students in the hallway because it was quieter than the office. I had one file cabinet drawer I could call my own, but I hauled all my papers and books back and forth from home to office and back each day because I couldn't work in the office, never knowing how many times I would have to jump up and answer the phone, and if I would have a desk to sit at. (Brady 2001: 147)

What might surprise full-time professors is the extent to which the adjunct writers feel they are engaged in a class war with full-timers—a war they are losing, as the adjuncts begin to comprise a majority of the instructors). Part of this involves the segregation of full-time and part-time instructors. There are few scheduled activities in which the two groups meet. Two excerpts illustrate the point:

At one college, I share office space one day a week with one of the full-time instructors. He put a sign with my name by the door as a sort of welcoming gesture. The next week, the secretary of the English Department

Photo: Ron Bull/GetStock.com

Have you been to this site? What do you think are some of the consequences of rating your instructors online? How are these consequences different for adjuncts and full-time professors?

wrote me a note. Two of the full-time teachers were in a fury at the arrogance of my putting up a nameplate. (Gale 2001: 13)

Once, in a heated personal discussion with a full-time colleague, she blurted out, 'Who the hell do you think you are? You're only an adjunct here!' (Werner 2001: 37)

These frustrations with colleagues are compounded by trying relationships with the students. Student evaluations are more important to the employment status of adjuncts than they are to the positions of full-time staff members. A poor evaluation won't get a full-timer fired, but it could cause an adjunct not to be hired back once the contract has ended. One writer explains:

If I have poor course evaluations, I will be out. . . . If my students complain about me, legitimately or otherwise, I will be out. If a full-time faculty member faces any of this, he or she will be supported, worked with, helped. Full-time tenured faculty may not even be evaluated, and . . . if their students complain about them, nothing affecting their employment or job security will be done. (Swift 2001: 3)

It should not be surprising, then, that adjunct professors have been organizing. There are adjunct associations, journals, and attempts to unionize. The kinds of conditions described above were a flashpoint in the strike by graduate student tutorial assistants and part-time instructors at York University in 2008–9. Of course, the media concentrated mainly on the money issues, not the working and hiring conditions.

Online Teaching: A Critical Sociological Approach

During the late 1990s and early 2000s, there was a push throughout North America to offer a drastically increased number of online courses, even to the point of offering online diplomas and degrees, in some cases through colleges and universities based entirely online. This was driven by technological improvements, certainly, but also by cuts to post-secondary education funding. The online movement was hyped with the allure of change as

progress, and played well to the susceptibility of educators to changes in intellectual fashion. It was also driven by private organizations specializing in delivering educational packages over the Internet, who coined or co-opted sexy terms like 'advanced learning' and 'open learning', in spite of their yet unproven ability to provide education that is either more advanced or more open. They invest heavily in hosting or attending 'educational' conferences (popular perks among post-secondary instructors), where they offer solicited and unsolicited product demonstrations.

The success of online education providers has come at a time when many colleges and universities, feeling the financial pinch, have turned to the private sector as a partial solution to an underfunded public system. The boosters of online education are more often administrators and educational companies looking for the government dollars that flow to public institutions than actual instructors, though the latter group does include believers. Student demand for these courses is more unsupported myth than documented fact.

In the world of post-secondary education, a magic word is **access**. Online courses promise to provide access to education for those who would find it difficult to attend college or university otherwise, the so-called 'non-traditional students' (a group that supposedly includes working parents, who have traditionally made good use of night school courses). As we have seen, **access without mobility** can readily reproduce the class system, while seeming to improve the lot of the more marginalized social groups.

From a sociological standpoint, how are online courses different from in-class courses? Before we tackle this question, it's worth noting that another flawed feature of many a North American university is the large lecture hall, which shares some weaknesses with online courses. One colleague of mine, who was a sessional instructor at the University of Toronto, had 900 students in his introductory class. One person lecturing to hundreds has to put on an amazing performance to engage students. It can be done, but it is difficult, and not the norm. The teacher–student relationship that is possible in smaller classes is replaced by a student's relationship with a teaching assistant (or TA), someone who may be at the university

The Point Is...

Online Education: A New Spin on a Failed Idea?

Historian David Noble (2002) reminds us that a movement similar to the online education movement happened from the 1880s to the 1930s, when correspondence courses—which enabled students to receive lessons and submit their work by mail—came into vogue. The movement began with independent, privately run schools, before the universities, fearing competition and eager to benefit from a relatively easy source of profit, got involved. People marketing the correspondence courses used a language that would be familiar to educators today, as they reached out to 'non-traditional students' with the promise of 'working on your own time'. Mostly, however, post-secondary administrators eyed not the chance to bring higher education to the masses but a good source of profit with relatively low overhead costs. Tuition was paid up front and was non-refundable, yet the dropout rate was high; indeed, the vast majority never completed their courses. Noble refers to the main source of profit as 'drop-out money'. At the same time, the faculty involved were under-paid, receiving between 25 and 35 cents a lesson. By the 1930s, although correspondence courses continued to be offered, the institutions involved were criticized for being 'diploma mills' serving up an inferior education.

The factors that sparked the establishment of correspondence courses in the late nineteenth century are similar to the ones that have created a favourable environment for the growth of online education today:

- the rise of credentialism (setting value on credentials such as certificates and diplomas)
- funding cuts, sending universities and colleges in search of new sources of revenue
- the development of private training companies
- the rapid development of information technology (then, of course, advances in mail delivery services).

Noble sees the contemporary movement, with the flood of online courses and of online universities, as suffering from the same flaws that plagued correspondence courses—profit considered over education, poorly paid staff with very little job security, and, on average, an inferior education when matched up against its in-class equivalent. Historian George Santayana famously said, 'Those who cannot remember the past are condemned to repeat it.' Shouldn't colleges and universities learn the lessons of history here?

only temporarily and is paid significantly less than a full-time, tenured lecturer. This arrangement that features massive classes supported by smaller tutorials is, like the online movement, driven by the perceived economics of post-secondary education. When we talk in this chapter about in-class teaching, we are referring to classes held in the more intimate classroom setting, not the lecture hall or theatre.

Critics of the online movement fear that it is driven mainly by economics rather than education. Interestingly, though, the savings supposedly achieved by online education may be more apparent than real: acquiring and upgrading expensive technical equipment combined with the hiring of additional technical and administrative staff can drastically reduce the profit margin. When boosting revenue becomes the main objective, it leads to

the **commodification** of education. Noble (2002) describes this as

the disintegration and distillation of the educational experience into discrete, reified, and ultimately saleable things or packages of things. In the first step toward commodification, attention is shifted from the experience of the people involved in the educational process to the production and inventorying of an assortment of 'course materials'; syllabi, lectures, lessons, exams. . . . As anyone familiar with higher education knows, these common instruments of instruction barely reflect what actually takes place in the educational experience, and lend an illusion of order and predictability to what is, at its best, an essentially unscripted and undetermined process.

Second, these fragments are removed or 'alienated' from their original context, the actual educational process itself, and from their producers, the teachers, and are assembled as 'courses,' which take on an existence independent of and apart from those who created and gave flesh to them. (Noble 2002: 3)

The concept of **alienation** is important. In the writings of Karl Marx, alienation involves the separation or disconnect between people and the work that they are paid to do. People working on an assembly line are disconnected from what they do, as it is work handed down to them by others; the workers themselves have no say in what they do or how they do it, and there is no personal footprint on their labour. Chefs who have signature dishes are closely connected with their work; people working the fry counter at McDonalds are not. In a similar way, instructors can become disconnected from their **intellectual property** when it is used as part of an online course. Noble elaborates on what this entails:

Once faculty put their course material online, . . . the knowledge and course design skill embodied in that material is taken out of their possession. . . . The administration is now in a position to hire . . . cheaper workers to deliver the technologically prepackaged course. It also allows the administration, which claims ownership of this commodity, to peddle the course elsewhere without the original designer's involvement or even knowledge, much less financial interest. The buyers of this packaged commodity, meanwhile, . . . are able thereby to contract out . . . the work of their own employees and thus reduce their reliance upon their in-house teaching staff. (Noble 1998)

Alienation involves the hierarchical control of a product, in which the boss has ultimate say in how it is developed, used, and distributed. With online courses, the potential for administrative monitoring and control is greatly increased. Instructors can be more closely supervised through the educational products they have supplied for the course's website. Online courses also allow administrators to measure instructor interactions with students: How often are instructors logging on? How responsive are they to students' online questions? This kind of supervision is also possible with course

Is online learning the way of the future? What are the pros and cons of teaching in a chatroom rather than a classroom?

Photo: Lucas Oleniuk/GetStock.com

components offered by means of packaged Web products like Blackboard (an American company that took over the University of British Columbia's WebCT software, thereby gaining a powerful foothold on post-secondary education in Canada).

Online universities like the University of Phoenix in the US and Athabasca University ('Canada's open university') are staffed with relatively few full-time instructors and many 'tutors'. Professors fear that this is the face of the future: part-time and limited-time contract staff dominating over full-time teachers. The following statement from Meritus University, which opened its virtual doors in September 2008 (headquartered in Fredericton, though its physical location is of very little importance), shows that they indeed have something to fear:

> While others established academic programs around tradition and tenure, Apollo has built programs in conjunction with the needs of business and industry—effectively translating those needs into clear and transparent learning objectives.

In its first semester, Meritus University had just four full-time teaching staff.

The online delivery of education depends, like many exploitative systems, on getting workers to do more than they are paid for, relying on dedicated teachers who improve a bad situation with their talent and their labour. But there are also those who 'work to rule', who calculate exactly how much work they have to do to get paid and do no more. (Anecdotally, we know of one case an instructor would do only three hours of work a week and would not answer e-mails after that point.) At that point, the system fails the student.

So what about the students? We know that these courses suffer from significant dropout rates. Students who succeed are typically highly motivated, highly disciplined people, who get through despite the flaws inherent in the method of delivery. The good marks these students get should not be used to argue that people do better in a work-at-home, online environment. They represent triumphs of individuals over systems.

Online education works better for some kinds of courses. It lends itself more to **instrumental education**, where courses are narrowly directed to particular sets of tasks, than to **critical education**, which involves analysis of ideas and, ideally, classroom discussion. With online courses, as the information flow is more one-directional than in the classroom, more controlled by the curriculum than by student–teacher interaction. Students have less input into how the course proceeds. Their instructors have less input as well, since they are typically part-timers who are more vulnerable to administrative control.

There is concern among educators and critics that a two-tiered, two-class system will develop, with the middle and upper classes attending in-class institutions ('brick universities') and preparing for jobs that will maintain their family's class standing, while those 'attending' the digital institutions ('click universities') will be lower-class students and others for whom regular college or university attendance is impossible (e.g. single mothers and other working parents); they will receive lower-cost virtual vocational training that will lead them to lower-level, lower-paying service jobs. These are also the people most likely to suffer, academically as well as socially, from the isolation that comes with online courses, and the ones who would most benefit from in-class discussions. In this way, the system will reproduce rather than challenge the North American class system.

● ● ● ● ● ● ● ● ● ● ● ● ● ● ● ● ● ● ●

What do YOU think?

1. What arguments would supporters of online education mount to combat the arguments given here?

2. Why do you think sociology professors might be more critical of online education than would professors of other disciplines (for instance, business)?

3. How could you do research that would test the effectiveness or ineffectiveness of online education?

● ● ● ● ● ● ● ● ● ● ● ● ● ● ● ● ● ● ●

Political Correctness and the College/University Campus

We're all familiar with **political correctness**. It generally refers to the well-intentioned, if sometimes somewhat misguided, attempts to limit speech and writing by censoring words and phrases that exhibit and promote racism, sexism, ableism, ageism, and other forms of discrimination. The basic idea is that people who have been negatively named should be treated with greater respect. Words that relate to specific groups can have a different sense or 'feel' to them depending on who uses them and to whom they are applied. If the term is used by those who are economically, socially, and politically dominant to apply to those who are minoritized (by being in a weaker economic, social, or political position), then the term has a different meaning to the dominant and to the minoritized. The emotional impact differs sharply. It is often difficult for members of the dominant group to understand the impact, because they don't feel it. It cannot hurt them. Members of the dominant group also have conversation-paralyzing 'word weapons' at their disposal that they can use to negate any complaint by the minoritized. They can belittle those who are offended by attributing any complaint to political correctness 'making a big deal over nothing' or an attempt to censor 'free speech'. Political correctness was essentially born and raised in post-secondary institutions, so the

academy is often accused of restrictively censoring 'free speech' or having 'no sense of humour'. Those who encourage or enforce political correctness on college and university campuses are sometimes negatively labelled as 'thought police'.

In *Patriotic Correctness: Academic Freedom and Its Enemies* (2008) John K. Wilson describes several conservative strains of political correctness, which he refers to generically as **patriotic correctness**. In the US, he explains, patriotic correctness greatly restricts academic freedom, by preventing people from expressing ideas or viewpoints that might be considered unpatriotic because they are critical of government policies, especially those relating to the 'war on terror'. For students, this means lack of exposure to a diversity of ideas: courses may be cancelled for political reasons, public speakers may be prevented from making speeches on campus, and student newspapers, websites, and behaviour may be strictly monitored and censored.

Another form of conservative political correctness Wilson discusses is **corporate correctness,** whereby instructors and students are restricted

Photo: © Scott Camazine/Alamy

At what age do you think students are able to recognize and evaluate politically loaded messages in the classroom?

from criticizing the corporations that give large donations to post-secondary institutions; this can include an element of **capitalist correctness**, where people are discouraged or prevented from criticizing the 'free-market' system and its excesses. Wilson also identified examples of **Christian correctness** in the many Christian post-secondary institutions that exist in the United States, where faculty and students have been prohibited from challenging a literal, conservative interpretation of the Bible (especially concerning evolution). For instance, some Catholic post-secondary institutions in the US restrict speakers on campus and try to block the hiring of professors who take a pro-choice stance with respect to abortion. We would add to Wilson's list **college correctness**, something he discusses throughout his book, though he does not name it as such. College correctness includes punishing teachers and students for publicly voicing criticisms of administrative policies or administrators, particularly effective in institutions in which tenured staff are in the minority or non-existent, and where unions do not exist.

● ● ● ● ● ● ● ● ● ● ● ● ● ● ● ● ● ● ●

What do YOU think?

1. What signs of political correctness have you seen on your campus? What category do they fall into? Are they more liberal or conservative?

2. Why do you think we hear less about the conservative than the liberal forms of political correctness?

● ● ● ● ● ● ● ● ● ● ● ● ● ● ● ● ● ● ●

Do You Want Fries with that Degree?

Students joke about the **McJob**—the low-paying, unskilled service job—they might be able to get with their undervalued degree once they've graduated. What the term really refers to is **underemployment**, which can have two meanings relevant to our discussion of education:

- involuntary part-time work for people seeking full-time employment
- low-wage, low-skill employment for people with valuable skills, experience, or academic credentials.

Statistics Canada, since 2005, has defined 'underemployed as 'seeking full-time work but finding only part-time work'. The category does not include those who have been unable to work full-time for health or other personal reasons, nor does it acknowledge the problem of an over-skilled workforce. Underemployment is the result of several factors, including

- the rate of unemployment,
- regional disparity (lack of employment opportunities and resources like training and childcare in economically depressed areas), and
- discrimination based on ethnicity, gender, disability, or lack of 'appropriate' credentials.

How does this apply to post-secondary students? Those who hold high-quality skills and academic credentials become underemployed when there is low marketplace demand—a demand determined not just by the strength or weakness of the Canadian or global economy, but, in the case of Canada, demographics. The demographic bulge caused by the baby boomers means that access to employment is cut off for those newly entering the workforce, many of whom are better qualified than their predecessors. Moreover, the instrumental and utilitarian pragmatics of **neoliberal** economics means that despite the fact that having a degree is a prerequisite for almost any job, degrees in the social sciences, humanities, and especially fine arts and classics are valued poorly within the marketplace. Sustained underemployment also means that skills acquired from one's degree (critical and analytical thinking, writing, researching, etc.) can wither from disuse.

During the 1990s, according to Statistics Canada, universities produced 1.2 million graduates, but only 600,000 jobs requiring university-level credentials were created during that same period. Currently, there are about one million students in the post-secondary system. If job creation remains the same as it did in the 1990s, then several hundred thousand graduates each year will be pursuing fewer than 100,000 job openings. This could effectively increase the structural underemployment rate from the 50 per cent level found in the 1980s and 1990s to 75 per cent.

In the case of highly trained immigrants, their level of education is used as part of a point system that determines who can and cannot immigrate to Canada. However, while their level and type of education is used to determine their worthiness for immigration, their foreign credentials as well as their work experience are not recognized or accepted in their new country due, in part, to **cultural racism**. Those educated in the developing world, whether engineers or medical doctors, are seen to have a substandard education, which in most cases is not true. The standard of education in many non-Western countries is at least equal to that in Canada.

In the case of new college and university graduates, underemployment can result from a lack of practical experience, even for those who have technical training in a specific field or who are seeking employment when the job market is strong. As a result, recent graduates may be forced to work in low-paying or part-time jobs until they find work in their field. Studies between 1982 and 2004 in Canada show that while post-secondary education attainment has increased for various occupational classes, so too has the underemployment rate for those same occupational classes. The same research also shows that the rate of underemployment is greater than the underqualified rate. Forty-five per cent of those aged 18–24 see themselves as being overqualified for their current jobs as opposed to 25–22 per cent of those 40 and over (Livingstone 2004). Among the solutions that have been proposed to reduce skill-based underemployment are government-imposed restrictions on enrolment in post-secondary courses and programs with low labour market demand. However, the university system would be unable to support such a proposal, as it would reduce student enrolment and, therefore, revenues.

James Côté and Anton Allahar (2007), in their book *Ivory Tower Blues: A University System in Crisis*, take a close look at underemployment. They note, as we've mentioned here, that some underemployment is structural: there are simply not enough jobs for our university and college graduates. Post-secondary graduates, however, are less likely to be unemployed because they will take jobs requiring lower levels of education, leaving high school and community college graduates in an even worse predicament than was

the case before so many began taking the university route to compete for entry-level positions. This predicament is referred to as the 'downward cascading effect' of credential over-production (Côté and Allahar 2007).

The Sociology of Plagiarism

Ask any professor about the problems of teaching at a post-secondary institution, and he or she will talk about **plagiarism**. This is particularly true of instructors teaching courses in the social sciences and the humanities, including literature courses—in other words, those courses with a heavy grade component based on essay writing.

Carol Thompson, in her insightful article 'Unintended Lessons: Plagiarism and the University', defines plagiarism as 'the wholesale copying of another's work or the collaging of several papers (or Web sites) via the Internet'. (2006). Basically, it involves passing off someone else's ideas or work as your own. The ideas and words aren't yours, and the sources of those ideas and words aren't properly identified or even mentioned.

Thompson adopts a sociological approach to address why plagiarism has become such a common phenomenon. She emphasizes the influence of **role models**, asserting that students have the very patterns of behaviour they're warned not to fall into modelled for them by professors, school administrators, and even famous writers and academics, like American historian Stephen Ambrose (who acted as historical consultant for Stephen Spielberg's *Saving Private Ryan*) and the Pulitzer Prize–winning Doris Kearns Goodwin. In Canada the list could include Prime Minister Stephen Harper, whose speech in 2003 supporting the American attack on Iraq was copied almost word for word from a speech made by Australian Prime Minister John Howard two days earlier. These role models are not necessarily the kinds of **significant others** (see Chapter 4) who would have an important impact on college and university students. Yet they do show that there is some kind of acceptance of plagiarism by the 'leaders' of society. More influential could be parents, who have often helped students in writing and assembling their projects in high school, and who may get involved in their children's post-secondary

The Point Is...

You Are Not as Smart as You Think You Are: Grade Inflation

In their book *Ivory Tower Blues: A University System in Crisis*, Côté and Allahar uncover an interesting trend in post-secondary education over the last 20 years: grade inflation, the gradual rise in grades awarded to students. Part of this trend has come as a result of changing student expectations, which they summarize in the following passage:

> The traditional standard for an average performance was a C, but that is now a thing of the past in most of our educational institutions. Many students now expect B's for putting out a modicum of effort that produces mediocre work, and A's if they do any more than this. Failure is a thing of the past in many schools.

The Canadian university system emerged out of the British system, where no more than 5 per cent of students were awarded A's, and 30 per cent were given B's. That means that just one-third of the student population would have been judged to be above average, and between 30 and 40 per cent would have been judged as average. Currently, at least twice as many students are receiving A's and B's in Canadian universities and high schools. Côté and Allahar note a recent survey of first-year university students, which found that 70 per cent of respondents rate themselves as above average.

The practice of grade inflation has consequences for both individuals and society. It is bad for bright students, because they aren't challenged and, in turn, don't develop their intellectual potential in ways that would both enrich their lives and contribute to the Canadian economy. Inflated grades are also bad for those students who are average or below, in that they are given higher marks than they deserve and therefore aren't encouraged or told how to improve. When we ask less of students, many simply drift through the education system and into the workforce without building or maximizing their intellectual potential. Those high-school students who do go on to higher education on the strength of inflated grades are often ill prepared.

According to Côté and Allahar, the current grading system developed more as a means of keeping students in school than as a way to maintain standards and promote excellence. They believe that an open public discussion about the grading practices and the history of grading practices is needed, explaining that a problem critics face when discussing the current crisis is that most people are unfamiliar with the history of grading practices and the meaning of the standards they represent. Many younger teachers and administrators themselves went through the system when grades were increasing and performance expectations were decreasing. According to Côté and Allahar, the crisis is coming to a head because so much of the current cohort are arriving at university with a sense of 'grade entitlement', or what has also been called a 'degree purchasing' attitude, meaning that they believe that simply paying their tuition entitles them to receiving good grades.

work as well. The idea that the work submitted does not have to have been prepared entirely on one's own could stem from that experience of having received help from parents.

In a capitalist society, plagiarism can be seen as something profitable, 'good for business', an example of free enterprise. In fact, it has spawned two booming industries. One is the essay industry, represented by a number of websites such as SchoolSucks, Genius Papers, and AcaDemon that sell students ready-composed or, for a higher fee, customized papers. These companies are not engaged in anything that is technically against the law, although the means they sometimes use to obtain papers do involve theft of academic property. Copyright laws are fuzzy about academic work. A colleague of ours wrote an anti-racist feminist piece for a university newspaper when she was a graduate student; the article now appears for sale by three Web-based companies that cater to university students. The fact that there are numerous companies of this kind out there, set up to accept your credit card number or payment via PayPal, might make the practice seem legitimate.

The industry does benefit graduate students, who are often desperate for money and will take cash for their writing. Writing articles for academic journals may be good for a graduate student's career, it doesn't pay anything, and grad students are not trained to write for magazines and newspapers that pay. They are trained to write academic papers. In this sense, by selling their services to Web-based essay providers, they are capitalizing on their hard-earned skills in an industry in which these skills are valued.

Another group of businesses that profit from plagiarism are those that claim to be able to catch the plagiarizers, with companies such as Turnitin.com selling their services to colleges and universities. You have to wonder how many people working on this side of the business once worked on the other side, like the reformed hackers who become computer security specialists. Could they work for both sides? Think of the free material they get from the post-secondary institutions that send them student papers to be checked for plagiarism. The more institutions a company like this sells their services, the larger their database of student essays will become.

A potential social factor in the willingness to plagiarize is **social distance**. If you know your instructors, and they recognize you by name or by sight, then you are less likely to submit a plagiarized essay, since it would be like cheating a friend or lying to a parent. However, if your professor is just a blurry face at the front of a crowded lecture hall, or an even more anonymous presence online, the social distance is far greater. Plagiarism, then, is more like stealing from a large corporation; it becomes a 'victimless crime', since there is no identifiable injured party. This would make for interesting sociological research: Is there more plagiarism in lower-level courses than in upper-level courses (where the classes are smaller and less likely to be offered online)? In larger institutions than in smaller ones? Would comparing colleges and universities be useful here, the former having a lower student-to-teacher ratio?

Cultures of Education

It's also worth considering plagiarism in terms of **cultures of education**. In mainstream Western culture there is a tendency to emphasize the individual's competition with others. This emphasis is made stronger when, for instance, a large first-year course is known to allow a fixed number of students to graduate with A's, or is marked on a bell curve. This makes these precious marks more valuable by putting them in limited supply (rather like gold, with the available amount artificially limited). Honours students have their names posted in front of department offices. Students receive awards primarily for individual performance.

Other cultures put a greater emphasis on the group. Aboriginal students, for example, have traditionally not wanted to be singled out in class. They will whisper answers to peers who have been asked to reply to teacher questions, so that there will be no embarrassment for a classmate who doesn't know the answer. Research has shown that they are typically more likely to share answers on tests, the same way they would help their family members and friends. The cultural value of sharing is higher than in mainstream Canadian culture.

The Western culture of education also emphasizes putting what you say 'in your own words'. While that may seem natural and normal to most Canadian students reading this book, think about the following parallels: most Canadians do not program their own computers 'with their own programs', or fix their cars 'with their own parts' or 'to their own design'. They turn to experts, the masters and the patterns they have set. There are cultural traditions in which 'repeating the words of the master' is more valued than personalizing an answer. When foreign students come to Canada (paying much more for their education than Canadian citizens, incidentally), they are unlikely to have been told about how education in Canada follows a different model. There might be a class component here as well. In Anyon's 1980 work on the class-based hidden curriculum in education, working-class schools were taught to copy steps, while the middle-class schools stressed finding the right answer; only at the affluent professional or elite executive schools were students encouraged to put things 'in their own words'. Is it possible that plagiarism as defined by one class and culture may be a perfectly appropriate answer in another class or culture? (For the record, we are *not* encouraging you to plagiarize, or to attempt to excuse yourself from charges of plagiarism on the basis of your class or cultural

What in this ad makes this service seem morally legitimate and socially acceptable?

status. Underlying causes are one thing, but there is no excuse for cheating.)

Another influential aspect of the Western culture of education is the increasingly corporatized nature of post-secondary institutions, where students are viewed as customers or clients (or 'stakeholders'—a hideous term). Students, in turn, may feel that it is their right as consumers to appeal grades or even to sue. As long as school administrators feel that their institutions are competing for students, they may be reluctant to cultivate an unfavourable reputation by aggressively pursuing plagarizers, risking law suits and bad publicity. And with the increased level of credentialism—the emphasis on 'getting the piece of paper', a physical consumer product—rather than on learning, a more abstract entity, it's understandable that students may act more like customers than like learning apprentices. Should we be surprised, then, when the resourceful student buys a term paper over the Internet?

The corporate culture of the post-secondary institution is also expressed and experienced internally, within the institution, and can have an influence on how plagiarism is treated and judged. Remember that plagiarism doesn't reflect well on anyone—student, department, or institution. Department where students write a lot of essays (say, sociology, anthropology, history, literature, or philosophy) are probably more involved in providing electives to students who are studying in different programs than in training majors in their field of study. Pressure can be brought to bear on a department's administrator by administrators of the students' programs to 'just let my student pass,' rather than doggedly pursuing cases of plagiarism. Remember, too, that the competition for students goes on within colleges and universities, as different departments attempt to draw students to take their electives. A popular course gains status for the department and can be used to justify new hires and a higher budget; a course with a high rate of catching plagiarism offenders is not popular. The increased use of temporary, sessional, or adjunct professors, who typically don't want to 'rock the boat' with administrators, also weakens the impulse to take a firm stand against plagiarism: they want to be seen as 'team players' so that they will get hired again, maybe even full-time. Finally, as Thompson notes, when it comes to plagiarism, word gets around. Those schools that have a clear policy of dealing strictly with plagiarism have fewer instances of the offence. Where people often 'get away' with it, student culture might simply become supportive of plagiarism.

● ● ● ● ● ● ● ● ● ● ● ● ● ● ● ● ●

What do YOU think?

1. Why do you think that plagiarism is on the rise at post-secondary institutions in Canada?

2. Do you accept the idea that students should be able to draw on the work of experts without reshaping it, or should students always be encouraged to put things 'in their own words'?

● ● ● ● ● ● ● ● ● ● ● ● ● ● ● ● ●

Summary

We live in a time in which there are a number of important choices to make concerning the future of our education system. The sociology of education can help make those choices truly informed and democratic. At the elementary and secondary level, we need to change the curriculum so that marginalized peoples get to read and hear about people like themselves. The effects of 'streaming' (or 'tracking') must be seriously studied. At the post-secondary level, we need to look critically at such practices as the increasing dependence on adjuncts, on corporate sponsorship, and on online education to uncover the potential harm as well as benefits that they may bring.

Question for Critical Review

1. Summarize the factors that contribute to the growing problem of plagiarism. Which factors make plagiarism possible? Which ones encourage it? Are there any factors that legitimize it?

Suggested Readings

Côté, James, & Anton Allahar (2007). *Ivory Tower Blues: A University System in Crisis*. Toronto: University of Toronto Press.

Dei, George (1996). *Anti-Racism Education: Theory and Practice*. Halifax: Fernwood Publishing.

———, & Agnes Calliste (2000). *Power Knowledge and Anti-Racism Education: A Critical Reader*. Halifax: Fernwood Publishing.

———, Irma James, L. Karumanchery, S. James-Wilson, & J. Zine (2000). *Aboriginal Margins: The Challenges and Possibilities of Inclusive Schooling*. Toronto: Canadian Scholars' Press.

Dubson, Michael, ed. (2001). *Ghosts in the Classroom: Stories of College Adjunct Faculty—and the Price We All Pay*. Boston: Camel's Back Books.

Oakes, Jeannie (2005). *Keeping Track: How Schools Structure Inequality*, 2nd edn. New Haven: Yale University Press.

Richards, John, Jennifer Hove, & Kemi Afolabi (2008). *Understanding the Aboriginal/Non-Aboriginal Gap in Student Performance: Lessons from British Columbia*. Toronto: C.D. Howe Institute.

Suggested Websites

Trends in Higher Education: A Report Prepared for the UNESCO 2009 World Conference on Higher Education
http://unesdoc.unesco.org/images/0018/001831/183168e.pdf

Ivory Tower Blues: A University System in Crisis (blog)
www.ivorytowerblues.com

Canadian Education Association
www.cea-ace.ca/foo.cfm?subsection=lit&page=pol&subpage=lan&subsubpage=abo

Key Terms

- absolutist
- alternative (or complementary) medicine
- Arctic hysteria

- Big Pharma
- biomedicine
- brain drain
- clinical iatrogenesis

- commodification
- cultural iatrogenesis
- cultural syndromes
- cultures of medicine

10

Health and Medicine

LEARNING OBJECTIVES

After reading this chapter, you should be able to

> discuss the significance of the social course of disease;

> outline the various aspects of biomedicine;

> contrast Aboriginal concepts of medicine with those of biomedicine;

> discuss how the process of medicalization takes place;

> articulate the different views surrounding the accreditation of immigrant doctors; and

> outline Ivan Illich's critique of modern medicine.

iatrogenesis	• posttraumatic stress disorder	• sick role (or patient role)	**Key Names**
inverse care law	• psychoneuroimmunology	• social course (of disease)	• Talcott Parsons
medicalization	• radical monopoly	• social iatrogenesis	• Ivan Illich
medical sociology	• reductionist		

Photo: Trevor Snapp/Corbis

A trash can for biological and infectious waste, outside a feedlot run by Granjas Carroll de Mexico Farms, one of a number of industrial pig farms in Mexico owned or partly owned by Smithfield Foods. The lake contains the excrement and urine of 1,500 pigs, as well as other waste.

FOR Starters

Swine Flu: Big Farm Meets Big Pharma

We will remember 2009 as the year of the swine flu scare. Or, given that the H1N1 virus never quite lived up to the fear-mongering hype, maybe we won't. But whether or not you or someone you know came down with a bout of swine flu, it had a huge impact on a couple of industries: we call them Big Farm and Big Pharma.

Big Farm

To analyze the swine flu of 2009 from a sociological perspective, we have to examine the practices—social and environmental—of the industrial farm in La Gloria, Mexico, where the H1N1 virus emerged. It was run by Smithfield Foods Inc., an American company based in Virginia, the world's largest 'producer and processor' of pork, operating in 29 states and 9 countries. The company has a horrible environmental record. In 1997 it was fined $12.6 million—then the third-largest fine in the history of the Environmental Protection Agency—for violating the US Clean Water Act. The company's industrial farm practices include keeping a high concentration of pigs (typically within the small stalls used to confine pregnant and nursing sows) and dumping hog feces into nearby rivers with little attempt at treating the material to make it less polluting. These practices have made Smithfield the target of numerous accusations by farm workers and nearby residents, who blame the company for creating health problems. In the face of public opposition in its home country, it is little wonder that Smithfield found nearby Mexico, with its relative lack of environmental controls, an attractive site for its commercial farming.

Smithfield's labour practices also have an odour. It took 15 years for the United Food and Commercial Workers Union to establish a local union for Smithfield workers, despite strong employee interest. One Illinois packing facility not only demands long working days and weeks, but also has a point system that penalizes employees one point per day for being sick with doctor's excuse or for going to any appointment, or for having to take a day off to care for a sick child; the accumulation of a specified number of points leads to automatic firing. (Note that they're in the US, where unions are much stronger than they are in Mexico.)

As critical sociologists we suggest that swine flu and the greater danger of workers and locals contracting serious illnesses are products of the practices and attitudes of industrial farms and the governments they deal with. We'd like to add that we read little to nothing about Smithfield Foods during the H1N1 scare of 2009.

Big Pharma

The term **Big Pharma** is used to refer to the world's large pharmaceutical companies, which reap enormous annual profits to develop and manufacture the drugs used to fight and manage disease. Take Roche, the owners of the patent for Tamiflu, the main vaccine used against swine flu (the generic name of the drug is oseltamivir). During the 2005 scare surrounding avian (bird) flu (another pandemic that failed to live up to the hype), Canada, the US, Britain, Israel, and Australia bought billions of dollars' worth of Tamiflu to stockpile 'just in case' of a serious outbreak. The money was mostly wasted on a pandemic that never emerged (you can look at it as a really expensive insurance policy). Meanwhile, countries that couldn't afford the expensive patented vaccine, and companies that wanted to provide generic versions of oseltamivir, had to fight to make the cheaper versions of the vaccine available. It wasn't until 2009 that an Indian company (Cipla Ltd) won the right to produce an alternative version of Tamiflu, called Antiflu.

Big Pharma benefits when the media uncritically spreads fear over pandemics, which sends you to the nearest public health clinic for a shot. Curiously, the same drug companies that market and sell anti-viral drugs seem immune to media criticism. The flu shot sold in Canada hadn't been through a complete set of clinical trials when it was distributed in the fight against H1N1; this means that possible side effects and risks to people with certain pre-existing conditions weren't completely known when the vaccine began to be used. Yet, in Canada and the US, governments granted GlaxoSmithKline (GSK, a manufacturer of an approved anti–swine flu vaccine) indemnity, meaning that the government (that is you, the taxpayer) would cover the cost of any lawsuit filed against the drug maker. GSK is essentially taking no financial risk while profiting hugely, making an estimated $1.66 billion (US) per year.

● ●

What do YOU think?

Did you read or hear anything related to Big Farm or Big Pharma in the news in 2009? If you did, in what context? Why do you think these social organizations did not become a bigger part of the reporting of the scare?

● ●

Medical sociology is based on the view that medical practices and beliefs are intensely social. A large part of it is policy sociology, involving health professionals such as doctors and professors of nursing, pharmacy, and medicine. Among the principal aims of medical sociology is to improve the delivery of health services through sociologically informed research. Critical sociology contributes significantly as well, especially when the practices of multinational pharmaceutical companies, medical schools (particularly when they raise their fees), and privately run, profit-making hospitals are objects of study. Healing is achieved through social means, so it's natural that sociology has a lot to contribute to our understanding of the field of medicine. Race, gender, ethnicity, age, and class—all social factors—affect an individual's experience of the medical professions.

Sociological factors will affect the treatment you receive from your doctor. Let's say you're a middle-aged woman living outside the city, suffering from intensely sore feet. You go to your family doctor. She is of South Asian descent and was educated in Britain, having moved to Canada just five years ago. She can't find a cause for your ailment, so she recommends a number of specialists. Which specialists she recommends will depend on her social network, the circle of people she knows and trusts. This network depends on such social factors as the location of her practice (outside the city) and the level of status she has a doctor (itself possibly determined by how long she has been practising and the degree to which she has been politically active in medical associations). Religion can be a factor, since certain hospitals are governed by specific religious groups. Her gender alone might be a factor, as men are still more prominent in medicine than women.

For contrast, imagine that you are a very successful businessperson with a prominent white male doctor who has hospital privileges at one of the best hospitals in the city. Your doctor has been head of the provincial medical association and is often asked to present papers at medical conferences around the world. Imagine how his social network might differ from that of the doctor discussed in the preceding paragraph, and how your treatment might differ as a result.

Sick Role

American sociologist **Talcott Parsons** (1902–1979) came up with perhaps the first medical sociology term when, in his book *The Social System* (1951), he developed the concept of the **sick** (or **patient**) **role**. Like other sociological roles, he argued, being sick came with certain expectations—four, to be exact. In his thinking, two relate to what the sick person can expect from society, two to what society should expect of the sick person. The four expectations are outlined as follows. The person engaged in the sick role:

1. should expect to be granted 'exemption from normal social responsibilities'. In other words, the sick patient should not be expected to have to work, either at home or at his or her job, while he or she recovers.
2. should expect to be 'taken care of' rather than having to take care of him- or herself.
3. is socially obligated to try to 'get well' rather than remain in the undesirable state of being ill.
4. is socially obligated to 'seek technically competent help' (in other words, the help of a qualified health professional).

The sick role, according to Parsons, gave the individual licence to be temporarily 'deviant' (Parsons' own choice of word) with regards to the first two expectations provided that he or she acts in accordance with the second two.

Parsons' work is considered the epitome of structural functionalism, both its strengths and (to a greater extent, in the view of many contemporary sociologists) its weaknesses. Structural functionalism presumes a social uniformity that conflict or critical sociologists would challenge. You have to ask yourself whether you think the sick role is the same for everybody.

The first challenge to the uniformity of the structural-functionalist model came quickly. In 1954, just three years after Parsons' *The Social System*, E.L. Koos published *The Health of Regionalville: What the People Thought and Did About It*. It was based on research he carried out between 1946 and 1950 in order to look at differences in what people thought and did about their health depending on their class. What he found was that people in higher occupational groups were better able to afford to play the sick role, a privilege less available to those of lower occupational groups.

Similar arguments against the uniformity of the sick role applied other standard sociological factors, such as gender, ethnic background, and age. Societies have different expectations for, as one TV commercial calls her, 'Dr Mom' than they have for Dad. When children are sick, it is usually the mother who is expected to take time off work to look after them. And who is *least* likely to be able to play the sick role if the whole family gets sick? We can also look at people with chronic illnesses or disabilities. Are they to be considered permanently 'deviant' according to Parsons' model?

When looking critically at Parsons' model of the sick role, not only is it hard to defend its universal applicability, but it is clear that the model changes over time. In his article 'Patients in the New Economy: The "Sick Role" in a Time of Economic Discipline' (2002), Ivan Emke proposes that in Canada at the turn of the twenty-first century there are five new expectations of the patient role. Two of these are central. The first is that 'patients in the New Economy are responsible for their own illnesses.' Emke's point is that instead of looking at social causes of sickness (pollution, unsafe working and living conditions, stress through overworking,

economic insecurity, and social disruption), we've become more inclined to blame individual and debatable 'choices' (smoking, drinking, not belonging to a health club, not making time for exercise, eating foods with transfats). Emke notes that the bulk of cancer information currently provided in ads and public health materials focuses on individual risk factors rather than those presented by society. This expectation, by lowering society's sense that everyone is equally entitled to free healthcare (e.g. we may have more sympathy for the non-smoking cancer patient), is born at least in part of the search for ways to lower rising healthcare costs in Canada. You can see how those who buy into this expectation might use the underlying argument to justify charging 'user fees' for some medical services.

The second new expectation we'd like to highlight is really a conflation of two expectations Emke identified: 'the patient in the new economy is instructed to tread lightly on the system,' and 'patients in the new economy are not to be trusted.' We could recast it: 'patients are assumed to be abusing the system.' Emke raises it in connection with the increasing 'public education' campaign to encourage people to use as few medical services as they can. He cites as an example a 1994 pilot project by the Ontario government designed to encourage residents of the city of London to stop going to their family doctor for relatively minor

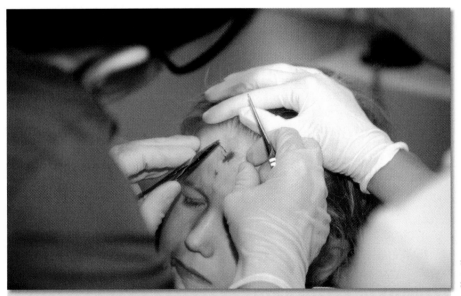

Photo: Alamy

A nurse practitioner and a nurse attend a young child with a head injury. Should this kind of procedure be left to doctors?

• Our Stories •

The Social Course of Tuberculosis among the Inuit

Ethnic background can be a powerful factor affecting the social course of a disease. Witness, for example, the treatment of Inuit with tuberculosis. At the beginning of the twentieth century, tuberculosis was responsible for the deaths of tens of thousands of Canadians, especially immigrants living in squalid conditions that fostered the disease. In 1908, the annual rate of tuberculosis-related deaths was 165 per 100,000 population; since the country's population was about 6,625,000 in 1908, that meant that over 7,500 Canadians died from tuberculosis that year alone.

By 1949, new antibiotics combined with improved sanitation, screening, and treatment helped reduce the rate in Canada to about 33 deaths per 100,000. But at the same time, the rate among Canada's Inuit population was rising dramatically, peaking at an alarming 569 per 100,000 (then the highest in the world) in 1952. To get a feel for how high that is, compare it with the high rate of TB found in prisons in post-Communist Russia: 484 per 100,000. In that year, 54 of the roughly 10,000 Canadian Inuit died.

There were a number of reasons for the high rate of TB among Canada's Inuit. First, the severe cold of the Arctic—though not cold enough to kill the tuberculosis bacillus—made the Inuit especially susceptible to respiratory problems. The intimate closeness of the Inuit in their igloos facilitated the spread of tuberculosis from one family member to another. More significant were the causes related to the increasing contact with people from the rest of Canada. Pat Grygier, in *A Long Way from Home: The Tuberculosis Epidemic among the Inuit*, explains that

> as the Inuit adapted to accommodate the desires of the newcomers, trapping to exchange furs for store goods or working for the RCMP or on military construction sites for cash, their highly nutritious fresh-meat or fish diet and their warm caribou-skin clothing were grad-ually exchanged for a diet largely of white flour, lard, tea, jam, and canned goods, and for much less warm southern clothing. When the caribou declined or the pattern of migration changed (possibly as a result of the incursions of military and mining into the North), mal-nutrition occurred. (Grygier 1994: 55)

Arguably as devastating as the disease, however, was the way in which Inuit TB sufferers were treated. At the time, the standard treatment for tuberculosis involved a period of confinement—from six months to two years—in a hospital or sanatorium. These were not to be built in the Arctic, so the Inuit with tuberculosis were brought (or, more accurately, taken, since many were most reluctant to leave their homes) to southern Canada. Grygier eloquently describes what would happen once health professionals, brought north by ship, had conducted their patient examinations:

> When the doctors had made their final decision on whether an individual should go to hos-pital for treatment or stay in the North, the evacuees were sent down to the Inuit quarters in the prow of the ship and the rest were sent ashore. The evacuees were not allowed to go ashore to collect belongings, to say goodbye, or to make arrangements for their families or goods. If a mother was judged sick but her children were not infected, the children (some-times including unweaned babies) were given to an Inuk woman going ashore. Fathers had no chance to arrange for someone to hunt for food for their families or to look after their

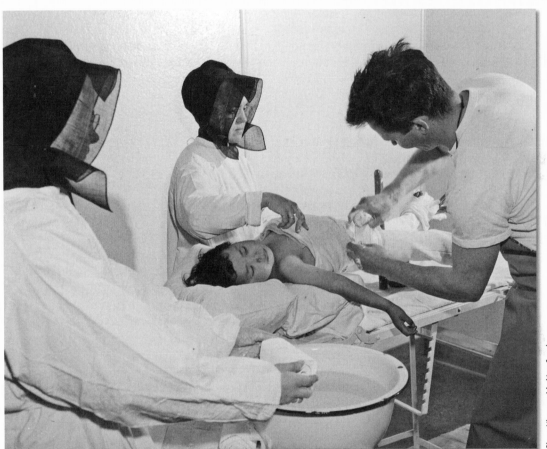

Photo: Library and Archives Canada

Sisters J. Marchand (left) and M. Lachambie assist Dr L.J. Mulvihill, superintendent of Indian Health Services, place a cast on an Aboriginal boy suffering from tuberculosis of the hip c. 1949.

dogs and equipment. Mothers had no chance to arrange for someone to care for their children or to sew and process the skins needed to keep the family warm. . . . Those needing hospital treatment were kept on board, the rest sent ashore, and on sailed the ship to the next settlement. (Grygier 1994: 96)

The tuberculosis rate among the Inuit dropped during the 1950s to a low of 53 per 100,000 (just 5 in number) in 1959, but the effects of the separation were to last. Many families were never reunited, often because a sick loved one died, but even, in many cases, when the TB-suffering family member recovered.

complaints. No research had been done before to see if people were 'abusing' the system, but the assumption underlying the project was clearly that escalating healthcare costs can be attributed to a large number of billable visits to family doctors, some—if not many—of which could be avoided. Perhaps, though, rising healthcare costs are actually the result of building huge technology-intensive hospitals that are less cost-effective than having a greater number of small-town and community-based medical centres. Perhaps nurses, who make less than doctors do, should be permitted to perform basic medical procedures (stitching wounds, for example) that doctors are normally responsible for, so that the same work can be done more efficiently and at lower cost.

● ● ● ● ● ● ● ● ● ● ● ● ● ● ● ● ● ● ● ●

What do YOU think?

1. How do you think factors such as gender and ethnicity might affect the universality of Parsons' sick role?

2. Do you believe that people who smoke are entitled to free healthcare? What about people who eat badly?

3. Have you seen evidence of the new trends Emke identified in Canadian healthcare? Do you agree with them?

4. Could you argue that the social nature of healthcare—how it reflects social factors such as economics and ethnicity—abuses the system more than its users do? In what way?

● ● ● ● ● ● ● ● ● ● ● ● ● ● ● ● ● ● ● ●

The Social Course of Disease

One of the medical breakthroughs of the nineteenth century was the realization that every disease has a natural, or biological, course it goes through, a lifespan during which you catch the disease, suffer through it, and gradually get well (or, in some cases, sicker). It depends on the virus or bacteria, and the way the human body reacts to it. Think of a cold virus: doctors can prescribe medicine to help alleviate the symptoms and speed up recovery, but they can't fundamentally change the natural course of the illness.

Likewise, we can speak of the **social course** that diseases and disorders go through, a course affected by sociological factors such as ethnic background, culture, class, age, and gender of the people most commonly affected. Leading medical anthropologist Arthur Kleinman demonstrates this convincingly in his discussion of the social course of epilepsy in China:

The social course of epilepsy indicates that epilepsy develops in a local context where economic, moral, and social institutional factors powerfully affect the lived experience of seizures, treatment, and their social consequences. The social course of epilepsy, furthermore, is plural, heterogeneous [i.e. there is more than one course that it can take], and changing. It is as distinctive as are different moral worlds, different social networks, different social histories. . . .

Framing epilepsy in terms of its social course suggests that to improve the quality of life and reduce disability, it is essential that health and social policy address the context of social experience. Stigma, institution discrimination, the relatively high cost of care in a setting of chronic deprivation, and the other specific social consequences we have delineated, including the social resistance put up by sufferers, are as important for health and health policy as are basic medical services. Indeed, they are as salient for the content of medical care as are diagnosis and pharmacology. The social course of illness constitutes much of what is meant by prognosis. Health education, disability laws and services, community action projects, and work- and family-based rehabilitation programs are essential to this orientation. (Kleinman 1995: 171–2)

The box on pages 272–3 provides another example of factors that affect the social course of a disease. It's good to keep in mind that the social course of a disease, just like physical factors such as medicine, clean living conditions, rest, and so on, can help or hinder the healing process.

Biomedicine

Biomedicine involves the application of standard principles and practices of Western scientific disciplines, particularly biology, in the diagnosis and treatment of symptoms of illness and disease. It uses physical tests to find defined, purely physical entities (such as bacteria, viruses, and trauma) and then applies purely physical medicines and therapies to counteract them. Sometimes described as 'conventional medicine', it is the dominant practice in Western society.

When, suffering from migraine headaches, you visit your family doctor and she prescribes medication to reduce the severity of your symptoms, you have experienced biomedicine. If you've grown up in Canada or the US, this is likely the approach you expected—even hoped for—when you booked your appointment. But there are other approaches to treatment that fall outside of mainstream medical practice. We refer to these approaches collectively as **alternative** (or **complementary**) **medicine**. Your doctor, for instance, might have recommended acupuncture for your migraines. Or she might have recommended massage therapy or yoga as means of reducing the stress that may have contributed to your headaches. She might have tried to discover any environmental causes—bright lights in the area where you read or study, for example—of your condition. These would all be considered alternative approaches.

Alternative approaches are used to treat the gamut of medical ailments. Recent research in **psychoneuroimmunology**—the study of the effect of the mind on health and resistance to disease—has shown links between a person's psychological state and his or her ability to fight diseases such as cancer. A study at the University of Texas monitored the spread of cancer in two groups of mice. One group was placed in small plastic chambers for several hours at a time, which caused a surge in their stress hormones. Tumours in these mice grew more quickly and in greater number than those in the mice that were not confined,

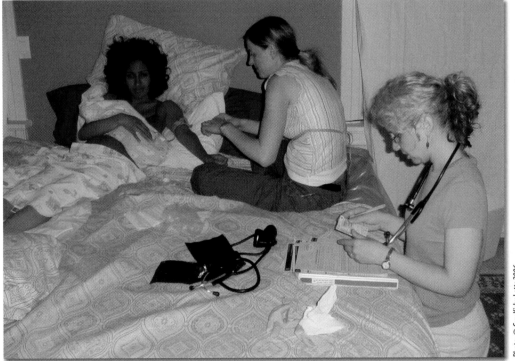

When you see this picture, do you think that the woman is being treated by 'health professionals'? An illegal practice less than 20 years ago, midwives are now an integral part of the medical system. Why was midwifery illegal?

Photo: © Guy Kirby Letts 2006

suggesting a link between stress and the spread of the disease. As the *Globe and Mail*'s Margaret Philip (2006) reports, the study is one of a number that have caused oncologists to consider more holistic approaches to treating cancer sufferers, using massage, meditation, music therapy, and support groups to help reduce tension.

A good example of divergent biomedical and alternative approaches to health is childbirth. Most North American women choose to deliver their infants at a hospital under the care of a team of medical professionals including an obstetrician, an anaesthesiologist, and several nurses. Increasingly, however, women are choosing to stay at home to give birth under the care of a midwife and/or a doula. There are good reasons to recommend the latter approach. For one thing, many people find hospitals uncomfortable. Some women do not want to be separated from their families, especially if they have other young children, and knowing they will remain at home eliminates stressful contemplation of the hurried trip to the hospital once the contractions begin. Many new mothers-to-be find that a doula is more available to provide support and answer questions than is an obstetrician. And, it's important to point out, for thousands of years and in many parts of the world today, giving birth at home was and is the only option. On the other hand, there are many advantages to having a hospital birth, including ready access to doctors and medical equipment in the event that either the mother or the infant requires immediate care for life-threatening complications. It's worth noting that some women choose to combine these approaches by having a hospital birth attended by the midwife or doula who has guided them through their pregnancy. In cases such as this, the term 'complementary medicine' is really more apt: biomedicine and alternative medicine do not need to be mutually exclusive.

Biomedicine remains the norm in North American society, but it is increasingly called into question by those who endorse a more holistic approach to diagnosis and treatment. Biomedicine has been criticized for looking at health from a **reductionist** perspective that attributes medical conditions to single factors treatable with single remedies; it fails to take into account the broader set of circumstances surrounding a person's health or illness. Those involved in biomedicine are sometimes accused of being **absolutist**, of failing to recognize that just as there are cultures of business, policing, and clothing, there are **cultures of medicine**, each with a unique approach to interpreting medicine in ways that reflect and reinforce other aspects of the culture from which it is derived. Every patient, critics argue, should be treated in the context of his or her culture; no single treatment should be applied universally across all cultures.

In Chapter 3 we touched on Anne Fadiman's study of the Hmong people living in the United States (Fadiman 1997). Originally from China, the Hmong people were forced to flee their homeland after resisting the Chinese government and encouraging the participation of the United States in the Southeast Asian wars of the 1960s and 1970s. Fadiman's study shows how Hmong refugees suffered because of narrow Western medical practices that did not respect their cultural beliefs. She cites, as just one example, the failure of North American doctors to take into account the fear—widespread among the Hmong people—of losing their soul. The Hmong wear (and put on their infants) neck-rings and cotton-string spirit bracelets to combat their fear of soul-loss, and

QUICK HITS

Hallucinations and Visions: Two 'Views'

As evidence that medicine has distinct cultures, consider the following descriptions of 'hallucinations', from a biomedical perspective, and 'visions', from an Aboriginal perspective. Are they really different, or is it only in how we look at them?

Hallucinations
- things that are seen but are not physically there
- associated with drug use, nervous disorders, stress
- sign of mental or emotional instability.

Visions
- pictures, words, tunes, dances coming from a quest for visions
- associated with inspiration, intuition, 'sixth sense'
- sign of spiritual health, creativity.

they rely on their spirit doctors or shamans, the *tsiv neebs*, to address and help them overcome these fears. Problems occurred when Hmong patients arriving at a refugee camp in Ban Vinai, Thailand, had their spirit strings cut by American health workers, who claimed they were unsanitary. The neck-rings thought to hold intact the souls of babies were also removed, placing this especially vulnerable (in the eyes of the Hmong) group in graver danger of soul-loss.

Cultural Syndromes

Another way in which Western medicine has marginalized minority cultures is by inventing **cultural syndromes**—disorders believed to afflict people of only certain ethnicities—in order to psychologize problems brought on by Western colonial control. Cultural syndromes are responsible for establishing or perpetuating stereotypes that can be difficult to stamp out. (Consider, as an example, the condition known as 'amok', a term used by the Portuguese to describe the homicidal frenzy supposedly typical of the Malayan people; the term survives in the English expression 'to run amok'.)

A classic example of a cultural syndrome is '**Arctic hysteria**', a condition first identified and described by the wife of Arctic explorer Robert Peary in 1892. In her journal, Josephine Peary described the 'crazy' acts of Inuit women who would suddenly scream, tear their clothes off, imitate the sound of some bird or animal, or run in circles—apparently for no reason—to the point of collapse. White visitors to the Arctic began to record this phenomenon as *pibloktuq* (or any one of a number of linguistically challenged variations of this).

The term *pibloktuq* first entered the historical record, then the psychiatric medical record, as a form of 'Arctic hysteria' (Brill 1913). It still exists as a psychological disorder legitimated by a medical name, authenticated by case studies. It also became enshrined in anthropology textbooks (e.g. Harris 1987: 328–9, and Barnouw 1987: 207) as one of a number of culture-specific syndromes or psychoses.

In a 1995 article entitled '"Pibloktoq" (Arctic Hysteria): A Construction of European–Inuit Relations?', historian Lyle Dick challenged the existence of the phenomenon as a part of traditional Inuit culture. He offers his opinion (with which I agree) that it is more likely the product of the White–Inuit power imbalance embodied in such contexts as the obsessively driven Robert Peary forcing the Inuit to take unwise risks in exploration, and the sexual abuse by white men of Inuit women.

Medicalization

An effect associated with the biomedical approach to medicine is the phenomenon known as **medicalization**. Chang and Christakis, sociologists at the University of Chicago, define medicalization in the following way:

> Medicalisation refers to the process by which certain behaviours or conditions are defined as medical problems (rather than, for example, as moral or legal problems), and medical intervention becomes the focus of remedy and social control. (Chang and Christakis 2002: 152)

The point of reference for Chang and Christakis's discussion of medicalization is obesity. The two authors were summarizing the results of a content analysis aimed at investigating how the discussion of obesity had changed between 1927 and 2000 in a widely consulted American medical textbook, the *Cecil Textbook of Medicine*. They found that although the textbook was consistent over time in citing, as the root cause of obesity, the factor of caloric intake exceeding energy expenditure, it had medicalized obesity through its successive editions. Early editions of the textbook identified 'aberrant individual activities such as habitual overeating' as being of great significance; they placed blame for the condition squarely on the individual. Later editions looked more to genetic and social environmental factors (for instance, the increased availability of fast food and the decreased amount of physical labour required in many jobs).

Critics of the health industry's tendency to medicalize conditions describe the practice as a form of reductionism that reduces medical conditions to biomedical causes without examining possible

Members of the Princess Patricia's Canadian Light Infantry carry the casket of a fallen comrade to a plane at Kandahar Airfield to be returned home to Canada. The soldier was one of four killed by a bicycle suicide bomber. Would you consider symptoms of posttraumatic stress disorder among Canadian soldiers a natural consequence of their work? What do you think are the consequences of how PTSD is viewed for the treatment (and funding of treatment by the federal government) of soldiers returning from Afghanistan?

Photo: Rick Madonik/GetStock.com

sociocultural or political factors. A second, and related, criticism is that Western health professionals are too quick to situate the problem exclusively or primarily in the individual human body, not, say, in an oppressive social or political system. Medicalization, by ascribing conditions like alcoholism to genetic factors, does excuse the sufferer by removing individual blame, but at the same time it portrays the sufferer as a genetic 'victim' who can be saved only by the medical profession; in this way, it takes away the individual's ability to make empowering choices that will affect the outcome of his or her condition. 'You can't stop overeating,' says the medicalizing health professional, 'it's in your genes. Your only recourse is a tummy tuck.' This leads to a further criticism: that medicalization promotes the **commodification** of healthcare by identifying certain conditions that might be considered normal (though slightly regrettable) as diseases that may be treated with 'commodity

cures' (such as certain drugs or procedures). Part of this commodifying process involves turning conditions that might be, in medical terms, relatively normal into deviant disorders (to use sociological terms). Examples for the aging male include obesity, male pattern baldness, increasingly frequent nighttime trips to the bathroom, and erectile 'dysfunction'. A current advertising campaign assures men that embarrassing excess breast tissue (there's even a medical name for it: gynecomastia) can be removed. These are not diseases; they are relatively normal aspects of the aging process and do not need to be medicalized. If it ain't broke (just a little bent), don't fix it.

Government agencies and health professionals are sometimes guilty of medicalizing disorders that can be traced to complicated social or environmental factors much more difficult to address than the purely medical factors. Medical journalist Lynn Payer offers an example in her eye-opening work

The Point Is...

Illich Quotations Concerning Medicalization

What do you think Illich meant by each of the following statements? Do you agree with him?

The fact that the doctor population is higher where certain diseases have become rare has little to do with the doctors' ability to control or eliminate them. It simply means that doctors deploy themselves as they like, more so than other professionals, and that they tend to gather where the climate is healthy, where the water is clean, and where people are employed and can pay for their services. (1976: 21–2)

In a complex technological hospital, negligence becomes 'random human error' or 'system breakdown', callousness becomes 'scientific detachment', and incompetence becomes 'a lack of specialized equipment'. The depersonalization of diagnosis and therapy has changed malpractice from an ethical into a technical problem. (1976: 30)

In every society, medicine, like law and religion, defines what is normal, proper, or desirable. Medicine has the authority to label one man's complaint a legitimate illness, to declare a second man sick though he himself does not complain, and to refuse a third social recognition of his pain, his disability, and even his death. It is medicine which stamps some pain as 'merely subjective', some impairment as malingering, and some deaths—though not others—as suicide'. (1976: 45)

Medicine always creates illness as a social state. The recognized healer transmits to individuals the social possibilities for acting sick. Each culture has its own characteristic perception of disease and thus its unique hygienic mask. Disease takes its features from the physician who casts the actors into one of the available roles. To make people legitimately sick is as implicit in the physicians power as the poisonous potential of the remedy that works. (1995: 44)

Disease-Mongers: How Doctors, Drug Companies, and Insurers Are Making You Feel Sick (1992):

When . . . a child died of lead poisoning in Michigan, there was a call for screening for lead poisoning. But when you read the circumstances, you found that the child was homeless, living in an abandoned building. Calling for blood testing was obviously easier than calling for a policy of providing safe and low-cost shelter for the poor, but who can doubt which policy would really benefit such children more? (Payer 1992: 39)

Posttraumatic stress disorder is another condition that is often medicalized (see Kleinman 1995). Suffered especially by those who have experienced the extreme violence of warfare (as soldiers or civilians), violent political oppression, or crime, PTSD was first diagnosed by Western psychiatrists who traced its origins to bleak, unstable environments

in countries such as Cambodia, El Salvador, Tibet, and the former Republic of Yugoslavia. Gradually, though, the focus of treatment has shifted from the pathology of the environment to the pathology of the individual. Patients are treated as though their psychobiological reactions to these harrowing circumstances are not normal; they are labelled 'victims', deprived of social agency. To be clear, it is not wrong to help people by recognizing that they have suffered psychological trauma, but it is misleading to remove from an individual's story the sociopolitical situation in which that person fought and survived, won freedom, and maybe lost loved ones.

Ivan Illich: Pioneering Critic of Medicalization

Ivan Illich (1927–2002) introduced the notion of medicalization in his highly creative and popular work. Although he was trained as a medieval historian, theologian, and philosopher, sociologists stake claim to him as a public sociologist.

Illich developed the concept of medicalization as part of a general critique of what he called 'radical monopolies' in industrial societies. He defined **radical monopoly** as follows:

> A radical monopoly goes deeper than that of any one corporation or any one government. It can take many forms. . . . Ordinary monopolies corner the market; radical monopolies disable people from doing or making things on their own. . . . They impose a society-wide substitution of commodities for use-values by reshaping the milieu and by 'appropriating' those of its general characteristics which have enabled people so far to cope on their own. Intensive education turns autodidacts [people who teach themselves] into unemployables, intensive agriculture destroys the subsistence farmer, and the deployment of police undermines the community's self control. The malignant spread of medicine has comparable results: it turns mutual care and self-medication into misdemeanors or felonies. (1995: 42)

In *Medical Nemesis: The Limits of Medicine*, which opens with the claim, 'The medical establishment has become a major threat to health' (1976: 1), Illich identified a 'doctor-generated epidemic' that was harming the health of people in industrialized society by taking away people's freedom to heal themselves or prevent their illnesses, as well as their freedom to criticize industrial society for the ills of stress, pollution, and general danger he said was 'sickening' (i.e. making sick) the people. Illich's term for this was **iatrogenesis**, and he distinguished three different kinds:

- clinical iatrogenesis,
- social iatrogenesis, and
- cultural iatrogenesis.

Clinical iatrogenesis refers to the various ways in which diagnosis and cure cause problems that are as bad or worse than the health problems they are meant to resolve. This occurs, for example, when a patient enters hospital for treatment of one ailment and becomes infected with a virus originating in the hospital. **Social iatrogenesis**, of greater interest to sociologists (unless they're in hospital), is the action of hiding or obscuring political conditions that 'render society unhealthy' (1995: 9). **Cultural iatrogenesis** takes place when the knowledge and abilities of the medical community are extolled or mythologized to the point where the authority of the health profession 'tends to mystify and to expropriate the power of the individual to heal himself and to shape his or her environment' (1995: 9); in other words, the patient is given no credit for his or her role in the recovery.

Ethnicity and Medical Sociology

Unemployed Immigrant Doctors: A Problem with Many Standpoints

The Canadian healthcare system is currently facing a shortage of doctors in some communities. At the same time, the country is welcoming immigrants with medical degrees and general credentials that are considered insufficient to qualify them to practise medicine in this country. It is a perplexing issue, one that must be considered from a number of standpoints (perspectives shaped by social location). The sections that follow outline four of these differing standpoints.

1. Immigrant Doctors

As an immigrant doctor, you have come to a country that offers a greater financial opportunity for you and your family. On the strength of skills and experience gained in your home country, you have scored highly in the 'point system', by which the worthiness of candidates for immigration is judged. It seems as though the Canadian government is encouraging you to come.

As soon as you arrive in Canada, the problems hit you in the face. If you have chosen to settle in Toronto—as many do—you encounter a two-step problem. First, your skills and knowledge must be assessed through a training program. The Ontario International Medical Graduate Program takes 48 weeks—close to a year—and has limited entrance. Assuming you manage to gain entrance and do well in the program, you still face a second, even

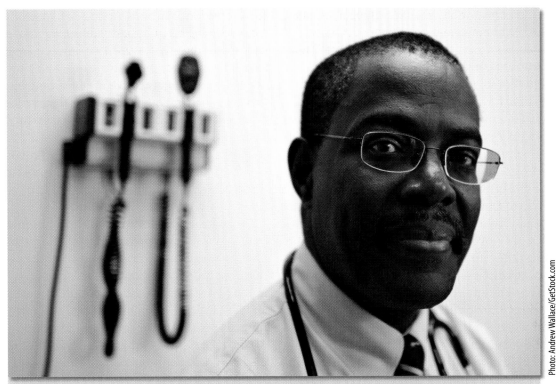

Photo: Andrew Wallace/GetStock.com

Dr Munini Mulera, a Newmarket pediatrician, left Uganda in 1981. How long do you think it might have taken him to gain accreditation to practise in Canada? What challenges do you think he faced?

higher hurdle: you must go through a residency program of several years in which you essentially relearn everything you needed to know to earn your medical qualifications in the first place. But like many others in your position, you accept this and are eager to get on with it. However—and this is the biggest problem you face—there are so very few residency positions available. You are one of more than 1,100 immigrant doctors in Ontario competing for just 36 spots open each year in the residency program.

In the meantime, your family must eat. If you are fortunate, you may get a job in the medical field, possibly (with training) as a lab assistant. But it is more likely you will end up working as a telemarketer, driving a taxi, delivering pizza, or doing manual labour in factories. Your dream of practising your chosen profession in this country supposedly rich in opportunity has proven elusive.

2. Rural Communities

You live in a community that is home to fewer and fewer doctors. The older ones retire, the young graduates opt to take up medical work in the big city. Your family doctor has retired and closed her practice, and you, like her other patients, are scrambling to find another doctor to take you on. But most family doctors are already seeing more patients than they can handle. You once laughed at the joke that the best way to find a family doctor with an opening was to check the obituaries, but you're desperate enough that you might resort to this tactic in earnest. The trouble is you're older, and, face it, older people have more complicated and time-consuming medical problems, so you're not the most attractive candidate even if you managed to find a doctor taking new patients. So you put up with minor complaints, knowing that anything more serious will require a trip down to the big city, where the bigger research hospitals and more lucrative practices are.

Occasionally you wonder whether there's something your town should be doing to attract doctors. You don't very much care where they come from. In Ontario, 136 communities have been designated as 'underserved' by the provincial ministry of health. Saskatchewan and Newfoundland and Labrador have higher percentages of foreign-trained doctors than other provinces. The reason: not as many obstacles for immigrant doctors.

3. Countries of Origin of Internationally Trained Doctors

You think *you're* underserved. In developing countries, especially in rural areas, there are fewer doctors per population than there are in Canada's rural communities. The cost of educating medical professionals is prohibitively high. It is much more likely that your country will lose trained doctors to emigration than benefit from an influx of health professionals. In post-apartheid South Africa, the government decided to block doctors immigrating from other African nations to halt the **brain drain**—the exodus of educated professionals—eroding the healthcare systems of those countries. Canada experiences a bit of that brain drain when some of its medical specialists go to the US—but it's nothing compared to the brain drain of doctors leaving developing countries for North America.

4. Doctors' Associations

Placing restrictions on internationally trained medical graduates gives Canadian-trained doctors more power as a sociopolitical body of professionals. As Linda McQuaig explains in her commentary on a doctors' strike in New Brunswick in 2004,

> Doctors have managed to maintain enormous bargaining power in Canada by threatening, from time to time, to abandon us for more prosperous climes. But these threats only have teeth because doctors can rely on the fact that there is no one here to replace them if they go—even when potential replacements are already here and desperate to get to work. (McQuaig 2004)

On the other side, consider the Ontario Medical Association's 'Position Paper on Physician Workforce Policy and Planning', dated 4 April 2002. It's a document addressing the OMA's concerns about 'the problem of inadequate physician human resources, and the related consequences for public access to medical treatment'. One of the 18 recommendations in the report was to 'Temporarily increase the number of fully qualified international medical graduate

(IMG) positions'. In a 20 April 2004 speech, OMA president Dr Larry Erlick, addressing the same problems, noted that

> We . . . need more foreign-trained physicians to practice in Ontario. The fact that we have relied on foreign trained physicians in the past should come as no surprise, as 25% of physicians practicing today in this province are in fact international medical graduates! Some of the red tape has to be cut.

Still, in both documents, helping foreign-trained physicians gain accreditation to practise in Canada was clearly viewed as a secondary solution. The words 'temporarily' and 'fully qualified' in the first statement leaves holes in that support, and Dr Erlick's recommendation was one of a number of 'short-term recommendations', given decidedly less priority than bringing back Ontario medical graduates now practising elsewhere.

● ● ● ● ● ● ● ● ● ● ● ● ● ● ● ● ● ● ●

What do YOU think?

1. Are there any other 'stakeholders' in this issue who should be considered?

2. What do you think the position of Canadian universities with medical schools would be?

3. Why do you think the word 'temporarily' was put into Dr Erlick's recommendation?

4. What is your position on the subject of immigrant doctors?

● ● ● ● ● ● ● ● ● ● ● ● ● ● ● ● ● ● ●

Quebec

As we have seen elsewhere, Quebec, from a sociological point of view, is quite different from other provinces in Canada. Here are four areas in the sociology of health and medicine that illustrate this point:

- the relative number of male nurses
- the number of female medical students
- the number of people without regular doctors
- the cost of tuition fees for medical students.

In 2002, there were 219,161 women registered nurses (RNs) in Canada, compared with just

The homepages for two Canadian schools of nursing. What messages does each convey? How do they differ?

Photos: Courtesy of the Faculty of Nursing, Université Laval and Lawrence S. Bloomberg, Faculty of Nursing, University of Toronto.

11,796 male registered nurses (about 5.4 per cent of the total). In Quebec, the 5,272 male RNs make up roughly 9.8 per cent of the total (59,193). A more striking statistic is that approximately 45 per cent of the male nurses in Canada were working in Quebec.

It should not be surprising, then, that there is also a difference in non-traditional gender with Quebec medical students. The number of female medical students is consistently higher in Quebec than elsewhere in Canada. In 1997, 59 per cent of the students at Quebec's four medical schools were women, compared with 46 per cent in the 12 schools throughout the rest of the country. That year, the University of Sherbrooke had the highest proportion of women starting medical school—71 per cent—compared with the lowest figure (just 30 per cent), at the University of Manitoba. In the 2003–4 academic year, the Université de Laval had the highest percentage of female first-year medical students, with 74 per cent; the University of Saskatchewan had the lowest, with 43 per cent. Overall, 68 per cent of all medical students in Quebec in 2003–4 were women.

The third factor, relating to people without regular doctors, is borne out by a 1994–5 study of Canadians over the age of 20. About 14 per cent of the people studied were without regular doctors, but the figure for Quebec residents without regular doctors was 25.6 per cent, by far the highest of any province (with the exception of Newfoundland and Labrador, which ranked a fairly close second).

The fourth factor is the cost of a medical degree, which is much lower at universities in Quebec than in medical schools elsewhere in Canada. Compare the recent figures in Table 10.1, presented in order of most to least expensive. It should also be noted that with the exception of Newfoundland and Labrador, whose medical school tuition fees have

Table 10.1 Average annual cost of attending medical school, by province, 2003–4	
Ontario	$14,878
Nova Scotia	$10,460
Saskatchewan	$9,774
British Columbia	$8,876
Alberta	$7,493
Manitoba	$6,693
Newfoundland and Labrador	$6,250
Quebec	**$2,781**

not risen for four years, and Manitoba, where fees dropped in 2000–1 and then held constant for the next three years, Quebec has the slowest growth rate in medical school fees, rising by just $200 between 1999–2000 and 2003–4 (compare that with the $6,216 rise in Ontario, where medical school fees are the highest in Canada).

The Intersection of Race and Medicine

From a sociological perspective, one of the most interesting points of intersection between race and the medical professions in Canada is the issue of nurses who are not white. The following two sections take a closer look at this issue.

The Filipino Nurses

Filipinos were later than other Asian immigrant groups—Chinese, Japanese, Koreans, and South Asians—to come to Canada. It was only after some of the more overt forms of discrimination in Canada's immigration policy were abolished in 1962 and the points system, rewarding candidates with desirable skills and education, was established in 1967 that Filipino immigration to this country became significant.

In 1967, the demand for nurses in Canada outstripped the field of qualified nursing professionals. That year, 4,262 nurses were allowed to immigrate to Canada; 1,140 of them—roughly 27 per cent—were Filipino. (In fact, an astonishing 43.3 per cent of the 2,632 immigrants from the Philippines were nurses.) Over the next three years, 2,002 of the 8,897 immigrant nurses—22.5 per cent—were Filipinos. While the numbers dropped slightly in the following years, in total more than a thousand Filipino nurses entered the country over the next five years.

Filipino health professionals did not come to Canada only. Indeed, during the same period, the United States also accepted a large number of Filipino nurses. However, the American approach to immigration was different from the Canadian in one crucial regard: whereas Canada limited the immigration of Filipinos to those with nursing experience or training, the US welcomed all manner of Filipino health professionals, including physicians, surgeons, and dentists. In 1970, for example, 968 Filipino physicians, surgeons, and dentists entered the US, compared with 954 nurses; that same year, all but 53 of the 571 Filipino health professionals to enter Canada were nurses.

Given that most of the Filipino nurses coming to Canada were young women in their twenties, Canada's immigration policy resulted in a huge gender imbalance among the Canadian Filipino population during the early years of Filipino immigration. The sex ratio of males to females among immigrants from the Philippines between 1967 and 1969 was about 1 to 2.75, with 2,293 men and 6,380 women coming to Canada during that time. While this rate would even out over the next two decades, with the percentage of male Filipino immigrants rising to 74 per cent of the total in 1971, 90 per cent in 1975, and 86 in 1979, a second wave of large-scale immigration would lower it again, so that by 1992 it was back down to 50 per cent.

Sociological studies suggest that because they were fluent English speakers and Christians, coming from a capitalist country where they were very familiar with Western culture, the Filipino immigrants adapted more easily to life in Canada than other Asian groups. Even so, Winn (1988), in a study of 15 ethnic groups in Canada, demonstrated that while the Filipinos ranked the highest in college or university education, their ranking dropped when it came to income return on university education. Imagine, as well, the effect on

Telling It Like It Is

An Account of Systemic Racism from a Black First-Year Nursing Student

Unfortunately, I regret to say that I have had my first clinical experience in the nursing profession and I feel I have already been subjected to systemic racism. Examples of this include disciplinary actions that are different from other student nurses such as when myself and a non-Black student returned late from break. I was pulled aside and it was stated that the teacher felt sorry for the other student. When I asked 'why', it was implied that I coerced her into returning late against her will. Also, vague work appraisals are given and no specific areas of improvement are suggested. Comments such as, 'You seem like a very angry person,' and 'I have a hard time approaching you and can only imagine how the residents feel,' or 'Any monkey can be trained to take a blood pressure' are an every day occurrence. There are many cases where my mistakes are far more noted and exaggerated than those of other students. When defending myself (as I feel I am performing equally well to everyone else), I am labelled as not being 'self-aware' and not accepting feedback. Yet, when feedback is taken and changes are made, I am told I take things too literally. As a result, I can do no right.

It is sad to say that events like these are commonplace. As a result, promotions as well as workload may not be fairly distributed.

—Nadine Smith

women coming from a culture where family is an extremely strong social element to one where they would often have to delay marriage until eligible Filipino immigrants arrived. Others, married in their home country, had to leave their husbands behind until, years later, they could sponsor them.

The Racialization of Disease

We describe an illness or disease as having been 'racialized' when it has become strongly associated with people of a particular ethnic background. The result is that we may treat all people sharing this ethnicity, whether or not they have the ailment, differently because of their supposed connection to it. Here we're thinking not of illnesses such as German measles or the Spanish flu—most of us don't avoid people of Spanish or German background for fear of catching these viruses. A better example is severe acute respiratory syndrome, or SARS, an ailment that, during a 2003 outbreak, afflicted Canadians of all ethnic backgrounds but became primarily associated with two.

SARS: The Racialization of Disease

Canadians first began hearing about severe acute respiratory syndrome in March 2003, and throughout the spring and early summer it became the focus of widespread media attention. Over the course of this period, the disease became racialized. Because it originated in China, and because a Filipino Catholic charismatic community (Bukas-Loob Sa Diyos) had members who contracted it, the disease took on a racial identity. Chinese and Filipino Canadians became targets of discrimination.

In a Web-published report released in June 2004, researchers Carrianne Leung and Jian Guan noted, among other things, how the mainstream media racialized SARS by portraying Asians as carriers of disease in a way that spread fear among non-Asian Canadians. Table 10.2 summarizes Leung and Guan's findings about the content of pictures featured with SARS articles in four national newspapers and periodicals (Leung and Guan 2004: 9, 10).

Leung and Guan found that photographs accompanying stories about SARS tended to feature Asians, particularly Asians wearing masks to

Table 10.2 Photographic treatment of SARS in the national media, 2003

NEWSPAPER/ MAGAZINE	NUMBER OF PICTURES	SHOWING PEOPLE	SHOWING ASIANS	SHOWING ASIANS WITH MASKS
National Post	120	95 (82.0%)	65 (54.2%)	60 (50.0%)
Globe and Mail	119	68 (57.1%)	52 (43.9%)	41 (34.45%)
Maclean's	27	17 (63.0%)	8 (29.6%)	6 (22.2%)
Time (Canada)	17	15 (88.2%)	8 (47.0%)	6 (35.3%)

Source: Carrianne Leung and Jian Guan, 'Yellow Peril Revisited: Impact of SARS on the Chinese and Southeast Asian Canadian Community' (Toronto: Chinese Canadian National Council, 2004).

THURSDAY, APRIL 3, 2003 ★ **TORONTO STAR** ★ B3

SARS Outbreak

China admits wider spread of SARS

12 more deaths reported among inland provinces

First cases found in Latin America and Israel

ANN PERRY
STAFF REPORTER

The global death toll from Severe Acute Respiratory Syndrome jumped yesterday as China broke its silence and admitted it had more cases in more provinces than it had previously revealed.

The South China Morning Post reported today that the first victims of the deadly illness were people in China's southern province of Guangdong who ate or handled wild game, confirming earlier reports linking the disease to ducks.

China said it had 1,190 suspected cases through the end of March, and 46 deaths instead of the 34 it had admitted. Cases were reported in Guangxi, Hunan and Sichuan provinces as well as Guangdong for the first time.

In total, the World Health Organization estimated that SARS has infected more than 2,200 people worldwide and killed an estimated 78.

Brazil reported its first suspected case, which, if confirmed, would be the first in Latin America. Israel also reported its first suspected case.

China agreed yesterday to let a team of WHO investigators visit the southern province of Guangdong, where the disease is believed to have started.

The four-member international team, which will leave Beijing today, will take samples from suspected patients to help identify a culprit virus and assess how infectious and virulent it is.

And, for the first time in its 55-year-history, WHO recommended that travellers avoid part of the world because of an infectious disease: Hong Kong and adjoining Guangdong province.

In the first public statement by a senior leader, Chinese Health Minister Zhang Wenkang said the outbreak was "under effective control."

He said 80 per cent of those diagnosed with SARS have recovered.

For weeks, U.N. agency officials have appealed for more cooperation from China.

"Because the mainland is not sharing information . . . the outbreak has been lengthened," Taiwan's Mainland Affairs Council said in a recent report.

Laboratories around the world are racing to come up with a test for SARS.

The U.S. Centers for Disease Control has issued two tests that health officials can give to patients with suspected SARS. Dr. Julie Gerberding, the director of the Atlanta-based centre, said until a large number of people are tested, no one can say whether the disease is caused by the main suspect — a coronavirus.

But she said so far 400 healthy people had been tested for the virus, a previously unknown relative of one of the common cold viruses, and all had tested negative.

Several patients with SARS have tested positive.

"It is not yet proof. There are other viruses still under investigation," she said. In Toronto, Dr. Raymond Tellier of the Hospital for Sick Children, has developed a test that detects this new species of coronavirus. It is currently being used here.

A top health expert in China told a newspaper the earliest SARS patients in Guangdong had close and continuous contact with chickens, ducks, pigeons and owls.

"We will explore further if the disease was passed to human beings from wild animals. You know, Guangdong people like eating exotic animals and I don't find it a healthy practice," said Bi Shengli, a vice-director at the Chinese Centre for Disease Control and Prevention.

The earliest cases of the disease were traced to either chefs or bird vendors, Bi said.

In Thailand yesterday, the government said it would turn back foreigners suspected of having SARS and would force those allowed in from affected countries to wear masks in public.

In the Philippines, which has no confirmed cases, President Gloria Macapagal Arroyo put in place a contingency plan — including air and seaport checks — to prevent an outbreak. Health officials in New Zealand urged indigenous Maori tribesmen to forgo their traditional "hongi" nose-rubbing greeting for visiting Chinese at a convention.

In Hong Kong, the Roman Catholic Church ordered priests to wear masks during Communion and put wafers in the hands of the faithful rather than on the tongue.

FROM STAR WIRE SERVICES

REUTERS
With Hong Kong being the global centre of the SARS outbreak, face masks are common on the city's streets. Some residents strive for their own style amid the crisis. Chinese officials are reporting there are more cases and more deaths than they previously admitted.

Photo: Courtesy Toronto Star Archives

Telling It Like It Is

SARS and Being Chinese

POINT OF VIEW

Around the time of the SARS crisis, being Chinese made people look at me in a different way, whether it was at school, work, or in public places such as the subway and buses. It did not bother me at first, but as more and more individuals died due to SARS, the more I kept my eyes open for tainted looks darting in my direction.

Around that time in school, it wasn't so much the looks, but comments made in class about the situation. What I have learned and understood in this game we call life is that everyone is entitled to his or her opinion. I have also learned and understood that not all opinions are necessarily right or wrong. Unfortunately, not all people feel that their opinions are wrong, hurtful, disrespectful, condescending, and rude.

One incident happened in my math class at college. Our class got off topic, and our focus was turned from present and future value to SARS. Our teacher was reminding us that proper hand washing helps in preventing the spread of infection. One obnoxious fellow who felt he was the class clown replied to our teacher's comment and stated that to prevent the spread of infection, we need to stay away from all those darn Chinese people. His language use and vocabulary was a little cruder. Being the only Asian person in the class, everyone turned and looked in my direction as if they were expecting me to curse at him. I was beside myself and decided to let the one and only authority figure take care of his biased opinion. However, our teacher said absolutely nothing, except to get on with the lesson. His comments offended me and our teacher not correcting him hurt my feelings. It made me pay more attention to the things that were being said in all the rest of my classes. The impact it had on my school life made me more defensive towards what my peers had to say about those of Asian descent. . . .

Ethnicity is a sociological factor that made an impact on my life within the last year. Because I have been on the end of a biased opinion at school and indirect discrimination at work, I have further learned another aspect of the game of life; the value and meaning of equality and fairness and that even though there are different ethnicities and races, we are all part of one race called the human race.

—Karin Koo

What do YOU think?

1. Do you think we can assign blame for the racialization of a disease like SARS? If so, where?

2. Does blame lie with the media, for exaggerating the facts surrounding the outbreak and feeding public fears? Or is it the media's responsibility to make people aware of the gravest possible outcomes of an event?

3. Does blame lie with individuals, for succumbing to fearmongering? Can regular patrons of Chinatown businesses be blamed for altering their purchasing habits if there's any chance at all that not doing so will increase their odds of contracting the virus? Should people be expected to weigh decisions about their personal health against the greater economic and social impact of their decisions?

reduce the spread of the disease. The researchers noted that the exaggerated use of frightening words and unreasonable parallels drawn between SARS and the Spanish influenza pandemic of 1918–19 (in which at least 20 million people died over an 18-month period) were also part of media fearmongering. SARS had a devastating economic impact on parts of Canada where the outbreak was prevalent, notably Toronto and, in particular, its various Chinatowns. Commentators were quick to note that many of the patrons suddenly avoiding Chinese business communities and restaurants were themselves Chinese, as though this fact somehow justified similar acts of discrimination on the part of non-Asian Canadians. But whether the economic losses can be attributed more to a drop in Chinese Canadian patronage or to decreased patronage by non-Chinese Canadians makes little difference. The fact is that the loss of business occurred, and it did so because the disease was racialized to the point where many Canadians, of all ethnic backgrounds, temporarily changed their purchasing habits as a precaution against contracting the virus in communities where it was thought to be prevalent.

Throughout their report, Leung and Guan note the effect of acts of discrimination, large and small, on individuals of Asian ancestry. In the narrative on page 286, one student tells her story.

Whose Diseases are Important? An Exercise in Medical Ethnocentrism

The most devastating disease in history was the bubonic (or black) plague that occurred in the fourteenth century (see Weatherford 2004: 242–50). During the period of its most powerful effect, it may have reduced the world's population from about 450 million to somewhere between 350 and 375 million. It affected Africa, Asia, and Europe equally. China, where it began, may have suffered a population loss of close to 60 million, reducing the overall population from 123 to 65 million. The population of Europe, where the plague spread next, fell from about 75 million to perhaps as low as 50 million. Africa, the next continent to be hit, lost 12 million of its approximately 80 million inhabitants.

Ethnocentrism is an excessive focus on one culture as a model or standard. Eurocentrism occurs when this focus is placed on the European situation or standpoint as if it were the only important one. Now, if you were to do an Internet search using the words 'Black Plague', what you would find are stories of what happened in Europe, nowhere else. The only mention of places outside of Europe are brief and occasional references to China or Asia as the point of origin.

● ● ● ● ● ● ● ● ● ● ● ● ● ● ● ● ● ● ● ●

What do YOU think?

1. Do your own Internet search on 'Black Death' or 'Bubonic Plague' and briefly summarize the results. Can you account for the ethnocentric perspective of these reports?

2. What effect do you think this presentation of knowledge would have on students of history in secondary or post-secondary schools?

3. Can you think of any contemporary diseases that might receive a similarly ethnocentric treatment?

● ● ● ● ● ● ● ● ● ● ● ● ● ● ● ● ● ● ● ●

Gender and Medical Sociology

Physicians and Gender

Both the number and the percentage of women in and graduating from medical schools in Canada is increasing. In 1959, women accounted for just 6 per cent of medical school graduates; forty years later, they made up 44 per cent of the graduating class. According to Burton and Wong, authors of a paper called 'A Force to Contend With: The Gender Gap Closes in Canadian Medical Schools' (2004), Canadian medical school classes today 'have a range of 43%–74% women (mean 58%), compared with a range of 26%–57% men (mean 42%)'. The percentage of women graduating from medical school and entering the health profession will only increase in the coming years, as the majority of doctors approaching retirement are men. Male doctors in Canada make up 74 per cent of physicians aged between 45 and 65, and 90 per cent of those over 65.

How might this trend affect the profession? How are women physicians different from their male counterparts? A number of features have been regularly noted in the literature. Here are a few examples: women doctors are more likely to

- screen their patients for preventable illnesses,
- spend time counselling about psychosocial issues,
- enter primary care (i.e. become family physicians),
- work fewer hours and see fewer patients, and
- leave the profession sooner.

Women doctors are less likely to

- become surgeons,
- be sued for malpractice, and
- join professional organizations.

What do YOU think?

1. How much do you think this changing gender dynamic will affect the practice of medicine in Canada?

2. Do you think this could lead to a reduction in the power differential between doctors and nurses in Canadian hospitals?

Pharmacy Professors in Canada and Gender

In an article detailing the practices of departments of pharmaceutical sciences at Canadian colleges and universities during the 1990s, sociologist Linda Muzzin noted several gender-based patterns. To gain a proper perspective on these patterns, it's important to know that there is an almost class-like distinction between the two kinds of jobs held by pharmacy professors. The first position involves basic science teaching and some molecular biology research. This position offers a lighter teaching load and tends to be a 'tenure-stream' position, making it more highly valued than the second class of jobs, which Muzzin describes as the 'professional caring' or clinical and social-administrative jobs. The distinction between the two kinds of position within the department falls along gender lines. Consider the following points, noted by Muzzin:

- In 1996, a substantially higher proportion of the professional caring jobs were held by women, except in smaller universities, where a higher percentage of the professional caring jobs are tenured or tenure-stream positions—in these cases, the jobs were more likely to be held by men.
- The majority (86 per cent) of the basic science jobs were tenured or tenure-stream positions, while only 37 per cent of the professional caring jobs were.
- Only 15 of the 112 (13 per cent) tenured or tenure-stream basic science jobs were held by women.
- A majority (65 per cent) of the contract or part-time staff of the professional caring jobs were held by women.

What do YOU think?

1. How could you argue that these findings prove that women pharmacology professors are being discriminated against?

2. How might university presidents or department heads explain the distribution of jobs in a way that sounds reasonable?

Class and Medical Sociology

The Inverse Care Law

Dr Julian Tudor Hart's parents were doctors. He himself studied medicine at Cambridge and interned at the equally prestigious St George's Hospital. A natural career move for a British doctor on that path would have been to serve the needs of the middle class or the rich in London or some other big city. Instead, he moved to Glyncorrwg, to dedicate his life to helping the

Photo: M-J Milloy © 2006

Journalists at a homeless protest are called over by a man revealing festering sores on his hands and arms, which he says doctors refuse to treat because he's on methadone. Why is this man being refused medical treatment? Does our healthcare system discriminate against different segments of society?

citizens of a working-class mining village in south Wales. Dr Hart became famous among medical sociologists for the introductory paragraph to an article he wrote in 1971 and published in the venerable British medical journal *The Lancet*. In it he introduced the idea of the **inverse care law**:

> The availability of good medical care tends to vary inversely with the need for it in the population served. This inverse care law operates more completely where medical care is most exposed to market forces, and less so where such exposure is reduced. The market distribution of medical care is a primitive and historically outdated social form, and any return to it would further exaggerate the maldistribution of medical resources. (Hart 1971: 405)

Hart was describing a system that had, for almost 20 years, experienced socialized healthcare similar to what we know in Canada, a system markedly different from the private or market-force system in the United States. What the inverse care law meant in terms of the Britain he was describing can be seen in a series of statistics concerning infant mortality from the years

1949–53. From Hart's perspective, these statistics

> showed combined social classes I and II (wholly non-manual) with a standardised mortality form all causes 18% below the mean, and combined social classes IV and V (wholly manual) 5% about it. Infant mortality was 37% below the mean for social class I (professional) and 38% about it for social class V (unskilled manual). (Hart 1971: 405)

In other words, the lower classes experienced a greater likelihood of infant mortality (i.e. death of an infant during the first year of life). This, of course, would tend to reflect both the working and living conditions of the different classes, as well as differences in medical care in areas where the various classes live, work, and see doctors. Regarding doctors, which were the main focus of his article, Hart observed the following trends:

> In areas with most sickness and death, general practioners have more work, larger lists [of patients], less hospital support, and inherit more clinically ineffective traditions of consultation [e.g. short visits with little listening to patients' problems] than in the

healthiest areas; and hospital doctors shoulder heavier case-loads with less staff and equipment, more obsolete buildings, and suffer recurrent crises in the availability of beds and replacement staff. (Hart 1971: 412)

● ● ● ● ● ● ● ● ● ● ● ● ● ● ● ● ● ● ●

What do YOU think?

1. Do you think that the inverse care law holds in Canada? How would you, as a sociologist, go about trying to prove or disprove it?

2. How do you think class affects the social course of disease?

3. What was your reaction to news that some NHL players and hospital administrators (who do not come into direct contact with the sick) received H1N1 shots before the general Canadian population? Is this an example of class trumping need in healthcare?

● ● ● ● ● ● ● ● ● ● ● ● ● ● ● ● ● ● ●

Rising Tuition Fees and Medical Students

Most students can relate to the effects of rising tuition fees. How does that affect medical students? A study conducted by Kwong et al. in early 2001 compared tuition costs in Ontario with costs in the rest of Canada (except for Quebec, which, as is so often the case, was excluded). The reason for highlighting Ontario tuition costs is that medical students in that province had the greatest hike in tuition fees in Canada from 1997–8 to 2000–1. The cost of tuition at the University of Toronto, for example, nearly tripled over that period, from $4,844 per year to $14,000.

The researchers contrasted people in their fourth year with those in their first, because they represented the two extremes. They found that there were three differences between the two academic cohorts that were unique to Ontario. First, the proportion of respondents with a family income of less than $40,000 declined significantly, from 22.6 per cent to 15.0 per cent; the same figure among non-Ontario schools stayed just about the same (decreasing slightly from 16.0 per cent to 15.8 per cent). The figure of $40,000 was chosen to represent 'low income', as it was beneath the median family income of $46,951 in Canada in 1996. Another difference between the

groups was that the median debt level anticipated upon graduation by first-year medical students in Ontario was $80,000; the debt anticipated by the graduating class was a lower, but still nasty, $57,000; no such contrast existed in the other provinces. The problem here for the sociologist is that there are no earlier studies with which to compare these findings. What if first-year medical students often project a higher figure than their more experienced graduating colleagues? Is the control group sufficient here for comparative purposes? What do you think?

Finally, first-year medical students in Ontario were more likely than fourth-year students to report that their financial situation was 'very' or 'extremely' stressful (20.5 per cent vs 17.5 per cent; the reverse was true in other provinces: 11.9 per cent vs 15.8 per cent). They were also more likely to cite financial considerations as having a major influence on their choice of speciality or practice location (25.4 per cent vs 13.3 per cent, compared with a reverse ratio of 21.4 per cent to 26.0 per cent in the other provinces). Again, is this a cohort problem or a stage problem somehow conditioned by being in Ontario?

Final Thoughts: Twelve Sociological Tips for Better Health

In 1999, British sociologist David Gordon drew up the following list of 'Alternative 10 Tips for Better Health'; it was meant as an alternative to the British Medical Officer's 10 health tips, which included the usual things about smoking, eating right, drinking in moderation, driving safely, and so on:

1. Don't be poor. If you can, stop. If you can't, try not to be poor for long.
2. Don't have poor parents.
3. Own a car.
4. Don't work in a stressful, low paid manual job.
5. Don't live in damp, low quality housing.
6. Be able to afford to go on a foreign holiday and sunbathe.
7. Practice not losing your job and don't become unemployed.

8. Take up all benefits you are entitled to, if you are unemployed, retired or sick or disabled.
9. Don't live next to a busy major road or near a polluting factory.
10. Learn how to fill in the complex housing benefit/asylum application forms before you become homeless or destitute. (Quoted in Pohlmann 2002)

This tongue-in-cheek but accurate appraisal has been adapted a number of times. In a speech he delivered on 8 May 2003, Roy Romanow, author of the Romanow Report on Canada's healthcare, adapted this list to include two additional items:

11. Graduate from high school and then go on to college or university. Health status improves with your level of education.
12. Be sure to live in a community where you trust your neighbours and feel that you belong. A civil and trusting community promotes health and life expectancy.

What do YOU think?

How do these 'health tips' reflect William Ryan's idea of 'blaming the victim'?

This student works 20 hours a week at the University of Toronto's athletic complex to supplement his student loans. He expects to graduate $40,000 in debt and worries rising costs will deter his younger siblings from seeking a post-secondary education. Should medical students expect to graduate with higher debts given the greater earning potential their degree confers?

Photo: Rene Johnston/GetStock.com

Questions for Critical Review

1. Take a particular disease or injury that you have experienced and discuss the social course that you went through to get cured or healed. Where did you go? Who treated you? How were you socially processed?
2. Identify what biomedicine is and talk about its weaknesses and strengths. In terms of its weaknesses, think of what happens when a Western practitioner of medicine encounters non-Western people or Aboriginal people who have different medical traditions and explanations.
3. How and why does medicalization take place during the treatment of a particular physical condition? When is medicalization more harmful than helpful?
4. How do you think the question of immigrant doctors should be handled?
5. How does Ivan Illich critique modern medicine? Do you agree or disagree with his views? Why?

Suggested Readings

Das Gupta, Tania *Real Nurses and Others: Racism in Nursing*. Halifax: Fernwood Publishing, 2009.

Foucault, Michel (1973). *The Birth of the Clinic: An Archaeology of Medical Perception*. A.M.S. Smith trans. New York: Vintage Books.

Goffman, Erving (1961). *Asylums: Essays on the Social Situation of Mental Patients and Other Inmates*. New York: Doubleday.

Lorde, Audre (1980). *The Cancer Journals*. San Francisco: aunt lute books.

Turner, Bryan (1984). *The Body and Society: Explorations in Social Theory*. London: Sage.

Wertz, Richard W., & Dorthy C. Wertz (1989). *Lying-In: A History of Childbirth in America*. New Haven: Yale UP.

Yalom, Marilyn (1997). *A History of the Breast*. New York: Harper Collins.

Suggested Websites

Children's Environmental Health Project
www.cape.ca/children/index.html

National Aboriginal Health Organization
www.naho.ca/english/

The Canadian Women's Health Network
www.cwhn.ca/indexeng.html

World Health Organization
www.who.int/en/

Key Terms

- American Dream
- aristocrats
- blaming the victim
- Brahmins
- capital
- capitalists (bourgeoisie)
- caste (varna)
- class

- class consciousness
- class reductionism
- corporate (or organic) identity
- counter ideology
- Dalits (Untouchables)
- deciles
- dominant capitalist class
- dominant ideology

- false consciousness
- food bank
- hegemony
- Highland Clearances
- ideology
- Indo-European
- Kshatriyas
- liberal ideology

12

'Race' and Ethnicity: Sites of Inequality

LEARNING OBJECTIVES

After reading this chapter, you should be able to

> discuss the extent to which race, ethnicity, and gender are social constructs;

> distinguish between different forms of racism;

> explain four 'mind traps' of studying blacks in Canada;

> demonstrate how, historically, Canadian laws can be said to be racist; and

> contrast the social inequality in Quebec before and after the Quiet Revolution.

- prejudice
- primordialism
- Quiet Revolution
- racial bigotry
- racialization
- registered Indian
- relational accountability

- scrip
- social constructivism
- systemic (or institutional) racism
- token
- urban reserve
- vertical mosaic

Key Names
- Franz Fanon
- Albert Memmi
- Everett C. Hughes
- John Porter
- W.E.B. DuBois
- Daniel G. Hill

Photo: CP Photo/Andrew Vaughan

The home crowd at a Calgary Flames game represents 'the invisibility of whiteness', which speaks both to a homogeneous demographic and to a society that is constructed around white beliefs, values, and ideals—anything other than white becomes 'visible'.

FOR Starters

The Invisibility of Being White

Most white people living in North America are for all intents and purposes invisible. That invisibility affords a safety that is easily taken for granted.

In the 1960s, I—a white male—became visible for a time because of my long hair. With this status I took a few baby steps down the long path of unmasked prejudice. Police, folks from small towns, and denizens of Toronto's 'greaser' neighbourhoods all made me highly aware of my visibility, causing me to feel vulnerable to the emotions of others. Once, waiting for a bus in northern Ontario, dark from a summer's work in forestry, straight hair hanging well below my shoulders, one of the people working at the bus depot thought I was Native. I got a brief glimpse of what it was like to be the object of racial disdain.

My hair remains long, but age and a respectable career have made me invisible again. That is, unlike a young black male, I am not watched carefully in convenience stores, nor stopped for no apparent reason while driving. White people, even when they are visible, do not lose status; on the contrary, in many cases, with greater visibility comes a rise in status. When I went to Taiwan, I had visibility with prestige. Children watched me with respect. They would practise English with 'the expert'. Among school children on a trip to the museum, I became a walking exhibit of the West. They passed me with deference, my 'Hi, how are you?' spoken to their face-covering hands.

When I took the train south to the mid-sized city of Hualien, my visibility helped me, when the person who was supposed to meet me failed to turn up. Taxi drivers helped me use the phone (I was unsure of which coins to use), even when I told them I wouldn't be needing a ride. Would a Taiwanese person in a mid-sized, racially homogeneous city in Canada have been served that well?

For the first time in my life, on that trip, I went an entire day without seeing another white person. Far from being able to disappear anonymously into crowds, I parted the throngs like Moses through the Red Sea (the beard might have helped). I felt as though I was always on stage, but with a friendly audience.

Coming back, I needed to get a taxi from the station to the airport. I knew the name of the airport, but that didn't help me as I passed from taxi to taxi trying to communicate what I needed, each time to baffled looks. Knowing that fluency in English and administrative status often went hand in hand in Taiwan, I went to the office of the station manager, who wrote down what I wanted so that I could show it to one of the taxi drivers. Can you imagine a non-English speaker, non-white person doing that in Canada? Imagine the response.

It was a good lesson for me to be visible, even if the experience of visibility was not a negative one. It helped me imagine what it would be like if the roles were reversed.

Introduction to 'Race'

The term 'race' was first applied to humans in the context of Spanish and English colonial expansion during the sixteenth and seventeenth centuries. Use of the term reflected—and still does reflect—beliefs about natural or biological superiority and inferiority in the context of colonial power. It does not boil down to the formula 'lighter skin = good, pure / darker skin = bad, corrupt'—witness, for example, Russian racism directed at Siberian peoples speaking languages related to Finnish and Hungarian, and Japanese racism towards their indigenous people (the Ainu and the Okinawans), and the racism of the Chinese concerning Tibetans and the Turkic-speaking, Muslim Uygurs. However, white supremacy—which amounts to discrimination against anyone not of western European ethnic background—has been the prevailing pattern since people began discussing humans in terms of different 'races', each with its own set of qualities and characteristics.

Why do we put quotation marks around 'race'? It's important to understand that as biological entities, races do not exist among humans. When early scientists tried to divide humans into three 'races'—Caucasian (named after the mountains in which 'pure' whites were supposed to live), Mongoloid, and Negroid—there were always peoples left over. Where do you file the Ainu of Japan, the Aborigines of Australia, the peoples of various physical differences living in the South Asian subcontinent? Differences *within* supposed races often outnumbered those *between* races. 'Negroid' people included both the tallest and shortest people in the world, and people of greatly varying skin colour. English-born anthropologist Ashley Montagu published a landmark argument against the existence of separate human races in *Man's Most Dangerous Myth: The Fallacy of Race*, first printed in 1942. Since then, science has shown that there is but one human species, albeit one that displays variation among its members—rather like *Ursus americanus*, the black bear, which can be black, cinnamon brown, and even white.

Racialization, though, does exist. It is a social process in which people are viewed and judged as essentially different in terms of their intellect, their morality, their values, and their innate worth because of differences of physical type or cultural

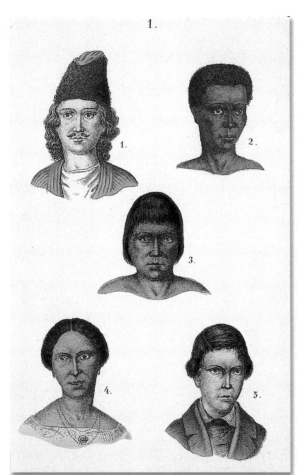

This frontispiece from an 1862 English translation of *Martin's Natural History* shows three of five supposed principal 'races' together with two mixed races: (1) the white, or Caucasian, race; (2) the black, or Negro, race; (3) the American, or Red, race; (4) the Mulatto mixed race; and (5) the Mestizza mixed race. The other two principal races identified in the book are the Yellow, or Mongolian, race and the Brown, or Malayan, race. (From S.A. Myers, trans., *Martin's Natural History*, First Series, New York: Blackeman & Mason, 1862: frontispiece.)

heritage. In this chapter we will examine some of the contexts in which this process plays out, and the effects it creates.

A Sociological Profile of Canada's Native People

Racialization occurs in Canada, as elsewhere. It is perhaps most evident in the way Native people have been and still are treated. The racialization of North American Native people began in the sixteenth century in Europe with a discussion of whether or not Aboriginal people were even human and had souls. To western Europeans they were an 'Other' that needed to be explained, and racialization was part of that explanation. A few facts from the sociological profile of Canada's Native People shows how this racialization has occurred.

First, Native people have been living in what is now Canada for a very long time: a conservative estimate is 12,000 years. If you figure that the first Europeans (the Norse explorers, or Vikings) visited Canada's eastern shores about 1,000 years ago (and left shortly afterwards), we can say that roughly 92 per cent of Canadian history is Aboriginal history alone. The first non-Native settlements in Canada were founded just 400 years ago. That means that non-Aboriginal people have lived continuously in this country for only 3.3 per cent of its history.

Second, from a sociological perspective, Aboriginal people have been studied primarily as social problems. Aboriginal writers have been loud in their criticism of this preoccupation and have called for a more balanced approach. Métis writer Emma LaRoque expresses her own criticism as follows:

> Several years ago in a sociology class on social problems, I recall wondering if anyone else was poor, because the professor repeatedly referred to Native people as statistical examples of poverty. . . . Not for one moment would I make light of the ugly effects of poverty. But if classroom groups must talk about Indians and poverty, then they must also point out the ways in which Native people are operating on this cancer. To be sure, the operations are always struggles and sometimes failures, but each new operation is faced with more experience, more skill, more confidence and more success. (LaRoque 1993: 212)

LaRoque here calls for a perspective that attempts to balance how people are seen, a perspective based on what Wilson and Wilson (1998) refer to as **relational accountability**. This is an approach that balances the social portrayal of a people so that both strengths and weaknesses, problems and successes can be seen.

Third, Aboriginal voices have barely been heard in the sociological study of their people in

Canada (Steckley 2003). Unfortunately, as Aboriginal people have only recently been able to take advantage of graduate-level work in Canadian universities, and as sociology, like anthropology, has been tainted as an outsider-privileged research area, it will be a while yet before these voices speak loudly in Canadian sociology.

Fourth, Aboriginal people are defined by a complex system of legal status that separates them in a number of ways from non-Aboriginal people, and from each other. The main designations, as defined in Canadian legislation, are:

- **registered Indian**
- Bill C-31 Indian
- band member
- reserve resident
- treaty Indian (and each treaty is different)
- Métis
- Eskimo.

The legal differences come from the Indian Act, which is administered by the federal Department of Indian Affairs. Passed in 1876, the Indian Act enshrined a sexist definition of 'Indian' as any man of 'Indian blood' reputed to belong to a particular band, any child of such a man, or any woman married to such a man. A man kept his status no matter whom he married, but a woman, if she married someone not legally an Indian, lost her status, and her children would share that fate. Ironically, a non-Native woman could gain Indian status by marrying an Indian man. This discriminatory law was in force until 1985, when Bill C-31 was passed, enabling people who had lost their Indian status through marriage or through the marriage of their mother to apply to be reinstated.

Inuit (from a word in their language meaning 'people'; the singular is 'Inuk') differ from Indians, having been in Canada for a shorter time, somewhere between 5,000 and 10,000 years. It was not until 1939, when the federal government wanted to assert territorial claims in the Arctic, that Canada officially took responsibility for the Inuit. Each Inuk was given a metal disc with a number that was to be used as a **token** of their status. Today, about 60 per cent of Inuit have disc numbers. The lives of Canada's Northern Aboriginal population changed on 1 April 1999, when the territory of Nunavut (meaning 'Our Land') came

into being. More than 80 per cent of Nunavut's 25,000 residents are Inuit. They own 18 per cent of the land, have subsurface rights to oil, gas, and other minerals for about 2 per cent of Nunavut, and will receive royalties from the extraction of those minerals from the rest of the territory. They do not require a licence to hunt or fish to meet their basic needs.

The term **Métis** is used in two ways. It is commonly used, often with a lowercase *m*, to refer to anyone of mixed Native and non-Native heritage. With an uppercase *M* it usually refers to the descendants of French fur traders and Cree women. Starting in the late eighteenth century, the Métis developed a culture that brought together European and Native elements. Over time, they came to regard themselves as a nation, having achieved a sense of solidarity from their shared legal struggles with the Hudson's Bay Company (HBC) over the HBC's trade monopoly. The HBC owned most of the prairies and about half of present-day Canada thanks to a 1670 charter granted by the English King Charles II, who little knew what he was signing away. In 1867, the HBC negotiated the sale of most of its lands to the Government of Canada, which, with no regard for Métis land rights, moved to set up a colony in Manitoba. In 1869, led by 25-year-old, college-educated Louis Riel, the Métis achieved a military takeover in the colony and set up an independent government to negotiate with Ottawa. The *Manitoba Act* of 1870 established the province and recognized the rights of the Métis. The Métis were given **scrips**, certificates declaring that the bearer could receive payment in land, cash, or goods. But government officials and land speculators swindled the Métis out of their land by buying up the scrips for next to nothing. Most Métis simply moved west. In 1885, with western expansion again threatening their rights to the land, the Métis, led still by Louis Riel, set up an independent government in Saskatchewan. Federal Canadian forces attacked and defeated them, and this time Riel was hanged for treason.

The Métis settled in a patchwork of rural prairie communities and nearly disappeared altogether. But during the 1930s, Alberta Métis pushed for the creation of communal settlements similar to reserves. In 1938, eleven Métis 'colonies' were formed (eight remain today). These colonies carry some political rights, making them more like rural municipalities; however, the Métis do not have rights to the royalties for oil and gas extracted from the land. Beyond the colonies, the Métis are represented by the Métis National Council and provincial organizations in Ontario and the Western provinces. These organizations suffer from difficulties of legal definition and lack of recognition.

In the 2006 census, 389,785 people identified themselves as Métis, representing a 91 per cent increase from 1996 and nearly doubling their overall recognized population. The Métis also upped their percentage of the Aboriginal population during that time, from 26 per cent to 34 per cent. The main reason for this increase likely is a heightened tendency to self-identify as Métis, which is due to an increase in Métis political and cultural activities.

Two Recent Changes in Aboriginal Canada

In 1993, two Métis men, Steve Powley and his son, were charged with unlawfully hunting and possessing a moose. They fought the case on the grounds that it was their right as Aboriginal people to hunt for food. On 23 September 2003, the Supreme Court of Canada upheld Powley's right to hunt for food out of season and without a provincial licence. The case helped establish the **Powley test**, used to determine whether Native and Métis people can lawfully hunt without a licence. According to the test, a person must be able to show that he or she has been identified as Métis for a long time and is accepted as a member in a community that was historically and is currently Métis. Powley and his community of 900, just outside of Sault Ste Marie in northwestern Ontario, qualified. The Powley case has been used by the Métis to obtain hunting rights in parts of British Columbia, Alberta, and Saskatchewan.

Recently, the province of Saskatchewan has become home to a number of newly established **urban reserves**. These reserves, located on lands within a municipality or northern administrative district, have been given official reserve status to compensate Native peoples who were promised land more than 100 years ago. The main function of these urban reserves is to provide central urban locations for Aboriginal businesses. More than 1,350 people work in the businesses set up in Saskatchewan's 28 urban reserves.

Muskeg Lake Cree Nation was the first band to develop an urban reserve. The band has about 1,200 members, most living off reserve. They were granted 33 acres of land in Saskatoon. In 1993, they signed a services agreement with the city, under which the band makes an annual payment for municipal services such as snow and garbage removal; electricity and water charges are billed directly to individual customers on the reserve. Businesses operating there are almost all owned by Aboriginal people, and nearly all of the 300 employees are Native.

What do YOU think?

1. Who would oppose the successful invocation of the Powley test?

2. How could this opposition be overcome?

3. Native people have made up a disproportionately high percentage of the poor in Canadian cities. Do you think that turning city neighbourhoods into urban reserves will change this significantly? Are their drawbacks you can think of?

Blacks in Canada

Black communities have existed in Nova Scotia since the British Proclamation of 1779 offered freedom to slaves who left their American masters to fight on the British side in the American Revolution. Over 3,000 African Americans moved north, followed 20 years later by 2,000 more, who came to the Maritime colonies when they were offered their freedom by the British government during the War of 1812, in which Britons and Canadians fought Americans (Conrad and Hiller 2001: 103, 111). They were offered significantly less land and fewer opportunities than white immigrants were (see Whitfield 2004), and they endured incredible hardship and prejudice.

The black population of Canada has declined several times. In 1792, nearly 1,200 black Loyalists left the Atlantic colonies for the new African colony of Sierra Leone (Conrad and Hiller 2001: 103), and many more returned to the United States following the Civil War. Between 1871 and 1911 there was a slow decline in the population of black people in Canada, from 21,500 to 16,900,

Photo: CP Photo/Halifax Chronicle Herald

A young woman walks along the tracks in Africville, a black Loyalist community settled on the outskirts of Halifax, Nova Scotia, which was demolished, its residents relocated, between 1964 and 1967 to make room for urban development.

Photo: CP Images/Peter McCabe

Radio host Yvon Chery brings updates on the January 2010 earthquake in Haiti to listeners of CPAM, the Haitian community radio station in Montreal. The city is home to 83 per cent of Canada's Haitian community, which makes up the tenth-largest non-European ethnic group in Canada (Statistics Canada 2007). Do you think most Canadians were aware of the country's large Haitian community before the earthquake? Why do you think that this was the case?

and a further drop—from 22,200 to 18,000—between 1941 and 1951. It wasn't until the 1970s, when the population rose from 34,400 in 1971 to 239,500 by the end of the decade, that the number of black Canadians began to increase consistently (Milan and Tran 2004: 3).

In 2006 there were an estimated 783,795 blacks living in Canada, making them the country's third highest visible minority behind Chinese people (1,216,570) and South Asians (1,262,865). In three provinces—Nova Scotia, New Brunswick, and Quebec—they are the leading visible minority, and in only one province—British Columbia—do they rank last among the six 'official' visible minorities (Chinese, South Asians, blacks, Filipinos, Latin Americans, and Southeast Asians). The high population of blacks in Nova Scotia and New Brunswick is largely a result of eighteenth- and nineteenth-century immigration, whereas in Quebec it is due to more recent immigration from a number of former French colonies, including Haiti, Chad, and Cameroon.

● ●

What do YOU think?

Why do you think the number and percentage of black people are so low in British Columbia?

● ●

The Point Is...   Blacks in Canada: Four Mind Traps

There are several 'mind traps'—misconceptions or unsubstantiated generalizations—that you may encounter, and must be careful to avoid, when studying blacks in Canada. Here are four to watch out for:

- ✗ Canada's black population consists mostly of recently arrived immigrants.
- ✗ Canada's black community has a relatively brief history.
- ✗ The vast majority of blacks coming to Toronto are from Jamaica.
- ✗ A black student who receives a post-secondary education has just as good a chance of succeeding in Canada as a non-black student.

While there is a tendency to think of black Canadians as immigrants, almost half of Canada's black population was born in this country. The tendency of Torontonians (whose city is home to nearly half of Canada's black population) to think of all black immigrants as 'Jamaicans' is also flawed, as there is a growing number arriving from African countries. Of the roughly 139,800 black immigrants who came to Canada between 1991 and 2001, only 20 per cent came from Jamaica; 12 per cent came from French-speaking Haiti (settling mostly in Montreal), while 23 per cent came from three African countries: Somalia (10 per cent), Ghana (8 per cent), and Ethiopia (5 per cent).

Education does not seem to benefit black people as much as it does others. In 2001, Canadian-born blacks between the ages of 25 and 54 were just as likely as other Canadian-born citizens to be university graduates (21 per cent), and slightly more likely to have a college diploma (23 per cent compared with the national average of 20 per cent). Still, the average income of Canadian-born blacks was substantially lower than the average for all Canadian-born people ($29,700 versus $37,200). Some analysts have tried to 'explain away' this discrepancy by arguing that the majority of working black citizens are relatively young, earning the lower incomes typical of younger workers. Yet when the income of Canadian-born blacks is age-standardized to overcome the statistical bias, the result is an annual income of $32,000, which is still significantly lower than the national average.

● ●

What do YOU think?

1. How do you account for the prevalence of the four 'mind traps' noted above? Do you think they are honest mistakes or myths perpetuated by certain groups that stand to benefit from the misinformation?

2. Why do you think black university graduates earn considerably less than non-white graduates?

● ●

Racism

Four Elements of Racism

Racism can be understood as the product of four linked elements. The first is the construction of certain groups of people as biologically superior or inferior. This fosters ideas of relative worth and quality, which leads to the second element, **prejudice**, the 'pre-judgment' of others on the basis of their group membership. The third element is **discrimination**, which includes acts by which individuals are treated differently—rewarded or punished—based on their group membership. Finally, there is power, which is manifested when institutionalized advantages are regularly handed to one or more groups over others. Tatum, addressing the question *Can non-White people be racist?*, touches on the importance of power in this equation when she writes:

> People of color are not racist because they do not systematically benefit from racism. And equally important, there is no systematic cultural and institutional support or sanction for the racial bigotry of people of color. In my view, reserving the term 'racist' only for behaviors committed by whites in the context of a white-dominated society is a way of acknowledging the ever-present power differential afforded whites by the culture and institutions that make up the system of advantage and continue to reinforce notions of white superiority. (Quoted in Codjoe 2001: 287)

Those who share this position believe that without power, non-white people in Canada cannot, strictly speaking, be racist. They can be prejudiced. They can perform discriminatory acts. But they cannot be racist without institutional, structural, ideological, and historical support. Certainly this is true of systemic racism, which by definition involves power. But this view does not adequately account for situations in which one racialized group that lacks power puts down another. In such an instance, both groups are sharing in the racism of the dominant 'race'. Cree leader David Ahenakew's public—and much publicized—anti-Jewish statements in 2002 are a case in point. Both Aboriginal and Jewish people have been and continue to be victims of racism in Canada. But

although it would be mistaken to call Aboriginal people in Canada racists, Ahenakew contributed to anti-Jewish racism with his prejudiced remarks.

There are different kinds of racism. **Racial bigotry** is the open, conscious expression of racist views by an individual. When racist practices, rules, and laws become institutionalized, made 'part of the system' (no matter how aware or unaware people are of their discriminatory nature), then we have **systemic** (or **institutional**) **racism**. Sometimes, racism can be subtle, hidden in a way behind a smile or words that seem friendly to the perpetrator. This is called **friendly** (or **polite** or **smiling**) **racism**. Henry Martey Codjoe provides an example:

> Canada's 'smiling racism' was with me until the very day I left the country. The realtor who showed our house to prospective buyers quietly hinted that if I wanted my house to sell quickly, I would have to remove all traces of anything that indicated that Blacks had lived in the house: no family pictures, no African art or crafts, everything Black or African must go, and we must be out of the house before he showed the house to prospective buyers. He would call and let us know. No matter what we were doing, we must leave. One time we were late in getting out and we ended up hiding in our minivan in the garage. When he showed the garage, we ducked. It was a shameful and degrading experience. The house sold, but my wife and I never did meet the family that bought it. (Codjoe 2001: 286)

Master Narratives and Buried Knowledge

In the **master narratives** that countries construct about themselves, which get repeated in textbooks and in the stories people (especially politicians) tell about their country, racism is often downplayed or altogether omitted. Stories about the mistreatment of minorities, stories that make the dominant culture or their ancestors look bad, are often excluded. For example, the master narrative of early Canadian history describes how Native people co-operated with Europeans to make the fur trade successful, by obtaining the furs, teaching Europeans how to use canoes and snowshoes, and providing the Europeans with new foods (such as pemmican and corn). This 'official' version of the story often appears in elementary and middle-school textbooks; it overlooks the exploitation and social destruction that occurred when Europeans introduced alcohol into the fur trade. To use Michel Foucault's terminology, that story is 'buried knowledge'.

Canada's master narrative depicts a country that is more multicultural than the United States. While there is some evidence to support this, the master narrative does not include some buried knowledge about the history of certain racial groups in Canada. The following three stories are part of that buried knowledge.

1. Defending the Women: An Act to Prevent the Employment of Female Labour

The head tax of $500 imposed on Chinese immigrants beginning in 1903 had a dramatic effect on immigration to Canada. For the overwhelmingly

• Going Global • • • • • • • • • • • • • • •

The Day I Learned that Libyans Were Human Beings: Lessons in Globalization

It was early 1983, and I was teaching English as a Second Language at a private school in Toronto, a job I had held for about a year. At the time, most of my students had been Venezuelans. Then a group of Libyan students arrived. I imagine they came to us because they weren't allowed into the US. Libyans were portrayed in the media as the great enemy of the West during the 1980s. 'Libyan' became a kind of shorthand for 'terrorist'. Even the 1985 movie *Back to the Future* featured Libyan terrorists with automatic weapons to play the role of evil gunmen whose motives did not have to be explained. Libyan terrorists; story told. Libyan leader then and now Mu'ammar Gaddafi was the Osama bin Laden of his day.

Despite my sociological training, I couldn't help feeling a bit suspicious of the new students. Growing up in Toronto in the 1950s and 1960s, I had only encountered a few Arabs: a geography teacher and two schoolmates—a brother and sister—in high school. In my first few classes with the Libyans, I found them quieter than the students I was used to, and I didn't know how to read that quiet. I half-wondered whether some of them were involved in or somehow connected with terrorism. I was different too. Humour is a teaching tool I fall back on regularly, but I was hesitant to use it. I didn't want to offend.

Our school was right beside a subway stop. One morning, as I began the long climb out of the station, I met one of my Libyan students. We greeted each other politely and walked together with few words. Then we faced the long double escalator, flanked on either side by a set of stairs that is so seldom used it seems reserved for emergencies. He turned to me and said, 'Come on, we are both still young men.' We took the stairs at a run, together. At that moment, our common age and gender (and male pride) were all that mattered. It was a lesson for me.

I grew fond of my Libyan students. They reminded me of conservative Christians I had met: they didn't drink and were very polite. My humour re-entered the classroom ('Is that your father?' I asked when someone showed me a picture of Qaddafi). I learned about the beauty and creativity of Arab poetry, and how it could be chanted (the kind of chanting I had heard before only on TV when Arab 'terrorists' were being portrayed). I missed them when they left.

—J.S.

male population of Chinese immigrants who had already settled in Canada, it meant the chances of marrying a Chinese woman were greatly reduced. Many Chinese-Canadian men were forced to lead a bachelor's life, and this made them a threat to white women in the eyes of some European Canadians. This prejudice brought about Saskatchewan's *Act to Prevent the Employment of Female Labour in Certain Capacities* on 5 March 1912. It declared that

> No person shall employ in any capacity any white woman or girl or permit any white woman or girl to reside or lodge in or to work in or, save as a *bona fide* customer in a public apartment thereof only, to frequent any restaurant, laundry or other place of business or amusement owned, kept or managed by any Japanese, Chinaman or other Oriental person. (Quoted in Backhouse 1999: 136)

In May 1912, Quong Wing was convicted and fined for employing two white women in his restaurant. His appeals to the Supreme Court of Saskatchewan and of Canada failed.

In 1924 in Regina, Yee Clun, owner of the Exchange Grill and Rooming House, challenged the law. He had strong personal support in the city from members of both the Chinese and non-Chinese communities. Two white women who ran the Chinese mission spoke of his upstanding moral character. But local newspapers were spreading poorly researched stories of Chinese men bringing opium into Saskatchewan and turning white women into 'drug fiends'. Clun won the case in court but found his efforts foiled by the Saskatchewan Legislature, which simply passed another statute authorizing any municipal council to revoke the court ruling. The Act wasn't repealed until 1969.

2. Punished for Success:
Japanese-Canadian Fishers

What happens when a group that considers itself superior begins losing a competition with one it deems inferior? In the competition for fish in early twentieth-century British Columbia, the answer was that the rules were changed to favour the 'superior race'.

In 1919, the Federal Department of Marine and Fisheries responded to growing concern that Japanese-Canadian gill net salmon fishers were 'taking over' at the expense of white Canadian fishers. In the ironic words of Major R.J. Burde, MP for Port Alberni, reported in the Victoria *Colonist* on 22 May 1920, 'they have become so arrogant in their feeling of security that many white settlers are reaching the limit of tolerance' (Adachi 1977: 105). The government reacted by drastically reducing the number of licences that Japanese-Canadian fishers could obtain (see Table 12.1).

In just three years, white fishers gained 493 licences, an increase of 33.5 per cent; Aboriginal fishers gained 215 (up 20.8 per cent). Japanese fishers, by contrast, lost 974 licences, a drop of 48.9 per cent. Japanese-Canadian fishers in the north Skeena area were even prohibited from using power boats between 1925 and 1930. The rules had been changed, and the playing field was no longer level.

3. Not Wanted on the Voyage:
The *Komagata Maru*

Most of the first South Asians to come to Canada, in the late nineteenth century, were Sikhs, who had been given special status by the British as soldiers and police serving imperial purposes throughout the world. In 1904 they began to arrive in small numbers, many of them settling in Port Moody, east

Table 12.1 Salmon gill net licences issued, 1922–5

	TO WHITES	TO INDIANS	TO JAPANESE	TOTAL
1922	1,470	1,032	1,989	4,491
1923	1,642	1,122	1,193	3,957
1925	1,963	1,247	1,015	4,225

Source: *Report on Oriental Activities within the Province*, British Columbia Archives NW 305.895R425.

of Vancouver. By 1906, those small numbers had increased considerably, with as many as 5,000 Sikhs entering the country between 1905 and 1908 (Johnston 1989: 5; Burnet with Palmer 1988: 31). They were young men, most of them single, though a good number had wives back in India, and they arrived at a time when there was a shortage of labourers in British Columbia willing to work in the sawmills, on the roads, and in the bush cutting wood and clearing land. They were greeted with a measure of respect, as many were British army veterans, and they soon earned a reputation for working hard for low wages. An October 1906 report in the Vancouver *Daily Province* quoted one employer as saying, 'I would

have White labourers of course if I can get them. . . . But I would rather give employment to these old soldiers who have helped fight for the British Empire than entire aliens.'

BC's natural resources-based economy has long fluctuated between periods of wild success, with employers happy to hire anyone willing to work hard, and short periods of unemployment, in which newcomers are seen as taking jobs from whites. It wasn't long before the initial acceptance of the hard-working Sikh immigrants was undermined by a growing unease over their rise in numbers. The local press fuelled the simmering discord with stories about the unfamiliar cultural practices of these 'Hindus' (as South Asians collectively were

Telling It Like It Is

AN AUTHOR POV

Racialized Views of a Canadian Institution

POINT OF VIEW

According to CBC hockey analyst Don Cherry, he had told us all along that Russians were 'quitters'. He was referring to an apparent threat by the Russian team to pull out of the 2002 Winter Olympics in Salt Lake City over alleged bias in drug testing. 'I've been trying to tell you people for so long about the Russians, what kind of people they are,' Cherry told *Hockey Night in Canada* viewers, 'and you just love them in Canada with your **multiculturalism**.'

Cherry's comments sparked an angry reaction among many Canadians. Nevertheless, he stood by his comments, although he issued a statement a week later to 'clarify' his remarks. According to Cherry, he was referring not to the Russian people as a whole but to the Russian delegation, 'who threatened to pull out of the Olympics because they got caught with drugs and were losing'. Anyone who heard the statement, however, knew that Cherry had been addressing what he considered an essential and long-held character trait of the Russian people.

Among those in Canada stunned by Cherry's comments was Maia Master, publisher of the *Russian Express*, a Toronto-based newspaper serving the needs of the city's 160,000 Russian Canadians, who was flooded with calls com-

plaining about the remarks. During an interview shortly afterwards on *CBC NewsWorld*, Master was informed by a smirking Dennis Trudeau that Cherry was still popular enough to remain on the air despite having insulted other groups before (including Quebecers, whom he described on air in 1998 as 'whiners'). Trudeau's suggestion that Don Cherry was simply being himself and that his comments should not be taken personally was nearly as disturbing as Cherry's original views. Russian Canadians, he seemed to suggest, should simply put up with such slights, like all immigrants and minorities in Canada.

Canadian corporate mass media continues to be an active agent in perpetuating a cohesive social order based on affluence, while simultaneously telling us that 'good' people tolerate prejudice, discrimination, racism, and other forms of repression. Yet we must be intolerant of intolerance. Russian Canadians, like all immigrants and minorities, have a right to complain and to speak out as Canadian citizens about those things that are unacceptable in what is supposed to be a multicultural society. To capitulate to the tyranny of silence is to capitulate to one's own repression.

—G.L.

called, regardless of their actual religion). 'Hindus Cover Dead Bodies with Butter' announced a headline in the 20 October 1906 edition of Vancouver *Daily Province* (Johnston 1989: 3).

Vancouver police began taking Sikh immigrants directly from the immigration shed to the BC interior to keep them out of the city. In spite of the mounting effects of racism and the deplorable accommodations in which they were placed—some were housed in an abandoned cannery with no running water and little electricity—the Sikhs showed tremendous resilience, as Johnston records:

> Two thousand had arrived during the latter half of 1906. By the end of December, with the exception of some 300 who had taken steamers for Seattle and San Francisco, all but fifty or sixty had found employment in British Columbia, most of them in saw mills. The authorities would gladly have deported any convicted of vagrancy, but there were few such cases; those who were out of work were looked after by their companions, and . . . none became a public charge. (Johnston 1989: 3)

Facing pressure both from white British Columbians disconcerted by the influx of Sikh immigrants and from British government officials in India, who wanted to curtail emigration, the Canadian government responded with clever discrimination. They passed a law requiring that all Asian immigrants entering Canada possess at least $200—a large sum for people who typically earned about 10 to 20 cents a day. They also prohibited the landing of any immigrant arriving directly from any point outside of India—significant because most Sikhs were making the journey from Punjab province by way of Hong Kong—while pressuring steamship companies not to provide India-to-Canada service or to sell tickets to Canada from Indian ports. These measures brought Sikh immigration to a halt. Unable to bring their wives and families over, denied the right to vote or hold public office, and facing open discrimination from local leaders, Canada's Sikh population became discouraged. Dr Sundar Singh, in an address at the Empire Club in Toronto on 25 January 1912, articulated the frustration many Sikhs were feeling:

> Just at present there are two Sikh women confined on board a boat at Vancouver. . . . One is the wife of a merchant, the other is the wife of a missionary. These men have been settled in this country for five years, and are well spoken of. They went back some time ago to bring out their wives and children. . . They came to Hong Kong, and the steamship company refused to sell them tickets; they waited there since last March and last month the CPR sold them tickets. On the 22nd, they arrived here, and the men were allowed to land, but the ladies are still confined as if they were criminals.
>
> We have the promise of Queen Victoria that all British subjects, no matter what race or creed they belong to, shall be treated alike. . . . The Indian people are loyal British subjects. They are as loyal as anybody else. Why should there be such a difference in the treatment of these loyal people?
>
> We appeal to you, gentlemen, to say that in any country, under any conditions, the treatment of the Sikhs are receiving is not fair. . . . You may well imagine the feeling of these two men, who are suffering as I have described, for no fault at all, except that they are Sikhs. (www.empireclubfoundation.com/details.asp?SpeechID=2519&FT=yes)

But opposition to Sikh immigration only continued to grow. On 1 December 1913, the Vancouver *Province* claimed that the 'Hindu problem' had assumed 'a most serious and menacing aspect' (Johnston 1989: 22), even though only 39 Sikhs had entered the area that year. The following spring, on 3 May 1914, the Japanese steamship *Komagata Maru* left Yokohama headed for Canada. Rented by a 55-year-old Sikh, Bhai Gurdit Singh, the ship contained 376 passengers: 340 Sikhs, 24 Muslims, and 12 Hindus. News of the ship's approach was announced in headlines such as 'BOAT LOADS OF HINDUS ON WAY TO VANCOUVER' and 'HINDU INVASION OF CANADA' in British Columbia dailies. When the ship reached Vancouver on 23 May 1914, the local

Sikh passengers aboard the *Komagata Maru*. The treatment of what was called 'the Hindu problem' has left a dark legacy in Canada's history. Despite that fact that Sikhs have been in Canada since 1904, their 'visibility' still prompts the question: *Where are you from?*

South Asian community was ready with lawyers, funds, and food to assist the passengers. Local immigration officials, politicians, and vigilante groups were also ready. For about two months, the ship's passengers were forced to endure legal battles, severe shortages of food and water, and a confrontation with the *H.M.C.S. Rainbow*. Finally, on 23 July 1914, the *Komagata Maru* was forced to leave. Only 24 passengers were permitted to enter Canada.

On 26 September, as the ship approached Calcutta, the remaining passengers were told that they would have to be put on a special train taking them to the Punjab area. Amidst confusion and frustration, a riot ensued. Twenty of the passengers were killed; others were imprisoned or became fugitives. Gurdit Singh was a fugitive for more than seven years before being captured and imprisoned for five years. In his early seventies he was elected to the All-India Congress.

Little changed afterwards. After 1918, a few of the men were able to bring over to Canada their long absent wives and children, but most could not afford such an expense. By 1941, there were no more than 1,500 South Asians in Canada. Most were men, many aged between 50 and 65. Only when India was granted its independence from British imperial control in 1947 were South Asians given the vote and full citizenship status.

On 3 August 2008, in a park in Surrey, BC—a city with a large South Asian population—Prime Minister Stephen Harper issued an apology to South Asians for the *Komagata Maru* affair. He left immediately after representatives of the South Asian community received the apology with an officially approved thank-you speech. Once the PM was gone, a South Asian leader addressed the crowd of roughly 8,000 and asked whether they accepted the apology. Most did not, and the Indian media widely condemned the apology because it had not been presented in Parliament to be written into the official record; this made it, in the eyes of its critics, a second-class apology. Some have called Harper's apology, like the one he made

• Our Stories • • • • • • • • • • • • • • • • • • •

A Minoritizing Episode

On 21 August 1914, shortly after the start of World War I, a group of Canadians was **minoritized** through the War Measures Act, which would be used as an instrument of discrimination against Japanese Canadians nearly 30 years later and then, almost another 30 years after that, against French Canadians.

As with South Asian ethnic groups—Sikhs, Hindus, and Muslims—that were lumped together as 'Hindoos' and, decades later, as 'Pakis', the chosen identity of this minoritized group was ignored for another, 'alien' one. Like Aboriginal people in both world wars, members of this minoritized group would sometimes have to pass as Canadian to be able to join up to fight, lying about their identity and changing their names. And like the Chinese, South Asians, Native people, and women of their time, many would be denied the federal vote. During the Second World War they were put into concentration camps, like the Japanese.

Surprisingly, the members of this group were white.

Britain and her allies, including Canada, were fighting Germany and the decrepit Austro-Hungarian empire. The latter was home to a people who thought of themselves as Ukrainians by nationality, even though their official citizenship was 'Austrian'. The War Measures Act led to the internment of 8,579 people labelled 'enemy aliens' in 24 camps spread across Canada. More than 5,000 of them were Ukrainians, though they were called Ruthenians, Galicians, and Bukovynans.

Another 80,000—again, most of them Ukrainians— had to register as 'enemy aliens'. More than 10,000 Ukrainians enlisted in the Canadian military, some by faking their names and identity to conceal their true ethnicity. Among them was Filip Konoval, one of only 83 Canadians to be awarded the prestigious Victoria Cross. Still, the War Elections Act denied most Ukrainians the right to vote.

Those who spent time in internment camps worked hard, developing Banff National Park, logging, working in mines and in steel mills. One hundred and seven internees died. Tuberculosis killed twenty-six, pneumonia, twenty-two. Six were shot to death trying to escape camp; three committed suicide. An undetermined number died due to unsafe working conditions. One hundred and six were sent to mental institutions, all but three of whom were eventually deported. There was a riot in Kapuskasing, Ontario. In Sydney, Nova Scotia, there was a hunger strike. Running the camps cost Canadian taxpayers $3.2 million.

The effects of the discrimination did not end with the war. Some of the land, valuables, and money possessed by Ukrainian Canadians and confiscated by the Canadian government 'disappeared'. Internment and suspicion killed the spirit of many who had been keen to contribute to the growth of Canada, who had nurtured high hopes for their new home.

Photo: Library and Archives Canada/C-063254

A young 'Galician' immigrant in Saint John, New Brunswick, May 1905. Ukrainians began to settle in Canada during the 1890s; today, in spite of the discriminatory and dispiriting measures they were subjected to during the First World War, Canada's Ukrainian population is among the highest in the world outside of Ukraine and Russia. In 1990, Ray Hnatyshyn, a Ukrainian Canadian, became Governor General of Canada.

that same year for the Chinese head tax, a political stunt designed to improve the Conservative Party's standing among non-White voters, who traditionally support either the Liberals or the NDP (see, for example, Walla 2008).

● ● ● ● ● ● ● ● ● ● ● ● ● ● ● ● ● ● ● ●

What do YOU think?

How can we evaluate official apologies by Canadian governments? Do some come across as being more sincere, more genuine than others? Do some seem staged or designed merely for political vote-gaining with a marginalized group?

● ● ● ● ● ● ● ● ● ● ● ● ● ● ● ● ● ● ● ●

Ethnicity

Everyone belongs to at least one ethnic group. But understanding ethnicity is not just a matter of collecting social traits—language, clothing, religion, foods, and so on—and applying the appropriate ethnic label. This would not help us understand conflict between closely related ethnic groups, nor would it help us understand why 'ethnic pride' surfaces in certain times and situations, and not during others.

There are various ways of theorizing ethnicity. We will confine our discussion to five approaches. Political sociologists often divide theoretical approaches to ethnicity into three categories: **social constructivism**, **instrumentalism**, and **primordialism**. Wsevolod W. Isajiw, in *Understanding Diversity: Ethnicity and Race in the Canadian Context*, discusses primordialism in relation to the **epiphenomenal** approach, which will be helpful to consider here as well. To this list we will add one more approach, **anti-colonialism**, because it is essential to understanding ethnicity in the context of the case study we are about to present.

One of the most savage and destructive ethnic conflicts of recent times—and, in fact, one that is still ongoing—involves rival Hutu and Tutsi tribes in Rwanda, as well as in neighbouring Burundi. The history of Rwanda since it gained independence in 1962 has been punctuated by uprisings of the disenfranchised Hutu majority against the ruling Tutsi elite, which have brought about the deaths of hundreds of thousands of civilians in both groups. The violence reached a bloody peak during the spring and summer of 1994, when Hutu military forces massacred between 500,000 and 1,000,000 of the Tutsi minority, sending more than a million destitute Hutu civilians, fearing reprisals from the surviving Tutsi population, fleeing to refugee camps in neighbouring Zaire (now the Democratic Republic of the Congo) and Tanzania. It is easy to dismiss the conflict as just another instance of tribal violence in Africa, but this is far from the truth. What happened presents a challenge of interpretation that can be facilitated by looking at it through the lens of various theories of ethnicity.

Primordialism

Primordialism (sometimes referred to as 'essentialism') is the view that every ethnic group is made up of a 'laundry list' of traits that have been carried down from the past to the present with little or no change. Adopting this view uncritically leads to believing that the tribal conflicts in Africa have a deep history that existed long before **colonialism**, and that these conflicts are reignited only once the 'stabilizing influence' of the colonial power has left. It does not allow for conflicts to arise during colonization. It absolves colonial powers of any blame for regional conflicts.

Primordialism presents a static, as opposed to a dynamic, view of culture. In this view, culture does not seem to change from the inside; change is ascribed primarily or entirely to outside forces. 'Modernization', for example, is credited solely to colonial outsiders. Primordialism is a kind of functionalist theory, displaying one of the weaknesses of functionalism: that it poorly explains the development of conflict.

Anti-Colonialism

Colonialism is the economic and political exploitation of a weaker country or people by a stronger one. Typically—historically—it involves the domination by a European state of an African, Asian, or American people; however, it is not limited to this. The Chinese have exercised and continue to wield colonial control over Tibetans and Uighurs. **Internal colonialism** is colonialism of one people by another within a single country. The history of Canada involves the internal colonialism of Aboriginal peoples by European settlers and their governments.

Anti-colonialism (or **post-colonialism**) is a theoretical framework that analyzes the destructive impact colonialism has on both the colonizer and the colonized. It was first developed by writers such as **Franz Fanon** (1925–1961) and **Albert Memmi** (b. 1920) to examine French colonies in North Africa and their fight for independence from France. Fanon, born in the French colony of Martinique in the West Indies, was radicalized by his experience as a black intellectual in France and by his work as a doctor and psychiatrist in Algeria during the fight for independence there. His influential works *Black Skin, White Masks* (1952) and *The Wretched of the Earth* (1961) deal with the psychological effects of colonization and have inspired considerable sociological study. Albert Memmi was a Jew born in the predominately Muslim Tunisia, which gained its independence in 1956 (six years before neighbouring Algeria). His major work, *The Colonizer and the Colonized* (1957), demonstrated how the two groups negatively conditioned each other, and how no party could be 'neutral' in the relationship between the two.

Anti-colonialism theory as it applies to ethnicity involves identifying colonialism as a factor in the development or escalation of conflict between ethnic groups. In Canada, for example, anti-colonialism theory could be used to explain the increasing conflict between the Huron and Iroquois during the 1640s in terms of the former group's connections with the French and the latter's ties with the English. In the African context, it is usefully applied to study situations involving the concept of **indirect rule**, the policy in which a European nation uses the members of a particular ethnic group as its intermediaries in ruling an area of Africa. (Here we prefer the term 'area' to 'nation' because the territorial boundaries were often defined or altered by colonizing European powers.)

One problem with anti-colonialism as a theory is that it can attribute every negative change in a colonized area to outside forces. It does not leave much room for agency of one or more of the colonized groups. A corrective for this is **dual colonialism**, the idea that under a colonial regime, the most oppressed groups suffer both at the hands of the colonizing outsider group and at the hands of a local group that is given privilege and power by the outsider group. Political scientist Catharine Newbury applies this idea well in her discussion of Rwanda in *Cohesion of Oppression* (1988).

Primordialism, Anti-Colonialism, and Rwanda

As you read the following description of ethnic conflict in Rwanda, consider how well the theories of primordialism and anti-colonialism apply.

In Rwanda three main ethnic groups are currently recognized: Hutu, Tutsi, and Twa. Numerically, the Hutu are by far the dominant group. The 1956 census lists 83 per cent of the population as Hutu, with 16 per cent Tutsi and 1 per cent Twa (Newbury 1988:3). Yet from at least the eighteenth century onwards, the Tutsi have been the group with the most power. If we consider a list of typical 'ethnic traits'—including physical attributes, language, religion, kinship structure, occupation, and economic circumstances—we gain some interesting findings about Rwanda prior to colonization.

PHYSICAL APPEARANCE

Tutsi and Hutu tended to differ in their physical appearance. The former were typically portrayed as being taller and thinner than the latter, with longer and thinner faces. One study (Chrétien 1967) found that the Tutsi averaged 1.75 metres in height, the Hutu 1.66 metres. We must note that before and during the colonial period, intermarriage was not uncommon. The physical differences combined with the fact that the Tutsi appear to have come later to Rwanda than the Hutu led colonial administrators and social scientists to draw otherwise unfounded conclusions about the Tutsi being a 'superior, conquering race'. This helped justify European colonial support of the Tutsi elite.

OCCUPATION

Concerning occupation and labour, the Tutsi were, in the pre-colonial period, primarily pastoralists—that is, they herded cattle. The Hutu, on the other hand, were primarily agriculturalists, growing crops. The division was not absolute: some Hutu, particularly those heading up the richer lineages, herded cattle, and some Tutsi were agriculturalists. Passing from one group to the other was not uncommon. But during the colonial period, the more powerful Tutsi took advantage of their enhanced privileges to gain a greater share of the cattle.

LANGUAGE

The people of Rwanda all speak the same language, with regional dialect variants. The language, belonging to the local Bantu group of languages, was likely spoken in Rwanda before the Tutsi moved into the area (probably from Ethiopia).

RELIGION

In terms of religion, the Tutsi and Hutu did not differ historically, and during the colonial period most were converted to Christianity by Catholic missionaries. However, religion would, through the education system, come to have a powerful effect on the development of a strong sense of ethnicity in Rwanda by entrenching the ethnic-based class system that placed the Tutsi at the top and the Hutu at the bottom. Established in 1932 and recognized as the best school in Rwanda, the Groupe Scolaire played a part in promoting class and ethnic divisions, as Newbury explains. One of the goals of this school was to create a 'new social class',

> and in accordance with this goal . . . very few Hutu were admitted; indeed, after World War II *the school even had a minimum height requirement for admission.* Graduates of the Groupe Scolaire considered themselves superior to other educated Rwandans, . . . and their diplomas were accorded greater value by the Belgian [colonial] administration. Thus, in theory because of their professional qualifications but in reality because they were overwhelmingly drawn from among the families of Tutsi chiefs, the graduates of the Groupe Scolaire enjoyed the benefits of both the 'traditional' economic structures, and of the higher status jobs and better pay available in the 'modern' sector. (Newbury 1988: 116) [emphasis added].

IDENTITY

Identity is difficult to characterize historically. It seems that prior to the colonial period, sense of identity was derived mainly from lineage, clan, chiefdom, or kingdom, and from a general sense of being Rwandan. Of the kin groups, the two that were of the greatest significance (and remain important today) are lineage and clan. Lineage heads were important figures, and a person's primary identity came from lineage. Clan was less important, but, interestingly, a single clan could include members of all three Rwandan ethnic groups.

Under colonialism lineage heads lost power, being replaced by centrally appointed chiefs who were overwhelmingly Tutsi. The distinction between Tutsi and Hutu, which was of less significance in the time before the colonial period, became much more of a factor, its importance reinforced by the fact that Rwandan citizens now had to carry identification cards with 'Hutu', 'Tutsi', or 'Twa' written on them.

The growing central authority of the king during the colonial period also helped to enhance the status of the Tutsi. During the reign of Kigeri Rwabugiri (*c.* 1860–1895), the king's central authority grew to encompass chiefdoms and kingdoms, some of them Hutu, that until then had been relatively independent. The colonial administration and the Tutsi elite collaborated to take away the more diverse traditional government forms through which the Hutu in particular could play one authority against another into a more simplified and powerful system. A system of taxes payable either in money or with labour was developed and exploited, with colonial support, by unscrupulous Tutsi chiefs who took advantage of free labour from Hutu civilians.

Altogether we see a situation that is not well explained by primordialism, but which fits well with dual colonialism theory. How do other theories fit into this situation?

Ethnicity as Epiphenomenal

The word 'epiphenomenal' describes a secondary effect or phenomenon that arises from, but does not causally influence, a separate phenomenon. Marx was the first to apply it in a sociological context. He believed that economic structure was the main causal factor in society, and everything else was epiphenomenal or insignificant.

When applied to ethnicity, the epiphenomenal theory suggests that any ethnic conflict is really just a byproduct of the struggle between economic classes. Thus, the strife in Rwanda stems from a situation in which the country's rich and powerful (the Tutsi elite) were exploiting its poor (the Hutu and the poorer Tutsi). Ethnicity was just a smokescreen, a false consciousness that made it impossible for poorer Hutu and Tutsi with shared class interests to overcome oppression by the Tutsi elite. This lasted through the 1950s, when Hutu of all classes shared what Newbury termed a 'cohesion of oppression', until 1962, when the country became independent and witnessed a social revolution that replaced the Tutsi elite with a Hutu one. The Hutu elite used the pretense of democracy to gain broader Hutu support. There is a measure of truth in the epiphenomenal explanation, yet it fails to fully account for why the poor would identify with the rich.

Instrumentalism

Traditionally presented in direct opposition to primordialism and compatible with the epiphenomenal approach is instrumentalism, which focuses on emerging ethnicity rather than on long-established ethnic characteristics. It acknowledges that elites can mobilize others who identify with them ethnically. Ethnic identification and action come from a competition for scarce resources for and by the elite. In Newbury's words, ethnic groups are created or transformed when

> groups gain self-awareness (become 'self-conscious communities') largely as the result of the activities of leaders who mobilize ethnic followings in order to compete more effectively. Improved communications and the spread of writing are important in this process; so is 'ethnic learning', where groups develop ethnic awareness as a result of seeing others using ethnic solidarities to compete. The state is important, instrumentalists suggest, as an arena in which competition between these groups occurs (the state controls many of the scarce resources over which elites are competing), and also because government policies can significantly affect the strategies chosen by ethnic leaders. (Newbury 1988: 15)

Elite members who mobilize ethnicity for personal gain are called **ethnic entrepreneurs**. Examples of ethnic entrepreneurship include Adolph Hitler's construction and manipulation of the German 'Aryan race', and Slobodan Milosevic's use of Serb ethnic symbols to achieve and maintain dictatorial power in the former Yugoslavia. An instrumentalist approach better explains how a frustrated Hutu leadership could invoke the injustice of Tutsi elite oppression to draw poorer Hutu into their political parties and their acts of revolution.

Social Constructivism

Social constructivism is the view that ethnicity is constructed by individuals for varying social purposes. Instrumentalism can be considered a partly formed social constructivism in that it shows how ethnicity is constructed by the elite; however, it suffers as a theory of ethnicity and ethnic action by overstating the influence and impact of the elite. It generally fails to attribute the non-elite members any agency, any power to choose and act without being manipulated. A social constructivist theory of ethnicity would look to the motivations of the broader group.

The social constructivist approach makes sense in the case of Rwanda, where it helps to explain why the general rural population of the Hutu became so thoroughly engaged in driving off and killing local Tutsi (often neighbours). Rwanda was, for most of the twentieth century, a very crowded land, with many people, particularly Hutu, being regularly malnourished because their working farms were insufficient for their needs. Unlike in the nineteenth century, when there was considerably more space and people could move to new land in difficult situations, during the twentieth century people suffered through various famines and cattle diseases while the country's rise in population shrunk farm size. Drive your neighbours out and your family has an improved chance of survival.

Summary

So what can our five approaches to studying ethnicity tell us about the Hutu and Tutsi in Rwanda? We can say that by the middle of the nineteenth

A refugee camp in Goma, Zaire, July 1994, where thousands of Rwandans sought refuge from the fighting in Rwanda. Many became sick and died of cholera.

century, some people in the area were taller and were more likely to herd cattle, but being a member of an ethnic group was not a major part of the day-to-day lives of most Rwandans—not like lineage, region, and sometimes individual chiefdom or kingdom. First with the growth in power and widespread influence of the king (who was Tutsi) and his court working toward the development of a modern state, and then, more tellingly, from the effects of colonialism (first German, then Belgian), a dual colonialism developed in which Europeans and elite Tutsi collaborated to put social, economic, and political substance to an increasingly rigid 'ethnic' divide between Hutu and Tutsi. And when, in the 1950s, European colonialism began to fade in Rwanda, the common experience of oppression experienced by Hutu of all classes, particularly the peasant class, led to a social revolution in which the majority Hutu overthrew their oppressors, only to set up an ethnic dictatorship of their own. Ethnic violence was a not surprising effect, and an easily

fanned racial hatred, with fuel piled high during colonial times, combined with a powerful need for land led in 1994 to the massacre of the Tutsi.

Ethnicity in Canada: Classic Studies

Ethnic Class: English and French in Quebec

When **Everett C. Hughes** (1897–1983) entered the sociology department at McGill in 1927, the focus of his research became the 'ethnic division of labour' between the English, who held positions of power, and the French, who occupied the lowest rung of the employment ladder. This was a wrong that he wished to right.

In *French Canada in Transition*, Hughes studied the small industrial city of Drummondville during the 1930s. He noted two types of industries there. First, there were small, local, French-Canadian–run industries, which 'do not make the town grow but proliferate and grow with it' (Hughes 1963: 47). Second, and more important, were what he called '*nos grandes industries*'. The top nine of these eleven 'big industries' had headquarters in Montreal, England, and the United States; their managers were Americans, English Canadians, and Brits. In 1937, the largest of these industries, a textile company, employed 389 'English and Others' and 2,337 French workers. The former group occupied 24 of the 25 positions above the foreman level and 57 of the 82 foreman's jobs. The vast majority of the French employees (1,882) were on the 'factory floor', involved directly in textile production (Hughes 1963: 55).

In a 1954 study of intergenerational (father to son) occupational mobility, Yves de Jocas and Guy Rocher (1957) found that Anglophones in Quebec cities scored much higher than Francophones (11.8 per cent versus 3.2 per cent) in the occupational category they called 'professional, proprietor, manager', and that the discrepancy among their sons was even greater (17.3 per cent versus 6.8 per cent; in Langlois 1999: 73). This suggested that the ethnic division of labour was increasing. John Porter, in *The Vertical Mosaic*, observed a similar growing separation (see Table 12.2). French-Canadian sociologists Jacques Dofny and Marcel Rioux (1962) described this separation as the phenomenon of **ethnic class**, in which people of a particular ethnicity belong predominantly to one class.

During the 1960s the balance shifted somewhat with the **Quiet Revolution**, which represented an attempt by a growing educated, skilled, and urban middle class to overthrow three social bodies that combined to restrict the people: (1) the English-dominated large businesses; (2) the Union Nationale, a provincial political party that exerted great conservative control through the rurally supported premier Maurice Duplessis (1936–9 and 1944–59); and (3) the Catholic Church, which had a firm grip on education, the press, and the unions. In large measure, the decrease in inequality between French and English was brought about by provincial policies and practices, designed in part by sociologists, enacted as part of a concerted effort to make French Canadians '*maîtres chez nous*' ('masters in our own house').

John Porter and the Vertical Mosaic

The best-known book of Canadian sociology is *The Vertical Mosaic: An Analysis of Social Class and Power in Canada* (1965) by **John Porter** (1921–1979). Porter's title derives from the often-stated notion that Canadian society is a **cultural mosaic** rather than a **melting pot**. The term 'cultural mosaic' applies to societies in which individual ethnic, cultural, and religious groups are able to maintain separate identities (a mosaic is a type of artwork made up of many tiles that lend different colours to the picture). The opposite model is the 'melting pot', where immigrating ethnic, cultural, and religious groups are encouraged to assimilate into their new society; it is the term typically used to describe American society.

Porter's **vertical mosaic** refers to a hierarchy, or ranking, of higher and lower ethnic, cultural, and religious groups. To keep with the metaphor of the mosaic, Porter found that the different tiles were stacked, not placed evenly, so that the white-Anglo-Saxon-Protestant tiles are on top.

Table 12.2 French and British in the professional and financial occupation

YEAR	FRENCH	BRITISH	DIFFERENCE
1931	6.2%	7.1%	0.9%
1951	6.0%	7.2%	1.2%
1961	7.8%	9.3%	1.5%

Source: Truncated table reprinted with permission of the publisher from *The Vertical Mosaic* by John Porter. Original data taken from the following volumes of *The Census of Canada*: 1931, vol. 7, Table 49; 1951, vol. 4, Table 12; and 1961, vol. 3.1–15, Table 22.

Telling It Like It Is

Ethnicity and Class in Sept-Îles During the 1960s and 1970s

Sept-Îles is located on the north shore of the Gulf of St Lawrence, in Quebec. During the 1960s and early 1970s it was often described in superlatives, thanks to a couple of American-owned mining companies. Iron ore had been discovered in the 1950s in the Quebec–Labrador peninsula. Consequently, the Iron Ore Company of Canada and Wabush Mines set up shop. The Quebec North Shore and Labrador Railway delivered the ore to Sept-Îles from the mines nearly 600 kilometres north of town. Sept-Îles was for a while the richest city in Canada in per capita income and the biggest port in terms of sheer tonnage shipped.

Originally a fishing village with a few hundred people, it grew rapidly. At its peak, it had a population of about 35,000, about 85–90 per cent French-speaking and about 10 per cent English-speaking. A small minority were Innu. They had a reserve in town and another about 15–20 kilometres east of town.

Many of the English-speaking population came from Atlantic Canada. Many were Newfoundlanders and those who were known as 'Coasters', people who came from further along the coast as it stretched toward Labrador. They sought employment outside their traditionally impoverished areas. There were also many Europeans and Americans. The former brought skilled trades and professional training with them. Many of the French-speaking population were from Gaspé and the south shore of the St Lawrence.

Even as a young boy, I could discern disparities within the community. There were two better neighbourhoods in town, known locally as 'Executive Point' and 'the Wabush Ghetto'. These areas were where the executives of the two companies lived. Although small—only a dozen or so houses in each—they were the most desirable areas of town. They were where power and money resided in the community. The residents were almost entirely English-speaking.

Within the companies, it seemed that there were unwritten rules. Unilingual French speakers could not aspire to a position above foreman within the companies and they would be very lucky indeed to reach assistant foreman-level speaking only French. The opposite was true with unilingual English speakers: the sky was the limit. The top executives, more often than not, were brought in from the parent companies, i.e. from the United States.

I spent two summers working on the railroad and got to see these disparities first-hand. Most of the foremen were English-speaking, some were bilingual, and some were not. The French-speaking foremen inevitably spoke English as well as their native tongue. Unfortunately, there were many people who simply did not think they had to learn French. They believed it was up to French-speaking Quebecois to learn English. I knew far too many such people.

There were a number of French-speaking schools and two English-speaking school systems: public and Catholic. The Protestant schools, which I attended, were Fleming Elementary and Queen Elizabeth High School ('Queenie' to her students). When I graduated, Fleming and Queenie had a total student population of fewer than 300. When I was a teenager, there was not a lot of dating among the groups. A few people dated students from the English Catholic school, fewer still who dated French-speaking students. However, it did exist. My sister married a French Canadian. Her children are all fluently bilingual. Two are with French-Canadian girls.

There was a movement, initiated by my dear old mother, to have a school uniform. The daughters of Executive Point made monthly trips on the company plane to Montreal, 1,000 kilometres away, to buy clothes. Keeping up with the daughters of the executives was a costly prospect, so a school uniform was adopted. There were blue blazers, white shirts and ties and grey flannel pants for boys, and kilts and white blouses for girls.

The uniform had a number of unintended consequences. It enhanced school pride. There was a levelling effect, with less competition over fashionable clothing. But, I cannot help but think that the school uniform, so visible as we walked home and to the shopping centre after school each day, contributed to a sense of divisiveness within the community. It was clear that the ASPs held the best jobs and, in some cases, lived in the best neighbourhoods. Here was the symbolic marker, paraded by their youths.

—Bryan Cummins

Sociologists of Colour

As we have seen earlier, standpoint theory suggests that sociological researchers bring a different perspective to their work based on their 'social location'—their gender, age, ethnicity, and sexual orientation. This does not mean that male and female sociologists may study only their own gender. It means that the pioneers in the sociological study of specific groups—women, for instance, or black people—are often those who belong to the group themselves, and that they have unique and valuable insights that everyone can learn from.

W.E.B. DuBois: First Black Sociologist

W.E.B. DuBois (1868–1963) was the first African-American sociologist. He researched and wrote about the major problems and concerns of Africans, both those living in the United States and those living in the rest of the world. He can be called a '**pan-Africanist**', one who sees the connection between the oppression or success of Africans and that of their descendants around the world.

DuBois's sociology had a definite applied perspective to it. He was one of the founders of the NAACP (National Association for the Advancement of Colored People). He used his position as editor-in-chief of their magazine, *Crisis*, to advocate for such varied causes as opening up black officer training schools and initiating legal action against white people who lynched African

Americans. He was a prolific writer, known for several landmark studies, including his doctoral thesis, *The Suppression of the African Slave Trade in America* (1896); his comprehensive study for

W.E.B. DuBois, after receiving an honorary degree from the University of Ghana, Accra, on the afternoon of his ninety-fifth birthday, 23 February 1963.

Photo: Special Collections Department, W.E.B. Du Bois Library, University of Massachusetts—Amherst

the University of Pennsylvania of Philadelphia's black slums, *The Philadelphia Negro* (1896); *The Souls of Black Folks* (1903); *Black Reconstruction* (1935); and *Dusk of Dawn* (1940). The following captures the oratorical power and sense of fairness of his writing:

> [I]t is the duty of black men to judge the South discriminatingly. The present generation of Southerners are not responsible for the past, and they should not be blindly hated or blamed for it. . . . The South is not 'solid'; it is a land in the ferment of social change, wherein forces of all kinds are fighting for supremacy; and to praise the ill the South is today perpetrating is just as wrong as to condemn the good. Discriminating and broad-minded criticism is what the South needs—needs it for the sake of her own white sons and daughters, and for the insurance of robust, healthy mental and moral development.
>
> Today even the attitude of the Southern whites toward the blacks is not, as so many assume, in all cases the same; the ignorant Southerner hates the Negro, the workingmen fear his competition, the money-makers wish to use him as a laborer, some of the educated see a menace in his upward development, while others . . . wish to help him to rise. National opinion has enabled this last class to maintain the Negro common schools, and to protect the Negro partially in property, life, and limb. Through the pressure of the money-makers, the Negro is in danger of being reduced to semi-slavery . . . ; the workingmen, and those of the educated who fear the Negro, have united to disfranchise him . . . while the passions of the ignorant are easily aroused to lynch and abuse any black man. To praise this intricate whirl of thought and prejudice is nonsense; to inveigh indiscriminately against 'the South' is unjust. . . . (DuBois 1903)

QUICK HITS
Who Has the Right to Vote?

1867	Canadian federal and provincial vote given only to white men with property.
1875	Chinese denied the provincial vote in British Columbia.
1885	'Indians' west of Ontario are denied the vote; eastern 'Indian' males are given the vote only if they own land separate from the reserve and have made at least $150 worth of improvements.
	Chinese denied the federal vote.
1895	Japanese denied the provincial vote in BC.
1898	'Indian' males east of Manitoba denied the federal vote regardless of property.
	White males without property given the vote federally and provincially.
1907	South Asians denied the federal vote.
1908	Chinese denied the provincial vote in Saskatchewan.
1917	People born in 'enemy countries' (i.e. Ukrainians) are denied the vote.
	Japanese-Canadian war veterans are promised the federal vote.
1931	Japanese-Canadian war veterans actually receive the federal vote.
1947	Chinese and South Asians get the federal vote and the provincial vote in British Columbia.
1948	Japanese Canadians get the federal vote.
1949	'Indians' get the provincial vote in British Columbia and Newfoundland.
	Japanese Canadians get the provincial vote in British Columbia.
1951	Chinese get the provincial vote in Saskatchewan.
1952	'Indians' get the provincial vote in Manitoba.
1954	'Indians' get the provincial vote in Ontario.
1960	'Indians' get the federal vote, and also get the provincial vote in Yukon and Saskatchewan.
1963	'Indians' get the provincial vote in New Brunswick and Nova Scotia.
1965	'Indians' get the provincial vote in Alberta.
1969	'Indians' get the provincial vote in Quebec.

What do YOU think?

There is an American organization called The Association of Black Sociologists, founded in 1970 'by women and men of African descent', but which is not confined in its membership to people of African descent.

1. Why do you think the founders of this organization felt it was necessary?

2. Do you think it is important that such an organization exists?

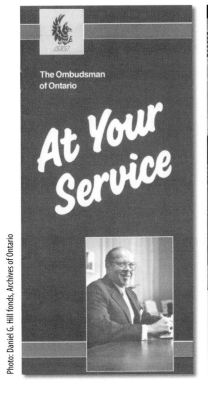

Photo: Daniel G. Hill fonds, Archives of Ontario

Photo: Al Dunlop/Getstock.com

[*Left*] In his work as director of the Ontario Human Rights Commission and, later, as ombudsman of Ontario, Daniel Hill reached out to Ontarians of all ethnic and cultural backgrounds. The pamphlet shown here testifies to the importance he placed on the accessibility of his position to all citizens of the province. [*Top*] Daniel G. Hill, ombudsman of Ontario, circa 1985.

Daniel G. Hill: First Black Canadian Sociologist

The face of sociology in Canada has been almost exclusively a white face. Finding a South Asian, black, East Asian, or Aboriginal sociologist who has had an impact is not easy. **Daniel G. Hill** (1923–2003) is an exception. Although he was not born in Canada, he is considered the first black Canadian sociologist.

Hill studied sociology at the University of Toronto, receiving his MA in 1951 and his PhD in 1960. His primary writings include his doctoral dissertation, *Negroes in Toronto: A Sociological Study of a Minority Group* (1960), and *The Freedom Seekers: Blacks in Early Canada* (1981). But it is mainly in applied work that Hill's sociology is expressed. He was a researcher for the Social Planning Council of Metropolitan Toronto (1955–8), executive secretary of the North York Social Planning Council (1958–60), and assistant director of the Alcoholism and Drug Addiction Research Foundation (1960). In 1962, Hill became the first full-time director of the Ontario Human Rights Commission, and 10 years later,

he became Ontario Human Rights Commissioner. He formed his own human rights consulting firm in 1973, working at various times for the Metropolitan Police Service, the Canadian Labour Congress, and the government of British Columbia. From 1984 to 1989, he served as Ontario Ombudsman, fielding complaints from people concerning their treatment by provincial government agencies. In 1999 he was made a Member of the Order of Canada.

What do YOU think?

1. Why is it more likely that a black Canadian sociologist would get involved in human rights work than a white Canadian sociologist would?

2. How could you determine whether Hill served as a token (i.e. as a black person hired merely so that the committees he was involved with could point to him as proof of their commitment to addressing the concerns of the black community) or as a meaningfully employed member of the social committees he was on?

Questions for Critical Review

1. Discuss the extent to which race, ethnicity, and gender are social constructs.
2. Explain what is meant by a white person being 'invisible' in Canada.
3. How is institutional, or systemic, racism different from other forms of discrimination?
4. What groups have been discriminated against by voting laws in Canada?
5. How did the Quiet Revolution change the social position of Francophones in Quebec?
6. How were Ukrainians minoritized during World War I? What effect do you think that had on their participation in Canadian society for the period that immediately followed?

Suggested Readings

Anderson, Kay J. (1991). *Vancouver's Chinatown: Racial Discourse in Canada, 1875–1980*. Montreal: McGill-Queens UP.

Bannerji, Himani, ed. (1993). *Returning the Gaze: Essays on Racism, Feminism and Politics*. Toronto: Sister Vision Press.

Calliste, Anges, & George J. Sefa Dei, eds. (2000). *Anti-Racist Feminism: Critical Race and Gender Studies*. Halifax: Fernwood.

Goldberg, David Theo (1993). *Racist Culture: Philosophy and the Politics of Meaning*. Cambridge: Blackwell.

hooks, bell (1992). *Black Looks: Race and Representation*. Toronto: Between the Lines.

Paul, Daniel N. (2000). *We Were Not the Savages: A Mi'kmaq Perspective on the Collision between European and Native American Civilizations*. Halifax: Fernwood.

Suggested Websites

Canadian Race Relations Foundation
www.crr.ca

The Metropolis Project
www.canada.metropolis.net

Canadian Heritage/Patrimoine canadien
www.pch.gc.ca/index-eng.cfm

PART FOUR | SOCIAL DIFFERENCE

Key Terms

- *boyat*
- complicit masculinity
- dragon lady
- feminist essentialism
  (or essentialist feminism)
- feminist liberalism
  (or liberal feminism)
- feminist postmodernism
  (or postmodernist feminism)
- feminist socialism
  (or socialist feminism)
- feminization
- geisha
- gender
- gendered
- gender roles
- hegemonic masculinity
- ideology of fag
- Indian Princess
- lotus blossom baby
- marginalized masculinity

Gender and Sexuality

LEARNING OBJECTIVES

After reading this chapter, you should be able to

> outline the feminist work done by early women sociologists;

> compare and contrast the four different categories of feminism outlined in this chapter;

> contrast the effects of biological and sociological influences on the gender of David Reimer;

> explain what is meant by the 'gendering' and 'feminization' of work;

> compare and contrast the four masculinities outlined in the section on male daycare workers; and

> discuss the stereotyping involved in the intersection of female gender and minoritized ethnicity/race.

- pay equity
- queer theory
- scientific management
- sex
- squaw
- subordinate masculinity
- tabula rasa

Key Names
- Harriet Martineau
- Annie Marion MacLean
- Aileen Ross
- Helen C. Abell

- Henrietta Muir Edwards
- Nellie McClung
- Louise McKinney
- Emily Murphy
- Irene Parlby

Photos: [*left*] 12/Alamy, [*right*] © John Steckley

A portrait of the author as he sees himself.

A portrait of the author as he is.

FOR Starters

What it Means to Be a Man

How flexible are we concerning gender roles?
   Most of us like to think we're very flexible, both in the way we act and in the way we perceive others. But I have to be honest: although I feel 'secure in my masculinity', as they say, there are a number of things I—a Toronto-bred white man in my fifties—will not do because they're inconsistent with my own sense of being male, and with the sense of maleness I wish to project for others. For instance, I will not

- carry or use an umbrella (in part from having lived in Newfoundland, where a 'real man' is not afraid of getting wet).
- use a hair dryer (despite having rather long hair—it seems effeminate to me to blow your hair around like you're in a shampoo commercial).
- use one of those convenient book and file carriers on wheels, the ones that remind me of a flight attendant's suitcase (a man should carry a briefcase).
- cry at the microphone during a press conference (all right, I don't do a lot of press conferences, but when I was growing up, athletes didn't cry when they announced their retirement).
- wear clothes that are yellow, orange, or pink (high-school classmates of mine wearing those colours were given a hard time).
- use a snow blower instead of a shovel (real men aren't afraid of getting wet *or* heaving snow).
- spend longer than five minutes getting dressed or fifteen minutes in any one clothing store (maybe this reflects my male body image hangup).

- clip favourite recipes from a magazine (man's food is that which may be fried, barbecued, or nuked in a microwave).
- shake hands in a 'wimpy way' (a man is still judged by how strong his handshake is; I don't make a contest of it—as some do—but I try to meet a minimum standard).
- wear a cologne or 'body spray' (women should smell good; men should just try not to smell bad).
- dye my hair (or my beard).
- use the word 'lovely' without being sarcastic.
- have a manicure.

And of course, real men don't eat quiche or ask directions, so I don't do those things either. And when I first became a stepfather and my very shy eight-year-old stepson wanted to hold my hand in public, I felt *extremely* uncomfortable (but I still did it). It's important to point out that this list reflects my own assumptions, as a white middle-aged man, of what my gender role is.

I'd like male readers to think about this list. Do you share my inflexibility on these issues? Be honest. What other things will you not do out of male pride? Women readers can set us straight: would you be bothered if you knew the young man sitting next to you has weekly manicures?

Now comes the critical question: why do we feel the way we do, and how flexible are we really when it comes to gender? Here are two other scenarios to consider:

1. *How would you feel if your son took an interest in figure skating rather than hockey?* One of my nephews, when he first learned to skate, became really interested in figure skating and adopted Elvis Stojko as a hero. He took lessons for two years before he eventually quit, in large part, I suspect, because his father (my brother-in-law) didn't encourage him in this interest. To give my brother-in-law credit, he never made fun of the sport, but I don't think he gave his budding figure skater the kind of support he might have given a budding hockey player.
2. *What is your reaction to a man who wants to become a nurse?* Nursing programs are dominated by women; men are few and far between. Male students get asked questions like 'Why don't you want to be a doctor?', a question less often asked of female nursing students.

Compare notes on the topics above with your classmates, and you're likely to find a fair bit of disagreement. That's because as inflexible as we might be when it comes to how we see gender, we all—men and women, homosexuals and heterosexuals, blacks and whites and Arabs and Asians, and so on and so on—see gender differently. How do you see your own gender role?

Introduction to Gender

Gender is a highly contested area within sociology today. Sociologists theorizing about gender and gender roles differ sharply, particularly on the degree to which gender is determined by either culture or biology. Even the absolute duality (male–female) of gender is contested. Not surprisingly, the greatest part of the critical work on gender has been carried out by feminist scholars, reflecting the (now) obvious fact before the 'Women's Movement' of the 1960s and 1970s, male sociologists had done an inadequate job on the subject.

Gender is different from **sex**. British sociologist Ann Oakley formally stated the distinction between sex and gender when she argued that the former refers 'to the biological division into male

"Sex brought us together, but gender drove us apart."

and female' while the latter refers to 'the parallel and socially unequal division into femininity and masculinity' (Oakley 1972 in Marshall 1998: 250). 'Gender', in other words, is a sociological term that refers to the roles and characteristics society assigns to women and men, and carries with it notions of men and women's inequality; 'sex' refers merely to anatomical or biological characteristics of women and men.

Another key term to establish here is **gender role**. A gender role is a set of expectations concerning behaviour and attitudes that relates to being male or female. It may be useful here to think of a gender role as being similar to a movie role: it is a part we're assigned at birth, and how we play it reflects what we understand about what it means to act as either a girl/woman or a boy/man. Gender roles differ across cultures, both in content—in the specific expectations society holds for each sex—and in the severity or permissiveness with which society treats those whose behaviour contravenes the expectations for their gender.

The 'Founding Mother of Sociology' and the Sociology of Gender

British writer **Harriet Martineau** (1802–1876) can be called the founding mother of sociology. She wrote over 6,000 articles, many of them on the social condition of women in her time. In 1834 she began a two-year study of the United States, which she documented in *Society in America* (1837) and *Retrospect of Western Travel* (1838). Her feminist thinking can be seen in her comparison of women to slaves in a chapter of the 1837 volume revealingly called 'The Political Non-Existence of Women'. Martineau's feminist attitudes combined with her opposition to slavery made her unpopular in the United States. After travelling to the Middle East, she published *Eastern Life Past and Present* (1848), in which she struggled between her intended sociological spirit of impartiality and her moral condemnation of polygyny (one husband with more than one wife).

Three Early Women Sociologists and the Writing of Gender in Canada

Annie Marion MacLean

Annie Marion MacLean (*c.* 1870–1934) was the first Canadian woman to obtain a PhD in sociology. Born in Prince Edward Island, she received her first two degrees form Acadia University before earning the PhD at the University of Chicago. She went on to teach at the University of Chicago, although, despite her excellent qualifications, in a very subordinate position.

MacLean pioneered the sociological study of women, especially in her study *Wage-Earning Women*, which was based on a survey of some 13,500 women. She conducted her research while working in department stores, toiling in 'sweat shop' factories, and picking hops in rural Oregon. She also sent out a team of women to discover more about the unfair and unsafe conditions in which women were forced to work. The titles of her articles tell you a lot about her research. Though Canadian by birth, she was never hired by a Canadian university.

Aileen Ross

The first woman hired as a sociologist at a university in Canada was **Aileen Ross** (1902–1995), a native of Montreal who taught sociology at the University of Toronto for three years, from 1942 to 1945, before joining the faculty at McGill University. She took her first degree at the London School of

• Our Stories •

David Reimer: Assigning Gender

In May 2004, 38-year-old David Reimer of Winnipeg committed suicide. His decision to take his life was likely influenced by his separation from his wife, the loss of his job, and the suicide death of his twin brother two years earlier. But there is a deeper, older cause that must be cited, too. David was the victim of a medical accident that was compounded by an unsuccessful social experiment.

During his first year of life, David and his brother were both circumcised electronically using an experimental method. During David's circumcision, too much electricity was applied, and his penis was badly burned; there was no chance it could be even surgically repaired. Desperate for a solution, David's parents consulted numerous doctors and specialists. At the time, a psychological school of thought known as behaviourism, which emphasized the power of socialization (nurture) over biology (nature), was popular. It was held in especially high regard by feminist psychologists (both male and female), as it supported the notion that gender and gender roles were not 'natural' but taught. In its extreme version, behaviourism advanced the theory that each of us starts out as a **tabula rasa**, or blank slate, on which our social environment writes our lives. A proponent of this school, the psychologist Dr John Money of Johns Hopkins University in Baltimore, was one of the specialists contacted by David's parents. He persuaded them to have David castrated and given female hormones, and to rename their child 'Brenda', to be raised as a girl.

Money's articles made the 'John/Joan' case study famous. The doctor claimed that David was adapting successfully to his new gender, socially taught and hormonally enhanced. But his view of the situation was, as it turns out, based more on wishes than on facts. In a journalistic biography, *As Nature Made Him*, writer John Colapinto shows that David's childhood was highly conflicted. He felt he was male, not female, and preferred to play with boys than with girls. He wasn't told he had been born male until he was 13, when his parents, under pressure from Dr Money, approached him about allowing surgeons to create a vagina. David rebelled and attempted suicide a number of times. He abandoned his female identity and sought out surgery, which he eventually received, to have his male sex restored. He later married and had stepchildren, but the effects of both the accident and the social experiment never left him.

David Reimer's tragic case illustrates that while gender is a social construct, it has a strong biological component. It also shows, as recent research confirms (Kruijver et al. 2000), that gender has a neurological component in addition to the biological features of genitals and hormones: the brain helps to shape our gender. It also clearly demonstrates the dangers of allowing social theory to impose itself into unthinking social practice.

• •

What do YOU think?

1. In what way(s) can we say that David Reimer was neurologically male? How could we argue that he was not a gender 'tabula rasa'?

2. How could we study individuals to determine the extent to which their gender roles are natural versus taught/learned?

• •

QUICK HITS

Selected Articles by Annie Marion MacLean

1897–8	'Factory Legislation for Women in the United States'. *American Journal of Sociology* 3: 183–205.
1898	'Two Weeks in a Department Store'. *American Journal of Sociology* 4: 721–41.
1899–1900	'Faculty Legislation for Women in Canada'. *American Journal of Sociology* 5: 172–81.
1903–4	'The Sweat Shop Summer'. *American Journal of Sociology* 9: 289–309.
1908–9	'Life in the Pennsylvania Coal Fields'. *American Journal of Sociology* 14: 329–51.
1909–10	'With the Oregon Hop Pickers'. *American Journal of Sociology* 15: 83–95.
1923	'Four Months in a Model Factory'. *Century* 106 (July): 436–44.

Economics, and got her MA (1941) and PhD (1950) from the University of Chicago. A founding member of the Canadian Human Rights Foundation, Ross devoted her books to two of her foremost concerns: women and India. The last book she published was *The Lost and the Lonely: Homeless Women in Montreal* (1982). Upon retirement, she had helped to organize a shelter for homeless women in her hometown, and wrote the book to enable them to tell their stories. Her second book, *The Hindu Family in an Urban Setting* (1962), was the product of several years' research in India. She also wrote a series of articles about Indian businesswomen (1976, 1977, and 1979).

Helen C. Abell

Helen C. Abell (b. 1917) was born in Medicine Hat, Alberta, and grew up in Toronto. She has been called the founder of rural sociology in Canada. After receiving a degree in human nutrition at the University of Toronto (1941), she worked as a nutritionist for the Ontario Department of Agriculture, then as an officer in the Canadian Women's Army Corps during World War II. She received her PhD in rural sociology (the first Canadian to do so) in 1951. She then established a rural sociology research unit in the Federal Department of Agriculture. Her role as a sociologist is summarized by Jenny Kendrick as follows:

Helen Abell's research played an important role in identifying systematically the roles women played on the farm. This was an invaluable contribution to the policy arena, virtually forcing society and policymakers to lay aside their stereotypes of the marginal contributions of farm women to agriculture. (Quoted in Eichler 2001: 382)

● ● ● ● ● ● ● ● ● ● ● ● ● ● ● ● ● ● ●

What do YOU think?

Why do you think these early women sociologists wrote primarily about women? Does that say something about the gender role of a female sociologist?

● ● ● ● ● ● ● ● ● ● ● ● ● ● ● ● ● ● ●

Feminism and Gender Theory: Four Categories

In 'Feminist Social Theories: Theme and Variations' (2003, orig. 1995), Beatrice Kachuck usefully divides feminist theories into four broad categories, each with several variations:

- feminist liberalism
- feminist essentialism
- feminist socialism
- feminist postmodernism.

We'll examine each of these in turn.

Feminist Liberalism

Feminist liberalism (or **liberal feminism**), Kachuck explains, 'identifies women as a class entitled to rights as women' (Kachuck 2003: 81). In terms of gender roles, this approach values the contributions of women in the public realm of the workplace and examines whether women receive fair pay for the work they do. In this sense, it is associated with the fight for **pay equity**, the guarantee that women in traditionally female-dominated industries (nursing, childcare, library science, for instance) receive compensation similar to the salaries of those working in comparable (in terms of educational qualifications required, hours worked, and social value) professions that are typically dominated by men. Think of it this way: if we value our children so much, why do we pay so little to those in primary and early childhood education, who play such an important role in the social and educational development of our children? Feminist liberalism is credited with securing benefits for women on maternity leave, including the rights to claim employment insurance and to return to the same or an equivalent job in the same company after a fixed period of time (up to a year in Canada).

Criticism of feminist liberalism and its view of gender roles centres around the idea that it universalizes the position of white, middle-class, heterosexual, Western women. It fails to recognize that the social location of this category of women enables them to receive benefits not available to other women. White, middle-class women in Europe and North America are the main beneficiaries of the gains that feminist liberalism has obtained; it has been considerably less successful in promoting the interests of women who differ in terms of class, ethnicity, sexual orientation, and country.

Feminist Essentialism

While feminist liberalism concentrates essentially on making women equal to men in terms of employment opportunities and salary, **feminist essentialism** (or **essentialist feminism**) looks at differences between the way women and men think, and argues for equality—or female superiority—in that difference. Women's morality (Gilligan 1982) and their 'maternal thinking' (Ruddick 1989) involve social norms that are more or less 'natural' to them. Added to this is the idea that this morality is negatively valued in a patriarchal society. For Kachuck, feminist essentialism is useful in that it 'generates profound questions. Should we understand women in terms of patriarchal constructions or value their models of human ideals? How is women's sexuality to be

How do you measure the social value of the work done by an early childhood educator (ECE) versus that of an investment banker, or a professional athlete, or a sociology professor? (Did you assume that the ECE was a woman and the investment banker a man? If so, would your answer be different if the opposite were true?)

Photo: Monkeybusinessimages/Dreamstime.com

comprehended outside of patriarchal visions? How do women resist control?' (Kachuk 2003: 66–7).

Kachuk presents the criticisms of the feminist essentialist approach to gender thinking in terms of what other Western feminists think and also in terms of what feminists in India have to say. In the eyes of the first, she writes, feminist essentialism has the following shortcomings:

- It universalizes women, assuming erroneously that all experience gender alike.
- It confuses natural phenomena with women's strategies for coping with patriarchal demands.
- It invites continued perceptions of women as social housekeepers in worlds that men build. (Kachuk 2003: 66)

She adds that feminists in India have their own concerns about feminist essentialism:

Indian feminists deplore assumptions of women's inherent caring function as an ideology that impedes their full human development. Thus, essays on education critique practices that socialize girls for dedication to family service. . . . This puts them [Indian feminists] in opposition to calls for women's devotion to families as their national identity. (Kachuk 2003: 66)

In sum, then, while feminist essentialism speaks constructively about the potential for women's differences from men to be positively valued, it can fall into the trap of generalizing from the Western

---

The Point Is...   Gender and the Bible

The holy books of the largest established religious traditions were developed in the context of specific cultures. The Judeo-Christian and Islamic sacred texts were developed in cultures that valued pastoralism (the herding of animals such as sheep, goats, camels, or cows as the primary means of obtaining food). Pastoral cultures are most often patriarchal in ideology, with males significantly dominant over females, and some theorists attribute a perceived patriarchal bias concerning gender roles in the holy books to the patriarchal ideology prevalent at the time the books were written.

The Words of Paul the Apostle

- 'A man . . . is the image and glory of God; but woman is the glory of man. For man was not made from woman, but woman from man. Neither man created from woman, but woman for man.' (1 Corinthians 11: 7–9)

- 'As in all the churches of the saints, the women should keep silence in the churches. For they are not permitted to speak, but should be subordinate, as even the law says. If there is anything they desire to know, let them ask their husbands at home. For it is shameful for a woman to speak in church.' (1 Corinthians 14: 33–5)

- 'Wives, be subject to your husbands, as to the Lord. For the husband is the head of the wife as Christ is the head of the church. . . . As the church is subject to Christ, so let wives also be subject in everything to their husbands.' (Ephesians 5: 22–4)

- 'Let a woman learn in silence with all submissiveness. I permit no woman to teach or to have authority over men; she is to keep silent. For Adam was formed first, then Eve; and Adam was not deceived, but the woman was deceived and became a transgressor. Yet woman will be saved through bearing children, if she continues in faith and love and holiness, with modesty.' (1 Timothy 2: 11–15)

● ● ● ● ● ● ● ● ● ● ● ● ● ● ● ● ● ● ● ●

What do YOU think?

1. What do these statements say about the culture that Paul was part of?

2. Do you think that statements such as these have influenced the fact that the Catholic Church does not allow women to hold mass or have any position of power? How else do you think statements such as these have been used to influence Western thought concerning gender roles?

● ● ● ● ● ● ● ● ● ● ● ● ● ● ● ● ● ● ● ●

model—a trap that Western social scientists of all stripes have often fallen into.

Feminist Socialism

Feminist socialists (or **socialist feminists**), according to Kachuk, have to 'revise their Marxism so as to account for gender, something that Marx ignored. They want sexuality and gender relations included in analyses of society' (Kachuk 2003: 67). There is insight to be gained from looking at the intersections of oppression between class and gender. The struggles faced by and resources available to lower-class women can be different from those of middle- and upper-class women, and feminist socialism is useful in identifying these. Still, there is the danger that factors such as race, ethnicity, and sexual orientation get overlooked in the focus on class. Black women in North America face some of the same difficulties of prejudice and stereotyping regardless of whether they come from the upper or lower classes.

• Going Global • • • • • • • • • • • • • •

Defying Gender Expectations through Gender Performance: Boyat in the UAE

An anonymous woman journalist published an article with this title in the 23 February 2009 edition of *The Globe and Mail*. She was writing about *boyat* (singular *boyah*), a traditional name for tomboys in the United Arab Emirates. As the journalist encountered them, *boyat* were young women who dressed up as men, with short hair, Rolex watches, Ray Ban sunglasses, and military-style clothes. The journalist expressed her view that these young Arab women were participating in cross-dressing and disguise so that they could show strength rather than the passive, gentler qualities associated with (and expected of) women in the Arab world. Facebook, she argued, facilitated the process by providing a venue where *boyat* could interact anonymously, or seek out likeminded others operating group pages with names like *McBoyah* or *Hot Boyah*. The journalist described the *boyat* lifestyle this way:

> Many of the girls live double lives. After leaving home, they undergo a radical transformation, changing their clothes at school or a friend's house. While in transit, they run no real risk of being caught because, while in public, Emirates women are required to wear the national dress—a long black over-garment called an *abaya*, which makes it easier to switch roles without drawing attention.
>
> Because they focus on themselves, not the opposite sex, the *boyat* spend much time reading, philosophizing and analyzing international events. They also meet regularly to recite poetry about things that have 'touched' them.
>
> But it was clear to me that they consider what they do a way of life, not just a game. Gatherings sometimes turned into therapy sessions in which each *boyah* spoke openly about her fears and problems.
>
> It is a dangerous gender role to play, as they risk prison if caught.

• •

What do YOU think?

1. Why do you think the *boyat* phenomenon is so popular with girls in the United Arab Emirates?

2. Do you think this phenomenon will last more than 10 years? Explain.

• •

Feminist Postmodernism

Feminist postmodernism (or **postmodernist feminism**) takes the strongest social constructionist position, a position almost diametrically opposed to that of feminist essentialism. Some postmodernists even contest the widely held view that all women are biologically all female, and all men are all male. Feminist postmodernists refer to women more as subjects than as objects of sociological study, allowing the perspective of the women studied to guide their research. Standpoint theory is an important aspect of this category of feminism.

Another methodology that fits within the broad-ranging perspective of feminist postmodernism is **queer theory**, first articulated in the book *Gender Trouble* (1990) by Judith Butler, professor of comparative literature and rhetoric at the University of California, Berkeley. Queer theory rejects the idea that male and female gender are natural binary opposites. It disputes the idea that gender identity is connected to some biological 'essence', arguing instead that gender identity is related to the dramatic effect of a gender performance. Gender is seen not as each of two categories—male and female—but as a continuum with male and female at the extremes; individuals act, or perform, more one way or another along the continuum at different times and in different situations.

Cultural configurations and norms of gender keep us from playing out a broader variety of gender performances. In this sense, gender performances are restricted by sanctions. Consider the gender performance of a male athlete crying in public, as he apologizes for having failed a drug test or having cheated on his wife. The monologue by a late-night comedian/talkshow host or the between-period comments by a former coach turned pundit might provide opportunities for popular commentators to issue negative sanctions of that kind of gender performance. Professional sport—in fact, sport in general—because it is a prominent theatre for gender performance, is a breeding ground for negative sanctions. In hockey, refusing to drop the gloves against a taunting opponent and donning a protective visor are just two actions that could incur negative sanctions drawn from what is known as the **ideology of fag**. This is a set of beliefs and sanctions that is invoked throughout society to keep people in line: if you violate a gender role, then you *must* be gay. The negative way in which this suggestion (or accusation) is presented makes it a very powerful sanction.

Kachuck's main criticism of feminist postmodernism (criticism that could just as easily be applied to many forms of postmodernism) is that it leads to no conclusions. It merely problematizes other people's conclusions and generates no solid criteria for judging better or worse positions, but satisfies itself with 'constructing a "feminine" space where intellectuals aggressively play out tentative ideas' (Kachuck 2003: 81).

Gendered Occupation and Education

Certain jobs, and the college and university programs preparing people to work in those jobs, are **gendered**. That means two things. First, one gender will be prevalent among the people employed in certain kinds of work or among the students in a particular program. When we talk about 'gender prevalence' or 'gender dominance', we mean that as many as 85 per cent of students or employees may be either female or male. Second, as Sargent puts it, 'the work itself is typically imbued with gendered meanings and defined in gendered terms' (Sargent 2005). What this means is that, for example, the gendered profession of nursing is associated with words like 'caring' and 'nurturing' that are typically associated with women; nursing is thus characterized as a natural offshoot of the mother role. By contrast, the job of police officer (still often called 'policeman') is described in terms of 'toughness' and the 'brotherhood' of officers.

In 2001, men outnumbered women by a ratio of at least 3 to 1 in the following occupations categorized by Statistics Canada:

- the primary industries of forestry, fishing, mining, and oil and gas
- the utilities
- construction
- transportation and warehousing.

In the prestigious occupational fields of 'profession-al, scientific and technical services', men outnum-bered women by 14 per cent (567,800 to 431,700); in the administrative category of 'business, build-ing, and other support services', men outnumbered women by 10 per cent (352,200 to 287,000).

Telling It Like It Is

A STUDENT POV

Gender Roles and Being Lesbian

POINT OF VIEW

People in my life in the past have tended to believe that because I am a lesbian, I auto-matically have more male-specific interests, and that I do not enjoy typical girl-oriented activ-ities. Shortly after I told my brother, he invited me to a football game, stating, 'you like football now don't you?' Although he was joking at the time, this is an example of a very typical com-ment often made to me. Although I may enjoy fixing things around the house, my partner is a sports fanatic, and while I like to sew and knit, she enjoys cooking and romantic comedies. The gender stereotyping, which is exactly what this comes down to, even goes so far as to include the style of clothes I wear. I remember one time that I went into work wearing a baseball cap, although I usually do not wear a hat to work, as I find it unprofessional. This particular day I was coming from school and in a rush. Immediately after entering work I began to hear comments and mutters from my co-workers. It seemed that in their eyes because I was wearing a hat, I was portraying a male characteristic and they assumed that being a lesbian is the next closest thing to being a male.

There is a significant difference between sexual orientation and gender identity. All of the gay people that I know, including myself, are very happy with their sex. They just hap-pen to be attracted to the same sex as well. I am proud to be a woman and I enjoy it and would not want to change that. This leads me to my next point. For one reason or another people with little understanding of the gay popula-tion seem to need a definite clarification of 'who's the man and who's the woman', which is a question that I have been asked on too many occasions to count. The truth is that in many gay relationships there are no specific roles, and each individual's identity is not masculine or feminine, but it slides on a continuum. It is almost ridiculous to assume that there is a male and female figure in the relationship, after all, if I wanted a male–female partnership, I wouldn't be gay.

Another opinion that I have found many people have is that gay people, male or female, are involved in a sexual scene full of promis-cuity, voyeurism, and ménages à trois. This is evidenced by the number of people that have made suggestive comments to me about non-committed casual sexual encounters. Although these beliefs are positive in one aspect as they break down the very untrue opinion that women cannot have the high sex drive that men are more known for, it also reflects a lar-ger belief that being in a gay relationship is all about the sex. This leads people to believe that gay people do not commit and take part in stable, settled relationships. I remember talking with my father once about the relationship I was in and he responded, 'It's alright if that's what you want, but it's unfortunate because those relationships don't last, they just don't settle.' Ironically, I must say that gay relationships in fact have very little to do with sex. As a hetero-sexual relationship has many dimensions, so does the homosexual one, encompassing all one's needs such as emotional support, com-panionship, the sharing of values and spiritual-ity, and of course, physical attraction does play its role as well. I once saw an advertisement that mocked this expectation of such extravagant sex lives. The poster was in a bookstore located in a gay community. The caption read: 'What do lesbians do in bed?' and the picture had two women in bed wearing flannel pajamas, one watching television and the other reading a book. I saw this as an accurate portrayal and a clever way to challenge this opinion.

By comparison, women outnumbered men in the following categories:

- finance, insurance, real estate, and leasing
- educational services
- accommodation and food services
- health care and social assistance.

In the last of these categories, the dominance was more than 4 to 1.

Sociology students need to look at what might cause these gender specializations to occur. A place to start would be post-secondary education, where men and women typically take different routes. In both community college and university, men greatly outnumber women as graduates in the engineering and applied sciences programs.

For instance, in 1998–9, almost four times as many men as women received diplomas in these disciplines, and the difference grew by slightly more than 3,000 students from 1994 to 1995. In 1999–2000, men received slightly more than three times as many university degrees in the area than women did, the difference dropping slightly from 1995–6. Similarly, more than twice as many men as women received degrees in mathematics and physical sciences in 1999–2000.

On the other hand, women greatly outnumber men in college diplomas and university degrees in health professions and related occupations. This is true especially of college diplomas (where the difference is growing), which typically qualify students for less prestigious and more poorly paid occupations, such as pharmacy assistants

Photo: Juergen Hasenkopf / Alamy

Serena Williams returns a shot during a match at the 2009 US Open. Although the game is becoming more and more about power rather than strategy, women tennis players are frequently subject to negative sanctions by fans and media alike for grunting, arguing with officials, and other on-court behaviour deemed 'unladylike'. What does this tell you about female gender performance in a sport like tennis?

Photo: CP Images/Maclean's Magazine/Andrew Tolson

McMaster's Nick Bontis teaches a course on strategic market leadership to a group of male students on the university's Allan Gould Trading Floor, an actual trading room that does real-time stock trading on world markets. While the number of women attending university in Canada has increased from 10 per cent of the total in 1970 to over 50 per cent as of 2005, women are still underrepresented in disciplines such as business management, engineering, math, and physics. What are some of the barriers preventing women from entering those fields?

and nursing assistants. Similarly, women dominate in fields such as social sciences and services at the community college level, and education at the university level.

In sum, there appear to be separate spheres of post-secondary education for men and women, with no sign that the trend is changing. On the contrary, in several areas—engineering and applied sciences, health sciences, and social sciences and services in community colleges—the disparity seems to have grown since the early 1990s.

In Chapter 4 we looked at some of the factors that lead men and women into different programs. As Table 13.1 shows, men and women, because they typically take different routes through education, are presented with different employment opportunities once they graduate. In all age groups, there are more men than women working at full-time jobs, and more women than men working at part-time jobs. This difference is on the rise for the age groups 15–24, and 45+, especially

for the latter group; only in the group aged 24–44 is the gap between the two genders narrowing.

When looking at gender difference in occupations it is important, too, to consider relative earnings. In this area, the overall ratio does not appear to be changing. From 1992 to 2001 the earnings ratio for women to men has varied slightly from a low of 62.0 per cent in 1994 (when women earned 62 per cent of what men earned) to a high of 64.8 per cent in 1995. The ratio in 2001 was 64.2, slightly below the high.

The disparity in relative earnings decreases when education is taken into account. For instance, in 1993, women aged 25–34 with a university degree earned 84 per cent of what male degree-holders in the same age bracket earned. However, women aged 45–54 with university degrees earned less—just 72 per cent of what their male counterparts earned. It is interesting to note that relative earnings do not vary with age to the same degree among people holding community

Table 13.1   Full- and part-time gender employment in 2007 (x 1,000)

AGE	FULL-TIME EMPLOYMENT			PART-TIME EMPLOYMENT		
15–24	**1999**	**2007**	**CHANGE**	**1999**	**2007**	**CHANGE**
Males	712.5	828.5	116.0	428.5	484.8	56.3
Females	510.5	606.6	96.1	554.9	669.5	114.6
Difference	202.0	221.9	–19.9	126.4	184.7	+58.3
25–44	**1999**	**2007**	**CHANGE**	**1999**	**2007**	**CHANGE**
Males	3,908.0	3,840.2	–67.8	184.3	192.5	8.2
Females	2,751.6	2,934.2	182.6	790.8	692.0	–98.8
Difference	1,156.4	906.0	+250.4	606.5	499.5	–90.6
45+	**1999**	**2007**	**CHANGE**	**1999**	**2007**	**CHANGE**
Males	2,431.7	3,241.3	803.6	200.9	301.7	100.8
Females	1,534.9	2,352.4	817.5	522.6	722.8	200.2
Differences	896.8	888.9	+13.9	321.7	421.1	99.4

± The plus or minus refers to a gain or loss by women in this category.

Source: Adapted from www.statcan.ca/english/Pgdb/labor (2 Feb. 2004), www40.statcan.ca/101/cst01/labor12.htm.

college diplomas rather than university degrees: women diploma-holders aged 25–34 earned 75 per cent of what men earned, while those aged 45–54 earned 73 per cent.

Feminization of Occupations

The **feminization** of an occupational sphere occurs when a particular job, profession, or industry comes to be dominated by or predominantly associated with women. Since the start of the First World War, when women began to work outside the home in greater numbers, many occupations have become feminized, including bank teller and secretary (or, now, administrative assistant), but there are instances of job feminization occurring well before that, as the first of the two examples below describes. Typically, the feminization of an industry works to the disadvantage of those involved in it, who earn lower salaries with fewer protections and benefits than those enjoyed by workers outside the feminized occupational sphere.

Women's Work During the London 'Gin Craze' of the Eighteenth Century

Beginning around 1720 there was a sudden rise in the sale and consumption of gin in London, England. During the so-called 'gin craze', which lasted until the middle of the century, the liquor was sold not just in bars but in the streets, from wheelbarrows and baskets, in alleyway stalls, in shady one-room gin shops, and from boats floating on the Thames.

Anyone selling gin without a licence was operating illegally. This was the case for the majority of the thousands of women involved in the gin trade, who couldn't afford the expensive licence. They operated at great risk, and were primary targets of

Photo: Burstein Collection/Corbis

English artist William Hogarth became famous for engravings that satirized the vices of high and low society in mid-eighteenth-century London. What does this one, *Gin Lane* (1851), tell you about his impressions of the London gin trade? Would he have been sympathetic to or critical of the London gin sellers?

the Gin Acts, which were passed chiefly to restrict the selling of gin to bars owned predominantly by middle-class men. Women were more likely than men to be arrested, and also were more likely to be put in prison if convicted.

Why take the chance? At the time, thousands of young women were immigrating to London from Scotland, Ireland, and rural England, looking for jobs and for husbands. The quality and availability of both turned out to be greatly lacking. So why turn to hawking gin? Historian Jessica Warner gives three reasons:

[I]t required little or no capital; it did not require membership in a professional organization; and it was one of the few occupations from which women were not effectively or explicitly excluded. It was, in other words, a means of economic survival. (Warner 2002: 51)

The Gin Acts often pitted women against women. Enforcement depended heavily on the accusations of paid informants, half of whom were women. The harsh economics that drove these women to rat out illegal gin sellers is well described by Warner:

Consider the options of a young woman newly arrived in London in 1737 or 1738. She could work for a year as a maid and earn £5 in addition to receiving room and board, or she could inform against one gin-seller, and upon securing a conviction collect a reward of £5. There were two ways to make money, one hard, the other easy, and many people naturally chose the latter. Most did so only once, collecting their reward and then attempting to hide as best they could. (Warner 2002: 137)

This could be called danger pay, as informers were not well liked.

Women's Clerical Work in Canada, 1891–1971

The early twentieth century saw spectacular growth of clerical workers in the Canadian labour force. It also saw the feminization of the position, along with the degradation of the position, as measured in terms of wages, skill level, and opportunity for promotion. How all three trends—growth, feminization, and degradation—mesh together is a story that gives insight on both the past and the present.

Clerical work was traditionally a man's job. The male bookkeeper's varied duties required a lot of what we would call now multitasking. As companies grew in size, there was much more clerical work that needed to be done, and businesses moved towards a system of **scientific management** (see Chapter 5), which was seen as a more rationalized and efficient approach to task management. It involved the rapid performance of repeated simple tasks, and it created a kind of assembly-line office work, with few opportunities to move up in the company. The growing belief, based on assumptions about women's limited capabilities, that this was ideal work for women, who were supposed to be wives and mothers first and workers second, was reinforced by discrimination that allowed them few alternatives. The thinking of the time is illustrated in William Leffingwell's *Office Management, Principles and Practice*, published in 1925:

A woman is to be preferred for the secretarial position for she is not averse to doing minor

The secretary pool in a scene from the TV series *Mad Men*, about an advertising agency in the 1960s. What does the current popularity of the show, among both female and male viewers, say about our view of the gendered division of labour it presents? Could it be that we're a little nostalgic for a time when men's and women's roles—in the office as well as the home—were so clearly defined?

Photo: The Kobal Collection/PictureDesk.com

tasks, work involving the handling of petty details, which would irk and irritate ambitious young men, who usually feel that the work they are doing is of no importance if it can be performed by some person with a lower salary. Most such men are also anxious to get ahead and to be promoted from position to position, and consequently if there is much work of a detail character to be done, and they are expected to perform it, they will not remain satisfied and will probably seek a position elsewhere. (1925: 116)

This job transformation got a big push during World War I (1914–18), when women seized the opportunity to enter the workforce to replace men who had gone overseas to serve in Europe. The number of clerical workers in Canada jumped by 113,148—around half of them women. The percentage of women clerks working for the Bank of Nova Scotia's Ontario region jumped from 8.5 per cent in 1911 to 40.7 per cent in 1916. Although it fell somewhat when the men returned from the war, the number of women clerical workers remained high and steadily grew (see Table 13.2).

What do YOU think?

1. How do the gin business in the eighteenth century and the rise of clerical work in the early twentieth century demonstrate what is meant by the 'feminization of occupation'?

2. To what extent is the feminization of occupation occurring in Canada today? Where, if at all, can we find evidence of it?

3. Could we say that the reverse happens, that an occupation 'masculinizes', acquiring greater prestige and, of course, greater pay? (Think, perhaps, of the teaching profession.)

Being a Gender Minority in a Gendered Occupation

When individuals find themselves in gendered jobs and they are of the minority, or 'wrong', gender, it can have a profound effect on their gender performance on the job. Paul Sargent discusses the phenomenon with great clarity in his look at men in early childhood education (which, for Sargent's purposes, includes the lower grades

Table 13.2 Feminization of clerical workers in Canada

YEAR	CLERICAL WORKERS	WOMEN CLERICAL WORKERS	
		NUMBER	PERCENTAGE
1891	133,017	4,710	14.3
1901	57,231	12,660	22.1
1911	103,543	33,723	32.6
1921	216,691	90,577	41.8
1931	260,674	117,637	45.1
1941	303,655	152,216	50.1
1951	563,083	319,183	56.7
1961	818,912	503,660	61.5
1971	1,310,910	903,395	68.9

• Our Stories •

The Famous Five and the 'Persons' Case

'The famous five' is the name given to five Canadian women who fought for equal rights during the first half of the twentieth century. They are **Henrietta Muir Edwards** (1849–1931), **Nellie McClung** (1873–1951), **Louise McKinney** (1868–1931), **Emily Murphy** (1868–1933), and **Irene Parlby** (1868–1965). Among their distinguished achievements is their successful campaign to have women awarded the status of 'persons' under British and Canadian law.

When Emily Murphy, in 1916, was named the first woman police magistrate in Alberta, her appointment was challenged on the grounds that women were not 'persons' under the British North America (BNA) Act, which had officially created the Dominion of Canada in 1867. It was understood, when the BNA Act was written, that 'persons' meant 'men', for women were not allowed to vote or hold public office. In 1917, the Supreme Court of Alberta ruled that women were, in fact, 'persons' in that province, and Emily Murphy became officially the first woman magistrate in the British Empire. In order to advance the cause of women aspiring to hold public office at the federal level, she then had her name put forward as a candidate for the Canadian Senate, only to have the Conservative prime minister Robert Borden, invoking the BNA Act and its reference to 'persons', reject her bid.

In the years that followed, the fight to have women in the Senate was taken up by numerous women's groups across the country. In 1927, Murphy and the other four members of the famous five, all of them prominent women's rights activists in Alberta, petitioned the Supreme Court of Canada with the question *Does the word 'persons' in Section 24, of The British North America Act, 1867, include female persons?* The Court answered that it did not. At that time there were no women in the British House of Lords, so the notion that there might be female members in the Canadian Senate was easily dismissed. But the famous five were undeterred and took their case to a higher court of appeal: the Judicial Committee of the Privy Council in Britain. On 18 October 1929, the Lord Chancellor of the Privy Council announcing the judicial committee's decision, ruled that 'women are persons . . . and eligible to be summoned and may become Members of the Senate of Canada.' In their decision, the committee stated 'that the exclusion of women from all public offices is a relic of days more barbarous than ours. And to those who would ask why the word "persons" should include females, the obvious answer is, why should it not?'

The following year, 1930, Montreal-born Cairine Reay Wilson became the first woman appointed to the Senate of Canada.

of primary school as well as the daycare profession, where most ECE teaching jobs are found). Sargent incorporates R. Connell's (1995) four performances of masculinity, four ways in which men act out gender roles. These are

- **hegemonic masculinity**,
- **subordinate masculinity**,
- **marginalized masculinity**, and
- **complicit masculinity**.

Sargent explains them this way:

Hegemonic masculine practices are those that serve to normalize and naturalize men's dominance and women's subordination. Subordinate masculinities are those behaviors and presentations of self that could threaten the legitimacy of hegemonic masculinity. Gay men, effeminate men, and men who eschew competition or traditional

In her popular writing, Nellie McClung often drew her readers' attention to the hard-working reality of farm women. During the early 1920s, she was a Member of the Legislative Assembly in Alberta.

QUICK HITS

Granting the Provincial and Federal Vote to Women

1867	Canadian federal and provincial vote given only to white men with property.
1916	Women in Manitoba, Saskatchewan, and Alberta get the provincial vote.
1917	World War I nurses and the female relatives of soldiers get the federal vote. Women in British Columbia and Ontario get the provincial vote.
1918	Women in Canada get the federal vote. Women in Nova Scotia get the provincial vote.
1918	First woman provincial cabinet minister (Mary Ellen Smith, BC).
1919	Women in New Brunswick get the provincial vote.
1921	First woman federal cabinet minister (Mary Ellen Smith).
1922	Women in Prince Edward Island get the provincial vote.
1925	Women in the British colony of Newfoundland get the vote.
1930	First woman senator in Canada (Cairine Wilson).
1940	Women in Quebec get the provincial vote.
1951	First woman mayor in Canada (Charlotte Whitten, Ottawa).
1991	First woman provincial premier (Rita Johnson, BC).
1993	First woman prime minister (Kim Campbell).

definitions of success are examples frequently cited. . . . These men are vulnerable to being abused and ridiculed by others. Marginalized masculinities represent the adaptation of masculinities to such issues as race and class. For example, a Black man may enjoy certain privileges that stem from success as a small business owner, yet still find himself unable to hail a cab. . . . Finally, complicit masculinities are those that do not embody hegemonic processes *per se*, but benefit from the ways in which hegemonic masculinities construct the gender order and local gender regimes. (Sargent 2005)

Using these terms, Sargent argues that men who work in early childhood education are caught up in a conflict between performing a *subordinate masculinity* (for example, by being 'nurturing'), which would make them good teachers, and more

Telling It Like It Is

On-the-Job Training: Making the Right Impression in a Male-Defined Business

I was on my very first job as a criminologist. I had gone through years of school to learn theories, statistics, research methods—everything that I *thought* was necessary before going out into the field.

I had been hired as a research assistant to make observations and conduct interviews at a law enforcement conference. This was the first time that I was actually going to be around the law enforcement community, and I was eager to make a good impression on my new colleagues.

I got to the conference a bit early and waited for the rest of the research team to arrive for our scheduled meeting. We were meeting near the entrance of the venue, where most people would be entering and exiting the premises. It was quite early, and not many people were around.

A gentleman came up and introduced himself to me as a fellow conference attendee. We chatted for a minute or so before I noticed that he was staring at the ring on my finger. Next thing I knew, he was asking me questions about whether or not I was happy in my relationship. That's when I realized that this man was not being kind or professional—he was hitting on me!

I made it very clear that I was only at the conference as a researcher, and then excused myself from the conversation. Just then, someone from my team walked through the door and I quickly went over to say hello.

I was a little thrown by the whole incident at first. While it might not seem like a big deal, I want you to consider this: imagine that you are a brand-new graduate from your field of study—who happens to be a woman. You have been given an opportunity to begin your career. On your very first day, instead of being met with professionalism, you are met with sexist attitudes that see every woman as an 'available' woman.

How did I deal with this? I had brushed it off by the time the rest of the team arrived and was ready to get back to work.

As the conference continued, I started to hear that other women (researchers, attendees, and keynote speakers alike) were having similar experiences. Law enforcement is a male-dominated field, and at least 70 per cent of the people at this conference were men; women stood out.

I discussed my concerns with my supervisor and learned that my experiences were not atypical of the experiences of women criminologists. My supervisor was a wonderful source of information and support. I quickly learned how to react appropriately to inappropriateness—there's a fine line between a reaction that will enable you to work with people who have just offended you, and putting up walls that get in the way of your research objectives.

In fact, over the years, I have informally gathered similar stories from other women in the field.

Now, I do not want to paint a picture of the male law enforcement community as predators or convey any other negative stereotype. Most of the people at the conference (both men and women) were there to learn and share ideas with other professionals. However, there were a few people who made one thing very clear: the professional world is not a completely level playing field—not yet anyway. Being a woman does matter.

—Rhea Adhopia

What do YOU think?

How is the author being sanctioned for being deviant?

stereotypical masculinity performances, which are imposed on them by the gendered nature of the job. The male gender images involved here are 'homosexual-pedophile' and 'man as disciplinarian'. Male ECE teachers are not allowed the caring physical contact that female teachers are encouraged to have. As one male teacher, in a narrative, explains, 'Women's laps are places of love. Men's are places of danger.' This stems from the popularly reproduced image of the homosexual–pedophile, which mistakenly conflates, or links, two different sexualities. As a result, male teachers are reduced to less threatening performances of complicit masculinity, which include 'high fives' and handshakes rather than hugs, and rewarding children with prizes and names written on the board rather than physical contact. This can be demoralizing for the male early childhood educator. As one male teacher wrote in a narrative, 'I sometimes feel really inadequate when I watch the kids draped all over the women and all I'm doing is keeping them busy, handing out trinkets, or slapping high fives.'

The 'man as disciplinarian' gender image also restricts the performance of male gender roles in the ECE environment. Because it is assumed that men more naturally perform discipline, they are assigned greater responsibility for monitoring the behaviour of 'problem kids'. Classrooms occupied by male teachers then become seen as sites of discipline. No matter what the particular male's natural inclinations or teaching styles are—whether or not they are more nurturant or 'female defined'—these teachers are forced to conform to a masculinity performance that reinforces male authoritarian stereotypes.

Men in early childhood education are expected to want to move into occupational positions more in keeping or complicit with male hegemony: administrative positions in ECE organizations and higher grades in elementary schools. Sargent's study did not verify this trend, but we could argue that a longitudinal approach, looking at male teachers' careers over time, would yield evidence of men 'moving up' in the system. We might find, too, that this kind of trend is as much or more the product of the gendered nature of the organizations as of the individuals' actual intent.

● ● ● ● ● ● ● ● ● ● ● ● ● ● ● ● ● ●

What do YOU think?

In some ways it's easier to examine the impact on men of working in a female-gendered occupation because it is much less common than the reverse: women working in male-dominated occupations. Think of three jobs defined as male. What would restrict female performance of gender in these jobs?

● ● ● ● ● ● ● ● ● ● ● ● ● ● ● ● ● ●

Race and Gender: Intersecting Oppression

Race and gender can intersect as forms of oppression. Racial prejudice and discrimination can often reinforce gender bias, and vice versa. In some cases, opposing gender/race stereotypes can affect an oppressed group, as in the case of Asian women, described below.

Opposing Gender/Race Stereotypes

There is a tendency to stereotype visible minority women into two extremes. So, for example, Renee Tajima (1989) writes about how an East Asian woman may be stereotyped either as the 'Lotus Blossom Baby' or as the 'Dragon Lady'. In Tania Das Gupta's words, the former stereotype 'encompasses the images of the China doll, the geisha girl and shy Polynesian beauty. The latter includes prostitutes and "devious madams"' (Das Gupta 1996: 27). Any fan of the TV series M*A*S*H would recognize both stereotypes. Popular during the 1970s and 1980s, the show, which revolved around a unit of American doctors and nurses stationed near Seoul during the Korean War in the early 1950s, featured numerous sly allusions to geisha girls and occasional appearances by Asian women who periodically became involved with the leading male characters. It also featured characters who fit the 'Dragon Lady' stereotype, including the sharp businesswoman Rosie, of Rosie's Bar and Grill, and a woman who threatens the male character Klinger with a pitchfork when she believes he is fooling around with her daughter.

The stereotype of the Lotus Blossom Baby, which gained popularity during the American occupation of Japan after World War II, has contributed to the image, prevalent in the West, of a geisha as an expensive prostitute. This is a narrow view, as Mineko Iwasaki makes clear in *Geisha, A Life* (2002). Born in 1949, Iwasaki was Japan's foremost geisha, having begun her training at the age of four and retired wealthy at 29. She entertained such prominent Western figures as the British royal family and the American General Douglas MacArthur. In her book, she describes her strict training in calligraphy, dance, music, serving tea, and the other hostess functions of a geisha. She dispels the stereotype of 'geisha as prostitute', explaining that there were occasionally 'romantic entanglements' between rich patrons and geisha artists, leading to marriage, affairs, or 'heartache', but that 'in the same way that a patron of the opera does not expect sexual favors from the diva', a rich and powerful man would more often support a prominent geisha 'solely because of the artistic perfection that she embodied and the luster that she lent to his reputation' (Iwasaki 2002: 51–2).

Black women also face discrimination on the basis of opposing race/gender stereotypes. Das Gupta describes the double image as follows:

> On the one hand there was the slow, de-sexed, 'cow-like' mammy, evolved into the 'Aunt Jemima figure'—familiar to many from older boxes of pancake mix—a servile and contented image which brings together gender and race ideologies. On the other hand, there was the sexual objectification of Black women's bodies, or body parts to be more exact. (Das Gupta 1996: 27)

The sexually objectified black woman is a familiar figure in music videos, but the brief and supposedly inadvertent exposure of black singer Janet Jackson's breast on TV during the halftime show at

This scene from the movie *Memoirs of a Geisha* (2005) hints at the kind of romantic attachment that often developed between Japanese geishas and the men they were paid to entertain. The term *geisha* translates literally as 'hostess' or 'artist'. Why do you think many Westerners have difficulty seeing the role as anything other than that of a prostitute?

Photo: Photos 12/Alamy

the 2004 Super Bowl sparked an astonishing level of outrage among scandalized American viewers (not to mention all of those who had merely heard about the incident). Why the big fuss? The sudden appearance in prime time of the sexually objectified black woman experiencing a 'wardrobe malfunction' seemed to have caught a largely white middle-class audience by surprise. Were these viewers right to object? Or is the North American viewing public guilty of a double standard, finding it okay for the sexually objectified woman to appear in videos on MTV, but not on 'family entertainment' on CBS?

The Indian Princess and the Squaw

Aboriginal women have long been subject to the opposing gender/race stereotypes of the 'Indian princess' and the 'squaw'. In the United States, the Indian princess is a heroine that forms an integral part of the American story of how their country was built. She is the beautiful Pocahontas of Disney's

Photo: Library and Archives Canada, C-14141

The daughter of an English mother and a Mohawk father, E. Pauline Johnson played up her mixed heritage in her popular performances, often appearing for the first part of a show in traditional Native costume before changing into a formal evening dress for the remainder of the performance.

QUICK HITS

The *Ninauposkitzipxpe*, or 'Manly-Hearted Women', of the Peigan

About a third of elderly (sixty years or older) North Piegan women in 1939, and a few younger women, were considered manly-hearted. . . . Such women owned property, were good managers and usually effective workers, were forthright and assertive in public, in their homes, and as sexual partners, and were active in religious rituals. They were called 'manly-hearted' because boldness, aggressiveness, and a drive to amass property and social power are held to be ideal traits for men. . . . [T]he manly-hearted woman is admired as well as feared by both men and women. (Kehoe 1995: 115)

What do YOU think?

How do we in Canadian society tend to characterize women who are bold, aggressive, and career-oriented? Can we say that we think of them as positively as the traditional Blackfoot did?

worldview, saving the handsome John Smith from certain death, in the process abandoning her people to serve the interests of the incoming colonial power. She is Sacajawea, the Shoshone woman who aided the Lewis and Clark Expedition from 1804 to 1806, helping to open the West to 'civilization' and the eventual reservation entrapment of her people and their Plains neighbours.

The Indian princess is not part of the founding mythology, or master narrative, of Canada. Still, she is found here and there across the country. Emily Pauline Johnson, popular Mohawk poet and novelist at the turn of the twentieth century, was frequently billed as 'The Mohawk Princess' to audiences in North America and Britain, for whom she performed her poetry. Catharine Sutton, a heroic Ojibwa woman of the nineteenth century, is known in Owen Sound, Ontario, as 'the Indian Princess' (see Steckley 1999).

While the stereotype of the Indian princess has been used as a metaphor for the supposed open-armed acceptance by North American Native people of European colonizers, the squaw is a figure that has been used by white writers (including

American presidents Thomas Jefferson and Theodore Roosevelt) to characterize Aboriginal people as savages, providing ample justification for white colonial dominance (Smits 1982). The image summarizes the impressions of Aboriginal culture as brutal and barbaric, with lazy, abusive Native men overworking and generally mistreating their wives, sisters, mothers, and daughters.

The squaw figure is a familiar one in the Canadian literature on Aboriginal women (see McLean 1970: 148–9 and Jenness 1932: 403). The way the distorted depiction of the lives of Aboriginal women was used to justify white colonialism is clearly seen in the following passage, written by a nineteenth-century missionary, Egerton R. Young:

> Marvelous were the changes wrought among these Indians when they became Christians. And in no way was the change greater or more visible than in the improved conditions of women. In paganism she has not the life of a dog. She is kicked and cuffed and maltreated continually. She is the beast of burden and has to do all the heavy work. . . . Very quickly after they become Christians does all this

The Point Is...

Indian Princesses and Cowgirls: Stereotypes from the Frontier

Pocahontas, Calamity Jane, and Annie Oakley. When we think of women in the Wild West, these are the images that come to mind. The Indian princess is a serene, noble savage, while the cowgirl is a smart-talking, gun-slinging dynamo. These stereotypes are so deeply ingrained in our popular culture that we scarcely give them a second thought.

A recent exhibit of popular-culture images of Indian and western women from the nineteenth and twentieth centuries unveiled and challenged these representational stereotypes. *Indian Princess and Cowgirls: Stereotypes from the Frontier*, shown across Canada between 1997 and 2000, featured over 200 photographs, postcards, calendars, and other historical images of 'Indian princesses' and 'cowgirls' that graphically depict the historical representation of women, race, and the colonial west. Together, the images demonstrated how European notions of femininity and wild savagery were grafted onto First Nations and frontier women, bringing civilization to the wild and the wild to civilization in a more palatable form. In essence, Native women were whitened up and made more 'feminine', while white women of the frontier were made wilder and more Native.

According to Gail Valaskakis, one of two curators of the exhibit, 'The discourse of the Indian as noble and savage, the villain and the victim . . . is threaded through the narratives of the dominant culture and its shifting perceptions of the western frontier as a land of savagery and a land of promise.' Like the cultural narratives of the western frontier that sustained them, textual representations of real First Nations peoples reveal stories of conquest and its legacies. For Valaskakis, this ambiguous representation of Native women 'has been with us since the earliest colonization of the Americas'. As representations changed, the images of First Nations women as Indian princesses who embodied mystery and exoticism began to emerge. During the post–World War I era, the Indian princess was repeatedly portrayed alone in the pristine wilderness, scantily clad in a buckskin or tunic dress, sporting a jaunty feather over two long braids. Most striking, the models in the images are notably white-skinned.

Meanwhile, the masculine transgression of cowgirls in Wild West fiction depicted the romanticism of their underlying 'Indian nature'. Pictures of cowgirls, adventure heroines, and outlaw women were first produced for rodeo and vaudeville shows, dime novels, and monograms as a means to promote sales. But in actual frontier society, many women deliberately took on this fictional role by 'playing Indian'. Playing Indian gave white women the opportunity to escape the conventional and often restrictive boundaries of society. Rodeo shows frequently featured women in pants performing death-defying stunts on horseback, performances that mimicked the fantasy of the Native huntress and warrior as imagined by nineteenth-century onlookers.

change. Then happy homes begin. Mother and wife and sister and daughter are loved and kindly cared for. (Young 1970: 148–9)

In contemporary society, the squaw image is often blended with the stereotype of the 'drunk Indian', with tragic consequences. Consider the case of Minnie Sutherland, a 40-year-old Cree woman who was struck by a car in downtown Hull (Gatineau), Quebec, while walking with her cousin on New Year's Eve, 1989. The car was driven by two white nurses, who quickly stopped and got out of their car, and were soon joined by two white police officers and three university students who were witnesses to the incident. The students explained that Minnie had been hit by a car, but according to John Nihmey, who had access to the transcript of the hearing that would follow, the officers 'were perplexed by what seemed to be an overreaction to a drunk woman who had either slipped on an ice patch and fallen, or walked into a car that couldn't have been going very fast given all the traffic' (Nihmey 1998: 82–3). In communication with police headquarters, the officers referred to Minnie as 'the squaw' (Nihmey 1998: 84).

With Minnie barely conscious, the police and students left. An attending paramedic arriving with another police officer concluded that Minnie was drunk and suggested that she be taken to a detoxification centre. However, when the officer brought her to a detox centre, she was turned away on the grounds that the facility would not admit non-ambulatory people. The officer eventually drove Minnie to a nearby hospital, where she died 11 days later as the result of a blood clot in the back of her brain caused by her accident. The doctors, unaware of the blood clot, hadn't considered her case serious enough to warrant an MRI. On 17 January, a doctor from the hospital sent the following letter to the Hull police:

There is no doubt that the lack of information about the traumatic event was of great significance in making the initial diagnosis of the abnormality and in following this up to a logical conclusion which may have been able to prevent her demise. . . . In particular, if the allegations of the conduct of the Hull Police are correct, then a serious error

in judgment has been made by the officers concerned and this should be investigated. (Nihmey 1998: 163)

A coroner's jury ruled that the Hull police should offer compulsory courses to sensitize officers to the needs of visible minorities. At the same time, four out of five jurors felt that racism was not a factor in the case. The Quebec Police Commission cleared its officers of racism charges.

Aboriginal women may be the ones to lose out when efforts are made to counter racial discrimination, as Brenda Comaskey and Anne McGillivray (2001) explain. Well-meaning attempts to divert some Aboriginal offenders from prisons by reducing their sentences have placed the wives and girlfriends of abusive offenders in a dangerous position. The women need to feel safe from harm, but the justice system's determination to treat male Aboriginal defendants more leniently has sometimes produced situations that are unsafe and frightening for Aboriginal women.

Gender and Immigration

There have been several instances in Canadian history when only the men or the women of a particular ethnic group were permitted or encouraged to immigrate. We have seen, in Chapter 12, that Chinese and South Asian women were effectively blocked from entering Canada for significant parts of the twentieth century. In the section that follows, we will see the difficulties Filipino women faced when they made up the majority of those allowed to immigrate to Canada from the Philippines.

Filipino Immigrants: A Second Wave of Pioneering Women

Filipino immigration to Canada is unique in that women have been the 'pioneers'—arriving first before their husbands and other male family members, sending most of their money together with care packages of bargain-hunted goods back home to their families, sponsoring relatives and providing them with a place to stay. There have been two waves of Filipino immigration. The first wave, discussed in Chapter 10, brought nurses, mostly women, while the second wave brought nannies, who suffer more from the inequalities of gender and race than did the earlier generation of Filipino immigrants.

In 1981, the Canadian government instituted its Foreign Domestic Movement Program (FDMP) to address the growing need for in-house childcare that was created as more and more women began working outside the home. In 1992, the FDMP was replaced by the more restrictive Live-In Caregiver Program, which required selected immigrants to commit to 24 months of domestic work within a three-year period, during which time they were also required to 'live in' with the family. Nannies came mainly from three countries: the Philippines, Jamaica, and the United Kingdom. Filipino nannies dominated the figures, the percentage of domestics coming from the Philippines rising between 1982 and 1990 from 10.60 per cent to 50.52 per cent. This trend occurred not just in Canada but in Hong Kong, Singapore, Saudi Arabia, Britain, and the United States. The political and economic unrest that surrounded the fall of the corrupt Marcos government made the Philippines a place many wanted to leave if they could.

The women of the second wave of Filipino immigration were older than their compatriots who had migrated earlier: those aged 30–34 predominated, with those aged 25–29 and 35–39 forming smaller but roughly equal groups, and those aged 20–24 and 50–54 sharing about the same low percentage. It was more difficult for this generation of Filipino immigrants. They were better educated than immigrating British and Jamaican nannies: among those receiving temporary employment authorization as nannies between 1982 and 1990, 8 per cent held bachelor's degrees, 7 per cent had at least some university education, 17 per cent had some trade and technology training, and 12 per cent had other non-university training. Working as nannies made these women

grossly underemployed, as sociologist Anita Beltran Chen argues (1998). Yet domestic work was the only kind of work that could bring them to Canada, so they took their chances.

As women, as visible minorities, and as temporary and poorly paid employees subject to few industrial controls, the women were vulnerable to exploitation and physical, emotional, and sexual abuse. Those who had been trained in a specific field such as nursing also had to fight losing their skills through disuse. Between 15 and 20 per cent were married and had to endure separation from their husbands and, in many cases, children. Those who were single returned a large portion (estimates vary around 75 per cent) of their income to their family back home, holding onto little money to look after themselves. In short, they are restricted by the stereotypes of race and gender that treat Asian women as caregivers, overlooking skills that might make them productive in other areas of Western society.

Summary and Conclusions

You need be neither a woman nor a feminist to recognize that feminization of an occupation—in the sense of making it unrewarding in terms of pay, power, and social status—helps to create inequality between men and women. This inequality, reflected in pay ratio and in the greater likelihood of women working part-time, is changing very little. As sociologists, we need to investigate why this is so, and look for ways to address the inequity. We also must ask ourselves whether the separate paths that men and women take in post-secondary education lead to social inequality or just difference, an issue we raised in Chapter 4, on socialization.

Questions for Critical Review

1. To what extent can a man be considered a feminist? How would that define his role as a sociologist?
2. A metrosexual is loosely defined as a heterosexual male who has the fashion sense of a gay male. Do you think that men in twenty-first-century Canada are comfortable identifying themselves publicly as metrosexual?
3. Do you think that the stereotype, popular in North American culture, of male nurses as gay can be changed? What would it take to change it?
4. Describe how gender and ethnicity intersect in creating female stereotypes.

Suggested Readings

Chodrow, Nancy J. (1994). *Femininities, Masculinities, Sexualities: Freud and Beyond*. Lexington, KY: The UP of Kentucky.

Comaskey, Brenda, & Anne McGillivray (1999). *Black Eyes All of the Time: Intimate Violence, Aboriginal Women, and the Justice System*. Toronto: University of Toronto Press.

Eliot, Lise (2009). *Pink Brain, Blue Brain: How Small Differences Grow Into Troublesome Gaps—And What We Can Do About It*. Boston: Houghton Mifflin Harcourt.

Fausto-Sterling, Anne (1985). *Myths of Gender: Biological Theories about Women and Men*. New York: Basic Books.

Foucault, Michel (1978). The *History of Sexuality: An Introduction*, vol. 1. R. Hurley, trans. New York: Vintage.

Medovarski, Andrea, & Brenda Cranney, eds. (2006). *Canadian Women Studies: An Introductory Reader*, 2nd edn. Toronto: INANNA.

Seidman, Steven, ed. (1996). *Queer Theory / Sociology*. Cambridge: Blackwell.

Silman, Janet (1987). *Enough is Enough: Aboriginal Women Speak Out*. Toronto: Women's Press.

Suggested Websites

Canadian Woman and Internet Association
www.herplace.org/

Gender Watch
http://www.genderwatch.com/products/pt-product-genderwatch.shtml

International Gay & Lesbian Human Rights Commission
http://www.iglhrc.org/

Andrea Dworkin Online Library
http://www.nostatusquo.com/ACLU/dworkin/

Key Terms

- barbarism
- civilization
- conservatism
- cultural norms
- cycle of civilization
- democracy

- digital divide
- evolution
- fashion
- Islamist
- Luddites
- modernism

- narrow vision
- oligarchy
- particularist protectionist
- political globalization
- polyarchy
- postmodernism

14

Social Change
and the Future

LEARNING OBJECTIVES

After reading this chapter, you should be able to

> outline and contrast five different models of social change;

> discuss the application of the cycle of civilization to the United States;

> summarize the social changes to which the Luddites were reacting;

> outline and discuss the applicability of Kroker's idea of the virtual class; and

> distinguish between cultural and statistical norms.

- reference group
- relative deprivation
- savagery
- slippery slope
- social change

- social Darwinism
- statistical norms
- survival of the fittest
- universalist protectionist
- virtual class

Key Names
- Georg Wilhelm Friedrich Hegel
- August Comte
- Herbert Spencer

- Lewis Henry Morgan
- Robert A. Dahl
- George Grant
- Arthur Kroker

Protesters outside the security fence at the Summit of the Americas in Quebec City, April 2001. Can it be reasonably argued that 'Capitalism is Organized Crime'?

Photos: CP Photo/Jonathan Hayward

FOR Starters

Raging Against the Machine

The following are the words of an English cropper (an independent producer of woollen cloth) from the county of Yorkshire in 1802, describing the desperate straits of people in his position, and what he wanted to do to the machines that were, in part, the cause of their difficulty:

> The burning of Factorys or setting fire to the property of People we know is not right but Starvation forces Nature to do that which he would not, nor would it reach his Thoughts had he sufficient Employ. We have tried every Effort to live by Pawning our Cloaths and Chattles so we are now on the brink for the last struggle. (Quoted in Sale 1995: 71)

People sharing this view would later be known as Luddites. Compare his attitude with the one expressed in the lyrics to the song 'Take the Power Back' by the American band Rage Against the Machine, from their self-titled album released in 1992:

The present curriculum
I put my fist in 'em
Eurocentric every last one of 'em
See right through the red, white
    and blue disguise
With lecture I puncture the
    structure of lies
Installed in our minds and
    attempting
To hold us back
We've got to take it back

'Cause holes in our spirit causin'
    tears and fears
One-sided stories for years and
    years and years
I'm inferior?
Who's inferior?
Yeah, we need to check the interior
Of the system that cares about only
    one culture
And that is why
We gotta take the power back . . .

Predicting the Future: A Fool's Game

What do we mean by **social change**? We mean that a group of people has experienced dramatic change in one part of their lives, and must make adjustments in other areas of their lives in order to adapt. The central fact about society today is that it is changing. Things are not what they used to be, even just a few short years ago. Think just of personal technology change: we need think back only a few years to remember our first time using a number of items that then seemed gimmicky and now seem indispensible—cellphones, iPods, BlackBerries, digital cameras, and so on. Some of us can even remember life before touching a computer keyboard.

Throughout much of this textbook we've reviewed trends and events that triggered, exemplified, or proceeded from social change. We've tried to show that these trends and events are subject to different and equally valid interpretations by groups examining them from different standpoints, depending on such factors as gender, ethnicity, class, and so on. In other words, examining social change in the past is no straightforward exercise. Imagine, then, the difficulty of predicting social change in the future.

Ultimately, we concede, it's a fool's game. In 1987, no one could have predicted that the divorce rate would peak that year, and then decline over the next 20 years. (For that matter, sixteen years

ago, I could not have predicted that I would get married for a third time—and have that marriage last; two years ago, I couldn't have predicted that I would now have four parrots!) At the start of the twenty-first century, no 'futurist' (a consultant who studies trends and gets paid a lot of money to present predictions that generally don't come true—think of a psychic with an MBA or other degree) predicted that within 10 years there would be a black president of the United States, that General Motors would crash, that the Canadian and American governments would bail out and impose tight conditions on the automotive industry (once thought to be the ultimate capitalist industry), or that Ontario would join the club of Canada's 'have-not' provinces because of unemployment in the manufacturing sector. Of course, no one on New Year's Day 2001 could have foreseen the extraordinary set of social changes that would be sparked by the events of that infamous date just eight months and eleven days later.

Another cautionary note concerning any discussion of social change: it is important to recognize that as rapid as change is today, with advances in technology in particular enabling us to chart new territory in our social world, it would be wrong to say that earlier society was primarily static, sitting still. Think, for instance, of the Austronesian-speaking people who, perhaps as far back as 2,000 years ago, travelled from mainland Southeast Asia to the far-flung islands of Taiwan, Malaysia, Indonesia, Hawaii, Easter Island, New Zealand, and even Madagascar, hundreds of years

Photo: Photodisc

Do you think the gentleman in the photo looks as cool as he must have thought he did when this mobile phone was the model of convenience and technological sophistication?

before the era of modern travel—all in relatively small outrigger canoes. Think, too, of fourteenth-century China, Africa, and Europe, whose populations, recovering from the devastating effects of the Black Plague, saw their cultures change on a large scale. In Europe, traditional religious views were challenged, and surviving labourers of the plague-ravished workforce, in accordance with the principle of supply and demand, were able to charge more for their work. We can also cite those cultures of South and Central America, Africa, Asia, and Europe that, thousands of years ago, began to practise agriculture, changing the landscape forever. Dramatic social change, certainly a defining feature of our present age, is nevertheless not unique to it.

We can look at social change as affecting three areas of life: the material, the social, and the intellectual. This is clear when we take a look at the changes experienced by the person starting college or university. The student may have to move to another area to be closer to the school, or she

may have to travel farther, by a different means of transportation. The cost of just about every aspect of life will go up. Books surround her life. These are all material changes.

In the social sphere, the student will encounter new groups of classmates, leaving behind some or all of the people she grew up with. If the college is located in the city and if the student is coming from a rural community, she may experience different ethnicities for the first time. Some of the students she shares classes with might be significantly older, and her relationships with instructors will be different from those she had with teachers in high school.

The student's intellectual sphere, her world of ideas, will change dramatically as well, and not just with the knowledge and new ideas she is exposed to in class. As just one example, the student learns to think of time in a different way. She may have more free time or spares outside of the classroom, but has to learn to budget that time to deal with a greater workload.

Thus, it's easy to see how one major change—starting college—necessitates changes in all areas of the student's life—material, social, and intellectual.

Five Interpretations of Social Change

Any one instance of social change may be interpreted in a number of different ways. No single model of interpretation is the 'right' one all the time. The five we are considering here have varying degrees of applicability at different times. They are

1. **modernism**,
2. **conservatism**,
3. **postmodernism**,
4. **evolution**, and
5. **fashion**.

As we present each one, we will point out situations where it is and is not likely to apply. First, though, we offer a disclaimer concerning sociological models based on analogy. It comes from American sociologist Robert A. Nisbet in his classic study *Social Change and History: Aspects of the Western Theory of Development*:

> No one has ever seen a civilization die, and it is unimaginable, short of cosmic disaster or thermonuclear holocaust, that anyone ever will. Nor has anyone ever seen a civilization—or culture or institution—in literal process of decay and degeneration, though there is a rich profusion of these words and their synonyms in Western thought from [the Greek writer] Hesiod to [the early twentieth-century historian] Spengler. Nor, finally, has anyone ever seen—actually, empirically seen, as we see these things in the world of plants and animals—growth and development in civilizations and societies and cultures, with all that is clearly implied by these words: change proceeding gradually, cumulatively, and irreversibly, through a kind of unfolding of internal potentiality, the whole moving toward some end that is presumably contained in the process from the start. We see none

of these in culture: death, degeneration, development, birth. (Nisbet 1969: 3)

1. Modernism

Modernism and the discipline of sociology have long been connected. Modernism holds that change equals progress, that what is modern or new will automatically be better than the older thing it replaces. It views society as advancing along a straight path from primitive to more sophisticated, from out-of-date to up-to-date, from worse to better. This change is usually portrayed as a single line, not being very open to different paths of development. Seen in its best light, the modernist view is the view of the future long envisioned by Gene Roddenberry, creator of *Star Trek*. Seen in a more sinister light, it reduces progress to a formula that equates 'new' with 'better' and simultaneously 'more expensive'. Education technology has co-opted the term 'advanced learning' without even having to demonstrate that it is in any way more 'advanced' or 'better' than traditional methods of instruction. Teachers using older methods are portrayed as educational dinosaurs, even though they may be more effective educators than their pyrotechnically inclined colleagues (known by nicknames including 'Twitter Tutor', 'Facebook Facilitator', 'Blackboard Blogger', and 'Peter Power Pointer').

The German philosopher **Georg Wilhelm Friedrich Hegel** (1770–1831), who strongly influenced Marx and many other early sociological thinkers, adopted a modernist view that history represented a steady progress in the freeing of the spirit, from freedom for the few to freedom for all, and that this reflected a geographical movement, over time, from East (i.e. China and India) to West (from Greece and Rome to Germany):

> The History of the World travels from East to West, for Europe is absolutely the end of History, Asia the beginning. . . . The History of the World is the discipline of the uncontrolled natural will, bringing it into obedience to a Universal principle and conferring subjective freedom. The East knew and the present day knows only that *One* is Free; the Greek and Roman world, that *some* are

free; the German World knows that *All* are free. The first political form therefore which we observe in History, is *Despotism*, the second *Democracy* and *Aristocracy*, the third *Monarchy*. (Hegel 1956: 103–4)

French thinker, **August Comte** (1798–1857), often identified as the father of sociology, was also a cheerleader for modernism, as we can see in the following quotation:

The true general spirit of social dynamics [i.e., sociology] then consists of each . . . social [state] as the necessary result of the preceding, and the indispensable mover of the following, according to the axiom of Leibniz—the present is big [i.e., pregnant] with the future. In this view the object of science is to discover the laws which govern that continuity. (Comte 1853; quoted in Nisbet 1969: 159)

Positivism, which characterized Comte's view and dominated much of the early history of sociology, is an aspect of modernism. Positivism, as we defined it in Chapter 2, involves a belief that the rules, methods, and presumed objectivity of the natural sciences can be applied to the social sciences with no accommodation made for the biases, or subjectivity, or personality of the social scientist.

Along with Charles Darwin's theory of evolution came the idea, often referred to as **social Darwinism** or social evolution, that societies naturally proceed from simple (and inferior) to complex (and superior), and that only the strongest societies triumph. This notion of progress was articulated by **Herbert Spencer** (1820–1903), who coined the expression **survival of the fittest** (in his *Social Statics*, 1851), later borrowed by Darwin—in a solely biological sense—to refer to societies. The idea that society progresses through stages was developed and put forward by anthropologist **Lewis Henry Morgan** (1818–1881), who identified the three stages of **savagery**, **barbarism**, and **civilization**. These, he felt, could be established by looking at seven different aspects of any society: subsistence, government, language, the family, religion, house life, and architecture

and property (Morgan 1964: 12). In the following passage, from the opening chapter of the aptly named *Ancient Society or Researches in the Lines of Human Progress from Savagery through Barbarism to Civilization*, Morgan sets out his aim of tracing human development through the three stages:

The latest investigations respecting the early condition of the human race are tending to the conclusion that mankind commenced their career at the bottom of the scale and slowly worked their way up from savagery to civilization through the slow accumulations of experimental knowledge.

As it is undeniable that portions of the human family have existed in a state of savagery, other portions in a state of barbarism, and still other portions in a state of civilization, it seems equally so that these three distinct conditions are connected with each other in a natural as well as necessary sequence of progress. Moreover, that this sequence has been historically true of the entire human family, up to the status attained by each branch respectively, is rendered probable by the conditions under which all progress occurs, and by the known advancement of several branches of the family through two or more of these conditions.

An attempt will be made in the following pages to bring forward additional evidence of the rudeness of the early condition of mankind, of the gradual evolution of their mental and moral powers through experience, and of their protracted struggle with obstacles while winning their way to civilization. It will be drawn, in part, from the great sequence of inventions and discoveries which stretches along the entire pathway of human progress; but chiefly from domestic institutions, which express the growth of certain ideas and passions. (Morgan 1964 [1877]: 11)

The influence of Morgan's three-tiered view of human development would last well into the twentieth century. Vestiges of it can be seen in Émile Durkheim's *Elementary Forms of Religious Life* and in the writings of influential (but now largely vilified) conservative American sociologist

Talcott Parsons, who, in his *Societies: Evolutionary and Comparative Perspectives*, divided societies into the supposedly less judgmental but nevertheless still misleading 'primitive', 'intermediate', and 'modern' (Parsons 1966).

From the nineteenth to the mid-twentieth century, a key aspect of modernism was the belief that science and technology would combine to create a material heaven on earth. Science would become a rational, hard evidence–based religion to supersede the traditional religions built on faith, on unproven and unprovable beliefs. Technology would free people from having to perform hard physical labour on the job and at home, while we humans, freed from tedious labour, would have plenty of leisure time to spend as we pleased. It's easy to smirk at the idealism of the 1950s and early 1960s, but how different is that from the message we hear in TV and radio ads today about how new time-saving technology will keep us more 'connected' with the world?

Modernist theories of politics incorporate the idea that societies are constantly improving. In this view, societies are believed to be becoming more democratic, while respect for human rights is on the rise and the barriers between societies are falling, all of which will help to eradicate the threat of war. Indeed, this was the premise behind the founding of the United Nations after World War II (and its precursor, the League of Nations, after

Photo: Colin Young-Wolff/Photo Edit Inc.

Rosie the Robot gets her hands dirty on the cover of a *Jetsons* comic book from 1963. Do you think the artist expected that by now every home would have its own domestic robot?

Going Global

Political Globalization and the Spread of Democracy

Political globalization, as defined by Steger, is 'the intensification and expansion of political interrelations across the globe' (Steger 2003: 56). These interrelations tend to range across whole groups of countries. They include the United Nations and its affiliated organizations as well as regional coalitions such as the European Community and NATO (the North Atlantic Treaty Organization); they also include NGOs (non-government organizations) such as Amnesty International and Greenpeace.

Champions of globalization, taking a modernist view of change, argue that it benefits many countries by spreading democracy (Steger 2003: 110). The validity of this claim depends on how you define **democracy**. At the foundation of a democracy is a government elected by its citizens. But this is a rather thin definition; merely holding a vote for a leader does not guarantee true democracy. Think of the former Soviet Union, where citizens would go through the exercise of voting for the one name on the ballot. And how many people must be allowed to vote in order for there to be a true democracy? A broader definition of democracy might include such features as the following:

- a broad-based electorate in terms of gender, class, ethnicity, and race
- freedom of the press and freedom of speech
- freedom of association and of travel (within and between countries)
- the presence of a viable opposition (and one that does not literally fear for its life)
- a system of education in which people can teach and take courses that can be critical of society's institutions
- protection of the rights of minorities
- relative equality of men and women

Thin democracy might be spreading, but broad democracy really is not.

Around the time of the US-led invasion of Iraq in 2003, there was a joke going around that George W. Bush was trying to bring democracy to Iraq— and if it worked there, he was going to try to bring it to Florida (the deciding state in the 2000 presidential election, which became the focus of allegations of voter fraud). The joke raises an interesting question: When do we have democracy? A typical definition of democracy involves some notion of government by citizens—note the Greek root of the word, *demos–*, meaning 'the people'. But the ancient Greeks, who coined the term, can hardly be said to have had democracy themselves. After all, women and the large class of slaves were excluded from having a voice.

What are the analytical alternatives to 'democracy' when describing a society? In *A Preface to Democratic Theory* (1956), American political scientist and sociologist **Robert A. Dahl** (b. 1915) suggested that modern industrial states were governed by **polyarchies,** shifting coalitions of powerful interest groups. But in *Power Elite*, published that same year, C. Wright Mills disagreed, arguing that the power elite, who ran the big companies and had the most significant say in government, was governing, and that its governance was relatively stable. In essence, he claimed that there was an **oligarchy**, rule by

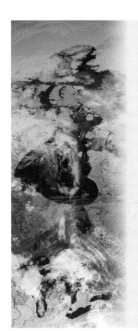

a few powerful individuals or groups. Kirkpatrick Sale (1980) has argued that democracy cannot exist in a population over 10,000, so that we can only have relative degrees of democracy in state-level societies. While the actual number might be somewhat higher, the basic premise seems sound.

What do YOU think?

1. What features would have to be in place in a society that can be considered relatively 'democratic'? In what ways would you consider Canada 'democratic' and 'undemocratic'?

2. Do you think that political globalization, around the world, fits the modernist model?

World War I). A glimpse of the spirit of that postwar feeling comes from the general introduction to a series of philosophical and religious works that was put together by liberal, religious-minded Oxford scholars during the 1950s:

> Read and pondered with a desire to learn, they will help men and women to find 'fullness of life', and peoples to live together in greater understanding and harmony. Today the earth is beautiful, but men are disillusioned and afraid. But there may come a day, perhaps not a distant day, when there will be a renaissance of man's spirit: when men will be innocent and happy amid the beauty of the world, or their eyes will be opened to see that egoism and strife are folly, that the universe is fundamentally spiritual, and that men are the sons of God. (The Editors 2002: 8)

This view is one that is not likely to be echoed by their peers of the early twenty-first century. It is easy for the leaders of developing empires to use modernist principles to justify their decisions on the grounds that their latest achievement represents the culmination of progress and that whatever is in the best interests of their country is in the best interests of humankind. Noam Chomsky, in a number of best-selling publications, has expressed his concern that his country's

presidents and policy makers and their supporters have taken this approach, wrapping American policy in the flag of modernism. In *Hegemony or Survival: America's Quest for Global Dominance*, he describes the modernist thinking of the American power elite:

> [T]here is a guiding principle that 'defines the parameters within which the policy debate occurs,' a consensus so broad as to exclude only 'tattered remains' on the right and left and 'so authoritative as to be virtually immune to challenge'. The principle is '*America as historical vanguard*': 'History has a discernible direction and destination. Uniquely among all the nations of the world, the United States comprehends and manifests history's purpose.' Accordingly, US hegemony is the realization of history's purpose, and what it achieves is for common good, the merest truism, so that empirical evaluation is unnecessary, if not faintly ridiculous. (Chomsky 2004: 42–3)

Chomsky here identifies one of the flaws of the modernist model, namely its **narrow vision**, roughly cast as 'Whatever innovation benefits the dominant class is justifiable on the grounds of progress.' Today, we are often skeptical of modernism. Science and technology have enabled us to create problems of pollution that we need to solve more by how we live than by adding more technology. Commercials for SUVs promise personal freedom, yet if we in North America did not manufacture vehicles with such low fuel efficiency, our demands for oil and the damage to our environment would be less.

Meanwhile, human leisure time is not increasing. People with jobs seem to be working harder than in decades past in spite of labour-saving technology. The office is now a virtual space, as advances in telecommunications make it more difficult for people to leave their work at the end of the day. 'Crackberries' enable bosses to get their employees to do more work for the company on weekends. In politics, governments with little respect for democracy, human rights, or peace abound in countries that talk of protecting those ideals.

So where might the modernist view be valid? When asked this question in the classroom, students typically point to medical technology. Certainly diagnostic and life-saving technology has become more sophisticated, and in this sense it

validates a modernist view of progress. At the same time, we must accept that reliance on this technology as an alternative to adopting preventative social practices is not a social improvement. The old saying 'an ounce of prevention is worth a pound of cure' would seem to hold.

2. Conservatism

Another interpretation of social change is conservatism. Conservative thinkers see social change as potentially more destructive than constructive, especially in emotionally charged areas of life such as family, gender roles, sexuality, and the environment.

It would be easy to dismiss conservatism as an 'unrealistic' interpretation of social change held by old-timers or religious fanatics romanticizing the past, by red-necked reactionaries gazing down the gun barrel at anyone attempting to interfere with their rights, or by anti-business, tree-hugging nature 'freaks'. It would, however, be often inaccurate to do so. Some values and

Photo: iStockphoto/David H. Lewis

An automated external defibrillator (AED) hangs ready for use on the wall of an airport in Texas. This piece of medical technology is an increasingly common sight in public spaces, where it enables private citizens to save lives before emergency personnel arrive on the scene. Do you think it would be better to concentrate on improving the health (e.g. by targeting high cholesterol foods—Texas is the home of the chicken-fried steak) of North Americans to reduce the risk of heart attacks?

Going Global

Opposing Globalization: A Conservatist Stance

There are fundamentally two kinds of opposition to globalization: particularist protectionism and universalist protectionism. **Particularist protectionist** opponents of globalization focus on the socio-economic, political, and cultural problems caused in their home territory by increasing processes of globalization. In Steger's words,

> Fearing the loss of national self-determination and the destruction of their cultures, they pledge to protect their traditional ways of life from those 'foreign elements' they consider responsible for unleashing the forces of globalization. (Steger 2003: 114)

This is a mixed group. It includes **Islamists**—people like Osama bin Laden and his Al-Qaeda network, who oppose globalization with narrow-minded and distorted fundamentalist notions of Islam. It also includes European ethnic entrepreneurs, who use principles of particularist protectionism to defend their campaign for 'racial/national purity' (examples include Jean-Marie Le Pen's French National Front, which strongly opposes any manifestation of Islam in France). The group of particular protectionists even includes Americans who argue that skilled and unskilled tradeworkers are losing their jobs to citizens of the developing world, and are not benefiting from economic globalization like the power elite are. While they sometimes identify 'big business' as the culprit, it is often easier to blame Japanese-owned firms. Sociologist Roland Robertson, who teaches in the United States, wrote the following for a Japanese publication in 1997:

> I can assure you that the *anti*-global sentiment is very, very strong in the United States of America. It is playing a key part in the current campaign to decide which candidate should run for president from the Republican Party; the phrase 'anti-globalism' is a significant one in American politics; there are numerous movements which are directed in opposition to the teaching of the subject of globalization, to so-called 'international educa-tion'; there have been people protesting at school boards all over America about American children learning about other countries; they fear that if they learn about ancient Greek philosophy or about Japanese religion or French philosophy, that their minds will be destroyed, in other words, that their views will be relativized. (Robertson 1997)

But from a Canadian perspective, a certain amount of particularist protection would seem necessary. Only about 2 per cent of the movies we watch are Canadian, despite the fact that there is a relatively booming movie production business in Toronto and Vancouver. Think of how many times you have seen someone play the part of an American president in a movie. Can you ever remember seeing a movie with someone cast as the Canadian prime minister? Our stories are simply not being told on film, except in Quebec, where French-language films are being produced for the domestic market. Canadian content rules and specially funded programs have helped many of our musicians begin careers in the face of the competition from the loud voices to the south.

While particularist protectionists argue that globalization causes social, cul-tural, and political problems in their own countries, **universalist protectionists**, as Steger describes them, promote the interests of the poor and marginalized groups worldwide (Steger 2003: 115). Amnesty International, Doctors Without Borders, World Wildlife Federation, and similar organizations can be seen as univer-salist protectionist, taking up the cause of those hurt by globalization worldwide.

customs, like community and 'neighbourliness', need to be preserved. Their loss is neither inevitable nor desirable.

Conservatism as it relates to social change should not be confused with the political principles of right-wing, large-C Conservative parties in Canada, Britain, Australia, and New Zealand. An excellent example of small-c conservatism is found in the nationalist sentiment of **George Grant** (1918–1988), one of Canada's foremost conservative public intellectuals. Grant taught philosophy at a number of Canadian universities, including McMaster, Dalhousie, and Queen's, and his *Lament for a Nation* (1965), recently republished on its fortieth anniversary, is widely recognized as a landmark of Canadian writing. His concern, as expressed in *Lament* and in *Technology and Empire* (1969), was that the technology,

culture, and sense of progress emanating from the US would lead to the destruction of Canada as a place that cultivated and cherished an alternative to the American vision. A man of deep religious convictions, he inspired Canadian nationalists from the political left to the political right. Conservative prime minister Stephen Harper and NDP leader Jack Layton would both agree with points made by George Grant.

We mentioned in the previous section the modernist belief that science will ultimately replace traditional religion. So far this has not happened, and we cast our bets on the side of its not happening. Humans, it would appear, have spiritual needs, however they might be defined, that science cannot completely address. We see in the growing strength of conservative religion in the United States and in the battles that proponents

Photo: Big Valley Creation Science Museum, Alberta

The Big Valley Creation Science Museum opened its doors in Big Valley, Alberta, in 2008. Exhibits such as this one make the unscientific claim that they provide 'considerable evidence that not only did dinosaurs exist recently, but that humans existed with them' (www.bvcsm.com/). How do you account for the recent establishment of galleries like this one and the Creation Museum in Petersburg, Kentucky (where 'Children play and dinosaurs roam near Eden's Rivers'—http://creationmuseum.org/), which use 'scientific evidence' to support the biblical account of creation?

of 'intelligent design' or 'scientific creationism' are mounting against the basic scientific tenet of evolution that the modernist vision of the new religion of science has not overcome the old religions of faith.

One of the ideas closely associated with conservatism is that of the **cycle of civilization**. This is the belief that civilizations rise and fall in a somewhat predictable cycle. It is an old idea, one that was articulated, for example, by Greek historian Polybius (*c.* 200–*c.* 118 BC) in explaining to his fellow Greeks how the Roman Empire came to have dominance over them while warning the Romans about the potential for their collapse. In his words:

> [T]he destruction of the human race, as tradition tells us, has more than once happened, and as we must believe will often happen again, all arts and crafts perishing at the same time, then in the course of time, when springing from the survivors as from seeds men have again increased in numbers. (Quoted in Nisbet 1969: 34)

Historian Oswald Spengler, in his pessimistically titled *The Decline of the West* (1918–22), took a similar view when he wrote that civilization was passing 'through the age-phases of the individual man. It has its childhood, youth, manhood, and old age' (quoted in Nisbet 1969: 8). Adherents of conservatism are sometimes guilty of the logical fallacy known as **slippery slope** reasoning. This occurs when they cite one instance of social change—say, for example, gay marriage—as evidence of the imminent collapse of the entire social order (including, to keep with this particular example, polygamy and bestiality). It amounts to an overreaction. As applied to the conservatism model, slippery slope reasoning consists of saying that if one small change I disapprove of (like gay marriage) is permitted to occur, then huge negative changes will necessarily follow (e.g. marriage to multiple partners, sex with animals).

Another pitfall of the conservative position is a tendency to project backwards an idealized picture of social life from which the modern world is said to have fallen. For instance, people who bemoan what they consider the rampant sexual promiscuity occurring today speak in idealized terms of a time when couples would not engage in sex before marriage. In holding this view, they would be rather misinformed, as British social historian Peter Laslett could attest. In *The World We Have Lost* (1971), he writes about how it was common in the late sixteenth century for couples to contract marriage (like our engagement) and then immediately live together for months, with full sexual benefits. In his conclusion to a discussion of the county of Leicester, Laslett observes that 'Brides in Leiceistershire at this time must normally have gone to their weddings in the early, and sometimes in the late, stages of pregnancy' (Laslett 1971: 150). He also points out that in Colyton, 46 per cent of first baptisms between 1538 and 1799 were recorded within the first eight months after the wedding ceremony of the parents (Laslett 1971: 148).

Sometimes modernism and conservatism combine in theories that view signs of decline as indications that progress is on the horizon. In Marx's thinking, the worse capitalism got, with the shrinking of the bourgeoisie and the growth of the proletariat to include a falling middle class, the more likely capitalism would altogether collapse, leading to the ultimate social change, the communist revolution. With a similar perspective, albeit from a very different position, conservative Americans who believe in a fundamentalist form of Christianity often look upon environmental, economic, political, and social (i.e. moral) decline in their country as a sign that the world is on the verge of the apocalypse, which will bring the second coming of Jesus. Think of the movies and TV shows that reflect that perspective. Kirkpatrick Sale (2005) cites a survey, commissioned by *Time* and CNN, that indicates 59 per cent of Americans polled believe the apocalypse is just around the corner.

Case Study in Social Change and Conservatism: The Luddites

From spring 1811 to spring 1813, beginning in the industrializing area of Nottinghamshire and spreading to Yorkshire and Manchester, a group of independent textile workers took desperate measures into their hands by destroying what would today amount to millions of dollars' worth of property. In the words of American writer Kirkpatrick Sale, author of the book from which much of the following description will come, they were 'rebels

The Point Is...

The Impending Collapse of the American Empire?

A good example of modern conservatist thinking appears in 'Imperial Entropy: Collapse of the American Empire' (2005), by Kirkpatrick Sale. Sale regards the United States as an empire, and therefore subject to what he believes is the inevitable fate of empires: collapse. He explains:

> [T]hey all fell, and most within a few hundred years. The reasons are not really complex. An empire is a kind of state system that inevitably makes the same mistakes simply by the nature of its imperial structure and inevitably fails because of its size, complexity, territorial reach, stratification, heterogeneity, domination, hierarchy, and inequalities. (Sale 2005)

Sale points to four things that will help to bring about the collapse of the American empire, like all empires in his thinking:

- environmental degradation,
- economic meltdown (through excessive resource exploitation),
- military overstretch, and
- domestic dissent and upheaval.

● ● ● ● ● ● ● ● ● ● ● ● ● ● ● ● ● ● ● ●

What do YOU think?

1. Do you think that the United States can be considered an empire like the Greek, Roman, Mongol, Ottoman, British, and Soviet regimes were?

2. Do you agree with Sale that the decline or collapse of the United States is inevitable?

● ● ● ● ● ● ● ● ● ● ● ● ● ● ● ● ● ● ● ●

against the future' (Sale 1996). Part of a larger movement occurring at the time in Britain, France, Germany, and the United States, they made night-time raids to destroy machinery, sent anonymous threatening letters to known industrialists, stockpiled weapons, and participated in food riots in the marketplace.

They were called **Luddites**, after a mythical, Robin Hood–like figure, Edward (Ned) Ludd, whose precise origin is not known. They were skilled tradesmen—croppers (finishers of wool cloth), wool combers (not as easy a job as it sounds), handloom wool weavers—who in the late eighteenth century worked out of their homes, often assisted by family members, and made good wages. They had leisure time probably similar to that of most Canadians today, and were part of strongly linked small communities.

But the work of the Luddites was becoming obsolete. While there were about 5,000 croppers in Yorkshire in 1812, within a generation there were virtually none. New kinds of machinery owned by the rising class of factory owners combined with new business practices were changing the working and social world. Even with the earliest generation of machines, one person could

do the work of five or six. It is important to note that contrary to the tradition surrounding the old-fashioned machine-hating Luddites, the social practices accompanying the machines were just as much the enemy. A typical workday in the new factories averaged 12 to 14 hours in length, sometimes as many as 16 to 18, and there was at this time no five-day work week. Children as young as four and women were hired in preference to men and made up a great majority of the workforce (80 per cent, according to Sale). Women and children received about a third of a man's wages, and were thought to be less likely than men to resist oppression by the owners.

Desperate poverty for millions of people was the not unpredictable result. Life expectancy dropped drastically. In the rough statistics for 1830, it was reckoned that 57 per cent of the people of Manchester died before the age of five. While the life expectancy at birth for people throughout England and Wales was a lofty 40, for labourers in the textile manufacturing cities of Manchester and Leeds, it was reckoned to be about 18 (Sale 1995: 48).

Working conditions were not the only social change the Luddites were rebelling against. They also opposed the manufacturing of need. One of the most profound social changes accompanying the Industrial Revolution and the manufacture of consumer goods was the sudden creation of a need where people had once been mostly self-sufficient. Food and clothing, for instance, now had to be purchased rather than produced at home. The social change this brought about was neatly summed up by nineteenth-century British writer Thomas Carlyle in *The Gospel of Mammonism* (1843), when he stated, 'We have profoundly forgotten everywhere that *Cash-payment* is not the sole relation of human beings' (quoted in Sale 1995: 39). This trend, described by French historian Fernand Braudel as 'a revolution in demand', extended from Britain to the colonies, particularly India, where millions of consumers were created by the dumping of manufactured cloth from Britain. It was not until the 1930s and 1940s, when Gandhi and the less lauded Muslim Pathan Badshah Khan (leader of the non-violent protest movement the Khudai Khidmatgar) intervened, that the people of India began to boycott British cloth and make their own, as had been their tradition.

A remarkable aspect of the Luddite social movement was its solidarity. Despite the rich rewards paid to those who would inform on their neighbours, despite the torture alleged to have been used on those who were caught, there were very few informers. In all, 24 Luddites were hanged, and about an equal number died in the raids; a similar number were put in prison, while at least 37 were sent to Australia.

What did they ultimately achieve? There were a few short-term gains for the Luddites. Wages were raised slightly in areas where the Luddites had been the most active. Social reform got on the political agenda, although it would be a long time before significant changes were made. And the 'poor laws', which administered what we might today call social welfare, received more attention and greater funding, although charities continued to carry the greater part of the welfare load.

Perhaps the main accomplishment of the Luddites lies in what they can teach us today about social change and what Sale calls the 'machine question'. We need to realize that machines are not socially neutral, and may be more likely to destroy than to create jobs. The Luddites were not backward-looking 'loonies' refusing to face the inevitability of

technological 'progress'. They wanted an alternative future, an alternative modern. That progress can take many forms is perhaps the most important lesson of the Luddite movement.

● ● ● ● ● ● ● ● ● ● ● ● ● ● ● ● ● ● ●

What do YOU think?

1. Why can it be said that technology is not neutral in terms of social change?

2. Why do you think the Luddites are usually cast merely as people who destroyed machines because they could neither face nor understand 'progress'?

3. What do you consider the most important message of the Luddite movement?

4. Do you think that assembly line workers in the automotive industry are in a position like that of the Luddites?

● ● ● ● ● ● ● ● ● ● ● ● ● ● ● ● ● ● ●

3. Postmodernism

Postmodernism as a theory relates largely to voice. It challenges the notion that, for example, researchers can speak for peoples that they study without letting the people studied have a voice, or speak, in some way. Postmodernism challenges the notion that anyone can, with any authority, talk of 'progress' or 'decline' across all society. Instead, a sociologist with a postmodernist perspective on social change might ask, 'Progress *for which group(s)?*' or 'Decline *for which group(s)?*'. The same sociologist, hearing conservatives complain about how Canadian values are eroding, might wonder if what they really mean is that *their* ethnic group with *its* set of values is no longer dominating like it once was.

Think of how modernist media usually present computers and computer-related products and services as bringing about benefits to everyone. But how often do you hear or read the opinions of those, even within Canada, who cannot afford a (decent) computer or the education necessary to make use of one? This is creating what has been called a **digital divide**, a socio-economic gap separating those nations and groups within nations that are 'haves' from those that are 'have nots' where up-to-date computer technology and reliable Internet access are concerned. One person known for thinking this is way is futurist Arthur Kroker.

Students in Lagos, Nigeria, learn computer skills on a older-model Pentium III computer. Given the pace of technological advances, which can make a 10-year-old piece of hardware almost obsolete, is an old computer better than no computer?

Photo: Peter Essick/Aurora Photos/GetStock

Arthur Kroker and the Virtual Class

Arthur Kroker, of the University of Victoria's political science department, is a Canadian 'futurist' who advanced the notion of the **virtual class** in the mid-1990s to articulate his conservativist position. His innovative writing combines Marxist views on class with a lot of postmodernist wordplay (which can make him hard to read). His work is difficult to summarize in an introductory textbook because it depends on a great deal of jargon that would need to be explained in order for any summary to be intelligible. However, we can give you a taste of what Kroker has to say.

The virtual class, according to Kroker, is a class of visionary capitalists, or as he calls them,

> visionless-cynical-business capitalists, and the perhaps visionary, perhaps skill-oriented, perhaps indifferent techno-intelligentsia of cognitive scientists, engineers, computer scientists, video-game developers, and all the other communication specialists, ranged in

hierarchies, but all dependent for their economic support on the drive to virtualization. (Kroker and Weinstein 1995: 15–16)

We will briefly outline three ways in which this diverse group acts like a class. First, says Kroker, this class is responsible for the loss of jobs by those who do not belong to the class. This group supports the goals of **neoliberalism** that promote the interests of big business. This is how Kroker accounts for the corporate downsizing that became a widespread cost-saving strategy among North America businesses during the early 1990s:

> Against economic justice, the virtual class practices a mixture of predatory capitalism and gung-ho technical rationalizations for laying waste to social concerns for employment, with insistent demands for 'restructuring economies', 'public policies of labor adjustment', and 'deficit cutting', all aimed at maximal profitability. (Kroker and Weinstein 1995: 5)

Another example of the virtual class's move for power has to do with its role in the way the Internet, once democratic and freely accessible, became restricted by the authoritarian 'digital superhighway' ever more controlled by what Kroker calls 'privileged corporate codes'. To use an example familiar to the authors of this textbook, online access to sociological journals is being more and more limited to those who possess expensive memberships or those who are affiliated with universities and not community colleges.

The third defining characteristic of the virtual class is the way this group, according to Kroker, restricts the freedom of creativity, promoting instead 'the value of pattern-maintenance (of its own choosing)' (Kroker and Weinstein 1995: 5). Have you ever noticed how computer-generated monsters, ghosts, and aliens all look remarkably alike? How often have you seen black smoke issuing from people possessed by demons? This is an example of 'pattern maintenance': the tools of the trade are controlled by but a few companies. Compare that with the situation faced by the Luddites.

● ● ● ● ● ● ● ● ● ● ● ● ● ● ● ● ● ● ● ●
What do YOU think?

1. How does Kroker portray the virtual class as a class in the Marxist sense?

2. Do you think that Kroker leans a little too far towards conspiracy theory in his view?

● ● ● ● ● ● ● ● ● ● ● ● ● ● ● ● ● ● ● ●

4. Evolution

Evolution is perhaps the most misused of all scientific concepts. The biological term does not refer to general progress or improvement of a species. What it really means is adapting well to particular circumstances. Darwin's use of Spencer's phrase 'survival of the fittest' is best interpreted as 'survival of the *best fit*'—in other words, the one best suited to the environment. It was not about the biggest, the meanest, the fastest, and so on.

Jonathan Weiner, in *The Beak of the Finch: A Story of Evolution in Our Time* (1995), provides an example of evolution when he explains that guppies swimming in the rivers of Venezuela come in two basic colour patterns. High in the hills, where

the rivers are little more than streams, the guppies are brightly coloured. They compete in terms of sexual selection, with the most colourful having the greatest chance of attracting a mate. The bright colours are the result of the competition. In the waters down in the valleys, the guppies swim where predators feed upon those guppies that are easily seen. Not surprisingly, the guppies there are less brightly coloured. The competition has less to do with attracting a mate, more to do with not being seen. Neither colour pattern is a general improvement in the species. Each is a better fit in the local environment.

How does this apply to social change? We can look at the history of the family structure in Canada as an example. At different times, the number of children born to parents has varied. In times and places where agriculture is the primary source of income, the number of children is relatively high, since children make good unpaid help to work the land. During the 1950s and early 1960s, the number of children went up, going against the trend of previous decades, because it was a time of prosperity. People could afford to have more children. The 'ideal' number of children changes with the circumstances—just like the colours of the Venezuelan guppies.

5. Fashion

Sometimes a change is just a change—change solely for the sake of change. We seek and discover novelty, and the result is neither an improvement nor a turn for the worse. And it does not reflect some deeper meaning, or a value shift. In this case, we have the **fashion** model of change. In *A Matter of Taste: How Names, Fashions and Cultures Change* (2000), Montreal-born, American-raised sociologist Stanley Lieberson argues that the change in North American baby names falls into the category of fashion. Consumer companies likewise profit from this desire for the new, and it's not just clothing companies, either. Tweaking an automotive design, or the 'look' of a team uniform, or the advertised attributes of a popular brand of beer can help a company make money on people's desire for the new.

Education involves fashion changes as well. Buzzwords like 'whole language', 'collaborative

In 1978 the NHL's Vancouver Canucks replaced their conservative blue-and-green sweaters with a new colour scheme meant to look more aggressive and intimidating. The unconventional and widely derided fashion was scrapped in the mid-1980s. After a series of new designs, the team has returned to its 'vintage' jersey, sporting the same logo and colour scheme as the sweaters the team wore in its inaugural season (1970–1). Once considered plain and simplistic, the 'new look' is popular among fans as well as consumers. How do you think sports merchandisers play to the fan's desire for fashion change?

learning', and 'advanced learning' are used to promote new styles in education, but they merely reflect people's need to feel they have a fresh approach to an ages-old problem. Education fashions come and go, but real improvement or decline is hard to measure. The culture around education changes and has an impact on the scores that quantify educational 'excellence'. Declining marks in North American literacy tests may reflect educational changes, but they might also reflect an increase in students whose first language is not English, and a decrease in reading as a leisure activity. Increase in literacy may reflect being part of the 'Harry Potter cohort'.

The narrative in the box on page 395 is a look at a social change that separates generations. When you read it, we want you to consider whether this follows a fashion model or has deeper sociological meaning.

Technology and Social Neutrality

As we can see from the situation of the Luddites, and from the ideas of George Grant and Arthur Kroker, it would be misleading to assume that technology is socially neutral. A change in technology always benefits some, and places others at a disadvantage. The beneficiaries can act like social predators, and the ones who lose out can become social prey. Imagine, for example, that you have been running printing presses for a major newspaper for 30 years and have developed an expertise with your machinery that is highly valued and (hopefully) well rewarded. One day your newspaper changes over to computer-run presses, contracting a new company to do that work. Suddenly all of your expertise, knowledge, and

Telling It Like It Is

AN AUTHOR POV

The F-Word and Social Change

POINT OF VIEW

I don't remember the first time I heard the 'f-word' used, but I do recall that in the suburban, middle-class junior high school that I attended in the early 1960s, there was one real tough guy, feared by everyone, who seemed to use it in every sentence he spoke. He was eventually expelled for hitting a teacher.

The first movie I heard the f-word uttered in was the 1970 film *Joe*. It was carefully and deliberately used for shock effect by Peter Boyle's character, a working-class guy who stuns his polite upper-middle-class companions by shouting 'F&%$ing right!'.

The one and only time I heard the word spoken in a university classroom was when a very well-spoken classmate of mine used it (with implied quotation marks around it) after the word 'mind', to refer to someone trying to psyche someone out. Her male classmates were dumbstruck.

As far as I can remember, the mores, or customs, surrounding the use of the word as I was growing up in my middle-class neighbourhood were these: I could, as a teenaged boy, use the word (but not too frequently) with my buddies, but never with my parents or teachers (no matter how tempted I was on occasion to tell them all to 'f—' off). I would not use the word in front of a girl or woman, ever. Generally, use of the f-word in front of a woman was considered a vile offence committed by a man too drunk, too stoned, or too angry to realize what he was doing. Use of the word by a woman would normally illicit shock and disgust.

That was a different time. Now, and in the Toronto college where I teach, use of the word seems to depend on social location. It was in the general concourse that I first started hearing the word regularly, between 10 and 15 years ago, and it is where I still hear it used most often. True it is on the premises of the college, but it isn't really a site of education; it is more of a public place. Recently I've begun to hear the f-word in the halls between classrooms. Five years ago I heard the word spoken for the first time in my classroom. It wasn't spoken in anger, but it was

Photo: Digital Vision

used for effect by someone with a reputation for brash attention-seeking behaviour.

Over the past five years, I've found that the f-word is relatively commonplace in the concourse and still not infrequent in the halls, used with no apparent concern that 'the teacher walking past might hear'. I have heard it in the classroom in general conversation during breaks, and used about as often by women as by men.

—J.S.

What do YOU think?

1. How have the rules, or mores, surrounding use of the f-word changed, according to the writer of the narrative?

2. What would it take for these mores to change back? Could they change back?

3. Could this kind of language use be considered a verbal 'fashion statement'?

seniority mean nothing. Either you are replaced by someone younger who is paid less, or else you accept a lower salary to start over.

Agricultural technology is biased against small farmers. The technology needs of the modern farm (some of which are mandated by governments with a poor sense of the technological bias) put small farm owners out of business. Education technology could pose a similar threat to college and university instructors. It fosters a class system among instructors, with full-time, tenured professors providing the technological 'show' for large numbers of students, and graduate students and part-time faculty earning less to do the 'dirty work' of marking the massive number of papers generated.

Relative Deprivation, Absolute Deprivation, and Movements for Social Change

Situations like the ones just described tend to create in one group—the disadvantaged group—a feeling of **relative deprivation**, a sense of having less or enjoying fewer benefits than another group. Relative deprivation refers to negative feelings experienced when individuals compare themselves with others. They lack something others have, and that lack is meaningful to them, as the ones they are comparing themselves with are significant others seen as equals or betters; they constitute a significant **reference group.**

As Marshall (1998: 152) explains, the depth of a person's sense of relative deprivation will always depend on the particular reference group to which it compares itself. If the reference group is seen as comparatively quite well off, the person experiencing relative deprivation may be moved to protest. This is what happened with the Luddites, who watched the rising class of factory owners thrive under conditions that greatly threatened their own livelihoods.

The concept of relative deprivation is useful in looking at people's experience of poverty. As we saw in Chapter 2, on sociological research methods, poverty is difficult to define, in part because many sociologists believe that the subjective experience of 'feeling poor' should be considered a factor. If you are a teenager living in a relatively well-to-do bedroom community on the outskirts of a big city, it is easy for you to feel poor if your parents' income is less than that of many others in your town. Your reference group includes your peers in high school who have greater access to desired goods (for instance snowboarding equipment and associated branded clothing). With these peers as your reference group, you may well feel relatively deprived, and therefore 'poor'.

Social Change in China during the 1980s and 1990s

A good application of the theory of relative deprivation is social change in China during the 1980s and 1990s. As Joshua Harman (1998) explains, rapid social change led to Chinese workers' awareness of a new reference group, the existence of which sparked feelings of relative deprivation that eventually led to the 1989 Tiananmen Square protests:

> In order to understand how and why Chinese workers reached a state of relative deprivation, one must first examine Deng Xiaoping's rise to political preeminence. Deng's rise brought with it the promise of a better material life for the general population as well as the potential for economic discord. Both of these aspects of the reform movement were recognized during the 1980s and the 1990s, and both are primary reasons for the Chinese workers' relative deprivation and political unrest.
>
> Deng's reform coalition used a three-pronged approach to shore up its claim to legitimacy. First, it actively sought to increase the people's awareness of their own relative backwardness. Second, the coalition raised demand for new consumer goods and services. Finally, as it sought to raise consumer demand, it also promised to deliver these goods to the people. (Harman 1998)

Before the 1980s, there were few televisions and few foreign shows available in China. Most programming featured documentaries about the

A Beijing man parks his bike in front of a billboard advertising televisions and washing machines in 1983. What message is the ad trying to convey to China's new consumer class? Why is the image of the iconic Great Wall used?

Photo: Kelly-Mooney Photography/Corbis

country's supposed economic progress. In 1979, the Chinese government loosened cultural restrictions on programming, and American and British television programs were suddenly let loose on the Chinese airwaves. By 1991, 12 per cent of total air time and more than 25 per cent of air time for entertainment (rather than news) was taken up by foreign shows. At the same time and at about the same pace, television ownership in China was growing. In 1979, there was 1 television set for every 240 people in the cities, and only 1 per 1,000 in rural areas. By 1988, 1 in every 2.6 city dwellers and 1 in every 15.2 rural citizens owned a TV. A new, foreign reference group had been created, with print media helping to promote this new reference group through increased advertising for Western consumer goods.

As workers' pay increased, there was a drastic increase in consumer spending on relatively 'big ticket' items (see Table 14.1). But the late 1980s brought layoffs and growing job insecurity. The

Table 14.1 Urban household possession of durable consumer goods (per 100 households)

	1981	1989
refrigerators	0.2	36.5
washing machines	6.3	76.2
electric fans	42.6	128.7
tape recorders	13.0	67.1
cameras	4.3	17.3
bicycles	135.9	184.7
watches	240.9	290.1
sofas	89.3	150.0
wardrobes	86.1	100.0

Source: Harman 1998.

cost of living went up. On 20 April 1989, the Beijing Workers' Autonomous Union declared:

> The entire population of China now faces an intolerable situation. Long accustomed to bureaucratic–dictatorial forms of control, they now live with uncontrolled inflation and declining living standards. . . . We earnestly demand the following: a wage increase, price stabilization, and a publication of the incomes and possessions of government officials and their families.

In the spring of 1989, crowds of protesters gathered in Tiananmen Square, many of them college and university students and urban workers. The protest ended with a military show of force: it's possible that as many as 2,600 protesters were shot and killed. Despite the clampdown on worker protest, strikes and slowdowns occurred in previously unheard-of numbers throughout the early 1990s. Significant numbers of Chinese citizens now had reference groups that made them feel relatively deprived: their wealthier fellow citizens, themselves in earlier times, and the supposedly typical Westerners they watched on imported TV sitcoms.

What do YOU think?

The Chinese government restricts the websites its country's users have access to. This effectively limits the exposure of Chinese citizens to other reference groups. What effect do you think this might have on the people of China? Can you compare the situation to that of pre-1980s China, when foreign television programs weren't available?

Weaknesses in the Relative Deprivation Theory

One weakness in the theory of relative deprivation lies in the issue of how to distinguish, in practice, between *absolute* deprivation (however that is established) and *relative* deprivation. Take the earlier example of the teenager in the bedroom community. Say the teenager's only computer access is to an outmoded PC with low-speed Internet connections giving slow, intermittent access to the Web. Having an up-to-date computer and reliable Internet access is important, even essential, for achieving success in high school. Achieving good marks in high school might, in turn, determine whether or not she goes to college or university. Who is then to determine whether the teenager merely *feels* poor because the other kids have better computers or genuinely *is* poor because access to goods and services that enhance educational opportunities is part of determining class status in Canada?

Perhaps a more serious problem with the theory is that it can be used to conduct relatively superficial 'sociology-of-the-moment' that focuses on what is happening now without examining a current situation's roots in the past. In this sense, relative deprivation can trivialize both historical and contemporary grievances. Take the example of the 1990 Oka crisis, discussed in Chapter 6. The conflict surrounded a land rights issue that stretched back to the early 1700s. Causes included nearly 200 years of colonial oppression of the Oka Mohawk by federal and provincial policing agencies, as well as several decades of failing to recognize local Aboriginal political and policing agencies in several communities. To examine the Mohawk protest only through the lens of relative deprivation, as some recent sociology textbooks have done (see Steckley 2003), is to treat the matter in an overly simplistic way.

Understanding Social Change Through Cultural Norms and Statistical Norms

Oftentimes there are differences in a culture between **cultural norms**, which are the generally expected and *stated* rules of behaviour, and **statistical norms**, which reflect what people actually do. The latter are quantifiable and can therefore be measured by sociologists. In a way this discrepancy reproduces the distinction, noted in Chapter 3, between ideal and real culture. While a cultural norm may show little difference from its corresponding statistical norm, in many cases there are discrepancies. And as we will see from the following example, these discrepancies can sometimes be useful, as a group's discovery of a significant gap between expectation and action might spark social change in the cultural norm.

The Dobe !Kung: Differences in Cultural and Statistical Norms

The Dobe !Kung are a hunting society of the Kalahari Desert in southwestern Africa. As documented by anthropologist Lorna Marshall and corroborated with archaeological evidence from the 1940s found by John Yellen, the Dobe !Kung had observed a cultural norm of sharing their collective resources. But in the 1960s, with the coming of a money economy to the people, especially to those working for their agriculturalist or farming neighbours, came an increase in the production and supply of consumer goods. There was also a growing distance between houses (many enclosed in fences), and accompanying this came a gradual increase in hoarding. But even amid the locked metal trunks crammed full of unshared possessions, the Dobe !Kung continued to claim sharing as a cultural norm: 'Bushmen share things,' John Yellen was told. 'We share things and depend on each other, help each other out. That's what makes us different from the black people [i.e. their Bantu-speaking agriculturist neighbours]' (Yellen 1985; quoted in Hanna and Cockerton 1990: 74).

This kind of contradiction can be readily found in most cultures. Canadians raised in neighbourhoods with a reputation for a strong sense of community will often speak fondly of the importance of being close to their neighbours, though they controvert these statements when responding to simple questions such as *How many of your neighbours' homes have you been inside?*, *How many of your neighbours have you had inside your home?*, *How many of your neighbours do you know the phone numbers of?*, and *'Have you ever left your neighbours' phone numbers with your children when you are away from home for a long period of time?* It's not that people are hypocrites. It is just that change takes place, driven by a number of factors that are beyond the immediate control of individuals (such as the fast turnover of homes when house prices are high and mortgage rates are low), and it affects behaviour before it does stated values.

Social Changes in Canada: Two Case Studies

Canadians have been and are experiencing social change in many forms. We touched in earlier chapters on the tremendous changes that occurred in the province of Quebec beginning in the 1960s with the Quiet Revolution, but other large-scale changes have been taking place across Canada. Farmers, especially those on the prairies, are finding that the family farm (as opposed to the corporate 'factory farm') is becoming very difficult to maintain. Cattle producers, who have been particularly hard hit, are still recovering from recent bans on exports to the US because of concerns about the spread of mad-cow disease. At the same time, Alberta has been enjoying booming conditions because of the success of the oil industry. Immigration to the province is up significantly. According to Statistics Canada's bulletin *The Daily*, issued on 23 June 2009, Alberta's 0.59 per cent rise in population during the first quarter of 2009 (January to the end of March) exceeded that of all other provinces, and more than doubled Canada's overall increase of 0.26 per cent.

The following sections examine two striking, and very different, examples of recent social change in Canada.

Fisheries Change on the Northern Peninsula of Newfoundland

One of the most devastating social changes to hit any part of Canada in recent decades is the loss of the longstanding cod fishery in Newfoundland and Labrador. A recent article by sociologists Lawrence Hamilton and Cynthia Duncan and biologist Richard Haedrich describes the ways that change has affected communities along the province's Northern Peninsula (2004).

The most fisheries-dependent part of the province, the Northern Peninsula was hardest hit by the closure of the cod fishery, which had sustained the region for centuries. The first signs of trouble appeared in the 1970s, when it became apparent that cod stocks were diminishing, owing largely to overfishing by foreign (mostly Russian and Portuguese) vessels and mismanagement of the resource.

When, in 1976, the 200-mile economic exclusion zone was declared, reserving waters within 200 nautical miles of the shore for Canadian fishers, many in Newfoundland and Labrador thought that the troubles were over. People who had left the province returned, and the fishing population grew.

Sociologically and technologically, there were two different cod fisheries in Newfoundland: the dragger, or long-liner, fishery and the in-shore fishery. The first involved larger boats, more technology, and longer trips. Traditionally, both profited from the rich fishery, and the fishing community overall was very egalitarian. And in the 'glory years' following the establishment of the 200-mile line, the dragger fleet increased, as did the catch, which reached unprecedented levels. Dragger captains made huge profits, some as much as $350,000–600,000 a year, and even sharemen (often the teenaged sons of dragger boat owners) could earn $50,000 a year. But the in-shore fishery was suffering. In the words of one interviewed fisher, 'Guys were makin' big bucks and the other guys were just survivin'. Just livin' from day to day, where the other guys were drivin' fancy skidoos and two vehicles' (quoted in Hamilton et al. 2004). The community was more financially divided than ever before.

Eventually, the cod fishery crashed, after a decade-and-a-half of harvesting groundfish, including cod, beyond their sustainable limits. In 1992, the federal government declared a two-year moratorium on the fishery from the Labrador coast to the southeastern tip of Newfoundland, temporarily suspending cod fishing in this part of the province; the following year the closure area was expanded to include the southern shore of the island. Although it was supposed to be in effect for just two years, the moratorium has yet to be lifted.

It was not just fishers and their families who were hit by the moratorium but others along the chain of the fishing industry. At a local fish-processing plant on the Northern Peninsula, 400 workers were laid off. Different adaptations were made by the people in the area. For instance, the birth rate went down, from one of the highest in Canada to just slightly above the national average. Some of the dragger captains were well placed to shift their prey species from fish to invertebrates, such as snow crab, northern shrimp, and the more

traditional lobster. Fortunately for them, government money was available to make the transition easier. This new fishery brought revenues comparable to those of the glory days of the cod fishery, but these were distributed across a much smaller segment of the local population. Many, forced out of their livelihood, had to leave the province to look for a new line of work. Others who remained could not afford to become involved in the new fishery, yet refused to move off the island because they didn't feel they could leave their home. A growing percentage of the local income came from government transfer payments in the form of employment insurance and welfare.

● ● ● ● ● ● ● ● ● ● ● ● ● ● ● ● ● ● ● ●

What do YOU think?

1. What adaptations did the people of Newfoundland and Labrador make with the loss of the cod fishery?

2. Do you think that the changes that took place were inevitable?

● ● ● ● ● ● ● ● ● ● ● ● ● ● ● ● ● ● ● ●

Religious Change: Islam as a Canadian Religion

According to statistics from 2001 (the last year for which we have precise data), Islam is the fastest-growing organized religion in Canada. The number of Canadian Muslims rose by 128.9 per cent from 1991 to 2001, more than twice the increase for the period 1981 to 1991. In 2001 the Muslim population of 579,640 made up 2 per cent of the total Canadian population. Most of that population (352,525) was concentrated in Ontario, where over the same 10-year period it had grown by 142.2 per cent. Islam was the sixth largest religion in the country, just a little behind the Baptist and Lutheran churches, and way behind the 'big three'—the Catholic Church, the United Church, and the Anglican Church. But in contrast to these, Islam was the religion with the youngest median age: its followers averaged just 28.1 years. Muslims come from a broad variety of ethnic backgrounds and countries, including Iran, Iraq, Pakistan, India, Afghanistan, Turkey, Somalia, Bosnia, and Indonesia.

Rukhsana Khan reads from her book *Coming to Canada* to students at a public school in Markham, Ontario, north of Toronto. What do you think it would take for Canada to be considered, at least in part, a 'Muslim country'?

Photo: Toronto Star/GetStock.com

While there isn't what could be called a 'Muslim tradition' in Canada, the faith is not entirely new to the country. In 1871, according to that year's census, there were 13 Muslims living in Canada. The first mosque in Canada—in all of North America, in fact—was Al Rashid, built in Edmonton in 1938, funded by local Muslims, Arab Christians, and Jews.

● ● ● ● ● ● ● ● ● ● ● ● ● ● ● ● ● ●

What do YOU think?

1. Do you think that the variety of ethnic backgrounds among Muslims will lead to the development of 'Canadianized' multicultural mosques?

2. Canadian introductory sociology textbooks often present Muslims, even those living in Canada, as 'them', an other. What are the effects on non-Muslim students of reading this treatment of Muslims?

● ● ● ● ● ● ● ● ● ● ● ● ● ● ● ● ● ●

Social Change and Sociology in Canada

Like all academic disciplines, sociology must change, and it must do so in a way that involves all five of the models of change discussed above. It needs to improve, to get better, in a modernist sense. Perhaps some of this improvement will come in the way sociology is presented to students of the discipline, just as we've tried to fashion something a little different with this textbook. But sociology also needs a touch of conservatism not to stray too far from the early vision that gave it perception; otherwise, it will diminish. It must constantly have postmodern eyes, using fly-like, multi-dimensional perception to look at who has benefited and who hasn't from sociology as it has been traditionally practised and written about. And it must adapt, evolve.

Telling It Like It Is

AN EXPERT POV

Irshad Manji on the Gender Challenge for Canadian Muslim Women

POINT OF VIEW

Recently the Government of Ontario considered allowing sharia, or Islamic, law to be applied in family law cases involving Muslims. It was strongly opposed by most Muslim women as well as by more liberal Muslim groups. The Canadianization of Islam poses a considerable gender challenge, as the Muslim writer of the excerpt below, Irshad Manji, explains. Born in Uganda in 1972, Manji and her family emigrated to Canada when she was four, during the expulsion of Uganda's South Asian population under Idi Amin. As an activist and a lesbian, Manji has faced considerable opposition from within her Muslim community. In her provocative book *The Trouble with Islam: A Wake-Up Call for Honesty and Change* (2003)—a Canadian bestseller—Manji describes how she discovered, at the madressa (the Muslim school she attended on weekends), that the separation and inequality of the genders found in strict Muslim countries were being reproduced in Canada. That this situation was not being challenged but obeyed without question conflicted with what she was learning about the importance of individuality and equality she was taught in the regular school system. In the following passage she describes the conflict that led her to leaving the madressa:

> The trouble began with *Know Your Islam*, the primer that I packed in my madressa bag every week. After reading it, I needed to know more about 'my' Islam. Why must girls observe the essentials, such as praying five times a day, at an earlier age than boys? Because, Mr Khaki [her nickname for her teacher] told me, girls mature sooner. They reach the 'obligatory age' of practice at nine compared to thirteen for boys.
>
> 'Then why not reward girls for our maturity by letting us lead prayer?' I asked.
> 'Girls can't lead prayer.'
> 'What do you mean?'
> 'Girls aren't permitted.'
> 'Why not?'
> 'Allah says so.'
> 'What's His reason.'
> 'Read the Koran.' (Manji 2003: 13–4)

She did not find an answer there that satisfied her Western-trained (and somewhat Western-biased) mind. Still, she remains a Muslim, and later in the book, she makes the following statement:

> Had I grown up in a Muslim country, I'd probably be an atheist in my heart. It's because I live in this corner of the world, where I can think, dispute, and delve further into any topic, that I've learned why I shouldn't give up on Islam just yet. (Manji 2003: 228)

Concerning that last point, sociology in Canada, and probably elsewhere, is facing some serious challenges. One indication of this was noted by Robert J. Brym in 2003. In an article in *The Canadian Journal of Sociology*, he remarked on the fact that while the Canadian Sociology and Anthropology Association (CSAA) is the official organization of Anglo-Canadian sociology, it has been losing members, even while the number of faculty members in sociology and anthropology has been growing. Membership peaked at 1,165 in 1993 and within 10 years had dropped by 39 per cent. Brym has his explanations for this phenomenon, including (1) external competition from American sociological organizations, (2) internal competition from the *Canadian Journal of Sociology*, (3) a changing organizational environment, and (4) unprofessionalism. On the second-to-last point he notes reform movements that are 'left-leaning' and 'feminist'. Those he names might argue that they left or never even joined because the organization had become an old boys' club that failed to represent their interests.

Whichever way you interpret it, Canadian sociology needs to change. What follows is a personal narrative that suggests one aspect of that change.

Concluding Narrative: Where Does Sociology Go from Here?

We have had narratives throughout this textbook, so it is only fitting that the book should end with a narrative. At the end of my doctoral dissertation on how Canadian introductory sociology textbooks present information about Aboriginal people, I argued that in order for textbook writers to present the information in a way that is worthy of the best aims and works of the discipline, they must engage in what can be called 'Aboriginal sociology'. We could generalize this approach to a broader category of 'minorities sociology', but here I will speak in terms of the minority I know best.

This Aboriginal sociology, as I envisioned it, must begin by recognizing the inadequacy of traditional methods of sociological knowledge production concerning Aboriginal people. The voices of the people need to be heard. I warned that if the writers of these textbooks continue to ignore Aboriginal voice in their knowledge production, they will continue to be complicit in the colonialist practices of governments. They are not being neutral, objective, or distanced. They are taking a side.

Equally important is the related recognition that the non-Aboriginal cultural background of the writers of introductory sociology textbooks permits them but a limited perspective, one that, as Dorothy Smith (1990) informs us, will miss core concepts that are intrinsically important to understanding Aboriginal people from an Aboriginal standpoint. The important place of elders in Aboriginal society is one of these core concepts. Elders are involved in all the social institutions of Aboriginal life—education, justice, religion, and politics, for example—and anyone in any way involved in Aboriginal society is aware of their significance. But people coming from other cultures that diminish the role of the elderly could easily miss this important point. Indeed, they have missed it. Spirituality is another such core concept, one that tends to be erased in sociology textbooks. The reserve is a

Photo: © Sonny Assu; photo by Guy Letts

'Enjoy Colonialism' is a Coast Salish parody displayed at the UBC Museum of Anthropology in Vancouver. What is the artist trying to communicate with this piece of work?

spiritual centre, often (one can probably say usually) the location of a number of sacred sites of significance, and yet in sociology textbooks it is only a site for sorry statistics and horror stories.

More generally, the development of an Aboriginal sociology entails the recognition that non-sociologists have authority in talking about Aboriginal life. There are very few Aboriginal sociologists, something that the discipline should note and rectify. For the Aboriginal standpoint to be represented, the knowledge production of Aboriginal journalists, educators, filmmakers, elders, and literary writers should be sought out and respected. All of them have voices that are valued in Aboriginal society. That alone should guarantee their inclusion in introductory sociology textbooks.

In my first year of university, sociology opened my eyes to a world of understanding that changed my perception forever. Every semester I teach introductory sociology, I tell my students that my goal in teaching the course is to change how they think. I quote, with pride, a former sociology student of mine, a Brazilian nun, who said that my course had 'ruined her' by forcing (enabling?) her to question her previous perception of society. I am a believer in the discipline. But I strongly believe that it needs to change its textual presentation of Aboriginal people, and its presentation of other groups that do not belong to the dominant culture in ways as radical as how the discipline itself altered my viewpoint. It requires more voices to thrive in Canada in the twenty-first century.

Questions for Critical Review

1. Compare and contrast the five different models of social change presented in this chapter.
2. Outline the features of the cycle of civilization, and discuss the degree to which it might apply to the United States.
3. Explain who the Luddites were, and outline the social changes to which they were reacting.
4. Outline Arthur Kroker's idea of the virtual class.
5. Distinguish between cultural and statistical norms.

Suggested Readings

Alinsky, Saul D. (1971). *Rules for Radicals: A Pragmatic Primer for Realistic Radicals*. New York: Vintage Books.

Freire, Paulo (1970). *Pedagogy of the Oppressed*. M.B. Ramos, trans. New York: Continuum.

Grant, George. *Lament for a Nation*. Montreal: McGill/Queen's University Press, 2005.

Lummis, C. Douglas (1996). *Radical Democracy*. Ithaca: Cornell UP.

Merchant, Carolyn ed. (1994). *Ecology*. New Jersey: Humanities Press.

Schumacher, E.F. (1973). *Small Is Beautiful: Economics As If People Mattered*. New York: Harper/Perennial.

Suggested Websites

Citizenshift (Free Range Media for Social Change)
http://citizen.nfb.ca/onf/info

Greenpeace International
www.greenpeace.org

Institute for Anarchist Studies
www.anarchist-studies.org/

Glossary

Aboriginal visions meaningful inspirations, often experienced during a **vision quest** or dream. The individual may hear a song or chant in his or her head, see an animal that might take on a role as spiritual guardian, or in some other way perceive something that enables the individual to better understand his or her life and future.

absolute poverty poverty calculated in absolute material terms. To exist in absolute poverty is to be without sufficient nutritious food, clean and safe shelter, access to education, etc. *Compare* **relative poverty**.

absolutist holding or having to do with the view that certain things are always right, good, moral, modern, or beautiful. Ethnocentrism is a negative example of an absolutist position.

age group a group composed of people of a particular age (e.g. teenagers, 'tweens', twentysomethings), studied over time.

agency the capacity to influence what happens in one's life. *Compare* **victimology**.

agent a person who does take or is capable of taking an active role in the events and circumstances that shape her or his life.

agents of socialization the groups that have a significant influence on a person's socialization. Examples include family, **peer group**, community, school, mass media, the legal system, and culture generally.

American Dream the mostly unrealistic belief that one can become rich and successful through hard work and determination. A naïve belief in the American Dream is sometimes used to justify punishing others for being poor.

anomie (as described by Durkheim) a societal state of breakdown or confusion, or a more personal one based on an individual's lack of connection or contact with society.

anti-colonialism (as described by Fanon and Memmi) a theoretical framework used to analyze the destructive impact colonialism has on both the colonizer and the colonized. *Also called* **post-colonialism**.

archaeology of knowledge (as described by Foucault) the process of 'digging down' to find out how a piece of information was constructed, typically in order to discover or expose flaws in the way supposed facts or truths were established.

Arctic hysteria a **cultural syndrome** that was conjured up by white colonizers of the Arctic to explain behaviour that might better be explained as a product of colonialism. *Also called* **pibloktuq**.

aristocrats (in Marxist theory) the landowner class of feudal times, who owned the land worked on by the peasants.

assimilation the process in which minorities, indigenous peoples, and immigrants lose their distinctive cultural characteristics to become like members of the dominant culture.

authenticity the quality of being true to the traditions of a people. Authenticity is often **contested** by the modern representatives of the people themselves and 'experts' from outside the community.

barbarism (as described by L.H. Morgan in the nineteenth century) the second stage of social evolution on the way to modern civilization. It was identified as one of a series of stages all societies were thought to pass through in their natural development. *Compare* **civilization**, **savagery**.

bar mitzvah (in the Jewish tradition) a **rite of passage** for a boy becoming a man.

bat mitzvah (in the Jewish tradition) a **rite of passage** for a girl becoming a woman.

behaviourism a school of thought in psychology, which emphasizes that behaviour can be studied and explained scientifically, not in terms of internal mental states (unlike **psychoanalysis**) but through observing how people's actions are supposedly conditioned by earlier actions and reactions.

best practices strategies with a proven history of achieving desired results more effectively or consistently than similar methods used in the past by a particular organization or currently by other organizations in the same industry.

biomedicine the application of standard principles and practices of Western scientific disciplines (particularly biology) in the diagnosis and treatment of symptoms of illness.

blaming the victim (as described by W. Ryan) the process of assigning individuals responsibility for harmful events or circumstances that have broader social causes.

bodily stigma *see* **stigma**.

bopi (in Mbuti culture) a playground that is almost exclusively the territory of children.

bourgeoisie *see* **capitalists**.

brain drain the exodus of scientists, doctors, and other skilled professionals from a country.

broad socialization socialization in which individualism and independence are promoted. *Compare* **narrow socialization**.

capital (as described by Marx) the funds and properties necessary for the large-scale manufacture and trade of goods.

capitalists (as described by Marx) the owners of the means of production (or 'capital', as these were known during the industrial era). *Also called* **bourgeoisie**.

case study approach a research design that explores a social entity or phenomenon by examining a single representative case or a few selected examples.

caste each of the hereditary classes of Hindu society, distinguished by relative degrees of ritual purity and social status. Members of different castes are traditionally born into the unequal possession of specific occupations, dharma (duty in life), rights to foods, colours in clothing, religious practices, and imputed personal qualities. *Also called* **varnas**.

catharsis   emotional relief through the release of built-up energy or tension.

civilization   (as described by L.H. Morgan in the nineteenth century) the third and final stage of social evolution of all societies, viewed by European and North American thinkers as best exemplified by European and North American culture. *Compare* **barbarism**, **savagery**.

class   (as described by Marx) a socioeconomic group defined either relationally—that is, in Marxist terms, with respect to their relationship to the **means of production** (e.g. owner, worker)—or absolutely, in terms of access to socially valued goods such as money, education, and respect (e.g. lower class, middle class, upper class).

class consciousness   (as described by Marx) awareness of what is in the best interests of one's class.

class reductionism   the intellectual fallacy that all forms of oppression are just about class, a view that wrongly downplays the role of factors such as race, ethnicity, gender, and age.

clinical iatrogenesis   (as described by Illich) the ways in which diagnosis and cure cause problems that are equal to or greater than the health problems they are meant to resolve. An example would be catching a virus while in hospital for minor surgery.

cluttered nest   a situation in which adult children continue to live at home with their parents. *Compare* **empty nest**.

cohort   a group of people with a common statistical characteristic. Examples include baby boomers, who were born during the same period, and the frosh of 2010, who entered college or university in the same year.

colonialism   the policy or practice of acquiring full or partial control over another country, occupying it with settlers, and exploiting it economically or culturally.

commodification   the tendency to treat something as though it were an object to be bought or sold. For example, the commodification of medicine involves identifying certain conditions that might be normal (though slightly regrettable) as diseases that may be treated with 'commodity cures' (such as drugs or surgical procedures).

companionate roles   the overlapping **conjugal roles** of partners in a marriage who both work outside the home and do work around the house. *Compare* **complementary roles**.

complementary roles   the **conjugal roles** of partners in a marriage when one (traditionally the husband) does paid work, while the other (traditionally the wife) does the unpaid work of childcare and housework. *Compare* **companionate roles**.

complex household   a household in which there are two or more adults who are related but not married to each other.

complicit masculinity   forms of masculinity that do not contribute to or embody male hegemony yet still benefit from it.

confirmation   (in the Christian tradition) a **rite of passage** in which a person—usually an adolescent—who has been baptized affirms his or her belief and is admitted as a full member of the Church.

conflict deviance   behaviour that is subject to debate over whether or not it is deviant. Examples of conflict deviance include marijuana use and 'creative accounting' on tax returns.

conflict theory   a sociological perspective espousing the view that complex societies are made up of groups in conflict, with one or more groups dominating or oppressing the others.

conjugal roles   the distinctive roles of the husband and wife that result from the division of labour within the family.

conservatism   a view of social change as potentially more destructive than constructive, especially in emotionally charged areas of life such as family, gender roles, sexuality, and the environment.

content analysis   a study of a set of cultural artifacts (e.g. children's books, newspaper articles) or events by systematically counting them and interpreting the themes they reflect.

contested   describing a practice whose moral goodness or badness, normalcy or deviance, etc., is disputed by some members of society.

corporate crimes   (as described by Clinard and Quinney) (1) offences committed by corporate officials on behalf of the corporation they represent, or (2) the offences of the corporation itself.

corporate identity   the shared sense of common membership and common purpose that a social group can have. *Also called* **organic identity**.

countercultures   groups that reject selected elements of the dominant culture, such as clothing styles or sexual norms. *Compare* **subculture**.

counter ideology   a set of beliefs that challenges or contests the **dominant ideology** put forward by the dominant culture and the ruling classes.

covert characteristics (of deviance)   the unstated qualities that might make a particular group a target for sanctions. *Compare* **overt characteristics (of deviance)**.

critical sociology   sociology that challenges both established sociological theories and the research that sociologists do.

crude marriage rate   the number of marriages per 1,000 people in a population.

cultural globalization   (as described by Manfred Steger) the intensification and expansion of the flow of culture across the world in a process that involves media and patterns of consumption.

cultural iatrogenesis   (as described by Illich) a situation in which the knowledge and abilities of health professionals have become so mythologized that individuals lose the capacity to heal themselves.

cultural mosaic a metaphor for any society in which individual ethnic groups are able to maintain distinctive identities. Compare **melting pot**.

cultural norms generally expected and stated rules of behaviour. These may reflect the **ideal culture** more than they do the **real culture**.

cultural relativism the view that any aspect of a culture, including its practices and beliefs, is best explained within the context of the culture itself, not by the standard or ways of another culture.

cultural studies a field drawing on both the social sciences (primarily sociology) and the humanities (primarily literature and media studies) to cast academic light on the meanings expressed in popular culture and their significance.

cultural syndromes disorders thought to afflict people of only certain ethnicities. They are often invented to psychologize problems brought on by Western colonial control.

culture a social system (sometimes **contested**) comprising behaviour, beliefs, knowledge, practices, values, and material such as buildings, tools, and sacred items.

culture and personality (as described by R. Benedict) a now discredited school of thought that argued that every culture has a distinct personality that is encouraged by cultural practices and beliefs.

culture industry an industry that produces commodities and services that in some way express a way of life (such as the film and TV industry) or that occupy a special place in the social communications system (such as advertising or the media).

cultures of medicine the recognition that different cultures have different ways of practising medicine, including different **social courses of disease**, different techniques, and different physical remedies.

cycle of civilization the supposed rise and fall of **civilizations** in somewhat predictable cycles. The term has been applied to the Roman Empire, the Mongol Empire, the Ottoman (Turkish) Empire, and the American Empire.

Dalits the lowest and most discriminated against group in the traditional Hindu **caste** system. *Also called* **Untouchables**.

deciles ranked groups each making up 10 per cent of a total population, used for statistical analysis of such things as household income.

delinquent subculture (as described by A. Cohen) the **subordinate culture** of teenage gangs.

democracy a political system that involves a broad-based voting electorate, an opposition that is free to criticize the group in power without fear, freedom of the press and of speech, protection of the rights of minorities, and relative equality of men and women.

desensitization theory the idea that increased exposure to media violence (e.g. from television, movies, and video games) blunts, or desensitizes, natural feelings of revulsion at the sight or thought of violence.

developed nations the wealthier nations of the world, typically including the United States, Canada, the western European nations, and the more financially successful countries of Asia, Africa, and the Americas.

developing nations the world's poorer nations that are seeking to become more advanced economically and socially. The label is **contested** by some critics of globalization, who prefer the term 'underdeveloping nations' to better reflect the status of these countries as they become poorer as a result of exploitation by **developed nations**.

dialect a version of a language, usually with a unique set of features (in terms of vocabulary, grammar, and pronunciation) and a socially identifiable group of speakers.

digital divide the situation in which citizens of the world's wealthier nations, as well as richer citizens of the poorer nations, have an access to computers and related technology that gives them an enormous social, economic, and political advantage over the poorer citizens of the richer nations and most people in the poorer countries.

discourse a conceptual framework with its own internal logic and underlying assumptions. Different disciplines, such as sociology and psychology, have their own discourses.

discourse analysis an approach to analyzing a conversation, a speech, or a written text. More recently the scope of discourse analysis has broadened, with **discourse** now taken to mean such things as entire academic disciplines, like sociology and political philosophy.

discrimination acts by which individuals are differentially rewarded or punished based on their membership in a social group defined by class, sexual orientation, ethnicity, and so on.

disjuncture a gap between knowledges produced from two or more different perspectives (e.g. those of management and employees).

dominant culture the culture that through its political and economic power is able to impose its values, language, and ways of behaving and interpreting behaviour on a given society.

dominant ideology a set of beliefs put forward by and in support of the dominant culture and/or ruling classes within a society, to help them justify their dominant position and dominating practices.

dominants the group within a society that has the most political and social power, whose culture or subculture is seen as 'the' culture of a country.

Dragon Lady (as described by R. Tajima and T. Das Gupta) a stereotype of East Asian women as tough, ruthless, and mercenary. The stereotype is seen in film and TV portrayals of hardened prostitutes and madams, and women who fight with nasty, angry facial expressions.

dramaturgical approach (as described by Goffman) a way of approaching sociological research as if everyday life were taking place on the stage of a theatre.

dual colonialism a situation that occurs when the most oppressed groups (e.g. Rwanda's Hutu) are colonized both by the colonizing outsider group (the Belgians) and by a local group that is given privilege and power by the outsider group (the Tutsi).

dynamic denoting a social situation in which groups are subject to change. *Compare* **static**.

ego (as described by Freud) the conscious aspect of the individual personality. *Compare* **id**, **superego**.

embedded journalist a journalist who travels with and is protected by the military, but who is, in turn, authorized or led to express views sympathetic to the military's purposes.

empty nest a situation in which the children of an older couple have grown up and moved out of the family home. *Compare* **cluttered nest**.

endogamy the practice of marrying within one's class, 'race', or ethnic group. *Compare* **exogamy**.

epiphenomenal denoting a factor of secondary significance to a more significant cause. For Marx, race and ethnicity were epiphenomenal to economic structure.

eros (as described by Freud) the 'sexual' or 'life' instinct within the **id**.

essentialism *see* **primordiality**.

ethnic class (as described by J. Dofny and M. Rioux) a class system that exists when members of different ethnic groups adopt occupations that are ranked differently (e.g. administration versus labourers). An ethnic class system has existed in Quebec for most of the twentieth century.

ethnic entrepreneurs individuals who manipulate symbols with strong meaning to their ethnic group in order to gain and wield personal power. Examples include Adolf Hitler and Slobodan Milosevic.

ethnocentrism the belief that one culture (often one's own, occasionally another considered more powerful) is the absolute standard by which other cultures should be judged.

ethnography a research method, shared by sociology and social anthropology, in which communities or groups are studied through extensive fieldwork. Ethnography requires the researcher to participate daily in the lives of the subjects, observing their actions and asking questions.

eugenics the science of improving a population by controlled breeding. The idea was especially popular in the early twentieth century, when people believed that 'good traits' and 'bad traits' were inherited, and that the poor, the colonized, and other marginalized people should be sterilized to prevent them from reproducing.

evolution (as described by Darwin) a model of **social change** in which change is seen as an adaptation to a set of particular circumstances (i.e. 'survival of the best fit').

exogamy the practice of marrying outside of one's class, 'race', or ethnic group. *Compare* **endogamy**.

exoticism the process of making peoples from other cultures seem more exotic or 'strange', more different from one's own culture than they actually are or were.

extended family the family beyond mother, father, and children. Use of this term reflects the user's belief that the **nuclear family** is the model of a 'normal' family.

fact something that has been observed, and that as far as can be proven is believed to be true.

false consciousness (as described by Marx) the belief that something is in the best interests of one's class (e.g. religion, racism) when it is not.

fashion a model of **social change** that promotes change for its own sake, not for better (**modernism**), not for worse (**conservatism**), not even for adaptation (**evolution**). Fashion change may occur because a manufacturer wants consumers to believe a product has been improved (though it hasn't), or it may occur because people desire something different.

fecundity a woman's ability to conceive, which changes with age.

feminist essentialism a feminist approach that involves looking at differences between the way women and men think while arguing for the equality—and sometimes female superiority—in that difference. *Also called* **essentialist feminism**.

feminist liberalism a feminist approach that typically involves working towards **pay equity** for women. This form of feminism is criticized as reflecting more the concerns of white middle-class Western women than the women of different ethnicities and classes. *Also called* **liberal feminism**.

feminist postmodernism a feminist approach that involves looking at women more as subjects (i.e. people with **voices** and **standpoints** of interpretation) who guide research, rather than as objects being researched. *Also called* **postmodernist feminism**.

feminist socialism a feminist approach that involves looking at the intersections of oppression between class and gender, focusing mainly on the struggles faced by lower-class women. *Also called* **socialist feminism**.

feminization the process whereby an occupational sphere becomes dominated by and associated with women (e.g. secretaries, clerical workers). Feminized occupations are usually rewarded with lower salaries and fewer benefits.

First World a term used prior to the collapse of the USSR in the late twentieth century to refer to the world's rich, capitalist countries.

folk society (as described by R. Redfield) a rural, small-scale, homogeneous society imbued with a strong sense of the sacred and the personal, usually in contrast to an urban society.

folkways (as described by W. Sumner) **norms** that in the usual course of events one *should* not (rather than *must* not) violate. They are the least respected and most weakly sanctioned norms.

food bank a central clearing house run by a non-profit organization to collect, store, and distribute food free of charge to the poor.

Frankfurt School a school of social philosophers (including Adorno, Horkheimer, and Marcuse) who, beginning in the 1920s, applied the insights of Nietzsche, Marx, and Freud to their critical writing on fascism, communism, and capitalism.

free-floating statistic a statistic created in a particular context of time and place that is repeated outside of that context.

friendly racism (as described by H. Codjoe) a form of racism that is subtle and seemingly (to the perpetrator) harmless.

functionalism a sociological approach that involves explaining social structures in terms of their functions (i.e. what they do for society).

game stage (as described by G.H. Mead) the third stage of intellectual development, in which the child considers simultaneously the perspective of several roles.

geisha a traditional occupation for Japanese women. Geishas are expected to be well trained in the arts and capable of intelligent conversation so that they can entertain well-to-do customers in the geisha house.

gender (as described by A. Oakley) the socially constructed and socially unequal division of masculinity and femininity, as opposed to the biological division of **sex**.

gendered denoting occupations or post-secondary programs dominated by either men or by women. Examples include early childhood education and interior design for women, fire fighting and industrial design for men.

gender role the role that a culture or society assigns as 'normal' for boys/men and girls/women.

genealogy a form of **discourse analysis** that involves tracing the origin and history of modern **discourses** (e.g. the importance of light-coloured skin in South Asian culture). The term is sometimes considered interchangeable with the **archaeology of knowledge**.

general intelligence the largely mistaken idea that people have a single intelligence level that applies to many areas of life, skills, and abilities. Belief in general intelligence would lead one to conclude that a boy who does not earn high marks at school is stupid.

generalized others (as described by G.H. Mead) the attitudes, viewpoints, and general expectations of the society that a child is socialized into.

genocide a set of social practices designed to eliminate or exterminate a people. These practices include warfare, displacement from a homeland, enforced sexual sterilization, separation of family members, and banning languages and other culturally identifiable features, all of which were committed against Aboriginal people in Canada.

globalism (as described by M. Steger) an ideology that links globalization with neoliberalism.

globality (as described by M. Steger) a set of social conditions of globalization at a particular time and place.

globalization the worldwide process or policy of making the realms of communication and commerce more international in scope.

glocalization (as described by R. Robertson) the process of tailoring globalization to local needs and tastes. Glocalization is done either by **transnational companies** bent on increasing their globalized sales and influence, or by the local culture filtering the effects of globalization.

habitus (as described by P. Bourdieu) a set of class-affected or culturally affected and socially acquired characteristics (e.g. opinions, definitions of 'manners' and 'good taste', leisure pursuits).

hallucination an image of something that is not considered to be 'objectively' there (not to be confused with an **Aboriginal vision**).

hegemonic masculinity (as described by R. Connell) practices and beliefs that normalize and naturalize men's dominance and women's subordination.

hegemony (as described by A. Gramsci) a set of relatively non-coercive methods of maintaining power used by the dominant class (e.g. through the various media and the legal system). Often the terms *hegemony* and *hegemonic* are used to refer just to the possession and exercise of power (see, for instance, **hegemonic masculinity**).

heteronormative denoting or relating to the norms, mores, rules and laws that uphold heterosexual standards of identity and behaviour and heterosexuality as natural and universal.

high culture the culture deemed to be sophisticated, civilized, and possessing great taste within a society.

Highland Clearances the eviction by land-owning aristocrats of tenant farmers in the late eighteenth and early nineteenth centuries. The clearances, which were carried out to make room for sheep, helped aristocrats capitalize on the rapidly growing textile industry.

hijab an Arabic word for the veil or headscarf worn by Muslim women for religious and cultural reasons.

hyperglobalists people who are uncritical of globalization and dismissive of its negative effects; they champion the process of globalization as good for everyone.

hypothesis a statement that is verifiable/falsifiable (i.e. that can be proven true or false) and that proposes a specific relationship between or among variables. An example of a hypothesis: 'Playing violent video games makes a person more violent or antisocial.'

iatrogenesis (as described by Illich) health problems that are supposedly caused by health professionals. See **clinical iatrogenesis**, **cultural iatrogenesis**, **social iatrogenesis**.

id (as described by Freud) the instinctive part of the subconscious. (Remember it by the term **i**nner **d**emons.)

ideal culture social life and institutions as they ought to exist, based on our social norms, values, and goals. *Compare* **real culture**.

ideology a relatively coherent set of interrelated beliefs about society and the people in it. Examples include **dominant ideology**, **counter ideology**, and **liberal ideology**.

ideology of fag (as described by G. Smith) the use of such label as 'gay' and 'lesbian' pejoratively as a way to make people conform to strictly proscribed gender roles (e.g. telling a young man who expresses interest in poetry, interior design, or figure skating, 'You're so gay').

impression management (as described by Goffman) the ways in which people present themselves publicly in specific roles and social circumstances. Goffman first used the term to discuss the differences between how restaurant staff presented themselves to customers and how they presented themselves to one another behind the kitchen door.

Indian Princess an Aboriginal woman portrayed or seen as beautiful, submissive to white men, and ready to betray her nation for the love of a European man. The classic example is Disney's Pocahontas.

indigeneity the end-result of the process of refashioning indigenous identities according to alternative knowledges rather than those traditionally produced by outsider experts.

indirect rule a colonial policy in which a European nation uses members of a particular ethnic group as its intermediaries in ruling an area. The policy often leads to **dual colonialism** and **internal colonialism**.

informant a person knowledgeable in his or her own culture who provides his or her views of the culture to an outside researcher (either a sociologist or an anthropologist).

insider perspective the viewpoint(s) of those who experience the subject being studied or written about. *See* **standpoint theory**, **subjective**. *Compare* **outsider perspective**.

institutional ethnography a form of ethnography that challenges the need for a neutral stance in sociological research, claiming instead that any institution or organization can be seen as having two sides: one representing the **ruling interests** of the organization, one representing the interests of those working for the organization (typically in a non-administrative capacity).

institutional racism *see* **systemic racism**.

instrumentalism a sociological approach that focuses on situations in which ethnic leaders mobilize groups in order to develop the groups' political and social strength.

intelligences the idea that we have differing intelligence levels in different areas of life.

internal colonialism a situation that occurs when people within a country are colonized or put in a subordinate position (e.g. Aboriginal people in Canada; the Karen in Myanmar).

internalize incorporate the norms and values that one observes.

Inuit (*singular* **Inuk**) a people indigenous to Canada, Alaska, Greenland, and Siberia, who have been in Canada for a shorter time (between 5,000 and 10,000 years) than earlier indigenous people. They speak related languages and share various aspects of an Arctic-adapted culture.

inverse care law (as described by J.T. Hart) the view that the availability of good medical care varies inversely with the need for it in the population served.

Islamists people who oppose globalization and Western culture generally with narrow-minded and distorted fundamentalist notions of Islam.

jihad a term generated from an Arabic word meaning 'to struggle, strive'; it has several different forms and interpretations: *see* **jiha-i-akbar**, **jihad-i-asghar**, and **ummaic jihad**.

jihad-i-akbar the personal **jihad**, which represents the perpetual struggle to purge oneself of baser instincts such as greed, racism, hedonism, jealousy, revenge, hypocrisy, lying, and cheating.

jihad-i-asghar (*literally* 'the smaller, lower, or lesser jihad') the struggle against aggressors who are not practising Muslims. **Islamists** practise a distorted version of this.

joint conjugal roles **conjugal roles** in which many tasks, interests, and activities are shared. *Compare* **segregated conjugal roles**.

liberal ideology a set of beliefs that focuses on the individual as an independent player in society, not as a member of a class or an ethnic group. Components of this set include a strong belief in the potential for **social mobility** in the individual (as seen in the **American dream**) and a tendency towards **blaming the victim**.

liberalism (as described by A. Smith) the belief that 'the market' should be completely free to expand and grow without any governmental interference. In the writing of nineteenth-century thinker John Stuart Mill, it referred to a belief in the freedom of the individual from both government and the dominant culture (the 'tyranny of the majority').

longitudinal study a study that continues over time as the subjects get older.

Lotus Blossom Baby (as described by R. Tajima and T. Das Gupta) a stereotype of East Asian women as childlike, sexually available, and respectful of men. Evidence of this stereotype may be found in the China doll and in Western notions of the Japanese **geisha**.

Low Income Cutoffs (LICOs) a measure of poverty derived by calculating the percentage of a family's income spent on food, clothing, and shelter.

Low Income Measure (LIM-IAT) a measure of poverty calculated by identifying those households with total incomes (after taxes) half that of the median income in Canada (with some adjustments made for family size and composition).

Luddites British members of an early anti-industrial movement in Europe, in which craftspeople who had lost their work with the introduction of labour-saving machines protested by destroying the new machinery. The term is used today to refer to people who resist new technology.

Lumpenproletariat (as described by Marx) the group of people in capitalist society who neither own capital nor participate in wage labour. For the most part they get by with casual/occasional labour, scavenging for food and articles to sell, and crime.

macro-sociology an approach that involves looking at the large-scale structure and dynamics of society as a whole.

marginalization the experience of being treated as insignificant or of being moved beyond the margin of mainstream society.

marginalized masculinity (as described by R. Connell) those forms of masculinity that, owing to class, race, sexual orientation, and ethnicity, are accorded less respect than other forms of masculinity.

marked term a term with a qualifying or distinguishing label added to it (e.g. *field* hockey or *lite* beer), showing that it is not the usual form. *Compare* **unmarked term**.

Market Basket Measurement (MBM) an estimate of the cost of a specific basket of goods and services for a given year, assuming that all items in the basket were entirely provided for out of the spending of the household. Having an income lower than the MBM constitutes low income or poverty.

mass culture the **culture** of the majority, when that culture is produced by big companies and powerful governments.

master narrative a story that a nation or a people constructs about itself. A master narrative typically makes one group (the group that produced it) look heroic while casting other peoples, including minorities within the group, as bad or invisible.

matrilineal denoting kinship determined along the mother's line.

matrilocal denoting a situation in which a man and a woman live together in or near the mother's family residence(s).

means of production (as described by Marx) the main social means for producing wealth (e.g. land in feudal times; capital—wealth, machinery—during the industrial period).

medicalization the process by which certain behaviours or conditions are defined as medical problems (rather than, say, social problems), and medical intervention becomes the focus of remedy and social control.

melting pot a metaphor for a country in which immigrants are believed or expected to lose their cultural distinctiveness and assimilate into the dominant society. *Compare* **cultural mosaic**.

Métis a people of mixed Aboriginal and European ethnicity (usually Cree or Saulteaux and French) that developed in the late eighteenth century and grew to take on a sense of nationality as well as a distinct legal status.

micro-sociology an approach to sociology that focuses not on the grand scale of society but on the plans, motivations, and actions of the individual or a specific group. *Compare* **macro-sociology**.

minoritized denoting an identifiable social group that is discriminated against by mainstream society or the **dominants**.

misogyny (*adjective* **misogynous**) practices or beliefs in a patriarchal culture that show contempt for women.

mobility sports sports such as soccer and boxing that provide access to socioeconomic mobility for the poorest groups in society. These sports do not require significant funds or access to resources, but can be played with little or no equipment.

modernism an optimistic view of **social change** that envisions it as producing a world better than what preceded it.

moral entrepreneur someone who tries to convince others of the existence of a particular social problem that he or she has defined.

moral stigma *see* **stigma**.

mores (as described by W. Sumner) rules that one 'must not' violate. Some of these are enshrined in the criminal code as laws; violation often results in shock, severe disapproval, or punishment.

multiculturalism the set of policies and practices directed towards the respect for cultural differences in a country.

narratives stories that reflect the lives and views of the tellers.

narrow socialization socialization in which obedience and conformity to the standards and expectations of the community are emphasized, and punishment for deviation is practised. *Compare* **broad socialization**.

narrow vision (as described by Chomsky) a shortsighted view, held by those who believe in **modernism**, that whatever innovation benefits the dominant class is justifiable on the grounds of progress.

national character a now discredited belief, belonging to the **culture and personality** school of thought, that people of different countries have distinct personalities unique to their country (e.g. Italians are passionate, Germans are cold).

negative sanctions ways of punishing people who 'break the rules' of the cultural norms. Examples of negative sanctions include laughing at or isolating an individual.

neoliberalism policies that involve shrinking the public sector (through privatization of public enterprises, tax cuts, the reduction of public spending, and the downsizing of government) and increasing freedom for big business (through deregulation of the economy, control of organized labour, the expansion of international markets, and the removal of controls on global financial flows). *Also called* **neoconservativism**.

noble savage the romantic belief that indigenous people, or 'savages', are superior in outlook and lifestyle because they don't live in the industrialized and urbanized environment of the person invoking the image.

non-utilitarian denoting actions that are not designed to gain financial rewards or desired possessions.

normalized made to seem 'normal', 'right', and 'good'.

norms rules or standards of behaviour that are expected of a group, society, or culture.

North, the the wealthiest nations of the world, previously termed the **First World** or the **developed nations**. It refers to the fact that the majority of rich countries are located in the northern hemisphere.

nuclear family a family comprising a mother, a father, and children. The term is used to describe what is typically considered a 'normal' family.

objectivity (*adjective* **objective**) a supposed quality of scientific research that is not influenced by emotions, personality, or particular life experiences of the individual scientist. It better applies to the physical sciences—physics, chemistry, biology, etc.—than to the social sciences.

observational learning theory the theory that children acquire 'aggressive scripts' for solving social problems through watching violence on television.

occupational crimes (as described by Clinard and Quinney) offences committed by individuals for themselves in the course of their occupations, or by employers against their employees.

occupational segregation (as described by R. Beaujot) the situation in which women choose (or end up in) occupations that afford them some flexibility and greater tolerance of childcare-related **work interruptions**.

oligarchy rule of a country by a few powerful individuals or groups.

operational definition the definition of an abstract quality (e.g. poverty, abuse) in such a way that it can be counted for statistical purposes.

organic identity *see* **corporate identity**.

Orientalism (as described by Said) a **discourse** about the Middle East and the Far East constructed by outsider 'experts' from the West.

other, the an exotic, often fearful image conjured up by the dominant culture of a racialized subordinate culture, or by a colonizing nation of the colonized.

outsider perspective the viewpoint(s) of those outside of the group or culture being studied. The outsider perspective was once considered a privileged position, with the outsider viewed as an expert. *Compare* **insider perspective**.

oversocialized (as described by D. Wrong) a misleading conception of humans as passive recipients of socialization.

overt characteristics (of deviance) actions or qualities taken as explicitly violating the cultural norm. *Compare* **covert characteristics**.

participant observation a form of research in sociology and anthropology that entails both observing people as an outsider would and actively participating in the various activities of the studied people's lives. It is usually employed in undertaking an **ethnography**.

patriarchal construct a set of social conditions structured in a way that favours men and boys over women and girls.

patriarchy a social system in which men hold political, cultural, and social power. Patriarchy is visible in societies where only male political leaders are elected and where the media and the arts are dominated by male views.

patrilineal kinship determined along the father's line.

pay equity compensation paid to women in traditionally female-dominated industries (e.g. childcare, library science, nursing, and secretarial work) where salaries and benefits have been lower than those given to employees in comparable (in terms of educational qualifications, hours worked, and social value) professions dominated by men.

peasants (in Marxist thinking) the people who in feudal times worked the land but did not own it.

peer group the social group to which one belongs, or to which one wishes to belong, as a more-or-less equal.

peer pressure the social pressure put on an individual to conform to the ways of a particular group that the individual belongs to or wishes to belong to.

petty bourgeoisie (as described by Marx) the sub-class made up of small-time owners with little capital.

pibloktuq *see* **Arctic hysteria**.

play stage (as described by G.H. Mead) the second developmental sequence for child socialization, in which pretending is involved. See **role taking**.

polite racism *See* **friendly racism**.

political economy an interdisciplinary approach that involves sociology, political science, economics, law, anthropology, and history. It looks primarily at the relationship between politics and the economics surrounding the production, distribution, and consumption of goods.

popular culture commercial culture based on popular taste.

positive sanctions ways of rewarding people for following the norms of a society (e.g. inclusion into a desired group, career success).

post-colonialism *see* **anti-colonialism**.

postmodernism a model of **social change** that recognizes that change can benefit some while harming others (e.g. a **digital divide**).

Potlatch any of various traditional ceremonies of Aboriginal groups of the Northwest Coast. It involves reaffirming traditional values and stories through speaking, acting, dancing, and singing important stories, and reflecting the traditional value of generosity through large-scale giveaway of cherished items.

poverty a state of doing or being without what are considered essentials.

poverty line the arbitrary dividing point, usually based on household income, that separates the poor from the rest of society. It can differ according to the cost of living in the studied environment, and it may differ for urban and rural communities. It will also vary according to the political biases of the person drawing the line

power elite (as described by Mills) the people wielding significant economic and political power.

Powley test a set of questions used to determine whether Métis and other Native people can lawfully hunt without a licence.

prejudice the pre-judging of people based on their membership in a particular social group.

preparatory stage (as described by G.H. Mead) the first developmental sequence of child socialization, which involves pure imitation.

preventive war a military campaign justified on the grounds of preventing an attack on one's own country.

primary socialization the earliest socialization that a child receives.

primordiality the view that every ethnic group is made up of a list of readily identifiable traits that have been passed down from the past to the present with little or no change. *Also called* **essentialism**.

professionalization the process of turning work done by volunteers into paid work.

professional sociology sociology that involves research typically designed to generate highly specific information, often with the aim of applying it to a particular problem or intellectual question. Its usual audience is the academic world of sociology departments, academic journals, professional associations, and conferences.

proletariat *see* **workers**.

Protestant (work) ethic (as described by Weber) a set of values embodied in early Protestantism, believed to have led to the development of modern capitalism.

psychoanalysis (as described by Freud) an approach to psychological study that involves hypothesized stages of development and components of the self (see **id**, **ego**, **eros**, **superego**, and **thanatos**). It is used by sociologists to look at individual relationships to society and at cultural expression.

public sociology (as described by H. Gans) sociology that addresses an audience outside of the academy. It is presented in a language that can be understood by the college-educated reader, without the dense style of the academic paper or journal, and expresses concern for a breadth of sociological subjects.

qualitative research the close examination of characteristics that cannot be counted or measured.

quantitative research the close examination of social elements that can be counted or measured, and therefore used to generate statistics.

queer theory (as described by J. Butler) an approach that rejects the idea that gender identity is connected to some biological essence, proposing instead that gender reflects social performance on a continuum, with 'male' and 'female' at opposite poles.

quintile each of five ranked groups making up 20 per cent of a total population, used for statistical analysis of such things as household income.

racial bigotry the open, conscious expression of racist views by an individual.

racialization a social process in which groups of people are viewed and judged as essentially different in terms of their intellect, morality, values, and innate worth because of differences of physical type or cultural heritage.

racializing deviance the creation of a connection, through various media (television, movies, textbooks), between a racialized group and a form of deviance or crime (e.g. Latinos and drug dealing, black people and prostitution).

racial profiling actions undertaken supposedly for reasons of safety, security, or public protection, based on racial stereotypes, rather than on reasonable suspicion.

radical monopoly (as described by Illich) a situation in which professional control work is deemed socially important (e.g. teachers in education; doctors/nurses in healthcare).

real culture social life and institutions as they really exist. *Compare* **ideal culture**.

reductionist denoting any unrealistic statement or theory that attempts to explain a set of phenomena by referring to a single cause. In sociology, this includes **class reductionism**, or reducing all inequality to gender, race, or ethnicity.

reference group a group perceived by another group to be equal but better off.

registered Indian an Aboriginal person who bears federal government recognition of his or her legal right to the benefits (and penalties) of being 'legally Indian'. *Formerly called* **status Indian**.

relational denoting the relationship between a class and the means of producing wealth.

relational accountability an approach that balances the social portrayal of a people so that both strengths and weaknesses, problems and successes are seen.

relations of ruling (as described by D. Smith) the dominance of the individual or group by large government and large business. Smith argues that these are reinforced by uncritical sociological analysis.

relative deprivation a situation in which an individual or the members of a group feel deprived compared to a **reference group** that they see as having no greater entitlement to their relatively better situation.

relative poverty a state of poverty based on a comparison with others in the immediate area or country. *Compare* **absolute poverty**.

replacement rate the rate at which children must be born in order to replace the generation before them.

reproduction (as described by P. Bourdieu) the means by which classes, particularly the upper or dominant class, preserve status differences between classes.

residential schools a system of educating Aboriginal children that involved removing them from their homes and communities, isolating them from their culture, and often abusing them physically, emotionally, and sexually. Underfunded by the federal government, the schools were run by a number of church groups, primarily the Roman Catholic, Anglican, and Presbyterian churches. The system, which began in the late nineteenth century and was formalized in 1910, ended slowly between the 1960s and the 1980s.

resocialization the process of unlearning old ways and learning new ways upon moving into a significantly different social environment.

reverse ethnocentrism a situation in which individuals set up a culture other than their own as the absolute standard by which to judge their own culture. *Compare* **ethnocentrism**.

rhetoric the study of how people use language to persuade others or to put together an argument.

risk behaviour behaviour with a relatively high chance of harming an individual. Examples include driving at unsafe speeds, practising unsafe sexual activities, and abusing drugs and alcohol.

rite of passage (as described by Van Gennep) a ceremonial or ritualized passage from one stage of life to another. Examples include Christian **confirmation** and the Aboriginal **vision quest**.

ritual degradation a rite of passage in which the person is stripped of his or her individuality (e.g. hazing).

role the function assumed or the part played by a person in a particular situation.

role taking (as described by G.H. Mead) the stage at which children assume the perspective of **significant others**, imagining what they are thinking as they act the way they do.

ruling interests the interests of the organization, particularly its administration, or the interests of those who are dominant in society.

ruling relations the conformity of workers to the rules and practices of the organization they work for; ruling relations are activated when workers fulfill the organization's **ruling interests.**

Sapir-Whorf hypothesis (as described by Sapir and Whorf) the theory that the structure of a language determines a person's perception of experience. A milder version argues for linguistic relativity, the view that language and culture have a unique relationship in each society.

savagery (as described by L.H. Morgan) the supposed first stage of social evolution toward modern civilization. *Compare* **barbarism**, **civilization**.

scientific classism the use of flawed, pseudoscientific ideas (e.g. eugenics) to justify discriminatory actions against poor people.

scientific racism the use of flawed, pseudoscientific ideas (e.g. eugenics, measuring brain sizes) to justify discriminatory actions against certain racialized groups.

scrips certificates issued to Métis in the latter part of the nineteenth century, which declared that the bearer could receive payment in land, cash, or goods. The legal status of these certificates was abused by government officials and land speculators.

secondary socialization any socialization that occurs later than the **primary socialization** in the life of a child.

Second World (prior to the collapse of the USSR in the late 1980s) a term used to refer to the Soviet Union and the eastern European countries under its power.

segregated conjugal roles **conjugal roles** in which tasks, interests, and activities are clearly different. *Compare* **joint conjugal roles**.

semiotics the study of signs, symbols, and signifying practices.

sex the biological differences between boys/men and girls/women, as opposed to the sociological differences (which come under the term **gender**).

sick role (as described by T. Parsons) the set of expectations that surround a sick person and the experience of being sick.

sign communication made up of a **signifier**, which carries meaning, and a **signified**, the meaning that is carried.

significant others (as described by G.H. Mead) those key individuals—primarily parents, to a lesser degree older siblings and close friends—whom young children imitate and model themselves after.

simple household a household consisting of unmarried, unrelated adults with or without children.

simulacra (as described by J. Baudrillard) cultural images, often in the form of stereotypes, that are produced and reproduced like material goods or commodities by the media and sometimes by academics.

Sixties Scoop the removal, between the 1960s and the early 1980s, of thousands of Aboriginal children from their families, their communities, their home provinces (particularly Manitoba), and sometimes their home country, to place them in non-Aboriginal homes.

skeptical globalizers those who see globalization as a process that is potentially dangerous to the environment and to the economies and social welfare of the 'have-not' countries.

slippery slope the logical fallacy that one small change will automatically snowball into the collapse of the entire social order. Slippery-slope arguments are often voiced by adherents of **conservatism**.

smiling racism *see* **friendly racism**.

social change the set of adjustments or adaptations made by a group of people in response to a dramatic change experienced in at least one aspect of their lives.

social constructionism the idea that social identities such as gender, ethnicity, and 'race' do not exist 'naturally' but are constructed by individuals or groups for different social purposes. **Instrumentalism** is an example of social constructionism.

social course of disease the social interactions that a sick person goes through in the process of being treated.

social Darwinism the application, in the late nineteenth and early twentieth centuries, of the principle of **survival of the fittest** to human groups, used to justify the power held by Europeans and the upper classes on the grounds that they were the strongest and the best.

social gospel a movement in the late nineteenth and early twentieth centuries in Canada, the United States, and various European countries to apply the human welfare principles of Christianity to the social, medical, and psychological ills brought on by industrialization and uncontrolled capitalism.

social iatrogenesis (as described by Illich) the deliberate obscuring of political conditions that render society unhealthy.

social inequality the long-term existence of significant differences in access to goods and services among social groups defined by class, ethnicity, etc.

social mobility the movement from one class into another (usually higher) class.

sociolinguistics (as described by W. Labov) the study of language (particularly **dialect**) as a social marker of status or general distinctiveness, or the study of how different languages conceptualize the world (e.g. the **Sapir-Whorf Hypothesis**).

sociological imagination (as described by Mills) the capacity to shift from the perspective of the personal experience to the grander, societal scale that has caused or influenced that personal experience.

sociological poetry (as described by Mills) the writing of sociology in such a way that it is beautifully crafted and readily understood. *Compare* **public sociology**.

sociology the social science that studies the development, structure, and functioning of human society.

South, the the poorer nations of the world, previously known either as the **Third World** or the **developing nations**.

spurious reasoning the perception of a correlation between two factors that are wrongly seen as cause and effect.

squaw a stereotype of the Aboriginal woman as lazy, drunken, and abused by Aboriginal men. *Compare* **Indian Princess**.

standpoint theory (as described by D. Smith) the view that knowledge is developed from a particular lived position, or 'standpoint', making **objectivity** impossible.

staples (as described by Innis) natural resources such as fish, fur, minerals, and crops, upon which countries such as Canada built their economy.

statistical norms norms that reflect, statistically, what people actually do, in distinction to **cultural norms**, which are what people claim to do.

statistics a science that, in sociology, involves the use of numbers to map social behaviour and beliefs.

status the relative social standing of a person or group, typically when it is highly regarded.

status frustration (as described by A. Cohen) a feeling of failure to succeed in middle-class terms or institutions, leading to participation in **delinquent subculture**.

status Indian *see* **registered Indian**.

stigma (as described by Goffman) a human attribute that is seen to discredit an individual's social identity. **Bodily stigmata** are any of various physical deformities. **Moral stigmata** are perceived flaws in the character of an individual. **Tribal stigmata** relate to being of a particular lineage or family that has been stigmatized (e.g. the family of a murderer or gang member).

strata social classes in ranked layers, with no specific relationship to the means of producing wealth.

subculture a group that is organized around occupations or hobbies differing from those of the dominant culture but that is not engaged in any significant opposition to the dominant culture.

subjective denoting theories, beliefs, and opinions influenced by emotions, personality, and particular life experiences of the individual. The term is used in opposing ways: some sociologists discredit observation that is 'merely subjective' rather than 'objective fact'; others argue that all 'facts' are to some degree subjective but hide behind the mask of objectivity.

subordinate cultures groups who feel the power of the dominant culture and exist in opposition to it.

subordinate masculinity (as described by R. Connell) behaviours and presentations of self that can threaten the legitimacy of hegemonic masculinity. The usual examples given are gay or effeminate men, and those whose lives and beliefs challenge traditional definitions of male success.

superego (as described by Freud) the human conscience or moral sense.

survival of the fittest (as described by Spencer) the principle, wrongly attributed to Darwin, that only the biggest and strongest survive, both in nature and in human society.

swaddling hypothesis (as described by J. Richman and G. Gorer) a hypothesis that attributed the presumed 'moodiness' of Russian citizens to their having been too tightly swaddled or wrapped up as infants.

symbol an aspect of a culture that has many strings of meaning that are unique to that culture. Examples include the flag for Americans, hockey for Canadians, songs of the early fourteenth century for Scots.

systemic racism racist practices, rules, and laws that have become institutionalized or made 'part of the system'. People who benefit from this type of racism tend to be blind to its existence. Also called **institutional racism**.

taboo a **norm** so deeply ingrained that the mere thought or mention of it is enough to arouse disgust or revulsion. An example is incest.

tabula rasa the idea that every human is born as a 'blank slate' upon which the culture writes or inscribes a personality, values, and/or a set of abilities.

terrorism the intentional use or threat of violence against civilians in order to attain political objectives (e.g. freeing 'political' prisoners, establishing an independent country, or destabilizing a political regime in another country in order to produce a regime change).

thanatos (as described by Freud) the violent 'death instinct' within the **id**.

theory an attempt to explain something that has been observed.

third variable a **variable** that causes two more variables to correlate.

Third World a twentieth-century term used to refer to the poorer nations of the world. *Compare* **First World**, **Second World**.

total fertility rate an estimate of the average number of children that a woman between the ages of 15 and 49 will have in her lifetime if current age-specific fertility rates remain constant during her reproductive years.

total institutions (as described by Goffman) institutions such as the military, hospitals, and asylums that regulate all aspects of an individual's life.

totalitarian discourse any **discourse** that makes a universal claim about how all knowledge and understanding can be achieved.

transnational corporation a company operating in countries around the world, typically based in the United States, Europe, or Japan.

triangulation the use of at least three narratives, theoretical perspectives, or investigators to examine the same phenomenon.

tribalism a movement to promote the cause of a small nation that is usually not represented as having a country of its own.

tribal stigma see **stigma**.

trickle-down theory the misleading social theory that if the rich are free to earn as much money as they can, the benefits will 'trickle down' to society's poorer citizens.

unmarked term a term without any distinguishing or delimiting term added; the usual form, as opposed to a marked term. Examples include 'hockey' (versus 'ice hockey', 'field hockey', 'table hockey', etc.) and 'anthropology' (versus 'cultural anthropology' or 'physical anthropology').

Untouchables see **Dalits**.

urban reserve a parcel of land within an urban area reserved for Aboriginal-run businesses and services.

values those features held up by a culture as good, right, desirable, and admirable. Values are typically **contested**.

variable a factor or element that is likely to vary or change according to the circumstances governing it.

vertical mosaic (as described by J. Porter) a metaphor used to describe a society or nation in which there is a hierarchy of higher and lower ethnic groups.

victimology either (1) the study of people who are victims of crime, or (2) an outlook that undervalues the victims of crime by portraying them as people who cannot help themselves, who cannot exercise **agency**.

virtual class (as described by A. Kroker) a **class** of people who control and are dependent for their jobs and economic well-being on digital technologies and the Internet.

vision quest (in traditional North American Aboriginal culture) a **rite of passage** in which an adolescent leaves the community for a brief period and goes without eating or sleeping in order to have a vision (*see* **Aboriginal vision**) that will teach him or her such things as what guardian spirit he or she may have and what songs he or she would have as personal songs.

voice the expression of *a* (not *the*) viewpoint that comes from occupying a particular social 'location' (e.g. gender, ethnicity, sexual orientation, age, class).

white collar crime (as described by E. Sutherland) non-violent crime committed by a person of the middle or upper middle class in the course of his or her job. Examples include embezzlement and fraud.

workers (as described by Marx) the people who work for wages and do not own capital, the means of production, in an industrial, capitalist society. *Also called* **proletariat**.

work interruptions (as described by J. Baudrillard) time taken off work, typically by a woman, to care for an infant (i.e. during maternity or paternity leave) or a child who is sick.

xenocentrism a preference for foreign goods and tastes based on the belief that anything foreign must be better than the same thing produced domestically.

XYY males men and boys who differ from the 'normal' XY chromosome pattern. They are associated with above-average height, a tendency to have acne, and somewhat more impulsive and antisocial behaviour and slightly lower intelligence than 'normal' men and boys.

Credits

Jean Anyon, excerpts from 'Social Class and the Hidden Curriculum of Work', *Journal of Education*, 162, 1 (1980): 67–92.

Caledon Enterprise, 'Boys Must Read to Catch Up to Girls', from *Caledon Enterprise*, editor Marney Beck (26 January 2005).

Velma Demerson, excerpt from *Incorrigible* (Wilfrid Laurier Press, 2004). Reproduced by permission.

W.E.B. Du Bois, excerpt from *The Souls of Black Folk* by W.E.B. Du Bois, introduction by Donald B. Gibson, notes by Monica E. Elbert (London: Penguin Classics, 1989). Copyright © the Estate of W.E.B. Du Bois 1903. Introduction copyright © Viking Penguin, a division of Penguin Books USA Inc., 1989. Reproduced by permission of Penguin Books Ltd. US reprint rights granted by Random House, Inc.

Michael Dubson, excerpts from *Ghosts in the Classroom: Stories of College Adjunct Faculty—and the Price We All Pay* (Camel's Back Books, 2001).

Émile Durkheim, excerpts from *The Elementary Forms of Religious Life*, by Émile Durkheim, translated by Karen E. Fields. Translation, Copyright © 1995 by Karen E. Fields. All rights reserved. Reprinted with the permission of The Free Press, a Division of Simon & Schuster, Inc.

David Elkind, exerpts from *Technology's Impact on Child Growth and Development* (CIO.com, 22 September 2003).

David Flint, excerpts from *The Hutterites: A Study in Prejudice* © 1975 Oxford University Press Canada. Reprinted by permission.

The Globe and Mail, excerpt from Globe and Mail/CTV/Ipsos-Reid poll.

Pat Grygier, excerpts from *A Long Way from Home: The Tuberculosis Epidemic Among the Inuit* (Montreal: McGill–Queen's University Press, 1994).

Everett C. Hughes, excerpts from 'Dilemmas and Contradictions of Status', *American Journal of Sociology*, 50, 5 (1945): 353–359. University of Chicago Journals.

Margaret Humphreys, excerpts from *Empty Cradles* (Transworld Publishing, 1996).

Carl James and Adrienne Shadd, excerpts from *Talking About Identity: Encounters in Race, Ethnicity, and Language* (Toronto: Between the Lines, 2001).

Diamond Jenness, exerpts from *Arctic Odyssey: The Diary of Diamond Jenness, 1913–1916* © Canadian Museum of Civilization.

Jenny Joseph, excerpt from 'Warning', from *Rose in the Afternoon, and Other Poems* (J.M. Dent, 1974).

Ibn Khaldūn, excerpt from *The Muqaddimah*, translated by Franz Rosenthal © 2005 by Princeton University Press. Reprinted by permission of Princeton University Press.

Mary-Ann Kirkby, excerpts from *I Am Hutterite* (Polka Dot Press, 2007). Reproduced with permission.

Arthur Kleinman, excerpts from *Writing at the Margin: Discourse Between Anthropology and Medicine* (Berkeley: University of California Press, 1997). Copyright © 1997 by The Regents of the University of California.

David R. Maines, excerpt from 'Narrative's Moment and Sociology's Phenomena', *Sociological Quarterly*, 34, 1 (1993): 17–37. Published by Blackwell Publishing Ltd.

Henry Lewis Morgan, excerpts reprinted by permission of the publisher from *Ancient Society* by Henry Lewis Morgan, edited by Leslie A. White (Cambridge, MA: The Belknap Press of Harvard University Press). Copyright © 1964 by the President and Fellows of Harvard College.

Serena Nanda, excerpt from *Cultural Anthropology*, 5th edn. Copyright © 1994 Wadsworth, a part of Cengage Learning, Inc. Reproduced by permission. www.cengage.com/

Catherine Newbury, excerpts from *The Cohesion of Oppression*, by Catharine Newbury. Copyright © 1993 Columbia University Press. Reprinted with permission of the publisher.

Robert A. Nisbet, excerpts from *Social Change and History: Aspects of the Western Theory of Development* (Oxford University Press, 1970). Reprinted by permission of Oxford University Press, Inc.

Rage Against the Machine, lyrics from 'Take the Power Back', from *Rage Against the Machine* (Epic Associated Records, 1992).

George Ritzer, excerpts from *The McDonaldization of Society* (Sage Publications, 2004). Reproduced by permission.

John R. Seeley, Alexander Sim, and Elizabeth Loosley, excerpt from *Crestwood Heights: A Study of the Culture of Suburban Life* (Toronto: University of Toronto Press, 1956). Reprinted with permission of the publisher.

Sundar Singh, excerpt from 'The Sikhs in Canada', an address delivered to the Empire Club of Canada on 25 January 1912. The Empire Club of Canada.

Jessica Warner, excerpts from *Craze: Gin and Debauchery in the Age of Reason* (Random House, 2003).

Additional photo credits: p. iv: Guy Letts; p. vi: © Sophia Fortier; p. xi: Bill Ivy Images; p. 2: iStockphoto.com/dwphotos; p. 32: Toronto Star/GetStock.com; p. 64: © Picture Hooked/Loop Images/Corbis; p. 94: © Erica Shires/Corbis; p. 122: Dreamstock/Dreamstime.com; p. 152: Leah Warkentin/DesignPics; p. 176: © Image Source/Alamy; p. 202: © Michele Falzone/JAI/Corbis; p. 234: Bill Ivy Images; p. 266: © Christopher Morris/Corbis; p. 294: David Cooper/Toronto Star/GetStock.com; p. 322: Vince Talotta/Toronto Star/GetStock.com; p. 350: Darren Greenwood/DesignPics; p. 378: Tory Zimmerman/GetStock.com

References

Abdo, Nahla, ed. (1996). *Sociological Thought: Beyond Eurocentric Theory*. Toronto: Canadian Scholars' Press.

Abu-Laban, Yasmeen (1986). 'The Vertical Mosaic in Later Life: Ethnicity and Retirement in Canada'. *The Journal of Gerontology* 41 (5), pp. 662–71.

Adachi, Ken (1976). *The Enemy That Never Was: A History of Japanese Canadians*. Toronto: McClelland & Stewart.

Adams, Carol, ed. (1993). *Ecofeminism and the Sacred*. New York: The Continuum Pub. Co.

Adams, Howard (1975). *Prison of Grass: Canada From the Native Point of View*. Toronto: New Press.

Adams, Michael (2003). *Fire and Ice: The United States and the Myth of Converging Values*. Toronto: Penguin Canada.

Aguiar, Luis (2001). '"Whiteness" in White Academia'. In Carl James & Adrienne Shadd, eds, *Talking About Identity: Encounters in Race, Ethnicity and Language*, 2nd edn, pp. 177–92. Toronto: Between the Lines.

Akard, Patrick J. (1992). 'Corporate Mobilization and Political Power: The Transformation of US Economic Policy in the 1970s'. *American Sociological Review* 57 (Oct.), pp. 597–615.

Alberta Advanced Education & Career Development (AAECD) (1993). *Adult Learning in Alberta: Budget Roundtable Workbook*. Edmonton: Alberta Dept. of Advanced Education and Career Development (Nov.).

Allen, Michael Patrick (1978). 'Economic Interest Groups and the Corporate Elite Structure'. *Social Science Quarterly* 58 (4), pp. 597–615.

Allen, Peter M. (1994) 'Evolution, Sustainability and Industrial Metabolism'. In R.U. Ayres & U. Simonis, eds, *Industrial Metabolism: Restructuring for Sustainable Development*. Tokyo: United Nations UP.

Allen, Richard (1971). *The Social Passion: Religion and Social Reform in Canada 1914–28*. Toronto: U of Toronto P.

Ames, Herbert Brown (1972 [1897]). *The City Below the Hill*. Toronto: U of Toronto P.

Anderson, Karen (1996). *Sociology: A Critical Introduction*. Toronto: Nelson.

Anyon, Jean (1980). 'Social Class and the Hidden Curriculum of Work'. *Journal of Education* 162 (1), pp. 67–92.

Aristotle (2000). *Politics*. Mineola, NY: Dover Publications.

Armstrong, Karen (2005 [1981]). *Through the Narrow Gate: A Memoir of Life in and Out of the Convent*. Toronto: Vintage Canada.

Arnett, Jeffrey (1995). 'Broad and Narrow Socialization: The Family in the Context of a Cultural Theory'. *Journal of Marriage and the Family* 57 (3), pp. 617–28.

Arnett, Jeffrey, & Lene Balle-Jensen (1993). 'Cultural Bases of Risk Behavior: Danish Adolescents'. *Child Development* 64, pp. 1842–55.

Aujla, Angela (1998). 'The Colour Bar of Beauty'. *The Peak* 1 (99), pp. 1–5.

Axelrod, Paul (1982a). 'Businessmen and the Building of Canadian Universities'. *Canadian Historical Review* 63, pp. 202–22.

——— (1982b). *Scholars and Dollars: Politics, Economics, and the Universities of Ontario, 1945–1980*. Toronto: U of Toronto P.

Backhouse, Constance (1999). *Colour-Coded: A Legal History of Racism in Canada, 1900–1950*. Toronto: U of Toronto P.

Banerjee, Mukulika (2000). *The Pathan Unarmed*. Karachi & New Delhi: Oxford UP.

Barber, Benjamin (1992). 'Jihad vs McWorld'. *The Atlantic Monthly* March 1992.

Barnouw, Victor (1987). *An Introduction to Anthropology: Ethnology*, vol. 2, 5th edn. Chicago, IL: The Dorsey Press.

Barrowcliffe, Mark (2008). *The Elfish Gene: Dungeons, Dragons and Growing Up Strange—A Memoir*. London: Soho Press.

Barthes, Roland (1957). *Mythologies*. London: Paladin/HarperCollins.

Baskin, Cyndy (2003). 'Structural Social Work as Seen from an Aboriginal Perspective'. *Emerging Perspectives on Anti-Oppressive Practice*. W. Shera, ed. Toronto: Canadian Scholars' Press.

Battiste, Marie (1997). 'Mi'kmaq Social-ization Patterns'. In L. Choyce & R. Joe, eds, *Anthology of Mi'kmaq Writers*. East Lawrencetown, NS: Pottersfield Press.

Baudrillard, Jean (1983). *Simulations*. Trans. Paul Foss, Paul Patton, & Philip Beitchman. New York: Semiotext[e].

Beaujot, Rod (2000). *Earning and Caring in Canadian Families*. Peterborough: Broadview Press.

——— (2004). 'Delayed Life Transitions: Trends and Implications'. *Vanier Institute of the Family* (June 15, 2009), http://www.vifamily.ca/library/cft/delayed_life.html.

Becker, Howard (1963). *Outsiders: Studies in the Sociology of Deviance*. New York: The Free Press.

Bellegarde-Smith, Patrick (2004). *Haiti: The Breached Citadel*. Toronto: Canadian Scholars' Press.

Benedict, Ruth (1946). *The Chrysanthemum and the Sword*. Boston: Houghton Mifflin.

Benton-Banai, Edward (1988). *The Mishomis Book: The Voice of the Ojibway*. St Paul, MN: Red School House, Indian Country Communications.

Berry, Wendell (1992). *Sex, Economy, Freedom & Community*. New York: Pantheon.

Best, Joel (2001). *Damned Lies and Statistics: Untangling Numbers from the Media, Politicians, and Activists*. Berkeley and Los Angeles: U of California P.

Beverly, J. (1978). 'Higher Education and Capitalist Crisis'. *Socialist Review* 8 (6), pp. 67–91.

Bezlova, Antoaneta (2002). 'Young Workers Toil to Churn Out Santa's Toys'. *Inter Press Service* 19 (23 Dec.), www.commondreams.org/headlines02/1223-01.htm.

Bibby, Reginald Wayne (1995). *The Bibby Report: Social Trends Canadian Style*. Toronto: Stoddard.

Biehl, Janet (1991). *Rethinking Ecofeminist Politics*. Boston: South End Press.

Bissell, Tom (2003). *Chasing the Sea: Lost Among the Ghosts of Empire in Central Asia*. New York: Pantheon.

Bloom, Allan (1988). *The Closing of the American Mind*. New York: Simon & Schuster.

Bohannan, Laura (1966). 'Shakespeare in the Bush', *Natural History* (Aug./Sept.). Reprinted in E. Angeloni (Ed.), *Annual Editions Anthropology, 1995/1996*, 65–9.

Bolaria, B. Singh, & Peter S. Li (1985). *Racial Oppression in Canada*. Toronto: Garamond.

Bott, Elizabeth (1957). *Family and Social Networks: Roles, Norms of External Relationships in Ordinary Urban Families*. London: Tavistock.

Bourdieu, Pierre (1970). *La reproduction: Eléments pour une théorie d'enseignement*. Paris: Éditions de Minuit.

——— (1988). *Homo Academicus*. Trans. P. Collier. Stanford, CA: Stanford UP.

——— (1996). *On Television*. New York: New Press.

Bourdieu, Pierre, & Jean-Claude Passeron (1990). *Reproduction in Education, Society and Culture*. Thousand Oaks, CA: Sage.

Bowles, S., & H. Gintis (1976). *Schooling in Capitalist America: Educational Reform and Contradictions of Economic Life*. New York: Basic Books.

Boyd, Monica, & Doug Norris (1995). 'Leaving the Nest? Impact of Family Structure'. *Canadian Social Trends* 38, pp. 14–17.

Briggs, Jean (1970). *Never in Anger: Portrait of an Eskimo Family*. Cambridge: Harvard UP.

——— (1998). *Inuit Morality Play: The Emotional Education of a Three-Year-Old*. New Haven, CT: Yale UP.

Brookes, Martin (2004). *Extreme Measures: The Dark Visions and Bright Ideas of Francis Galton*. London: Bloomsbury Publishing Ltd.

Brym, Robert J., ed. (1985). *The Structure of the Canadian Capitalist Class*. Toronto: Garamond.

——— (2000). 'Note on the Discipline: The Decline of the Canadian Sociology and Anthropology Association'. *The Canadian Journal of Sociology* 28 (3), pp. 411–26.

Buchbinder, Howard, & Janice Newson (1985). 'Corporate–University Linkages and the Scientific-Technical Revolution'. *Interchange* 16 (3), pp. 37–53.

Budgell, Janet (1999). *Our Way Home: a Report to the Aboriginal Healing and Wellness Strategy: Repatriation of Aboriginal People Removed by the Child Welfare System: Final Report*. Prepared by Native Child and Family Services of Toronto, Sevenato and Associates. Toronto: Native Child and Family Services of Toronto.

Bullivant, Brian (1981). *The Pluralist Dilemma in Education: Six Case Studies*. Sydney: Allen & Unwin.

Burawoy, Michael (2004). 'The World Needs Public Sociology'. *Sosiologisk tidsskrift (Journal of Sociology, Norway)* 3.

Burnet Jean R., & Howard Palmer (1988). *'Coming Canadians'. An Introduction to a History of Canada's Peoples*. Ottawa: Ministry of Supply and Services.

Burton, Kirsteen R., & Ian K. Wong (2004). 'A Force to Contend With: The Gender Gap Closes in Canadian Medical Schools'. *Canadian Medical Association Journal* 170 (9) (17 April).

Bushman, Brad J., & L. Rowell Huesmann (2001). 'Effects of Televised Violence on Aggression'. In D. Singer & J. Singer, eds, *Handbook of Children and the Media*, pp. 223–54. Thousand Oaks, CA: Sage.

Butler, Judith (1990). *Gender Trouble: Feminism and the Subversion of Identity*. London: Routledge.

Buttel, Frederick, & Kenneth Gould (2004). 'Global Social Movement(s) at the Crossroads: Some Observation on the Trajectory of the Anti-corporate Globalization Movement'. *Journal of World Systems Research* 10 (1), pp. 51–2.

Campbell, Marie, & Frances Gregor (2002). *Mapping Social Relations: A Primer in Doing Institutional Ethnography*. Aurora: Garamond.

Canada (1884). An Act to Further Amend the Indian Act 1880. *Statutes of Canada*, 47 Vict. c 27.

Canadian Association of Food Banks (2004). *Poverty in a Land of Plenty: Towards a Hunger-Free Canada*. Toronto.

Cardinal, Harold (1969). *The Unjust Society: The Tragedy of Canada's Indians*. Edmonton: New Press.

——— (1977). *The Rebirth of Canada's Indians*. Toronto: New Press.

Carroll, William (1982). 'The Canadian Corporate Elite: Financiers or Finance Capitalists'. *Studies in Political Economy* 8, pp. 89–114.

Casey, Catherine (1992). 'Restructuring Work: New Work and New Workers in Post-Industrial Production'. *Rethinking Vocationalism: Whose Work Life is it?* R.P. Coulter & I.F. Goodson, eds. Toronto: Our Schools, Our Selves.

Cavan, Ruth (1965 [1928]). *Suicide*. New York: Russell and Russell.

Certeau, Michel de (1984). *The Practice of Everyday Life*. Trans. S. Rendell. Berkeley, CA: U of California P.

Chaitin, Gilbert (1996). *Rhetoric and Culture in Lacan*. Cambridge: Cambridge UP.

Chang, Virginia, & Nicholas Christakis (2002). 'Medical Modelling of Obesity: A Transition from Action to Experience in a 20th Century American Medical Textbook'. *Sociology of Health and Illness* 24 (2), pp. 151–77.

Chen, Anita Beltran (1998). *From Sunbelt to Snowbelt: Filipinos in Canada*. Calgary: Canadian Ethnic Studies Association.

Chodrow, Nancy (1978). *The Reproduction of Mothering: Psychoanalysis and the Sociology of Gender*. Berkeley: U of California P.

——— (1994). *Femininities, Masculinities, Sexualities: Freud and Beyond*. UP of Kentucky.

Chomsky, Noam (2004). *Hegemony or Survival: America's Quest for Global Dominance*. New York: Henry Holt and Company.

Clark, S.D. (1962). *The Developing Canadian Community*. Toronto: U of Toronto P.

——— (1976). *Canadian Society in Historical Perspective*. Toronto: McGraw-Hill.

Clinard, M., & R. Quinney (1973). *Criminal Behavior Systems: A Typology*, 2nd edn. New York: Holt, Rinehart, and Winston.

Codjoe, Henry M. (2001). 'Can Blacks Be Racist? Further Reflections on Being "Too Black and African"'. In Carl James & Adrienne Shadd, eds, *Talking About Identity: Encounters in Race, Ethnicity and Language*, pp. 277–90. Toronto: Between the Lines.

Cohen, Albert K. (1955). *Delinquent Boys: The Culture of the Gang*. Glencoe, IL: Free Press.

Colapinto, John (2000). *As Nature Made Him: The Boy Who Was Raised as a Girl*. New York: HarperCollins.

Comaskey, Brenda, & Anne McGillivray (1999). *Black Eyes All of the Time: Intimate Violence, Aboriginal Women, and the Justice System*. Toronto: U of Toronto P.

Comte, Auguste (1830–42). *Cours de Philosophie Positive*. Paris: Librairie Larousse.

——— (1851–4). *Système de Politique Positive*.

——— (1853). *The Positive Philosophy of August Comte*. Trans. and ed. Harriet Martineau.

——— (1877). *The System of Positive Polity*. London: Longmans, Green.

Connell, R.W. (1995). *Masculinities*. Berkeley: U of California P.

Conrad, Margaret R., & James K. Hiller (2001). *Atlantic Canada: A Region in the Making*. Toronto: Oxford UP.

Cordell, Arthur J. (1993). 'The Perils of an Information Age'. In P. Elliot, ed., *Rethinking the Future*. Saskatoon: Fifth House.

Côté, James, & Anton Allahar (2007). *Ivory Tower Blues: A University System in Crisis*. Toronto: U of Toronto P.

Craib, Ian (1989). *Psychoanalysis and Social Theory: The Limits of Sociology*. Amherst: U of Massachusetts P.

Crehan, Kate (2002). *Gramsci, Culture and Anthropology*. Berkeley: U of California P.

Crozier, Michel (1964). *The Bureaucratic Phenomenon*. Chicago: U of Chicago P.

Curtis, James, Edward Grabb, & Neil Guppy, eds (1999). *Social Inequality in Canada: Patterns, Problems and Policies*, 3rd edn. Scarborough: Prentice Hall.

Dahl, Robert A. (1956). *A Preface to Democratic Theory: How Does Popular Sovereignty Function in America?* Chicago: U of Chicago P.

Dasgupta, Sathi (1992). 'Conjugal Roles and Social Network in Indian Immigrant Families: Bott Revisited'. *The Journal of Comparative Family Studies* 23 (3), p. 465.

Das Gupta, Tania (1996). *Racism and Paid Work*. Toronto: Garamond.

Dawson, Carl A., & Warren E. Getty (1948). *An Introduction to Sociology*, 3rd edn. New York: The Ronald Press.

d'Eaubonne, Françoise (1974). *Le féminisme ou la mort (Feminism or Death)*. Paris: P. Horay.

Dei, George (1996). *Anti-Racism Education: Theory and Practice*. Halifax: Fernwood Publishing.

Dei, George, & Agnes Calliste (2000). *Power Knowledge and Anti-Racism Education: A Critical Reader*. Halifax: Fernwood Publishing.

Dei, George, Irma James, L. Karumanchery, S. James-Wilson, & J. Zine (2000). *Aboriginal Margins: The Challenges and Possibilities of Inclusive Schooling*. Toronto: Canadian Scholars' Press.

Dei, George, M. James, S. James-Wilson, L. Karumanchery, & J. Zine (2000). *Removing the Margins: The Challenges and Possibilities of Inclusive Schooling*. Toronto: Canadian Scholar's Press.

Demerson, Velma (2004). *Incorrigible*. Waterloo: Wilfrid Laurier UP.

Diamond, Irene, & Gloria Feman Orenstein, eds (1990). *Reweaving the World: The Emergence of Ecofeminism*. San Francisco: Sierra Club Books.

Dick, Lyle (1995). '"Pibloktoq" (Arctic Hysteria): A Construction of European–Inuit Relations?'. *Arctic Anthropology* 32 (2), pp. 1–42.

Dickason, Olive (2002). *Canada's First Nations: A History of Founding Peoples from Earliest Times*, 3rd edn. Toronto: Oxford UP.

Dofny, Jacques, & Marcel Rioux (1962). 'Les classes sociales au Canada français'. *Revue français de sociologie* 111 (3), pp. 290–303.

Dollard, John (1937). *Caste and Class in a Southern Town*. New Haven, CT: Yale UP.

Dosman, Edgar J. (1972). *Indians: An Urban Dilemma*. Toronto: McClelland & Stewart.

Du Bois, W.E.B. (1896). *The Suppression of the African Slave Trade in America*. New York: Longmans, Green.

—— (1903). *The Souls of Black Folk*. Chicago: A.C. McClurg.

—— (1935). *Black Reconstruction: An Essay toward a History of the Part which Black Folk Played in the Attempt to Re-construct Democracy in America*. New York: Harcourt Brace.

—— (1940). *Dusk of Dawn*. New York: Harcourt, Brace & World.

—— (1967 [1899]). *The Philadelphia Negro: A Social Study*. New York: Schocken Books.

Dubson, Michael, ed. (2001). *Ghosts in the Classroom: Stories of College Adjunct Faculty—and the Price We All Pay*. Boston: Camel's Back Books.

Dumas, Jean, & Alain Bélanger (1996). *Report on the Demographic Situation in Canada, 1995*. Ottawa: Statistics Canada, cat. no. 91–209.

Dunfield, Allison (2005). 'Why Do Women Always Pay More?'. *Globe and Mail*, 15 March.

Dupuy, Alex (1997). *Haiti in the New World Order: The Limits of the Democratic Revolution*. Boulder, CO: Westview.

Durkheim, Émile (1938 [1895]). *Rules of the Sociological Method*. Chicago: U of Chicago P.

—— (1951 [1897]). *Suicide: A Study in Sociology*. Trans. John A. Spaulding & George Simpson. New York: The Free Press of Glencoe.

—— (1965 [1912]). *The Elementary Forms of Religious Life*. New York: The Free Press of Glenco.

—— (1995 [1912]). *The Elementary Forms of the Religious Life*. Trans. Karen Fields. New York: Simon and Schuster.

Dusenberry, Verne (1998). *The Montana Cree: A Study in Religious Persistence*. Norman OK: U of Oklahoma P.

Ebaugh, Helen Rose Fuchs (1988). *Becoming an EX: The Process of Role Exit*. Chicago: U of Chicago P.

Eichler, Margrit (2001). 'Women Pioneers in Canadian Sociology: The Effects of a Politics of Gender and a Politics of Knowledge'. *Canadian Journal of Sociology* 26 (3) (Summer), pp. 375–404.

Elkind, David (2001). *The Hurried Child: Growing Up Too Fast Too Soon*, 3rd edn. Cambridge, MA: Perseus.

—— (2003). 'The Reality of Virtual Stress'. *CIO* Fall/Winter. www.cio.com/archive/092203/elkind.

Emke, Ivan (2002). 'Patients in the New Economy: The "Sick Role" in a Time of Economic Discipline'. *Animus: A Philosophical Journal for Our Time* 7.

Erlick, Larry (2004). Untitled speech to the Economic Club of Toronto. www.oma.org/pcomm/pressrel/economicspeech04.htm.

Esar, Evan (1943). *Esar's Comic Dictionary of Wit and Humour*. New York: Horizon.

Fadiman, Anne (1997). *The Spirit Catches You and You Fall Down. A Hmong Child, Her American Doctors, and the Collision of Two Cultures*. New York: Farrar, Straus and Giroux.

Fanon, Franz (1965 [1961]). *The Wretched of the Earth*. New York: Grove.

—— (1967 [1952]). *Black Skin, White Masks*. New York: Grove.

Fleras, Augie, & Jean Elliott (1999). *Unequal Relations: An Introduction to Race, Ethnic, and Aboriginal Dynamics in Canada*, 3rd edn. Scarborough, ON: Prentice-Hall, Allyn & Bacon.

Fiske, John (1989). *Understanding Popular Culture*. London: Routledge.

Fletcher, S.D. (2000). 'Molded Images: First Nations People, Representation and the Ontario School Curriculum.' In T. Goldstein & D. Selby, eds, *Weaving Connections: Educating for Peace, Social and Environmental Justice*. Toronto: Sumach Press.

Food Banks Canada (2009). 'HungerCount 2009: A comprehensive report on hunger and food bank use in Canada, and recommendations for change'. http://foodbankscanada.ca/documents/HungerCount2009NOV16.pdf.

Foucault, Michel (1961). *Madness and Civilisation: A History of Insanity in the Age of Reason*. New York: Vintage.

—— (1975). *Discipline and Punish: The Birth of the Prison*. New York: Vintage.

—— (1977). *Discipline and Punish: The Birth of the Prison*. New York: Pantheon Books.

—— (1978). *The History of Sexuality. Vol. 1: An Introduction*. New York: Pantheon Books.

—— (1980). 'Two Lectures'. In Colin Gordon, ed., *Power/Knowledge*, pp. 78–108. New York: Pantheon Books.

—— (1994 [1972]). *The Archaeology of Knowledge*. Trans. from *L'archéologie du savoir* (1969). London: Routledge.

Fowles, Jib (1999). *The Case for Television Violence*. London: Sage.

—— (2001). 'The Whipping Boy: The Hidden Conflicts Underlying the Campaign against TV'. *Reason* March.

Frank, David, & Nolan Reilly (1979). 'The Emergence of the Socialist Movement in the Maritimes, 1899–1916'. In Robert J. Brym & R. James Sacouman, eds, *Underdevelopment and Social Movements in Atlantic Canada*, pp. 81–106. Toronto: New Hogtown Press.

Freud, Sigmund (1977 [1916–17]). *On Sexuality*, vol. 7. London: Penguin.

Friedman, Thomas L. (2000). *The Lexus and the Olive Tree: Understanding Globalization*. New York: Anchor Books.

Gallagher, James E., & Ronald D. Lambert, eds (1971). *Social Process and Institution: The Canadian Case*. Toronto: Holt, Rinehart and Winston.

Gans, Herbert (1989). 'Sociology in America: The Discipline and the Public'. *American Sociological Review* 54 (February), pp. 1–16.

Garigue, Philippe (1964). 'French Canada: A Case-Study in Sociological Analysis'. *Canadian Review of Sociology and Anthropology* 1 (4), pp. 186–92.

Gephart, Robert (1988). *Ethnostatistics: Qualitative Foundations for Quantitative Research*. London: Sage.

Gerth, Hans, & C. Wright Mills (1958 [1946]). *The Sociology of Max Weber*. New York: Vintage Books.

Giles, Philip (2004). 'Low Income Measurement in Canada'. www.statcan.ca/english/research/75F0002MIE/75F0002MIE2004011.pdf.

Gilligan, Carol (1982). *In a Different Voice: Psychological Theory and Women's Development*. Cambridge, MA: Harvard UP.

—— (1990). *Making Connections: The Relational Worlds of Adolescent Girls at Emma Willard School*. Cambridge, MA: Harvard UP.

Giroux, Henry A. (2004). *The Terror of Neoliberalism: Authoritarianism and the Eclipse of Democracy*. Boulder, CO: Paradigm Publishers.

—— (2005). *Against the New Authoritarianism: Politics After Abu Ghraib*. Winnipeg: Arbeiter Ring Publishing.

—— (2007). *The University in Chains: Confronting the Military-Industrial-Academic Complex*. Boulder, CO: Paradigm Publishers.

—— (2008). *Against the Terror of Neoliberalism: Politics Beyond the Age of Greed*. Boulder, CO: Paradigm Publishers.

Goffman, Erving (1959). *The Presentation of Self in Everyday Life*. New York: Anchor Books.

———— (1961). *Asylums: Essays on the Social Situation of Mental Patients and Other Inmates*. New York: Anchor Books.

———— (1963). *Stigma: Notes on the Management of Spoiled Identity*. Englewood Cliffs, NJ: Prentice-Hall.

———— (1976). *Gender Advertisements*. New York: Harper Torchbooks.

Goldscheider, Frances, & Regina Bures (2003). 'The Racial Crossover in Family Complexity in the United States'. *Demography* 40 (3), pp. 569–87.

Gomm, Roger, & Patrick McNeill (1982). *Handbook for Sociology Teachers*. London: Heineman.

Gorer, Geoffrey, & John Rickman (1949). *The People of Great Russia: A Psychological Study*. New York: Norton.

Gramsci, Antonio (1992). *Prison Notebooks*, vol. 1. Ed. Joseph A. Buttligieg. New York: Columbia UP.

Grant, George (1965). *Lament for a Nation: The Defeat of Canadian Nationalism*. Toronto: McClelland & Stewart.

———— (1969). *Technology and Empire: Perspectives on North America*. Toronto: House of Anansi.

Grattan, E. (2003). 'Social Inequality and Stratification in Canada'. In Paul Angelini, ed., *Our Society: Human Diversity in Canada*, 2nd edn, pp. 61–86. Scarborough, ON: Thomson-Nelson.

Griffith, Alison, & L. Andre-Bechely (2008). 'Standardizing parents' educational work'. In Marjorie DeVault, ed., *Embodied Workers*, New York: NYU Press.

Griswold, Wendy (1994). *Cultures and Societies in a Changing World*. London: Sage.

Gross, Bertram (1980). *Friendly Fascism: The New Face of Power in America*. Montreal: Black Rose.

Grygier, Pat (1994). *A Long Way from Home: The Tuberculosis Epidemic among the Inuit*. Montreal: McGill–Queen's UP.

Haedrich, Richard L., & Cynthia M. Duncan (2004). 'Above and Below the Water: Social/Ecological Transformation in Northwest Newfoundland'. *Population and Environment* 25 (3), pp. 195–215.

Hale, Sylvia (1992). 'Facticity and Dogma in Introductory Sociology Texts: The Need for Alternative Methods'. In William K. Carroll, Linda Christiansen-Ruffman, Raymond F. Currie, & Deborah Harrison, eds, *Fragile Truths: 25 Years of Sociology and Anthropology in Canada*, pp. 135–53. Ottawa, ON: Carleton UP.

Hall, Elaine J. (1988). 'One Week for Women? The Structure of Inclusion of Gender Issues in Introductory Textbooks'. *Teaching Sociology* 16 (4), pp. 431–2.

Hamilton, Lawrence, Cynthia Duncan, & Richard Haedrich (2004). 'Social/Ecological Transformation in Northwest Newfoundland'. *Population and Environment* 25 (3), pp. 195–215.

Hamilton, Roberta (1996). *Gendering the Vertical Mosaic: Feminist Perspectives on Canadian Society*. Toronto: Pearson Canada.

Hanna, William R., & Clive Cockerton (1990). *Humanities: A Course in General Education*. Toronto: Thompson Educational.

Hanson, Glen R., Peter J. Hanson, Peter J. Venturelli, & Annette E. Fleckenstein (2009). *Drugs and Society* (10th edn). New York: Jones and Bartlett.

Harley, David (n.d.). 'Witchcraft and the Occult, 1400–1700: Gender and Witchcraft'. www.nd.edu/~harley/witchcraft/homepage.html.

Harman, Joshua (1998). 'Relative Deprivation and Worker Unrest in China'. 1998 Esterline Prize Winner, Asian Studies on the Pacific Coast.

Harris, Marvin (1987). *Cultural Anthropology*, 2nd edn. New York: Harper & Row.

Harrison, Deborah (1999). 'The Limits of Liberalism in Canadian Sociology: Some Notes on S.D. Clark'. In Dennis W. Magill & William Michelson, eds, *Images of Change*. Toronto: Canadian Scholars' Press.

Hart, Julian Tudor (1971). 'The Inverse Care Law'. *The Lancet* 27 Feb., pp. 405–12.

Hegel, Georg Wilhelm Friedrich (1956). *The Philosophy of History*. Trans. J. Sibree. New York: Dover.

Helmes-Hayes, Rick, & James Curtis, eds (1998). *The Vertical Mosaic Revisited*. Toronto: U of Toronto P.

Henry, Frances, & Carol Tator (2006). *The Colour of Democracy: Racism in Canada*. Toronto: Nelson Thomson.

Hill, Daniel (1960). *Negroes in Toronto: A Sociological Study of a Minority Group*. Unpublished doctoral dissertation.

———— (1981). *The Freedom Seekers: Blacks in Early Canada*. Agincourt: Book Society of Canada.

Hiller, Harry H., & Linda Di Luzio (2001). 'Text and Context: Another "Chapter" in the Evolution of Sociology in Canada'. *Canadian Journal of Sociology* 26 (3), pp. 487–512.

Hiller, Harry H., & Simon Langlois (2001). 'The Most Important Books/Articles in Canadian Sociology in the Twentieth Century: A Report'. *Canadian Journal of Sociology/Cahiers canadiens de sociologie* 26 (3), pp. 513–16.

Hitchcock, John T., & Leigh Minturn (1963). 'The Rajputs of Khalapur'. In B. Whiting, ed., *Six Cultures: Studies of Child Rearing*, pp. 203–362. New York: John Wiley & Sons.

Hoebel, E. Adamson (1965 [1954]). *The Law of Primitive Man, A Study in Comparative Legal Dynamics*. Cambridge, MA: Harvard UP.

Hofley, John R. (1992). 'Canadianization: A Journey Completed?'. In William K. Carroll, et al., eds, *Fragile Truths: 25 Years of Sociology and Anthropology in Canada*, pp. 102–22. Ottawa: Carleton UP.

Hoodfar, Homa (2003). 'More Than Clothing: Veiling as an Adaptive Strategy'. In Sajida Alvi, H. Hoodfar, & Sheila McDonough, eds, *The Muslim Veil in North America: Issues and Debates*, pp. 3–40. Toronto: Women's Press.

Horowitz, Irving Louis, ed. (1971). *People, Power and Politics: The Collected Essays of C. Wright Mills*. New York: Oxford UP.

Huesmann, L. Rowell, & L.D. Eron (1986). *Television and the Aggressive Child: A Cross-national Comparison*. Lawrence Erlbaum Associates.

Huesmann, L. Rowell, & L. Miller (1994). 'Long Term Effects of Repeated Exposure to Media Violence in Children'. In L.R. Huesmann, ed., *Aggressive Behavior: Current Perspective*, pp. 153–86. New York: Plenum Press.

Huesmann, L. Rowell, J. Moise, C.P. Podolski, & L.D. Eron (2003). 'Longitudinal Relations between Childhood Exposure to Media Violence and Adult Aggression and Violence: 1977–1992'. *Developmental Psychology* 39 (2), pp. 201–21.

Hughes, Everett C. (1945). 'Dilemmas and Contractions of Status'. *American Journal of Sociology*. 50 (5), pp. 353–9.

———— (1963 [1943]). *French Canada in Transition*. Chicago: U of Chicago P.

Human Resources and Skills Development Canada (HRSDC) (2003). 'Market Basket Measure Report.' http://www.hrsdc.gc.ca/eng/cs/comm/news/2003/030527.shtml.

Humphreys, Margaret (1995). *Empty Cradles*. London: Transworld Publishing.

Hurtig, Mel (1992). *A New and Better Canada: Principles and Polices of a New Canadian Political Party*. Toronto: Stoddart.

Husain, Mir Zohair (1995). *Global Islamic Politics*. New York: HarperCollins.

Iker, Jack (2003). 'A Church's Choice'. *WCNY Online NewsHour* (1 Aug.), http://www.pbs.org/newshour/bb/religion/july-dec03/episcopalian_8-1.html.

Illich, Ivan (1976). *Medical Nemesis: The Limits of Medicine*. London: Penguin.

Isajiw, Wsevolod W. (1999). *Understanding Diversity: Ethnicity and Race in the Canadian Context*. Toronto: Thompson Educational.

Iwasaki, Mineko (2002). *Geisha: A Life*. New York: Washington Square Press.

Jenkins, Richard (1992). *Pierre Bourdieu*. London: Routledge.

Jenness, Diamond (1932). *Indians of Canada*. Ottawa: King's Printer.

Jenness, Stuart (1991). *Arctic Odyssey: The Diary of Diamond Jenness, 1913–1916*. Ottawa: Canadian Museum of Civilization.

Jhally, Sut (1990). *The Codes of Advertising: Fetishism and the Political Economy of Meaning in the Consumer Society*. New York: Routledge.

Jocas, Yves de, & Guy Rocher (1957). 'Inter-generation Occupational Mobility in the Province of Quebec'. *The Canadian Journal of Economics and Political Science* 25 (1), pp. 57–68.

Johnston, Hugh (1989). *The Voyage of the Komagata Maru: The Sikh challenge to Canada's Colour Bar*. Vancouver: U of British Columbia P.

Kachuck, Beatrice (2003 [1995]). 'Feminist Social Theories: Themes and Variations'. In Sharmila Rege, ed., *Sociology of Gender: The Challenge of Feminist Sociological Knowledge*. New Delhi: Sage.

Kaizuka, Shigeki (2002 [1956]). *Confucius: His Life and Thought*. Mineola, NY: Dover.

Kane, P.R., & A.J. Orsini (2003). 'The Need for Teachers of Color in Independent Schools'. In P.R. Kane & A.J. Orsini, eds, *The Colors of Excellence: Hiring and Keeping Teachers of Color in Independent Schools*, pp. 7–28. New York: Teachers College Press.

Keay, John (2000). *India: A History*. London: HarperCollins.

Kehoe, Alice (1995). 'Blackfoot Persons'. In L. Klein & L. Ackerman, *Women and Power in Native North America*. Norman, OK: U of Oklahoma P.

Kimelman, Edwin C. (1985). *No Quiet Place: Review Committee on Indian and Metis Adoption and Placements*. Manitoba Community Services.

King, Alan, Wendy Warren, & Sharon Miklas (2004). 'Study of Accessibility to Ontario Law Schools'. Executive Summary (Social Program Evaluation Group, Queen's University).

Kirkby, Mary-Ann (2007). *I Am Hutterite*. Prince Albert, SK: Polka Dot Press.

Klein, Naomi (2000). *No Logo*. Toronto: Vintage Canada.

——— (2002). *Fences and Windows: Dispatches from the Frontlines of the Globalization Debate*. Toronto: Vintage Canada.

Kleinman, Arthur (1995). *Writing at the Margin: Discourse Between Anthropology and Medicine*. Berkeley: U of California P.

Klopfenstein, Kristin (2005). 'Beyond Test Scores: The Impact of Black Teacher Role Models on Rigorous Math-Taking'. *Contemporary Economic Policy* 23, pp. 416–28.

Knockwood, Isabelle (1992). *Out of the Depths: The Experiences of Mi'kmaw Children at the Indian Residential School at Shubenacadie*. Lockeport, NS: Roseway.

Koos, E.L. (1954). *The Health of Regionsville: What the People Thought and Did About It*. New York: Columbia UP.

Krause, Elliott (1980). *Why Study Sociology?* New York: Random House.

Kroker, Arthur, & Michael A. Weinstein (1995). *Data Trash: The Theory of the Virtual Class*. Montreal: New World Perspectives.

Langlois, Simon (1999). 'Empirical Studies on Social Stratification in Quebec and Canada'. In Y. Lemel & N. Noll, eds, *New Structures of Inequality*. Montreal: McGill–Queen's UP, and www.soc.ulaval. ca/corps/langlois/empirical.pdf.

LaRocque, Emma (1975). *Defeathering the Indian*. Agincourt, ON: Book Society of Canada.

——— (1993). 'Three Conventional Approaches to Native People'. In Brett Balon & Peter Resch, eds, *Survival of the Imagination: the Mary Donaldson Memorial Lectures*, pp. 209–18. Regina: Coteau Books.

Laslett, Peter (1971). *The World We Have Lost*. London: Methuen.

Lawrence, Bonita (2004). *'Real' Indians and Others: Mixed-Blood Urban Native Peoples and Indigenous Nationhood*. Vancouver: U of British Columbia P.

Leah, Ronnie, & Gwen Morgan (1979). 'Immigrant Women Fight Back: The Case of the Seven Jamaican Women'. *Resources for Feminist Research* 7 (3), pp. 23–4.

Lebkowsky, J. (1997). 'It's Better to be Inspired than Wired: An Interview with R.U. Sirius'. *Digital Delirium*. A. & M. Kroker, eds. Montreal: New World Perspectives.

Le Bourdais, C., & N. Marcil-Gratton (1996). 'Family Transformations Across the Canadian/American Border: When the Laggard Becomes the Leader'. *Journal of Comparative Family Studies* 27 (3) (Fall), pp. 417–36.

Leffingwell, William (1925). *Office Management: Principles and Practice*. Chicago: A.W. Shaw Co.

Leiss, William, Stephen Kline, & Sut Jhally (1988). *Social Communication in Advertising: Persons, Products, and Images of Well-Being*. Toronto: Nelson.

Lieberson, Stanley (2000). *A Matter of Taste: How Names, Fashions and Cultures Change*. New Haven, CT: Yale UP.

Lipset, Seymour Martin (1990). *Continental Divide: Values and Institutions of the United States and Canada*. New York: Routledge.

Livingstone, David W. (2004). *The Education-Jobs Gap: Underemployment or Economic Democracy*, 2nd edn. Toronto: Garamond Press.

Lockhart, Alexander (1979). 'Educational Opportunities and Economic Opportunities—The 'New' Liberal Equality Syndrome'. *Economy, Class and Social Reality: Issues in Contemporary Canadian Society*. J. Allan Fry, ed. Toronto: Butterworths, pp. 224–37.

Lowe, Kevin, Stan Fischler, & Shirley Fischler (1988). *Champions: The Making of the Edmonton Oilers*. Scarborough: Prentice-Hall Canada.

Lundy, Katherina, & Barbara Warme (1986, 1990). *Sociology: A Window on the World*. Toronto: Methuen.

Lyotard, Jean-Francois (1984). *The Postmodern Condition: A Report on Knowledge*. Minneapolis, MN: U of Minnesota P.

McGillivray, Anne, & Brenda Comaskey (1999). *Black Eyes All of the Time: Intimate Violence, Aboriginal Women and the Justice System*. Toronto: U of Toronto U.

McKay, Ian (1998). 'Changing the Subject(s) of the "History of Canadian Sociology": The Case of Colin McKay and Spencerian Marxism, 1890–1940'. *Canadian Journal of Sociology* 23 (4).

MacLean, Annie Marion (1897–8). 'Factory Legislation for Women in the United States'. *American Journal of Sociology* 3, pp. 183–205.

——— (1898). 'Two Weeks in a Department Store'. *American Journal of Sociology* 4, pp. 721–41.

——— (1899–1900). 'Faculty Legislation for Women in Canada'. *American Journal of Sociology* 5, pp. 172–81.

——— (1903–4). 'The Sweat Shop Summer'. *American Journal of Sociology* 9, pp. 289–309.

——— (1908–9). 'Life in the Pennsylvania Coal Fields'. *American Journal of Sociology* 14, pp. 329–51.

——— (1909–10). 'With the Oregon Hop Pickers'. *American Journal of Sociology* 15, pp. 83–95.

——— (1910). *Wage-Earning Women*. New York: Macmillan.

——— (1923). 'Four Months in a Model Factory'. *Century* 106 (July), pp. 436–44.

Maclean, John (1970 [1889]). *The Indians of Canada: Their Manners and Customs*. Toronto: Coles.

McLeod, Linda (1980). *Wife Battering in Canada: The Vicious Circle*. Hull, QC: Canadian Government Publishing Centre.

McQuaig, Linda (2004). 'Closed Shop Gives Doc the Hammer in New Brunswick Strike'. *Straight Goods*. www.straightgoods. com/McQuaig/010122.shtml.

Maines, D.R. (1993). 'Narrative's Moment and Sociology's Phenomena—Toward a Narrative Sociology. *Sociological Quarterly* 34 (1), pp. 17–37.

Maioni, Antonia (2004). 'New Century, New Risks: The Marsh Report and the Post-War Welfare State in Canada'. *Policy Options* August 2004, pp. 20–3.

Mandell, Nancy, & Ann Duffy (1995). *Canadian Families: Diversity, Conflict and Change*. Toronto: Harcourt, Brace & Company.

Manji, Irshad (2003). *The Trouble with Islam: A Wake Up Call for Honesty and Change*. Toronto: Random House Canada.

Maracle, Brian (1996). *Back on the Rez: Finding The Way Home*. Toronto: Viking Penguin.

Maracle, Lee (1992). *Sundogs*. Penticton, BC: Theytus Books.

Marcuse, Herbert (1964). *One Dimensional Man*. Boston: Beacon.

Marshall, Gordon (1998). *Oxford Dictionary of Sociology*. New York: Oxford UP.

Martineau, Harriet (1848). *Eastern Life Past and Present*. London: Moxon.

——— (1962 [1837]). *Society in America*. Garden City, NY: Doubleday.

——— (2005 [1838]). *Retrospect of Western Travel*. Honolulu: UP of the Pacific.

Marx, Karl (1967 [1867]). *Capital: A Critique of Political Economy*. Ed. F. Engels. New York: International Publishers.

Marx, Karl, & Friedrich Engels (1967 [1848]). *The Communist Manifesto*. New York: Pantheon.

——— (1970 [1845–6]). *The German Ideology*, part 1. Ed. C.J. Arthur. New York: International Publishers.

Mazón, Mauricio (1984). *The Zoot-Suit Riots: The Psychology of Symbolic Annihilation*. Austin: U of Texas P.

Mead, George Herbert (1934). *Mind, Self, and Society*. Chicago: U of Chicago P.

Memmi, Albert (1991 [1957]). *The Colonizer and the Colonized*. Boston: Beacon.

Merton, Robert K. (1968 [1949]). *Social Theory and Social Structure*. New York: The Free Press.

Michaels, Eric (1986). *The Aboriginal invention of television in Central Australia, 1982–6*. Canberra: Australian Institute of Aborigine Studies.

Mies, Maria, & Vandana Shiva (1993). *Ecofeminism*. Halifax: Fernwood Pub.

Milan, Anne, & Kelly Tran (2004). 'Blacks in Canada: A Long History'. *Canadian Social Trends* Spring 2004, pp. 2–7.

Miller, J.R. (1996). *Shingwauk's Vision: A History of Native Residential Schools*. Toronto: U of Toronto P.

Mills, Albert J., & Tony Simmons (1995). *Reading Organization Theory: A Critical Approach*. Toronto: Garamond.

Mills, C. Wright (1948). *The New Men of Power: America's Labor Leaders*. Harcourt Brace & Company.

——— (1951). *White Collar: The American Middle Classes*. New York: Oxford UP.

——— (1956). *The Power Elite*. New York: Oxford UP.

——— (1958). *The Causes of World War Three*. London: Secker & Warburg.

——— (1959). *The Sociological Imagination*. New York: Oxford UP.

——— (1960). *Listen Yankee: The Revolution in Cuba*. New York: Ballantine Books.

——— (1962). *The Marxists*. New York: Dell Publishing.

Mills, Kathryn, ed. (2001). *C. Wright Mills: Letters and Autobiographical Writings*. Berkeley and Los Angeles: U of California P.

Miner, Horace (1963 [1939]). *St Denis: A French Canadian Parish*. Chicago: U of Chicago P.

Montagu, Ashley (1942). *Man's Most Dangerous Myth: The Fallacy of Race*. New York: Columbia UP.

Monture-Angus, Patricia (1995). *Thunder in My Soul: A Mohawk Woman Speaks*. Halifax: Fernwood.

Morehead Phillip, & Albert Morehead (1981). *Roget's College Dictionary*. New York: Penguin.

Morgan, Lewis Henry (1964 [1877]). *Ancient Society or Researches in the Lines of Human Progress from Savagery through Barbarism to Civilization*. Cambridge, MA: Harvard UP.

Murdoch, Michelle (2005). *Women with Disabilities and Adaptive Technology in the Workplace: Participatory Action Research and Applied Principles of Independent Living*. St John's, NL: Independent Living Resource Centre.

Murphy, Emily (1973 [1922]). *The Black Candle*. Toronto: Coles.

Muzzin, Linda J. (2001). 'Powder Puff Brigades: Professional Caring vs Industry Research in the Pharmaceutical Sciences Curriculum'. In Eric Margolis, ed., *The Hidden Curriculum in Higher Education*, pp. 135–54. London: Routledge.

Myers, S.A., trans. (1862). *Martin's Natural History*, First Series. New York: Blackeman & Mason.

Nakhaie, M. Reza (1995). 'Housework in Canada: The National Picture'. *Journal of Comparative Family Studies* 23 (3), pp. 409–25.

Nanda, Serena (1994). *Cultural Anthropology*, 5th edn. Belmont, CA: Wadsworth.

Newbury, Catharine (1993). *The Cohesion of Oppression*. New York: Columbia UP.

Newson, Janice, & Howard Buchbinder (1988). *The University Means Business: Universities, Corporations and Academic Work*. Toronto: Garamond.

Nietzsche, Frederick (1968 [1901]). *Will to Power*. Trans. Walter Kaufmann. New York: Vintage.

——— (1996 [1878]). *Human, All Too Human*. Trans. Marion Faber & Stephen Lehmann. Cambridge, MA: Cambridge UP.

——— (2003 [1887]). *The Genealogy of Morals*. New York: Dover.

——— (2006 [1882]). *The Gay Science*. New York: Dover.

Nihmey, John (1998). *Fireworks and Folly: How We Killed Minnie Sutherland*. Ottawa: Phillip Diamond.

Niosi, Jorge (1981). *Canadian Capitalism: A Study of Power in the Canadian Business Establishment*. Trans. R. Chodos. Toronto: James Lorimer & Co.

——— (1985). *Canadian Multinationals*. Trans. R. Chodos. Toronto: Between the Lines.

Nisbet, Robert A. (1969). *Social Change and History: Aspects of the Western Theory of Development*. Oxford: Oxford UP.

Noble, David (1998). 'Digital Diploma Mills: The Automation of Higher Education'. *Science as Culture* 7 (3), pp. 355–68.

——— (2002). *Digital Diploma Mills: The Automation of Higher Education*. Toronto: Between the Lines.

Nock, David. A. (1993). 'Star Wars in Canadian Sociology': Exploring the Social Construction of Knowledge. Halifax: Fernwood.

——— (2001). 'Careers in Print: Canadian Sociological Books and Their Wider Impact, 1975–1992'. *Canadian Journal of Sociology/Cahiers canadiens de sociologie* 26 (3), pp. 469–85.

Oakes, Jeannie (2005). *Keeping Track: How Schools Structure Inequality*, 2nd edn. New Haven: Yale UP.

Ontario Federation of Labour (1992). 'Education and Training: A Policy Adopted at the 33rd Annual Convention of the Ontario Federation of Labour, November, 1989'. *Our Schools, Our Selves* 4 (2), pp. 87–103.

Ontario Human Rights Commission (2003). 'Paying the Price: The Human Cost of Racial Profiling'. www.ohrc.on.ca/english/consultations/racial-profiling-report.pdf.

Ontario Medical Association (2002). 'Position Paper on Physician Workforce Policy and Planning'. Document addressing concerns of the Ontario Medical Association (OMA).

Ornstein, Michael (1984). 'Interlocking Directorates in Canada: Intercorporate or Class Alliance?' *Administrative Science Quarterly* 29, pp. 210–31.

——— (1988). 'Corporate Involvement in Canadian Hospital and University Boards, 1946–1977'. *Canadian Review of Sociology and Anthropology* 25 (3) pp. 365–88.

Park, Robert, & Ernest Burgess (1921). *Introduction to the Science of Sociology*. Chicago: U of Chicago P.

——— (1967 [1925]). *The City*. Chicago: U of Chicago P.

Parsons, Talcott (1951). *The Social System*. New York: Free Press.

——— (1966). *Societies: Evolutionary and Comparative Perspectives.* Englewoods Cliff, NJ: Prentice-Hall.

Patai, Raphael (2002). *The Arab Mind.* New York: Random House.

Payer, Lynn (1992). *Disease-Mongers: How Doctors, Drug Companies, and Insurers Are Making You Feel Sick.* New York: John Wiley & Sons.

Philip, Margaret (2006). 'Cancer in the Mind's Eye'. *Globe and Mail,* 9 Dec. www.theglobeandmail.com/servlet/story/RTGAM.20061208.cover09/BNStory/cancer/home

Pohlmann, Lisa (2002). 'Inequality is Bad for your Health'. www.mecep.or/MEChoices02/ch_029.htm.

Porter, John (1965). *The Vertical Mosaic: An Analysis of Social Class and Power in Canada.* Toronto: U of Toronto P.

Rajulton, Fernando, T.R. Balakrishnan, & Zenaida R. Ravanera (1990). 'Measuring Infertility in Contracepting Populations'. Presentation, Canadian Population Society Meetings. Victoria, BC, June.

Rege, Sharmila (2003). 'Feminist Challenge to Sociology: Disenchanting Sociology or "For Sociology"?'. In S. Rege, ed., *Sociology of Gender: The Challenge of Feminist Sociological Knowledge,* pp. 1–49. London: Sage.

Reid, Anna (2002). *The Shaman's Coat: A Native History of Siberia.* London: Weidenfeld & Nicolson.

Reiman, Jeffrey (1998). *The Rich Get Richer and the Poor Get Prison: Ideology, Class and Criminal Justice.* Boston: Allyn & Bacon.

Reinharz, Shulamit (1992). *Feminist Methods in Social Research.* New York: Oxford UP.

Richards, John, Jennifer Hove, & Kemi Afolabi (2008). *Understanding the Aboriginal/Non-Aboriginal Gap in Student Performance: Lessons from British Columbia.* Toronto: C.D. Howe Institute.

Richardson, Jack R. (1992). 'Free Trade: Why Did It Happen?' *Canadian Review of Sociology and Anthropology* 29 (3), pp. 307–28.

Riesman, David (1950). *The Lonely Crowd: A Study of the Changing American Character.* New Haven, CT: Yale UP.

Ritzer, George (2004). *The McDonaldization of Society,* revised edition. Newbury Park, CA: Pine Forge Press.

Robertson, Roland (1997). 'Comments on the "Global Triad" and "Glocalization"'. In Inoue Nobutaka, ed., *Globalization and Indigenous Culture.* Institute for Japanese Culture and Classics, Kokugakuin University.

Robinson, Angela (2005). *Ta'n Teli-ktlamsitasit (Ways of Believing): Mi'kmaw Religion in Eskasoni, Nova Scotia.* Toronto: Pearson.

Rochelau, Dianne, Barbara Thomas-Slayter, & Esther Wangari, eds. (1996). *Feminist Political Ecology: Global Issues and Local Experiences.* London: Routledge.

Ross, Aileen (1962). *The Hindu Family in Its Urban Setting.* Toronto: U of Toronto P.

——— (1976). 'Changing Aspirations and Roles: Middle and Upper Class Indian Women Enter the Business World'. In Giri Raj Gupta, ed., *Main Currents in Indian Sociology,* 103–32. Bombay: Vikas Publishing House Pvt Ltd.

——— (1977). 'Some Comments on the Home Roles of Businesswomen in India, Australia and Canada'. *Journal of Comparative Family Studies* 8 (3), pp. 327–40.

——— (1979). 'Businesswomen and Business Cliques in Three Cities: Delhi, Sydney, and Montreal'. *Canadian Review of Sociology and Anthropology* 16 (4), pp. 425–35.

——— (1982). *The Lost and the Lonely: Homeless Women in Montreal.* Montreal: Canadian Human Rights Commission.

Ruddick, S. (1989). *Maternal Thinking: Towards a Politics of Peace.* Boston: Beacon.

Ruether, Rosemary Radford (1993). 'Ecofeminism: Symbolic and Social Connections of the Oppression of Women and the Domination of Nature'. *Ecofeminism and the Sacred,* Carol Adams, ed. New York: The Continuum Pub. Co.

Ryan, William (1976 [1971]). *Blaming the Victim.* New York: Pantheon.

Said, Edward (1979). *Orientalism.* New York: Pantheon.

Sale, Kirkpatrick (1980). *Human Scale.* New York: Coward, McCann & Geoghegan.

——— (1996). *Rebels Against the Future: The Luddites and Their War on the Industrial Revolution—Lessons for the Computer Age.* Cambridge, MA: Perseus.

——— (2005). 'Imperial Entropy: Collapse of the American Empire'. *CounterPunch* 22 Feb. 2005.

Sargent, Paul (2005). 'The Gendering of Men in Early Childhood Education'. *Sex Roles: A Journal of Research,* Feb.

Sata, T.K. Nonaka, T. Miura, & K. Peter (1994). 'Trends in Cohort Fertility of the Dariusleut Hutterite Population'. *Human Biology* 66 (3) pp. 421–32.

Saussure, Ferdinand de (1966). *Course in General Linguistics.* New York: McGraw-Hill.

Schecter, Stephen (1977). 'Capitalism, Class, and Educational Reform in Canada'. *The Canadian State: Political Economy and Political Power.* L. Panitch, ed. Toronto: U of Toronto P.

Seeley, John, R. Alexander Sim, & Elizabeth Loosely (1956). *Crestwood Heights: A Study of the Culture of Suburban Life.* Toronto: U of Toronto P.

Shiva, Vandana (1988). *Staying Alive: Women, Ecology and Development.* London: Zed Books.

Shrimpton, Gordon (1987). 'The Crisis in Canadian Universities'. *The Political Economy of Canadian Schooling.* T. Wotherspoon, ed. Toronto: Methuen.

Siddiqui, Haroon (2006). *Being Muslim.* Toronto: Groundwood Books.

Simmel, Georg (1890). *On Social Differentiation.* Leipzig: Duncker & Humbolt.

——— (1908). *Sociology: Investigations on the Forms of Socialization.* Lepizig: Duncker & Humbolt.

——— (1990 [1900]). *The Philosophy of Money.* Ed. David Frisby. New York: Routledge.

Slaughter, Sheila (1990). *The Higher the Learning & Higher Technology: Dynamics of Higher Education Policy Formation.* New York: State U of New York P.

Smith, Dorothy (1987). *The Everyday World as Problematic: A Feminist Sociology.* Boston: Northeastern UP.

——— (1990). *The Conceptual Practices of Power: A Feminist Sociology of Knowledge.* Toronto: U of Toronto P.

Smith, George W. (1998). 'The Ideology of "Fag": The School Experience of Gay Students'. *The Sociological Quarterly* 39 (2), pp. 309–35.

Smits, David D. (1982). 'The "Squaw Drudge": A Prime Index of Savagism'. *Ethnohistory* 29 (4) (Autumn 1982), pp. 281–306.

Spencer, Herbert (1862). *First Principles.* http://praexology.net/HS-SP-FP-pref1.htm.

——— (1896). *Social Statics, Abridged & Revised Together with Man Versus the State.* New York: D. Appleton & Company.

——— (1896 [1880]). *The Study of Sociology.* New York: D. Appleton & Company.

Spengler, Oswald (1918–22). *The Decline of the West.* New York: Alfred A. Knopf.

Starhawk (1979). *The Spiral Dance: A Rebirth of the Ancient Religion of the Great Goddess.* San Francisco: Harper.

——— (1982). *Dreaming the Dark: Magic, Sex, and Politics.* Boston: Beacon.

——— (2002). *Webs of Power: Notes from the Global Uprising.* Victoria: New Society Pub.

Statistics Canada (2001). 'Religions in Canada: Highlight Table, 2001 Census'. Cat # 97F0024XIE2001015. http://www12.statcan.gc.ca/English/census01/products/highlight/religion/Index.cfm?Lang=E.

——— (2007). 'The Haitian Community in Canada'. 28 August. http://www.statcan.gc.ca/pub/89-621-x/89-621-x2007011-eng.htm.

——— (2009). 'Household Size Declining'. *Canada Year Book Overview. 2008.* http://www41.statcan.gc.ca/2008/40000/ceb40000_000-eng.htm.

Steckley, John L. (1999). *Beyond Their Years: Five Native Women's Stories*. Toronto: Canadian Scholars' Press.

——— (2003). *Aboriginal Voices and the Politics of Representation in Canadian Sociology Textbooks*. Toronto: Canadian Scholars' Press.

Steckley, John, & Bryan Cummins (2001). *Full Circle: Canada's First Nations*. Toronto: Prentice-Hall.

——— (2008). *Full Circle: Canada's First Nations*, 2nd edn. Toronto: Pearson.

Steckley, John, & Brian Rice (1997). 'Life-long Learning and Cultural Identity: A Lesson from Canada's Native People'. In Michael Hatton, ed., *Lifelong Learning: Policies, Programs & Practices*, pp. 216–29. Toronto: APEC.

Steger, Manfred B. (2003). *Globalization: A Very Short Introduction*. Oxford: Oxford UP.

Stewart, Susan (1996). 'A Day in the Life of Two Community Police Officers: The Aboriginal Police Directorate Takes a Look at the First Nations Policing Policy in Action'. *First Nations Policing Update, March 1996. No. 4*, www.sgc.gc.ca/whoweare/aboriginal/newsletter/no4/no43.htm.

Stewart, Walter (2003). *The Life and Political Times of Tommy Douglas*. Toronto: McArthur & Company.

Stiglitz, Joseph E. (2003). *Globalization and Its Discontents*. New York: Norton.

Sutherland, Edwin (1940). 'White Collar Criminality'. *American Sociological Review* 5 (1), pp. 1–12.

——— (1949). *White Collar Crime*. New York: Holt, Rinehart and Winston.

Tajima, E. Renee (1989). 'Lotus Blossoms Don't Bleed: Images of Asian Women'. In Asian Women United of California, ed., *Making Waves: An Anthology of Writings by and About Asian American Women*, pp. 305–9. Boston: Beacon.

Talbot, Yves, E. Fuller-Thomson, F. Tudiver, Y. Habib, & W.J. McIsaac (2001). 'Canadians Without Regular Medical Doctors: Who are They?'. *Canadian Family Physician* 47 (January), pp. 58–64.

Tepperman, Lorne, & Michael Rosenberg (1998). *Macro/Micro: A Brief Introduction to Sociology*, 3rd edn. Scarborough, ON: Prentice Hall, Allyn & Bacon Canada.

Thomas, W.I. (1966). *W. I. Thomas on Social Organization and Social Personality. Selected Papers*, Morris Janowitz, ed. and intro. Chicago: U of Chicago P.

Thomas, W.I., & Florian Znaiecki (1996 [1918–20]). *The Polish Peasant in Europe and America*. Urbana: U of Illinois P.

Thorndike, Edward (1999 [1911]). *Animal Intelligence: Experimental Studies*. Piscataway, NJ: Transaction Publishers.

Tuhiwai Smith, Linda (1999). *Decolonizing Methodologies: Research and Indigenous Peoples*. London: Zed Books.

Turnbull, Colin (1961). *The Forest People*. New York: Simon & Schuster.

Urmetzer, Peter, & Neil Guppy (1999). 'Changing Income Inequality in Canada'. In J. Curtis et al., eds, *Social Inequality in Canada*, pp. 56–65. Scarborough, ON: Prentice Hall.

Useem, Michael (1979). 'The Social Organization of the American Business Elite and Participation of Corporation Directors in the Governance of American Institutions'. *American Sociological Review* 44 (Aug.), pp. 553–72.

——— (1981). 'Business Segments and Corporate Relations with US Universities'. *Social Problems* 29 (2), pp. 129–41.

Varadarajan, Dhulasi Birundha (2002). 'Women and Environment Eco-feminists' Perspectives.' *Empowerment of Women and Ecological Development*, A. Ranga Reddy, ed. New Delhi: Serials Publications.

Veblen, Thorstein (1904). *The Theory of Business Enterprise*. New York: Charles Scribner's Sons.

——— (1912 [1899]). *The Theory of the Leisure Class*. New York: Macmillan.

Waldrop, M. Mitchell (1992). *Complexity*. New York: Simon and Schuster.

Walla, Harsha (2008). 'Komagata Maru and the Politics of Apologies'. *The Dominion: News from the Grassroots* (11 Sept.). www.dominionpaper.ca/articles/2014.

Walton, John (1984). *Reluctant Rebels: Comparative Studies of Revolution and Underdevelopment*. New York: Columbia UP.

Warner, Jessica (2003). *Craze: Gin and Debauchery in an Age of Reason*. New York: Random House.

Watkins, Mel (1992). *Madness and Ruin: Politics and the Economy in the Neoconservative Age*. Toronto: Between the Lines.

Watson, John B. (1925). *Behaviorism*. New York: Norton.

Weatherford, Jack (2004). *Genghis Khan and the Making of the Modern World*. New York: Crown Publishing.

Weber, Max. (1930 [1904]). *The Protestant Ethic and the Spirit of Capitalism*. Trans.

Talcott Parsons. New York: Charles Scribner's Sons.

——— (1968 [1914]). *Economy and Society: An Outline of Interpretive Sociology*. New York: Bedminster Press.

Weiner, Jonathan (1995). *The Beak of the Finch: A Story of Evolution in Our Time*. New York: Alfred A. Knopf.

Weir, Ruth (1994). 'Attacking the Deck: The Streaming of Working Class Kids in Ontario Schools'. *The Spark* (Feb.), pp. 11–12.

Weyer, Edward M. (1962 [1932]). *The Eskimos: Their Environment and Folkways*. Hamden, CT: Archon Books.

Whiting, Beatrice B. (1963). *Six Cultures: Studies of Child Rearing*. New York: John Wiley.

Whyte. William F. (1955). *Street-Corner Society: The Social Structure of an Italian Slum*, 2nd edn. Chicago: U of Chicago P.

Williamson, Judith (1978). *Decoding Advertisements: Ideology and Meaning in Advertising*. London: Marion Boyars.

Willis, Paul E. (1977). *Learning to Labour: How Working Class Kids Get Working Class Jobs*. New York: Columbia UP.

Wilson, John K. (2008). *Patriotic Correctness: Academic Freedom and Its Enemies*. St Paul, MN: Paradigm Publishing.

Wilson, Stan, & Peggy Wilson (1998). 'Relational Accountability to All Our Relations'. *Canadian Journal of Native Education* July.

Winn, Conrad (1988). 'The Socio-economic Attainment of Visible Minorities: Facts and Policy Implications'. In J. Curtis et al., *Social Inequality in Canada: Patterns, Problems, Policies*, pp. 195–213. Scarborough: Prentice-Hall.

Woolf, H. Bosley (1974). *The Merriam-Webster Dictionary*. New York: G & C Merriam Company.

Wrong, Dennis (1961). 'The Oversocialized Conception of Man in Modern Sociology'. *American Sociological Review* 26 (2), pp. 183–93.

Yalnizyan, Armine (1998). *The Growing Gap: A Report on Growing Inequality between the Rich and Poor in Canada*. Toronto: Centre for Social Justice.

Yellen, John (1985). 'Bushmen'. *Science 85* (May).

Young, Egerton R. (1974 [1893]). *Stories from Indian Wigwams and Northern Campfires*. Toronto: Coles.

Index